Introducing
New York Math A

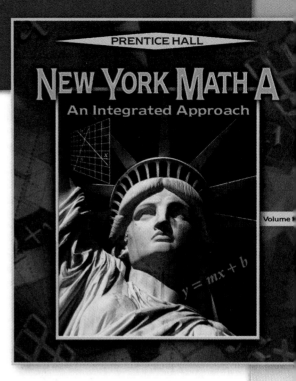

Contents

Test-Taking Strategies for the Math A Exam

The Math A Ex

Introduction

The Regents High School Examination for Mathematics A is developed by the Board of Regents of the University of the State of New York. The examination covers concepts and skills in a curriculum designed to raise standards in high school mathematics. The key ideas and performance indicators for this curriculum are outlined on the next two pages.

A specified minimum score on one of the Regents exams in mathematics is necessary for a high school diploma in New York State.

Math A and the Prentice Hall Math Course

This is the first volume of a two-volume mathematics course. Taken together, the two volumes cover all of the content assessed on the Mathematics A exam. The primary emphasis of this volume is algebra. Geometry, statistics, probability, and trigonometry are woven through the chapters to provide an integrated approach. In contrast, the primary emphasis of Volume 2 is geometry. In that text, algebraic topics and content from the other strands are integrated throughout.

As you can see from the lesson and page references on the next two pages, you will have studied most of the Math A curriculum when you have completed this text, which usually takes at least two semesters. The rest of Math A is covered in Volume 2.

Most students will take the exam after three or four semesters of Math A. Some students will wait until they have completed five or six semesters. Your mathematics teachers or counselors will be the best guides as to when *you* should take the Math A exam.

Volume 1

Volume 2

Options for Taking the Math A Exam

| Semester 1 | Semester 2 | Semester 3 | Semester 4 | Semester 5 | Semester 6 |

Math A Exam   Math A Exam   Math A Exam   Math A Exam

Math A: Key Ideas and Performance Indicators

The learning objectives for Mathematics A are organized under seven Key Ideas. Each Key Idea includes Performance Indicators that describe skills, concepts, and procedures in mathematics.

Following each performance indicator is a list of the lessons in this volume that cover all or part of the indicator. The indicators not covered in this text are covered in Prentice Hall *New York Math A/B, Volume 2*.

Correlation of Prentice Hall *New York Math A: An Integrated Approach, Volume 1* to New York Core Curriculum

Key Idea 1
Mathematical Reasoning

1A Construct valid arguments.
Page 201; New York 1 (page 594)

1B Follow and judge the validity of arguments.
Page 133

Key Idea 2
Number and Numeration

2A Understand and use rational and irrational numbers.
Lessons 1-6, 3-5, 3-7, 3-8, 7-4, 9-4, 9-5

2B Recognize the order of real numbers.
Lessons 1-4, 1-6, 4-3, 4-5, 4-6, 4-7, 4-8, 4-9, 7-4

2C Apply the properties of real numbers to various subsets of numbers.
Lessons 1-6, 3-4, 7-4, 9-5

Key Idea 3
Operations

3A Use addition, subtraction, multiplication, division, and exponentiation with real numbers and algebraic expressions.
Lessons 1-2, 1-3, 1-4, 1-5, 1-6, 3-4, 4-4, 8-1, 8-4, 8-6, 8-7, 8-8

3B Use integral exponents on integers and algebraic expressions.
Lessons 8-1, 8-4, 8-5, 8-6, 8-7, 8-8

3C Recognize and identify symmetry and transformations on figures.
Lessons 2-4, 2-5, 2-6, 2-7, 4-4, 5-4, 5-7

3D Use field properties to justify mathematical procedures.
Page 35; Lessons 3-2, 3-4, 4-2, 10-2, 10-6

Key Idea 4
Modeling/Multiple Representation

4A Represent problem situations symbolically by using algebraic expressions, sequences, tree diagrams, geometric figures, and graphs.
Lessons 1-1, 1-2, 1-8, 1-9, 2-1, 2-2, 2-3, 2-8, 3-1, 3-2, 5-1, 5-4, 5-5, 5-6, 7-2, 7-3, 9-1, 9-2, 10-6, 10-7, 11-6

4B Justify the procedures for basic geometric constructions.

4C Use transformations in the coordinate plane.
Lessons 2-7, 7-2

4D Develop and apply the concept of basic loci to compound loci.

4E Model real-world problems with systems of equations and inequalities.
Lessons 6-1, 6-2, 6-3, 6-4, 6-5, 6-6, 6-7, 6-8

Key Idea 5
Measurement

5A Apply formulas to find measures such as length, area, volume, weight, time, and angle in real-world contexts.
Lessons 4-1, 5-3, 8-5, 10-2

5B Choose and apply appropriate units and tools in measurement situations.
Lessons 4-1, 9-1, 9-2, 9-3

5C Use dimensional analysis techniques.
Page 219

5D Use statistical methods including the measures of central tendency to describe and compare data.
Lessons 1-1, 2-1, 5-6; New York 2 (page 598)

5E Use trigonometry as a method to measure indirectly.
Lesson 9-3

5F Apply proportions to scale drawings and direct variation.
Lessons 4-1, 5-2, 5-3

5G Relate absolute value, distance between two points, and the slope of a line to the coordinate plane.
Lessons 4-3, 5-1, 5-4, 5-5, 5-8, 9-2

5H Explain the role of error in measurement and its consequence on subsequent calculations.
New York 4 (page 605)

5I Use geometric relationships in relevant measurement problems involving geometric concepts.
Lessons 9-1, 9-2, 9-3

Key Idea 6
Uncertainty

6A Judge the reasonableness of results obtained from applications in algebra, geometry, trigonometry, probability, and statistics.
Lessons 1-7, 2-1, 2-8, 4-9, 9-3, 11-6, 11-7

6B Use experimental and theoretical probability to represent and solve problems involving uncertainty.
Lessons 1-7, 2-8, 3-6

6C Use the concept of random variable in computing probabilities.
Lessons 2-8, 3-6; New York 3 (page 602)

6D Determine probabilities, using permutations and combinations.
Lessons 11-6, 11-7

Key Idea 7
Patterns/Functions

7A Represent and analyze functions, using verbal descriptions, tables, equations, and graphs.
Lessons 2-4, 2-5, 2-6, 2-7, 2-8, 5-2, 5-4, 5-7, 6-8, 7-1, 7-2, 7-3

7B Apply linear and quadratic functions in the solution of problems.
Lessons 5-5, 5-8, 5-9, 7-5, 7-6, 7-7

7C Translate among the verbal descriptions, tables, equations, and graphic forms of functions.
Lessons 2-4, 2-5, 2-6, 2-7, 2-8, 5-2, 5-4, 5-7, 7-1, 7-2, 7-3

7D Model real-world situations with the appropriate function.
Lessons 2-4, 2-6, 2-7, 5-5, 7-1, 7-5, 7-7, 8-1, 8-2, 8-3, 9-7, 11-1, 11-2, 11-3

7E Apply axiomatic structure to algebra.
Lessons 3-1, 3-2, 3-3, 3-5, 3-7, 4-1, 4-2, 4-3, 4-5, 4-6, 4-7, 4-8, 6-1, 6-2, 6-3, 6-4, 6-5, 6-6, 6-8, 10-6

The Exam: Facts and Parts

Facts About the Math A Exam

The Regents High School Examination for Mathematics A covers the skills and concepts in the Math A curriculum. The Performance Indicators on the previous two pages give you an idea of the kinds of topics the exam will cover. Here are some important facts about the Math A exam.

- It is a 3-hour exam.
- You can answer the problems in any order you like. For example, you could answer Part IV first if you wished.
- Scrap paper is not permitted. Work must be done on the pages of the test booklet. One piece of scrap graph paper is provided, although you may request more graph paper.
- Scientific calculators, straightedges, compasses, and extra graph paper will be provided. The use of a graphing calculator is optional.
- Graphs and drawings must be done in pencil. All other work must be done in ink. Bring several pencils, several pens, and a good eraser.
- If you skip a question, you receive 0 points, but no points are subtracted for wrong answers. You should answer all the questions.
- Copies of previous Math A exams can be downloaded from the Web site of the New York State Education Department at **www.nysed.gov**.

The Parts of the Math A Exam

The Regents High School Examination for Mathematics A has four parts. The questions in Part I are in multiple-choice form. The questions in Parts II, III, and IV are not in multiple-choice form.

- There are a total of 85 possible credits. The four parts do not contribute equally to the total number of credits.

Part I	Part II	Part III	Part IV
20 questions	5 questions	5 questions	5 questions
2 credits each	2 credits each	3 credits each	4 credits each
40 credits possible	10 credits possible	15 credits possible	20 credits possible
47.1% of total	11.8% of total	17.6% of total	23.5% of total

- Answers for Part I are written on a separate answer sheet. Answers for Parts II, III, and IV are written in the test booklet.
- For Parts II, III, and IV, you MUST show your work. A correct answer without any work shown will receive only 1 credit.
- For Parts II, III, and IV, partial credit will be awarded according to the Exam's Scoring Key.

Part I: Strategies and Examples

General Strategies

- Bring a watch so you can keep track of the time. Be sure to leave enough time for Parts II, III, and IV.
- Write the Part I answers on the separate answer sheet. Use a pen to mark the answer sheet.
- Any marks or answers on the test pages do not count for your score. Do your computation in pencil on the test pages. If you need more space, you can erase previous work.
- Mark any questions you might want to re-check later.
- You can do the test problems in any order you like. Some students find multiple-choice questions to be difficult. If you wish, you can do Parts II, III, and IV before you do Part I, but make sure you allow plenty of time for Part I. The most credits can be earned from Part I.
- Answer ALL the Part I multiple-choice questions. There is no advantage in leaving an answer space blank. If you are not sure of the answer, use the strategies on the next few pages to make an educated guess.

Remember to sign the statement at the bottom of the answer sheet when you are finished.

This section includes some test-taking strategies for Part I. (Since the questions for Parts II, III, and IV are not in multiple-choice form, different strategies are appropriate for those parts of the test.) Each strategy that follows has an example and a practice problem for you to try. The examples come from actual questions on past Math A exams.

Use the Answer Choices

For any multiple-choice math question, read the question and all the answer choices before you begin. The answers may give you some valuable information, or hints as to how to approach the problem.

> **Example**
>
> The expression $\frac{y}{x} - \frac{1}{2}$ is equivalent to ■.
>
> (1) $\frac{2y - x}{2x}$ (3) $\frac{1 - y}{2x}$
>
> (2) $\frac{x - 2y}{2x}$ (4) $\frac{y - 1}{x - 2}$

Strategy Three of the four answer choices have the denominator $2x$. This may remind you that you must use a common denominator when subtracting fractions. It also allows you to eliminate choice (4).

Which expression is equivalent to 6.02×10^{23}?

(1) 0.602×10^{21} (3) 602×10^{21}

(2) 60.2×10^{21} (4) 6020×10^{21}

1. What is the second factor in all four answer choices? Describe a strategy suggested by this fact.

2. Use answer choice (4). Divide the first factor by 100. Multiply the second factor by 100. What happens? What strategy does this suggest?

3. The Think and Discuss question deals with scientific notation. Use the Index at the back of your book to find a lesson that covers this topic.

Answer Every Question

Answer ALL the Part I multiple-choice questions. There is no advantage in leaving an answer space blank.

Example

Which equation is an illustration of the additive identity property?

(1) $x \cdot 1 = x$ (3) $x - x = 0$

(2) $x + 0 = x$ (4) $x \cdot \frac{1}{x} = 1$

Strategy Assume that you do not know what the *additive identity property* is. Therefore, you will have to guess. Look over the answer choices. Notice that only one has a plus sign. Since *additive* might have something to do with addition, you could guess choice (2).

When the point $(2, -5)$ is reflected in the x-axis, what are the coordinates of its image?

(1) $(-5, 2)$ (3) $(2, 5)$

(2) $(-2, 5)$ (4) $(5, 2)$

1. Assume that you do not know what *reflected in the x-axis* means. You will have to guess. You sketch a graph, plot $(2, -5)$, and decide the answer should be above the x-axis. What should you do now?

2. If you had to guess an answer, which choice would you pick and why?

3. The Think and Discuss question deals with graphing ordered pairs. Use the Index at the back of your book to find a lesson that reviews this topic.

Use Elimination

If you do not know how to work a problem, you may be able to eliminate one or more possible answers before you make an educated guess. Cross out the answers you eliminate in the test booklet. Remember, only the answer sheet for Part I is scored.

Example

Which number has the greatest value?

(1) $1\frac{2}{3}$ (3) $\frac{\pi}{2}$

(2) $\sqrt{2}$ (4) 1.5

Strategy Assume you are not certain of the values for $\sqrt{2}$ and $\frac{\pi}{2}$. You can, however, still compare choices (1) and (4). Choice (4) is less than choice (1), so you can eliminate choice (4). You might then guess among the remaining three choices.

THINK AND DISCUSS

The formula $C = \frac{5}{9}(F - 32)$ can be used to find the Celsius temperature (C) for a given Fahrenheit temperature (F). What Celsius temperature is equal to a Fahrenheit temperature of 77°?

(1) 8°   (3) 45°
(2) 25°   (4) 171°

1. A student subtracts 32 from 77 to get 45. Even before multiplying $\frac{5}{9}$ times 45, the student eliminates choices (3) and (4). Explain the student's reasoning.

2. A student happens to remember that water boils at 100° C. What answer choice does this eliminate?

3. A student uses choice (4) and substitutes to get $171 = \frac{5}{9}(77 - 32)$. Without computing, tell why 171 is not a reasonable answer.

4. The Think and Discuss question deals with substituting numbers to evaluate algebraic expressions. Use the Index at the back of your book to find a lesson that covers evaluating expressions.

Use Estimation

Using estimation may help you find the answer, check the answer, or eliminate one or more answer choices.

Example

The expression $\sqrt{50}$ can be simplified to ▓.

(1) $5\sqrt{2}$ (3) $2\sqrt{25}$

(2) $5\sqrt{10}$ (4) $25\sqrt{2}$

Strategy Assume that you do not know how to simplify $\sqrt{50}$. However, you do know that $\sqrt{49} = 7$. So, $\sqrt{50}$ is a little more than 7. Since choice (2) is greater than 15, choice (3) equals 10, and choice (4) is greater than 25, the answer must be choice (1).

THINK AND DISCUSS

During a recent winter, the ratio of deer to foxes was 7 to 3 in one county of New York State. If there were 210 foxes in the county, what was the number of deer in the county?

(1) 90   (3) 280

(2) 147   (4) 490

1. A student makes this chart.

deer	foxes
7	3
	210

Why does the chart help eliminate choices (1) and (2)?

2. Since 7 is more than twice as large as 3, the number of deer must be more than twice the number of foxes. Why does this eliminate choice (3)?

3. The Think and Discuss question deals with solving a proportion for a missing term. Use the Index at the back of your book to find a lesson that covers solving proportions.

Make Sketches or Drawings

Making a sketch can sometimes help you estimate an answer to a problem, particularly if the problem is geometrical. You can request another sheet of graph paper to use for making sketches.

Example

A plot of land is in the shape of rhombus *ABCD* as shown below.

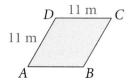

Which can *not* be the length of diagonal *AC*?

(1) 24 m   (3) 11 m
(3) 16 m   (4) 14 m

Strategy You know that all four sides of the rhombus are 11 m long. You make some sketches like the ones below showing points *D* and *B* getting closer and closer together. When point *D* coincides with point *B*, the diagonal *AC* will be 22 m, the sum of the two 11-m sides. So the diagonal (the shortest distance between points *A* and *C*) must be less than 22 m. Since 24 m is greater than 22 m, you know that (1) 24 m cannot be the length of the diagonal.

THINK AND DISCUSS

What is the perimeter of an equilateral triangle whose height is $2\sqrt{3}$?

(1) 6   (3) $6\sqrt{3}$
(2) 12   (4) $12\sqrt{3}$

1. Sketch the triangle. Explain how your sketch helps you solve the problem.

2. Using the square root key on a calculator, you will find that $2\sqrt{3}$ is about 3.5. How does knowing this eliminate choice (1)?

3. The Think and Discuss question involves simplifying radicals. Use the Index at the back of your book to find the lesson that covers simplifying radicals.

Parts II, III, and IV: Scoring Keys

The Math A Regents Exam is scored by committees of teachers. For Parts II, III, and IV of the exam, the teachers are given scoring keys. Each key describes how many credits should be awarded for different types of answers.

Example (2-credit question) ·····················

The graph shows the hair colors of all the students in a class. What is the probability that a student chosen at random from this class has black hair?

Scoring Key

[2] $\frac{6}{20}$ and appropriate work is shown.

[1] $\frac{6}{20}$ and no work is shown *or* a fraction with correct numerator or denominator and some work is shown.

[0] The response is completely incorrect, irrelevant, or incoherent *or* is a correct response arrived at using an obviously incorrect procedure.

A student can get 0, 1, or 2 credits for this question. Notice particularly the first 1-credit answer above. It includes the phrase *and no work is shown.* If you write only a correct answer and show no work, you can get only 1 credit—even for a 4-credit question. Compare these three responses and then answer the questions below.

0 credits	1 credit	2 credits
6 students have black hair.	total students = 9+8+7+6+5+4+3+2+1= 45 6 students have black hair. $\frac{6}{45}=\frac{2}{15}$	total students = 2+3+6+9=20 6 students have black hair. $\frac{6}{20}$

THINK AND DISCUSS

1. Compare the 1-credit response with the 2-credit response. What is the difference?

2. Why is the 0-credit response completely wrong?

General Strategies

Parts II, III, and IV each have five questions that are not in multiple-choice format. A Part II question is worth a maximum of 2 credits, a Part III question is worth a maximum of 3 credits, and a Part IV question is worth a maximum of 4 credits.

■ Watch your time. Remember, each Part II question is worth the same number of points as one of the multiple-choice questions in Part I. It is easy to spend too much time on the Part II questions.

■ You should spend about 20 minutes on Part II, 30 minutes on Part III, and 40 minutes on Part IV.

■ Remember, you can do the test questions in any order. You may want to do Part IV, then Part III, and then Part II. If you are a good reader, quickly read the 15 problems in these sections of the test. Do the ones you are certain of first.

■ Write your answer in ink on the same page as the test question. Be sure to cross out any wrong solutions so they do not affect your score.

■ The test directions will tell you: Use ink for answers and computation. Use pencil for graphs and drawings.

■ You will be given one sheet of scrap graph paper, but you can ask for more. Any work on this graph paper does NOT count towards your score.

■ It's sometimes good to skip a question. If you skip a question, there is no penalty. If you know nothing about a question, it may be better to skip it than to take too much time trying to answer it. Come back to the question after you have finished the other questions.

■ You must show your work to get maximum credit. Even if your answer is correct, you will get only 1 credit if you do not show your work.

■ If you skip a question, you will get 0 credits for it. There is no other penalty.

■ Some questions will have more than one part. Even if you can't answer part (a), you may be able to answer part (b) or part (c). Each part is probably worth at least 1 credit.

■ You may lose a credit if you forget to label an answer with the unit of measure. Even if a question asks something like, "How many square feet are in the area?" it is still a good idea to label your answer with "square feet."

■ In general, the Part IV questions are the most difficult. However, it depends on what you know. If you know a topic for a Part IV question well, that question will be easier for you than a Part II question about which you know little.

The next section describes test-taking strategies that will help you with Parts II, III, and IV.

Show Your Work

Even if an answer is obvious to you, you must show your work to get the maximum number of credits.

Example

Paloma has 3 jackets, 6 scarves, and 4 hats. Determine the number of different outfits consisting of a jacket, a scarf, and a hat that Paloma can wear.

Strategy This is a Part II question, so it is worth a maximum of 2 credits. You might use mental math to multiply the three numbers and get the correct answer, 72. However, writing "72" gives you only 1 credit. You must show work or describe a method to get the full 2 credits.

0 credits	1 credit	2 credits
$3+6+4=13$	72 outfits	$3 \times 6 \times 4 = 72$ 72 possible outfits I used the Multiplication Counting Principle to find the number of possible outcomes.

THINK AND DISCUSS

Which number below is irrational?

$$\sqrt{\tfrac{4}{9}}, \ \sqrt{20}, \ \sqrt{121}$$

Why is the number you chose an irrational number?

1. The correct answer is $\sqrt{20}$. How many credits would a student get if he or she circled $\sqrt{20}$?

2. A student wrote, "The square root of $\frac{4}{9}$ is $\frac{2}{3}$, and the square root of 121 is 11. So, the answer must be the square root of 20." Does this response completely answer the question? Explain.

3. Would guessing help you on this question? Explain.

4. The Think and Discuss question requires the definition of an irrational number. Where in this book can you find that definition?

Cross Out Wrong Answers

If you write two solutions for the same question, one completely correct and one completely wrong, you will not score the maximum credits possible. Be sure to cross out an incorrect solution.

Example

Judy needs a mean (average) score of 86 on four tests to earn a midterm grade of B. If the mean of her scores for the first three tests was 83, what is the *lowest* score on a 100-point scale that she can receive on the fourth test to have a midterm grade of B?

Strategy This is a Part III question, so it is worth a maximum of 3 credits. One way to do this problem is to multiply 86 by 4, then multiply 83 by 3, and then subtract the products. This correct method is shown in the chart under the 3-credit response. Notice that the 1-credit response has both the correct approach and an earlier, incorrect response.

1 credit	2 credits	3 credits
$86 + 83 = 169$ $169 \div 2 = 84.5$ 86 83 $\times 4$ $\times 3$ $\overline{344}$ $\overline{249}$ 344 -249 $\overline{95}$	86 83 $\times 4$ $\times 3$ $\overline{344}$ $\overline{249}$ 344 -249 $\overline{105}$	$\cancel{86 + 83 = 169}$ $\cancel{169 \div 2 = 84.5}$ 86 83 $\times 4$ $\times 3$ $\overline{344}$ $\overline{249}$ 344 -249 $\overline{95}$

THINK AND DISCUSS

1. Why must you cross out wrong trials rather than erasing them?

2. What is the difference between the 2-credit response and the 3-credit response?

3. The Example question deals with a type of average called a mean. Use the Index at the back of your book to find the lesson that covers finding the mean.

Describe a Method

You may be able to get 1 credit for describing a correct method—even if you do not completely finish the problem and get a correct answer.

Example

The midpoint M of line segment $\overline{AB}$ has coordinates $(-3, 4)$. If point A is the origin, $(0, 0)$, what are the coordinates of point B?

Strategy This is a Part II question, so it is worth a maximum of 2 credits. Assume you are not completely sure how to solve this problem. You could write, "I will use the midpoint formula for segment AB and substitute the given coordinates to solve the problem." You might get 1 point just for writing this much. You have nothing to lose by trying!

One correct approach is to double the coordinates to get the solution $(-6, 8)$. Compare these different responses.

0 credits	1 credit	2 credits
I divided each coordinate in half like this: $-3 \div 2 = -1.5$ $4 \div 2 = 2$ $(-1.5, 2)$	$(-6, 8)$	Doubling the coordinates will give the correct answer. $(-3, \quad 4)$ $\times 2 \quad \times 2$ $(-6, \quad 8)$

THINK AND DISCUSS

1. Why does the response on the left earn 0 credits?

2. Why does the middle response earn only 1 credit?

3. Suggest another approach to solving the problem.

4. This example deals with the midpoint of a line segment. Use the Index at the back of your book to find the lesson that explains the midpoint formula.

Include Units of Measure

You may lose a credit if you forget to label an answer with the unit of measure. Even if a question asks something like, "How many square feet are in the area?" it is still a good idea to label your answer with "square feet."

Example

The cross section of an attic is in the shape of an isosceles trapezoid as shown in the accompanying figure. If the height of the attic is 9 feet, $BC = 12$ feet, and $AD = 28$ feet, find the length of $\overline{AB}$ to the *nearest foot*.

Strategy This is a Part IV question, so it is worth a maximum of 4 credits. Read the 4-credit response below. Notice the student starts by describing the method to be used. This is a good idea because you might get credit for the method even if you do not carry the solution out to a correct answer.

2 credits	3 credits	4 credits
To find the length of $\overline{AB}$, I need to find the length of $\overline{AE}$. $28-12=16$ $16 \div 2 = 8$ $AE = 8$ $AB^2 = 9^2 + 8^2$ $AB^2 = 81 + 64$ $AB^2 = 145$ $AB = 145$ feet	To find the length of $\overline{AB}$, I need to find the length of $\overline{AE}$. $28-12=16$ $16 \div 2 = 8$ $AE = 8$ $AB^2 = 9^2 + 8^2$ $AB^2 = 81 + 64$ $AB^2 = 145$ $AB = \sqrt{145}$ $\sqrt{145} = $ about 12 $AB = 12$	To find the length of $\overline{AB}$, I need to find the length of $\overline{AE}$. $28-12=16$ $16 \div 2 = 8$ $AE = 8$ $AB^2 = 9^2 + 8^2$ $AB^2 = 81 + 64$ $AB^2 = 145$ $AB \sqrt{145}$ $\sqrt{145} = $ about 12 $AB = 12$ feet

THINK AND DISCUSS

1. Compare the 3-credit response and the 4-credit response. How are they different?

2. Read the 2-credit response. What mistake did this student make?

3. The example question involves the Pythagorean theorem. Use the Index at the back of your book to find the lesson that covers the Pythagorean theorem.

PRENTICE HALL

NEW YORK MATH A

An Integrated Approach

Volume 1

Prentice Hall dedicates
this mathematics program
to New York mathematics
educators and their students.

Prentice
Hall

Needham, Massachusetts
Upper Saddle River, New Jersey
Glenview, Illinois

AUTHORS

Allan Bellman

Sadie Chavis Bragg

Suzanne H. Chapin

Theodore J. Gardella

Bettye C. Hall

William G. Handlin, Sr.

Edward Manfre

Geometry Authors

Laurie E. Bass

Art Johnson

Basia Rinesmith Hall

Dorothy F. Wood

Contributing Author

Simone W. Bess

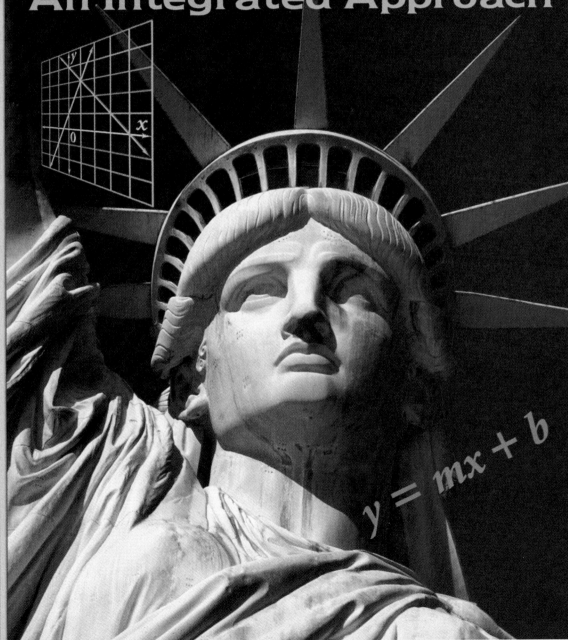

PRENTICE HALL

NEW YORK MATH

An Integrated Approach

$y = mx + b$

Authors, Algebra & Advanced Algebra

Allan Bellman
Blake High School
Silver Spring, Maryland

Sadie Chavis Bragg, Ed.D.
Borough of Manhattan
Community College
The City University of New York
New York, New York

Suzanne H. Chapin, Ed.D.
Boston University
Boston, Massachusetts

Theodore J. Gardella
Formerly, Bloomfield Hills
Public Schools
Bloomfield Hills, Michigan

Bettye C. Hall
Mathematics Consultant
Houston, Texas

William G. Handlin, Sr.
Spring Woods High School
Houston, Texas

Edward Manfre
Mathematics Consultant
Albuquerque, New Mexico

Authors, Geometry

Laurie E. Bass
The Fieldston School
Riverdale, New York

Basia Rinesmith Hall
East District
Houston Independent School District
Houston, Texas

Art Johnson, Ed.D.
Nashua High School
Nashua, New Hampshire

Dorothy F. Wood
Formerly, Kern High School District
Bakersfield, California

Contributing Author
Simone W. Bess, Ed.D.
University of Cincinnati
College of Education
Cincinnati, Ohio

ISBN: 0-13-053614-8

1 2 3 4 5 6 7 8 9 10   04 03 02 01 00

R E V I E W E R S

New York Math A

A. Rose Primiani, Ed.D., Program Consultant/Planner for Prentice Hall Math A

Howard Brenner, Assistant Principal, Mathematics, Fort Hamilton High School, Brooklyn, New York

William Caroscio, Elmira City School District, Elmira Southside High School, Elmira, New York

Raymond Ruby, Mathematics Curriculum Coordinator, Averill Park Central School District, Averill Park, New York

Joseph G. Ryan, Cardinal Hayes High School, Bronx, New York

Series Reviewers

James Gates, Ed.D.
Executive Director Emeritus, National Council of Teachers of Mathematics, Reston, Virginia

Vinetta Jones, Ph.D.
National Director, EQUITY 2000, The College Board, New York, New York

Algebra

John J. Brady III
Hume-Fogg High School
Nashville, Tennessee

Elias P. Rodriguez
Leander Junior High School
Leander, Texas

Dorothy S. Strong, Ed.D.
Chicago Public Schools
Chicago, Illinois

Art W. Wilson, Ed.D.
Abraham Lincoln High School
Denver, Colorado

Advanced Algebra

Eleanor Boehner
Methacton High School
Norristown, Pennsylvania

Laura Price Cobb
Dallas Public Schools
Dallas, Texas

William Earl, Ed.D.
Formerly Mathematics Education Specialist
Utah State Office of Education
Salt Lake City, Utah

Geometry

Sandra Argüelles Daire
Miami Senior High School
Miami, Florida

Priscilla P. Donkle
South Central High School
Union Mills, Indiana

Tom Muchlinski, Ph.D.
Wayzata High School
Plymouth, Minnesota

Bonnie Walker
Texas ASCD
Houston, Texas

Karen Doyle Walton, Ed.D.
Allentown College of
Saint Francis de Sales
Center Valley, Pennsylvania

Contents

Tools of Algebra

Connections
and Applications

. . . and More!

CHAPTER 2 Functions and Their Graphs

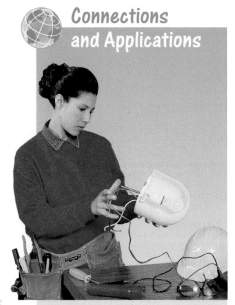

Algebraic Concepts and Simple Equations

Connections and Applications

. . . and More!

Equations and Inequalities

Connections and Applications

. . . and More!

Chapter Project
No Sweat!
Creating an Exercise Plan

Graphing and Writing Linear Equations

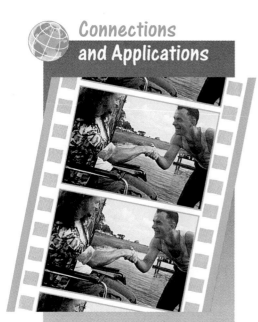

**Connections
and Applications**

. . . and More!

Systems of Equations and Inequalities

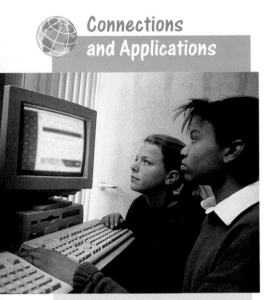

Connections and Applications

CHAPTER
7

Quadratic Equations and Functions

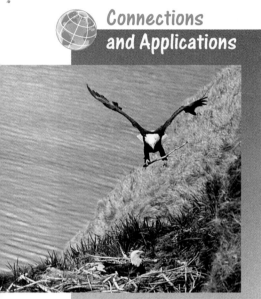

Connections and Applications

Exponents and Exponential Functions

Connections
and Applications

. . . and More!

NEW YORK
MATH A

Right Triangles and Radical Expressions

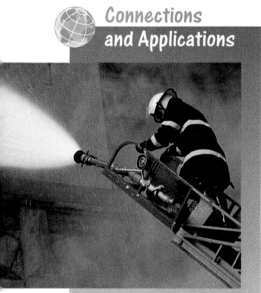

Connections and Applications

CHAPTER

10 Polynomials

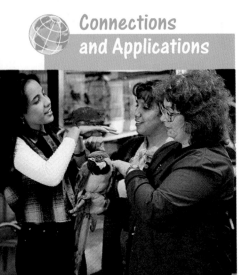

Connections and Applications

Rational Expressions and Functions

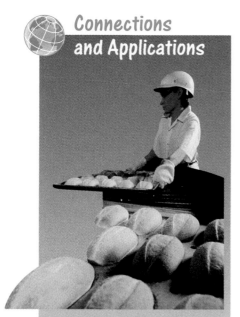

Connections
and Applications

. . . and More!

Chapter Project **Good Vibrations**
Examining and Creating Musical Pitch

To the Student

Students like you helped Prentice Hall develop this program. They identified tools you can use to help you learn now in this course and beyond. In this special "To the Student" section and throughout this program, you will find the **tools you need to help you succeed.** We'd like to hear how these tools work for you. Write us at Prentice Hall Mathematics, 160 Gould Street, Needham, MA 02494 or visit us at http://www.phschool.com.

"... Instead of problem after problem of pointless numbers, we should have a chance to think and to truly understand what we are doing. I personally think that we all should be taught this way."

Chris, Grade 9
Carson City, NV

"... I like to review what I learn as I go, rather than cramming the night before a test."

Ali, Grade 10
St. Paul, MN

"... I learn mathematics best when I draw a diagram or make a graph that helps show what the problem is that I will solve."

Amy, Grade 11
Columbia, SC

LEARN About Learning!

What comes to your mind when you hear the word **style**? Maybe it's hair style, or style of dress, or walking style. Have you ever thought about your learning style? Just like your hair or your clothes or your walk, everybody has a learning style that they like best because it works best for them. Look around you now. What do you see? Different styles … some like yours, some different from yours. That's the way it is with learning styles, too.

What's Your Best Learning Style?

I understand math concepts best when I...

❑ **A.** Read about them.

❑ **B.** Look at and make illustrations, graphs, and charts that show them.

❑ **C.** Draw sketches or handle manipulatives to explore them.

❑ **D.** Listen to someone explain them.

When I study, I learn more when I...

❑ **A.** Review my notes and the textbook.

❑ **B.** Study any graphs, charts, diagrams, or other illustrations.

❑ **C.** Write ideas on note cards; then study the ideas.

❑ **D.** Explain what I know to another person.

When I collaborate with a group, I am most comfortable when I...

❑ **A.** Take notes.

❑ **B.** Make visuals for display.

❑ **C.** Demonstrate what I know to others.

❑ **D.** Give presentations to other groups or the whole class.

Look for a pattern in your responses.

"A" responses suggest that you learn best by reading;

"B" responses indicate a visual learning style;

"C" responses suggest a tactile, or hands-on, learning style;

"D" responses signal that you probably learn best by listening and talking about what you are learning.

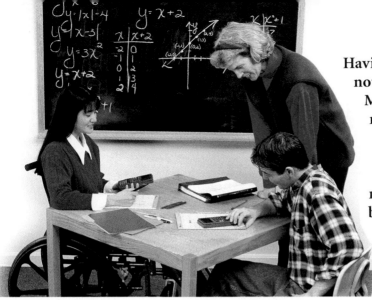

Having a preferred learning style does not limit you to using just that one. Most people learn by using a combination of learning styles. You'll be amazed by the ways that knowing more about yourself and how you learn will help you be successful — not only successful in mathematics, but successful in all your subject areas. When you know how you learn best, you will be well equipped to enter the work place.

Use this chart to help you strengthen your different learning styles.

Learning Style	Learning Tips
Learning by **reading**	✳ Schedule time to read each day.
	✳ Carry a book or magazine to read during wait time.
	✳ Read what you like to read—it's OK not to finish a book.
Learning by using **visual** cues	✳ Visualize a problem situation.
	✳ Graph solutions to problems.
	✳ Let technology, such as computers and calculators, help you.
Learning by using **hands-on** exploration	✳ Make sketches when solving a problem.
	✳ Use objects to help you solve problems.
	✳ Rely on technology as a tool for exploration and discovery.
Learning by **listening and talking**	✳ Volunteer to give presentations.
	✳ Explain your ideas to a friend.
	✳ Listen intently to what others are saying.

Most important, believe in yourself and your ability to learn!

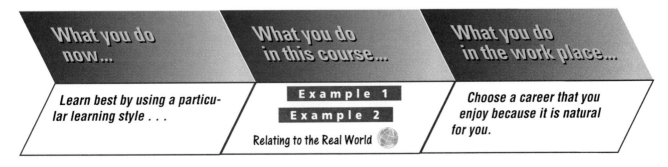

What you do now...	What you do in this course...	What you do in the work place...
Learn best by using a particular learning style . . .	**Example 1** **Example 2** Relating to the Real World 🌐	*Choose a career that you enjoy because it is natural for you.*

Help Teamwork Work for YOU!

Each of us works with other people on teams throughout our lives. What's your job? Your job on a team, that is. Maybe you play center on your basketball team, maybe you count votes for your school elections, perhaps you help decorate the gym for a school function, or maybe you help make scenery for a community play. From relay races to doing your part of the job in the work place, teamwork is required for success.

TEAMWORK CHECKLIST

☑ Break apart the large task into smaller tasks, which become the responsibility of individual group members.

☑ Treat the differences in group members as a benefit.

☑ Try to listen attentively when others speak.

☑ Stay focused on the task at hand and the goal to be accomplished.

☑ Vary the tasks you do in each group and participate.

☑ Recognize your own and others' learning styles.

☑ Offer your ideas and suggestions.

☑ Be socially responsible and act in a respectful way.

What you do now...	What you do in this course...	What you do in the work place...
Play on a team, decorate the gym, or perform in the band...	WORK TOGETHER	Collaborate with coworkers on projects.

Reading + Writing + Talking + Listening:
It's All COMMUNICATION

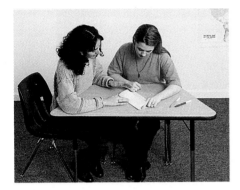

We communicate in songs. We communicate in letters. We communicate with our body movements. We communicate on the phone. We communicate in cyberspace. It's all talking about ideas and sharing what you know. It's the same in mathematics — we communicate by reading, writing, talking, and listening. Whether we are working together on a project or studying with a friend for a test, we are communicating.

Ways to Communicate What You Know and Are Able to Do

✔ Explain to others how you solve a problem.

✔ Listen carefully to others.

✔ Use mathematical language in your writing in other subjects.

✔ Pay attention to the headings in textbooks — they are signposts that help you.

✔ Think about videos and audiotapes as ways to communicate mathematical ideas.

✔ Be on the lookout for mathematics when you read, watch television, or see a movie.

✔ Communicate with others by using bulletin boards and chat rooms found on the Internet.

What you do now…

Teach a young relative a sport…

What you do in this course…

THINK AND DISCUSS

What you do in the work place…

Written and verbal communication at work.

Solving PROBLEMS — *a* SKILL You USE Every DAY

Problem solving is a skill — a skill that you probably use without even knowing it. When you think critically in social studies to draw conclusions about pollution and its stress on the environment, or when a mechanic listens to symptoms of trouble and logically determines the cause, you are both using a mathematical problem-solving skill. Problem solving also involves logical reasoning, wise decision making, and reflecting on our solutions.

Tips for Problem Solving

Recognize that there is more than one way to solve most problems.

When solving a word problem, read it, decide what to do, make a plan, look back at the problem, and revise your answer.

Experiment with various solution methods.

Understand that it is just as important to know how to solve a problem as it is to actually solve it.

Be aware of times you are using mathematics to solve problems that do not involve computation, such as when you reason to make a wise decision.

What you do now...	What you do in this course...	What you do in the work place...
Make decisions based on changing conditions, such as weather...	PROBLEM SOLVING	*Synchronize the timing of traffic lights to enhance traffic flow.*

Studying for the TEST — Whatever It May Be

SATs, ACTs, chapter tests, and weekly quizzes — they all test what you know and are able to do. Have you ever thought about **how** you can take these tests to your advantage? You are evaluated now in your classes and you will be evaluated when you hold a job.

Pointers for Gaining Points

◆ Study as you progress through a chapter, instead of cramming for a test.

◆ Recognize when you are lost and seek help before a test.

◆ Review important graphs and other visuals when studying for a test, then picture them in your mind.

◆ Study for a test with a friend or study group.

◆ Take a practice test.

◆ Think of mnemonic devices to help you, such as **P**lease **E**xcuse **M**y **D**ear **A**unt **S**ally, which is one way to remember order of operations (**p**arentheses, **e**xponents, **m**ultiply, **d**ivide, **a**dd, **s**ubtract).

◆ Reread test questions before answering them.

◆ Check to see if your answer is reasonable.

◆ Think positively and visualize yourself doing well on the test.

◆ Relax during the test… there is nothing there that you have not seen before.

What you do now...	What you do in this course...	What you do in the work place...
Study notes in preparation for tests and quizzes...	**How am I doing?** SELF ASSESSMENT	*Prepare for and participate in a job interview.*
	Exercises ON YOUR OWN	
	Exercises CHECKPOINT	

Relating to the Real World

Algebra is the basic language of mathematics. With algebra, you can describe and predict relationships about money, population, temperature, size—anything that uses numbers. Algebra saves time!
Architects use algebra to design before they build, computers use the shorthand of algebra, and every time you use a formula, so do you.

Displaying Data Relationships with Graphs	*Modeling Relationships with Variables*	*Order of Operations*	*Adding and Subtracting Integers*	*Multiplying and Dividing Integers*

Lessons	1-1	1-2	1-3	1-4	1-5

The BIG DIG!

Y our bones tell a lot
about your body.
Archaeologists and forensic scientists
study bones to estimate a person's
height, build, and age. These data are
helpful in learning about ancient people
and in solving crimes. The lengths of
major bones such as the humerus,
radius, or tibia can be substituted into
formulas to find a person's height.

As you work through the chapter, you
will collect data about bones from your
classmates and from adults. You will use
formulas to analyze the data and predict
heights. Then you will decide how to
organize and display your results in
graphs and spreadsheets.

humerus
radius
tibia

To help you complete the project:

Real Numbers and Rational Numbers	*Experimental Probability and Simulations*	*Organizing Data in Matrices*	*Variables and Formulas in Spreadsheets*
1-6	1-7	1-8	1-9

What You'll Learn

- Finding the mean, median, and mode of sets of data
- Drawing and interpreting graphs

...And Why

To analyze real-world data, such as age and employment statistics

1-1 Displaying Data Relationships with Graphs

WORK TOGETHER

Work in groups.

Line plots are simple graphs that help you see the relationship between data items. At the right is the start of a line plot for data collected on birth months of a group of students. Each × represents one student.

Birth Month Line Plot
```
 X
 X           X
 X    X      X
Jan. Feb. Mar.
```

1. What do you think a line plot for the birth months of the students in your class would look like?

2. **a.** Data Collection Find the birth month of each student in your group. Share this information with other groups.
   b. Draw a line plot of your class data.
   c. Does the line plot of your class data look similar to what you expected? Explain.

THINK AND DISCUSS

Finding Mean, Median, and Mode

You can use a line plot or *histogram* to show the frequency, or number of times, a data item occurs. The data item with the greatest frequency is the **mode.**

Birth Months of Presidents of the United States

There are no spaces between the bars in a histogram.

3. What is the mode of the data in the histogram above?

4. In which months were the fewest Presidents born?

5. **a.** Draw a histogram of the data you collected in the Work Together.
   b. Can you predict birth-month patterns for all the people in the United States based on your class data? Why or why not?

6. What is the mode (or modes) of your class data?

Mount Rushmore in South Dakota has carvings of four Presidents: Washington, Jefferson, T. Roosevelt, and Lincoln. Washington's head is as tall as a five-story building.

Age When Elected

First Presidents	Recent Presidents
Washington—57	Ford—61
J. Adams—61	Carter—52
Jefferson—57	Reagan—69
Madison—57	Bush—64
Monroe—58	Clinton—46

Do you think that the ages of the Presidents have changed a lot since the beginning of the United States in 1776? One way to find out is to compare the mean ages of the first Presidents with those of recent Presidents. Use this ratio to find the mean.

$$\text{Mean} = \frac{\text{sum of the data items}}{\text{total number of data items}}$$

7. **a.** Find the mean of each group of ages.
   b. Has there been much change in the mean age of the Presidents? Explain.

8. Would the mode be as useful as the mean in comparing the ages of the first Presidents to recent Presidents? Explain.

A third type of measure is the median. The **median** is the middle value in an ordered set of numbers. The mean, median, and mode may give a different picture of data—sometimes slightly different, sometimes very different.

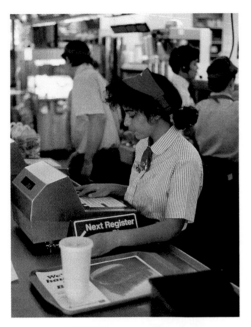

QUICK REVIEW

You can indicate multiplication of two numbers in any of these ways:

6(5.25)   (6)(5.25)
6 · 5.25   6 × 5.25

Example 1   Relating to the Real World

Jobs Find the mean, median, and mode of the data below.

What Employees Earn at a Local Fast Food Restaurant

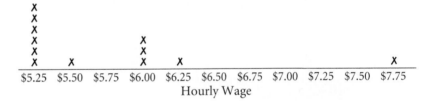

You can multiply 6 times 5.25 as a shortcut for adding 5.25 + 5.25 + 5.25 + 5.25 + 5.25 + 5.25.

Mean: $\dfrac{6(5.25) + 5.50 + 3(6.00) + 6.25 + 7.75}{12} = 5.75$

total number of employees

Median: 5.25 5.25 5.25 5.25 5.25 5.25 5.50 6.00 6.00 6.00 6.25 7.75

For an even number of data items, find the mean of the middle terms. $\dfrac{5.25 + 5.50}{2} \approx 5.38$

Mode: 5.25 ◀— the data item that occurs most often

The mean is $5.75/h. The median is about $5.38/h.

The mode is $5.25/h.

9. **Try This** Suppose the worker earning $7.75/h resigns. Her replacement earns $5.75/h. How does this change affect the mode? the median? the mean?

10. *Critical Thinking* Does the mean, median, or mode best describe the set of wages in the line plot? **Justify** your answer.

Drawing and Interpreting Graphs

Bar graphs are useful when you wish to compare amounts. Whenever you make a graph to display data, you must choose an appropriate scale so that the graph is neither too big for your paper nor too small to read.

> **Example 2** Relating to the Real World
>
> *Social Studies* Draw a multiple bar graph for the median income data.

Median Household Income				
	1987	1989	1991	1993
Calif.	$37,231	$37,348	$34,677	$33,083
Conn.	$40,586	$47,884	$43,423	$38,369
Ind.	$27,812	$29,302	$27,904	$28,618
Tex.	$30,531	$29,289	$28,568	$27,892
Utah	$32,764	$34,755	$28,859	$34,746

Source: *U. S. Bureau of the Census*

The highest projected income is $47,884. So a reasonable range for the vertical scale is from 0 to $50,000 with every $5000 labeled on the axis.

To draw a bar on the graph, estimate its placement based on the vertical scale. The value $37,231 is a little less than $\frac{1}{2}$ the distance from $35,000 to $40,000.

A multiple bar graph must include a key.

11. **Try This** Suppose you were drawing a graph of the data. How would you estimate where to put the top of the bar showing the median income for Texas in 1991?

12. Why is the key necessary for the graph above?

13. **a.** Which states decreased in median income for each of the last two years shown on the graph?
    b. Did you use the table or the graph to answer part (a)? Why?

14. Critical Thinking The United States had an economic recession in the late 1980s and early 1990s. Which states seemed to be least affected by the recession? Explain.

Line graphs allow you to see how a set of data changes over time. You can use line graphs to look for trends in data.

Example 3 **Relating to the Real World**

Aluminum Soft Drink Cans (in billions)		
Year	Manufactured	Recycled
1989	45.7	27.8
1990	49.2	31.3
1991	53.0	33.0
1992	54.9	37.3
1993	58.0	36.6

Source: *Can Manufacturing Institute*

Recycling Make a double line graph of the table at the left.

The least and greatest numbers in the chart are 27.8 and 58.0. A reasonable vertical scale is from 20 to 60 with every 10 units labeled on the axis.

The zigzag line shows a break where an unused portion of the scale is not shown.

15. a. Describe the trend for the number of cans manufactured.
 b. Describe the trend for the number of cans recycled.

16. a. Critical Thinking Suppose you draw the graph without a break in the vertical scale. How would this affect the way the graph looks?
 b. Would drawing the graph without a break in the scale improve the graph? Why or why not?

17. Critical Thinking From 1989–1993, did the amount of waste from soft drink cans increase, decrease, or stay the same? Explain.

Exercises **ON YOUR OWN**

1. An interviewer asked 25 people, "How many children live in your home?" Here are their responses.
2, 1, 3, 0, 4, 2, 2, 1, 0, 3, 2, 6, 4,
3, 3, 2, 1, 1, 3, 0, 0, 2, 1, 1, 2
 a. Draw a line plot for the data. Include a title for the line plot.
 b. Find the mean, median, and mode of the data.

2. **a.** Entertainment Use the data about television viewing to draw a double line graph.
   b. What trend do you see in the total number of households viewing the top-rated program?
   c. What trend do you see in the number of households with TV?
   d. Critical Thinking What could explain the differing trends you see in your graph?

3. Standardized Test Prep Suppose your mean on four literature tests is 78. Which score would raise the mean to 80?
   A. 95   **B.** 80   **C.** 100   **D.** 88   **E.** not possible

TV Viewing 1970–1990 (in millions)

Year	Total Viewing Top-Rated Program	Households with TV
1970	28.0	60.1
1975	30.3	71.5
1980	41.5	77.8
1985	39.4	84.9
1990	39.0	92.1

Source: *Nielsen Media Research*

Find the mean, median, and mode of each set of data. Round to the nearest tenth.

4. 2, 6, 3, 2, 4

5. 10, 10, 20, 0

6. 80, 90, 85, 80, 90, 90, 40, 85

7. 25, 25, 25, 25

8. 22, 23, 28, 33, 24, 27, 24, 26, 23, 26, 25, 29, 21, 30

9. 35.2, 42.6, 41.0, 37.2, 34.5, 35.0, 36.8, 41.0, 37.9, 42.1, 41.5

10. **a.** Recording Industry Use a triple bar graph or a triple line graph to display the data at the right.
    b. Why did you choose the type of graph you did?
    c. Which type of music showed the most growth in sales over the six-year period? **Justify** your answer.

11. **a.** Sports The median height of the 21 players on a girls' soccer team is 5 ft 7 in. What is the greatest possible number of girls who are less than 5 ft 7 in. tall?
    b. Critical Thinking Suppose three girls are 5 ft 7 in. tall. How would this change your answer to part (a)? Explain.

12. **a.** Agriculture What trend do you see in the graph showing the number of farms in the United States?
    b. What trend do you see in the graph showing the average size of farms in the United States?
    c. Writing Do you think the two trends are related? Explain.

Recording Industry Sales (in millions of dollars)

Year	Rock	Country	Jazz
1989	$2823	$447	$375
1990	$2722	$724	$362
1991	$2726	$1003	$298
1992	$2852	$1570	$313
1993	$3034	$1879	$311
1994	$4236	$1967	$362

Source: *Recording Industry Association of America*

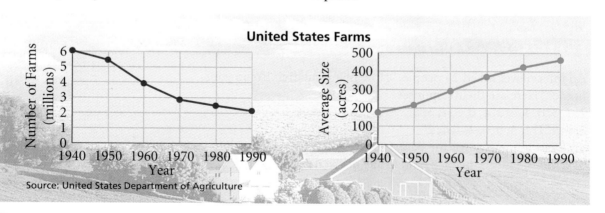

United States Farms

Source: United States Department of Agriculture

13. Languages Do Spanish words have more letters than English words? Compare the word lengths in the following excerpt from the Preamble to the United Nations Charter.

> We the peoples of the United Nations determined to save succeeding generations from the scourge of war, which twice in our lifetime has brought untold sorrow to mankind, and
>   To reaffirm faith in fundamental human rights, in the dignity and worth of the human person, in the equal rights of men and women and of nations large and small . . . have resolved to combine our efforts to accomplish these aims.

> Nosotros los pueblos de las Naciones Unidas resueltos a preservar a las generaciones venideras del flagelo de la guerra que dos veces durante nuestra vida ha infligido a la Humanidad sufrimientos indecibles,
>   a reafirmar la fe en los derechos fundamentales del hombre, en la dignidad y el valor de la persona humana, en la igualdad de derechos de hombres y mujeres y de las naciones grandes y pequeñas . . . hemos decidido aunar nuestros esfuerzos para realizar estos designios.

a. For each version, draw a line plot of word lengths.
b. Find the mean, median, and mode of the data in each line plot.
c. **Writing** Which language do you think has the longer word length? **Justify** your answer.

Open-ended Create a set of data for the given mean, median, and mode.

14. mean = 10, median = 10, mode = 10

15. mean = 100, median = 80, mode = 70

16. mean = 3, median = 2, no mode

17. mean = 5, median = 5, mode = 8 and 3

Chapter Project ▼ **Find Out by Graphing**

• Measure the length of your radius bone to the nearest half inch.

• Collect the data for the class, and display the data in a graph.

• Find the mean, median, and mode for the data you collected. Write a description of the data.

Exercises   MIXED REVIEW

Write as a decimal, a fraction or mixed number, and a percent.

18. $\frac{5}{8}$ **19.** 40%   **20.** 0.75   **21.** 25%   **22.** 4.6   **23.** $1\frac{4}{5}$

24. Open-ended Suppose a pair of shoes costs $25, a shirt costs $15, and a pair of pants costs $30. You have a budget of $100 and the sales tax is 6%. How many of each item would you buy? Explain.

Getting Ready for Lesson 1-2
Write the next three numbers in each pattern.

25. 1, 3, 5, ▦, ▦, ▦   **26.** 28, 25, 22, ▦, ▦, ▦   **27.** 4, 12, 36, ▦, ▦, ▦

Stem-and-Leaf Plots

After Lesson 1-1

For a class project, a student gathered data from her classmates. She made this request: "Tomorrow morning, find out how many minutes it takes you to get ready—from the time you get up until the time you leave your house for school." Here are the responses:

47 28 78 47 58 93 34 76 35 72 45 53 23

43 75 27 23 87 33 43 25 35 49 35 48 37 28

You can use a *stem-and-leaf plot* to give you a better picture of this information. A stem-and-leaf plot displays the data items in order. The digit (or digits) to the left is the *stem*. The digit farthest to the right is the *leaf*.

stem   leaf

For Exercises 1–4, use the stem-and-leaf plot at the right.

1. How many students responded?

2. What does the stem 2 and leaf 8 represent?

3. How many students took more than 50 min to get ready in the morning?

4. a. Explain how you would use the stem-and-leaf plot to find the median and the mode of the data.
   b. What is the median? the mode?

Time to Get Ready						
2	3	3	5	7	8	8
3	3	4	5	5	5	7
4	3	3	5	7	7	8 9
5	3	8				
6						
7	2	5	6	8		
8	7					
9	3					

key: 2|3 means 23 min

5. Consider the data on notebook prices.
   a. What would be the stems for the notebook data?
   b. What would be the key?
   c. Make a stem-and-leaf plot for this set of data.
   d. Find the median and mode of this set of data.

Notebook Prices			
$2.00	$2.50	$2.25	$2.50
$2.29	$1.97	$2.16	$2.49
$2.21	$2.36	$2.09	$1.95
$2.05	$2.57	$2.40	$1.99

6. **Writing** The two graphs below display the information on the time it takes to get ready in the morning. Compare the graphs with the stem-and-leaf plot. Describe the advantages and disadvantages of using each to display the data.

What You'll Learn

1-2

Modeling Relationships with Variables

- Describing relationships between sets of data
- Using variables as a shorthand way to express relationships

...And Why

To model relationships in areas such as geometry, music, and sales

T H I N K   A N D   D I S C U S S

Geometry The band Numerica is designing a stage to use in its new music video. Their set designer made the sketches shown below.

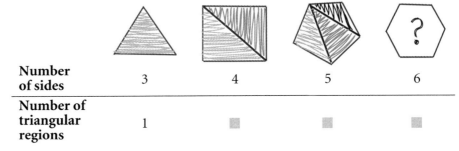

Number of sides	3	4	5	6
Number of triangular regions	1	▨	▨	▨

1. Use the sketches to help you complete the table.

2. **Analyze** the data in the table. What relationship do you see between the number of sides a stage has and the number of triangular regions created by the line segments?

3. Numerica plans to use a 12-sided stage. How many triangular regions can the designer form with the segments starting at one corner?

You could use the letter *s* to represent the number of sides of the stage. Since *s* can change in value, it is a **variable.** A **variable expression** is a mathematical phrase that contains at least one variable. The variable expression $s - 2$ is a short way to represent the number of triangular regions created by the segments.

4. Could you use a letter other than *s* to represent the number of sides of the stage? Explain.

terms

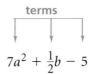

$$7a^2 + \tfrac{1}{2}b - 5$$

QUICK REVIEW

7a is a short way to write
$7 \times a$ or $7 \cdot a$.

Variable expressions are made up of one or more terms. A **term** is a number, a variable, or the product of numbers and variables.

5. How many terms does the expression $7a^2 + \tfrac{1}{2}b - 5$ have?

6. How many terms does the expression $s - 2$ have?

You can use variable expressions to write an equation. The **equation** $t = s - 2$ indicates that the two expressions t and $s - 2$ are equal.

Example 1   Relating to the Real World

Music   Each CD at Track One Records costs $12. Write an equation you can use to find the total cost when you know the number of CDs bought.

The plan below shows how you can go from a word problem to a short statement of the problem using variables.

Relate   The total cost is 12 times the number of CDs bought.

cost is 12 times a number

$$c = 12 \cdot n$$

$$c = 12n$$

7. What do the variables c and n represent in Example 1?

8. A worker at Track One Records says that 5 CDs cost $125 because $c = 12n$ and $n = 5$. Explain the worker's error.

9. Try This Suppose the manager at Track One Records raises the price of CDs to $15. Write an equation to find the cost of n CDs.

10. Suppose the manager at Track One Records uses the equation $c = 10.99n$. What does this mean?

Before writing an equation for data in a table, it is helpful to write a short sentence describing the relationship between the data. Then translate the sentence to an equation. Be sure to tell what each variable represents.

Example 2   Relating to the Real World

Sales   Write an equation for the data in the table.

Define c = cost of items purchased
          a = amount of change

Relate   Amount of change equals $20.00 minus cost of items purchased.

Write a =   20   − c

$$a = 20 - c$$

Change from a $20 Bill

Cost of Items Purchased	Amount of Change
$20.00	$0
$19.00	$1.00
$17.50	$2.50
$11.59	$8.41

11. Could you define the variables after writing the sentence describing the relationship between the data? Explain.

12. In Example 2, could the letter c represent the cost and also represent the change? Why or why not?

13. Suppose you wrote "The cost of items plus the amount of change equals $20" for the relationship between the data in the table. Model this statement with an equation.

State the number of terms in each expression.

1. $3x + 5y - 12$
2. $9x^3 + 2x^2 + 5x + 7$
3. $\frac{2}{5}y - 4$
4. 15

5. Open-ended Write an expression that has four terms.

6. Writing Use an example to explain the meaning of *variable*.

Use an equation to model each situation.

7. Total cost equals number of cans times $.70.

8. The perimeter of a square equals four times a side.

9. The total amount of rope, in feet, used to put up scout tents is 60 times the number of tents.

10. What is the number of slices of pizza left from an 8-slice pizza after you have eaten some slices?

Use an equation to model the relationship in each table.

11.

Hours	Distance
1	50 mi
2	100 mi
3	150 mi
4	200 mi

12.

Hours	Pay
4	$24
6	$36
8	$48
10	$60

13.

Days	Growth
1	0.165 in.
2	0.330 in.
3	0.495 in.
4	0.660 in.

14.

Tapes	Cost
1	$8.50
2	$17.00
3	$25.50
4	$34.00

15.

Workers	Radios
1	13
2	26
3	39
4	52

16.

Earned	Saved
$15	$7.50
$20	$10.00
$25	$12.50
$30	$15.00

17.

Number of Sales	Total Earnings
5	$2.00
10	$4.00
15	$6.00
20	$8.00

18.

Time (months)	Length (inches)
1	4.1
2	8.2
3	12.3
4	16.4

19. Open-ended Choose one table from Exercises 11–18. Describe a situation for which the data is reasonable.

20. Does each statement fit the data at the right? Explain.
   a. hours worked = lawns mowed · 2
   b. hours worked = lawns mowed + 3

Lawns Mowed	Hours
1	
2	
3	6

21. a. Which statement in Exercise 20 better describes the relationship between hours worked and lawns mowed? Explain.
   b. Use your answer to part (a). Copy and complete the table. How many hours would it take to mow 5 lawns?

Use the table at the right for Exercises 22 and 23. The table shows the result when a ball is dropped from different heights.

22. **a.** Write an equation to describe the relationship between the height of the first bounce and the drop height.
   b. Suppose you drop the ball from a window 20 ft above the ground. **Predict** how high the ball will bounce.

23. Suppose the second bounce is $\frac{1}{4}$ of the original drop height. Write an equation to represent the height of the second bounce.

Drop Height (ft)	Height of First Bounce (ft)
1	$\frac{1}{2}$
2	1
3	$1\frac{1}{2}$
4	2
5	$2\frac{1}{2}$

5 ft

$2\frac{1}{2}$ ft

24. *Standardized Test Prep* Compare the quantities in Column A and Column B.

Column A	Column B
the total cost of items bought by a customer	the change the customer receives when paying with a $10 bill

   A. The quantity in Column A is greater.
   B. The quantity in Column B is greater.
   C. The quantities are equal.
   D. The relationship cannot be determined from the information given.

25. **a.** Write an equation to show how the amount of money in a bag of quarters relates to the number of quarters in the bag.
   b. The bag contains 13 quarters. How much money is this?

Exercises   M I X E D   R E V I E W

26. For a project, a student asked 25 classmates the number of television news programs they watched in a week. She recorded these results:

   3 5 1 4 2 0 4 5 3 6 5 5
   2 0 0 1 2 5 3 1 1 4 6 3 1

   a. Make a histogram of the data.
   b. Find the mean, median, and mode(s) of the data.

27. List four prime numbers between 20 and 50.

28. Write the prime factorization of 105.

> **SELF ASSESSMENT**
>
> **FOR YOUR JOURNAL**
>
> Write a paragraph explaining what variables are and how you use them to model the relationship between sets of data.

Getting Ready for Lesson 1-3
Find the value of each expression.

29. $3 + 12 - 7$ 30. $4 \cdot 3 - 5$ 31. $15 \div 3 + 2$ 32. $6 \cdot 1 \div 2$ 33. $4 - 2 + 9$

What You'll Learn

- Using the order of operations
- Evaluating variable expressions

...And Why

To find the total cost of items with tax

What You'll Need

- calculator

Who? Astronaut Ellen Ochoa served on space flights in 1993 and 1994. She studied the solar corona and the effect of solar changes on Earth's environment.

1-3 Order of Operations

WORK TOGETHER

Work with a partner.

Geometry Two formulas for the perimeter of a rectangle are $P = 2l + 2w$ and $P = 2(l + w)$.

1. Let $l = 12$ and $w = 8$. Find the perimeter of the rectangle using each formula.

2. When you used the formula $P = 2l + 2w$, did you add first or did you multiply first?

3. When you used the formula $P = 2(l + w)$, did you add first or did you multiply first?

4. Which formula do you prefer to use? Why?

THINK AND DISCUSS

Evaluating Expressions

In the Work Together activity, you used your past experience to simplify the expressions to find the perimeter. Look at this new expression and the two ways that it has been simplified.

$$3 + 5 - 6 \div 2$$
$$8 - 6 \div 2$$
$$2 \div 2$$
$$1 \longleftarrow \text{Different results!}$$

$$3 + 5 - 6 \div 2$$
$$3 + 5 - 3$$
$$8 - 3$$
$$5 \longleftarrow \text{This one is correct.}$$

To avoid having two results for the same problem, mathematicians have agreed on an order for doing the operations when simplifying.

QUICK REVIEW

An **exponent** indicates repeated multiplication.

$$\text{base} \longrightarrow 3^4 = \underbrace{3 \cdot 3 \cdot 3 \cdot 3}$$

The base 3 is used as a factor four times.

You read 3^4 as "three to the fourth power."

Order of Operations

1. Perform any operation(s) inside grouping symbols.

2. Simplify any term with exponents.

3. Multiply and divide in order from left to right.

4. Add and subtract in order from left to right.

5. Which operation should you do first to simplify each expression?
   a. $3 + 6 \cdot 4 \div 2$ **b.** $3 \cdot 6 - 4^2$ **c.** $3 \cdot (6 - 4) \div 2$

You **evaluate** an expression with variables by substituting a number for each variable. Then simplify the expression using the order of operations.

Example 1 — Relating to the Real World

Sales Find the total cost of the sneakers shown in the ad. Use the expression at the right.

$$p + r \cdot p = 59 + (0.06)59 \quad \longleftarrow \text{Substitute 59 for } p. \text{ Change 6\% to 0.06 and substitute 0.06 for } r.$$
$$= 59 + 3.54 \quad \longleftarrow \text{Multiply first.}$$
$$= 62.54 \quad \longleftarrow \text{Then add.}$$

The total cost of the sneakers is $62.54.

6. Calculator Some calculators have the order of operations programmed into them. To check your calculator, use the key sequence below. Does your calculator use the order of operations? Explain.

59 [+] .06 [×] 59 [=]

Keep in mind that the base for an exponent is the number, variable, or expression directly to the left of the exponent.

Example 2

Evaluate $3a^2 - 12 \div b$ for $a = 7$ and $b = 4$.

$$3a^2 - 12 \div b = 3 \cdot 7^2 - 12 \div 4 \quad \longleftarrow \text{Substitute 7 for } a \text{ and 4 for } b.$$
$$= 3 \cdot 49 - 12 \div 4 \quad \longleftarrow \text{Simplify } 7^2.$$
$$= 147 - 3 \quad \longleftarrow \text{Multiply and divide from left to right.}$$
$$= 144 \quad \longleftarrow \text{Subtract.}$$

7. A student evaluated the expression above for $a = 8$ and $b = 6$. Her result is 94. Is her answer correct? If not, what error did she make?

8. Try This Evaluate $25 \div p + 2q^2$ for $p = 5$ and $q = 7$.

Example 3

Evaluate each expression for $c = 15$ and $d = 12$.

a. cd^2

$$cd^2 = 15(12)^2$$
$$= 15(144)$$
$$= 2160$$

b. $(cd)^2$

$$(cd)^2 = (15 \cdot 12)^2$$
$$= (180)^2$$
$$= 32{,}400$$

9. Write an expression for each phrase. Then simplify your expression.
a. four times three, squared
b. the square of three, times four

For practice with exponents, see Skills Handbook page 590.

CALCULATOR HINT

In part (b), you can use two different key sequences to find 180^2:

180 [x^2] [ENTER] or

180 [∧] 2 [ENTER] .

Evaluating Expressions With Grouping Symbols

When you evaluate expressions work within the parentheses first. A fraction bar is also a grouping symbol. Do any calculations above or below a fraction bar before simplifying the fraction.

Example 4   **Relating to the Real World** ·············

Community Students participating in a neighborhood clean-up project are cleaning a vacant lot, which has the shape of a trapezoid. They plan to turn the vacant lot into a park. Use the expression $h\left(\dfrac{b_1 + b_2}{2}\right)$ to find the lot's area.

$b_1 = 100$ ft

$h = 150$ ft

$b_2 = 290$ ft

$$h\left(\dfrac{b_1 + b_2}{2}\right) = 150\left(\dfrac{100 + 290}{2}\right) \quad \longleftarrow \text{ Substitute 150 for } h, \text{ 100 for } b_1,$$
$$\text{and 290 for } b_2.$$
$$= 150\left(\dfrac{390}{2}\right) \quad \longleftarrow \text{ Simplify the numerator.}$$
$$= 150(195) \quad \longleftarrow \text{ Simplify the fraction.}$$
$$= 29{,}250$$

The area of the lot is 29,250 ft².

PROBLEM SOLVING

Look Back You can also use the expression $\frac{1}{2}h(b_1 + b_2)$ to find the area of a trapezoid. Explain why $h(\frac{b_1 + b_2}{2})$ is equivalent to $\frac{1}{2}h(b_1 + b_2)$.

10. Would the result be the same if you substituted 290 for b_1 and 100 for b_2? Why or why not?

11. Describe the steps you would use to simplify $\dfrac{12 + 18}{3 + 9}$.

12. Explain the difference in the meaning of the expressions $5\frac{1}{6}$ and $5\left(\frac{1}{6}\right)$.

You can also use brackets [ ] as grouping symbols. When an expression has several grouping symbols, simplify the innermost expression first.

13. Try This Simplify each expression.
  a. $5[4^2 + 3(2 + 1)]$ **b.** $12 + 3[18 + 5(16 - 3^2)]$

Exercises   O N   Y O U R   O W N

Simplify each numerical expression.

1. $18 + 20 \div 4$

2. $(2.4 - 1.6) \div 0.4$

3. $\dfrac{6 \cdot 2 - 1}{9 + 2}$

4. $(5^2 - 3)6$

5. $(10 - 2)^2$

6. $6\left(\dfrac{4 + 10}{2}\right)$

7. $24.6 \div 2 \cdot 4.1$

8. $25 - [2(3 + 7)]$

9. $3 \cdot 5^2$

10. $(3 \cdot 5)^2$

11. $(5^2 + 3) \div 2$

12. $\dfrac{(2 + 3)^2}{2}$

13. Open-ended Write an expression that includes addition, subtraction, multiplication, and parentheses. Simplify your expression.

14. a. *Geometry* What is the volume of the juice can at the right? The formula for the volume of a cylinder is $V = \pi r^2 h$.
   b. About how many cubic inches does an ounce of juice fill?

Juice
12 oz.
$r = 1.4$ in.
$\leftarrow h = 5$ in.$\rightarrow$

Evaluate each expression.

15. $a - 7 \cdot 2$ for $a = 15$

16. $\dfrac{q}{q + 8}$ for $q = 4$

17. $r + 2s$ for $r = 5.2$ and $s = 3.8$

18. $5a^2 - 4$ for $a = 3$

19. $2b^2 + 4b$ for $b = 6.3$

20. $(5x)^2$ for $x = 3$

21. $2\left(\dfrac{5d - 6}{3}\right)$ for $d = 9$

22. $[(5.2 + a) + 4]10$ for $a = 3.5$

23. $\dfrac{m^2}{m + 9}$ for $m = 6$

Use grouping symbols to make each equation true.

24. $10 + 6 \div 2 - 3 = 5$

25. $14 - 2 + 5 - 3 = 4$

26. $8 + 4 \div 3 - 1 = 10$

27. *Critical Thinking* Use the problem solving strategy *Guess and Test* to find two values of n that make the equation $2n = n^2$ true.

28. a. *Entertainment* You can use the expression $2.4t + 0.779$ to model the number of subscribers, in millions, to cable television. Copy and complete the table.
   b. *Statistics* Use your table to draw a line graph.

Cable TV Subscribers (in millions)

Year	Subscribers
1970 ($t = 0$)	▪
1980 ($t = 10$)	▪
1990 ($t = 20$)	▪
2000 ($t = 30$)	▪

Writing Tell if each equation is *true* or *false*. If false, use the order of operations to explain why.

29. $3(2^3) = 6^3$

30. $2^4 = (1 + 1)^4$

31. $(4 + 5)^2 = 4^2 + 5^2$

32. *Calculator* Which key sequence could you use to simplify $\dfrac{3 + 8^2}{5}$? Explain why your choice works and the other choices do not.

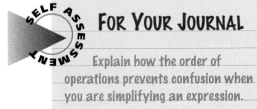

A. ⦗ 3 ⊞ 8 ⦘ ∧ 2 ÷ 5 ENTER   **B.** 3 ⊞ 8 ∧ 2 ÷ 5 ENTER

C. ⦗ 3 ⊞ 8 ∧ 2 ⦘ ÷ 5 ENTER   **D.** ⦗ 3 ⊞ 8 ÷ 5 ∧ 2 ⦘ ENTER

Exercises   M I X E D   R E V I E W

Write each fraction as a fraction or mixed number in simplest form.

33. $\dfrac{4}{6}$ **34.** $\dfrac{15}{10}$ **35.** $\dfrac{27}{6}$ **36.** $\dfrac{9}{12}$ **37.** $\dfrac{12}{15}$

Getting Ready for Lesson 1-4

Use the number line at the right.

38. What number corresponds to point A on the number line?

39. How far is B from zero?   **40.** How far is D from zero?

41. How far is C from zero?   **42.** How far is A from D?

A B C D
-5 0 5

SELF ASSESSMENT

FOR YOUR JOURNAL

Explain how the order of operations prevents confusion when you are simplifying an expression.

What You'll Learn

- Adding and subtracting with integers and decimals
- Finding absolute value
- Evaluating expressions

...And Why

To calculate with data that include negative numbers

1-4 Adding and Subtracting Integers

Science Work with a partner. Falling snow has chemical traces of the environmental events that occur each year. In 1994, scientists in Antarctica drilled a core of ice 7000 ft deep. The diagram shows some of what scientists found.

1. Draw a diagram. Place the events listed below where you think they would appear in the core of ice.
   a. 1906: San Francisco earthquake
   b. 1923: Tokyo earthquake and fires
   c. 1935–36: "Dust Bowl" of the U.S.
   d. 1986: nuclear accident at Chernobyl, in the former U.S.S.R.

2. **Open-ended** Name two other situations for which you would use negative numbers.

History in Ice

0 ft — 1994: ice surface

−26.6 ft — 1964: peak of radioactive fallout from atomic testing

−67.3 ft — 1883: eruption of Krakatoa, a volcanic island in Indonesia

Source: *Boston Globe*

Adding Integers and Decimals

A number line can help you see the relationship between numbers.

−4 is the opposite of 4.

−7 −6 −5 −4 −3 −2 −1 0 1 2 3 4 5 6 7

Two numbers are **opposites** if they are the same distance from zero on the number line. Since −4 and 4 are both a distance of 4 units from 0, they are opposites. **Integers** are whole numbers and their opposites.

QUICK REVIEW

Whole numbers are 0, 1, 2, 3 . . . .

3. **Try This** What is the opposite of 3? −5? −100? 0?

4. **Try This** Name the two integers that are a distance of 7 units from 0 on the number line.

Tiles to Represent Integers

■ 1   ■ −1

PROBLEM SOLVING

Look Back Which do you find more helpful when adding: using tiles or using a number line? Explain.

The sum of a number and its opposite, or *additive inverse*, is zero.

←— A positive tile and a negative tile make a zero pair.

$3 + (-3) = 0$

Example 1 Relating to the Real World · · · · · · · · · · · ·

Sports On two plays a football team gains 2 yd and then loses 7 yd. What is the result of the two plays? You need to find $2 + (-7)$.

Method 1: Use a number line.

Start at 0. Move right two units. ——

Then move left seven units.

−6 −5 −4 −3 −2 −1 0 1 2 3

└— The result is −5.

$2 + (-7) = -5$

Method 2: Use tiles.

Start with 2 positive tiles and 7 negative tiles.

Make zero pairs.

←— There are 5 negative tiles left.

$2 + (-7) = -5$

The result of the two plays is a loss of 5 yd.

5. Try This Use a model to find each sum.
  a. $-6 + 4$ **b.** $4 + (-6)$ **c.** $-3 + (-8)$ **d.** $9 + (-3)$

To understand the rules for addition, you need to be familiar with absolute value. The **absolute value** of a number is its distance from zero on a number line. Using symbols, you write "the absolute value of −6" as $|-6|$.

$|-5| = 5$ $|5| = 5$

←— The absolute value of a number is either zero or positive.

−6 −5 −4 −3 −2 −1 0 1 2 3 4 5 6

Absolute value symbols are also grouping symbols. Simplify expressions within absolute value symbols before finding the absolute value.

6. Try This Find the value of each expression.
  a. $|-12|$ **b.** $|2.5|$ **c.** $|-5 + 3|$ **d.** $|5 + (-5)|$

7. What is the sign of each sum?
  a. $6 + 4$ **b.** $4 + 6$ **c.** $-6 + (-4)$ **d.** $-4 + (-6)$

8. Use your answers to Question 7. When adding two numbers that have the same sign, how can you **predict** the sign of their sum?

9. For each expression below, which number has the greater absolute value? What is the sign of each sum?
  a. $6 + (-4)$ **b.** $-4 + 6$ **c.** $-6 + 4$ **d.** $4 + (-6)$

10. Use your answers to Question 9. When adding two numbers that have different signs, how can you **predict** the sign of their sum?

Addition Rules

To add two numbers with the same sign, *add* their absolute values. The sum has the same sign as the numbers.

Example: $3 + 5 = 8$ $\qquad$ $-3 + (-5) = -8$

To add two numbers with different signs, find the *difference* between their absolute values. The sum has the same sign as the number with the greater absolute value.

Example: $-3 + 5 = 2$ $\qquad$ $3 + (-5) = -2$

CALCULATOR HINT

To find $-12.5 + 4.8$, use this sequence:

(-) 12.5 + 4.8 ENTER

11. Try This Find each sum.
   a. $-12 + 4$ $\quad$ **b.** $26 + (-8)$ $\quad$ **c.** $-12.5 + 4.8$ $\quad$ **d.** $14.7 + (-8.3)$

12. Try This Evaluate each expression for $n = 3.5$.
   a. $5.2 + n$ $\quad$ **b.** $-5.2 + n$ $\quad$ **c.** $-n + 5.2$ $\quad$ **d.** $-n + (-5.2)$

Subtracting Integers and Decimals

Example 2

Find each difference.

a. $4 - 7$

Start with 4 positive tiles.

Add zero pairs until there are 7 positive tiles.

Remove 7 positive tiles.

There are 3 negative tiles left.

$4 - 7 = -3$

b. $3 - (-5)$

Start with 3 positive tiles.

Add zero pairs until there are 5 negative tiles.

Remove 5 negative tiles.

There are 8 positive tiles left.

$3 - (-5) = 8$

1 Which expression has a value of 16?
(1) $20 \div 5 + 4 \cdot 2$
(2) $4^2 \cdot 3 - 2$
(3) $21 \div 3 + (4 - 1)^2$
(4) $(7^2 - 11) \cdot 3$

2 Use an equation to model this situation: The total cost of a refrigerator is the cost of the item and the $39 delivery charge.

13. Use tiles to find each difference and sum.

    a. $2 - 6$ **b.** $5 - (-9)$ **c.** $-3 - 8$ **d.** $7 - 2$

        $2 + (-6)$ $5 + 9$ $-3 + (-8)$ $7 + (-2)$

14. Use your answers to Question 13. What do you notice about each pair of sums and differences?

The relationship you found between subtraction and addition is summarized in a rule for subtraction.

Subtraction Rule

To subtract a number, add its opposite.

Example: $3 - 5 = 3 + (-5)$
$$= -2$$

---

15. Try This Find each difference.

    a. $-6 - 2$ **b.** $8 - (-4)$ **c.** $7.1 - (-5.4)$ **d.** $11.5 - 15.6$

The expression $-n$ means the opposite of n. The expression $-n$ can represent a negative number, zero, or a positive number.

16. a. What is the value of $-n$ when $n = -4$?

    b. What is the value of $-n$ when $n = 4$?

    c. For what values of n will $-n$ be positive? negative?

Example 3

Evaluate $-a - b$ for $a = -3$ and $b = -5$.

$$-a - b = -(-3) - (-5) \quad \longleftarrow \text{Substitute –3 for } a \text{ and –5 for } b.$$
$$= \quad 3 \quad - (-5) \quad \longleftarrow \text{The opposite of –3 is 3.}$$
$$= \quad 3 \quad + \quad 5 \quad \longleftarrow \text{To subtract –5, add its opposite, 5.}$$
$$= \quad 8$$

17. Open-ended Choose negative values for a and b other than -3 and -5. Evaluate the expression in Example 3 using the values you chose.

Exercises   O N   Y O U R   O W N

1. Critical Thinking Which is greater, the sum of -227 and 319 or the sum of 227 and -319? Explain.

2. Open-ended Use a number line or tiles to show why the sum of a number and its opposite is zero.

Write *positive* or *negative* to indicate the sign of the sum or difference.

    3. $-6 + 13$ **4.** $6 - 13$ **5.** $-6 + (-13)$ **6.** $6 - (-13)$ **7.** $|-6 - 13|$

Evaluate each expression for $p = 4$ and $q = -3$.

8. $3 - q$

9. $3p - q$

10. $q - 7p$

11. $|p - 9|$

12. $|-12 + q|$

 Choose **Use a calculator, paper and pencil, or mental math to add or subtract.**

13. $-21 + (-14)$

14. $13 + (-9)$

15. $6 - (-5)$

16. $-12 + 12$

17. $-16 - 12$

18. $|-16 - 12|$

19. $|-16| - |12|$

20. $15 - 19$

21. $-18.6 - 25.3$

22. $14.4 - 19.7$

23. $|43.7 + (-45.2)|$

24. $-25.7 - (-18.3)$

25. $62.5 - 89.4$

26. $-54.1 + 99.4$

27. $|-28.2| + 17.5$

28. $-65.7 - 98.9$

Critical Thinking **Use the number line for Exercises 29 – 31.**

29. If P is the opposite of T, what is the value of S?

30. If Q is the opposite of T, is R positive or negative? Why?

31. If R is the opposite of T, which of the labeled points has the greatest absolute value? Why?

Paul Ching-Wu Chu (b. 1941) is a physicist who heads a research group at the University of Houston.

32. *Critical Thinking* Explain what is wrong with the reasoning in the statement: *Since 20 is the opposite of -20, then 20°F must be very hot, because -20°F is very cold.*

33. *Critical Thinking* Is $|a - b|$ always equal to $|b - a|$? Use examples to illustrate your answer.

34. *Physics* Superconductors allow for very efficient passage of electric currents. For practical use, a superconductor must work above -196°C (the boiling point of nitrogen). In 1987, Paul Chu discovered a new class of materials that conduct electricity at -178°C.
   a. At how many degrees above the boiling point of nitrogen did the new materials conduct electricity?
   b. In 1990, researchers created a miniature transistor that conducts electricity at a temperature that is 48°C above the boiling point of nitrogen. What temperature is this?

35. *Critical Thinking* In the cartoon below, does the total "12 27" make sense? Explain.

Frank & Ernest

36. Geography Suppose you travel from Park Headquarters to the floor of Death Valley.
   a. What is your change in elevation?
   b. Why does it make sense to write your change in elevation with a negative number?

37. Find the change in elevation from Telescope Peak to Death Valley.

38. Writing Suppose a friend missed class today. Write an explanation for adding two numbers with different signs.

Telescope Peak to Death Valley

Site	Elevation
Telescope Peak	11,049 ft
Park Headquarters	−190 ft
Floor of Death Valley	−282 ft

Evaluate each expression for $a = -2, b = 3$, and $c = -4$.

39. $6 - a$
40. $a - b + c$
41. $c - b + a$
42. $|-a + 2|$

43. $-|a|$
44. $|a| + |b|$
45. $|a + b|$
46. $-|3 + a|$

47. $a - b$
48. $b - a$
49. $4b - a$
50. $4b - |a|$

51. $a + 3b$
52. $|a| + |3b|$
53. $c + a + 5$
54. $|c + a + 5|$

55. Standardized Test Prep Evaluate $(a - b) - (c - d)$ for $a = -15, b = -8, c = 6$, and $d = 9$.
   A. -20
   B. -4
   C. -10
   D. -26
   E. none of these

56. Chemistry A charged particle of magnesium has 12 protons and 10 electrons. Each proton has a charge of $^+1$ and each electron a charge of $^-1$. What is the total charge of the particle?

Exercises   MIXED REVIEW

57. a. Statistics Draw a graph of the data in the table to show change in tuition from 1990 to 1993.
   b. Why did you choose the graph you drew?
   c. Open-ended **Predict** what the tuition will be for a 2-year public college and a 4-year public college the year you graduate from high school. Explain.

Yearly College Tuition 1990–1993

Year	Public 2-Year Colleges	Public 4-Year Colleges
1990	$ 756	$2035
1991	$ 824	$2159
1992	$ 937	$2410
1993	$1018	$2610

Evaluate each expression.

58. $5t + 6$ for $t = 2$
59. $18 - 7m$ for $m = 2$

Simplify.

60. $\dfrac{3 + 5}{6 + 10}$
61. $\dfrac{7 - 2}{12 + 8}$
62. $\dfrac{1 + 4}{21 - 6}$
63. $\dfrac{8 - 5}{16 - 7}$

Getting Ready for Lesson 1-5

Patterns Write the next three numbers in each pattern.

64. $-5, -1, 3, \blacksquare, \blacksquare, \blacksquare$
65. $9, 6, 3, 0, \blacksquare, \blacksquare, \blacksquare$
66. $-15, -10, -5, \blacksquare, \blacksquare, \blacksquare$
67. $6, 4, 2, \blacksquare, \blacksquare, \blacksquare$

What You'll Learn

1-5 **M**ultiplying and Dividing Integers

- Multiplying and dividing with integers and decimals
- Simplifying expressions with exponents
- Evaluating expressions

...And Why

To compute with real-world data, like temperatures, that are negative as well as positive

WORK TOGETHER

Work with a partner.

Space Flight When the space shuttle is in the first stage of its return to Earth, it descends about 3.5 mi/min. You can write the rate as -3.5 mi/min.

To find how far the shuttle descends in 10 min, you need to find $(-3.5)(10)$. You know that $(3.5)(10) = 35$.

1. Did the shuttle's altitude *increase* or *decrease* during the 10 min?

2. Which phrase better describes descending 35 mi? Why?
   A. a change in altitude of 35 mi   **B.** a change in altitude of -35 mi

3. Is the product $(-3.5)(10)$ equal to 35 or -35? Why?

4. Tell which result makes more sense and explain why.

	Situation	Expression	Result
a.	in football, the total of 2 penalties of 5 yd each	$2(-5)$	10 or -10?
b.	the average hourly decrease in temperature when it falls 20°F in a 4-h period	$\dfrac{-20}{4}$	5 or -5?
c.	the monthly income of a company with losses of \$48,000 for one year	$\dfrac{-48{,}000}{12}$	4000 or -4000?

5. **a. Generalize:** Is the product of a positive and a negative number *positive* or *negative*?
   b. Generalize: Is the quotient of a positive and a negative number *positive* or *negative*?

6. **Patterns** Use your knowledge of patterns to complete each column.
   a. $3 \cdot (-4) = \blacksquare$
   $2 \cdot (-4) = \blacksquare$
   $1 \cdot (-4) = \blacksquare$
   $0 \cdot (-4) = \blacksquare$
   $-1 \cdot (-4) = \blacksquare$
   $-2 \cdot (-4) = \blacksquare$
   $-3 \cdot (-4) = \blacksquare$

   b. $15 \div (-5) = \blacksquare$
   $10 \div (-5) = \blacksquare$
   $5 \div (-5) = \blacksquare$
   $0 \div (-5) = \blacksquare$
   $-5 \div (-5) = \blacksquare$
   $-10 \div (-5) = \blacksquare$
   $-15 \div (-5) = \blacksquare$

7. Use the patterns you developed in Question 6. Is the product or quotient of two negative numbers positive or negative?

8. Compare your results with another pair of students. If you do not have the same results, explain your reasoning to each other.

Multiplying and Dividing

The multiplication and division rules summarize what you discovered in the Work Together activity.

MULTIPLICATION AND DIVISION RULES

The product or quotient of two positive numbers is positive. The product or quotient of two negative numbers is positive.

Examples: $3 \cdot 5 = 15$ $-3 \cdot (-5) = 15$

$\frac{15}{5} = 3$ $\frac{-15}{-5} = 3$

The product or quotient of a positive number and a negative number is negative.

Examples: $-3 \cdot 5 = -15$ $3 \cdot (-5) = -15$

$\frac{-15}{5} = -3$ $\frac{15}{-5} = -3$

Example 1

Evaluate $\frac{-x}{-4} + 2yz$ for $x = -20$, $y = 6$, and $z = -1$.

$\frac{-x}{-4} + 2yz = \frac{-(-20)}{-4} + 2(6)(-1)$ ⟵ Substitute –20 for x, 6 for y, and –1 for z.

$= \frac{20}{-4} + 2(6)(-1)$ ⟵ The opposite of –20 is 20.

$= -5 + (-12)$ ⟵ Divide and multiply.

$= -17$ ⟵ Add.

9. **Try This** Evaluate the expression in Example 1 for $x = 8$, $y = -7$, and $z = -3$.

When you divide, sometimes you need to round your result. The number line shows that -5.8 is closer to -6 than to -5. So, you round -5.8 to -6.

Example 2   Relating to the Real World

Math in the Media Find the mean high temperature. Round to the nearest degree.

mean high temperature $= \frac{-17 + (-18) + (-9) + (-7) + (-6) + 4 + 1}{7}$

$= \frac{-52}{7}$

≈ -7.428571429

The mean high temperature is about $-7°$F.

10. **Try This** Find the mean low temperature to the nearest degree.

11. **a.** Suppose the temperature at 6 P.M. is $-8°$. Write an equation to find the temperature if the temperature falls $2°/\text{h}$. Let n represent the number of hours since 6 P.M.
    b. Find the temperature at 10 P.M.

12. **Try This** **Predict** whether the product of each expression is *positive* or *negative*. Then multiply.
    a. $(-1)(-2)$
    b. $(-1)(-2)(-3)$
    c. $(-1)(-2)(-3)(-4)$
    d. $(-1)(-2)(-3)(-4)(-5)$

13. Use your results in Question 12 to complete each statement.
    a. For an even number of negative factors, the product will be __?__.
    b. For an odd number of negative factors, the product will be __?__.
    c. For a product that includes negative and positive factors, do the positive factors affect the sign of the product?

Simplifying Expressions with Exponents

A term like -3^4 means the opposite of 3^4. Keep this in mind as you simplify expressions that have exponents and negatives.

Example 3

Use the order of operations to simplify each expression.

a. -3^4

$$-3^4 = -(3 \cdot 3 \cdot 3 \cdot 3)$$
$$= -81$$

b. $(-3)^4$

$$(-3)^4 = (-3)(-3)(-3)(-3)$$
$$= 81$$

QUICK REVIEW

1. Perform operations inside grouping symbols.
2. Simplify any terms with exponents.
3. Multiply and divide in order from left to right.
4. Add and subtract in order from left to right.

14. Evaluate each expression for $b = -2$.

    Sample: $b^2 = (-2)^2$
    $= 4$

    a. b^3
    b. b^4
    c. b^5
    d. b^6

15. *Critical Thinking* How can you use the exponent to predict whether an expression like $(-2)^{76}$ is positive or negative?

Exercises   ON YOUR OWN

Simplify.

1. $10(-12)$
2. $(-8)(-5)$
3. -9^2
4. $(-9)^2$
5. $18 \div (-3)$
6. $-18 \div (-3)$
7. $\dfrac{-36}{9}$
8. $(-20)(-5)$
9. $(-1)^{23}$
10. $-(-2)^3$
11. $(-2)(5)(-3)$
12. $3(-4)^3$
13. $|4 + 8(-6)|$
14. $13 - 3(6)$
15. $\dfrac{(3-14)}{-2}$
16. $(-5)(-1)^4$

17. Suppose a and b are integers.
    a. When is the product ab positive?   **b.** When is the product ab negative?

18. **a.** A parachutist opens her parachute at an altitude of 5000 feet. Her change in altitude is -25 ft/s. Write an equation to find her altitude at time t after she opens her parachute.
    b. How far has she descended in 12.5 s?
    c. What is her altitude 12.5 s after she opens her parachute?

Evaluate each expression for $m = -4, n = 3$, and $p = -1$.

19. mn **20.** mnp **21.** $3m - n$ **22.** $-5p^2$

23. $2m$ **24.** $7p - 2n$ **25.** m^3 **26.** $\frac{m}{p} - n$

27. $\frac{m}{n}$ **28.** $8p \div (-2n)$ **29.** $4n^3 \div m$ **30.** $m \div n + (-n)$

31. **Writing** In your own words, write the rules for adding, subtracting, multiplying, and dividing a positive number and a negative number. Write an example for each rule.

32. **Critical Thinking** Does $|ab|$ always equal $|a| \cdot |b|$? Explain.

Is the value of each expression *positive* or *negative*? Explain.

33. $(-3)^4$ **34.** $(-4)^3$ **35.** $(-3)^{103}$ **36.** $(10)^5$

37. $-(-3)^2$ **38.** $(-7)^2$ **39.** -5^{10} **40.** -5^{11}

Open-ended Use $a = -3, b = 2$, and $c = -5$ to write an expression that has each value.

41. 17   **42.** 0   **43.** -1 **44.** 1   **45.** 7

46. **Oceanography** To map the features of the ocean floor, scientists take several sonar readings. Find the mean of these readings: $-14{,}235$ ft; $-14{,}246$ ft; and $-14{,}230$ ft.

47. Complete each statement:
    a. $(-7)^n < 0$ if n is __?__.   **b.** $(-7)^n > 0$ if n is __?__.

48. **Entertainment** You can find the approximate height, in feet, above the ground of a roller-coaster car plunging down the hill of the roller coaster at the right. Use the formula $h = 155 - 16t^2$ where t is the number of seconds since the start of the descent.
    a. How far is a rider from the bottom of the hill after 1 s? 2 s?
    b. **Critical Thinking** Does it take more than or less than 4 s to reach the bottom? Explain.
    c. Use your calculator and the problem solving strategy *Guess and Test* to find the time the roller coaster descends to the nearest tenth of a second.

155 ft

Find Out by Calculating

Scientists use these formulas to approximate a person's height H, in inches, when they know the length of the tibia t, the humerus h, or the radius r.

- Use your tibia, humerus, and radius bone lengths to calculate your height. Are the calculated heights close to your actual height? Explain.
- An archaeologist found an 18-in. tibia on the site of an American colonial farm. Do you think it belonged to a man or a woman? Why?
- Choose one radius measurement from the data you collected for the Find Out question on page 9. Calculate the person's height. Can you tell whose height you have found? Explain.

Male
$H = 32.2 + 2.4t$
$H = 29.0 + 3.0h$
$H = 31.7 + 3.7r$
Female
$H = 28.6 + 2.5t$
$H = 25.6 + 3.1h$
$H = 28.9 + 3.9r$

Exercises   MIXED REVIEW

Statistics Use the line plot at the right.

49. How many people watched more than three hours of television?

50. What other kind of graph could you use for the data? Explain.

51. a. Find the mean, median, and mode of the data.
    b. Is the *mean*, *median*, or *mode* the most useful to describe people's viewing habits? Why?

Hours Spent Watching TV Each Day

```
X
X   X       X
X   X   X   X
X   X   X   X   X   X
1   2   3   4   5   6
```

Getting Ready for Lesson 1-6

Find each sum or difference.

52. $\frac{3}{8} + \frac{1}{4}$ **53.** $\frac{7}{12} - \frac{1}{3}$ **54.** $\frac{5}{6} + \frac{2}{3}$ **55.** $\frac{1}{2} - \frac{1}{6}$ **56.** $\frac{7}{8} - \frac{3}{5}$

Exercises   CHECKPOINT

Simplify.

1. $8 + 4 \cdot 3$ **2.** $(-3)^2 + (-5)$ **3.** $\frac{7 + 5}{7 - 5}$ **4.** $(9^2 - 60) \div 3$

Evaluate each expression for $a = -7$ and $b = 4$.

5. $-a$ **6.** a^2 **7.** $a + b$ **8.** $|a - b|$ **9.** $2b^2 + 3a$

10. Writing Is -5^2 positive or negative? Explain.

11. Find the mean, median, and mode. Round to the nearest tenth.
$-12, 15, 8, -4, -6, 7, -4, 8, -5, -12, 0, -2, 5, -4$

12. Write an equation to describe the relationship shown at the right.

boxes	tissues
1	175
2	350
3	525

What You'll Learn

- Comparing and ordering rational numbers
- Evaluating expressions with rational numbers

...And Why

To solve real-world problems, such as converting temperatures

What You'll Need

- calculator

1-6

Real Numbers and Rational Numbers

THINK AND DISCUSS

Comparing Rational Numbers

The Venn diagram shows the relationship of sets of numbers.

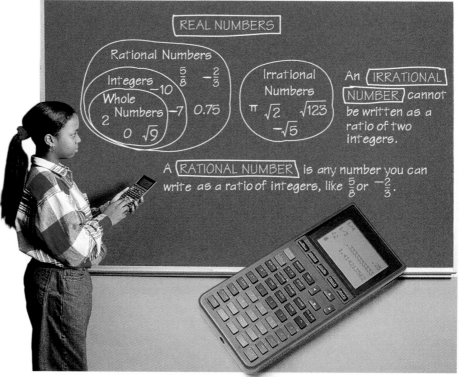

Integers are rational numbers because you can write them as ratios using 1 as the denominator: $7 = \frac{7}{1}$. Rational and irrational numbers make up the set of **real numbers**.

1. Write three numbers that are rational numbers but not integers. Choose numbers different from the ones in the diagram above.

2. Show that 0.75 is a rational number by writing it as a ratio.

3. *Open-ended* Where have you used irrational numbers?

4. *Calculator* Use a calculator to find the square root of the numbers 1 through 10. Which do you think are rational? irrational?

An irrational number expressed in decimal form is a nonterminating and nonrepeating decimal. If you use a calculator to express an irrational number as a decimal, the calculator gives you a decimal approximation.

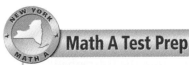

Math A Test Prep

1 What is the value of $|a - b|$ when $a = -2$ and $b = 6$?
(1) 4
(2) 8
(3) −4
(4) −8

2 The average temperature for one day is the mean of the day's high temperature and the day's low temperature. One January day, the high was 8°F and the low was −12°F. What was the average temperature for that day?

When you compare two real numbers, only one of these can be true:

$a < b$	or	$a = b$	or	$a > b$
less than		**equal to**		**greater than**

Example 1

Use a number line to compare $-\frac{1}{8}$ and $-\frac{1}{2}$.

$$-1 \qquad\qquad 0$$

⟵ Numbers are greater as you move to the right on the number line.

$$-\frac{1}{8} > -\frac{1}{2}$$

5. Rewrite the answer to Example 1 using the symbol for *less than*.

6. *Critical Thinking* Suppose you are comparing $-25\frac{1}{2}$ and $-25\frac{1}{8}$. Do you need a different number line from the one in Example 1 to determine which mixed number is greater? Explain.

Many ratios are not easy to compare using a number line. Another method is to write the ratios as decimals and then compare.

Example 2

Write $-\frac{3}{8}$, $-\frac{1}{2}$, and $-\frac{5}{12}$ in order from least to greatest.

Use a calculator to write the rational numbers as decimals.

$-\frac{3}{8}$	(-) 3 ÷ 8 ENTER	$-.375$
$-\frac{1}{2}$	(-) 1 ÷ 2 ENTER	$-.5$
$-\frac{5}{12}$	(-) 5 ÷ 12 ENTER	$-.4166666667$

$$-0.5 < -0.41\overline{6} < -0.375$$

From least to greatest the ratios are $-\frac{1}{2}$, $-\frac{5}{12}$, and $-\frac{3}{8}$.

7. Try This Write $\frac{1}{12}$, $-\frac{2}{3}$, and $-\frac{5}{8}$ in order from least to greatest.

Evaluating Expressions

You evaluate expressions using rational numbers by substituting and performing the indicated operations.

Example 3

Evaluate $a + 2b$ where $a = \frac{2}{3}$ and $b = -\frac{5}{8}$.

$$a + 2b = \frac{2}{3} + 2\left(-\frac{5}{8}\right) \quad\text{⟵ Substitute the values for } a \text{ and } b.$$
$$= \frac{2}{3} - \frac{5}{4}$$
$$= -\frac{7}{12}$$

CALCULATOR HINT

You can use this key sequence:

(2 ÷ 3) − (
5 ÷ 4) ENTER

1-6 Real Numbers and Rational Numbers   **31**

Example 4   **Relating to the Real World** 🌐 ....

Weather Use the expression $\frac{5}{9}(F - 32)$ to change from the Fahrenheit scale to the Celsius scale. What is 10°F in Celsius?

$\frac{5}{9}(F - 32) = \frac{5}{9}(10 - 32)$ ⟵ Substitute 10 for F.

$\qquad\qquad = \frac{5}{9}(-22)$

$\qquad\qquad \approx -12$

The temperature is about -12°C.

8. Find the Celsius temperature when the Fahrenheit temperature is 90°.

The **reciprocal,** or *multiplicative inverse,* of a nonzero number $\frac{a}{b}$ is $\frac{b}{a}$. Zero does not have a reciprocal because division by zero is undefined.

9. a. Patterns Complete the chart.
   b. What is the product of a number and its reciprocal?
10. Is a number's reciprocal the same as its opposite? Explain.

Number	Reciprocal	Product
3	$\frac{1}{3}$	$3 \cdot \frac{1}{3} = \blacksquare$
$\frac{1}{5}$	$\frac{5}{1}$ or 5	$\frac{1}{5} \cdot 5 = \blacksquare$
$-\frac{2}{3}$	$-\frac{3}{2}$	$-\frac{2}{3} \cdot \left(-\frac{3}{2}\right) = \blacksquare$

You know $12 \div 3 = 12 \cdot \frac{1}{3}$. This means that dividing by a nonzero number is the same as multiplying by its reciprocal.

$$a \div \frac{b}{c} = a \cdot \frac{c}{b} \text{ for } b \neq 0 \text{ and } c \neq 0$$

Example 5 ....

Evaluate $\frac{x}{y}$ for $x = -\frac{3}{4}$ and $y = -\frac{5}{2}$.

$\frac{x}{y} = x \div y$

$\quad = -\frac{3}{4} \div \left(-\frac{5}{2}\right)$

$\quad = -\frac{3}{4} \cdot \left(-\frac{2}{5}\right)$ ⟵ Multiply by $-\frac{2}{5}$, the reciprocal of $-\frac{5}{2}$.

$\quad = \frac{3}{10}$

11. Try This Evaluate the expression in Example 5 for $x = 8$ and $y = -\frac{4}{5}$.

Exercises   ON YOUR OWN

Use <, =, or > to compare.

1. $1\frac{2}{3} \ \blacksquare \ 1\frac{1}{6}$

2. $-1\frac{2}{3} \ \blacksquare \ -1\frac{1}{6}$

3. $\frac{15}{8} \ \blacksquare \ 1\frac{6}{8}$

4. $\frac{3}{5} \ \blacksquare \ 0.6$

5. $\frac{1}{2} \ \blacksquare \ \frac{1}{4}$

6. $0.14 \ \blacksquare \ \frac{1}{7}$

7. $-17\frac{1}{5} \ \blacksquare \ -17\frac{1}{4}$

8. $-3.02 \ \blacksquare \ -3.002$

Complete with a rational number that makes each statement true.

9. $\frac{3}{5} \cdot \blacksquare = 1$ **10.** $-4 \cdot \blacksquare = 1$ **11.** $\blacksquare \cdot \frac{7}{8} = 1$ **12.** $\blacksquare \cdot \left(-\frac{8}{3}\right) = 1$

Evaluate.

13. $x - \frac{3}{4}$ for $x = -1\frac{1}{4}$

14. $a - b$ for $a = -\frac{1}{2}, b = \frac{1}{5}$

15. rs for $r = \frac{2}{15}, s = 5$

16. $-p + t$ for $p = 1\frac{3}{8}, t = \frac{5}{8}$

17. $2xy$ for $x = -\frac{2}{3}, y = -\frac{3}{4}$

18. $\frac{v}{w}$ for $v = -\frac{5}{8}, w = -\frac{5}{6}$

19. ab for $a = 2\frac{1}{4}, b = -3$

20. $\frac{m}{n}$ for $m = -\frac{1}{2}, n = 5$

21. $\frac{1}{2}(q - p)$ for $q = 4, p = -\frac{1}{3}$

22. $4rs$ for $r = -3\frac{1}{4}, s = -\frac{1}{5}$

23. $b + c$ for $b = -2\frac{1}{3}, c = \frac{1}{4}$

24. $\frac{1}{5}z - y$ for $z = 1.5, y = 0.3$

Write each group of numbers in order from least to greatest.

25. $-\frac{1}{2}, -\frac{2}{3}, \frac{1}{4}$ **26.** $-1.5, -\frac{4}{3}, -1\frac{1}{4}$ **27.** $-9.7, -9\frac{7}{12}, -9\frac{3}{4}$ **28.** $-4.12, -4.22, -4.05$

29. Science Air temperature drops as altitude increases. In the formula $t = (-5.5)\left(\frac{a}{1000}\right)$, t is the approximate change in Fahrenheit temperature, and a is the increase in altitude in feet.
  a. Find the change in temperature for the balloon.
  b. Suppose the temperature is 40°F at ground level. What is the approximate temperature at the balloon?
  c. Research Find the height of a mountain that is near you or that you are interested in. Suppose the temperature at the base of the mountain is 80°F. What is the approximate temperature at the top of the mountain?

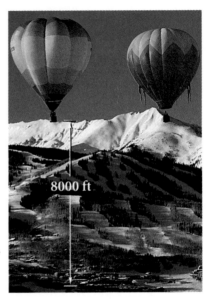

8000 ft

30. Weather In the formula $w = -39 + \frac{3}{2}t$, w is the approximate windchill temperature when the wind speed is 20 mi/h, and t is the actual air temperature. Find the approximate windchill temperature when the actual air temperature is 10°F and the wind speed is 20 mi/h.

Rewrite each expression using the symbol ÷, then find each quotient.

Sample $\dfrac{-\frac{7}{12}}{4} = -\frac{7}{12} \div 4$ ⟵ Rewrite as $-\frac{7}{12} \div 4$.

$\qquad = -\frac{7}{12} \cdot \left(\frac{1}{4}\right)$ ⟵ Multiply by $\frac{1}{4}$, the reciprocal of 4.

$\qquad = -\frac{7}{48}$

31. $\dfrac{\frac{3}{8}}{-\frac{2}{3}}$ **32.** $\dfrac{\frac{5}{4}}{\frac{9}{9}}$ **33.** $\dfrac{-\frac{5}{6}}{8}$ **34.** $\dfrac{-\frac{2}{5}}{-\frac{4}{5}}$

35. a. Open-ended Name a point between -2 and -3 on a number line.
  b. Name a point between -2.8 and -2.9.
  c. Name a point between $-2\frac{1}{16}$ and $-2\frac{3}{8}$.
  d. On a number line, is it possible to find a point between any two given points? Explain.

Evaluate.

36. $x + y$ for $x = \frac{13}{4}$, $y = -\frac{5}{2}$

37. $\frac{1}{5}(r - t)$ for $r = 6$, $t = -7$

38. $\frac{3}{4}w - 7$ for $w = 1\frac{1}{3}$

39. $\frac{x}{2y}$ for $x = 3.6$, $y = -0.4$

40. $\frac{3a}{b} + c$ for $a = -2$, $b = -5$, $c = -1$

41. $\frac{n}{m}$ for $n = -\frac{4}{5}$, $m = 8$

Writing Decide if each statement is *true* or *false*. Justify your answer.

42. All integers are rational numbers.

43. All negative numbers are integers.

44. All rational numbers are integers.

45. Some real numbers are integers.

Exercises   MIXED REVIEW

For Exercises 46–48, write an equation to model each situation.

46. the cost of several movie tickets that are $6.26 each

47. the change from a $10 bill after a purchase

48. the total cost of an item with a shipping fee of $3.98.

49. Real Estate Boulder City, Nevada, bought 107,500 acres of land in Nevada's Eldorado Valley from the United States government. The price was $12/acre. How much did the city pay for the land?

Getting Ready for Lesson 1-7

50. Probability How much of the spinner is red? yellow? blue?

A Point in Time

1000 B.C. 1000

2000 B.C. 0 2000

The Rhind Papyrus

A scroll discovered in Egypt shows that Egyptians were using symbols for plus, minus, equals, and an unknown quantity over 3500 years ago. Named for the British Egyptologist A. Henry Rhind, the papyrus is 18 ft long and 1 ft wide. It is a practical handbook containing 85 problems including work with rational numbers. In the Rhind Papyrus, rational numbers are written as unit fractions. A unit fraction has 1 as its numerator. Here are some examples.

$\frac{3}{4} = \frac{1}{2} + \frac{1}{4}$ $\frac{3}{8} = \frac{1}{4} + \frac{1}{8}$ $\frac{21}{30} = \frac{1}{6} + \frac{1}{5} + \frac{1}{3}$

Using Properties

After Lesson 1-6

These properties of mathematics help you to perform arithmetic and algebraic operations.

Commutative Properties of Addition and Multiplication

For all real numbers a and b:
$$a + b = b + a \qquad\qquad a \cdot b = b \cdot a$$
Examples: $\quad 2 + 3 = 3 + 2 \qquad\qquad 4 \cdot 5 = 5 \cdot 4$

Associative Properties of Addition and Multiplication

For all real numbers a, b, and c :
$$(a + b) + c = a + (b + c) \qquad (a \cdot b) \cdot c = a \cdot (b \cdot c)$$
Examples: $\quad (5 + 6) + 7 = 5 + (6 + 7) \qquad (2 \cdot 3) \cdot 4 = 2 \cdot (3 \cdot 4)$

Identity Properties of Addition and Multiplication

For every real number a:
$$a + 0 = a \quad \text{and} \quad 0 + a = a \quad a \cdot 1 = a \quad \text{and} \quad 1 \cdot a = a$$
Examples: $\quad 5 + 0 = 5 \quad \text{and} \quad 0 + 5 = 5 \quad 7 \cdot 1 = 7 \quad \text{and} \quad 1 \cdot 7 = 7$

Name the property that each exercise illustrates.

1. $1m = m$

2. $(-3 + 4) + 5 = -3 + (4 + 5)$

3. $3(8 \cdot 0) = (3 \cdot 8)0$

4. $2 + 0 = 2$

5. $np = pn$

6. $f + g = g + f$

Use the properties to simplify each expression.

7. $(5 \cdot 83) \cdot 2$

8. $47 + 39 + 3 + 11$

9. $25 \cdot 74 \cdot 2 \cdot 2$

10. $-5(7y)$

11. $8 + 9m + 7$

12. $4.75 + 2.95 + 1.25 + 6$

13. $6\frac{1}{2} + 4\frac{1}{3} + 1\frac{1}{2} + \frac{2}{3}$

14. $25 \cdot 1.7 \cdot 4$

15. $(3p)(4q)(6r)$

16. Writing Justify your answers to these questions: Is subtraction commutative? Is subtraction associative? Is division commutative? Is division associative?

What You'll Learn

1-7

Experimental Probability and Simulations

- Finding experimental probability
- Using simulations to find experimental probability

...And Why

To solve problems in business and sports

What You'll Need

- two number cubes

Work with a partner.

1. Suppose you roll two number cubes many times. Do you think that all of the sums will occur about the same number of times, or will some sums occur more often than others? Explain.

2. **Data Collection** Roll two number cubes sixty times. On a line plot numbered from 2 to 12, mark the sum of the cubes each time you roll.

3. How well do your results of rolling the number cubes match your **prediction** in Question 1? Explain.

THINK AND DISCUSS

Finding Experimental Probability

Probability measures how likely something, usually called an **event,** is to happen. For **experimental probability** you gather data through observations or experiments. Use this ratio to find experimental probability.

You read *P* (event) as "the probability of an event."

$$P(\text{event}) = \frac{\text{number of times an event happens}}{\text{number of times experiment is done}}$$

Suppose that in the Work Together activity, the sum 3 occurred five times. Then, $P(3) = \frac{5}{60}$, or $\frac{1}{12}$. Each time you repeat an experiment, the experimental probability of an event may vary. The more data you collect, the more reliable your results will be.

4. **a.** Use your Work Together data to find $P(2)$, $P(7)$, and $P(12)$.
   b. Which sum in part (a) has the greatest probability? Do you think this will be true if you repeat the experiment? Explain.

You can conduct an experiment by choosing items *at random*. This means that each item has an equal chance of being picked.

Example 1   Relating to the Real World

Business After receiving complaints, a retailer checked 100 light bulbs at random. Eighty of the bulbs worked. What is $P(\text{bulb works})$?

$$P(\text{bulb works}) = \frac{\text{number of times an event happens}}{\text{number of times the experiment is done}}$$

$$= \frac{80}{100} \quad \longleftarrow \text{The light bulbs worked 80 times.}$$

$$= \frac{4}{5} = 0.8 = 80\%$$

The probability that a light bulb works is 80%.

QUICK REVIEW

You can write $\frac{4}{5}$ as a fraction, decimal, or percent:
$\frac{4}{5} = 0.8 = 80\%$

5. There are 500 light bulbs in stock. **Predict** how many of the light bulbs will work. (*Hint*: Multiply the probability found in Example 1 by the number of light bulbs in the shipment.)

Conducting a Simulation

A **simulation** is a model of a real-life situation. One way to do a simulation is to use a table of numbers that a computer has picked at random.

Example 2 **Relating to the Real World** ················

Medical Technician According to the American Red Cross, 40% of the people in the United States have type A blood. What is the probability that the next two people who donate blood have type A blood?

Define how the simulation will be done.

Use a random number table.

Random Number Table

23948 71470 12573 05954
65628 22310 09311 94864
41261 09943 34078 79481
34831 94510 71490 93312

Let the numbers 0–3 in the random number table represent having type A blood. Let 4–9 represent not having type A blood. Since the simulation is for two people, list the numbers in pairs. Look at twenty pairs.

← 40% of the numbers must represent having type A blood.

Conduct the simulation.

23 94 87 14 70 12 57 30 59 54 65 62 82 23 10 09 31 19 48 64

The arrows point to pairs in which both "people" have type A blood.

Interpret the simulation.

Six pairs represent "both people have type A blood" because these pairs contain only the numbers 0–3.

$$P(\text{both have type A blood}) = \frac{\text{number of times an event happens}}{\text{number of times the experiment is done}}$$
$$= \frac{6}{20}$$
$$= \frac{3}{10} = 0.3 = 30\%$$

The probability that both of the next two people have type A blood is 30%. ■

6. For the simulation in Example 2, could you use any four numbers from 0–9 to represent having type A blood? Explain.

7. Try This In the United States, about 50% of the people have type O blood. Use the random number table above to find the probability that the next two donors have type O blood.

1. **a.** Group Activity What do you expect the probability is for getting heads when you toss a coin?
   b. Have each member in your group toss a coin 20 times, one person at a time. Use a table like the one below to record your data. After each person's turn, find the P(head) based on the total number of heads and the total number of tosses for your group.

Team Member	Number of Heads	Number of Tosses	Total Number of Heads	Total Number of Tosses	P(head)
1	■	20	■	20	■
2	■	20	■	40	■

   c. As the total number of coin tosses increases, does the probability get closer to what you expect? Explain.

A driver collects data on the color of a certain traffic light. When she arrives at the light, it is green 16 times, yellow 5 times, and red 9 times. Find each probability.

2. P(red)   3. P(green)   4. P(yellow)   5. P(not green)

6. Suppose you bought a box of marbles. You select twelve marbles at random and record the color. The results are at the right.
   a. Find P(red), P(green), P(blue), and P(yellow).
   b. Suppose the box contains 160 marbles. About how many blue marbles do you expect?
   c. Do you think there will be exactly 80 red marbles? Explain.

Suppose you grab a handful of coins from your change jar, and these coins are a random sample of the coins in your jar. You have 13 pennies, 3 quarters, 2 nickels, and 6 dimes. Find the probability that each is the next coin you select. Write each probability as a percent.

7. P(nickel)   8. P(penny)   9. P(coin worth less than 10¢)

10. **a.** A softball player is at bat 25 times. She gets a hit 7 times. What is the probability that she gets a hit the next time she comes to bat?
    b. Writing Suppose the player gets a hit the 26th time at bat. Explain how getting a hit changes the experimental probability.

11. Health The table shows the results of the 1954 trials for the Salk polio vaccine. To test the vaccine, researchers gave a test group shots with vaccine and a control group shots without vaccine. Compare the probability of developing polio in the test group and in the control group.

Results of Polio Vaccine Trials

Group	Number of Children	Number of Cases of Polio
Test	200,745	82
Control	201,229	162

Use the data in the line plot to find each probability.

12. $P(\text{Sunday})$ **13.** $P(\text{Tuesday})$ **14.** $P(\text{Wednesday})$

15. $P(\text{weekend day})$ **16.** $P(\text{weekday})$ **17.** $P(not \text{ Friday})$

Students' Birthdays

X					X	
X	X				X	X
X	X	X		X	X	X
X	X	X		X	X	X
Su	M	Tu	W	Th	F	Sa

18. Suppose you guess the answers to a two-question true/false test. Your probability of getting one answer correct is 50%. Do a simulation of this test by flipping a coin for each question. Let "heads" represent a correct answer and "tails" represent an incorrect answer. Simulate the test ten times and record the results. Find $P(\text{both answers are correct})$.

19. Suppose there are three stoplights on your way to school. Each one has a 30% chance of stopping you. Use the random number table on page 37 to do a simulation. Record your data and find $P(\text{stopped by all three lights})$. Write your probability as a decimal rounded to the nearest hundredth. Then write it as a percent. (*Hint*: Let the numbers 0–2 represent being stopped and 3–9 represent not being stopped.)

20. Critical Thinking Suppose you are taking a poll for student council elections. Which is the best method for choosing students at random? Explain your choice.
  A. You choose every 20th student on a list of all students.
  B. You choose students as they leave a band concert.
  C. You choose students in line at lunch.

21. Open-ended Conduct a simulation to find the experimental probability that exactly two children in a family of five children will be girls. Record the results of your simulation.

22. a. Data Collection Roll a number cube and record how often each of the numbers 1 through 6 occurs. Roll the cube 50 times.
  b. Find the experimental probability for each number.
  c. Are the probabilities for each number the same? Explain.

Chapter Project ▼ **Find Out by Analyzing**

When predicting height, scientists use different formulas for men and women.

• Review the data collected for the Find Out by Question on page 9. Separate the data by male and female.

• Organize and display the data to see if there are differences between the sexes.

Exercises   M I X E D   R E V I E W

Simplify each expression.

23. $13 + 16(-2)$ **24.** $36 \div (-4) - 2(-15)$

25. -7^2 **26.** $(-7)^2$

Getting Ready for Lesson 1-8

27. What number is in the first row, second column?

28. What number is in the second row, first column?

17	53.6	42
32	52.5	-7
4	98	5.6

FOR YOUR JOURNAL

Explain why the experimental probability of an event can vary each time you perform the same experiment.

What You'll Learn

1-8

Organizing Data in Matrices

• Adding and subtracting matrices

...And Why

To investigate real-world data, such as school enrollment and employee wages

1992 School Enrollment in the United States (in millions)

Level	Public	Private
Elementary	27.1	3.1
High School	12.3	1.0
College	11.1	3.0

Source: *Statistical Abstract of the United States*

THINK AND DISCUSS

A **matrix** is a rectangular arrangement of numbers. The numbers are arranged in rows and columns and are usually written inside brackets. The matrix below displays the school enrollment data at the left.

$$
\begin{array}{cc}
 & \text{Public} \quad \text{Private} \\
\begin{array}{c}\text{Elementary}\\\text{High School}\\\text{College}\end{array} &
\left[\begin{array}{cc} 27.1 & 3.1 \\ 12.3 & 1.0 \\ 11.1 & 3.0 \end{array}\right] \leftarrow \text{row}
\end{array}
$$

↑ column

You identify the size of a matrix by the number of rows and the number of columns. This matrix has 3 rows and 2 columns, so it is a 3 × 2 matrix. Each item in a matrix is an **entry.**

1. What entry is in row 1, column 2? in row 2, column 1?

2. *Open-ended* Make a 2 × 3 matrix.

Two matrices are equal if corresponding entries are equal.

corresponding entries

$$
\begin{bmatrix} 0.5 & \frac{3}{8} \\ \frac{1}{4} & 0.4 \end{bmatrix} \qquad \begin{bmatrix} \frac{1}{2} & 0.375 \\ 0.25 & \frac{2}{5} \end{bmatrix}
$$

3. Are the two matrices equal? Explain.

You can add or subtract matrices if they are the same size. You do this by adding or subtracting corresponding entries.

Example 1

Subtract the two matrices. $\begin{bmatrix} 7 & -4 & 11 \\ 6 & 5 & -1 \end{bmatrix} - \begin{bmatrix} 5 & 9 & 7 \\ 8 & -7 & -3 \end{bmatrix}$

$$
\begin{bmatrix} 7 & -4 & 11 \\ 6 & 5 & -1 \end{bmatrix} - \begin{bmatrix} 5 & 9 & 7 \\ 8 & -7 & -3 \end{bmatrix} = \begin{bmatrix} 7-5 & -4-9 & 11-7 \\ 6-8 & -(-7) & -1-(-3) \end{bmatrix}
$$

$$
= \begin{bmatrix} 2 & -13 & 4 \\ -2 & 12 & 2 \end{bmatrix}
$$

4. What size are the matrices in Example 1?

5. **Try This** Add the two matrices that were subtracted in Example 1.

Matrices are a handy way to organize real-world data so that you can add or subtract the data.

Example 2   **Relating to the Real World**

Environment Write each table as a matrix. Then add the matrices to find the total of endangered and threatened species.

Endangered Species

Species	United States Only	Both United States and Foreign	Foreign Only	Total
Mammals	36	20	251	307
Birds	57	16	153	226
Reptiles	8	8	63	79
Amphibians	6	0	8	14
Fishes	60	3	11	74

Threatened Species

Species	United States Only	Both United States and Foreign	Foreign Only	Total
Mammals	5	4	22	31
Birds	8	9	0	17
Reptiles	15	4	14	33
Amphibians	4	1	0	5
Fishes	32	6	0	38

What? The Endangered Species Act of 1973 protects plant and animal species. *Endangered* species are close to extinction. The survival of *threatened* species is of great concern.

$$\begin{bmatrix} 36 & 20 & 251 & 307 \\ 57 & 16 & 153 & 226 \\ 8 & 8 & 63 & 79 \\ 6 & 0 & 8 & 14 \\ 60 & 3 & 11 & 74 \end{bmatrix} + \begin{bmatrix} 5 & 4 & 22 & 31 \\ 8 & 9 & 0 & 17 \\ 15 & 4 & 14 & 33 \\ 4 & 1 & 0 & 5 \\ 32 & 6 & 0 & 38 \end{bmatrix} = \begin{bmatrix} 41 & 24 & 273 & 338 \\ 65 & 25 & 153 & 243 \\ 23 & 12 & 77 & 112 \\ 10 & 1 & 8 & 19 \\ 92 & 9 & 11 & 112 \end{bmatrix}$$

6. How many species of mammals are endangered or threatened?

7. Critical Thinking The grizzly bear is threatened in the United States but endangered in Mexico. So it is counted twice in the totals. There is a total of four mammal species counted twice. What is the actual total of endangered or threatened mammals?

Exercises   **ON YOUR OWN**

What is the size of each matrix?

1. $\begin{bmatrix} 5 & 4 & 7 \\ 6 & 9 & 8 \end{bmatrix}$
   2. $\begin{bmatrix} 4 & 1 \end{bmatrix}$
   3. $\begin{bmatrix} 1 & 2 \\ 3 & 4 \\ 5 & 6 \end{bmatrix}$
   4. $\begin{bmatrix} -8 \end{bmatrix}$
   5. $\begin{bmatrix} 16 & -22 & 24 & 35 \\ 17 & -35 & 19 & 41 \\ 28 & -10 & 15 & 50 \end{bmatrix}$

Mental Math Find each sum or difference.

6. $\begin{bmatrix} 1 & 2 \\ 5 & 3 \\ -1 & -4 \end{bmatrix} + \begin{bmatrix} 2 & 0 \\ 9 & 1 \\ 3 & -8 \end{bmatrix}$ 7. $\begin{bmatrix} 4 & 2 \\ 1 & -3 \end{bmatrix} + \begin{bmatrix} -4 & -2 \\ -1 & 3 \end{bmatrix}$ 8. $\begin{bmatrix} -6 & -1 & 7 \\ 3 & -2 & -5 \end{bmatrix} - \begin{bmatrix} -8 & 6 & -2 \\ 14 & -3 & 1 \end{bmatrix}$

9. What is the value of m, n, and p in the matrices?

$$\begin{bmatrix} 5 & -1 \\ m & 0 \end{bmatrix} = \begin{bmatrix} n & -1 \\ -6 & p \end{bmatrix}$$

Add each pair of matrices. Then subtract the second matrix from the first matrix in each pair.

10. $\begin{bmatrix} 16 & 11 & -20 \\ 22 & 8 & -10 \end{bmatrix}, \begin{bmatrix} 9 & 10 & 14 \\ -15 & -10 & 5 \end{bmatrix}$

11. $\begin{bmatrix} 42 & -36 \\ -10 & 54 \end{bmatrix}, \begin{bmatrix} 39 & 4 \\ 37 & 46 \end{bmatrix}$

12. $\begin{bmatrix} 3 & 2 & 1 \\ 4 & 2 & 0 \\ 0 & -2 & 5 \end{bmatrix}, \begin{bmatrix} 1 & -2 & 3 \\ -4 & 5 & -6 \\ 7 & -8 & 9 \end{bmatrix}$

13. $\begin{bmatrix} 3.4 & 2.1 \\ -6.4 & 5.7 \\ 8.8 & -9.3 \end{bmatrix}, \begin{bmatrix} 4.9 & -7.9 \\ 3.8 & -2.8 \\ 4.2 & 1.5 \end{bmatrix}$

14. $\begin{bmatrix} 5.0 & -1.7 \\ 1.2 & -3.8 \\ 1.5 & 2.4 \end{bmatrix}, \begin{bmatrix} 5.7 & 6.8 \\ -4.0 & -1.2 \\ 6.2 & 8.1 \end{bmatrix}$

15. $\begin{bmatrix} \frac{2}{3} & \frac{4}{5} \\ \frac{1}{8} & \frac{1}{6} \end{bmatrix}, \begin{bmatrix} \frac{1}{2} & \frac{2}{5} \\ \frac{3}{4} & 1 \end{bmatrix}$

16. $\begin{bmatrix} 356 & -190 & 171 \\ -256 & 321 & -150 \end{bmatrix}, \begin{bmatrix} 1 & 6 & -4 \\ -17 & -3 & 5 \end{bmatrix}$

17. $\begin{bmatrix} 3.5 & -0.2 \\ 0 & -7 \end{bmatrix}, \begin{bmatrix} -1 & 0.5 \\ -8.1 & 9.7 \end{bmatrix}$

18. a. *Sports* Write each table of data as a matrix.
    b. Make a matrix that shows the change in participation from 1987 to 1992.
    c. Did any categories lose participants? Which ones?
    d. In which category did the number of participants increase the most?
    e. *Writing* Suppose you have money to invest in sports equipment. In which sport would you invest? Use entries from your matrix to explain your choice.

19. *Critical Thinking* Suppose two matrices are equal. What will the matrix for their difference look like?

20. a. *Open-ended* Make two 3 × 5 matrices.
    b. Add your two matrices.
    c. Subtract your two matrices.

Participation in Sports Activities (in millions)

1987	Sport	7–11 yr	12–17 yr	18–24 yr
	Basketball	3.7	8.3	5.1
	Tennis	1.0	3.4	3.9
	Soccer	3.6	4.1	0.9
	Volleyball	2.0	6.6	4.7

1992	Sport	7–11 yr	12–17 yr	18–24 yr
	Basketball	5.5	8.2	4.9
	Tennis	1.4	3.2	3.9
	Soccer	4.2	3.8	1.3
	Volleyball	1.6	5.2	5.1

Simplify each entry in the matrix.

21. $\begin{bmatrix} \frac{5}{6} \div \frac{2}{3} & -4 - 2\frac{1}{2} \\ \left(3\frac{1}{3}\right)\left(\frac{3}{4}\right) & \frac{1}{2} - \left(\frac{2}{5}\right)\left(\frac{5}{4}\right) \end{bmatrix}$

22. $\begin{bmatrix} 8 + 2 \div 4 & 2^5 & -12 - 15 \\ 45 + 5(-13) & \frac{10 + 16}{4} & 4 - 2^2 \end{bmatrix}$

23. a. Jobs Create a matrix to find the total number of workers in each pay category for each work shift.
   b. How many weekend employees on the evening shift earn $5.50/h?
   c. Critical Thinking Suppose all employees work 8-h shifts both Saturday and Sunday. How could you use the matrix to find the total wages of the weekend employees?

Number of Employees

Saturday Schedule
Hourly Wage

Shift	$5.25	$5.50	$6.00	$6.50
Day	8	3	5	1
Evening	10	2	2	1
Night	4	1	0	1

Sunday Schedule
Hourly Wage

Shift	$5.25	$5.50	$6.00	$6.50
Day	5	2	1	1
Evening	8	2	0	1
Night	2	1	0	1

Multiply each matrix by the given value.

Sample $2\begin{bmatrix} 2 & -3 \\ 1 & 5 \end{bmatrix} = \begin{bmatrix} 2(2) & 2(-3) \\ 2(1) & 2(5) \end{bmatrix}$ ← Multiply each entry by the factor outside the matrix.

$= \begin{bmatrix} 4 & -6 \\ 2 & 10 \end{bmatrix}$

24. $3\begin{bmatrix} -9 & 2 \\ 6 & -12 \end{bmatrix}$

25. $-5\begin{bmatrix} 70 & 30 & -10 \\ 80 & 20 & -50 \end{bmatrix}$

26. $0\begin{bmatrix} -15 & 12 \\ 17 & 21 \end{bmatrix}$

Exercises MIXED REVIEW

Evaluate each expression for $a = -5$, $b = 2.4$, $c = -0.5$, and $d = 3.7$.

27. $a + (-b) +$

28. $2b + (-d) + ac$

29. $a \div c + 2d$

30. $a^2 + bc$

Getting Ready for Lesson 1-9
Geometry Use the formula $A = \frac{1}{2}bh$ to find the area of each triangle.

31. $b = 12$ in.
$h = 4$ in.

32. $b = 15$ cm
$h = 7$ cm

33. $b = 9.2$ m
$h = 14.8$ m

Exercises CHECKPOINT

Evaluate each expression.

1. $2a - b$ for $a = \frac{3}{4}$, $b = \frac{7}{8}$

2. $3m - 2n$ for $m = 3.5$, $n = -0.8$

3. $p \div q$ for $p = -\frac{5}{8}$, $q = -\frac{4}{5}$

Simplify.

4. $\begin{bmatrix} 3 & 5 \\ -4 & 2 \end{bmatrix} + \begin{bmatrix} \frac{1}{2} & -6 \\ 8 & -11 \end{bmatrix}$

5. $\begin{bmatrix} 3.3 & 0.4 & 3.0 \\ -1.7 & 9.6 & -6.5 \end{bmatrix} - \begin{bmatrix} -2.3 & 7.2 & -8.5 \\ 4.1 & 6.3 & 9.2 \end{bmatrix}$

6. Open-ended Write a problem you could solve by using a simulation. Describe how the simulation would be done.

Matrices

After Lesson 1-8

You can use your graphing calculator to add or subtract matrices. In the calculator, a matrix is named using a variable. Some calculators will put brackets, [ ], around a variable to indicate a matrix. Before entering the values for a matrix, you must enter the size of the matrix.

$$[A] = \begin{bmatrix} 1 & 2 & 3 \\ 4 & 5 & 6 \end{bmatrix} \quad [B] = \begin{bmatrix} 6 & 9 & 2 \\ -1 & 4 & -7 \end{bmatrix}$$

Remember that $[A]$ and $[B]$ can be added or subtracted because they are the same size, 2×3.

The key sequences below are for entering and adding two matrices. Do all the steps for matrix A, then for matrix B.

	Matrix A	**Matrix B**
To edit a matrix:	MATRX ▶ ▶ 1	MATRX ▶ ▶ 2
To enter matrix size:	2 ENTER 3 ENTER	2 ENTER 3 ENTER
To enter values for row 1:	1 ENTER 2 ENTER 3 ENTER	6 ENTER 9 ENTER 2 ENTER
To enter values for row 2:	4 ENTER 5 ENTER 6 ENTER	(−) 1 ENTER 4 ENTER (−) 7 ENTER
To go to the Home screen:	2nd QUIT	2nd QUIT

To add $[A]$ and $[B]$: MATRX 1 ＋ MATRX 2 ENTER

Your calculator screen will display the sum.

```
[A]+[B]
        [[ 7  11   5 ]
         [ 3   9  -1 ]]
■
```

Use a graphing calculator. Find $[A] + [B]$ and $[A] - [B]$.

1. $[A] = \begin{bmatrix} 3.8 & 2.1 \\ 1.5 & -0.8 \\ -1.4 & 1.9 \end{bmatrix}, [B] = \begin{bmatrix} 1.1 & -1.4 \\ 0.6 & 1.5 \\ -1.7 & 0.8 \end{bmatrix}$

2. $[A] = \begin{bmatrix} 123 & 87 \\ 112 & 63 \end{bmatrix}, [B] = \begin{bmatrix} 112 & 64 \\ 92 & 50 \end{bmatrix}$

3. $[A] = \begin{bmatrix} 5 & -4 & 7 & -13 \\ 4 & -9 & -10 & 5 \\ 6 & -7 & -6 & 12 \end{bmatrix}, [B] = \begin{bmatrix} -5 & 8 & 13 & -12 \\ 4 & 11 & 7 & 10 \\ -15 & 6 & -8 & -3 \end{bmatrix}$

4. $[A] = \begin{bmatrix} 122 & 48 & -63 \\ 95 & 167 & 78 \\ -110 & 59 & 45 \\ -87 & 114 & 132 \end{bmatrix}, [B] = \begin{bmatrix} -89 & 67 & -101 \\ 42 & -53 & 77 \\ -81 & 103 & 96 \\ 59 & 88 & -107 \end{bmatrix}$

5. a. Use the matrices in Exercise 1 to find $[B] + [A]$ and $[B] - [A]$.
   b. Writing Does changing the order of the matrices affect the result when you add matrices? subtract matrices? Explain.

1-9 **V**ariables and Formulas in Spreadsheets

What You'll Learn
- Using variables and formulas in spreadsheets

...And Why
To investigate real-world situations, such as television viewership

Math A Test Prep

1 Of the first 20 customers at a music store, 7 bought tapes, 10 bought CDs, and 3 bought neither. If this trend continues, what is the probability that the next customer will buy a tape or CD?

(1) $\frac{17}{20}$ (3) $\frac{3}{20}$

(2) $\frac{17}{3}$ (4) $\frac{7}{10}$

2 A report said that five salespeople earned bonuses of $300, $250, $325, $375, and $250. An error was found in the report. The fifth salesperson had actually earned a bonus of $350. How does the corrected amount affect the mean, median, and mode?

TECHNOLOGY HINT
A spreadsheet program allows you to put a formula in one cell and copy its format in other cells.

T H I N K   A N D   D I S C U S S

How much time do you spend watching television? Is it about average for a teenager? You can use the spreadsheet below to find out.

Like a matrix, a **spreadsheet** organizes data in rows and columns. A **cell** is a box where a row and column meet.

Hours of Weekly TV Viewing

	A	B	C	D
1	Viewing Group	Nov. 91	Nov. 93	Change
2	Children 2–5	26.4	21.5	–4.9
3	Children 6–11	21.2	20.0	–1.2
4	Female Teens	22.2	20.8	–1.4
5	Male Teens	22.7	21.2	–1.5
6	Women 18–24	28.9	25.7	–3.2
7	Men 18–24	23.0	22.5	–0.5
8	Women 25–54	32.8	30.6	–2.2
9	Men 25–54	28.1	28.1	0
10	Women 55 and over	43.5	44.2	0.7
11	Men 55 and over	39.8	38.5	–1.3

column ↓

cell B4

row ↑

1. **a.** Estimate About how many hours do you watch TV in a week?

    b. Compare your weekly TV viewing hours with the November 1993 average for your group.

You can use spreadsheet formulas to calculate the values in column D. The spreadsheet you see on a computer screen shows the value in the cell. The formula used to calculate the value is not shown in the spreadsheet.

Cell	Formula in Cell	Value Shown in Cell
D2	C2 − B2	−4.9
D3	C3 − B3	−1.2
D4	C4 − B4	−1.4
⋮	⋮	⋮

You can save time by using expressions to write formulas in cells. Suppose you change the value in cell B4. The computer will automatically evaluate the formula C4 − B4 and change the value in cell D4.

A computer spreadsheet program uses these operation symbols:

- To multiply: 3 * 5 means 3 · 5.
- To divide: 3/5 means 3 ÷ 5.
- To raise to a power: 3^5 means 3^5.

Example 1 ·········

Cell A2 contains a value for the variable *x*. Write a spreadsheet formula for cell B2 to evaluate the expression in cell B1.

	A	B	C	D	E
1	x	x^3	x – 3	3x	
2	–4				
3	–1				

Expression	Cell	Formula in Cell	Value Shown in Cell
x^3	B2	A2^3	–64

2. What formulas would the computer use to find the values in cells C2 and D2?

3. Write the formulas and find the values for cells B3, C3, and D3.

4. Suppose you use column E to evaluate $2x^3 - 5$. What spreadsheet formula would you use in cell E2?

Example 2   Relating to the Real World ·········

Package Delivery Both the United States Postal Service (USPS) and the United Parcel Service (UPS) add the girth of a package to its length to find its delivery size. Both USPS and UPS measure dimensions in inches.

Write a formula for cell D2 that will find the delivery size of a package. Then find the delivery size of the package in row 2.

	A	B	C	D
1	width	height	length	delivery size
2	5	10	20	
3	16	28	30	
4	18.5	20.5	26	

formula for cell D2:

$$\begin{aligned} &\quad\text{girth} \quad+\ \text{length} \\ &=\quad 2w \ +\ 2h \ +\quad l \\ &=\ 2 * A2 + 2 * B2 +\quad C2 \end{aligned}$$

delivery size:

$$\begin{aligned} &\quad 2 \cdot 5 \ +\ 2 \cdot 10\ +\quad 20 \\ &=\quad 50 \end{aligned}$$

The delivery size of the package in row 2 is 50 in.

girth = 2w + 2h

height
h

The length of a package is its longest dimension.

width
w

length
l

5. The maximum delivery size for packages sent by USPS is 108 in. For UPS the maximum delivery size is 130 in. Find the values in cells D3 and D4. Which package or packages qualify for UPS delivery but not for USPS delivery?

6. Critical Thinking Suppose for the package in row 4 you used 26 in. as the height and 20.5 in. as the length. Is this helpful to the person mailing the package? Explain.

Exercises   ON YOUR OWN

1. Critical Thinking How are spreadsheet formulas similar to other kinds of formulas you have used? How are they different?

2. Suppose you are an employer. You must find your employees' wages, taxes, and income after taxes. Can a spreadsheet program save you time? Explain.

Use the spreadsheet.

3. Write the formulas you would use in cells B2, C2, and D2 to evaluate the expressions in cells B1, C1, and D1.

4. Find the values for cells B2, C2, and D2.

5. Find the values for cells B3, C3, and D3.

6. Open-ended Write an expression of your own for cell E1. Then write the formula for cell E2 that you would use to evaluate your expression.

	A	B	C	D	E
1	x	4x^2	2x – 5	3x + 7	
2	7				
3	–2				

Evaluate each spreadsheet expression.

7. mean of three numbers: (A2 + B2 + C2)/3
   a. for A2 = −3, B2 = − 9, C2 = 3
   b. for A2 = −10.8, B2 = 4.5, C2 = 0.6

8. total of hourly wage minus deductions: A4 * B4 − C4
   a. for A4 = 6, B4 = 10, C4 = 20
   b. for A4 = 11.70, B4 = 40, C4 = 135

9. Geometry The formula for the volume of a rectangular prism is $V = lwh$. The spreadsheet gives the dimensions in feet for three rectangular prisms.
   a. Write a formula for cell D2 to find the volume of the rectangular prism in row 2.
   b. Find the volume of each rectangular prism.

	A	B	C	D
1	length	width	height	volume
2	20	12	8	
3	14.8	9.8	5	
4	30	25.4	7	

10. Writing You can find the volume of a cube using the formula $V = s^3$, where s is the length of a side. Explain how to set up a spreadsheet to find the volumes of cubes with sides 4, 12, 3.8, and 6.25.

11. **a. Business** Write a formula for cell D2 in the spreadsheet for Milo Construction Company.
    b. Find the values for cells D2, D3, D4, and D5.
    c. Suppose a worker earned the mean yearly wage in 1995. She worked 40 h each week and 50 weeks in a year. What was her hourly wage?

Milo Construction Company

	A	B	C	D
1	Year	Number of Workers	Total Wages Paid to All Workers	Mean Yearly Wage
2	1980	13	$241,400	▪
3	1985	20	$485,190	▪
4	1990	35	$969,570	▪
5	1995	39	$1,203,580	▪

Geometry **Evaluate each spreadsheet expression.**

12. area of a parallelogram: B2 * C2
    a. for B2 = 9, C2 = 12
    b. for B2 = 15.3, C2 = 8.9

13. surface area of a sphere: 4/3 * 3.14 * A2^3
    a. for A2 $= \frac{3}{4}$
    b. for A2 = 7.2

14. volume of a cylinder: 3.14 * B3^2 * C3
    a. for B3 = 5, C3 = 8
    b. for B3 = 3.5, C3 = 4.2

15. surface area of a rectangular prism:
    2 * B2 * C2 + 2 * B2 * D2 + 2 * C2 * D2
    a. for B2 = 2, C2 = 3, D2 = 4
    b. for B2 = 3.5, C2 = 5.8, D2 = 4.2

16. **a.** How are the values in column G below related to values in columns A and D?
    b. Write formulas to find the values of the cells in columns G and H.
    c. *Critical Thinking* How does this spreadsheet model adding matrices?

	A	B	C	D	E	F	G	H
1	−3	4		−2	−4		−5	0
2	0	5		−1	7		−1	12
3	3	−2		4	−6		7	−8

17. *Computer* Eva Arturo owns Shine On, a small shop in the mall. She buys earrings for $6.75 and sells them for $8.95. The store sold 127 pairs of earrings in January, 174 in February, and 156 in March. Create a spreadsheet to calculate each amount.
    a. the monthly earring sales
    b. the monthly profit from earring sales

18. *Critical Thinking* In Exercise 17, what computer formula could you use to find the total profit for all three months?

Population of Four Cities in the United States

	A	B	C	D	E	F
1	City	1950 Population	1990 Population	Population change (1950 to 1990)	Area (mi^2)	1990 Density (people/mi^2)
2	Fort Wayne, IN	133,607	172,971	■	62.7	■
3	Albuquerque, NM	96,815	384,619	■	132.2	■
4	Houston, TX	596,163	1,629,902	■	539.9	■
5	Norfolk, VA	213,513	261,229	■	53.8	■

Source: *The World Almanac* and *The Statistical Abstract of the United States*

19. Standardized Test Prep For the spreadsheet, which statements are correct?

   I. The formula for cell D2 is C2 − B2.

  II. In column D, negative entries indicate a population loss.

 III. The formula for cell F5 is B5/E5.

  A. I and III   **B.** II and III   **C.** I and II   **D.** I, II, and III

Chapter Project *Find Out by Creating*

- Measure the tibia, humerus, and radius bones and the height of several adults to the nearest half-inch.

- Create a spreadsheet. Organize the measurements. Use the formulas from the Find Out question on page 29 in your spreadsheet to predict the heights of the adults.

- Compare the predicted heights with the measured heights. Does one of the formulas predict heights better than the other formulas? Explain.

Exercises   **MIXED REVIEW**

Simplify each expression.

20. $8 - 14 \div 2$ **21.** $(8 - 14) \div 2$

22. $|8 - 32 \div 4| + 1$ **23.** $(20 - 12) \div (3 + 1)$

24. $9(3 + 5) + 6 \div 3$ **25.** $[9(3 + 5) + 6] \div 3$

26. $\dfrac{6 - 18}{2}$ **27.** $\dfrac{-5 - 4^2}{-7}$

28. $6 + 3^2 - 2 \cdot 5$ **29.** $10 - 4 \cdot 8 - 7^2$

30. a. A notebook costs $1.95. Write an equation to find the cost of any number of notebooks.

     b. What is the cost of three notebooks?

PORTFOLIO

Select one or two items from your work for this chapter. Consider:
- corrected work
- diagrams, graphs, or charts
- a journal entry

Explain why you have included each selection that you make.

Finishing the Chapter Project

The BIG DIG!

Questions on pages 9, 29, 39, and 49 should help you to complete your project. Assemble all the parts of your project in a notebook. Add a summary of what you have learned about using the height formulas. What difficulties did you have? Are there ways to avoid these problems? What advice would you give to an archaeologist or forensic scientist about predicting heights from bone lengths?

Reflect and Revise

Ask a classmate to review your project notebook with you. Together, check that your graphs are clearly labeled and accurate. Check that you have used formulas correctly and that your calculations are accurate. Is your spreadsheet well organized and easy to follow? Make any revisions necessary to improve your work.

Follow Up

Archaeologists and forensic scientists use many other formulas about the human body. Research these by contacting your local police department or by using one of the resources listed below.

For More Information

Avi-Yonah, Michael. *Dig This! How Archaeologists Uncover Our Past.* Minneapolis, Minnesota: Runestone, 1993.

Stones and Bones! How Archaeologists Trace Human Origins. Prepared by the Geography Department, Runestone Press. Minneapolis, Minnesota: Runestone, 1994.

"It's a Boy." *Scholastic Math Magazine* (April 1993):12–13.

"The Arm Bone's Connected to Math." *Scholastic Math Magazine* (October 1992): 8–9.

Key Terms

absolute value (p. 20)
bar graph (p. 6)
base (p. 15)
cell (p. 45)
entry (p. 40)
equation (p. 11)
evaluate (p. 16)
event (p. 36)
experimental
   probability (p. 36)
exponent (p. 15)
integers (p. 19)

irrational
   numbers (p. 30)
line graph (p. 7)
line plot (p. 4)
matrix (p. 40)
mean (p. 5)
median (p. 5)
mode (p. 4)
opposite (p. 19)
order of
   operations
   (p. 15)

rational
   numbers (p. 30)
real numbers (p. 30)
reciprocal (p. 32)
simulation (p. 37)
spreadsheet (p. 45)
term (p. 11)
variable (p. 11)
variable expression
   (p. 11)

How am I doing?

- State three ideas from this chapter that you think are important. Explain your choices.
- Describe the rules for the order of operations that you must use to simplify expressions.

SELF ASSESSMENT

Displaying Data Relationships with Graphs   1-1

You can use a **line plot** or **histogram** to show frequency, or the number of times a data item occurs. A **bar graph** compares amounts. A **line graph** shows how a set of values changes over time. **Mean, median,** and **mode** are three measures of central tendency.

Find the mean, median, and mode for each set of data.

1. 24, 45, 33, 27, 24

2. 80, 87, 81, 92, 87, 80, 83

3. 2.4, 2.3, 2.1, 2.5, 2.3, 2.2

Use the bar graph.

4. Find the difference between the 1996 and the 1997 sales for March.

5. Which month had the most sales in 1996?

6. Find the average number of video recorders sold during the first three months for each year.

Sales of Video Recorders

Variables, Order of Operations, Evaluating Expressions   1-2, 1-3

A **variable** represents changing values. To **evaluate** a variable expression, you substitute a given number for each variable. Then you simplify the expression using the **order of operations**.

Evaluate each expression for $a = 3$, $b = 2$, and $c = 1$.

7. $4a - b^2$

8. $9(a + 2b) + c$

9. $\dfrac{2a + b}{2}$

10. $2a^2 - (4b + c)$

11. Open-ended Use 3, −, 6, *x*, 5, and + to write a variable expression: Simplify your expression.

12. A data entry operator can input 140 records into a computer each day. The table shows the relationship between the number of days worked and the number of records entered.

  a. Write an equation to describe this relationship.

  b. How many records will be entered after 21 days? after 30 days?

Days	Records Entered
1	140
2	280
3	420
4	560

Adding and Subtracting Integers   1-4

Two numbers are **opposites** if they are the same distance from zero on the number line. Whole numbers and their opposites are **integers.** The **absolute value** of a number is its distance from zero on a number line.

To add two numbers with the same sign, *add* their absolute values. The sum has the same sign as the addends. To add two numbers with different signs, find the *difference* of their absolute values. The sum has the same sign as the number with the greater absolute value. To subtract a number, add its opposite.

Add or subtract.

13. $(-13) + (-4)$ **14.** $5 - 17$ **15.** $-12.4 + 22.3$ **16.** $|54.3 - 29.4|$ **17.** $-12 - (-7)$

Evaluate each expression for $a = -5, b = 8$, and $c = -7$.

18. $a + c$ **19.** $b - c$ **20.** $-a + b$ **21.** $|c - a|$ **22.** $-|b| + |c|$

Multiplying and Dividing Integers   1-5

The product or quotient of two integers with the same sign is *positive*. The product or quotient of two integers with different signs is *negative*.

Evaluate each variable expression for $x = 4, y = -2$, and $z = -3$.

23. $-3^2 + z^2$ **24.** $y + (-4)x$ **25.** $5xy$ **26.** $\frac{x}{-2} + 2z$ **27.** $\frac{x - y}{3}$

28. Evaluate $a^2 - 2b^3$ for $a = -5$ and $b = -3$. Choose the correct answer.

  A. -29 **B.** 79 **C.** 43 **D.** 241 **E.** -181

Real Numbers and Rational Numbers   1-6

A **rational number**, such as $\frac{5}{8}$ or $\frac{2}{3}$, is a ratio of two integers. An **irrational number** like π or $\sqrt{2}$, cannot be written as a ratio of integers. The product of a nonzero number and its **reciprocal** is 1.

Evaluate each expression for $a = \frac{5}{6}$ and $b = -\frac{2}{3}$.

29. $a - 3b$ **30.** $3a - 4b$ **31.** $6ab$ **32.** $a \div b$ **33.** $a + b^2$

Experimental Probability and Simulations

Experimental probability is based on data gathered through observations. The probability of an event, P(event), equals the number of times an event happens divided by the number of times the experiment is done.

34. The results of a blind taste test of fruit juices are at the right. Find each probability.

Brand A	Brand B	Brand C
̶H̶H̶ ̶H̶H̶		

   a. P (preferred Brand A)   b. P (preferred Brand B)
   c. P (preferred Brand C)   d. P (did *not* prefer Brand C)

Organizing Data in Matrices

A **matrix** is a rectangular arrangement of numbers in rows and columns. You can add or subtract matrices if they are the same size. You add and subtract matrices by adding or subtracting corresponding entries.

Find the sum of each pair of matrices. Then find the difference of each pair of matrices by subtracting the second matrix from the first matrix.

35. $\begin{bmatrix} 2 & -3 \\ 9 & -1 \end{bmatrix}, \begin{bmatrix} 5 & 10 \\ -11 & -9 \end{bmatrix}$

36. $\begin{bmatrix} 1.2 & -1.1 \\ 2.7 & 2.9 \\ -3.2 & -1.1 \end{bmatrix}, \begin{bmatrix} 3.1 & 1.7 \\ -1.7 & -3.2 \\ 1.5 & 2.3 \end{bmatrix}$

37. $\begin{bmatrix} -\frac{1}{2} \\ \frac{2}{5} \end{bmatrix}, \begin{bmatrix} \frac{5}{8} \\ -\frac{3}{4} \end{bmatrix}$

Variables and Formulas in Spreadsheets

You can use a **spreadsheet** to analyze data. A spreadsheet organizes data in rows and columns. A **cell** is a box where a row and column meet. Spreadsheets use formulas to calculate values.

38. **Writing** A. Jones earns \$5.85/h, and M. Vasquez earns \$6.30/h. Explain how you could use a spreadsheet to find each person's total wage.

Employee	M	T	W	TH	F
A. Jones	7.8	7.3	7.9	7.2	7.3
M. Vasquez	7.5	7.6	7.4	7.8	7.8

Getting Ready for .... CHAPTER 2

Evaluate each expression.

39. $3n + 2$ for $n = 1.2$ 40. $8(g + 1) - 3$ for $g = -2$ 41. $5.4b + 2.6b$ for $b = 10$

Complete the spreadsheet at the right for each value of x.

42.
43.
44.

	A	B	C	D	E
1	x	x + 2	2x	x^2	x^3
2	−2	▩	▩	▩	▩
3	0	▩	▩	▩	▩
4	4	▩	▩	▩	▩

Use an equation to model the relationship in each table.

1.

Number	Cost
1	$2.30
2	$4.60
3	$6.90

2.

Payment	Change
$1	$9
$2	$8
$3	$7

Simplify each expression.

3. $3 + 5 - 4$

4. $8 - 2^4 \div 2$

5. $\dfrac{2 \cdot 3 - 1}{3^2}$

6. $36 - (4 + 5 \cdot 4)$

Evaluate each expression for $x = 3, y = -1$, and $z = 2$.

7. $2x + 3y + z$

8. $-xyz$

9. $-3x - 2z - 7$

10. $-z^3 - 2z + z$

11. $\dfrac{xy - 3z}{-5}$

12. $x^2 + (-x)^2$

Find the sum or difference.

13. $\begin{bmatrix} 3 & 2 \\ -1 & 5 \end{bmatrix} + \begin{bmatrix} 8 & -5 \\ 3 & 0 \end{bmatrix}$

14. $\begin{bmatrix} 1 & 9 & -4 \\ 5 & 2 & -1 \\ -6 & -2 & -1 \end{bmatrix} - \begin{bmatrix} 2 & -6 & 7 \\ -8 & 3 & -3 \\ 4 & -7 & 9 \end{bmatrix}$

Explain why each statement is true or false.

15. All rational numbers are integers.

16. The absolute value of a number is always positive.

17. A random survey of 60 students showed that 36 students used calculators for computation. What is the probability that a student chosen at random uses a calculator for computation?

18. Complete the following: $3^2 \cdot \blacksquare = 1$

A. $\dfrac{1}{9}$ B. -3^2 C. 0   D. 2^3 E. $-\dfrac{1}{3}$

19. **Writing** Tell if each of the subtraction sentences would *always*, *sometimes*, or *never* be true. Support your answer with two examples.
 a. $(+) - (+) = (+)$ b. $(+) - (-) = (-)$
 c. $(-) - (-) = (-)$ d. $(-) - (+) = (+)$

20. **Open-ended** Write four rational numbers. Then use a number line to order them from least to greatest.

Evaluate each spreadsheet expression.

21. $(A3 + B1 + C2)/4$
 for A3 $= -5.3$, B1 $= 7.5$, C2 $= 6.48$

22. $A1 - B1 * C2$
 for A1 $= 16.09$, B1 $= 9.16$, C2 $= -5$

23. A softball player made a hit 54 times in the last 171 times at bat. Find the probability that the softball player will get a hit the next time at bat.

24. The double line graph shows the quarterly profit for a software company.

Company Profits

 a. In which quarter did the company have its lowest quarterly profit?

 b. Estimate the company's profit for each quarter. Then find the mean quarterly profit for each year.

25. **Writing** Explain why the equation below is not always true.
$$\left|\frac{a}{b}\right| = \frac{a}{b}$$

Part I

1   Tamara's teacher allows students to decide whether to use the mean, median, or mode for their test averages. Tamara will receive the highest average if she uses the mean. Which set of test scores could be Tamara's?

   (1) 95, 82, 76, 95, 96   (3) 65, 84, 75, 74, 65
   (2) 79, 80, 91, 83, 80   (4) 100, 87, 94, 94, 81

2   Which equation models the relationship in the table?

Speed s (mi/h)	Distance d (mi)
30	90
40	120
50	150
60	180

   (1) $d = s + 60$ (3) $d = 3s$
   (2) $d = \frac{1}{3}s$ (4) $d = s - 60$

3   The expression $2(5 - 3)^2 + 4 \div 2$ can be simplified to ▪.
   (1) 6   (3) 10
   (2) 8   (4) 18

4   Which is the greatest sum or difference?
   (1) $19.8 - (-2.4)$ (3) $37 + (-15)$
   (2) $-17 - 31$ (4) $-18.3 + 4.7$

5   What is the value of $\dfrac{3x - (-4)}{7}$ when $x = -6$?

   (1) 2   (3) -3
   (2) 3   (4) -2

6   Which of the following does *not* equal 27 when $x = -3$?
   (1) $-x^3$ (3) $-(-x)^3$
   (2) $-9x$ (4) $3x^2$

7   The Fuller Book Company inspects a sample of 860 books and finds that 172 books have defective bindings. What is the probability that a book has a defective binding?

   (1) $\frac{1}{4}$ (2) $\frac{1}{3}$ (3) $\frac{1}{2}$ (4) $\frac{1}{5}$

8   Which equation illustrates the identity property of addition?
   (1) $x + 0 = 0$ (3) $1 + x = x$
   (2) $0 + x = x$ (4) $x + 1 = 1$

Part II

9   Write the negation of the sentence: $30 \div 5 \geq 6$. Determine the truth value of the original sentence and its negation.

10   Simplify: $\dfrac{3^2 + 3^2 + 3^2}{4^2 + 4^2 + 4^2}$.

11   Evaluate $\frac{s}{t}$ for $s = \frac{3}{8}$ and $t = \frac{5}{16}$.

Part III

12   Write a formula for cells C2 and C3 in the spreadsheet. Then calculate the values for cells C2 and C3 using the formula.

Areas of Triangles

	A	B	C
1	base	height	Area
2	4	6	▪
3	5	9	▪

13   Write in order from least to greatest: $\frac{5}{6}, -\frac{6}{7}, 0.4, -0.75$.

Part IV

14   The table below shows the number of questions the students in Ms. Lee's class answered correctly on the quiz.

Correct Answers on Quiz

Number Correct	1	2	3	4	5
Frequency	1	5	6	7	3

   a   Draw a histogram of the data.
   b   What is the mode of the data?
   c   What is the median of the data?

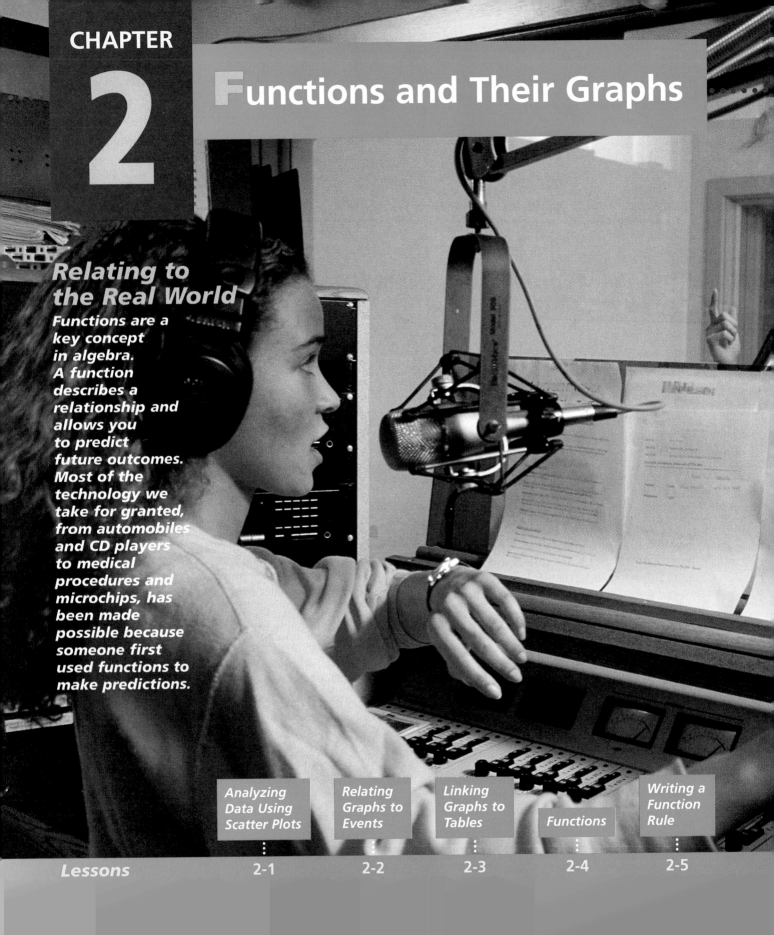

Relating to the Real World

Functions are a key concept in algebra. A function describes a relationship and allows you to predict future outcomes. Most of the technology we take for granted, from automobiles and CD players to medical procedures and microchips, has been made possible because someone first used functions to make predictions.

FAST TALKER

R adio announcers have to time their speech so that commericals and news updates are the correct length. Do you know how fast you talk? How about your friends? Try saying these tongue twisters: "The sunshade sheltered Sarah from the sunshine." — "Lavonne lingered, looking longingly for her lost laptop."

As you work through the chapter, you will time people as they say tongue twisters. You will use scatter plots and graphs to help investigate and display relationships in the data you collect. Then, using functions, you will summarize your findings and make predictions.

To help you complete the project:

The Three Views of a Function	Families of Functions	The Probability Formula
2-6	2-7	2-8

The Coordinate Plane

Before Lesson 2-1

The **coordinate plane** is formed when two number lines intersect at right angles. The horizontal axis is the **x-axis** and the vertical axis is the **y-axis.** The axes intersect at the **origin** and divide the coordinate plane into four sections called **quadrants.**

An **ordered pair** of numbers identifies the location of a point. These numbers are the **coordinates** of the point.

$(-2, 4)$

x-coordinate   **y-coordinate**

Name the point with the given coordinates in the graph at the right.

1. $(2, 3)$
2. $(-5, -3)$
3. $(-3, 2)$
4. $(0, -5)$

Name the coordinates of each point in the graph at the right.

5. A
6. F
7. D
8. I

The coordinates of point J are $(-3, 4)$.

$C(5, -3)$

Point C is 5 units to the right and 3 units down from the origin.

origin $(0, 0)$

Graph each point on a coordinate plane.

9. $(3, 0)$
10. $(-1, 8)$
11. $(-2, -3)$
12. $(7, -7)$

In which quadrant or on which axis would you find each point?

13. $(-10, 6)$
14. $(-12, 0)$
15. $(8, -18)$
16. $(0, 30)$

17. **a.** Graph each point on a coordinate plane.
    $(-4, 0), (0, 1), (1, 5), (2, 1), (6, 0), (2, -1), (1, -5), (0, -1), (-4, 0)$
   b. Connect the points in order and describe the figure formed.

18. **Writing** Write a sentence describing the x- and y-coordinates of all points in Quadrant IV.

What You'll Learn

- Drawing and interpreting scatter plots
- Analyzing trends in scatter plots

...And Why

To predict trends related to television and transportation

What You'll Need

- graph paper
- tape measure

2-1 Analyzing Data Using Scatter Plots

WORK TOGETHER

Work in groups.

1. **a.** Data Collection Measure the heights and arm spans for each member of your group.
   b. Write the measurements as ordered pairs (height, arm span).
   c. Graph the ordered pairs for your data. Label the graph as shown.

2. **a.** Data Collection Share your data with all other groups in your class.
   b. Graph the data for your entire class.

3. Critical Thinking Compare the graphs you drew in Questions 1(c) and 2(b). Why does the graph for the class show the relationship between height and arm span more clearly?

4. Discussion Describe the relationship between height and arm span.

TECHNOLOGY HINT

You can use spreadsheet software or a graphing calculator to make a scatter plot.

THINK AND DISCUSS

Drawing and Interpreting Scatter Plots

A **scatter plot** is a graph that relates data from two different sets. To make a scatter plot, the two sets of data are plotted as ordered pairs.

Example 1 **Relating to the Real World** ·················

Television A group of students set out to see if the hours of television they watched yesterday relates to their scores on today's test. They polled each student in the group. Draw a scatter plot of the data.

A Test of Television			
Hours Watched	Test Score	Hours Watched	Test Score
0	92	2	80
0	100	2.5	65
0.5	89	2.5	70
1	82	3	68
1	90	3.5	60
1	95	4	65
1.5	85	4.5	55
2	70	5	60

Plot as: (2, 80)

The highest test score is 100. So, a reasonable scale on the vertical axis is from 0 to 100 with every ten points labeled.

A Test of Television

5. Two students in the sample watched 2 hours of television. What does the graph tell you about the students' test scores?

6. a. A student in the sample scores 85 on the test. How many hours of television did this student watch?
   b. How can you tell by looking at the scatter plot?

7. **Try This** Each ordered pair represents (unit price, quantity sold) of various items for sale in a store. Draw a scatter plot of the data.
   ($5.00, 56), ($9.99, 4), ($8.49, 21), ($1.09, 71), ($.35, 92), ($5.00, 32)

Analyzing Trends in Data

You use scatter plots to investigate trends relating two sets of data. These trends show positive, negative, or no correlation.

A **trend line** on a scatter plot shows a correlation more clearly.

Positive correlation
In general, both sets of data increase together.

Negative correlation
In general, one set of data decreases as the other set increases.

No correlation
Sometimes data sets are not related.

Example 2   Relating to the Real World

Cars The scatter plot below shows information from newspaper advertisements for a particular car model. Is there a *positive correlation*, a *negative correlation*, or *no correlation* between the ages and asking prices of these cars? Explain.

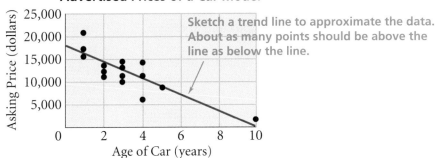

Sketch a trend line to approximate the data. About as many points should be above the line as below the line.

GRAPHING CALCULATOR HINT

You can use a graphing calculator to draw a trend line.

This trend line slants downward, so there is a negative correlation. As the age of the car increases, the price of the car decreases.

8. **Critical Thinking** What does each data point in Example 2 represent? Think of your answer in terms of (*x*–coordinate, *y*–coordinate).

9. **Predict** the asking price of a 7-year old car of the same model.

Exercises   ON YOUR OWN

Critical Thinking Would you expect a *positive correlation,* a *negative correlation,* or *no correlation* between the two data sets? Why?

1. Amount of Free Time vs. Number of Classes Taken

2. Air Pollution Levels vs. Number of Cars on the Road

3. Snow Shovel Sales vs. Amount of Snowfall

4. Length at Birth vs. Month of Birth

5. the Number of Gallons of Heating Oil Consumed vs. Average Daily Temperature

6. Number of Cavities vs. Number of Times you Floss Your Teeth

7. Cost of a Pair of Sneakers vs. Sneaker Size

8. Number of Calories Burned vs. Time Exercising

9. a. **Math in the Media** Think about the weather and its effect on voters. What correlation would you expect between inches of precipitation and voter turnout? Explain.
   b. Should candidates in the election be concerned about the weather forecast? Why or why not?

See special election-day supplement with complete guide to ballot questions.

The Daily Tribune

RAIN, HEAVY AT TIMES
CHANCE OF SNOW
HIGH: 38   LOW: 30
FULL REPORT ON PAGE 20

...ber 4, 1997

10. During one month at a local deli, the number of pounds of ham sold decreased as the number of pounds of turkey sold increased.
   a. Is this an example of a *positive correlation*, *negative correlation*, or *no correlation*?
   b. **Critical Thinking** Does this mean that fewer pounds of ham were sold *because* the deli sold more pounds of turkey? Could there be another reason? Explain.

11. a. **Nature** Use the data in the table to draw a scatter plot.
   b. Draw a trend line on the scatter plot. Describe the correlation, if any, between length and mass of a bird egg.
   c. Measure the length of the mallard duck egg at the right. **Predict** its mass.

Is there a *positive correlation*, a *negative correlation*, or *no correlation* between the two data sets in each scatter plot?

How Big Is a Bird Egg?

Type of Bird Egg	Length (cm)	Mass (g)
Swallow	1.9	2
Swift	2.5	3.6
Turtledove	3.1	9
Partridge	3.6	14
Barn owl	3.9	20.7
Arctic tern	4.0	19
Louisiana egret	4.5	27.5
Grey heron	6.0	60
Chicken (small)	5.3	42.5
Chicken (extra large)	6.3	63.8

12.

13.

14.

15.

16. **Open-ended** Describe three different situations: one that shows a positive correlation, one that shows a negative correlation, and one that shows no correlation.

Nutrition Use the table below for Exercises 17–18.

Calories and Fat in Some Common Foods

	Milk	Eggs	Chicken	Ham	Ice Cream	Corn	Ground Beef	Broccoli	Cheese
Grams of Fat*	8	6	4	19	14	1	10	1	9
Number of Calories*	150	80	90	245	270	70	185	45	115

*per serving

Source: *Home and Garden Bulletin No. 72*

17. a. Draw a scatter plot. Label the *x*-axis as Fat (g) and the *y*-axis as Number of Calories.
   b. Is there a *positive correlation*, *negative correlation*, or *no correlation* between calories and grams of fat?

18. a. **Writing** Write a statement to **generalize** the relationship between calories and grams of fat.
   b. **Critical Thinking** Do you think this statement is always true? **Justify** your answer with an example.

Toll Charges for 12 Vehicles on the Indiana Toll Road

Source: *Indiana Department of Highways*

Transportation Use the scatter plot above.

19. What does each data point in the scatter plot represent? Think of your answer in terms of (*x*-coordinate, *y*-coordinate).

20. How can you tell which vehicles traveled the same distance?

21. a. How can you tell which vehicles paid the same toll charge?
  b. *Open-ended* Why might two vehicles that travel different distances pay the same toll charge?

22. Is there a correlation between distance traveled and toll charges? Explain your reasoning.

Chapter Project **Find Out by Doing**

Work in a group. Choose a tongue twister from p. 57.

• Time one person saying the tongue twister. Record the time to the nearest tenth of a second.

• Time two people saying the tongue twister. Be sure they speak one after the other.

• Add more people. Make a table for the data you collect.

• Collect data from other groups.

• Draw a scatter plot for all the data. Describe any correlation you see.

Exercises   MIXED REVIEW

Evaluate each expression for $x = -3$, $y = 5$, and $z = 1$.

23. $3x + 2y - z$

24. $x^3 - 3z + y$

25. $\dfrac{y^2 + 2z}{x}$

26. $6x^2 - 4z^2$

27. $\dfrac{x + 6z}{2y}$

28. $z(y - 8)$

29. $x^2 + y^2 - z$

30. $z^3 - x^2$

31. *Critical Thinking* Is it easiest to find the mean, median, or mode of data in a line plot? Explain.

Getting Ready for Lesson 2-2

Use the graph at the right.

32. Describe the trend in minimum wage earnings.

33. Over which years did the minimum wage remain the same?

34. Over which years did the greatest increase in minimum wage occur? How do you know?

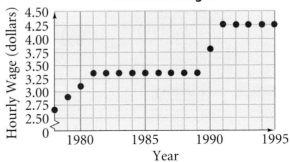

Minimum Wages

Source: *Statistical Abstract*

What You'll Learn

- Interpreting and sketching graphs from stories
- Classifying data as discrete or continuous

...And Why

To solve problems relating to travel and transportation

PROBLEM SOLVING

Look Back Another way to solve Example 1 is by writing a description. Write a short paragraph to describe the graph.

2-2 Relating Graphs to Events

THINK AND DISCUSS

Interpreting Graphs

Graphs can describe real situations. A graph is not a picture like a photograph. A graph shows a relationship between two variables.

Example 1 Relating to the Real World

Transportation A commute home from school combines walking with taking the subway. The graph describes the trip by relating the variables time and total distance. Describe what the graph shows.

A Commute Home

To describe a graph, you can label each part.

A Commute Home

walking
distance increases
slowly

taking the subway
distance increases quickly

waiting for the subway

1. **Critical Thinking** Explain why the section of the graph showing the person waiting for the subway is flat.

2. Why is the subway section steeper than the walking sections?

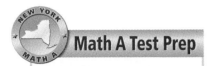
1 Between which two
data sets would you
expect a negative
correlation?
(1) Annual Income
vs.Years of Education
(2) Number of Vehicles
Passing through
Intersection vs.
Inches of Snowfall
(3) Math Test Scores vs.
Day of Birth
(4) Number of People at
Beach vs.
Temperature

2 This graph shows Dave's
morning run. Compare
and contrast the
intervals between times
10 and 15 and times 15
and 20.

Dave's Morning Run

This graph shows the relationship between time and speed on a bike ride.

Speed on a Bike Ride

3. A friend mistakenly states that this graph describes a person bicycling up and then down a hill. What would you say to this friend to help clear up the misconception?

Sketching Graphs

When you draw a graph without actual data, the graph is called a *sketch*. A sketch is useful when you want to get an idea of what a graph looks like.

Example 2 **Relating to the Real World**

Travel The Shermans are visiting friends several miles from home. On the way, they stop to buy juice drinks. After a few hours, they return home. Sketch a graph to describe the trip. Label the sections.

Choose two variables to explain the situation. Put one on the horizontal axis and the other on the vertical axis.

4. How is an increase in distance from home shown on the graph? a decrease?

5. Try This Sketch a graph to describe your height from the ground on a roller coaster ride. Explain the activity in each section of the graph.

Classifying Data

In this lesson you have worked with variables such as time and distance. Variables represent data values that are *discrete* or *continuous*. **Continuous data** usually involve a measurement, such as temperature, length, or weight. **Discrete data** involve a count, such as a number of people or objects.

Example 3

Classify the data as *continuous* or *discrete*. Explain your reasoning and sketch a graph of each situation.

a. height of a plant for five days   **b.** class attendance for five days

a. The plant height is continuous. The plant continues to grow between the times its height is measured.

b. The attendance is discrete. Each day's count is distinct. For example, there is no meaning for values between Monday's and Tuesday's counts.

6. a. Generalize how graphs of continuous and discrete data differ.
   b. Open-ended Give another example of each type of data.

WORK TOGETHER

Students get to school in a variety of ways. They may walk, drive, take a bus or subway, or ride a bike. The graph shows one student's daily trip.

Work with a partner.

7. Write a story describing how this student traveled to school and the events that took place during the trip.

8. Draw two new graphs to represent your daily trip and your partner's. Present your graphs to the class.

Exercises   ON YOUR OWN

Sketch a graph to describe each situation. Explain the activity in each section of the graph.

1. your distance from the ground as you jump rope   **2.** your energy level during one gym class

3. your pulse rate as you watch a scary movie   **4.** your speed as you skateboard downhill

5. Critical Thinking What is wrong with the graph at the right? Explain how you would fix this graph.

6. Meteorology The graph shows barometric pressure in Pittsburgh, Pennsylvania, during the blizzard of 1993. Describe what happened to pressure during the storm.

People in the Building

Blizzard of 1993

Source: *Purdue Weather Processor*

Classify the data as *discrete* or *continuous*. Explain your reasoning and sketch a graph of each situation.

7. your weight from birth to age 14

8. your algebra test grades for one term

9. the time you get up each morning for one week

10. temperatures throughout one week

11. number of books you bring home each day for a week

12. length of your hair between haircuts

13. your walking speed from this class to your locker

14. time you spend reading each day for a week

15. The graph at the right shows the weight of a baby and the weight of a puppy for their first two years.
  a. Which curve represents the puppy's weight? the baby's?
  b. Describe the growth patterns of the baby and the puppy.

Weight Gains

16. Open-ended Give an example of discrete data changing over time. Explain your reasoning and sketch a graph of the situation.

17. Cars On a highway, a driver sets a car's cruise control for a constant speed of 55 mi/h. Which graph shows the distance the car travels? Which graph shows the speed of the car? Explain your reasoning.

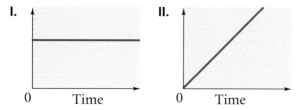

18. Use the cartoon at the right.
  a. What do you think the labels of the axes are?
  b. What is the presenter trying to imply with his graph?
  c. Why is his presentation misleading?
  d. Why might he want to do this?

"As you can see, our profit picture is steady."

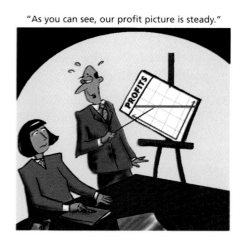

19. Writing Describe what the graph at the right shows about a student's in-line skating experience.

In-Line Skating After School

Exercises **MIXED REVIEW**

In Exercises 20–22, add or subtract.

20. $\begin{bmatrix} 2 & -3 \\ 0 & 8 \end{bmatrix} + \begin{bmatrix} -5 & 9 \\ 7 & -6 \end{bmatrix}$

21. $\begin{bmatrix} 18 & 26 \\ 37 & 12 \end{bmatrix} - \begin{bmatrix} 32 & 15 \\ 39 & 63 \end{bmatrix}$

22. $\begin{bmatrix} 2.3 & 7.5 \\ 0.9 & 8.1 \end{bmatrix} - \begin{bmatrix} 6.8 & 9.2 \\ 1.3 & 0.9 \end{bmatrix}$

23. a. Cooking A hotel kitchen uses 200 lb more vegetables than fruit each day. Write an expression for how many pounds of vegetables the kitchen uses.

b. Suppose the kitchen uses 1000 lb of fruit daily. How many pounds of fruit and vegetables does the kitchen use each week?

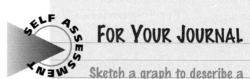

FOR YOUR JOURNAL

Sketch a graph to describe a situation that happened to you. Explain the activity in each section of the graph.

Getting Ready for Lesson 2-3

Graph each ordered pair on a coordinate plane.

24. $(0, 4)$ **25.** $(-9, 3)$ **26.** $(-3, -2)$ **27.** $(2.4, -6)$

Exercises **CHECKPOINT**

1. a. Statistics Use the data to draw a scatter plot.

b. Draw a trend line on the scatter plot. Describe the correlation, if any, between latitude and average low temperature.

c. What would you expect the average low temperature to be in a city at 20° north latitude?

2. Open-ended Describe a situation that shows a positive correlation.

3. Which graph shows your distance from home as you walk to the library and back? Explain.

City	Latitude (°N)	Average Daily Low Temperature in January (°F)
Miami, FL	26	59
Honolulu, HI	21	66
Houston, TX	30	40
Philadelphia, PA	40	23
Burlington, VT	44	8
Jackson, MS	32	33
Cheyenne, WY	41	15
San Diego, CA	33	49

Source: *Statistical Abstract of the United States*

A.

B.

C.

D.

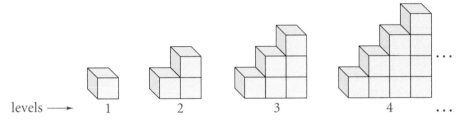
What You'll Learn

2-3 **L**inking Graphs to Tables

- Choosing a scale and graphing data in tables
- Identifying independent and dependent variables

...And Why

To solve problems that involve health and weather

What You'll Need

- blocks or tiles

Number of Levels	Number of Blocks
1	1
2	3
3	■
4	■
5	■
6	■

Target Heart Rates

Age in Years	Beats per Minute
15	143.5
20	140.0
25	136.5
30	133.0
35	129.5
40	126.0
45	122.5

Source: *World Almanac and Book of Facts*

WORK TOGETHER

Patterns Work with a partner to construct or sketch stairs out of blocks.

levels ⟶ 1   2   3   4   . . .

1. Copy and complete the table at the left.

2. **a.** Graph the data in the table. Plot the points as the ordered pairs (number of levels, number of blocks).
   b. Should the points be connected? Why or why not?
   c. Describe any trends you see between the number of levels and the number of blocks.

THINK AND DISCUSS

Health You use tables to organize data. Sometimes a graph shows patterns or trends in data better than a table does.

Heart rate is the **dependent variable** because it *depends* on the age of the person.

Target Heart Rate at 70% Level

The age of the person is the **independent variable**. Changes in age affect heart rate.

3. **Health** What is the target heart rate for a 70-year-old? Explain how you got your answer.

4. **Critical Thinking** Describe the relationship between the age of a person and the target heart rate.

5. Which axis relates to the independent variable? the dependent variable? Write a statement to **generalize** this.

6. **Try This** Identify the independent and dependent variables in the Work Together activity.

TECHNOLOGY HINT

You can use spreadsheet software to graph data in tables. You can improve the look of your graph by changing the scales on the x-axis and y-axis.

You can use data in tables to make graphs. You need to choose an appropriate scale so the data are easy to graph and understand.

Example   **Relating to the Real World**

Weather Graph the data in the table on a coordinate plane.

To draw a graph, first identify the least and greatest values for each set of data. Then, select a scale that includes these values and can easily be divided into equal sections.

How Altitude Affects Temperature

Altitude (meters)	Temperature (°C)
0	13.0
144	12.0
794	11.4
1501	11.4
3100	5.6
5781	−9.7
7461	−22.5
9511	−36.3
10,761	−44.9

Source: The University of Illinois at Urbana-Champaign's Web site *Weather World*

The y-values range from −44.9 to 13.0. So, choose a scale from −50 to 20 and label intervals of 10.

The x-values range from 0 to 10,761. So, choose a scale from 0 to 12,000 and label intervals of 2000. The x-axis is in thousands of meters to make graphing easier.

7. **Try This** Which variable is the dependent variable? the independent variable? Explain.

8. Were all four quadrants needed to graph the data? Why or why not?

9. Describe what happens to the temperature as the altitude increases.

10. **a. Open-ended** Write a question that might be of interest to a meteorologist and can be answered using the table or graph.
    b. Answer the question you wrote in part (a).

1. **a.** *Science* What scales do you need to graph the data in the table?

Weight on Earth (lb)	143	94	127	171
Weight on Moon (lb)	23.6	15.5	21	28.2

   b. Draw the graph.

   c. How can you use the graph to approximate your own weight on the moon?

Identify the independent and dependent variables.

2. hours worked, amount paid

3. area of a square, length of a side

4. weight of book, number of pages   5. weight of apples, cost of apples

6. For Exercises 2–5, write a statement using the word *depends*.

Match each table of data to its graph.

7.

x	y
−1	−1
0	0
1	−1
2	−4

8.

x	y
−2	$\frac{1}{4}$
−1	$\frac{1}{2}$
1	2
2	4

9.

x	y
−2	3
−1	1
0	−1
1	−3

A.

B.

C.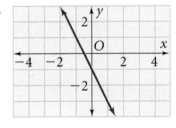

10. **Banking** Many people borrow money when they buy a car. The length of the loan might be anywhere from 2 to 6 years. The table shows the monthly payments on a loan of $10,000 at 9% interest.

Length of Loan (yr)	2	3	4	5	6
Monthly Payment ($)	456.95	318.08	248.92	207.64	180.31

   a. *Critical Thinking* What can you tell about the relationship between the length of the loan and the monthly payments?

   b. Identify the independent and dependent variables.

   c. Graph the data.

   d. Is it easier to see the relationship on a graph or in a table? **Justify** your answer.

11. **a.** Graph the data in the table at the right.

   b. What scales did you use and why?

High School Dance

Minutes Dancing	Admission
43	$5
12	$5
16	$5
111	$5
90	$5

12. Physics *Charles's Law* relates the volume of a gas to its temperature.
  a. What quadrant(s) do you need to draw to graph the data?
  b. Identify the dependent and independent variables.
  c. What happens to the volume of a gas as temperature increases?
  d. Graph the data.

Charles's Law

Temperature (°C)	Volume (m³)
−100	173
−50	223
0	273
50	323
100	373

13. Writing Define *dependent variable* and *independent variable* in your own words. Provide an example to illustrate your definitions.

14. Baseball In 1919, Babe Ruth broke the record for the longest home run.
  a. Graph the data in the table to approximate the path of the ball.
  b. Use the graph to estimate how far Babe Ruth hit the ball.
  c. In 1960, Mickey Mantle of the New York Yankees hit a home run 643 ft. Did he break Babe Ruth's record?
  d. **Research** How far would a home run need to be hit to clear the baseball stadium nearest you?

Babe Ruth's Record Home Run

Distance	Height
0	3
100	83
200	132
300	147
400	128
500	75
575	13

Chapter Project **Find Out by Graphing**

Sopchoppy, Florida, is the home of the Sopchoppy Shoe Shop. Time the tongue twister "The Sopchoppy Shoe Shop sells shoes" with a group of at least ten people. Use the same method you used in the Find Out question on page 63.
• Identify the dependent and independent variables.
• Record your data in a table.
• Display the data in an appropriate graph.

BABE RUTH
LIFETIME BATTING STATISTICS

1925

Exercises   MIXED REVIEW

Sketch a graph to describe each situation. Explain the activity in each section of the graph.

15. your speed as you march in a parade

16. the money you spend each day for a week

17. a. Statistics Make a line plot for the data: 33, 36, 32, 33, 35, 33, 36.
  b. What is the mode of the data?
  c. Open-ended What situation could the data represent?

Getting Ready for Lesson 2-4

Evaluate each expression.

18. $3a - 2$ for $a = -5$

19. $\dfrac{x + 3}{-6}$ for $x = 3$

20. $8p - p$ for $p = -11$

21. $3x^2$ for $x = 6$

22. $\dfrac{x + 5}{-2}$ for $x = 9$

23. $b^3 - 4b$ for $b = -1$

24. $7 - a$ for $a = -3$

25. $\dfrac{3b}{4}$ for $b = 12$

SELF ASSESSMENT

FOR YOUR JOURNAL

Record an example of anything you found difficult in today's lesson.

What You'll Learn

- Defining relations, functions, domain, and range
- Evaluating functions
- Analyzing graphs

...And Why

To solve problems involving money and exercise

2-4 Functions

T H I N K   A N D   D I S C U S S

Identifying Relations and Functions

Suppose your summer job pays $4.25 an hour. Your pay *depends* on the number of hours you work. The number of hours is the independent variable and pay is the dependent variable. So, you can say that pay *is a function of* the number of hours you work.

1. Identify the independent and dependent variables for each situation.
   a. number of magazines sold and the profit made selling magazines
   b. amount of money in the yearbook committee treasury and the number of days the committee can afford to rent camera equipment

2. Write each situation in Question 1 using the words *is a function of*.

Your Summer Job

Hours Worked	Pay
0	$0
1	$4.25
2	$8.50
3	$12.75

You can write the data in the table as a set of ordered pairs {(0, 0),(1, 4.25), (2, 8.50), (3, 12.75)}. Any set of ordered pairs is called a **relation.**

A **function** is a relation that assigns exactly one value of the dependent variable to each value of the independent variable. So, if x is the independent variable and y is the dependent variable, there can be only one y-value for each x-value.

PROBLEM SOLVING

Look Back Graph$(-2, -1)$ and $(-2, 1)$ on a coordinate plane. How are these points alike? How are they different?

Example 1

Determine if each relation is a function.

a.

x	y
11	−2	→ (11, −2)
12	−1	→ (12, −1)
13	0	→ (13, 0)
20	7	→ (20, 7)

The relation is a function because exactly one y-value is assigned to each x-value.

b.

x	y
−2	−1	→ (−2, −1)
−3	0	→ (−3, 0)
6	3	→ (6, 3)
−2	1	→ (−2, 1)

The relation is not a function because two y-values, −1 and 1, are assigned to one x-value, −2.

3. **a.** *Open-ended* Create a data table or set of ordered pairs that is a relation but *not* a function.

   b. *Open-ended* Create a data table or set of ordered pairs that is a function.

Evaluating Functions

QUICK REVIEW

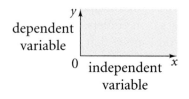

dependent variable

0   independent variable

A **function rule** is an equation that describes a function. If you know the input values, you can use a function rule to find the output values.

$$y = 3x + 4$$

The rule shows you that y is a function of x.

output values
dependent variable

input values
independent variable

QUICK REVIEW

Follow the Order of Operations.
1. Perform any operation(s) inside grouping symbols.
2. Simplify any terms with exponents.
3. Multiply and divide in order from left to right.
4. Add and subtract in order from left to right.

Example 2

Evaluate the function rule $y = 2x^2 - 7$ for $x = -4$.

$y = 2x^2 - 7$
$y = 2(-4)^2 - 7$ ← Substitute –4 for x.
$y = 2(16) - 7$ ← Find (–4)² first.
$y = 32 - 7$ ← Then multiply.
$y = 25$

When the x-value is –4, the y-value is 25.

4. **a.** Evaluate the function rule in Example 2 for $x = 4$.

   b. *Critical Thinking* Explain why $y = 2x^2 - 7$ is a function.

5. **Try This** Evaluate each function rule for $x = 6$.

   a. $y = x - 11$ **b.** $y = -3x^2 + 1$

   c. $y = \frac{1}{2}x^2$ **d.** $y = 1.5 + 2x$

Names Used with a Function

independent variable	dependent variable
input	output
domain	range
x-values	y-values

The **domain** of a function is the set of all possible input values. The **range** of a function is the set of all possible output values. You can write both the domain and the range using braces, {}. The summary box at the left shows some common names for the input and output values of a function.

Example 3

Find the domain and range of the function $\{(-2, 4), (-1, 1), (0, 0), (1, 1), (2, 4)\}$.

The domain is the set of all input values $\{-2, -1, 0, 1, 2\}$.

The range is the set of all output values $\{0, 1, 4\}$.

Example 4 Relating to the Real World ....

Bicycling The distance a wheel moves forward is a function of the number of rotations. The function rule $d = 7n$ describes the relationship between the distance d the wheel in the photo moves in feet and the number of rotations n. Find the range when the domain is $\{0, 2.5, 8\}$.

Substitute 0 for n.	Substitute 2.5 for n.	Substitute 8 for n.
$d = 7n$	$d = 7n$	$d = 7n$
$d = 7(0)$	$d = 7(2.5)$	$d = 7(8)$
$d = 0$	$d = 17.5$	$d = 56$

The range of the function is $\{0, 17.5, 56\}$.

One rotation is 7 ft.

6. Describe what the domain and the range represent in Example 3.

Analyzing Graphs

The domain and range values can be written as ordered pairs (x, y). These ordered pairs are points on the graph of a function. You can tell if a relation is a function by analyzing its graph. One way is to use the **vertical-line test.** If a vertical line passes through a graph more than once, the graph is not the graph of a function.

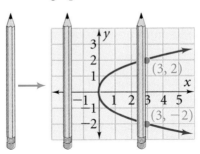

Pass a pencil across the graph as shown. Keep your pencil straight to represent a vertical line.

The pencil goes through more than one point on the graph. This graph is not the graph of a function because there are two y-values for the same x-value.

7. Why does the vertical-line test work? (*Hint*: How does the vertical-line test relate to the definition of a function?)

Work with a partner.

8. Use the vertical-line test to determine if the graphs are graphs of functions. Explain why or why not.

a.   b.   c.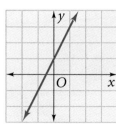

9. Can the graph of a function be a horizontal line? a vertical line? Why or why not?

Exercises   ON YOUR OWN

Evaluate each function rule for $x = -3$.

1. $y = x + 7$ 2. $y = 11x - 1$ 3. $y = x^2$ 4. $y = -4x$

5. $y = 15 - x$ 6. $y = 3x^2 + 2$ 7. $y = \frac{1}{4}x$ 8. $y = -x + 2$

Does each graph represent a function? Why or why not?

9.   10.   11.   12.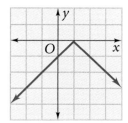

Which relations in Exercises 13–17 are functions? If the relation is a function, identify the dependent and independent variables.

13. number of tickets sold for a benefit play and amount of money made

14. students' heights and grade point averages

15. amount of your monthly loan payment and the number of years you pay back the loan

16. cost of electricity to run an air conditioner during peak usage hours and the number of hours it runs

17. time it takes to travel 50 miles and the speed of the vehicle

Determine whether each relation is a function. If the relation is a function, state the domain and the range.

18.

x	y
1	−3
6	−2
9	−1
10	0
1	3

19.

x	y
0	2
0	−2
3	1
3	−1
5	3

20.

x	y
2	12
1	5
0	0
−1	−3
−4	0

21.

x	y
−4	−4
−1	−4
0	−4
2	−4
3	−4

22. **Communications** The cost of a telephone call c is a function of the time spent talking t in minutes. The rule $c = 0.22t$ describes this function. At the right, a student calculates how much a 2-h phone call will cost.
   a. **Mental Math** Why does the student's answer seem unreasonable?
   b. What mistake(s) did the student make?
   c. How much does it cost to make a 2-h phone call?

$c = 0.22 \times 2$

$= 0.44$

$\$.44$ for 2 hours

23. a. **Open-ended** Sketch a graph of a relation that is not a function.
   b. **Writing** Explain why the graph you drew is not a function graph.

24. a. **Business** A store bought disposable cameras for $300. The store's profit p is a function of the number of cameras sold c. Find the range of $p = 6c − 300$ when the domain is {0, 15, 50, 62}.
   b. In this situation, what do the domain and range represent?

Find the range of each function when the domain is {−1, 0, 6}.

25. $g = 5 + r$

26. $b = \frac{1}{2}a + 110$

27. $w = \frac{11(h - 40)}{2}$

28. $y = x^2 + 1$

29. $q = 4p - 7$

30. $p = 2.4h$

31. $t = 6s^2$

32. $d = 60r$

33. $y = -x^3 + 6$

34. $d = 5t$

35. $y = x^2 - x$

36. $y = -\frac{x}{14}$

37. a. **Language Arts** Copy and complete the analogy:
   "Input value is to output value as independent variable is to ___?___.
   b. Write an analogy using *input, output, domain,* and *range.*

38. **Music** There are 52 white keys on a piano. The frequency of each key is the number of vibrations per second the key's string makes.
   a. Is this relation a function? Explain your reasoning.
   b. **Writing** Describe the patterns in the table.

Key Position	1	8	15	22	29	36	43
Frequency	27.5	55	110	220	440	880	1760

Evaluate each function rule for $x = 0.6$.

39. $y = x + 1.53$ **40.** $y = 3x^2$ **41.** $y = \frac{1}{3}x - 4.5$ **42.** $y = -4x$

43. $y = \frac{x^2}{9}$ **44.** $y = 34 - x$ **45.** $y = -x^2 + 2x$ **46.** $y = \frac{4x - 2}{7}$

Find the range of the function rule $y = x^2$ for each domain.

47. $\{0.5, 11\}$ **48.** $\{-1.2, 0, 4\}$ **49.** $\{-5, -1, 0, 2, 10\}$ **50.** $\left\{ -\frac{1}{2}, \frac{1}{4}, \frac{2}{5} \right\}$

51. Critical Thinking Suppose a classmate looks at the graph at the right and says, "This graph is not a function because both 2 and −2 have a y-value of 4." Explain what is wrong with this student's statement.

52. Science Light travels at a speed of approximately 186,000 miles per second. The function rule $d = 186,000t$ describes the relationship between distance d in miles and time t in seconds.
   a. How far does light travel in 20 seconds?
   b. How far does light travel in 1 minute?
   c. Make a table of values for this function rule.

53. Standardized Test Prep What is the range of the function $y = x^2 - 3$ when the domain is $\{2, 4, 6\}$?
   A. $\{-1, 1, 3\}$ **B.** $\{1, 5, 9\}$ **C.** $\{1, 1, 9\}$ **D.** $\{1, 13, 33\}$ **E.** $\{6, 10, 14\}$

Exercises   M I X E D   R E V I E W

54. a. Which variable is the independent variable? the dependent variable?
   b. Graph the data in the table.
   c. Use your graph to **predict** the retail price of an item with a $30 wholesale price.

Wholesale Price ($)	10.00	15.00	20.00	25.00
Retail Price ($)	17.50	26.25	35.00	43.75

Simplify each expression.

55. $72 \div (8 + 4)$ **56.** $5^2 + 9.5$ **57.** $86 - 18 \div 3$ **58.** $\frac{6 + 2}{4}$ **59.** $\frac{2}{5} - \frac{1}{2}$

Getting Ready for Lesson 2-5
Use an equation to model the relationship in each table.

60.

Number of People	Total Bill
1	$3.00
2	$6.00
3	$9.00
4	$12.00

61.

Amount Earned	Amount Spent
$15	$5
$30	$10
$45	$15
$60	$20

62.

Number of Days	Supplies Remaining
0	12 lb
2	10 lb
4	8 lb
6	6 lb

What You'll Learn

- Writing rules for functions from tables and words

...And Why

To solve problems related to computers and jobs

2-5 Writing a Function Rule

THINK AND DISCUSS

Understanding Function Notation

In the last lesson, you learned that a function rule is an equation that describes a function. Sometimes the equation is written using function notation. To write a rule in **function notation,** you use the symbol $f(x)$ in place of y. You read $f(x)$ as "f of x."

$$f(x) = 2x - 5$$

The rule shows you that $f(x)$ is a function of x.

output values
dependent variable

input values
independent variable

> **QUICK REVIEW**
>
> You can also write a function rule using "$y = .$" For example, $f(x) = 2x + 5$ is equivalent to $y = 2x + 5$.

Function notation allows you to see the input value. Suppose the input value above is -2. Here is how to find $f(-2)$.

$$f(-2) = 2x - 5$$
$$f(-2) = 2(-2) - 5$$
$$f(-2) = -9$$

Be careful: $f(x)$ does not mean "f times x"!

When the input value is -2, the output value is -9.

1. **Try This** Find $f(7)$ and $f(0)$.

2. **a.** Write an equation equivalent to $y = 7x + 6$ using function notation.
   b. Find the range of the function when the domain is $\{-1, 0, 5\}$.

> **QUICK REVIEW**
>
> domain = input values
> range = output values

Using a Table of Values

You can write a rule for a function by analyzing a table of values.

Example 1

Patterns Write a function rule for each table.

a.

x	$f(x)$
1	5
2	6
3	7
4	8

b.

x	$f(x)$
0	0
3	9
6	36
9	81

Look for a pattern relating x and $f(x)$. →

Ask yourself, "What can I do to 1 to get 5, 2 to get 6, . . . ?"

Relate	$f(x)$ equals	x	plus	four
Write	$f(x)$ =	x	+	4

Ask yourself, "What can I do to 3 to get 9, 6 to get 36, . . . ?"

$f(x)$ equals	x	times	itself
$f(x)$ =			x^2

Price	Tax
$5.00	$.25
$3.00	$.15
$2.00	$.10
$.60	$.03

3. a. Find $f(7)$ for parts (a) and (b) in Example 1.
  b. Did you use the function rule or the table in each case? Why?

4. a. Identify the independent variable and the dependent variable for the table at the left.
  b. Try This Let the independent variable be x and the dependent variable be $f(x)$. Write a function rule for the table.

Using Words to Write a Rule

You can also write a rule from a description of a situation. When you define variables, you may wish to use letters other than x and $f(x)$.

Example 2   **Relating to the Real World**

Computers The Computer Museum in Boston, Massachusetts, features an exhibit called The Walk-Through Computer™ 2000. You can walk on and through this giant computer and experience it firsthand. The exhibit is about 20 times larger than a normal-sized desktop computer. Write a function rule to describe this relationship.

Define $n =$ normal size
$\quad\quad\quad L(n) =$ larger size shown in museum exhibit

Relate	larger size	is	20	times	normal size
Write	$L(n)$	$=$	20	$\cdot$	n

The rule $L(n) = 20n$ describes the relationship.

5. The space bar in the normal-sized computer measures $4\frac{3}{8}$ in. $\times \frac{5}{8}$ in. Approximate the dimensions of the space bar in the museum exhibit.

6. Critical Thinking The keyboard in the exhibit is 20 ft long and 10 ft wide. Find the approximate dimensions in inches of the normal-sized keyboard.

Writing a rule from words may involve more than one operation.

Jobs Suppose you borrow money from a relative to buy a lawn mower that costs $245. You charge $18 to mow an average-size yard. Write a rule to describe your profit as a function of the number of lawns mowed.

Define l = number of lawns mowed
        $P(l)$ = total profit

Relate	total profit	is	$18	times	lawns mowed	minus	cost of mower
Write	$P(l)$	=	18	.	l	−	245

The function rule $P(l) = 18l - 245$ describes your profit.

7. *Critical Thinking* Find $P(9)$. What does $P(9)$ mean?

8. How many lawns would you need to mow to pay for the lawn mower?

Exercises   ON YOUR OWN

Find $f(-4)$ for each function.

1. $f(x) = x^2$
2. $f(x) = 5 - x$
3. $f(x) = 7(x + 2)^2$
4. $f(x) = -x^3$
5. $f(x) = -x - 2$
6. $f(x) = x^3 + 6$
7. $f(x) = x + 25$
8. $f(x) = 6x$

9. Laundry Use the function in the table at the right.
   a. Identify the dependent and independent variables.
   b. Write a rule to describe the function.
   c. How many gallons of water will you use for 7 loads of laundry?
   d. *Critical Thinking* In one month, you used 546 gal of water. How many loads did you wash? How did you find your answer?

Number of Loads	Gallons of Water Used
1	42
2	84
3	126
4	168

10. Food At a supermarket salad bar, the price of a salad depends on its weight. Salad costs $.19 per ounce.
    a. Write a rule to describe the function.   b. How much will an 8-ounce salad cost?

11. Writing What advantage(s) can you see of having a function rule instead of a table of values for a function?

Match each table of values with a rule at the right.

12.

x	$f(x)$
−2	−4
−1	−3
0	−2
1	−1

13.

x	$f(x)$
−1	−2
−2	−4
−3	−6
−4	−8

14.

x	$f(x)$
−1	−3
0	−4
1	−5
2	−6

A. $f(x) = 2x$
B. $f(x) = x - 2$
C. $f(x) = -4 - x$

Math in the Media Use the advertisement for Exercises 15–17.

15. a. Write a rule to find the total cost $T(a)$ for all the books a person buys through Book Express. Let a represent the additional books bought (after the first 6 books).
  b. Suppose a person buys 9 books in all. Find the total cost.

16. A bookstore sells the same books for an average price of $6 each.
  a. Suppose you plan to buy 12 books. What is the average cost per book as a member of Book Express?
  b. Is it less expensive to buy 12 books at the club or at a bookstore? **Justify** your answer.

17. a. Research Find an ad for another book club in a magazine.
  b. Select 9 books you would be interested in buying. Compare the cost of the 9 books you selected to the cost at Book Express.

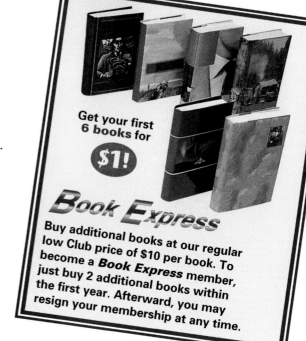

Get your first 6 books for

$1!

Book Express

Buy additional books at our regular low Club price of $10 per book. To become a **Book Express** member, just buy 2 additional books within the first year. Afterward, you may resign your membership at any time.

Find the range for each function when the domain is {–3, 0, 1.2, 5}.

18. $f(x) = x^3$
19. $C(g) = 15 - g$
20. $y = 1.3x$
21. $R(s) = -s^2$

22. $y = -4x$
23. $f(g) = g^2 + 1$
24. $G(n) = (n - 5)^2$
25. $f(x) = 6x - 4$

Patterns Write a function rule for each table.

26.

x	$f(x)$
1	0.5
2	1
3	1.5
4	2

27.

x	y
−2	−8
−1	−4
0	0
1	4

28.

x	y
3	9
6	18
9	27
12	36

29.

x	$f(x)$
1	1
2	8
3	27
4	64

30. Write another equivalent equation for each table in Exercises 26–29.

31. Food Kathy and Rheta share an 8-slice pizza. The number of slices Rheta can eat depends on how many slices Kathy eats. Write a function rule to describe this relationship. What are the domain and range?

For Exercises 32–33, write a function rule to describe each statement.

32. change from a one-dollar bill when buying pencils that cost 20¢ each

33. a worker's earnings when the worker is paid $4.25/h

34. Standardized Test Prep Compare the quantities in Column A and Column B.
  A. The quantity in Column A is greater.
  B. The quantity in Column B is greater.
  C. The quantities are equal.
  D. The relationship cannot be determined from the information given.

Column A	Column B
$f(3)$ when $f(x) = 4x - 12$	$f(0)$ when $f(x) = x + 1$

Chapter Project *Find Out by Writing*

The function $t(n) = 4.3n$ predicts the time t (in seconds) it takes n people in a row to say the tongue twister "A cricket critic cricked his neck at a critical cricket match."

• Find $t(5)$. Explain what it represents.

• What does $t(0) = 0$ mean?

• Suppose the output is 34.4 s. How can you find the input? What does the input represent?

• Make a table of values for the function and graph it.

Exercises   MIXED REVIEW

Evaluate each expression for $t = -2$, $m = 5$, and $s = 1.3$.

35. $m^2 + t$ **36.** $|s| - |t|$ **37.** $-mt$ **38.** $s^2 + t^2$ **39.** $\dfrac{m}{t}$

Getting Ready for Lesson 2-6

Graph the data in each table.

40.

x	y
−3	−7
−1	−1
0	2
2	8

41.

x	y
−3	4
−2	0
0	−2
2	4

42.

x	y
−4	−3
0	−2
2	−1.5
4	−1

43.

x	y
−2	0.5
1	2
4	3.5
7	5

Exercises   CHECKPOINT

1. a. The table at the right shows the number of words read within certain times. Identify the independent and dependent variables.
   b. Graph the data. What scales did you use and why?

2. Writing Define *relation* and *function* in your own words.

3. Explain how you would find $f(3)$ for $f(x) = 4x - 12$.

Number of Minutes	Number of Words Read
4	1100
8	2200
12	3300
16	4400

Write a function rule to describe each statement.

4. the price of rolls if they cost $.30 each   **5.** the cost of your dinner if you leave a 15% tip

Find the range of each function when the domain is {−7, 0, 1, 3}.

6. $y = 12(x - 3)$ **7.** $v = 9 - u^2$ **8.** $y = 4x + 2.5$ **9.** $t = s + 4$

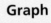

What You'll Learn

- Graphing a function
- Creating a table of values from a rule and a graph

...And Why

To solve problems involving electrician costs

2-6 **T**he Three Views of a Function

<hr />

THINK AND DISCUSS

You can model functions using rules, tables, and graphs. Suppose a car gets 30 mi/gal. Then the distance $d(g)$ that the car travels is a function of the number of gallons g.

Rule	Table of Values	Graph
$d(g) = 30g$	see below	see below

Table of Values

Gallons	Miles
g	$d(g)$
0	0
1	30
2	60
3	90

Graph

A function rule shows how the variables are related.

A table identifies specific values that satisfy the function.

A graph gives a visual picture of the function.

1. **a.** Suppose the car used 14 gal of gasoline. How far did the car travel?
   b. How did you find your answer to part (a)?
   c. Describe another method of solving the problem.

You can use a rule to model a function with a table of values and a graph.

Example 1 **Relating to the Real World**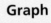

Electrician Suppose you hire an electrician to install an electrical outlet in a wall. The electrician charges $68 for materials plus $40 an hour for service. The total cost $C(h)$ is a function of the number of hours it takes to do the job. Use the rule $C(h) = 68 + 40h$ to make a table of values and then a graph.

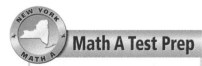
1 Which function is graphed below?

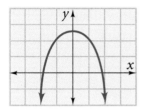

(1) $y = x + 1.5$
(2) $y = -1.625x^2 + 2.5$
(3) $y = 2x + 2.5$
(4) $y = -x^2 + 2.5$

2 A car ad costs $5.00 plus $.40 per word.
a Write a function rule for the cost of an ad.
b What is the cost of an ad that has 30 words?

STEP 1:
Choose values for h that seem reasonable, such as 1, 2.5, 4, and 7.

STEP 2:
Input the values for h. Evaluate to find $C(h)$.

STEP 3:
Plot the ordered pairs.

h	$C(h) = 68 + 40h$	$(h, C(h))$
1	$68 + 40(1) = 108$	$(1, 108)$
2.5	$68 + 40(2.5) = 168$	$(2.5, 168)$
4	$68 + 40(4) = 228$	$(4, 228)$
7	$68 + 40(7) = 348$	$(7, 348)$

2. a. What is the total cost of the job if it takes $5\frac{1}{2}$ hours?
   b. Did you use the rule, the table, or the graph to answer part (a)?

3. Why are the points on the graph connected by a line?

4. Are negative values for h reasonable? Explain.

5. Electrician Suppose this electrician tells you the job will take 2 to 6 hours to complete. What is the range of your costs?

6. Try This Model each rule with a table of values and a graph.
   a. $f(x) = -3x + 5$
   b. $f(x) = \frac{1}{2}x$

QUICK REVIEW

You can also write a function rule using "$y = $" form. For example, $f(x) = x^2 - x - 6$ is equivalent to $y = x^2 - x - 6$.

Some functions have graphs that are not straight lines. You can graph a function as long as you know its rule.

Example 2

Graph the function $y = x^2 - x - 6$.

First, make a table of values.

x	$y = x^2 - x - 6$	(x, y)
-2	$(-2)^2 - (-2) - 6 = 0$	$(-2, 0)$
-1	$(-1)^2 - (-1) - 6 = -4$	$(-1, -4)$
0	$(0)^2 - (0) - 6 = -6$	$(0, -6)$
1	$(1)^2 - (1) - 6 = -6$	$(1, -6)$
2	$(2)^2 - (2) - 6 = -4$	$(2, -4)$
3	$(3)^2 - (3) - 6 = 0$	$(3, 0)$

Then graph the data.

7. What advantage(s) does a rule have in describing a function?

8. Try This Graph each function.
   a. $y = -3x^2 + 1$
   b. $f(x) = x^2 - 4x - 5$

2-6 The Three Views of a Function   **85**

You can create a table of values from a graph.

Example 3

Make a table of values for the graph below.

Use the scale of the graph to find
ordered pairs.

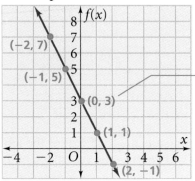

Put the ordered pairs
in a table.

x	$f(x)$
-2	7
-1	5
0	3
1	1
2	-1

Exercises   ON YOUR OWN

Model each rule with a table of values and a graph.

1. $y = -3x$

2. $y = x^2 - 4x + 4$

3. $f(x) = 2x - 7$

4. $y = 6x^2$

5. $f(x) = \frac{1}{3}x$

6. $f(x) = 8 - x$

7. $f(x) = x^2 - 2$

8. $y = 5 + 4x$

9. Patterns The table of values below describes the perimeter of each
figure in the pattern of blue tiles at the right. The perimeter P is a
function of the number of tiles t.

fig. 1   fig. 2   fig. 3   fig. 4

Number of Tiles (t)	1	2	3	4
Perimeter (P)	4	6	8	10

    a. Choose a rule to describe the function in the table.
      A. $P = t + 3$ **B.** $P = 4t$ **C.** $P = 2t + 2$ **D.** $P = 6t - 2$
    b. How many tiles are in the figure if the perimeter is 20?
    c. Graph the function.

10. Jobs Juan charges $3.50 per hour for baby-sitting.
    a. Write a rule to describe how the amount of money M earned is a
       function of the number of hours h spent baby-sitting.
    b. Make a table of values.
    c. Graph the function.
    d. Estimation Use the graph to estimate how long it will take Juan to
       earn $30.
    e. Critical Thinking Do you think of baby-sitting data as discrete or
       continuous? Explain your reasoning.

QUICK REVIEW

Continuous data are usually
measurements, such as
temperatures and lengths.
Discrete data are distinct
counts, such as numbers of
people or objects.

11. **Conservation** Use the data at the right.
   a. Write a function rule for a standard shower head.
   b. Write a function rule for a water-saving shower head.
   c. Suppose you take a 6-min shower as recommended and use a water-saving head. How much water do you save compared to an average shower with a standard head?
   d. Graph both functions on the same coordinate plane. What does the graph show you?
   e. **Open-ended** How much water did you use during your last shower? How did you find your answer?

How Long Does Your Shower Last?

 • average shower: 12.2 min

 • recommended shower: 6 min

• standard head uses 6 gal/min   • water-saving head cuts water flow in half

Source: *Opinion Research Corp.*

Graph each function.

12. $f(x) = x - 2$	**13.** $y = -10x$	**14.** $y = \frac{3}{4}x + 7$	**15.** $f(x) = x^2$
16. $y = x^2 - 3x + 2$	**17.** $f(x) = x$	**18.** $f(x) = x^2 - 9$	**19.** $y = 7 - 5x$
20. $f(x) = 6x + 1$	**21.** $f(x) = x - 3$	**22.** $y = x + \frac{1}{2}$	**23.** $y = 3.5x$
24. $f(x) = 4x$	**25.** $y = 1 - x^2$	**26.** $f(x) = 12 - x$	**27.** $f(x) = -5x^2$

Make a table of values for each graph.

28.

29.

30.

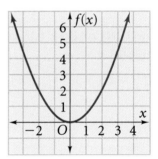

31. **Communications** The cost $C(a)$ of a call from Boston to Worcester, Massachusetts, is a function of the number of additional minutes a. The rule $C(a) = 0.27 + 0.11a$ closely models the cost.
   a. How much will a 5-min call cost? (*Hint:* The number of additional minutes is one minute less than the length of the call.)
   b. **Calculator** Make a table of values and graph the function.
   c. **Critical Thinking** Suppose you don't want to spend any more than $1.50 on this phone call. How many minutes can you talk?

32. **a.** **Research** Find the rate for weekday telephone calls in your area.
   b. Write a rule to describe the cost of the call. Be sure to define your variables.
   c. **Calculator** Make a table of values and graph the function.

33. **Standardized Test Prep** Which function is modeled by the table?
   A. $f(x) = x - 2$ **B.** $f(x) = 2x + 1$ **C.** $f(x) = 2x$
   D. $f(x) = -x + 1$ **E.** $f(x) = \frac{1}{2}x - 1$

x	$f(x)$
-3	-5
0	1
2	5
5	11

34. Geometry The function $A(l) = \frac{1}{2}l^2$ describes the area of an isosceles right triangle with leg l.
   a. Make a table of values for $l = 1, 2, 3, 4$.
   b. Graph the function.

35. Writing Suppose a student was not in class today. Describe to the student how to graph a function rule.

Exercises   **M I X E D   R E V I E W**

Use the scatter plot at the right.

36. What kind of correlation does the scatter plot show?

37. a. Open-ended Describe a situation the scatter plot might represent.
   b. What would you label your axes?

Find the range of each function when the domain is $\{-2, 0, 1, 4\}$.

38. $f(x) = x - 1$ **39.** $f(c) = 2c + 7$ **40.** $f(z) = \frac{1}{4}z$ **41.** $f(w) = -w + 2$ **42.** $f(t) = -2t$

Getting Ready for Lesson 2-7
Simplify each expression.

43. $-4|5|$ **44.** $|-5| + |-3.5|$ **45.** $|-8 + 4|$ **46.** $|-9.6|$ **47.** $3 - |-4|$

A Point in Time

1500 — 1600 — 1700 — 1800 — 1900 — 2000

Romana Acosta Bañuelos

In 1971, Romana Acosta Bañuelos became the first Mexican American woman to hold the office of United States Treasurer. Before her appointment to this post by President Nixon, she founded and managed her own multimillion-dollar food enterprise and established the Pan American National Bank of East Los Angeles. As a highly successful businesswoman, she had to work on a daily basis with interest rates, balance sheets, investments, and other functions used in the corporate world.

Graphing Functions

After Lesson 2-6

You can use a graphing calculator to graph a function. You can sketch a graph to record information about the function.

Example

Graph the function $y = x^2 - 9$. Use the standard setting for the range. Then sketch the graph on your paper.

STEP 1: Press [ZOOM] [6] to set the range at the **standard setting**. Press [WINDOW] to display the standard setting on the window screen.

STEP 2: Press [Y=] to go to the equation screen. Press [CLEAR] to get rid of any equation already in the calculator. Then press [X,T,θ] [x²] [−] [9] to enter the equation.

STEP 3: Press [GRAPH] to view the graph.

```
WINDOW FORMAT
Xmin = -10
Xmax = 10
X s c l = 1
Ymin = -10
Ymax = 10
X s c l = 1
```

```
Y1 ▱ X² – 9 ■
Y2 =
Y3 =
Y4 =
Y5 =
Y6 =
Y7 =
Y8 =
```

STEP 4: To sketch a graph that you see on your calculator screen, use the coordinates of at least three points. Plot these points on your paper and use them to make your sketch.

crosses the x-axis at (−3, 0) and (3, 0)

crosses the y-axis at (0, −9)

Graph each function on your graphing calculator. Use the standard setting for the range. Then sketch each graph.

1. $y = -2x + 4$
2. $y = \frac{1}{2}x - 2$
3. $y = x^2 + 2$
4. $y = x^3 - 1$
5. $y = 3x - 6$
6. $y = \frac{1}{3}x$
7. $y = 4 - x^2$
8. $y = 3x^2 - 7$

9. **Writing** Examine the Window screen and the Graph screen in the Example. Explain what the values Xmin, Xmax, Ymin, and Ymax represent on the graph.

What You'll Learn

- Identifying families of functions for equations and graphs

...And Why

To predict what the graph of an equation will look like

What You'll Need

- graphing calculator
- note cards

GRAPHING CALCULATOR HINT

Use the ABS key and the ( ) keys to enter the absolute value.

2-7 Families of Functions

WORK TOGETHER

Work with a partner.

1. Graphing Calculator Graph each equation using the standard range setting. To help you keep track, sketch each graph on a note card. Label it with the correct equation.

$y = x^2 - 6$ $y = x + 2$

$y = |x| - 4$ $y = 7x$

$y = |x - 3|$ $y = x^2 + 1$

$y = 3x^2$ $y = -3x$

2. a. Sort the cards into three categories by grouping graphs that look alike.
b. What similarities among the graphs in each category do you see?
c. What similarities among the equations in each category do you see?

The categories you made can help you make predictions.

3. What does the graph of $y = 2x^2$ look like?

4. Graphing Calculator What can you say about the equation of this graph?

THINK AND DISCUSS

Identifying the Family of an Equation

You've already seen how grouping functions that are alike can help you make predictions. These groups are called *families of functions*. You can identify what family a function belongs to by looking at its equation.

QUICK REVIEW

Remember that $x = x^1$. So, the power of x is 1.

Example 1

To what family of functions does each equation belong? Explain.

a. $y = 2x - 6$

Its highest power of x is 1.
So, $y = 2x - 6$
is a *linear function*.

b. $y = -8x^2$

Its highest power of x
is 2. So, $y = -8x^2$ is a
quadratic function.

5. The equation $y = |x + 7|$ is an *absolute value function*. What characteristic of the equation tells you this?

6. Try This To what family of functions does each equation belong? Explain.
   a. $y = 6x^2 + 1$
   b. $y = 3|x|$
   c. $y = x^2 + 3x + 2$

7. Open-ended Create three equations that belong to the quadratic family of functions.

Identifying the Family of a Graph

You can identify what family a function belongs to by looking at its graph.

Example 2

Graphing Calculator To what family of functions does each graph belong? Explain.

a.

b.

The graph is U-shaped. So,
it is a *quadratic function*.

The graph forms a "V." So,
it is an *absolute value function*.

8. a. The equation $y = -5x$ belongs to what family of functions? How do you know?
   b. Graphing Calculator Graph $y = -5x$.
   c. Look at your graph and **generalize**. What characteristic of a graph tells you it belongs to the *linear family of functions*?

9. Open-ended Sketch three graphs that belong to the absolute value family of functions.

The equations and graphs of functions that are in the same family are alike. Here are three families of functions.

Families of Functions

Linear Functions	Quadratic Functions	Absolute Value Functions
$y = 2x - 1$	$y = -3x^2 - x + 1$	$y = |x + 2|$
The highest power of x is 1.	The highest power of x is 2.	There is an absolute value symbol around a variable expression.

  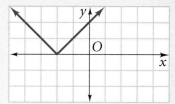

The graph forms a straight line.　The graph is a U-shaped curve that opens up or down.　The graph forms a "V" that opens up or down.

Exercises　ON YOUR OWN

To what family of functions does each equation belong? Explain.

1. $y = \frac{4}{7}x + 7$　　　　**2.** $y = 49 - x^2$　　　　**3.** $y = |2 + 3x|$

4. $y = -x^2 + 11$　　　**5.** $y = -6x^2 + 13x - 5$　　　**6.** $y = \frac{1}{4}x$

7. $y = 0.5x^2$　　　　**8.** $y = -2|x|$　　　　**9.** $y = |x - 2|$

Graphing Calculator **To what family of functions does each graph belong? Explain your reasoning.**

10.

11.

12.

13. Medicine The recommended dosage D in milligrams of a certain medicine depends on a person's body weight w in kilograms. To what family of function does the formula $D = 0.1w^2 + 5w$ belong? Explain.

14. Writing How are linear functions and absolute value functions alike? How are they different?

15. Define a *family of functions* in your own words.

16. Critical Thinking Why are these graphs *not* quadratic or absolute value functions?

17. Critical Thinking Is a vertical line the graph of a linear function? Why or why not?

18. Open-ended Write two linear, two quadratic, and two absolute value equations.

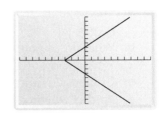

What characteristic do you look for to identify the family of each?

19. graph of a quadratic function

20. equation of a linear function

21. graph of an absolute value function

22. equation of a quadratic function

Critical Thinking Determine to which family of functions each graph belongs. Then sketch a graph to model each situation.

23. Income is a function of of hours worked.

24. Height of a fly ball is a function of time.

Graphing Calculator Predict the shape of the graph. Be as specific as you can. Graph each equation to verify your prediction.

25. $y = 7 - x$

26. $y = -4x^2$

27. $y = |1 - x|$

28. $y = 2x + 1$

29. $y = -|x| + 6$

30. $y = 2x^2 - 6$

31. $y = x^2 + 3$

32. $y = -x + 10$

33. $y = |-x| + 3$

To what family of functions does the function suggested by each picture belong? Explain your reasoning.

34.

35.

36.

37.

38. a. Make a table of values for each equation.
  I. $y = |x|$ **II.** $y = -x^2$
  b. What do you notice about the signs of the y-values?
  c. What quadrant(s) do you expect each graph to be in?
  d. Graph each function.
  e. Predict whether each graph will open up or down. Graph each function to test your prediction.
  I. $y = -|x|$ **II.** $y = x^2$

39. a. Predict the shape and opening of the graph $y = |x - 2|$.
  b. *Graphing Calculator* Test your prediction.

40. *Standardized Test Prep* Which equation is shown in the graph?
  A. $y = x + 2$
  B. $y = -|x| + 2$
  C. $y = -x^2 + 2$
  D. $y = x^2 + 2$
  E. None of these

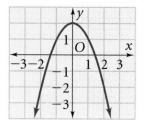

Chapter Project *Find Out by Analyzing*

Think of a tongue twister not yet used in this chapter. (You may know one in a language other than English.)

• Use a group of at least ten people. Use the same method to record times as you did for the Find Out question on page 63.

• Graph the data.

• Do your data points form a line? Explain.

• Write a function rule that you could use to predict the time for n people to say your tongue twister.

Exercises   MIXED REVIEW

Graph each function.

41. $f(x) = 5x - 1$ **42.** $f(x) = -3x^2$ **43.** $f(w) = 3w + 4.5$ **44.** $q(p) = 3p - 1$

45. $f(x) = x^2 + 7$ **46.** $f(t) = t + 2.5$ **47.** $d(t) = 55t$ **48.** $f(x) = \frac{1}{2}x + \frac{3}{2}$

49. a. Evaluate the function rule $f(x) = -2x^2 + 12$ for $x = -8$.
  b. Write the steps you used to evaluate the function.

50. *Probability* Use the random number table.
  a. *Open-ended* A sock drawer has an equal number of white and blue socks. Simulate choosing a sock without looking in the drawer. Which numbers will represent white? blue?
  b. Conduct the simulation. What is the experimental probability of drawing a blue sock?

Random Number Table

23948	71477	12573	05954
65628	22310	09311	94864
41261	09943	34078	70481

Getting Ready for Lesson 2-8

A bag of fruit has 5 apples, 6 bananas, 4 oranges, and one pomegranate. What fraction of the fruit does each represent?

51. apples   **52.** oranges   **53.** not pomegranates

54. bananas   **55.** not apples   **56.** bananas and apples

SELF ASSESSMENT **FOR YOUR JOURNAL**

Summarize what you understand about functions. Give examples of how to write them and how to use them. Be specific about how they relate to graphs.

What You'll Learn

- Finding theoretical probability
- Using a tree diagram and a sample space to find probability

...And Why

To make predictions about real-world situations such as mall promotions and game shows

2-8 The Probability Formula

Finding Theoretical Probability

To promote the new Westside Mall, the mall manager gives away a store gift certificate. The winning shopper chooses the store by picking a piece of paper from a box. The box contains the names of 170 stores.

1. What type of store is the winner most likely to pick? Explain.

In Chapter 1, you found experimental probability by conducting experiments. The possible results of an experiment are called **outcomes.** An event is any group of outcomes.

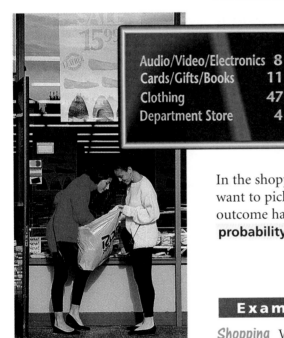

Stores at the Westside Mall					
Audio/Video/Electronics	8	Food	25	Health/Beauty	9
Cards/Gifts/Books	11	Footwear	16	Specialty Shops	10
Clothing	47	Home Furnishings	7	Toys/Hobby/Sport	9
Department Store	4	Jewelry	14	Other	10
		Total Number of Stores: 170			

In the shopping mall giveaway, each store represents an outcome. If you want to pick a food store, the 25 food stores are *favorable outcomes.* If each outcome has an equal chance of happening, you can find **theoretical probability** using this formula.

$$P(\text{event}) = \frac{\text{number of favorable outcomes}}{\text{number of possible outcomes}}$$

Example 1 Relating to the Real World

Shopping What is the probability of the winning shopper choosing a footwear store? Express your answer as a percent.

$$P(\text{footwear store}) = \frac{\text{number of favorable outcomes}}{\text{number of possible outcomes}}$$

$$= \frac{16}{170} \quad \longleftarrow \quad \text{There are 16 footwear stores in the mall and 170 stores in all.}$$

$$\approx 0.09 = 9\%$$

The probability of choosing a footwear store is about 0.09, or 9%.

For practice with percents, see Skills Handbook page 589.

2. *Calculator* Suppose you are the winning shopper. What is the probability you get a gift certificate to a jewelry store?

All probabilities range from 0 to 1.

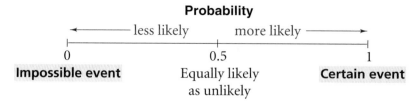

When you roll a number cube marked with numbers from 1 to 6, rolling a 7 is an impossible event. Rolling a number less than 7 is a certain event.

3. **Try This** Find each probability when rolling a number cube.
   a. $P(\text{even})$ **b.** $P(0)$ **c.** $P(5)$

4. **Open-ended** Suppose you chose a letter tile from a bag containing the letter tiles A, A, A, E, I, O, O, and U.
   a. Name a certain event.
   b. Name an impossible event.
   c. Name an event that is more likely than choosing the letter I.

The **complement of an event** consists of all possible outcomes not in the event. For example, when you roll a number cube, the complement of "rolling a 4 or less" is "rolling a 5 or 6." The sum of the probabilities of an event and its complement is 1. You can use this formula to find the probability of the complement of an event.

$$P(\text{complement of event}) = 1 - P(\text{event})$$

You can write $P(\text{complement of event})$ as $P(\text{not event})$.

Example 2   **Relating to the Real World** ··············

Games On a popular television game show, the winning contestant must choose from five envelopes. Each envelope contains a grand prize, such as a car or a trip.
a. What is the probability of choosing a particular grand prize?
b. What is the probability of not choosing that grand prize?

a. $P(\text{grand prize}) = \dfrac{\text{number of favorable outcomes}}{\text{number of possible outcomes}} = \dfrac{1}{5}$

The probability the contestant chooses a specific grand prize is $\frac{1}{5}$.

b. $P(\text{not grand prize}) = 1 - P(\text{grand prize})$

$$= 1 - \frac{1}{5}$$

$$= \frac{4}{5}$$

PROBLEM SOLVING

Look Back Describe another method you could use to find *P*(not grand prize).

The probability the contestant does not choose that grand prize is $\frac{4}{5}$. ■

5. Suppose you choose from three colored envelopes: red, orange, blue.
   a. What is $P(\text{blue})$?   **b.** What is $P(\text{not blue})$?

1 A nickel is flipped and a regular six-sided number cube is rolled. On the first flip and roll, what is the probability of rolling 1 and flipping heads?

(1) $\frac{2}{3}$ (3) $\frac{1}{6}$

(2) $\frac{1}{2}$ (4) $\frac{1}{12}$

2 Which value(s) of *x* *cannot* fill in the blank below, if the relation is a function?

x	y
2	4
6	11
▦	9
3	0
8	6

Using a Tree Diagram to Find a Sample Space

The set of all possible outcomes is the **sample space.** Displaying the sample space with a *tree diagram* can help you find the probability of an event.

Example 3   **Relating to the Real World**

Genetics What is the probability that there are at least two girls in a family of three children?

favorable outcomes: at least two girls

There are 8 possible outcomes.

$$P(\text{at least two girls}) = \frac{\text{number of favorable outcomes}}{\text{total number of possible outcomes}} = \frac{4}{8} = \frac{1}{2}$$

The probability that there are at least two girls is $\frac{1}{2}$ or 50%.

6. Try This What is the probability that there are exactly two girls in a family of three children?

Exercises   ON YOUR OWN

For Exercises 1–9, use the spinner at the right. Find each probability.

1. $P(\text{red})$

2. $P(\text{white})$

3. $P(5)$

4. $P(\text{even})$

5. $P(\text{red or blue})$

6. $P(\text{not 2})$

7. $P(\text{number} < 4)$

8. $P(\text{not blue})$

9. $P(8)$

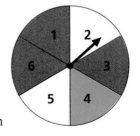

10. *Open-ended* Suppose your teacher chooses a student at random from your algebra class.
   a. What is the probability that you are selected?
   b. What is the probability that a boy is not selected?
   c. How did you find $P(\text{not boy})$ in part (b)? Describe another way.

11. *Critical Thinking* What is the difference between theoretical probability and experimental probability?

12. Suppose you have a 20% chance of being picked for a committee at school. What is the probability that you will not be picked? Express your answer as a percent.

13. a. Suppose you roll a number cube and toss a coin at the same time. Copy and complete the tree diagram to list the possible outcomes in the sample space.
   b. What is $P(4$ and heads$)$?
   c. What is $P($tails$)$?
   d. What is $P($even number and tails$)$?

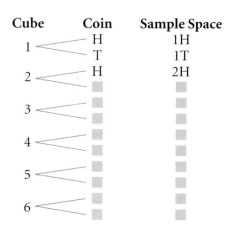

Cube	Coin	Sample Space
1	H	1H
	T	1T
2	H	2H
3		
4		
5		
6		

14. Music A disc jockey makes music selections for a radio program. For her first selection, she can choose from eight rock songs, three jazz pieces, five country-western ballads, and four rhythm and blues songs. Assume each selection has an equal chance of being chosen.
   a. What is the probability that she chooses a rock song?
   b. What is the probability that she does not choose a ballad?
   c. What is the probability that she chooses a classical symphony?

Discrete Math Suppose you select a 3-digit number at random from the set of all positive 3-digit numbers. Find each probability. (*Hint:* First find how many positive 3-digit numbers there are.)

15. $P($an odd number$)$

16. $P($number $> 900)$

17. $P($number $< 100)$

18. $P($number is a multiple of 30$)$

19. $P($number $< 500)$

20. $P($number $= 243$ or $244)$

21. On Cap Day each person who attends the baseball game receives a free cap. You have an equal chance of receiving any of the combinations at the right.
   a. Use a tree diagram to show the sample space.
   b. Find $P($yellow cap, green visor, team mascot$)$.
   c. Find $P($red cap, blue or green visor, team logo$)$

Team emblem:
• name
• logo
• mascot

Cap colors:

Visor colors:

22. Calculator Each day in the United States, about 713,263 people have a birthday. About 9630 people celebrate their 16th birthday each day. What is the probability that someone celebrating a birthday today will turn 16? Express your answer as a percent.

Use the sample space at the right. Find each probability for the sum of two number cubes.

23. $P(7)$

24. $P(2)$

25. $P($not 11$)$

26. $P(11$ or $12)$

27. $P($a multiple of 3$)$

28. $P(9)$

29. $P(15)$

30. $P($even number$)$

Sample Space for Two Number Cubes					
(1, 1)	(1, 2)	(1, 3)	(1, 4)	(1, 5)	(1, 6)
(2, 1)	(2, 2)	(2, 3)	(2, 4)	(2, 5)	(2, 6)
(3, 1)	(3, 2)	(3, 3)	(3, 4)	(3, 5)	(3, 6)
(4, 1)	(4, 2)	(4, 3)	(4, 4)	(4, 5)	(4, 6)
(5, 1)	(5, 2)	(5, 3)	(5, 4)	(5, 5)	(5, 6)
(6, 1)	(6, 2)	(6, 3)	(6, 4)	(6, 5)	(6, 6)

The outcome (2, 5) has a sum of 7.

Make a tree diagram to show the sample space for four tosses of a coin. Use the sample space to find each probability.

31. P(exactly 2 tails) **32.** P(exactly 3 heads) **33.** P(at least 2 heads) **34.** P(4 tails)

35. P(exactly 1 tail) **36.** P(no tails) **37.** P(5 tails) **38.** P(1 or 2 heads)

39. *Standardized Test Prep* You are going to roll a number cube once. Which has the same probability as P(not rolling a 4 or a 5)?
  A. P(rolling an even number) **B.** P(rolling a factor of 6) **C.** P(rolling a number less than 3)
  D. P(rolling a 1 or a 2) **E.** P(not rolling an odd number)

40. *Cars* A car dealer has an equal chance of receiving any of the colors or styles in the diagram. What is the probability that the next car the dealer receives is a red or black convertible with a gray interior?

Car Colors	Interior Colors	Style
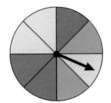		

Use the formula below to find the *odds in favor* of an event.

$$\text{Odds} = \frac{\text{number of favorable outcomes}}{\text{number of unfavorable outcomes}}$$

Sample Find the odds in favor of the spinner stopping on red.

$$\text{odds in favor of red} = \frac{\text{number of favorable outcomes}}{\text{number of unfavorable outcomes}} = \frac{3}{5}$$

41. Find the odds in favor of the spinner stopping on blue.

42. Find the odds in favor of the spinner not stopping on yellow.

43. *Writing* Explain how you can use odds to find probability. Include an example.

Exercises MIXED REVIEW

Simplify each expression.

44. $|-8 - 3| \times 3$

45. $(7^2 - 4) \div 9$

46. $-3\frac{1}{2} - 5\frac{1}{6}$

47. $5.6 \div 7 - 0.2$

48. $-9^2 + 5$

49. $-\frac{2}{3} \div 6$

50. a. Suppose you want a garden consisting of 8 tomato plants. Each plant costs $1.50. How much will you spend on tomato plants?
  b. A gardening "rule of thumb" is that for every dollar you spend on plants, you will spend three dollars on supplies. How much should you budget for supplies?
  c. Estimate the total cost of your tomato garden.

SELF ASSESSMENT

PORTFOLIO

For your portfolio, select one or two items from your work for this chapter. Here are some possibilities.
• corrected work
• most improved work
Explain why you have included each selection.

FAST TALKER

Questions on pages 63, 72, 83, and 94 should help you complete your project. Present your project as a poster or other visual display. For each tongue twister, show a scatter plot, a table and graph, or a function rule and graph. Your presentation should discuss correlation, input and output values, and how a function rule can be used to predict the time it will take *n* people to repeat a tongue twister consecutively.

Reflect and Revise

Show your project to an adult and review your work together. Are your graphs, tables, and other work easy to follow? Have you included all the required information? How can you modify your work to answer any questions that arise? Consider adding artwork or illustrations to your project. Make any revisions necessary to improve your work.

Follow Up

Most people cannot sustain speech at more than 300 words/min. Experiment with your own rate of speech. How will you measure it? You might compare familiar memorized speech, reading aloud, and saying tongue twisters. How can you express these rates as functions?

For More Information

Brandreth, Gyles. *The Biggest Tongue Twister Book in the World.* New York, New York: Sterling, 1978.

Schwartz, Alvin. *A Twister of Twists, a Tangler of Tongues.* Philadelphia, Pennsylvania: J. P. Lippincott, 1972.

Key Terms

absolute value function (p. 92)
certain event (p. 96)
complement of an event (p. 96)
continuous data (p. 65)
dependent variable (p. 69)
discrete data (p. 65)
domain (p. 74)
family of functions (p. 90)
function (p. 73)
function notation (p. 79)
function rule (p. 74)
impossible event (p. 96)

independent variable (p. 69)
linear function (p. 92)
negative correlation (p. 60)
no correlation (p. 60)
outcomes (p. 95)
positive correlation (p. 60)
quadratic function (p. 92)
range (p. 74)
relation (p. 73)
sample space (p. 97)
scatter plot (p. 59)
theoretical probability (p. 95)

tree diagram (p. 97)
trend line (p. 60)
vertical-line test (p. 75)

How am I doing?

SELF ASSESSMENT

- State three ideas from this chapter that you think are important. Explain your choices.
- Describe the different ways you can model a function.

Analyzing Data Using Scatter Plots   2-1

You use **scatter plots** to find trends in data. Two data sets that increase together show a **positive correlation.** There is a **negative correlation** when one data set increases as another decreases. If there is no trend, there is **no correlation.**

Would you expect a *positive correlation, negative correlation,* or *no correlation* between the two data sets. Why?

1. daily temperature vs. the sales of juice drinks

2. hours a swimmer trains each day vs. the time it takes to swim 100 m

3. *Open-ended* Describe two data sets that show a negative correlation.

Relating Graphs to Events   2-2

Graphs show a relationship between two variables. **Continuous data** usually involve measurements, such as temperatures, lengths, and weights. **Discrete data** involve a count, such as a number of people or objects.

Write a story to describe each graph.

4.

5.

6.
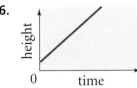

Sketch a graph to describe each situation. Explain the activity in each section of the graph.

7. the height of a sunflower over a summer

8. the number of people in a restaurant each hour

Linking Graphs to Tables 2-3

When you graph data from a table, put the **independent variable** on the horizontal axis and the **dependent variable** on the vertical axis. The dependent variable *depends* on the independent variable.

Cost of a Median Priced House

Year	1985	1986	1987	1988	1989	1990	1991	1992	1993	1994
Price	$75,500	$80,300	$85,600	$90,600	$93,100	$97,500	$99,700	$100,900	$106,100	$107,600

9. a. Which variable in the table is independent? dependent?
  b. Graph the data.
  c. What scales did you use for your axes? Explain why.

Functions 2-4

A set of ordered pairs is a **relation**. A **function** is a relation that has exactly one y-value for each x-value. A **function rule** is an equation that describes a function. The **domain** of a function is the set of all possible input values. The **range** of a function is the set of all possible output values. You can tell when a relation is a function by using the **vertical-line test**.

Find the range of each function when the domain is $\{-4, 0, 1, 5\}$.

10. $y = 4x - 7$ **11.** $m = 0.5n + 3$ **12.** $p = q^2 + 1$

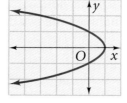

13. Use the vertical-line test to determine if the graph is a function.

14. Writing Explain when a relation is also a function.

Writing a Function Rule 2-5

A rule written using **function notation** allows you to see the input value. You can write a rule using a table of values or a description of a situation.

Write a function rule for each table of values.

15.

x	$f(x)$
2	3
4	5
6	7
8	9

16.

x	$f(x)$
-3	3
0	0
3	-3
6	-6

17.

x	$f(x)$
3.0	6.5
3.5	7.0
4.0	7.5
4.5	8.0

You can model functions using rules, tables, and graphs. Functions that are alike can be arranged into groups called *families of functions*. Some families are *quadratic, linear,* and *absolute value* functions.

Model each rule with a table of values and a graph.

18. $f(x) = 4x^2 - 3$ **19.** $f(x) = |x + 5|$ **20.** $f(x) = 2x + 1$ **21.** $f(x) = |x| - 7$

22. For Exercises 18–21, determine whether each equation is a quadratic function, a linear function, or an absolute value function. Explain.

You can find the **theoretical probability** of an event using this formula.

$$P(\text{event}) = \frac{\text{number of favorable outcomes}}{\text{number of possible outcomes}}$$

An **impossible event** has a probability of 0. A **certain event** has a probability of 1. The **complement** of an event consists of all outcomes not in the event. The set of all possible outcomes is the **sample space**.

Find each probability for one roll of a number cube.

23. $P(3)$ **24.** $P(\text{not } 5)$ **25.** $P(2 \text{ or } 6)$ **26.** $P(\text{number} \geq 7)$

27. Suppose you toss a coin 4 times.
 a. What is the probability that you toss exactly 3 heads?
 b. Explain what $P(\text{not 3 heads})$ means in your own words.

28. An astronomer calculates that the probability in favor of a visible meteor shower occurring in May is $\frac{3}{14}$. What is the probability that a visible meteor shower does not occur in May?
 A. 0   **B.** 1   **C.** $\frac{3}{14}$ **D.** $\frac{3}{17}$ **E.** $\frac{11}{14}$

Getting Ready for..▶ CHAPTER 3

Simplify each expression.

29. $\frac{7 + 9}{2}$ **30.** $3(2 + 1) - 4(2 + 1)$ **31.** $\frac{3}{4}(3 + 5)$

32. $\frac{7 - 4}{6}$ **33.** $5\left(\frac{6 + 1}{3 + 4}\right)$ **34.** $(4 - 4^2) \div 10$

Evaluate each expression for $m = 2, t = -3,$ **and** $w = 1.5.$

35. $t + 2$ **36.** $4m - 1$ **37.** $w(m + 1)$ **38.** $\frac{3}{2}w - t$

Is there a *positive correlation*, a *negative correlation*, or *no correlation* for the data sets in each scatter plot?

1.

2.

3.

4.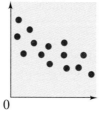

5. Which scatter plot above could be titled "Amount of Rain vs. Umbrella Sales"?

Classify the data as *discrete* or *continuous*.

6. your height from age 3 to age 14

7. the amount of money in a store's cash register during one day

Sketch a graph to describe each situation. Explain the activity in each section of the graph.

8. the speed of a bicycle during an afternoon ride

9. the amount of milk in your container over one lunch period

Determine if each relation is a function.

10.

x	y
−2	5
8	6
3	1.2
5	6

11.

x	y
9	6
3	8
4	9.5
9	2

12. Writing Explain how to use the vertical-line test to determine if a graph is a function graph.

Find the range of each function when the domain is {−3, −1.5, 0, 1, 4}.

13. $r = 4t^2 + 5$ **14.** $m = -3n - 2$

Write a function rule to describe each statement.

15. the cost of printing dollar bills when it costs 3.8¢ to make a dollar bill

16. the amount of money you earn mowing lawns at $15 per lawn

17. For Exercises 15 and 16, identify the independent and dependent variables.

Model each rule with a table of values and a graph.

18. $f(x) = 1.5x - 3$ **19.** $f(x) = -x^2 + 4$

20. Open-ended Describe a situation that could be modeled by the equation $y = 5x$.

21. Which graph is the graph of $y = -x + 2$?

A.

B.

C.

D.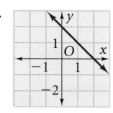

22. A vendor sells T-shirts in sizes small, medium, and large. The available colors are green, blue, red, purple, and black. All combinations of sizes and colors are equally likely.
   a. Draw a tree diagram showing all the possible combinations of sizes and colors.
   b. Find the probability of randomly selecting a black T-shirt that is size large.

Part I

1 Which title would be most appropriate for this scatter plot?

(1) Swimsuits Sold vs. Temperature
(2) Hourly Earnings vs. Teen's Age
(3) Coats Sold vs. Temperature
(4) Temperature vs. People Visiting the Beach

2 Which points lie on the graph shown?

(1) $(-1, 1), (1, 3)$
(2) $(0, -2), (0, 2)$
(3) $(-1, 2), (1, 1)$
(4) $(-1, -3), (1, -1)$

3 Which graph does *not* represent a function?

(1)   (3)

(2)   (4)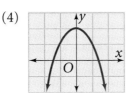

4 When $f(x) = -3x^2 + 4x$, $f(-2)$ is ■.
(1) 4   (3) -12
(2) -20 (4) 26

5 Find the range of $f(x) = |2x - 3|$ when the domain is $\{-5, -2, -1\}$.
(1) all integers   (3) $\{5, 7, 13\}$
(2) $\{-13, -7, -5\}$ (4) $\{1, 4, 7\}$

Part II

6 A vendor sells sweatshirts with the features described below. No sweatshirt is favored over any other sweatshirt by the customer.

Colors: white, blue, yellow
Emblem colors: black, red
Emblem designs: team name, team mascot

a What is the probability that the vendor sells a blue sweatshirt with a red team mascot?
b What is the probability that the vendor sells a sweatshirt with the team name in black?

Part III

7 Suppose your scores on four math tests were 95, 90, 88, and 90.
a Find the mean of your scores.
b Suppose your score on the fifth test was 88. Find the new mean.
c What score would you need on your sixth math test to raise the mean to 91?

8 The numbers in the box are the numbers of times some people in a survey said they ate dinner out last month.

7	2	11	25	3	16	14	16	3	11	8	17	6	12	21
21	6	12	10	12	30	7	15	9	19	5	11	10	14	20

a Make a cumulative frequency table for the data using intervals of 5 times.
b Make a cumulative frequency histogram.
c What percent ate dinner out more than 20 times last month?

Part IV

9 A pizza costs $8.00. Each topping costs an additional $.50.
a Identify the independent and dependent variables.
b Write a function rule for the cost of a pizza.
c Graph the function.

3

Algebraic Concepts and Simple Equations

Relating to the Real World

How do you solve a problem? Do you first decide what the problem really is, and then take a series of steps to improve the situation? In algebra, that's exactly what happens. To solve problems, many people, including pharmacists, marine biologists, and money managers, all use simple equations and step-by-step methods.

Modeling and Solving Equations	Modeling and Solving Two-Step Equations	Combining Like Terms to Solve Equations	Using the Distributive Property	Rational Numbers and Equations

Lessons   3-1   3-2   3-3   3-4   3-5

checks *and* balances

Sale! $99.99

Personal CD Player
with Headphones

- Rich, full sound
- 16-program mem

Take it anywhere!

(runs on 2 AA bat

When there is something you really want to buy, do you already have money saved for it? Or, do you put money aside each week until you can afford it? Maybe you just dream about it! A budget for your money can help you change dreams to reality.

As you work through the chapter, you will use equations to help model your personal finances. You will develop spreadsheets to analyze your weekly budget, including regular savings. You will use percents to create graphs. Then you will display and present your budget plan using the graphs and spreadsheets.

To help you complete the project:

▼ **p. 113** *Find Out by Researching*
▼ **p. 118** *Find Out by Modeling*
▼ **p. 123** *Find Out by Organizing*
▼ **p. 143** *Find Out by Graphing*
▼ **p. 150** *Finishing the Project*

Using Probability	Percent Equations	Percent of Change
3-6	3-7	3-8

What You'll Learn

- Solving one-step equations
- Using equations to solve real-world problems

...And Why

To organize your thoughts and your work

3-1 Modeling and Solving Equations

Solving Addition and Subtraction Equations

An equation is like a balance scale because it shows that two quantities are equal.

Equation: $20 + 30 = 50$

Equation: $x + 20 = 30$

To solve an equation containing a variable, you find the value (or values) of the variable that make the equation true. These values are called **solutions.**

1. **Mental Math** Solve each equation.
   a. $x + 5 = 6$ b. $y - 10 = 2$
   c. $-4 = -2 + b$

One way to solve an equation is to get the variable alone on one side of the equal sign. You can do this by using **inverse operations,** which are operations that undo one another.

Example 1   Relating to the Real World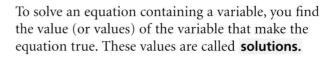

Veterinary Medicine A veterinary assistant holds a dog and steps on a scale. The scale reads 193.7 lb. Alone, the assistant weighs 135 lb. To find the weight of the dog, solve the equation $x + 135 = 193.7$.

$$x + 135 = 193.7$$
$$x + 135 - 135 = 193.7 - 135$$
$$x = 58.7$$

← The inverse operation for addition is subtraction. Subtract 135 from each side.

The dog weighs 58.7 lb.

Check $x + 135 = 193.7$
$58.7 + 135 \stackrel{?}{=} 193.7$ ⟵ Substitute 58.7 for x.
$193.7 = 193.7$ ✔

QUICK REVIEW

The expression $-a$ means the opposite of a.

2. Try This What is the inverse operation for subtraction? Use this operation to solve $a - 14 = -26$.

3. Mental Math Solve each equation by finding opposites.
a. $-x = 7$ **b.** $-y = -2$ **c.** $5 = -z$

Equivalent equations are equations that have the same solution. You can add or subtract the same number from each side of an equation to form an equivalent equation.

> ### Addition Property of Equality
> For any numbers a, b, and c, if $a = b$, then $a + c = b + c$.
> **Example:** Since $\frac{8}{2} = 4$, then $\frac{8}{2} + 3 = 4 + 3$.

> ### Subtraction Property of Equality
> For any numbers a, b, and c, if $a = b$, then $a - c = b - c$.
> **Example:** Since $\frac{15}{3} = 5$, then $\frac{15}{3} - 2 = 5 - 2$.

Solving Multiplication and Division Equations

For simple multiplication and division equations, you can use mental math to find the solutions.

4. Mental Math Solve each equation.
a. $4a = 12$ **b.** $20 = -2x$ **c.** $\frac{n}{6} = 5$

5. Mental Math Is -16 a solution to the equation $-3x = -48$? Explain.

Multiplication and division are inverse operations. You use multiplication to undo division and division to undo multiplication.

PROBLEM SOLVING

Look Back Show how you would check the solution.

Example 2

Solve $-\frac{r}{4} = -10.4$.

$-\frac{r}{4} = -10.4$ ⟵ The operation is division. Multiply to undo.

$-4\left(-\frac{r}{4}\right) = -4(-10.4)$ ⟵ Multiply each side of the equation by -4.

$r = 41.6$

The solution is 41.6.

1 Which equation is equivalent to $-3x = -6$?

(1) $\frac{x}{-9} = -2$

(2) $4x = 12$

(3) $5 + x = 3$

(4) $x - (-7) = 9$

2 It took Lana 9 hours to drive 522 miles. What was Lana's average speed? Write an equation to model this problem. Then solve it.

 6. a. Calculator Using his calculator to solve Example 2, Li got the answer 416. What error did he make?

b. Estimation How could Li use estimation to catch his error?

You can use multiplication and division to form equivalent equations.

Multiplication Property of Equality

For any numbers a, b, and c, if $a = b$, then $a \cdot c = b \cdot c$.

Example: Since $\frac{6}{2} = 3$, then $\frac{6}{2} \cdot 2 = 3 \cdot 2$.

Division Property of Equality

For any numbers a, b, and c, with $c \neq 0$, if $a = b$, then $\frac{a}{c} = \frac{b}{c}$.

Example: Since $3 + 1 = 4$, then $\frac{3 + 1}{2} = \frac{4}{2}$.

---

7. Try This Solve each equation.

a. $3.2m = 5.44$ **b.** $\frac{b}{4} = -18$ **c.** $100.8 = -16y$

8. Critical Thinking When you divide both sides of an equation by the same number, you cannot use the number zero. Explain what would result from the equation $3 \cdot 0 = 4 \cdot 0$ if you could divide both sides of the equation by zero.

Modeling by Writing Equations

A good strategy for solving a real-world problem is to model the problem with an equation. It organizes your thoughts and, of course, your work.

Average Annual Precipitation

46 in.

?

El Paso

Houston

Example 3 **Relating to the Real World**

Weather The average annual precipitation of Houston, Texas, is about 5.2 times that of El Paso, Texas. What is the average annual precipitation of El Paso?

Define $p = $ El Paso's precipitation

Relate Houston's precipitation is 5.2 times El Paso's precipitation

Write 46 $= 5.2$ $\times$ p

$$46 = 5.2p$$

$$\frac{46}{5.2} = \frac{5.2p}{5.2} \quad \longleftarrow \text{Divide each side by 5.2.}$$

$$8.8 \approx p$$

The average annual precipitation of El Paso is about 8.8 in.

9. a. Calculator What does your calculator display for 46 ➗ 5.2 [ENTER] ?

b. Critical Thinking Akira thinks that 8.846153846 more accurately describes El Paso's precipitation than 8.8 does. Abdul thinks that because of the phrase "about 5.2 times greater," 8.8 is a better answer. Do you agree with Akira or Abdul? Explain.

Exercises   ON   YOUR   OWN

1. Critical Thinking To solve $c - 3 = 12$, Kendra added 3 to each side of the equation. Ted subtracted 12 from each side, then added 15. Which method is better? Why?

2. Which property of equality do the balance scales model?

Mental Math **Solve each equation mentally.**

3. $4a = 24$ **4.** $-6 + y = -11$ **5.** $z - 8 = 0$ **6.** $\frac{x}{7} = -3$

7. $5 = -9 + v$ **8.** $36 = -4x$ **9.** $\frac{y}{5} = 100$ **10.** $-5 = n - 2$

11. Which equation is not equivalent to the others?
   A. $m + 7 = -4$ **B.** $7 + m = -4$ **C.** $-4 = m - 7$ **D.** $-4 = 7 + m$

12. Estimation Use estimation to check whether 96.26 is a reasonable solution for the equation $m - 62.74 = 159$. Explain your method.

Write an equation to model. Then solve each problem.

13. Geometry Suppose $\angle A$ and $\angle B$ are supplementary angles, and the measure of $\angle A$ is 109°. What is the measure of $\angle B$?

14. Wages Suppose you work as a carpenter's apprentice. You earn $93.50 for working 17 h. What is your hourly wage?

15. Physician's Assistant You measure a child and find that his height is $41\frac{1}{2}$ in. At his last visit, he was $38\frac{3}{4}$ in. tall. How much did he grow?

QUICK REVIEW

Two angles are *supplementary* if the sum of their measures is 180°.

Solve and check.

16. $5p = -75$ **17.** $2 = -2x$ **18.** $y - \frac{2}{3} = \frac{1}{3}$ **19.** $-8j = 12.56$

20. $-7 + a = 28$ **21.** $-\frac{p}{7} = 28$ **22.** $-7n = 28$ **23.** $y + 18 = 13.5$

24. $-3.4 + x = 9.5$ **25.** $10 = \frac{m}{-2}$ **26.** $\frac{t}{2} = 98$ **27.** $-5\frac{1}{3} = x + \frac{1}{2}$

28. $z - 0.35 = 1.65$ **29.** $a + 3\frac{1}{4} = 7\frac{1}{2}$ **30.** $6n = -120$ **31.** $-\frac{y}{7} = 35$

Use the cartoon for Exercises 32 and 33.

32. Writing Explain what the student does *not* understand about using letters in algebra.

33. What property of equality did the teacher use to solve the equation?

34. Standardized Test Prep Which equations are equivalent?

    A. II and III   **I.** $x - 5 = 10$

    B. II and IV   **II.** $4x = 20$

    C. I and V   **III.** $-\frac{x}{8} = -40$

    D. II, III, and IV   **IV.** $8 + x = 13$

    E. I, II, and IV   **V.** $-30 = 2x$

"Just a minute! Yesterday you said X equals two!"

Open-ended Describe a situation that can be modeled by each equation.

35. $\frac{m}{3} = 6$ **36.** $p - 0.5 = 19.5$ **37.** $14 + t = 16.1$ **38.** $0.25q = 10$

Choose Use a calculator, paper and pencil, or mental math to solve each equation. Check your solutions.

39. $z - 18 = 13.5$ **40.** $\frac{x}{18} = 13.5$ **41.** $-196 = m - 97$ **42.** $9\frac{2}{3} = a + 19$

43. $0.9x = 11.7$ **44.** $-6 = -3n$ **45.** $q - 28\frac{1}{2} = -12$ **46.** $-\frac{r}{3} = -101$

47. $-1\frac{3}{4} = p - \frac{1}{2}$ **48.** $\frac{m}{4} = -80$ **49.** $15x = 172.5$ **50.** $15.9 = r + 27.3$

Write an equation to model. Then solve each problem.

51. Parking In Los Angeles, the fine for illegally parking in a zone reserved for people with disabilities is $330. This is $280 higher than the fine in New York City. How much is the fine in New York City?

52. Recreation The federal government spends $25.2 million each year to operate parks and historic sites in Washington, D.C. This is $7.8 million more than it spends to run Yellowstone National Park. How much does it cost to run Yellowstone National Park?

53. Car Repair Your bill for a car repair is $166.50.
    a. One third of the bill is for labor. How much is the charge for labor?
    b. The mechanic worked on your car for 1.5 h. What is the hourly charge for labor?

54. Sports The total distance around a baseball diamond is 360 ft. What is the distance from third base to home plate?

Baseball Diamond

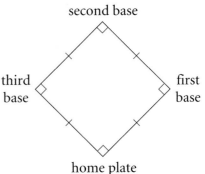

second base

third base   first base

home plate

Solve each equation.

55. $5 + v = -13$

56. $\frac{x}{6} = -10$

57. $8y = -64$

58. $m - 1.2 = -2.5$

59. $p + \frac{1}{4} = -3\frac{1}{2}$

60. $-\frac{a}{7} = 2.5$

61. $314 = n + 576$

62. $-1\frac{1}{3} = b - 5\frac{1}{2}$

63. $-3.2x = 14.4$

64. $32 = -0.8m$

65. $b + 6\frac{1}{8} = 5\frac{3}{4}$

66. $-\frac{p}{4} = 55$

67. $-1.05 = t - 6.17$

68. $-\frac{b}{3} = 107$

69. $6x = -\frac{1}{4}$

70. $-4.87 = x + 0.025$

Write an equation to model. Then solve each problem.

71. Geometry The Pentagon is the headquarters of the United States Department of Defense. Its shape is a regular pentagon, and its perimeter is about 1.6 km. How long is one side of the Pentagon?

72. Sports In 1994, German Silva of Mexico won the New York Marathon with a time of 2 h 11 min 21 s. In the same year, Cosmas N'Deti of Kenya won the Boston Marathon with a time that was 4 min 6 s faster than Silva's time in New York. How long did it take N'Deti to run the Boston Marathon?

> **QUICK REVIEW**
>
> A *regular pentagon* has five sides of equal length.

Chapter Project

Find Out by Researching

Think of several items you would like to buy for less than $150, such as a CD player, sports equipment, or some clothes.

• Price these items using ads or by visiting several stores.

• What factors other than price should you consider? Explain.

• After completing your research, choose one item as a goal to buy. Explain your decision.

Exercises   MIXED REVIEW

73. Find $f(2)$ when $f(x) = 3x + 2$.

74. Find the range of $f(x) = x^2 - 1$ when the domain is $\{-2, 1, 3\}$.

75. Cities The population of New York City is about 15 times the population of New Orleans, Louisiana. The population of New York City is about 7,300,000. What is the population of New Orleans?

Getting Ready for Lesson 3-2

Evaluate each expression.

76. $3n + 5$ for $n = -6$

77. $2.8 + 5x$ for $x = 7.9$

78. $3x - 7$ for $x = -12$

79. $-4w - 17$ for $w = -12$

80. $\frac{k}{5} + 3.8$ for $k = 14$

81. $8 - \frac{x}{2}$ for $x = -40$

> **SELF ASSESSMENT**
>
> **FOR YOUR JOURNAL**
>
> Describe some ways you can solve simple equations. Give a sample equation and solution for each method listed.

3-2 **M**odeling and Solving Two-Step Equations

WORK TOGETHER

Work in pairs. To model equations, use the ▮ tile to represent *x*.

$2x + 1 = -5$

$3x - 2$ is the same as $3x + (-2)$. ⟶

$3x - 2 = 4$

1. Write an equation for each model.

a.

b.

2. Use tiles to create a model for each equation.
   a. $2x = 8$ **b.** $x + 5 = -7$ **c.** $4x + 3 = -5$

THINK AND DISCUSS

Using Tiles

A **two-step equation** is an equation that has two operations. You can use tiles to model and solve a two-step equation.

Example 1   Relating to the Real World

Jobs Suppose you earn $4/h baby-sitting and pay $1 in bus fare each way. You want to buy a T-shirt that costs $10. To find the number of hours you must work to buy the T-shirt, solve the equation $4x - 2 = 10$.

Model the equation with tiles.
$$4x - 2 = 10$$

❶ Add 2 to each side of the equation. $4x - 2 + 2 = 10 + 2$

❷ Simplify by removing zero pairs. $4x = 12$

❸ Divide each side into four identical groups. $\frac{4x}{4} = \frac{12}{4}$

❹ Solve for $1x$.

$$1x = 3$$
$$x = 3$$

The solution is 3. You must baby-sit for 3 h to buy the T-shirt.

Check $4x - 2 = 10$

$4(3) - 2 \overset{?}{=} 10$ ⟵ Replace x with 3.

$12 - 2 \overset{?}{=} 10$

$10 = 10$ ✔

3. Which two operations were used to solve the equation? Why?

4. Try This Use tiles to model and solve each equation.
   a. $2y - 3 = 7$ **b.** $5 = 4m + 1$ **c.** $3z - 2 = -8$

Using Properties

To help you solve equations, you can write them in different ways. The variable x means $1x$. Similarly, $-x$ means $-1x$. Subtracting a variable is the same as adding its opposite. So, you can rewrite $4 - x$ as $4 + (-x)$.

5. It takes two operations to solve the equation $-x + 7 = 12$.
   a. Subtract 7 from each side of the equation.
   b. Multiply each side of the equation by -1. What is the solution?

6. Solve each equation.
   a. $-11 = -b + 6$ **b.** $-9 - m = -2$ **c.** $15 = 3 - x$

Example 2

Solve the equation $1 = -\frac{k}{12} + 5$.

$$1 = -\frac{k}{12} + 5$$

$$1 - 5 = -\frac{k}{12} + 5 - 5 \quad \longleftarrow \text{Subtract 5 from each side.}$$

$$-4 = -\frac{k}{12}$$

$$-12(-4) = -12(-\frac{k}{12}) \quad \longleftarrow \text{Multiply each side by } -12.$$

$$48 = k$$

The solution is 48.

7. a. Which operations would you use to solve $-4n + 20 = 36$?

   b. Try This Solve the equation and check your solution.

Example 3   Relating to the Real World

Money Suppose you have $18.75 to spend at Paradise Park. Admission is $5.50. How many ride tickets can you buy?

Define $r =$ number of ride tickets you can buy

Relate	entrance fee	plus	cost of ride tickets	equals	total cost
Write	5.5	+	1.5r	=	18.75

$$5.5 + 1.5r = 18.75$$

$$5.5 + 1.5r - 5.5 = 18.75 - 5.5 \quad \longleftarrow \text{Subtract 5.5 from each side.}$$

$$1.5r = 13.25$$

$$\frac{1.5r}{1.5} = \frac{13.25}{1.5} \quad \longleftarrow \text{Divide each side by 1.5.}$$

$$r \approx 8.8$$

You can buy 8 ride tickets.

8. Why should 8.8 be rounded to 8 in this situation?

9. If you buy 8 ride tickets, how much money do you have left?

CALCULATOR HINT

You can use a calculator to solve this equation. Write it in **calculator-ready form:**
$x = (18.75 - 5.5) \div 1.5$.
Use the sequence:

(18.75 − 5.5) ÷ 1.5
ENTER .

Exercises   ON YOUR OWN

Write an equation for each model.

1.

2.

3.

Use tiles to solve each equation.

4. $2n - 5 = 7$ **5.** $3 + 4x = -1$ **6.** $3b + 7 = -2$ **7.** $-10 = -6 + 2y$

8. $5y - 2 = -2$ **9.** $0 = 3x - 3$ **10.** $2z + 4 = -6$ **11.** $4x + 9 = 1$

Solve each equation. Check your solutions.

12. $3x + 2 = 20$ **13.** $-b + 5 = -16$ **14.** $\frac{y}{2} + 5 = -12$ **15.** $7 - 3k = -14$

16. $1 + \frac{m}{4} = -1$ **17.** $41 = 5 - 6h$ **18.** $1.3n - 4 = 2.5$ **19.** $\frac{x}{3} - 9 = 0$

20. $-t - 4 = -3$ **21.** $3.5 + 10m = 7.32$ **22.** $7 = -2x + 7$ **23.** $14 + \frac{h}{5} = 2$

Use an equation to model and solve each problem.

24. Farming An orange grower ships oranges in boxes that weigh 2 kg. Each orange weighs 0.2 kg. The total weight of a box filled with oranges is 10 kg. How many oranges are packed in each box?

25. Food Preparation Suppose you are helping to prepare a large meal. You can peel 2 carrots/min. You need 60 peeled carrots. How long will it take you to finish if you have already peeled 18 carrots?

26. You can find the value of each variable in the matrices at the right by writing and solving equations. For example, solving the equation $2a + 1 = 11$, you get $a = 5$. Find the values of x, y, and k.

$$\begin{bmatrix} 2a + 1 & -6 \\ -7 & -3k \end{bmatrix} = \begin{bmatrix} 11 & x - 5 \\ 5 - 2y & 27 \end{bmatrix}$$

Choose **Use a calculator, paper and pencil, or mental math to solve each equation. Check your solutions.**

27. $-y + 7 = 13$ **28.** $5 - b = 2$ **29.** $10 = 2n + 1$ **30.** $6 - 2p = 14$

31. $3x - 15 = 33$ **32.** $\frac{m}{3} - 9 = -21$ **33.** $14 - \frac{y}{2} = -1$ **34.** $\frac{x}{10} + 1.5 = 3.8$

35. $-7 = 11 + 3b$ **36.** $-6 + 6z = 0$ **37.** $\frac{a}{5} + 15 = 30$ **38.** $34 = 14 - 4p$

39. $4 = 4 - \frac{a}{9}$ **40.** $3x - 1 = 8$ **41.** $-8 - c = 11$ **42.** $\frac{m}{3} - 18 = 7$

43. $3x - 2.1 = 4.5$ **44.** $2 = -1 - \frac{k}{12}$ **45.** $\frac{m}{2} - 1.002 = 0.93$ **46.** $3 - 0.5c = 1.2$

47. Math in the Media You rent a car for one day. Your total bill is $60.
  a. Estimation You estimate your mileage to be about 100 mi. Does the bill seem reasonable? Explain.
  b. Exactly how many miles did you drive?

48. Insurance One insurance policy pays people for claims by multiplying the claim amount by 0.8 and then subtracting $500. If a person receives a check for $4650, how much was the claim amount?

49. Gardening Tulip bulbs cost $.75 each plus $3.00 for shipping an entire order. You have $14.00. How many bulbs can you order?

50. Open-ended Write a problem that you can model with a two-step equation. Define the variable and show the solution to the problem.

51. Critical Thinking If you multiply each side of the equation $0.24r + 5.25 = -7.23$ by 100, the result is an equivalent equation. Explain why it might be helpful to do this.

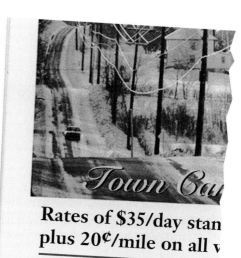

Town Ca

Rates of $35/day stan plus 20¢/mile on all v

20 U.S. TRAVEL TODAY

Calculator **Write each equation in calculator-ready form and solve.**

52. $1.2x + 0.6 = 32.4$ **53.** $2.8 = 1.34 + \frac{r}{2}$ **54.** $\frac{y}{4.5} - 9 = 3.5$ **55.** $0.05n - 0.5 = 8$

56. $9.007 - b = 8.32$ **57.** $5.3 - 0.8n = 7$ **58.** $0.3z + 0.91 = -0.08$ **59.** $3 - \frac{t}{2.5} = -7.06$

60. Temperature The formula for converting a temperature from Celsius, C, to Fahrenheit, F, is $F = 1.8C + 32$.

  a. Copy and complete the table. Round to the nearest degree.

  b. Mental Math To convert from Celsius to Fahrenheit, you can get an estimate by using this rule: multiply the Celsius temperature by 2, then add 30. Use this strategy to convert 4°C, 15°C, and 50°C.

Fahrenheit	Celsius	Description of Temperature
212°	▦	boiling point of water
▦	37°	human body temperature
68°	▦	room temperature
▦	7°	average January high in Baltimore
▦	0°	freezing point of water
19°	▦	average January low in Chicago

61. Writing Describe a situation that you can model with the equation $185 - 15n = 110$. Explain what the variable represents.

Chapter Project **Find Out by Modeling**

To make a successful budget, you need to think about savings.

- Geraldo has already saved $40 and wants to buy a CD player for $129 in about four months. To find how much he should save each week, he wrote $40 + 16x = 129$. Explain his equation.

- On page 113, you chose one item as the goal for your project. How much does it cost? When do you want to buy this item?

- Write and solve an equation to find how much you should save per week.

Exercises **MIXED REVIEW**

Solve each equation.

62. $4s = 18$ **63.** $x - 3 = 9$ **64.** $\frac{m}{5} = 3$ **65.** $-7 = n + 2$

66. In 1995, the Library of Congress had 110 million books and other items. It is projected to have about 117.2 million items in 1999. Write and solve an equation to find how many items the Library of Congress adds each year.

Getting Ready for Lesson 3-3

Simplify.

67. $8 - (-1)$ **68.** $9 - 11$ **69.** $-15 + (-5)$ **70.** $5 + (-12)$ **71.** $-6 - (-9)$

What You'll Learn

3-3 **C**ombining Like Terms to Solve Equations

- Combining like terms
- Solving equations by combining like terms

...And Why

To find the price of an item by using the total bill

What You'll Need

- tiles

QUICK REVIEW

▨ ■ represents zero.

W O R K   T O G E T H E R

Work with a partner. When you use tiles to model an expression, you can combine variable tiles and integer tiles to create a simpler expression. You can use the ▮ tile to represent $-x$.

$$2x - 5 - 3x + 1$$

 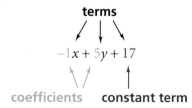

└─ Remove zero pairs. ──→ $-x - 4$

1. Model each expression. If possible, combine tiles and write a simpler expression.
   a. $4x - 2x$
   b. $5 + 2x - 1$
   c. $3x - 6x + 4$
   d. $8 + 3x - x - 6$
   e. $6 + 6x$
   f. $3x + 3x - x$
   g. $2x - 1$
   h. $-5 - x + 4x - 4$
   i. $x + x + 1 + x$

2. Which expressions in Question 1 could not be simplified? Explain.

T H I N K   A N D   D I S C U S S

QUICK REVIEW

A *term* is a number or a variable or the product of numbers and variables.

Combining Like Terms

If a term has a variable, the numerical factor is called the **coefficient.** To identify the coefficients of each term in the expression $-x + 5y + 17$, you can write the expression as $-1x + 5y + 17$.

terms

$$-1x + 5y + 17$$

coefficients   constant term

Terms are **like terms** if they have exactly the same variable factors. Terms like $5y$ and $2y^2$ are not like terms because their variable factors have different exponents. In the Work Together activity, you combined like terms using tiles. You can also combine like terms by adding coefficients.

Example 1

Simplify the expression $-2 + 6x + z - 2x + 8 - 4z$.

terms with x	terms with z	constant terms	←Group like terms.
$6x - 2x$	$1z - 4z$	$-2 + 8$	←Then add or subtract.
$4x$	$-3z$	6	

The simplified expression is $4x - 3z + 6$.

3. In Example 1, the term z was written as $1z$ before adding coefficients. Use tiles to verify that $z - 4z = -3z$.

4. Try This Combine like terms to simplify each expression.
  a. $9a + 10 - a + 3x - 5$ **b.** $-4 + y - 9m - m + 2y$

Solving Equations

You can combine like terms to solve equations.

Example 2 Relating to the Real World

Money Each used book at the library sale sold for the same amount. Suppose you bought 6 mysteries and 8 science-fiction books. Then you bought a poster for $2.40. You spent a total of $8.70. Solve the equation $6n + 8n + 2.40 = 8.70$ to find the cost of each book.

$$6n + 8n + 2.40 = 8.70$$
$$14n + 2.40 = 8.70 \qquad \longleftarrow \text{Combine like terms.}$$
$$14n + 2.40 - 2.40 = 8.70 - 2.40 \qquad \longleftarrow \begin{array}{l}\text{Subtract 2.40}\\\text{from each side.}\end{array}$$
$$14n = 6.30$$
$$\frac{14n}{14} = \frac{6.30}{14} \qquad \longleftarrow \text{Divide each side by 14.}$$
$$n = 0.45$$

Each book costs $.45.

5. Try This Solve each equation.
  a. $b + 5b = 42$
  b. $3x - 4x + 6 = -2$
  c. $7 = 4m - 2m + 1$

Example 3   **Relating to the Real World**

 The largest rock concert that has yet taken place was held on July 21, 1990, in Berlin, Germany, to celebrate German reunification.

Source: *The Guinness Book of Records*

Entertainment As a gift for your brother, you order two concert tickets. Two days before the concert a friend asks to join you. When you order the third ticket, there is a $12 charge for express delivery to be sure the ticket arrives on time. The total bill is $78. How much does each person owe?

Define c = charge for each of the original tickets
$c + 12$ = total charge for the late ticket

Relate
| charge for the original tickets | plus | total charge for the late ticket | is | 78 |

Write $\quad\quad\quad 2c \quad\quad\quad\quad + \quad\quad\quad c + 12 \quad\quad\quad = \quad 78$

$$2c + c + 12 = 78$$
$$3c + 12 = 78 \quad \longleftarrow \text{Combine like terms.}$$
$$3c + 12 - 12 = 78 - 12 \quad \longleftarrow \text{Subtract 12 from both sides.}$$
$$3c = 66$$
$$\frac{3c}{3} = \frac{66}{3} \quad \longleftarrow \text{Divide each side by 3.}$$
$$c = 22$$

You owe 2($22), or $44. Your friend owes $22 + $12, or $34.

Check $44 + $34 = $78 ✔

6. **Shopping** Suppose you buy 1.35 lb of apples and 3.55 lb of oranges. After you use a 50¢-off coupon, the total cost is $4.89. If apples and oranges sell for the same price, find their cost per pound.

Exercises   ON YOUR OWN

1. Use tiles to simplify $-y + 5 + 3y - 4$.

2. **Critical Thinking** Suppose you want to solve the equation $-3m + 4 + 5m = -6$. As a first step, would you combine $-3m$ and $5m$ or subtract 4 from each side of the equation? Why?

Simplify each expression.

3. $2n - 3n$
4. $28 - a + 4a$
5. $-4 + 3b + 2 + 5b$
6. $x + 1.3 + 7x$

7. $-x + 7n - 3x + n$
8. $4 + 5z + z - 6\frac{1}{2}$
9. $8 + x - 7x + m$
10. $2k - 5b - b - k$

Write and solve each equation modeled by tiles.

11.

12.

13.

Solve and check each equation.

14. $7x - 3x - 6 = 6$ **15.** $y + y + 2 = 18$ **16.** $-13 = 2b - b - 10$ **17.** $5 - t - t = -1$

18. $9 = -3 + n + 2n$ **19.** $13 = 5 - 13 + 3x$ **20.** $1.6y + 3.2y = 96$ **21.** $0.5t - 3t + 5 = 0$

Use an equation to solve each problem.

22. Geometry A rectangle has perimeter 42 cm. The length is 3 cm greater than the width. Find the width and length of the rectangle.

23. Entertainment Movie tickets for an adult and three children cost $20. An adult's ticket costs $2 more than a child's ticket. Find the cost of an adult's ticket.

24. Writing Three students simplify the expression $3p - 4p$. They get -1, $-p$, and $-1p$. State which answers are correct and explain why.

25. Open-ended Write an expression with four terms that can be simplified to an expression with two terms.

 Choose **Use a calculator, paper and pencil, or mental math to solve each equation. Check your answers.**

26. $4y - 2y = 18$ **27.** $-2b + 7b = 30$ **28.** $x + 3x - 7 = 29$ **29.** $6 - a + 4a = -6$

30. $1 - 6t - 4t = 1$ **31.** $s + s - 6\frac{2}{3} = 4\frac{1}{3}$ **32.** $72 + 4 - 14r = 36$ **33.** $a + 6a - 9 = 30$

34. $2 + 3n - n = -7$ **35.** $4x + 3.6 + x = 1.2$ **36.** $0 = -7n + 4 - 5n$ **37.** $3m + 4.5m = 18$

38. $x + x + 1 + x + 2 = -3.75$ **39.** $x + x + 2 + 3x - 6 = 31$

Use an equation to solve each problem.

40. Suppose you are fencing a rectangular puppy kennel with 25 ft of fence. The side of the kennel next to your house does not need a fence. This side is 9 ft long. Find the dimensions of the kennel.

41. Art An art gallery owner wants to frame a 30 in.-wide portrait of poet Maya Angelou. He wants the width of the framed poster to be $38\frac{1}{2}$ in. How wide should each section of the frame be?

Solve each consecutive integer problem.

Sample Find three consecutive integers with sum 219.

> *Consecutive integers* are integers that differ by one. Let the integers equal n, $n + 1$, and $n + 2$. Then solve this equation. $n + n + 1 + n + 2 = 219$

42. Find four consecutive integers with sum -362.

43. Three friends were born in consecutive years. The sum of their birth years is 5961. Find the year in which each person was born.

44. The sum of four consecutive even integers is 308. Find the integers.

Geometry Use equations to find the value of each variable.

45.

46.

QUICK REVIEW

The sum of the measures of the angles of a triangle is 180°. The sum of the measures of the angles of a quadrilateral is 360°.

47.

48.

49.

Chapter Project **Find Out by Organizing**

A spreadsheet can help you organize your information.

• Begin your budget by recording the amount of money you earn, the amount of money you save, and the amount of money you spend for two weeks.

• Analyze your expenses to plan how much you can spend each week, while still meeting your savings goal.

• Design a spreadsheet to show all the important categories in your budget plan. Include a column or row to show the total you will have saved after each week.

• Will you reach your savings goal when you hope to? Enter dollar amounts into your spreadsheet and verify that your budget works.

> what I earn (chores, job)
> what I save
> what I spend each week
>   (lunch, bus)
> what I spend occasionally
>   (movie, magazine)

Exercises   M I X E D   R E V I E W

Write a function rule for each table.

50.

x	y
3	7.5
4	10.0
5	12.5

51.

x	y
2	−4
4	−8
6	−12

52.

x	y
27	−3
28	−2
29	−1

53. Sketch a graph that shows your speed as you traveled to school today. Explain the activity in each section of the graph.

Getting Ready for Lesson 3-4
Simplify.

54. $2(3 + 7)$

55. $3(2 - 5)$

56. $-2(4 + 8)$

57. $-4(21 - 9)$

What You'll Learn

• Using the distributive property

• Solving equations that involve the distributive property

...And Why

To solve problems involving electricity

3-4 Using the Distributive Property

Sports A high school basketball court is 84 ft long by 50 ft wide. A college basketball court is 10 ft longer than a high school basketball court.

1. Work with a partner to evaluate each expression.
   a. $50(84 + 10)$ **b.** $50(84) + 50(10)$

2. Explain how each of the expressions in Question 1 represents the area of a college basketball court.

Simplifying Variable Expressions

Using two methods to find area illustrates the *distributive property*.

Distributive Property

For all real numbers a, b, and c:

$a(b + c) = ab + ac$ $(b + c)a = ba + ca$

$a(b - c) = ab - ac$ $(b - c)a = ba - ca$

Examples:

$5(20 + 6) = 5(20) + 5(6)$ $(20 + 6)5 = 20(5) + 6(5)$

$9(30 - 2) = 9(30) - 9(2)$ $(30 - 2)9 = 30(9) - 2(9)$

You can use the distributive property to simplify expressions.

$2(5x + 3) = 2(5x) + 2(3)$ $(3b - 2)\frac{1}{3} = 3b(\frac{1}{3}) - 2(\frac{1}{3})$

$\qquad\qquad = 10x + 6$ $= b - \frac{2}{3}$

To simplify an expression like $-(6x + 4)$, first rewrite it as $-1(6x + 4)$.

$$-(6x + 4) = -1(6x + 4)$$
$$= -1(6x) + (-1)(4)$$
$$= -6x - 4$$

$$-(2 - 9m) = -1(-2 - 9m)$$
$$= -1(-2) - (-1)(9m)$$
$$= 2 + 9m$$

3. **Critical Thinking** A student rewrote $4(3x + 10)$ as $12x + 10$. Explain the student's error.

4. **Try This** Use the distributive property to simplify each expression.
   a. $-3(2x - 1)$ b. $-(7 - 5b)$ c. $(3 - 8a)\frac{1}{4}$

Solving and Modeling Equations

Example 1   **Relating to the Real World**

Shopping Posters of astronaut Sally Ride were on sale for $3 off the regular price. Suppose you bought two posters and paid a total of $8. Solve the equation $2(x - 3) = 8$ to find the regular price of each poster.

Model the equation with tiles.

You represent $2(x - 3)$ as two groups of tiles each containing $x - 3$. $\longrightarrow$

$$2(x - 3) = 8$$

Rearrange tiles and use the distributive property.

$$2(x - 3) = 8$$
$$2x - 6 = 8$$

Add six to each side.

$$2x - 6 + 6 = 8 + 6$$
$$2x = 14$$

Divide each side into two identical groups.

$$\frac{2x}{2} = \frac{14}{2}$$

Solve for x.

$$x = 7$$

Each poster regularly costs $7.

You can use the distributive property to justify steps in combining like terms. For example :

$$3x - 5x = (3 - 5)x \qquad \longleftarrow \text{distributive property}$$
$$= -2x \qquad \longleftarrow \text{arithmetic}$$

You can use the distributive property to solve real-world problems.

Example 2   Relating to the Real World

Electricity Several 6- and 12-volt batteries are wired so that the sum of their voltages produces a power supply of 84 volts. The total number of batteries is ten. How many of each type of battery are used?

Define $x =$ number of 6-volt batteries
$\qquad$ $10 - x =$ number of 12-volt batteries

Relate	voltage from 6-volt batteries	plus	voltage from 12-volt batteries	equals	total voltage
Write	$6x$	$+$	$12(10 - x)$	$=$	84

$$6x + 12(10 - x) = 84$$
$$6x + 120 - 12x = 84 \qquad \longleftarrow \text{Use the distributive property.}$$
$$-6x + 120 = 84 \qquad \longleftarrow \text{Combine like terms.}$$
$$-6x + 120 - 120 = 84 - 120 \qquad \longleftarrow \text{Subtract 120 from each side.}$$
$$-6x = -36$$
$$\frac{-6x}{6} = \frac{-36}{-6} \qquad \longleftarrow \text{Divide each side by } -6.$$
$$x = 6$$

There are six 6-volt batteries.
$10 - x = 10 - 6 = 4$; there are four 12-volt batteries.

Check $6(6 \text{ volts}) + 4(12 \text{ volts}) \overset{?}{=} 84 \text{ volts}$
$\qquad\qquad$ $36 \text{ volts} + 48 \text{ volts} = 84 \text{ volts}$ ✔

5. a. Suppose you let x represent the number of 12-volt batteries. Write and solve a new equation that models the problem in Example 2.
   b. Do you get a different answer to the problem? Explain.

Exercises   ON YOUR OWN

Write and solve each equation modeled by tiles.

1.

2.

3.

4. Writing In your own words, explain what the word *distribute* means.

5. Critical Thinking Does $2ab = 2a \cdot 2b$? Explain your answer.

Use the distributive property to simplify each expression.

6. $7(t - 4)$

7. $-2(n - 6)$

8. $-(7x - 2)$

9. $(5b - 4)\frac{2}{5}$

10. $-2(x + 3)$

11. $\frac{2}{3}(6y + 9)$

12. $(4 - z)(-1)$

13. $(3n - 7)(6)$

14. $6x - x$

15. $-4b + 3b$

16. $4.8w - 2.5w$

17. $-8n - 3n$

Geometry **If a polygon has *n* sides, the sum of the measures of its interior angles is $(n - 2)180°$. Use this for Exercises 18–20.**

18. The sum of the measures of the interior angles of a pentagon is 540°. What is the value of *x* in the figure to the right?

19. A polygon has seven sides. What is the sum of the measures of its interior angles?

20. The sum of the measures of the interior angles of a polygon is 1440°. Use an equation to find the number of sides of the polygon.

Solve and check each equation.

21. $2(8 + w) = 22$

22. $m + 5(m - 1) = 11$

23. $-(z + 5) = -14$

24. $0.5(x - 12) = 4$

25. $8y - (2y - 3) = 9$

26. $\frac{1}{4}(m - 16) = 7$

27. $15 = -3(x - 1) + 9$

28. $\frac{3}{4}(8n - 4) = -2$

29. $5(a - 1) = 35$

30. $6(x + 4) - 2x = -8$

31. $-3(2t - 1) = 15$

32. $-8 = -(3 + y)$

33. $0 = \frac{1}{3}(6b + 9) + b$

34. $2(1.5c + 4) = -1$

35. $n - (3n + 4) = -6$

36. $-\frac{1}{5}(10d - 5) = 9$

In Exercises 37–40, use an equation to model and solve each problem.

37. Geography The shape of Colorado is nearly a rectangle. The length is 100 miles more than the width. The perimeter is about 1320 mi. Find the length and width of Colorado.

38. Geometry The formula for the area of a trapezoid is $A = \frac{1}{2}h(b_1 + b_2)$. The area of *ABCD* is 98 cm². Find the value of b_2.

39. Sports A baseball team buys 15 bats for $405. Aluminum bats cost $25 and wooden bats cost $30. How many of each type did they buy?

40. Business A company buys a copier for $10,000. The Internal Revenue Service values the copier at $10,000$(1 - \frac{n}{20})$ after *n* years. After how many years will the copier be valued at $6500?

41. Open-ended Describe a situation where you would use the distributive property to solve a real-life problem.

42. Standardized Test Prep If $y = 3x - 10$, what is the value of $\frac{y}{3}$?

   A. $-x + 10$ **B.** $x + \frac{10}{3}$ **C.** $x - \frac{10}{3}$ **D.** $-x + \frac{10}{3}$ **E.** $x - 10$

Mental Math You can use mental math and the distributive property to find prices quickly. Find each price.

43. 4($.99)

44. 6($1.97)

45. 5($5.91)

46. 7($29.93)

47. 3 computer games at $32.99 each

48. 4 cans of fruit punch at $.69 each

$$4(2.89) = 4(3.00 - 0.11)$$
$$= 4(3.00) - 4(0.11)$$
$$= 12 - 0.44$$
$$= 11.56$$

$11.56

Exercises   M I X E D   R E V I E W

Solve and check.

49. $m - 4m = 2$

50. $9 = -4y + 6y - 5$

51. $2t - 8t + 1 = 43$

52. $3.5 = 12s - 5s$

53. Technology Use the spreadsheet at the right.
   a. Write a formula for cell C2 if there are 250 million people in the United States.
   b. Use your formula to find the missing values in the spreadsheet to one decimal place.
   c. Suppose a gallon of cranberry juice costs about $4. How much do people in the United States spend on cranberry juice in one year?

Annual U.S. Fruit Juice Sales

	A	B	C
1	juice	gal (millions)	gal/person
2	orange	734	▨
3	apple	213	▨
4	cranberry	126	▨

Source: *Florida Dept. of Citrus*

Getting Ready for Lesson 3-5

Evaluate each expression.

54. $\frac{2}{3}n + 4$ for $n = -6$

55. $\frac{k}{5} + \frac{2k}{7}$ for $k = -35$

56. $\frac{3a + 1}{4}$ for $a = 7$

Exercises   C H E C K P O I N T

Solve and check.

1. $x - 7 = -6$

2. $\frac{w}{3} = 11$

3. $15 = 0.75v$

4. $2t - 1 = 4$

5. $\frac{b}{3} - 20 = 20$

6. $-12 - 4x + 3 = -1$

7. $10 = -5m - m - 2$

8. $3n + n - 8 = 32$

9. $-(z - 5) = -13\frac{1}{3}$

10. $-0.8 - y = 1.9$

11. $9(n + 7) = -81$

12. $x + 2(3 - x) = 4$

13. Sewing Suppose you are sewing a braid border on the edges of a quilt. The quilt is 20 in. longer than it is wide. You need 292 in. of braid to cover the edges of the quilt. What are the dimensions of the quilt?

14. Which equation has the greatest solution?
   A. $\frac{m}{4} = -12$
   B. $10 = 0.5(z + 3)$
   C. $4w - 5w + 9 = 8.4$
   D. $2c - 7 = 4$

What You'll Learn

What You'll Learn

• Solving equations involving rational numbers

...And Why

To solve nutrition and transportation problems

3-5 Rational Numbers and Equations

THINK AND DISCUSS

Multiplying by a Reciprocal

In Chapter 1 you learned that a rational number can be represented as a ratio of two numbers. You can use reciprocals to solve equations involving rational numbers.

Example 1 Relating to the Real World

Nutrition There are about 200 mg of calcium in 1 oz of cheddar cheese. How many milligrams of calcium are in 1 c of skim milk?

Define m = calcium (mg) in 1 c skim milk

Relate two-thirds calcium   equals   calcium in 1 oz
in 1 c skim milk   cheddar cheese

Write $\frac{2}{3}m$ =   200

$$\frac{2}{3}m = 200$$

$$\frac{3}{2}\left(\frac{2}{3}m\right) = \frac{3}{2}(200) \longleftarrow \text{Multiply each side by } \frac{3}{2}, \text{ the reciprocal of } \frac{2}{3}.$$

$$m = 300$$

There are about 300 mg of calcium in 1 c of skim milk.

Check Two-thirds of the calcium in 1 c skim milk is 200.

$$\frac{2}{3} \cdot 300 = 200 ✔$$

1. Solve the equation in Example 1 by multiplying each side by 3 and then dividing each side by 2. Which method do you prefer? Explain.

You can also use reciprocals to solve equations like $\frac{x}{5} = -7$. Write $\frac{x}{5}$ as $\frac{1}{5}x$ and multiply each side of the equation by 5, which is the reciprocal of $\frac{1}{5}$.

2. **Try This** Solve each equation.
   a. $\frac{2}{5}y = 1$ b. $-\frac{b}{8} = 2$ c. $-\frac{3}{4}x = 6$ d. $-2 = \frac{4c}{9}$

3. To solve $-\frac{1}{2}(3x - 5) = 7$, you can use the distributive property or you can multiply each side of the equation by –2, the reciprocal of $-\frac{1}{2}$. Explain why the second method is easier. Then solve the equation.

Multiplying by a Common Denominator

To simplify an equation containing a fraction, you can multiply each side by the denominator of the fraction. The resulting equation is easier to solve.

QUICK REVIEW

A *common denominator* of an equation is a multiple of all the denominators in the equation.

MILK
The Calcium Winner
One ounce of cheddar cheese has only two-thirds the calcium of one cup of skim milk.

SKIM MILK

Score	Grade
90–100	A
80–89	B
70–79	C
60–69	D

Example 2   **Relating to the Real World**

School   Your test scores are 92 and 75. Without extra credit, can you raise your test average to an A with your next test? Explain.

Define $x =$ your next test score

Relate   average of the scores   equals   lowest score for an A

Write $\dfrac{92 + 75 + x}{3}$ $=$ 90

$$\frac{92 + 75 + x}{3} = 90$$

$$3\left(\frac{92 + 75 + x}{3}\right) = 3(90) \qquad \longleftarrow \text{Multiply each side by 3.}$$

$$92 + 75 + x = 270$$

$$167 + x = 270 \qquad \longleftarrow \text{Simplify each side.}$$

$$167 + x - 167 = 270 - 167 \qquad \longleftarrow \text{Subtract 167 from each side.}$$

$$x = 103$$

Without extra credit the next test cannot bring your average to an A. ■

4. *Critical Thinking*   How is multiplying by the denominator in Example 2 similar to multiplying by a reciprocal?

CALCULATOR HINT

You can write the solution to this equation in calculator-ready form as $x = 3(90) - 92 - 75$. To calculate, use the sequence

3 ☒ 90 ⊟ 92 ⊟ 75 ENTER .

To solve an equation that has two or more fractions, multiply both sides of the equation by a common denominator.

Example 3   **Relating to the Real World**

Cars   You fill your car's gas tank when it is about $\frac{1}{2}$ empty. Later you fill the tank when it is about $\frac{3}{4}$ empty. You bought a total of $18\frac{1}{2}$ gal of gas on those two days. About how many gallons does the tank hold?

Define $x =$ amount of gas (gal) the tank holds

Relate   gallons from   plus   gallons from   equals   total
          first fill   ↓   second fill   ↓   bought

Write $\frac{1}{2} \cdot x$ $+$ $\frac{3}{4} \cdot x$ $=$ $18\frac{1}{2}$

$$\frac{1}{2}x + \frac{3}{4}x = 18\frac{1}{2}$$

$$4\left(\frac{1}{2}x + \frac{3}{4}x\right) = 4\left(18\frac{1}{2}\right) \qquad \longleftarrow \text{Multiply each side by 4.}$$

$$4\left(\frac{1}{2}x\right) + 4\left(\frac{3}{4}x\right) = 74 \qquad \longleftarrow \text{Use the distributive property.}$$

$$2x + 3x = 74 \qquad \longleftarrow \text{Simplify each term.}$$

$$5x = 74 \qquad \longleftarrow \text{Combine like terms.}$$

$$\frac{5x}{5} = \frac{74}{5} \qquad \longleftarrow \text{Divide each side by 5.}$$

$$x = 14.8$$

The gas tank holds about 14.8 gallons of gas. ■

5. What other common denominator could have been used in Example 3?

6. *Open-ended* Name a common denominator that you would use to solve each equation.

    a. $\frac{2}{3}x - \frac{5}{8}x = 26$ **b.** $\frac{y}{8} + \frac{y}{12} = -4$ **c.** $\frac{1}{2} = \frac{2}{3}b + \frac{1}{6}b$

Exercises   ON YOUR OWN

Mental Math **Solve each equation mentally.**

1. $\frac{3}{4}y = 9$

2. $-\frac{2}{3}x = 6$

3. $-4 = \frac{2}{5}a$

4. $\frac{b}{10} = 5$

5. $\frac{-7x}{8} = \frac{7}{8}$

6. $\frac{3}{7}y = 0$

7. $-\frac{n}{8} = 6$

8. $\frac{2}{3}c = -18$

9. *Critical Thinking* Explain the error in the student's work shown at the right.

10. *Jobs* Suppose you apply for a nurse's aide job that pays a \$12.90/h overtime wage. The overtime wage is $1\frac{1}{2}$ times the regular wage. What is the regular wage for the job?

$$\frac{3}{8}x - 1 = 4$$
$$3x - 1 = 32$$
$$3x = 33$$
$$x = 11$$

11. Suppose you buy $1\frac{1}{4}$ lb of roast beef for \$5. If p = price of the roast beef per pound, which equation models this situation?

    A. $1\frac{1}{4}p = 5$ **B.** $p = 5 \cdot 1\frac{1}{4}$ **C.** $5p = 1\frac{1}{4}$ **D.** $p = 1\frac{1}{4} \div 5$

12. *Geography* The area of Kentucky is about 40,000 mi². This is about $\frac{5}{7}$ the area of Wisconsin. What is the area of Wisconsin?

13. *Sewing* Suppose you buy $\frac{5}{8}$ of a yard of fabric for \$2.50. What is the price of the fabric per yard?

Choose **Use a calculator, paper and pencil, or mental math to solve each equation. Check your answers.**

14. $\frac{7}{8}x = 14$

15. $-\frac{2}{9}y = 10$

16. $\frac{x}{4} + \frac{3x}{5} = 17$

17. $\frac{z}{3} = -1$

18. $\frac{5a - 1}{8} = -5\frac{1}{4}$

19. $5 = -\frac{x}{6} + \frac{x}{2}$

20. $5 = \frac{a}{6}$

21. $\frac{y + 4}{3} = -1$

22. $12 = \frac{7}{5}y$

23. $5 = -\frac{1}{3}y + \frac{2}{7}$

24. $10 = -\frac{4}{3}d$

25. $\frac{-1 - 5x}{7} = 7$

26. $\frac{2x - 1}{5} = 3$

27. $-\frac{3x}{8} = -12$

28. $\frac{6a + 4}{3} = -14$

29. $2y - \frac{3}{8}y = \frac{3}{4}$

30. $\frac{3}{4} = \frac{3 - b + 4b}{12}$

31. $-\frac{n}{2} = 30$

32. $\frac{2x}{3} + \frac{x}{2} = 7$

33. $\frac{1}{3}x + \frac{1}{6}x = 27$

Travel **Solve each problem using the formula $d = r \cdot t$.**

34. If you drive 65 mi/h for 3 h, how far do you drive?

35. If you drive 200 mi in $3\frac{1}{4}$ h, how fast do you drive?

36. If you drive 210 mi at 60 mi/h, how long do you drive?

37. Work What would the average number of hours per week have to be in the 1990s, to make the average for the three decades be 35 h/wk?

38. Writing Explain how you can use common denominators to solve equations involving rational numbers. Give an example.

Choose Use a calculator, paper and pencil, or mental math to solve each equation. Check your answers.

39. $\frac{2x}{7} + \frac{x}{3} = -13$

40. $-\frac{1}{5}(3x + 4) = 1$

41. $\frac{2c - 1}{3} = 3$

42. $1 = \frac{a}{7} - \frac{a}{3}$

43. $-\frac{8}{11}b = 24$

44. $\frac{1}{2}(5d + 4) = 6$

45. $-1 = \frac{2x - 1}{3}$

46. $x - \frac{5x}{6} = -\frac{2}{3}$

47. $\frac{3}{8}y + \frac{2}{3}y = \frac{5}{8}$

48. $\frac{n}{60} + \frac{n}{15} = -1$

49. $\frac{7x}{3} = -21$

50. $\frac{3t}{2} - \frac{3t}{4} = \frac{3}{2}$

51. $\frac{3}{4}(2n - 5) = -1$

52. $\frac{5c - 8}{18} = \frac{2}{3}$

53. $\frac{b}{5} + \frac{5b}{3} = 2$

54. $-\frac{3t}{8} = \frac{3}{2}$

55. Entertainment As of 1994, the rental income for the movie *Back to the Future* was about $105.5 million. This was about three fourths the rental income for *Home Alone*. Find the rental income for *Home Alone*.

56. Family Budget A family allows $\frac{1}{3}$ of its monthly income for housing and $\frac{1}{4}$ of its monthly income for food. It budgets a total of $1050 a month for housing and food. What is the family's monthly income?

57. School Suppose that on an average day, you spend $\frac{1}{5}$ of your homework time on math and $\frac{1}{2}$ of your homework time on literature. The time for these subjects totals $1\frac{3}{4}$ h. How much time do you spend on your homework?

Exercises   MIXED REVIEW

Solve and check each equation.

58. $8h - 3 + 2h = 7$

59. $-x + 6x = -35$

60. $5k + 6 = -14$

61. $m - 7m + 3 = 0$

62. $y + 15 + 2y = 0$

63. $c - (5c - 1) = -47$

64. $9(w - 1) = -27$

65. $2j - 6j + 5 = 1$

66. Transportation On Atlanta's rapid rail system, the MARTA, trains leave Airport Station every 8 min from 7:11 A.M. to 6:31 P.M.
  a. You get to Airport Station at 7:55 A.M. How long will you have to wait for a train?
  b. The ride to Doraville Station takes 41 min. When will you arrive?

Getting Ready for Lesson 3-6

Probability You have five quarters in your pocket. Their mint dates are 1987, 1991, 1989, 1994, and 1991. You pick one. Find each probability.

67. P(mint date 1987)

68. P(a quarter)

69. P(mint date 1991)

70. P(a dime)

Problem Solving

Using Logical Reasoning

Before Lesson 3-6

You can use the strategy *Logical Reasoning* to solve problems. Organize what you know in a table. Use an X to eliminate an answer, and then draw conclusions.

Example

Space Exploration Astronauts Mae Carol Jemison, Ellen Ochoa, and Sidney M. Gutierrez flew separate space shuttle missions on the *Columbia*, the *Discovery*, and the *Endeavour*. Ellen Ochoa's mission occurred after the *Columbia's* mission. No crew member's initials were the same as the initial of his or her shuttle. On which shuttle did each person travel?

	M.C. Jemison	E. Ochoa	S.M. Gutierrez
Columbia	X	X	
Discovery			
Endeavour		X	

Ellen Ochoa's mission occurred after the *Columbia's*, so she was not on the *Columbia*.
Eliminate possibilities with matching initials.

In both the first row and the second column, only one possibility remains. Put a check in each box.

	M.C. Jemison	E. Ochoa	S.M. Gutierrez
Columbia	X	X	✓
Discovery		✓	
Endeavour	✓	X	

Sidney M. Gutierrez was on the *Columbia*.
Ellen Ochoa was on the *Discovery*.

Mae Carol Jemison was on the *Endeavour*.

Use the strategy *Logical Reasoning* to solve. Show your work.

1. The 1992 Olympic gold, silver, and bronze medals for soccer went to Ghana, Poland, and Spain, but not necessarily in that order. No country's medal began with the same letter as the country. If Ghana did not win the silver medal, what medal did each country win?

2. Latisha, Ken, and Ervin live on different floors of the same three-story building. The person on the third floor is the uncle of the person on the second floor. If Latisha lives on a higher floor than Ervin, where does each person live?

3. Coretta, David, Nando, and Helen live in Chicago, Dallas, New York, and Houston, but not necessarily in that order. No person's city begins with the same letter as his or her name. Coretta and Helen do not live in Texas. Where does each person live?

4. *Writing* You could have solved the space shuttle problem by using the problem solving strategy *Guess and Test* instead of *Logical Reasoning*. Which method do you prefer? Explain your reasons.

What You'll Learn

3-6 **U**sing Probability

- Finding the probability of independent and dependent events
- Using equations to solve probability problems

...And Why

To find probability in games of chance

What You'll Need

- colored cubes or chips
- bag

WORK TOGETHER

Work with a partner.
Play the game "Double Yellows." Put three yellow cubes and one red cube in a bag.

Partner X: Pick a cube. Put it back into the bag. Then pick again.

Partner Y: Pick a cube. Do not put it back into the bag. Then pick again.

Each partner takes turns choosing two cubes as described above. If a partner picks two yellow cubes, he or she scores a point.

1. Is the probability of choosing a yellow cube on the first pick the *same* or *different* for the two partners? Why?

2. Is the probability of choosing a yellow cube on the second pick the *same* or *different* for the two partners? Why?

3. **Predict** which partner is more likely to score points in "Double Yellows." Explain why.

4. Play the game with your partner. Have each partner take ten turns. How do your results compare with the prediction you made in Question 1?

THINK AND DISCUSS

Finding the Probability of Independent Events

In the game "Double Yellows" above, the two draws for Partner *X* are **independent events** because the result of the first draw does not affect the result of the second draw.

> ### Probability of Two Independent Events
>
> If *A* and *B* are independent events, you multiply the probabilities of the events to find the probability of both events occurring.
>
> $P(A \text{ and } B) = P(A) \cdot P(B)$

Example 1   Relating to the Real World ·············

Games In a word game, you choose a tile from a bag containing the letter tiles shown. You *replace* the first tile in the bag and then choose again. What is the probability of choosing an *A* and then choosing an *E*?

Since you replace the first tile, the events are independent.

$$P(A) = \frac{4}{15}$$ ←——There are 4 *A*'s in the 15 tiles.

$$P(E) = \frac{3}{15}$$ ←——There are 3 *E*'s in the 15 tiles.

$$P(A \text{ and } E) = P(A) \cdot P(E)$$
$$= \frac{4}{15} \cdot \frac{3}{15}$$
$$= \frac{4}{75}$$

The probability of choosing an *A*, then an *E* is $\frac{4}{75}$.

5. Write the answer to Example 1 as a decimal rounded to the nearest hundredth. Then write the decimal as a percent.

Finding the Probability of Dependent Events

When the outcome of one event affects the outcome of a second event, the events are **dependent events.** In the game "Double Yellows," if you choose a second cube without replacing the first cube, the events are dependent.

> **Probability of Two Dependent Events**
>
> If *A* and *B* are dependent events, then
> $$P(A \text{ and } B) = P(A) \cdot P(B \text{ after } A).$$

Example 2   Relating to the Real World ·············

Games Suppose you play the word game again. This time you *do not replace* the first tile before you choose the second tile. What is the probability of choosing an *A* and then choosing an *E*?

The events are dependent.

$$P(A) = \frac{4}{15}$$ ←——There are 4 *A*'s in the 15 tiles.

$$P(E \text{ after } A) = \frac{3}{14}$$ ←——There are 3 *E*'s in the 14 tiles left.

$$P(A \text{ and } E) = P(A) \cdot P(E \text{ after } A)$$
$$= \frac{4}{15} \cdot \frac{3}{14}$$
$$= \frac{2}{35}$$

The probability of choosing an *A* and then an *E* is $\frac{2}{35}$.

1 Michael said, "I solved this equation by adding 2 to 10 and dividing by 4." Which equation did Michael solve?

(1) $\frac{x}{4} - 2 = 10$

(2) $4x + 2 = 10$

(3) $\frac{x}{4} + 2 = 10$

(4) $4x - 2 = 10$

2 A basketball team buys 12 uniforms for $612. Each shirt costs $28. How much does each pair of shorts cost? Write an equation to model this problem. Then solve it.

 Most colorblind people have trouble recognizing red, brown, and green. About 8% of men and 0.5% of women are colorblind.

Source: *World Book Encyclopedia*

6. Write the answer to Example 2 as a decimal rounded to the nearest hundredth. Then write the decimal as a percent.

7. Try This What is the probability of choosing two *I*'s if you pick a tile, do not replace it, and pick again?

Finding Probability Using an Equation

You can write an equation to solve some probability problems. When you are given two probabilities, solve the equation for the missing probability.

Example 3

Kevin is colorblind, so he buys only white socks and black socks. The probability that he picks out a pair of white socks is $\frac{1}{3}$. The probability that he reaches in and grabs one white sock is $\frac{3}{5}$. What is the probability that he chooses the second white sock?

Define $n = P(\text{white after choosing white})$

Relate $P(\text{two white}) = P(\text{white}) \cdot P(\text{white after choosing white})$

Write $\frac{1}{3}$ $=$ $\frac{3}{5}$ $\cdot$ n

$$\frac{1}{3} = \frac{3}{5}n$$

$$\frac{5}{3}\left(\frac{1}{3}\right) = \frac{5}{3}\left(\frac{3}{5}n\right)$$ ← Multiply each side by $\frac{5}{3}$.

$$\frac{5}{9} = n$$

The probability that Kevin will get the second white sock after choosing a white sock is $\frac{5}{9}$.

8. The probability of Kevin choosing a white sock on his first try is $\frac{3}{5}$.

a. What does this tell you about the number of white socks he has?

b. *Critical Thinking* If Kevin has 10 socks altogether, how many of them are white?

Exercises   ON YOUR OWN

Are the two events *dependent* or *independent*? Explain.

1. Toss a coin twice.

2. Pick a vowel at random. Then pick a different vowel.

3. Pick a ball from a basket of both yellow and pink balls. Pick again.

4. *Gardening* A gardener's flat contains two plants with pink flowers, two with purple flowers, and two with white flowers. The plants have not yet flowered. You choose two plants from the flat. What is the probability that they both will have pink flowers?

You have three $1 bills, two $5 bills, and a $20 bill in your pocket. You choose two bills. Find each probability.

5. $P(\$5 \text{ and } \$1)$ with replacing

6. $P(\$1 \text{ and } \$20)$ without replacing

7. $P(\$20 \text{ and } \$1)$ with replacing

8. $P(\$1 \text{ and } \$1)$ without replacing

9. A and B are independent. $P(A \text{ and } B) = \frac{1}{4}$ and $P(B) = \frac{3}{5}$. Find $P(A)$.

10. Writing Use your own words to explain the difference between independent and dependent events. Give an original example of each.

You pick two marbles from the bag at the right. You replace the first one before you choose the second one. Find each probability.

11. $P(\text{red and green})$
12. $P(\text{two greens})$

13. $P(\text{blue and red})$
14. $P(\text{two yellows})$

15. $P(\text{blue and green})$
16. $P(\text{two reds})$

You pick two marbles from the bag at the right. You pick the second one without replacing the first one. Find each probability.

17. $P(\text{red and blue})$
18. $P(\text{two blues})$

19. $P(\text{blue and green})$
20. $P(\text{two reds})$

21. $P(\text{green and yellow})$
22. $P(\text{two greens})$

23. School Suppose you guess all the answers on a three-question "true or false" quiz. What is the probability you will guess them all correctly?
   A. $\frac{1}{2}$ **B.** $\frac{3}{2}$ **C.** $\frac{3}{8}$ **D.** $\frac{1}{8}$ **E.** $\frac{1}{3}$

24. A bag contains red cubes and blue cubes. You pick two cubes without replacing the first one. The probability of drawing two red cubes is $\frac{1}{15}$. The probability that your second cube is red if your first cube is red is $\frac{2}{9}$. Find the probability that the first cube you pick is red.

25. Open-ended Make up a game like "Double Yellows." Give rules for playing the game. Explain the probability of winning and the independence or dependence of the events in your game.

Government **Use the data at the right.**

26. An acre of land in Idaho is chosen at random. What is the probability that the land is owned by the federal government?

27. An acre of land is chosen at random from each of the three states listed. What is the probability that all three acres of land are owned by the federal government?

28. Research How many acres of land in your state are federally owned? What percent of the total land in your state is this?

State	Percent of Land Federally Owned
Idaho	62%
New Mexico	32%
Virginia	6%

29. Quality Control The probability that a spark plug is defective is 0.06. You need two new spark plugs for a motorcycle. What is the probability that both spark plugs you buy are defective?

A and B are independent events. Find the missing probability.

30. $P(A) = \frac{5}{8}$, $P(A \text{ and } B) = \frac{1}{4}$. Find $P(B)$.

31. $P(A) = \frac{1}{3}$, $P(B) = \frac{3}{5}$. Find $P(A \text{ and } B)$.

32. $P(A) = \frac{3}{20}$, $P(B) = \frac{5}{6}$. Find $P(A \text{ and } B)$.

33. $P(A) = \frac{1}{4}$, $P(A \text{ and } B) = \frac{3}{20}$. Find $P(B)$.

34. $P(A) = \frac{12}{35}$, $P(B) = \frac{7}{8}$. Find $P(A \text{ and } B)$.

35. $P(A) = \frac{2}{3}$, $P(A \text{ and } B) = \frac{8}{15}$. Find $P(B)$.

36. $P(A) = \frac{1}{20}$, $P(A \text{ and } B) = \frac{1}{50}$. Find $P(B)$.

37. $P(A) = \frac{7}{9}$, $P(A \text{ and } B) = \frac{21}{36}$. Find $P(B)$.

38. School A hat contains all the names of the students in a class that has 12 girls and 10 boys. To select representatives of the class, the teacher draws two names from the hat without replacing the first name.
  a. Find $P(\text{two girls})$.   **b.** Find $P(\text{two boys})$.
  c. Find $P(\text{boy, then girl})$.   **d.** Find $P(\text{girl, then boy})$.
  e. Predict the sum of the probabilities in parts (a)–(d). Check to see that the sum agrees with your prediction.

39. Standardized Test Prep You pick two balls from a bag containing balls of different colors. The bag contains at least two green balls. Compare the quantities in Column A and Column B.

Column A	Column B
$P(\text{two greens})$ with replacement	$P(\text{two greens})$ without replacement

  A. The quantity in Column A is greater.   **B.** The quantity in Column B is greater.
  C. The quantities are equal.   **D.** The relationship cannot be determined from the given information.

Exercises   M I X E D   R E V I E W

Solve each equation.

40. $3.2(m + 5) = 16$ **41.** $\frac{s}{5} - \frac{s}{3} = 8$ **42.** $w - 13w = 3$ **43.** $\frac{2c + 1}{7} = 3$

44. a. Communications Of the 99 million households in the United States in 1995, 35 million were not listed in phone books. Six million of these households did not have phones. How many households had phones, but did not list their numbers?
  b. Of the 35 million households not listed, $\frac{3}{7}$ had recently moved. How many households does this represent?

Getting Ready for Lesson 3-7
Write each number as a percent.

45. 0.45   **46.** $\frac{3}{4}$ **47.** 0.328

48. 1.2   **49.** $\frac{5}{5}$ **50.** 0.005

FOR YOUR JOURNAL

Describe a situation in your life in which you could find the probability of independent and dependent events.

3-7 Percent Equations

What You'll Learn
• Using equations to solve problems involving percents
• Finding simple interest

...And Why
To solve problems involving commission, interest, and circle graphs

What You'll Need
• protractor
• compass

QUICK REVIEW

A *percent* is a ratio that compares a number to 100. You can write a percent with the percent symbol or as a fraction or decimal. For example, you can write 40% as $\frac{40}{100}$ or as 0.40.

For more practice with percents, see Skills Handbook, page 589.

THINK AND DISCUSS

Solving Percent Equations

To model a percent problem with an equation, express each percent as a decimal. Three types of percent problems are modeled and solved below.

What is 40% of 8?	16 is 25% of what?	What percent of 40 is 5?
$n = 0.4 \times 8$ $n = 3.2$	$16 = 0.25 \times n$ $\frac{16}{0.25} = \frac{0.25n}{0.25}$ $64 = n$	$n \times 40 = 5$ $\frac{40n}{40} = \frac{5}{40}$ $n = 0.125$ $n = 12.5\%$

1. In the equations above, what symbol represents each of these words?
   a. is   **b.** of   **c.** what

2. Match each problem with the equation that models it.
   A. 15 is what percent of 12?   **I.** $n = 0.15 \times 12$
   B. What is 15% of 12?   **II.** $12 = 0.15n$
   C. 12 is 15% of what?   **III.** $15 = n \times 12$

3. Write an equation to model each question. Solve each equation.
   a. What is 25% of 80?   **b.** 3 is 75% of what?
   c. What percent of 44 is 11?   **d.** 16% of what is 200?

Writing Equations to Solve Percent Problems

Example 1   **Relating to the Real World** ············

Sales Suppose you work at a computer store. You earn 5% commission on everything you sell. How much do you earn on a computer you sell for $1900?

Define n = amount of your commission

Relate   Your commission is 5% of $1900.

Write $n = 0.05 \times 1900$
                 $n = 0.05(1900)$
                 $n = 95$

You earn $95 commission.

4. Tupi sells cars. He earns $145/wk in salary plus 8% commission. In one week he sells $36,000 worth of cars. How much does he earn?

You can use a circle graph to find data expressed in percents.

Example 2 **Relating to the Real World**

What Do You Think Is the Number One Problem in the World Today?

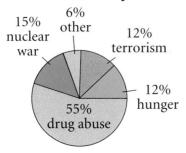

Source: *The Second Kids' World Almanac*

Surveys In a survey by *The Second Kids' World Almanac*, 1650 students said that drug abuse is the number one problem in the world today. How many students were surveyed?

Define n = the number of students surveyed

Relate 55% of the students surveyed is 1650.

Write $0.55 \times \quad n \quad = 1650$

$0.55n = 1650$

$\dfrac{0.55n}{0.55} = \dfrac{1650}{0.55}$ ← Divide each side by 0.55.

$n = 3000$

There were 3000 students surveyed.

Check 0.55 ⊠ 3000 ENTER

1650 ✓

5. How many students chose hunger as the number one problem?

Percents can be numbers greater than 100. Suppose you agree to do some yardwork with your grandfather for $20. You do such a good job that he pays you $30. A payment of $20 is 100% of what you expect. The payment of $30 is more than 100% of what you expect.

6. *Open-ended* Think of two more situations in which you would use a percent greater than 100%.

Math A Test Prep

1 A bag of marbles contains 3 red, 8 green, 3 yellow, 6 purple, and 4 black marbles. Find the probability of drawing a purple marble, and then another purple marble, without replacing the first.
(1) $\frac{5}{92}$ (3) $\frac{3}{46}$
(2) $\frac{1}{16}$ (4) $\frac{1}{12}$

2 Suppose you plan to tip 15% on a restaurant bill of $35.45. What is the total you will pay?

Example 3   Relating to the Real World

Community Service Suppose your school requires 36 hours of community service. You spent 56 hours volunteering at a hospital. What percent of the requirement have you fulfilled?

Define n = the percent of the requirement you have fulfilled

Relate 56 is what percent of 36?

Write $56 = n \times 36$

$$56 = 36n$$
$$\frac{56}{36} = \frac{36n}{36} \qquad \longleftarrow \text{Divide each side by 36.}$$
$$n = 1.555555555$$
$$n \approx 1.56$$

You have fulfilled about 156% of the community-service requirement. ■

7. **Mental Math** How many hours would fulfill 200% of the requirement?

Simple Interest

$I = prt$
I is the interest.
p is the principal.
r is the interest rate per year.
t is the time in years.

Today banks use *compound interest,* which you will study in Chapter 8. Compound interest is based on **simple interest.** Its formula is $I = prt$.

Example 4   Relating to the Real World

Finance Suppose you invested $900 for two years. You earned $67.50 in simple interest. What was the annual rate of interest?

$$I = prt \qquad \longleftarrow \text{Use the formula } I = prt.$$
$$67.50 = 900 \cdot r \cdot 2 \qquad \longleftarrow \text{Substitute 67.50 for } I, \text{ 900 for } p, \text{ and 2 for } t.$$
$$\frac{67.50}{1800} = \frac{1800r}{1800} \qquad \longleftarrow \text{Divide each side by 1800.}$$
$$r = 0.0375, \text{ or } 3.75\%$$

The annual rate of interest was 3.75%. ■

8. **Try This** Find the simple interest on $550 at 4.5% for one year.

QUICK REVIEW

central angle

radius

center

circle

WORK TOGETHER

Data Collection Work with a partner. Ask at least 10 people "How many pets do you have?" Complete these steps to construct a circle graph.

9. **a.** Find the percent of your data in each of these categories: no pets, one pet, two pets, three or more pets.
   b. Express each percent as a decimal and multiply by 360°. This gives the number of degrees in the central angle for each category.
   c. Draw a circle and use a protractor to draw each central angle.

Write an equation for each question. Do not solve the equation.

1. What is 4% of 150?

2. 32 is what percent of 40?

3. 24 is 150% of what?

Model with an equation. Then answer each question.

4. What percent of 51 is 17?

5. 10% of what is 8?

6. $7\frac{1}{2}$% of $200 is what?

7. 6% of what is 36?

8. 9% of 315 is what?

9. What percent of 45 is 18?

10. **Communications** There were 96 million households in the United States in 1994. How many households had two telephones?

11. **Finance** A bank pays $3\frac{1}{4}$ % simple interest annually. How much interest does $640 earn in three years?

12. **Estimation** Estimate a 15% tip for a restaurant bill of $7.25.

13. **Open-ended** What percent of your time do you spend sleeping? Describe the method you used to find this percent.

14. Choose the equation you would use to answer the question: What percent of 60 is 15?
    A. $15n = 60$
    B. $60(15) = n$
    C. $60n = 15$
    D. $n = \frac{60}{15}$

Number of Telephones in U.S. Households in 1994

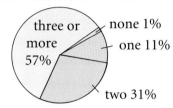

Choose Use a calculator, paper and pencil, or mental math to answer each question.

15. What is 25% of $80?

16. 1% of what is 7?

17. 5 is what percent of 10?

18. What percent of 27.7 is 1.8?

19. 80% of 49 is what?

20. 120% of what is 60?

21. 9 is what percent of 200?

22. 225% of 40 is what?

23. What is 55% of 600?

24. What percent of 150 is $7\frac{1}{2}$?

25. 5.4 is what percent of 9?

26. 95% of what is 83.125?

27. **Sales Tax** In Louisiana the state sales tax is 4%. If you buy a $2100 computer in Louisiana, how much tax will you pay?

28. **Geography** Alaska is the largest state in the United States, with an area of 570,374 mi². It accounts for about 15% of the country's area. Estimate the area of the United States.

29. **Finance** You received $41.60 in interest for a two-year investment at 6.5% simple interest. How much money did you invest?

30. **Geography** The information in the table gives the length of each of the four coastlines of the United States.
    a. How long is the coastline of the United States?
    b. Find the percent of the coastline of the United States that each coast represents. Round to the nearest hundredth of a percent.
    c. Draw and label a circle graph that represents the data.

U.S. Coastline Data

Coast	Miles
Arctic	1060
Atlantic	2069
Gulf	1631
Pacific	7623

Math in the Media   **Use the news article.**

31. What percent of residents of the United States are 65 or older?

32. About how many elderly residents live below the poverty level?

33. What percent of elderly residents' income is from Social Security?

34. Estimation   The population of Florida is about 13,000,000. Estimate the number of Florida residents who are 65 or older.

35. Writing   Explain how to use facts from the article to estimate the population of the United States in the year 2050.

Finance   **Use the formula for simple interest, $I = prt$. Find each missing value.**

36. $I = \blacksquare, p = \$340, r = 6\%, t = 3$ yr

37. $I = \$312.50, p = \blacksquare, r = 5\%, t = 5$ yr

38. $I = \$392, p = \$1400, r = \blacksquare, t = 4$ yr

39. $I = \$1540, p = \$22,000, r = 3.5\%, t = \blacksquare$

34 Million U.S. Residents are 65 or Older

Nearly 34 million of the 270 million residents of the United States have passed their 65th birthday. By the year 2050, roughly 20%, or 80 million people, will be 65 or older.

One of eight elderly residents lives below the poverty level. Two of every five dollars older residents earn are from Social Security.

Florida has the highest percent of elderly, with 18.4%. Alaska has the smallest share at 4.6%.

Chapter Project   **Find Out by Graphing**

····· Make a circle graph for the personal budget you created in the Find Out question on page 123. In a table, show the dollar amounts, percents, and angle degrees you used to create the graph.

Exercises   M I X E D   R E V I E W

Make a table, then graph each function.

40. $f(x) = 3x + 2$ **41.** $f(x) = 1.5x - 2$ **42.** $f(x) = \frac{4}{5}x - 0.5$ **43.** $f(x) = 4x + 1$

44. According to *USA TODAY*, children smile an average of 400 times a day. About how many times does a child smile in a week? in the month of October?

45. Find the range of the function $f(x) = |x| - 3$ when the domain is $\{-2, -1, 0, 1, 2\}$.

Getting Ready for Lesson 3-8

Simplify. Leave each answer in decimal form rounded to the nearest hundredth.

46. $\frac{45 - 35}{45}$ **47.** $\frac{100 - 25}{100}$ **48.** $\frac{80 - 21}{80}$ **49.** $\frac{32 - 4}{32}$

Solve.

1. $\frac{5w + 2}{3} = -4$ **2.** $\frac{3}{4}m = 7.2$ **3.** $\frac{t}{8} + \frac{t}{7} = 1$ **4.** $-\frac{4}{5}x - 2 = 7$ **5.** $6 = -\frac{1}{2}(3 - 5z)$

Suppose you have marbles in your pocket. One is red, three are blue, two are green, and three are yellow. You pick two marbles. Find each probability.

6. P(two yellow) with replacing

7. P(red and blue) without replacing

8. P(red and blue) with replacing

9. P(two green) without replacing

10. Writing Explain how P(yellow and blue) changes if you switch from replacing to not replacing.

11. Government A majority is any number greater than 50% of the total. When the 435 voting members of the House of Representatives use majority rule, how many members are needed to make a majority?

12. Open-ended Give an example of a situation in which you would use percents.

Algebra at Work

Media Researcher

Nielsen Media Research estimates the number of people who watch each network television show. The company polls a random sample of viewers. For national surveys, Nielsen polls about 10,000 viewers. For local surveys, they poll about 300 to 500 viewers. The results are then applied to the larger population. Nielsen Media Research estimates a 2–4% possible error for its local surveys, but only 1–2% for national polls. As you can see, the estimated error decreases as the sampling size increases.

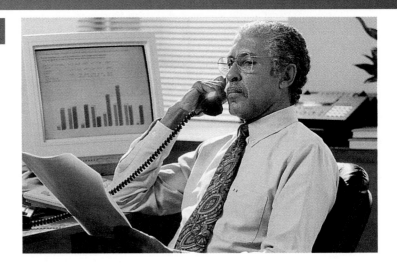

Mini Project: Describe how you would choose and contact a sample of 100 people to represent the entire population of your city.

Using a Graphing Program

After Lesson 3-7

In Chapter 1 you worked with graphs. In the last lesson you drew circle graphs. Computers can make graphing easier. To use a graphing program, you enter data in a spreadsheet. Then you choose the type of graph you want to draw. You must choose the type carefully because the computer will create the graph even if it is not appropriate for your data.

Instruments Played by Amateurs

	A	B
1	Instrument	People (millions)
2	Piano	24
3	Guitar	10
4	Flute	4
5	Drum	3

Source: *USA TODAY*

Instruments Played by Amateurs

A bar graph is a good choice for this set of data. You can use a bar graph to compare amounts.

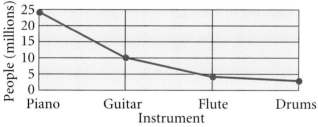

Instruments Played by Amateurs

A line graph is *not* a good choice for this set of data. A line graph shows a trend between two sets of data.

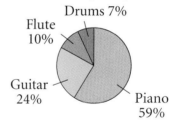

Instruments Played by Amateurs

A circle graph is *not* a good choice for this set of data. A circle graph displays parts of a whole.

Use a graphing program to make an appropriate graph for the data.

1. **Who Buys Take-Out Food?**

Age	18–29	30–44	45–59	60 plus
Percent	73%	64%	57%	39%

2. **People Who Telecommute**
(use a computer or a phone to work at home)

Year	1990	1991	1992	1993
People (millions)	4.0	5.5	6.6	7.6

3. "How often do you lose your television remote control each week?" Here is how people answered. Never: 44%, 1–5 times: 38%, Over 5 times: 17%, Don't know: 1%. Make a graph of this set of data.

4. Writing For Exercises 1–3, explain why you chose each type of graph.

What You'll Learn

3-8 **P**ercent of Change

- Finding percent of change
- Solving problems involving percent of change

...And Why

To solve problems involving careers in medicine and agriculture

Who? Dr. Graciela Solis Alarcón is a professor of medicine. Dr. Alarcón has won numerous awards for her research in rheumatology, which is the study of diseases of the muscles and joints.

THINK AND DISCUSS

News reporters often use statistics to present information. Here are two different ways a reporter related this fact: The number of female physicians in the United States increased from 25,400 in 1970 to 104,200 in 1990.

A: From 1970 to 1990, the number of female physicians more than quadrupled.

B: From 1970 to 1990, the number of female physicians increased about 310%.

Statement A is easy to verify by estimating: 104,200 is about 4 times 25,400, since 4(25,000) = 100,000.

To verify Statement B, you need to look at the percent of change in the data. The **percent of change** is the percent an amount changes from its original amount. The amount of change is the difference between these two values.

$$\text{percent of change} = \frac{\text{amount of change}}{\text{original amount}}$$

When a value increases from its original amount, you call the percent of change the **percent of increase.**

Example 1 Relating to the Real World

Medical Careers Verify statement B above by finding the percent of increase in the number of female physicians.

$$\text{percent of change} = \frac{\text{amount of change}}{\text{original amount}}$$

$$= \frac{104,200 - 25,400}{25,400} \quad \longleftarrow \text{Substitute.}$$

$$= \frac{78,800}{25,400} \quad \longleftarrow \text{Simplify the numerator.}$$

$$\approx 3.10, \text{ or } 310\% \quad \longleftarrow \text{Divide.}$$

The percent of increase is about 310%.

1. **a.** Explain why stating that an amount quadrupled is the same as stating that it increased 300%.
   b. What would an increase of 100% mean?

2. When you find the percent of change, why is it important to know which amount is the original amount?

3. **Try This** From 1970 to 1990, the total number of physicians in the United States increased from 334,000 to 615,400.
   a. Find the amount of change.
   b. Find the percent of increase.

When a value decreases from its original amount, you call the percent of change the **percent of decrease.**

Example 2   Relating to the Real World · · · · · · · · · · · · · ·

Agriculture   Changes in the economy have affected the location and number of farms in the United States. Find the percent of decrease in the number of farms from 1940 to 1990.

Changes in Farms in the United States

Year	Number of Farms (thousands)	Acres of Farmland (millions)
1940	6102	1065
1990	2140	987

Computer technology is used to vary the rate and type of fertilizer applied to a field.

$$\text{percent of change} = \frac{\text{amount of change}}{\text{original amount}}$$

$$= \frac{6102 - 2140}{6102} \quad \longleftarrow \text{Substitute.}$$

$$= \frac{3962}{6102} \quad \longleftarrow \text{Simplify the numerator.}$$

$$\approx 0.65, \text{ or } 65\% \quad \longleftarrow \text{Divide.}$$

The percent of decrease in the number of farms is about 65%.

4. **a.** Find the percent of decrease in the number of acres of farmland from 1940 to 1990.
   b. *Critical Thinking* While the number of farms decreased by 65%, the number of acres of farmland decreased by a much smaller percent. What can you conclude about the size of the average farm?

Exercises   **O N   Y O U R   O W N**

Choose **Use a calculator, pencil and paper, or mental math to find each percent of change. Describe the percent of change as a percent of increase or decrease. Round to the nearest percent.**

1. $12 to $9

2. 19 in. to 25 in.

3. $5\frac{1}{2}$ ft to $5\frac{3}{4}$ ft

4. 180 lb to 150 lb

5. 18 to $17\frac{1}{2}$

6. 15,000 to 12,000

7. $1.75 to $1.25

8. $6/h to $6.50/h

9. **Physical Therapy** Physical therapists measure strength on a dynamometer, which uses units called foot-pounds. Suppose you increase the strength in your elbow from 90 foot-pounds to 125 foot-pounds. Find the percent of increase.

10. **Environment** From 1987 to 1993, the number of days of unhealthy air quality in Atlanta dropped from 15 to 4. Find the percent of decrease in the number of days of unhealthy air.

Mental Math Find each percent of change.

11. 5 cm to 10 cm	**12.** $3.00 to $1.50	**13.** $10 to $4	**14.** 12 in. to 6 in.
15. 3 ft to 4 ft	**16.** $20,000 to $25,000	**17.** 2 m to 6 m	**18.** $15 to $5

19. **Open-ended** Choose an item that you buy that has changed in price. Give its original price and its new price. Find the percent of change.

20. **Sports** In the 1960 Olympics, Wilma Rudolph of the United States won the women's 100-m run in 11.0 s. In 1988, Florence Griffith-Joyner, also of the United States, won with a time of 10.54 s. Find the percent of decrease in the winning time.

21. **Writing** Suppose you increase the price of a product by 20%, then reduce the price by 20%. Is the resulting price greater than, less than, or equal to the price you started with? Explain your answer.

Calculator Find each percent of change. Describe the percent of change as a percent of increase or decrease.

22. $26 to $20	**23.** $8/h to $8.45/h	**24.** 21 in. to 54 in.	**25.** $4.95 to $3.87
26. 132 lb to 120 lb	**27.** $24,000 to $25,000	**28.** $8.99 to $3.99	**29.** 25 mi/h to 55 mi/h
30. $42.69 to $49.95	**31.** 2.3 cm to 2.8 cm	**32.** 10.5 km to 4.2 km	**33.** $3.99/lb to $2.89/lb

34. **Transportation** The number of cars in China increased from 1986 to 1993. Use the data at the right to find the percent of increase.

35. **Sales** Suppose that you are selling sweatshirts for a class fund-raiser. The wholesaler charges you $8 for each sweatshirt.
   a. You charge $16 for each sweatshirt. Find the percent of increase.
   b. **Generalize** your answer to part (a). Doubling a price is the same as a ___?___ percent increase.
   c. After the fund-raiser is over, you reduce the price on the remaining sweatshirts to $8. Find the percent of decrease.
   d. **Generalize** your answer to part (c). Cutting a price in half is the same as a ___?___ percent decrease.
   e. A few of the sale sweatshirts do not sell, so you give them away free to charity. Find the percent of decrease from the sale price.
   f. **Generalize** your answer to part (e). Reducing a price to zero is the same as a ___?___ percent decrease.

Passenger Cars in China

Source: *U.S. News & World Report*

36. Math in the Media Use the news article at the right.
  a. How does the information in the second sentence verify the "more than 40%" claim in the first sentence?
  b. In 1994, what percent of the people employed in the United States worked for businesses owned by women?

37. Standardized Test Prep All of the following are equal *except:*
  A. $100 increased by 50%   **B.** $150   **C.** 50% of $100
  D. 150% of $100   **E.** $100 increased by half

38. Animal Studies In 10 years, the African elephant population in Kenya decreased from 150,000 to 30,000.
  a. Find the percent of decrease.
  b. On average, how many fewer elephants were there each year?

Find the percent of change in each price.

39. $15 marked up to $24   **40.** $750 discounted to $600

41. $3500 marked up to $4000   **42.** $1.80 marked up to $2.20

43. $39.99 discounted to $19.99   **44.** $24 marked up to $36

45. a. Find the percent of change from 20 min to 25 min.
  b. Find the percent of change from 25 min to 30 min.
  c. Writing Explain why the percent of change is different for parts (a) and (b) even though the amount of change is the same.

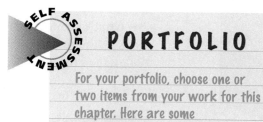

Women-Owned Businesses on the Rise

The number of businesses owned by women grew more than 40% in the three years from 1991 to 1994. The National Foundation for Women Business Owners reported that 7.7 million companies were owned by women in 1994, up from 5.4 million in 1991. In 1994, these businesses employed about 15.5 million of the 131 million people employed in the United States.

Exercises   MIXED REVIEW

Solve each equation.

46. $2 = \frac{c}{15}$ **47.** $8w = 12$ **48.** $z - 17 = -10$ **49.** $m - 4 = 9$

50. Health About 55 million Americans have foot problems. About 4.6 million of them have flat feet or fallen arches. What percent of people with foot problems have flat feet or fallen arches?

51. Probability You pick a colored chip from a bag, note its color, and replace it. You do this 20 times and get 7 red chips, 5 blue chips, and 8 green chips. What is the experimental probability that the next chip you choose will *not* be green?

52. Match each scatter plot correlation with the line that describes it.
  A. no correlation   **I.** downward slanted line (\)
  B. positive correlation   **II.** no line
  C. negative correlation   **III.** upward slanted line (/)

SELF ASSESSMENT

PORTFOLIO

For your portfolio, choose one or two items from your work for this chapter. Here are some possibilities:
● a journal entry
● corrected work
● a Find Out question
Explain why you include each selection you make.

Finishing the Chapter Project

checks *and* balances

Questions on pages 113, 118, 123, and 143 should help you to complete your project. Assemble all the parts of your project—the research on what you would like to buy, your expense record, your spreadsheet, and your circle graph. Are the expenses you recorded for two weeks typical for you? Does your budget support your purchase goal? Summarize what you think are the strengths and weaknesses of your budget.

Reflect and Revise

Present your budget and your purchase goal to a small group of classmates. Compare your decisions with theirs. Demonstrate to the group two equations of your own from the project. Check each other's work (including the circle graph) for reasonableness and accuracy. Use the comments and suggestions of your group to revise and improve your project.

Follow Up

Stick to your budget for several weeks. Are your savings on track? If not, what expenses can you reduce? Can you increase your income? Some of the resources listed below may give you ideas for a money-making project.

For More Information

Drew, Bonnie and Noel. *Fast Cash for Kids.* Hawthorne, New Jersey: Career Press, 1995.

Lamancusa, Joe. Kid Cash: *Creative Money-Making Ideas.* Blue Ridge Summit, Pennsylvania: TAB Books, 1993.

Spiselman, David. *A Teenager's Guide to Money, Banking, and Finance.* New York: J. Messner, 1987.

"The *Zillions* Allowance Survey." *Zillions* (April/May 1995): 14–17.

How am I doing?

- State three ideas from this chapter that you think are important. Explain your choices.
  - Describe several important rules that you must apply in order to solve equations.

SELF ASSESSMENT

Modeling and Solving Equations   3-1

The value (or values) of a variable that make an equation true are called **solutions.** To solve an equation you can use **inverse operations,** which are operations that undo one another. To solve an addition or subtraction equation, subtract or add the same value to each side of the equation. To solve a multiplication or division equation, divide or multiply each side of the equation by the same nonzero value.

Solve and check.

1. $y - 7 = 9$

2. $\frac{x}{12} = -3$

3. $w + 23 = 54$

4. $5d = 120$

5. $-9 + t = 35$

6. $c + 0.25 = 4.5$

7. $7b = 84$

8. $\frac{z}{4} = \frac{1}{2}$

Modeling and Solving Two-Step Equations   3-2

A **two-step equation** is an equation that has two operations. You can use tiles to model and solve a two-step equation. To solve a two-step equation, first add or subtract. Then multiply or divide.

Write and solve each equation modeled by tiles.

9.

10.

11.

For Exercises 12–19, solve and check each equation.

12. $8u + 2 = 6$

13. $7t - 3 = 18$

14. $-2q - 5 = -11$

15. $11y + 9 = 130$

16. $-z + 11 = -7$

17. $5x - 8 = 12$

18. $3m + 8 = 2$

19. $10h - 4 = -94$

20. Writing Describe a situation that you can model with $6m + 3 = 27$. Explain what the variable represents and solve the equation.

Combining Like Terms and Using the Distributive Property

3-3, 3-4

Terms with exactly the same variable factors are **like terms.** You can combine like terms and use the distributive property to simplify expressions and solve equations.

Simplify each expression.

21. $9m - 5m + 3$ **22.** $2b + 8 - b + 2$ **23.** $-5(w - 4)$ **24.** $9(4 - 3j)$

Solve and check each equation.

25. $6b + 4b = -90$ **26.** $-x + 7x = 24$ **27.** $2(t + 5) = 9$ **28.** $-2(r - \frac{1}{2}) = -2$

29. $2b + 5(b + 1) = -9$ **30.** $-(3 - 10y) = 12$ **31.** $x - (4 - x) = 0$ **32.** $1 = z + 3(z - 1)$

33. Geometry The width of a rectangle is 6 cm less then the length. The perimeter is 72 cm. Write and solve an equation to find the dimensions of the rectangle.

Rational Numbers and Equations

3-5

You can simplify an equation that has fractional coefficients by multiplying each side of the equation by a reciprocal or by a common denominator.

34. Which operation will solve the equation $\frac{3}{4}w = \frac{9}{8}$?

   A. Divide each side by $\frac{4}{3}$.   **B.** Subtract $\frac{4}{3}$ from each side.

   C. Multiply each side by $\frac{4}{3}$.   **D.** Add $\frac{4}{3}$ to each side.

Solve and check each equation.

35. $-\frac{2}{5}x = 18$ **36.** $\frac{2y}{3} + \frac{y}{4} = 22$ **37.** $\frac{3n - 2}{5} = -7$ **38.** $-\frac{1}{3}(4b + 1) = 5$

39. Suppose you spend $\frac{3}{5}$ of your monthly budget on food and $\frac{1}{4}$ on bus fare. Food and bus fare total $34/mo. What is your monthly budget?

Using Probability

3-6

Independent events do not affect one another. When the outcome of one event affects the outcome of a second event, the events are **dependent events.**

     For independent events A and B: For dependent events A and B:

     $P(A \text{ and } B) = P(A) \cdot P(B)$ $P(A \text{ and } B) = P(A) \cdot P(B \text{ after } A)$

For Exercises 40 and 41, you choose two numbers from a box containing tiles numbered 1–10. State whether the two events are *independent* or *dependent* and then find each probability.

40. $P(6 \text{ and an even number})$ without replacing   **41.** $P(1 \text{ and an odd number})$ with replacing

42. Writing Compare what the words *independent* and *dependent* mean in mathematics with what they mean in social studies.

Percent Equations

You can use an equation to solve a percent problem.

The formula to calculate **simple interest** is $I = p \cdot r \cdot t$, where I is the interest, p is the principal, r is the annual interest rate, and t is the time in years.

Write and solve an equation to answer each question. Check your answer.

43. What is 15% of 86?　　**44.** What percent of 5 is 40?　　**45.** 1.8 is 72% of what?

46. In one high school, 30 of the school's 800 students work on the school paper. What percent of the students work on the paper?

47. Finance You invest $2000 in a bank account paying 5.5% simple interest annually. How much interest will you receive after 2 yr?

Percent of Change

The **percent of change** $= \frac{\text{amount of change}}{\text{original amount}}$. If a value increases from its original amount, the percent of change is called the percent of increase. If a value decreases from its original amount, the percent of change is called the **percent of decrease.**

For Exercises 48–50, find each percent of change. Describe the percent of change as a percent of increase or decrease.

48. $75,000 to $85,000　　**49.** 20 ft to 15 ft　　**50.** 60 h to 40 h

51. In Irvine, California, parents donated 220,624 h of service to the schools in the 1993–1994 school year. This increased by about 60,000 hours the next year. Find the percent of increase of donated hours.

52. Open-ended Describe a situation that involves a percent of increase that is more than 100%.

Getting Ready for..▶ CHAPTER 4

Evaluate each expression.

53. $|-6| - |y|$ for $y = 8$　　**54.** $|t - 7|$ for $t = 5.6$　　**55.** $|c| + 9$ for $c = -10$

56. $|x| + 3$ for $x = -4$　　**57.** $3z - 4.5$ for $z = 3$　　**58.** $13 - 5y$ for $y = -1$

Solve and check.

59. $\frac{2}{3}k = \frac{1}{6}$　　**60.** $\frac{1}{2}b = \frac{4}{7}$　　**61.** $\frac{1}{3} = \frac{1}{9}d$　　**62.** $\frac{3}{2}l = \frac{2}{3}$

63. $5t + 4 = -16$　　**64.** $7 - m = 2$　　**65.** $2(w - 7) = 90$　　**66.** $3y + 8 = -1$

Solve and check each equation.

1. $5n = -20$
2. $t + 7 = 4$
3. $\frac{r}{3} = 21$
4. $u - 8 = -15$
5. $3q - 2 = 10$
6. $-2z + 1 = -9$

Write and solve each equation modeled by tiles.

7.

8.

Solve and check each equation.

9. $3w + 2 - w = -4$
10. $-9.5b + 4.5b = 25$
11. $\frac{1}{4}(k - 1) = 10$
12. $6(y + 3) = 24$
13. $\frac{5n + 1}{8} = \frac{1}{2}$

14. **Open-ended** Describe a situation that you can model with the equation $\frac{m}{5} = 4$.

15. If $2t + 3 = -9$, what is the value of $-3t - 7$?
    A. –6   B. 11
    C. –3   D. 2
    E. –9

16. Which equation is *not* equivalent to the equation $2x - 4 = -7$?
    A. $4 = -7 - 2x$ B. $-4 = -7 - 2x$
    C. $4 = 2x + 7$ D. $2x = -3$
    E. $-2x + 4 = 7$

Solve an equation to answer each question.

17. What is 16% of 250?

18. 8 is what percent of 12.5?

19. 19 is 95% of what?

20. **Finance** You invest $500 for three years and receive $60 in simple interest. What is the annual interest rate?

21. Suppose a person contributes 6% of her salary to her retirement account. She works 20 h/wk at $5.50/h. Find her weekly contribution.

Calculate the percent of change. Describe each as a percent of increase or a percent of decrease.

22. $4.50/h to $5/h   23. 60 km/h to 45 km/h

24. 150 lb to 135 lb   25. $18 to $24

26. The game Monopoly™ was introduced in 1935. The table shows how much some amounts in the game should have increased to have kept up with inflation.

	1935	1995
Total money in game	$15,140	$184,794
Amount each player starts the game with	1500	18,308
Park Place rent with no houses	35	428
Money collected when passing GO	200	2441

Source: Parker Brothers

a. Estimate the percent of inflation from 1935 to 1995 by finding the percent of increase in any one of the dollar amounts.
b. **Writing** Describe the steps you used to calculate your answer to part (a).
c. Explain another way to get the same result.

27. You have 8 red checkers and 8 black checkers in a bag. You choose two checkers. Find each probability.
    a. P(red and red) with replacing
    b. P(red and black) without replacing
    c. P(black and red) with replacing

28. **Open-ended** Write and solve a probability problem involving dependent events.

Part I

1 The table shows values for a linear function. Which equation describes the function?

x	1	2	3	4	5	6	7
$f(x)$	-2	-1	0	1	2	3	4

(1) $f(x) = -2x$ (3) $f(x) = x - 3$
(2) $f(x) = 2x$ (4) $f(x) = x + 3$

2 Which equation is equivalent to $s + 6 = 3$?

(1) $\frac{s}{2} = -3$ (3) $12 = 4s$

(2) $-7 = s - 4$ (4) $s + 5 = -2$

3 What is the solution of $-16 + \frac{n}{2} = -20$?

(1) $n = -4$ (3) $n = 2$
(2) $n = -2$ (4) $n = -8$

4 The expression $9a + 3b - 3 - 4a + 7 - 8b$ can be simplified to ▪.

(1) $5a - 5b + 4$ (3) $6a - 12b + 4$
(2) $5a + 11b - 10$ (4) $5a - 5b$

5 What is the solution of $4(z - 3) = -4$?

(1) $z = -13$ (3) $z = -4$
(2) $z = -1$ (4) $z = 2$

6 Which equation models "16 is 25% of what?"

(1) $16 = 0.25n$ (3) $n = 0.25(16)$

(2) $16 = \frac{n}{0.25}$ (4) $16 = 25n$

7 The graph shows the results of a survey of 2400 high school students. How many students worked 11–16 hours per week?

Hours Worked Weekly

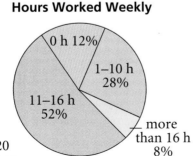

(1) 672   (2) 520
(3) 46   (4) 1248

8 What is the greatest possible percent of error for a measurement of 17.0 cm?

(1) 2.9%   (2) 50%   (3) 0.3%   (4) 0.6%

9 A bicycle is priced at $100. Then the price is raised by 10%. Then, during a sale, the price is lowered by 10%. The final price is ▪.

(1) $98   (3) $100
(2) $99   (4) $101

Part II

10 Suppose you can buy a pound of grapes for $1.36. How much would you pay for $1\frac{3}{4}$ pounds of grapes?

11 Suppose you received $67.50 for a 3-year investment at $4\frac{1}{2}$% simple interest. How much money had you invested?

Part III

12 The cost to mail a first-class letter in the U.S. in 1999 was $.33 for the first ounce, and $.22 for each additional ounce. If the cost to mail a letter was $.99, how much did the letter weigh? Write an equation to model this problem. Solve it.

13 Three coins are tossed.
  a Make a probability distribution table showing the probabilities of tossing 0, 1, 2, and 3 tails.
  b Make a histogram for the probability distribution.

Part IV

14 Three uncles were born in the same month in three consecutive years. The sum of their ages is 171. What are their ages? Write an equation to model this problem. Then solve it.

15 You have three red marbles, two blue marbles, and four green marbles in your pocket.
  a You pick one marble, replace it, and pick another marble. What is the probability that you pick a blue marble and a green marble?
  b You pick a marble, do *not* replace it, and pick again. What is the probability that you pick two green marbles?

CHAPTER 4

Equations and Inequalities

Relating to the Real World

You can use equations and formulas to model a variety of real-world problems. Business and industry, science, sports, travel, architecture, banking—these are some of the areas that rely on equations and inequalities to find solutions to problems, often by making comparisons and analyzing results.

Lessons	Using Proportions	Equations with Variables on Both Sides	Solving Absolute Value Equations	Transforming Formulas	Solving Inequalities Using Addition and Subtraction
	4-1	4-2	4-3	4-4	4-5

NO SWEAT!

Your good health and physical fitness will enhance your quality of life for years to come. As you grow older, your needs will change. How much exercise should you get? What should your blood pressure be? You can use formulas and inequalities to describe many aspects of good health.

As you work through the chapter, you will use formulas for physical fitness and health. You will work with equations and inequalities that allow for differences in weight, height, and age. Finally, you will design an exercise plan for yourself.

To help you complete the project:

▼ **p. 162** *Find Out by Calculating*
▼ **p. 178** *Find Out by Solving*
▼ **p. 194** *Find Out by Researching*
▼ **p. 200** *Find Out by Writing*
▼ **p. 205** *Find Out by Interviewing*
▼ **p. 206** *Finishing the Project*

Solving
Inequalities
Using
Multiplication
and Division

Solving
Multi-Step
Inequalities

Compound
Inequalities

Interpreting
Solutions

4-6   4-7   4-8   4-9

target range

$0.7(220-a) \le R \le 0.85(220-a)$

What You'll Learn

- Solving proportions
- Using proportions to solve real-world problems

...And Why

To solve problems by comparing and evaluating quantities

What You'll Need

- centimeter ruler
- calculator

1.5 m   4.5 m

3 m BATH

KITCHEN   6 m

scale
1 cm: ▇ m

4-1 Using Proportions

WORK TOGETHER

A **ratio** is a comparison of two numbers by division. For example, $\frac{3}{4}$ and $5 : 2$ are ratios. The **scale** of a blueprint is the ratio of a length on the blueprint to the actual length it represents.

1. **a.** Work with a partner. Measure the length and width of the two rooms in the apartment blueprint in centimeters.

   b. For the two rooms, record the measurements in a table like the one below. Complete the table by finding the ratios of the blueprint measurements to the actual measurements.

Length	Blueprint	Actual	Blueprint : Actual (cm : m)
	▇ cm	▇ m	▇ : ▇
Width	Blueprint	Actual	Blueprint : Actual (cm : m)
	▇ cm	▇ m	▇ : ▇

2. Use the ratios in your table to complete the blueprint scale.

THINK AND DISCUSS

Using Properties of Equality

A **proportion** is a statement that two ratios are equal. Another way to write the sample at the right is $3 : 4 = 12 : 16$. Read this "3 is to 4 as 12 is to 16."

$$\frac{3}{4} = \frac{12}{16}$$

To solve a proportion with a variable, you can use the multiplication property of equality.

QUICK REVIEW

Multiplication Property of Equality

For any numbers *a*, *b*, and *c*, if $a = b$, then $ac = bc$.

Example 1

Solve $\frac{t}{9} = \frac{5}{6}$.

$\frac{t}{9} \cdot 54 = \frac{5}{6} \cdot 54$ ◄— Multiply each side by a common denominator such as 54.

$6t = 45$

$\frac{6t}{6} = \frac{45}{6}$ ◄— Divide each side by 6.

$t = 7.5$

The solution is 7.5. The ratios $\frac{7.5}{9}$ and $\frac{5}{6}$ are equal.

3. Instead of 54, would another number have worked in Example 1? What number is the best choice? Why?

Using Cross Products

The numerators and denominators of the ratios that form a proportion have a special relationship. The **cross products** of a proportion are equal.

$$\frac{3}{4} = \frac{12}{16}$$

3 · 16 and 4 · 12 are cross products.
3 · 16 = 48 and 4 · 12 = 48

Cross Products of a Proportion

In a proportion, where $b \neq 0$ and $d \neq 0$; if $\frac{a}{b} = \frac{c}{d}$ then $ad = bc$.

Example: $\frac{2}{3} = \frac{8}{12}$ so $2 \cdot 12 = 3 \cdot 8$.

---

4. Use cross products to **justify** each statement.
  a. $\frac{8}{3}$ and $\frac{4}{1.5}$ form a proportion.   **b.** $\frac{5}{8}$ and $\frac{7}{10}$ do not form a proportion.

Another way to solve a proportion with a variable is to use cross products.

Example 2

Solve $\frac{y}{2.5} = -\frac{3}{4}$.

$$y(4) = (2.5)(-3) \quad \longleftarrow \text{Use cross products.}$$
$$\frac{4y}{4} = \frac{-7.5}{4} \quad \longleftarrow \text{Divide each side by 4.}$$
$$y = -1.875 \quad \longleftarrow \text{Simplify.}$$

The solution is -1.875.

PROBLEM SOLVING

Look Back **What steps would you take to solve this proportion using the multiplication property of equality?**

5. a. Is $-4 = \frac{x}{16}$ a proportion? Why or why not?
  b. Explain how to solve for x. Find x.

Similar figures are figures that have the same shape but not necessarily the same size. The corresponding angles of similar figures are equal and the corresponding sides are in proportion.

Example 3

Geometry In the figure, $\triangle ABC$ is similar to $\triangle DFE$. Find length DE.

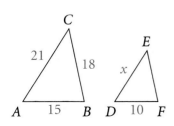

Define x = unknown length DE

Relate $\dfrac{\text{length } AB}{\text{length } DF} = \dfrac{\text{length } AC}{\text{length } DE}$

Write $\dfrac{15}{10} = \dfrac{21}{x}$ $\longleftarrow$ Write a proportion comparing the lengths of corresponding sides.

$$15x = 10(21) \quad \longleftarrow \text{Use cross products.}$$
$$\frac{15x}{15} = \frac{210}{15} \quad \longleftarrow \text{Divide each side by 15.}$$
$$x = 14$$

The length $DE = 14$. $\longleftarrow$ Simplify.

6. **a. Try This** Find length *EF* in the figure shown in Example 3.
   b. What is the perimeter of △*DFE*?
   c. Write a ratio comparing the perimeters of △*DFE* and △*ABC*.
   d. How does the ratio of the perimeters in part (c) compare with the ratio of length *DE* to length *AC*?

Solving Percent Problems Using Proportions

In Chapter 3 you used equations to solve problems involving percents. Recall that percent is a ratio that compares a number to 100. You can use proportions to solve word problems that involve percent.

| **Example 4** | **Relating to the Real World** |

Aquaculture In 1994, U.S. trout farms produced 52,100,000 lb of trout. Suppose a trout farmer raised 858,000 lb of trout. What percent of the 1994 U.S. trout production did the farmer raise? Round your answer to the nearest tenth of a percent.

Define n = the farmer's part of the trout production

Relate 858,000 is what percent of 52,100,000?

Write $\frac{858,000}{52,100,000} = \frac{n}{100}$ ←— part
←— whole

$858,000(100) = 52,100,000n$ ←— Use cross products.

$\frac{858,000(100)}{52,100,000} = \frac{52,100,000n}{52,100,000}$ ←— Divide each side by 52,100,000.

$\frac{858,000(100)}{52,100,000} = n$ ←— Write in a calculator-ready form.

$1.6468330134 = n$ ←— Use a calculator.

$1.6 \approx n$ ←— Round to the nearest tenth.

The farmer raised about 1.6% of the 1994 U.S. trout production.

7. **a.** A trout farm can produce 8800 lb/acre each year. At that rate, how many acres were needed to raise the 1994 U.S. trout production?
   b. How many acres did the farmer in Example 4 need?

8. *Critical Thinking* How are these three questions and their answers different from each other?
   - 10 is what percent of 25?
   - What number is 10% of 25?
   - 10% of what number is 25?

Which pairs of ratios could form a proportion? Justify each answer.

1. $\frac{6}{8}, \frac{15}{20}$　　　2. $\frac{9}{12}, \frac{4}{5}$　　　3. $-\frac{0.12}{0.15}, -\frac{0.4}{0.5}$　4. $\frac{5}{6}, \frac{20}{24}$　　　5. $-\frac{3}{100}, -\frac{1}{25}$　6. $\frac{51}{3}, \frac{17}{1}$

7. A canary's heart beats 130 times in 12 s. Use a proportion to find how many times its heart beats in 40 s.

8. **Open-ended** Write a problem that you can solve using the proportion $\frac{2}{5} = \frac{x}{9}$. Then show the solution to your problem.

Use a proportion to answer Exercises 9–20. Round your answer to the nearest tenth or to the nearest tenth of a percent.

9. Find 45% of $120.

10. What percent of 200 is 25?

11. 17 is what percent of 85?

12. 12.5 is 75% of what number?

13. What is $33\frac{1}{3}$% of 150?

14. 22 is 80% of what number?

15. What percent of 87 is 24?

16. 15 is 35% of what number?

17. Find 89% of 345.

18. What number is 75% of 250?

19. 12.5 is 80% of what number?

20. What is 23% of 27?

21. **Architecture** A blueprint scale is 1.5 in. : 6 ft. On the plan, the den measures 2.5 in. by 3 in. What are the actual dimensions of the den?

22. **Geometry** In the figure, $\triangle RST$ is similar to $\triangle XZY$. Find length ZY.

23. **Standardized Test Prep** Which equation does not have the same solution as $\frac{12}{x} = \frac{45}{60}$?

 A. $12 \cdot 60 = 45x$　**B.** $\frac{12}{45} = \frac{x}{60}$　　**C.** $\frac{x}{12} = \frac{60}{45}$　　**D.** $\frac{x}{60} = \frac{12}{45}$　　**E.** $\frac{60}{x} = \frac{12}{45}$

Mental Math **Solve each proportion mentally.**

24. $\frac{x}{6} = \frac{12}{18}$　　　25. $-\frac{12}{20} = -\frac{3}{y}$　　　26. $\frac{8}{d} = \frac{40}{30}$　　　27. $\frac{1}{2} = \frac{z}{25}$

▦ **Choose** **Use a calculator, paper and pencil, or mental math. Solve each proportion.**

28. $\frac{c}{6} = \frac{12}{15}$　　29. $\frac{21}{12} = \frac{7}{y}$　　30. $-\frac{37}{24} = \frac{k}{6}$　　31. $\frac{15}{n} = \frac{39}{13}$

32. $\frac{17}{51} = \frac{n}{1}$　　33. $-\frac{4.5}{x} = -\frac{1.8}{5}$　34. $\frac{q}{56} = \frac{15}{14}$　　35. $\frac{2.5}{1.8} = -\frac{1.2}{r}$

36. **a.** **Geometry** Rectangle $ABCD$ is 6 in. wide and 16 in. long. It is similar to rectangle $KLMN$, whose length is 24 in. What is the width of rectangle $KLMN$?
 b. Are the areas of the two rectangles proportional to the lengths of their corresponding sides? Explain.

37. **a.** Do the two phrases in the picture offer the same discount? Explain.
 b. **Open-ended** What would you expect to pay at the store's sale for a jacket regularly priced at $67? Explain.

38. a. Travel Use a ruler and the map at the right. Find the distance from each town to the others.

    b. A student lives halfway between Lincoln and San Paulo and goes by the shortest route to school in Duncanville. How far does the student travel each day to and from school?

39. Suppose $\frac{12}{72} = \frac{x}{24}$ and $\frac{x}{36} = \frac{y}{81}$. Find y.

40. Writing Write an explanation telling an absent classmate how to use cross products to solve a proportion. Include an example.

41. Hobbies Some model trains are built to $\frac{1}{87}$ of actual size. Suppose an actual boxcar is 40 ft long. How many *inches* long is the model?

42. Statistics In the southern United States, 68.6% of the population, or 58,656,000 people, live in urban areas. What is the total population of the southern United States?

43. In 1992, there were 255,082,000 people living in the United States. Of these, 18,100,000 were 10–14 years old. What percent of the population was this? Round your answer to the nearest tenth of a percent.

Chapter Project   ***Find Out by Calculating***

When you exercise, the number of calories you burn is roughly proportional to your weight.

• Write and solve a proportion to find how many calories you would burn if you performed one activity in the table for 60 min.

• Write and solve a proportion to find how many calories you would burn if you did the activity for 60 min three times in a week.

Calories Burned During Exercise	
(150-lb person exercising for 60 min)	
Exercise	**Calories**
Dancing	250
Biking, walking (3–5 mph)	300
Soccer, jogging (4–5 mph)	400
Swimming, skiing	500
Running (5–7 mph)	650

Exercises   M I X E D   R E V I E W

Add or subtract.

44. $\begin{bmatrix} 11 & -2 & 4 \\ 3.5 & 6.9 & 12.2 \end{bmatrix} + \begin{bmatrix} -5.4 & 3.2 & -8 \\ 7.6 & 2.3 & -9.7 \end{bmatrix}$

45. $\begin{bmatrix} -4.3 & 7.9 \\ 2.1 & -0.8 \end{bmatrix} - \begin{bmatrix} -3.1 & -6.7 \\ 3.5 & 4.9 \end{bmatrix}$

Find the value of each function when $x = 3$.

46. $f(x) = 4x - 1$ **47.** $f(x) = -1.5x - 7$ **48.** $f(x) = 8x + 2$

49. You have one foot of space left on a bookshelf, and your paperbacks are $\frac{3}{4}$ in. thick. How many more paperbacks can you fit on the shelf?

Getting Ready for Lesson 4-2

Solve and check each equation.

50. $7x + 4 - 15x = 36$ **51.** $w + (w + 2) = -27$ **52.** $6(7 - 2y) = 30$

What You'll Learn

4-2

Equations with Variables on Both Sides

- Solving equations with variables on both sides
- Identifying equations that have no solution or are identities

...And Why

To solve equations that model real-world situations, such as distance problems

What You'll Need

- tiles
- calculator

WORK TOGETHER

In Chapter 3 you used tiles and solved equations. Model each equation with tiles. Then solve.

1. $x - 4 = -9$ **2.** $-10 = 5y$ **3.** $3a + 8 = 2$ **4.** $-12 = 8 + 4b$

Now look at an equation with variables on both sides: $6x + 3 = 4x + 9$.

5. Model this equation with tiles.

6. Discuss how you might use tiles to solve the equation.

7. Use the problem solving strategy *Guess and Test* to solve the equation.

THINK AND DISCUSS

Using Tiles to Solve Equations

Some equations cannot be solved easily using the strategy *Guess and Test*. In this lesson you will learn how to solve equations with variables on both sides. First you will use tiles to help you understand the process.

Example 1

Solve the equation

$$5x - 3 = 2x + 12.$$

Model the equation with tiles.

$$5x - 3 = 2x + 12$$

Add $-2x$ to each side, and simplify by removing zero pairs.

$$5x - 3 - 2x = 2x + 12 - 2x$$
$$3x - 3 = 12$$

1 A scale drawing is made of a rectangular room whose dimensions are 18 ft by 24 ft. The scale is 3 ft = 1 in. What is the perimeter of the room in the scale drawing?
(1) 84 in.   (3) 28 in.
(2) 42 in.   (4) 14 in.

2 Beth said the equation $5v - 9 = 3(v - 3) + 2v$ is an identity. Explain what she meant by this. Show how she could reach this conclusion.

Add 3 to each side and simplify by removing zero pairs.

$$3x - 3 + 3 = 12 + 3$$
$$3x = 15$$

Divide each side into three identical groups.

$$\frac{3x}{3} = \frac{15}{3}$$

Solve for x.

$$x = 5$$

The solution is 5.

Check $5x - 3 = 2x + 12$
$5(5) - 3 \stackrel{?}{=} 2(5) + 12$ ◀— Substitute 5 for x.
$22 = 22$ ✔

8. Try This Use tiles to model and solve each equation.
   a. $6x - 2 = x + 13$ **b.** $4(x + 1) = 2x - 2$
   c. **Summarize** the steps you used to solve the equations.

Using Properties of Equality

You can use the properties of equality to get terms with variables on the same side of the equation.

Example 2

Solve $5t - 8 = 9t - 10$.
$5t - 8 + 10 = 9t - 10 + 10$ ◀— Add 10 to each side.
$\qquad 5t + 2 = 9t$ ◀— Simplify each side.
$5t + 2 - 5t = 9t - 5t$ ◀— Subtract $5t$ from each side.
$\qquad 2 = 4t$ ◀— Combine like terms.
$\qquad \frac{2}{4} = \frac{4t}{4}$ ◀— Divide each side by 4.
$\qquad \frac{1}{2} = t$ ◀— Simplify each side.
The solution is $\frac{1}{2}$.

GRAPHING CALCULATOR HINT

You can check your solution to Example 2 by using the TEST feature to see if $\frac{1}{2}$ is the solution of the equation.

9. Verify the solution of Example 2.

10. a. Suppose you began solving the equation in Example 2 by subtracting 9*t* from each side of the equation. Write the steps you would use to solve the equation.

 b. Compare your solution to the solution in Example 2. Does it matter that the variables are on different sides of the equal sign? Explain.

QUICK REVIEW

A formula for distance is distance = rate · time, or $d = rt$.

Equations are helpful when you solve distance problems.

Example 3   **Relating to the Real World** ················

Transportation Mary and Jocelyn are sisters. They left school at 3:00 P.M. and bicycled home along the same bike path. Mary bicycled at a speed of 12 mi/h. Jocelyn bicycled at 9 mi/h. Mary got home 15 min before Jocelyn. How long did it take Mary to get home?

PROBLEM SOLVING HINT

Draw a diagram to help you visualize the conditions of the problem in Example 3.

Mary's distance : 12t

Jocelyn's distance : 9(t + 0.25)

Define $t = $ Mary's time in hours
  $t + 0.25 = $ Jocelyn's time in hours

Relate   Mary's distance   equals   Jocelyn's distance
       (rate · time)   (rate · time)

Write $12t$ $=$ $9(t + 0.25)$

$$12t = 9(t + 0.25)$$
$$12t = 9t + 2.25 \qquad \longleftarrow \text{Use the distributive property.}$$
$$12t - 9t = 9t + 2.25 - 9t \quad \longleftarrow \text{Subtract } 9t \text{ from each side.}$$
$$3t = 2.25 \qquad \longleftarrow \text{Combine like terms.}$$
$$\frac{3t}{3} = \frac{2.25}{3} \qquad \longleftarrow \text{Divide each side by 3.}$$
$$t = 0.75 \qquad \longleftarrow \text{Use a calculator.}$$

It took Mary 0.75 h, or 45 min, to get home.

11. Critical Thinking To solve the problem in Example 3, Ben wrote the equation $12t = 9(t + 15)$. What mistake did he make?

Solving Special Types of Equations

An equation has **no solution** if no value makes the equation true.

Example 4 ···

Solve $6m - 5 = 7m + 7 - m$.
$$6m - 5 = 7m + 7 - m$$
$$6m - 5 = 6m + 7 \qquad \longleftarrow \text{Combine like terms.}$$
$$6m - 5 - 6m = 6m + 7 - 6m \quad \longleftarrow \text{Subtract } 6m \text{ from each side.}$$
$$-5 = 7 \qquad \text{Not true for any } m!$$

This equation has no solution.

12. Is an equation that has 0 for a solution the same as an equation with no solution? Explain.

An equation that is true for every value of the variable is an **identity.**

> ### Example 5
>
> Solve $10 - 8a = 2(5 - 4a)$.
>
> $$10 - 8a = 2(5 - 4a)$$
> $$10 - 8a = 10 - 8a \quad \longleftarrow \text{Use the distributive property.}$$
> $$10 - 8a + 8a = 10 - 8a + 8a \quad \longleftarrow \text{Add } 8a \text{ to each side.}$$
> $$10 = 10 \qquad \text{Always true!}$$
>
> This equation is true for any value of a, so the equation is an identity. ■

13. Could you have stopped solving the equation when you saw that $10 - 8a = 10 - 8a$? Explain.

14. *Mental Math* Without writing the steps of a solution, tell whether the equation has *one solution, no solution,* or is an *identity.*
   a. $9 + 5a = 5a - 1$ **b.** $5a + 9 = 2a$
   c. $9 + 5a = 2a + 9$ **d.** $9 + 5a = 5a + 9$

Exercises   O N Y O U R O W N

Write an equation for each model and solve.

1.

2.

3.

4.

Model each equation with tiles. Then solve.

5. $4x - 3 = 3x + 4$ **6.** $5x + 3 = 3x + 9$ **7.** $8 - x = 2x - 1$

Solve and check. If the equation is an identity or if it has no solution, write *identity* or *no solution.*

8. $3(x - 4) = 2x + 6$ **9.** $4x - 7 = x + 3(4 + x)$ **10.** $5x = 3(x - 1) + (3 + 2x)$

11. $0.5y + 2 = 0.8y - 0.3y$ **12.** $6 + 3m = -m - 6$ **13.** $3t + 8 = 5t + 8 - 2t$

Critical Thinking Find the mistake in the solution of each equation. Explain the mistake and solve the equation correctly.

14.
$$2x = 11x + 45$$
$$2x - 11x = 11x - 11x + 45$$
$$9x = 45$$
$$\frac{9x}{9} = \frac{45}{9}$$
$$x = 5$$

15.
$$4.5 - y = 2(y - 5.7)$$
$$4.5 - y = 2y - 11.4$$
$$4.5 - y - y = 2y - y - 11.4$$
$$4.5 = y - 11.4$$
$$4.5 + 11.4 = y - 11.4 + 11.4$$
$$15.9 = y$$

Mental Math Solve and check each equation.

16. $5y = y - 40$

17. $7w = -7w$

18. $r + 1 = 4r + 1$

19. $6t + 1 = 6t - 8$

20. $2q + 4 = 4 - 2q$

21. $3a + 1 = 9 - a$

Choose Use tiles, paper and pencil, calculator, or mental math to solve each equation. If appropriate, write *identity* or *no solution*.

22. $t + 1 = 3t - 5$

23. $7y - 8 = 7y + 9$

24. $0.5k + 3.6 = 4.2 - 1.5k$

25. $2r + 16 = r - 25$

26. $\frac{3}{4}x = \frac{1}{2} + \frac{2}{3}x$

27. $\frac{1}{3}(x - 7) = 5x$

28. $0.7m = 0.9m + 2.4 - 0.2m$

29. $14 - (2q + 5) = -2q + 9$

30. $0.3t + 1.4 = 4.2 - 0.1t$

31. Find the value of each variable in the matrices.
$$\begin{bmatrix} 2x + 1 & a - 1 \\ w - 4 & 9y \end{bmatrix} = \begin{bmatrix} -5x - 6 & 5a \\ 3w + 4 & -3y \end{bmatrix}$$

32. Business A toy company spends $1500 each day on plant costs plus $8 per toy for labor and materials. The toys sell for $12 each. How many toys must the company sell in one day to equal its daily costs?

33. Writing Describe the two situations you learned about in this lesson that cannot occur when you are solving an equation with the variable on only one side of the equal sign. Give examples.

34. Transportation A truck traveling 45 mi/h and a train traveling 60 mi/h cover the same distance. The truck travels 2 h longer than the train. How many hours did each travel?

35. Recreation You can buy used in-line skates from your cousin for $40, or you can rent them from the park. Either way you must rent safety equipment. How many hours must you skate at the park to justify buying your cousin's skates?

SKATE RENTALS

In-line skates and safety equipment $3.50/hour

Safety equipment $1.50/hour

Open-ended Write an equation with variables on both sides for each of the following solutions.

36. $x = 0$

37. x is a positive number.

38. x is a negative number.

39. All values of x are solutions.

40. $x = 1$

41. No values of x are solutions.

42. a. Technology Write formulas for cells B2 and C2 to evaluate the expressions at the top of Columns B and C.

	A	B	C
1	x	$5(x - 3)$	$4 - 3(x + 1)$
2	-5	-40	16
3	-4	-35	13
4	-3		

b. Enter the integers from –5 to 5 in Column A. Evaluate the expressions in Columns B and C using the values in Column A.

c. What is the value in Column A when the numbers in Columns B and C are equal?

d. What equation have you solved?

e. Use a spreadsheet to solve $5.2n - 9 = 11.2n + 3$.

43. Geometry $\triangle ABC$ is congruent to $\triangle DEF$. Find the lengths of the sides of $\triangle DEF$.

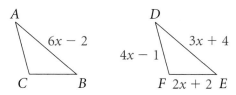

Solve each equation. Check your answers.

44. $2n - 5 = 8n + 7$

45. $3x + 4 = x + 18$

46. $3b + 5 - b = 4b$

47. $5a - 14 = -5 + 8a$

48. $4 - 6d = d + 4$

49. $-10t + 6.25 = t + 11.75$

50. $4x - 10 = x + 3x - 2x$

51. $6x = 4(x + 5)$

52. $\frac{3}{2}z - 2 = -\frac{5}{4}z - 4$

53. Standardized Test Prep Compare the quantities in Column A and Column B. Which statement is true for all values of x?

Column A	Column B
$5(x - 3)$	$7x - 12 - (2x + 3)$

A. The quantity in Column A is greater.

B. The quantity in Column B is greater.

C. The quantities are equal.

D. The relationship cannot be determined from the given information.

Exercises   MIXED REVIEW

Solve and check each equation.

54. $-\frac{12}{14} = \frac{-9}{m}$

55. $\frac{1}{3}(h - 5) = -11$

56. $2x = 7x + 10$

57. $\frac{w}{7} = \frac{11}{10}$

58. Money The sales tax in Austin, Texas, is 8%. How much would you pay for three $12 books and two $15 books in Austin?

Getting Ready for Lesson 4-3

Simplify.

59. $|15|$

60. $|-12|$

61. $|-34|$

62. $|18 - 12|$

63. $|9 + 2|$

64. $|-12 - (-12)|$

65. $-|-19|$

66. $-|32|$

67. $-|-10 + 8|$

SELF ASSESSMENT

FOR YOUR JOURNAL

Summarize what you know about solving equations with variables on both sides by writing a list of steps for solving this type of equation.

Using Graphs to Solve or Check Equations

After Lesson 4-2

You can use a graphing calculator to solve equations with variables on both sides. When you graph each side of an equation separately, the x-coordinate of the point where the graphs meet gives the solution to the equation.

Example

Find the solution of $-\frac{1}{2}c = \frac{1}{2}c + 5$ using a graphing calculator.

STEP 1: Press Y= to go to the equation screen. Press CLEAR to clear the first equation. Then press (−) · 5 X,T,θ to enter the left-hand side of the equation.

STEP 2: Press the down arrow once. Press CLEAR . Then press · 5 X,T,θ + 5 to enter the right-hand side of the equation.

STEP 3: Press GRAPH to view the graphs of the equations.

STEP 4: Press 2nd CALC 5 . Move the cursor near the point of intersection. Press ENTER three times to find the coordinates of the intersection point.

The x-coordinate of the point of intersection is -5. The solution of the equation $-\frac{1}{2}c = \frac{1}{2}c + 5$ is -5.

1. The graphing calculator screen at the right shows the solution of $2x - 1 = x + 1$.
   a. What two equations were graphed?
   b. What is the x-coordinate of the point where the graphs intersect?
   c. What is the solution of the equation?

2. David solved $3(a + 1) = 5a + 4$. His solution was $-\frac{3}{2}$. Graph $y = 3(x + 1)$ and $y = 5x + 4$. Use the CALC feature to find the x-coordinate of the intersection of the two lines. Is David's solution correct? Explain.

Use your graphing calculator to solve each equation.

3. $3d - 9 = 0$ **4.** $2n - 5 = 8n + 7$ **5.** $2x - 15 = 3(x - 15)$ **6.** $4 - 7q = -3$

Use your graphing calculator to check each solution.

7. $5(n + 1) = n + 2; \frac{1}{4}$ **8.** $2x - 9 = -3(x - 6); 5\frac{2}{5}$ **9.** $b - 0 = -2(b + 1); 3\frac{2}{3}$

10. Writing Explain the significance of the y-value of the point of intersection. (*Hint:* Use a pencil and paper to solve an equation and check the solution.)

What You'll Learn

4-3 **S**olving Absolute Value Equations

- Solving equations that involve absolute value
- Using absolute value equations to model real-world problems

...And Why

To solve problems involving opinion polls and quality control

WORK TOGETHER

Math in the Media Work with a partner to answer these questions.

1. The actual results could vary from the poll results by −3% to +3%.
   a. What is the greatest percent of voters who might vote for Blake?
   b. What is the least percent of voters who might vote for Cortez?

2. According to this poll, can Cortez get a majority of the votes? Explain.

3. *Open-ended* Write a short news article that includes numbers and a range around the numbers. (The article does not have to include percents and should not be about elections.)

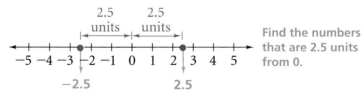

Poll Shows Cortez Leading

A telephone poll of likely voters in the senate race was conducted by this newspaper and radio station KLRW. The poll shows that Maria Cortez has 49% of the vote, James Blake has 42%, and 9% of those polled are undecided. The results are accurate to within 3%.

THINK AND DISCUSS

Solving Absolute Value Equations

Situations involving a range of numbers can often be represented by absolute value equations. You can use a number line and the definition of absolute value to solve these equations.

QUICK REVIEW

The *absolute value* of a number is its distance from 0 on a number line. The symbol for the absolute value of a is |a|.

An absolute value is either zero or a positive number.

Example 1

Use a number line to solve $|m| = 2.5$.

2.5 units   2.5 units

−5 −4 −3 −2 −1 0 1 2 3 4 5

−2.5   2.5

Find the numbers that are 2.5 units from 0.

The solution is −2.5 or 2.5.

4. **Try This** Use a number line to solve each equation.
   a. $|b| = 2$ b. $4 = |y|$ c. $|w| = 4.5$

5. Explain how the equations $|x| = 5$ and $x = |5|$ are different.

6. Critical Thinking Is there a solution for $|m| = -3$? Explain.

7. For what value of a does the equation $|x| = a$ have just one solution?

You can use the properties of equality to solve an absolute value equation. Remember that you must get the absolute value by itself on one side of the equation.

Example 2

Solve $|x| + 5 = 11$.

$$|x| + 5 = 11$$
$$|x| + 5 - 5 = 11 - 5 \quad \longleftarrow \text{Subtract 5 from each side.}$$
$$|x| = 6$$
$$x = 6 \text{ or } x = -6 \quad \longleftarrow \text{The value of } x \text{ is either 6 or } -6.$$

The solution is 6 or -6.

Check both solutions.

$$|x| + 5 = 11$$
$$|-6| + 5 \stackrel{?}{=} 11 \quad \text{or} \quad |6| + 5 \stackrel{?}{=} 11 \quad \longleftarrow \text{Substitute 6 and } -6 \text{ for } x.$$
$$6 + 5 = 11 \checkmark \qquad\qquad 6 + 5 = 11 \checkmark$$

8. What happens when you try to solve $|x| + 11 = 5$? Explain.

9. Try This Solve each equation.
   a. $3 = |w| - 4$ **b.** $4|n| = 32$ **c.** $-6 = \dfrac{|x|}{-2}$ **d.** $|x| - 5 = -9$

Sometimes the absolute value expression has more than one term. You can use what you know about absolute value to write and solve two equations. The solutions of both equations are solutions of the absolute value equation.

Example 3

Read the article from the Work Together again. The equation $|p - 9| = 3$ represents the maximum and minimum percent of people in the election poll who are undecided. Solve the equation.

$$|p - 9| = 3 \quad \longleftarrow \text{The value of the expression } p - 9 \text{ is 3 or } -3.$$
$$p - 9 = 3 \quad \text{or} \quad p - 9 = -3 \quad \longleftarrow \text{Write two equations.}$$
$$p - 9 + 9 = 3 + 9 \qquad p - 9 + 9 = -3 + 9$$
$$p = 12 \qquad\qquad p = 6$$

Anywhere from 6% to 12% of the voters polled are undecided.

Check both solutions.

$$|p - 9| = 3$$
$$|12 - 9| \stackrel{?}{=} 3 \quad \text{or} \quad |6 - 9| \stackrel{?}{=} 3 \quad \longleftarrow \text{Substitute 12 and 6 for } p.$$
$$|3| = 3 \checkmark \qquad\qquad |-3| = 3 \checkmark$$

10. Try This Solve and check. If there is no solution, explain why.
    a. $|c - 2| = 6$ **b.** $-5.5 = |t + 2|$ **c.** $|x + 8| = 5$
    d. $|7d| = 14$ **e.** $12.9 = |3b|$ **f.** $-6 = |x - 1|$

Modeling by Writing Equations

To maintain quality, a manufacturer sets limits for how much an item can vary from its specifications. You can use an absolute value equation to model a quality-control situation.

Example 4   Relating to the Real World

Manufacturing The ideal diameter of a cylindrical machine part is 12.000 mm. At the factory that makes the parts, the quality control inspector is told that the actual diameter can vary from the ideal by at most 0.017 mm. Find the maximum and minimum diameters of the part.

Define d = actual diameter in mm of the cylindrical part

Relate greatest difference between actual and ideal is 0.017 mm

Write $|d - 12.000| = 0.017$

PROBLEM SOLVING

Look Back Show how you could find the maximum and minimum diameters by sketching the situation.

$|d - 12.000| = 0.017$ ◄── The value of the expression $d - 12.000$ is 0.017 or -0.017.

$d - 12.000 = 0.017$ or $d - 12.000 = -0.017$ ◄── Write two equations.
      $d = 12.017$ or $d = 11.983$

The maximum diameter is 12.017 mm and the minimum is 11.983 mm. ■

11. a. *Critical Thinking* To solve the problem in Example 4, Mei wrote the equation $|d - 0.017| = 12.000$ and got the solution $d = 12.017$ or $d = -11.983$. Why is this solution not reasonable?
    b. How would you explain why her original equation was incorrect?

Exercises   ON YOUR OWN

Evaluate each expression.

1. $|x + 4|$ for $x = -1$ **2.** $|x - 7|$ for $x = -4$ **3.** $|8 - 2x|$ for $x = 3$ **4.** $|x| + 4$ for $x = 1$

5. $2|x|$ for $x = -3$ **6.** $|-3x|$ for $x = 2$ **7.** $6 - |x|$ for $x = -10$ **8.** $-|x|$ for $x = 7$

9. *Open-ended* Use each of the symbols $|\ \ |$, x, 5, 3, -12, $+$, and $=$ to write an absolute value equation. Then solve your equation.

10. a. *Graphing Calculator* Graph $y = 3|x| - 2$ and $y = 8$.
    b. Use the CALC feature of the calculator to identify the x-coordinates of the points where the graphs intersect.
    c. What absolute value equation have you solved?

Solve and check each equation. If there is no solution, explain.

11. $|n| - 8 = -2$ **12.** $\dfrac{|v|}{-3} = -4.2$ **13.** $\left|a + \frac{1}{2}\right| = 3\frac{1}{2}$ **14.** $3 = |u| + 9$

15. $|r - 8| = 5$ **16.** $|t| + 7 = 4.5$ **17.** $9 = |c + 7|$ **18.** $|n - 4| = 0$

19. $|m + 2| - 4 = 3$ **20.** $21 = |2d| + 3$ **21.** $|5p| = 3.6$ **22.** $3|v - 5| = 12$

Write an absolute value equation for each solution graphed below.

23.

24.

25.

26. Polling One poll reported that 53% of county residents favored building a recreation center. The polling service stated that this poll was accurate to within 4.5%. Use an absolute value equation to find the minimum and maximum percents of county residents who are in favor of building a recreation center.

27. Writing Describe how solving $3|c| - 4 = 9$ is similar to solving $3c - 4 = 9$ and how it is different.

28. Critical Thinking For what values of a and b will the equation $|x - a| = b$ have exactly one solution?

PROBLEM SOLVING HINT

Use the strategy *Guess and Test* in Exercise 28.

Write *true* or *false* for each statement. Justify your response.

29. If $|q + 4| = -1$, there is no solution.

30. If $|h| + 9 = 4$, then $h = 5$ or $h = -5$.

31. If $|3 + z| = 3$, then $z = -3$ or $z = 0$.

32. If $|6 - s| = 0$, then $s = 0$.

Mental Math Solve each equation. If there is no solution, explain.

33. $|b| = 12$ **34.** $|x| = 8$ **35.** $|m + 48| = 0$ **36.** $-2 = |b|$

37. $|n| - 3 = 7$ **38.** $|z| + 5 = 1$ **39.** $|2m| = 18$ **40.** $|b| - 10 = -1$

41. Meteorology A meteorologist reported that the previous day's temperatures varied 14°F from the normal temperature of 25°F. What were the maximum and minimum temperatures on the previous day?

42. Manufacturing A box of crackers should weigh 454 g. The quality control inspector weighs every twentieth box. The inspector sends back any box that is not within 5 g of the ideal weight.
  a. Write an absolute value equation for this situation.
  b. What are the minimum and maximum weights allowed?

43. a. Banking To check that there are 40 nickels in a roll, a bank weighs the roll and allows for an error of 0.015 oz in the total weight. What are the maximum and minimum acceptable weights if the wrapper weighs 0.05 oz?
  b. Critical Thinking If the roll weighs exactly 7.25 oz, can you be certain that all the coins are acceptable? Explain.

44. Standardized Test Prep Compare the quantities in Column A and Column B. Which statement is true for all numbers t?

Column A	Column B
$|t - 4|$	$|4 - t|$

- **A.** The quantity in Column A is greater.
- **B.** The quantity in Column B is greater.
- **C.** The two quantities are equal.
- **D.** The relationship cannot be determined from the information given.

Exercises   M I X E D   R E V I E W

Solve and check each equation.

45. $-3c + 7 = 25$

46. $\frac{1}{2}y = y - 6$

47. $9d + 3.5 = 2d$

48. $4x - 5 = \frac{2}{3}(6x + 3)$

49. $9.2t = 6.3t - 7.25$

50. $5.6m + 3.8 = 0.3$

51. Elio earns $2 per hour more than Ted. They each worked for 5 h. Together they earned a total of $65. What is each person's pay rate?

Getting Ready for Lesson 4-4

52. Geometry Explain how you can use the formula $C = \pi d$ to find the diameter of a tree without cutting down the tree.

53. Geometry The formula for the area of a rectangle is $A = lw$. A rectangular room is 28 ft long and its area is 672 ft^2. What is its width?

Algebra at Work

Cartographer

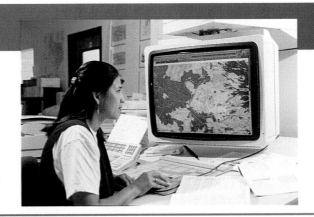

A cartographer, or map maker, makes exact measurements of the area being mapped. The cartographer uses these dimensions to create the scale of the map, showing the ratio of map distance to actual distance. Knowing the scale of a map means that you can use a proportion to calculate any distance on the map.

Mini Project: Find two maps of the same area that use different scales. Choose several points that are on both maps. Calculate the actual distance between each pair of points on both maps. Are the distances the same? What could account for any differences you find? Write a paragraph detailing your conclusions. Include the maps and your calculations.

What You'll Learn

- Using formulas to solve real-world problems
- Solving a literal equation for one of its variables

...And Why

To transform formulas for real-world situations, such as sports, wage, and temperature problems

4-4 **Transforming Formulas**

THINK AND DISCUSS

A formula shows the relationship between two or more variables. You can transform a formula to describe one quantity in terms of the others.

Example 1 **Relating to the Real World**

Sports Suppose a track coach wants to calculate the average speed of each track team member for an event. Transform the formula $d = rt$ to find a formula for the average speed r in terms of distance and time.

$$d = rt$$
$$\frac{d}{t} = \frac{rt}{t} \quad \longleftarrow \text{Divide each side by } t, t \neq 0.$$
$$\frac{d}{t} = r \quad \longleftarrow \text{Simplify.}$$

The formula for average speed is $r = \frac{d}{t}$.

PROBLEM SOLVING

Look Back **What property of equality was used to transform $d = rt$ into $r = \frac{d}{t}$?**

1. In 1994, Sevetheda Fynes took first place at the New England Track and Field Championships. Shown at the right, she ran 200 m in 23.10 s. Find her average speed.

Example 2 **Relating to the Real World**

Science The formula $C = \frac{5}{9}(F - 32)$ gives the Celsius temperature C in terms of the Fahrenheit temperature F. Transform the formula to find Fahrenheit temperature in terms of Celsius temperature.

$$C = \frac{5}{9}(F - 32)$$
$$\frac{9}{5} \cdot C = \frac{9}{5} \cdot \frac{5}{9}(F - 32) \quad \longleftarrow \text{Multiply each side by } \frac{9}{5}.$$
$$\frac{9}{5}C = F - 32 \quad \longleftarrow \text{Simplify.}$$
$$\frac{9}{5}C + 32 = F - 32 + 32 \quad \longleftarrow \text{Add 32 to each side.}$$
$$\frac{9}{5}C + 32 = F \quad \longleftarrow \text{Simplify.}$$

PROBLEM SOLVING

Look Back **Show how you can solve $C = \frac{5}{9}(F - 32)$ for F if you start by applying the distributive property to the right side of the formula.**

The formula for Fahrenheit temperature is $F = \frac{9}{5}C + 32$.

2. The highest temperature ever recorded in the state of Oklahoma occurred in Tishomingo on July 26, 1943, when the temperature reached 49°C. Find the equivalent Fahrenheit temperature.

J. E. MATZELIGER
LASTING MACHINE
No. 274,207.   PATENTED MAR. 20, 1883

Example 3   Relating to the Real World

History In 1883, Jan Matzeliger invented the shoe-lasting machine to attach the upper part of a shoe to its sole. Before that, each shoe was assembled and sewn by hand. Wages were calculated using this formula.

hourly wage in $\$ \longrightarrow$ $w = (0.34)(\frac{p}{t})$ $\longleftarrow$ price in $\$$ of a pair of shoes
$\longleftarrow$ time in minutes to assemble

Transform the formula to find the price of a pair of shoes in terms of the worker's hourly wage and the time needed to assemble the shoe.

$$w = (0.34)(\tfrac{p}{t})$$
$$w \cdot t = (0.34)(\tfrac{p}{t}) \cdot t \quad \longleftarrow \text{Multiply each side by } t.$$
$$wt = 0.34p \quad \longleftarrow \text{Simplify.}$$
$$\frac{wt}{0.34} = \frac{0.34p}{0.34} \quad \longleftarrow \text{Divide each side by } 0.34.$$
$$\frac{wt}{0.34} = p \quad \longleftarrow \text{Simplify.}$$

You can use the formula $p = \frac{wt}{0.34}$ to find the price of a pair of shoes. ■

3. **Try This** Transform the formula $w = (0.34)\frac{p}{t}$ to find a formula for time in terms of hourly wage and price.

4. In 1891 a worker who used the shoe-lasting machine could assemble one pair of shoes in two minutes and earned $.16/h. What was the price of a pair of shoes in 1891?

A **literal equation** is an equation involving two or more variables. Formulas are special types of literal equations. You solve for one variable in terms of the others when you transform a literal equation.

Example 4

Solve $ax + b = c$ for x in terms of a, b, and c.

$$ax + b = c$$
$$ax + b - b = c - b \quad \longleftarrow \text{Subtract } b \text{ from each side.}$$
$$ax = c - b \quad \longleftarrow \text{Simplify.}$$
$$\frac{ax}{a} = \frac{c - b}{a} \quad \longleftarrow \text{Divide each side by } a, a \neq 0.$$
$$x = \frac{c - b}{a} \quad \longleftarrow \text{Simplify.}$$

5. **Critical Thinking** Describe the approach you would use to solve each equation for m.
   a. $2n = 7(3 - m)$ b. $\frac{m - 5}{6} = -3x$ c. $\frac{2}{3}(2m + 4) = 9y$

6. Explain why you did or did not use the distributive property in each equation in Question 5.

Who? Jan Matzeliger (1852–1889) immigrated to the United States and worked in a shoe factory in Lynn, Massachusetts.

Solve each equation for the given variable.

1. $3r + 4 = s; r$

2. $c = \dfrac{d}{g}; g$

3. $\dfrac{m}{n} = \dfrac{p}{q}; p$

4. $ax + by = c; y$

5. $C = 2\pi r; r$

6. $5x - 2y = -6; y$

7. $3m = 2(4 + t); t$

8. $y = 3(t - s); s$

9. Geometry Suppose a and b are the coordinates of the endpoints of a line segment. To find the midpoint of the segment, you can use the formula $m = \dfrac{a + b}{2}$.

   a. Find the midpoint of a segment with endpoints 8.2 and 3.5.
   b. Transform the formula to find b in terms of a and m.
   c. Find the missing endpoint of a segment starting at −1.7 that has midpoint 2.1. Use the transformed formula from part (b).

Solve each equation for the given variable.

10. $x + y = 20; y$

11. $4m - n = 6; n$

12. $2(t + r) = 5; t$

13. $z - a = y; z$

14. $\pi = \dfrac{C}{d}; d$

15. $\dfrac{a}{2} = \dfrac{b}{7}; b$

16. $\dfrac{a + b}{c} = \dfrac{d}{4}; a$

17. $A = \dfrac{1}{2}bh; b$

18. $dx = c; x$

19. $V = lwh; h$

20. $V = \dfrac{1}{3}\pi r^2 h; h$

21. $|ap - b| = r; p$

22. a. Travel Manuel plans to drive to an amusement park. He will travel 121 mi on the highway at an average speed of 55 mi/h. Transform the formula $d = rt$ to find a formula for time.
   b. How much time does Manuel need for this part of his trip?

23. a. Recreation The aspect ratio of a hang glider measures its ability to glide and soar. The formula $R = \dfrac{s^2}{A}$ gives the aspect ratio R for a glider with wingspan s and wing area A. Solve this formula for A.
   b. Suppose you want to design a glider with a 9-ft wingspan and an aspect ratio of 3. Use the formula you found in part (a) to find the wing area.

24. Writing How is solving a literal equation similar to solving an equation with just one variable? How is it different?

25. Open-ended Write an equation using more than one variable. Solve the equation for each variable. Show all your steps.

26. a. Banking The formula $I = prt$ gives the amount of simple interest I earned by principal p at an annual interest rate r over t years. Solve this formula for p.
   b. Find p if $r = 0.035$, $t = 4$, and $I = \$420$. Write a sentence to explain the meaning of your answer.

27. a. Solve $2y + x = 4$ for y.
   b. Graphing Calculator Graph the equation you found in part (a).
   c. Use your graph and the TABLE feature of the calculator to find y when $x = 3$, $x = 4$, and $x = 5$.

Find Out by Solving

The volume of air an adult's lungs can hold decreases with age. The formula $V = 0.104h - 0.018a - 2.69$ estimates air volume V (in liters) of a person's lungs for someone of height h inches and age a years.

- Estimate your own lung volume. Then find 90% of your lung volume.

- Solve the formula for age a. Estimate how old you will be when your air volume is 90% of its current value. (Use your current height.)

- Substitute your current height for h in the original formula. Then graph the function to show how air volume changes as age increases.

Exercises M I X E D R E V I E W

28. 2.8 is what percent of 3.5? **29.** 70 is $12\frac{1}{2}\%$ of what number? **30.** What is 17% of 123?

31. a. Earnings Suppose you earn \$5.75/h and you work 12 h during one week. What are your earnings for the week?

  b. Write an equation that a worker paid hourly can use to find his or her earnings. Explain what each variable represents.

Getting Ready for Lesson 4-5

Complete each statement with $<$, $=$, or $>$.

32. $-3 \ \blacksquare \ -5$ **33.** $4.8 \ \blacksquare \ 4.29$ **34.** $-1 - 2 \ \blacksquare \ 6 - 9$ **35.** $-\frac{3}{4} \ \blacksquare \ -\frac{4}{5}$ **36.** $\frac{1}{2} + \frac{1}{2} \ \blacksquare \ \frac{1}{3} + \frac{1}{3}$

Exercises C H E C K P O I N T

Solve for the given variable.

1. $s = n - 90$; n **2.** $y = mx + b$; b **3.** $L = \frac{2b^2}{a}$; a **4.** $W = fd$; f

Solve and check each equation. If there is no solution, explain.

5. $\frac{6}{30} = \frac{m}{84}$ **6.** $-4(t + 1) = 4 - 4t$ **7.** $|x| = -7$ **8.** $8w = 6w$

9. $|n| + 2 = 10$ **10.** $y + 21 = 4y - 8$ **11.** $5(2w - 4) = 6w$ **12.** $|y - 4.5| = 3$

13. Maps The scale on a map is 3 cm : 10 km. On the map, the distance between two cities is 5.2 cm. What is the actual distance?

14. Geometry $P = 2l + 2w$ gives the perimeter P of a rectangle of length l and width w. Suppose a rectangle has perimeter 14.48 cm and length 4.16 cm. Which key sequence could you use to find the width?

  A. 2 ✕ 14.48 ➕ 2 ✕ 4.16 [ENTER]

  B. 14.48 ➖ 2 ✕ 4.16 ➗ 2 [ENTER]

  C. (14.48 ➖ 2 ✕ 4.16) ➗ 2 [ENTER]

  D. (2 ✕ 4.16 ➖ 14.48) ➗ 2 [ENTER]

What You'll Learn

- Using addition and subtraction to solve one-step inequalities
- Using inequalities to model real-world problems

...And Why

To solve inequalities that model real-world situations such as checking accounts

QUICK REVIEW

< is less than
≤ is less than or equal to
> is greater than
≥ is greater than or equal to
≠ is not equal to

4-5 Solving Inequalities Using Addition and Subtraction

WORK TOGETHER

Work with a partner.

1. Define a variable and write an inequality for each sign.

a.

b.

c.

2. Define a variable and write an inequality for each situation.
   a. Persons under 17 are not admitted.
   b. Visibility at the airport is less than two miles.
   c. You must be more than 36 in. tall to ride an amusement park ride.

3. *Open-ended* Describe three other situations that involve inequalities. Write an inequality for each situation.

THINK AND DISCUSS

Graphing and Writing Inequalities

Some inequalities contain a variable. Any value of the variable that makes the inequality true is called a **solution of the inequality.** The solutions of the inequality $x < 3$ are all the numbers less than 3.

4. Tell whether each number is a solution of $x < 3$.
   a. 1   b. −7.3   c. 9.004   d. 0   e. 3

The number lines show the solutions of $x < 3$ along with the graphs of three other inequalities comparing x and 3.

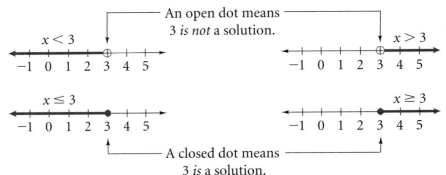

An open dot means 3 *is not* a solution.

$x < 3$

$x > 3$

$x \leq 3$

$x \geq 3$

A closed dot means 3 *is* a solution.

5. Explain how the inequality $x < 3$ is different from the equation $x = 3$.

6. *Critical Thinking* Describe how you can display the solutions of the inequality $x \neq 3$ on a number line.

PROBLEM SOLVING HINT

When the variable is on the left, the inequality symbol points in the same direction as the graph.

7. You can rewrite an inequality like $4 > n$ as $n < 4$. Rewrite each inequality so that the variable is on the left, then graph the solutions.
   a. $2 < x$ **b.** $-5 \geq b$ **c.** $0 \leq r$

Using Addition to Solve Inequalities

The solutions of an inequality like $x < 3$ are easy to recognize. To solve some other inequalities, you may need to find a simpler, equivalent inequality. **Equivalent inequalities** have the same set of solutions.

Consider the inequality $-4 < 1$. The number line shows what happens when you add 2 to each side of the inequality.

$-4 < 1$

$-4 + 2 < 1 + 2$

$-2 < 3$

$+2$ $+2$

$-5\ -4\ -3\ -2\ -1\ \ 0\ \ 1\ \ 2\ \ 3\ \ 4\ \ 5$

Notice that addition does not change the relationship between the numbers or the direction of the inequality symbol.

Addition Property of Inequality

For all real numbers a, b, and c, *if* $a > b$, then $a + c > b + c$.

Example: $5 > -1$, so $5 + 2 > -1 + 2$

For all real numbers a, b, and c, *if* $a < b$, then $a + c < b + c$.

Example: $-4 < 1$, so $-4 + 2 < 1 + 2$

8. What number would you add to both sides of each inequality to get a simpler, equivalent inequality?
   a. $x + 3 > -2$ **b.** $0 < -\frac{4}{3} + g$ **c.** $1.6 \geq z - 4.3$

You can use the Addition Property of Inequality to solve inequalities.

Example 1

Solve $x - 3 < 5$. Graph the solutions on a number line.

$$x - 3 < 5$$
$$x - 3 + 3 < 5 + 3 \quad \longleftarrow \text{Add 3 to each side.}$$
$$x < 8 \quad \longleftarrow \text{Combine like terms.}$$

The solutions are all numbers less than 8.

9. **a.** Substitute a number greater than 8 for x in the inequality $x - 3 < 5$. Is your result true?
   b. Substitute 8 for x in the inequality $x - 3 < 5$. Is your result true?
   c. Substitute a number less than 8 for x in the inequality $x - 3 < 5$. Is your result true?
   d. Parts (a), (b), and (c) can serve as a check for Example 1. **Generalize** the steps you can use to check the solutions of an inequality.

10. **a. Try This** Solve the inequality $f - 2 > -4$. Graph the solutions on a number line.
    b. Use the steps from Question 9, part (d), to check your work.

Using Subtraction to Solve Inequalities

Just as you can add the same number to each side of an inequality, you can subtract the same number from each side. The order, or direction, of the inequality is not changed.

Subtraction Property of Inequality

For all real numbers a, b, and c, if $a > b$, then $a - c > b - c$.
Example: $3 > -1$, so $3 - 2 > -1 - 2$
For all real numbers a, b, and c, if $a < b$, then $a - c < b - c$.
Example: $-5 < 4$, so $-5 - 2 < 4 - 2$

11. Solve and check the inequality $y + 2 < -6$. Graph the solutions on a number line.

12. What number would you subtract from both sides of each inequality to get a simpler, equivalent inequality?

    a. $w + 2 > -1$ **b.** $8 < \frac{5}{3} + r$ **c.** $5.7 \geq k - 3.1$

You can use inequalities to model real-world problems.

Example 2 **Relating to the Real World**

Banking The First National Bank offers free checking for accounts with a balance of at least $500. Suppose you have a balance of $516.46 and you write the check at the left. How much must you deposit to avoid being charged a service fee?

Define d = the amount you must deposit

Relate	current balance	minus	amount of check	plus	amount of deposit	is at least	$500
Write	516.46	−	31.50	+	d	≥	500

$$516.46 - 31.50 + d \geq 500$$
$$484.96 + d \geq 500 \quad \longleftarrow \text{Combine like terms.}$$
$$484.96 + d - 484.96 \geq 500 - 484.96 \quad \longleftarrow \text{Subtract 484.96 from each side.}$$
$$d \geq 15.04 \quad \longleftarrow \text{Simplify.}$$

You must deposit at least $15.04 in your account. ∎

13. **a.** Check the answer to Example 2 by choosing three values and checking the values in the original inequality.
   b. *Critical Thinking* Explain why checking the values in the inequality does not guarantee that your solution is correct.

14. Explain how the phrases "at least" and "at most" affect the inequality you write when you model a real-world problem.

Exercises ON YOUR OWN

Define a variable and write an inequality to model each situation.

1. A bus can seat 48 students or fewer.

2. There are over 20 species of crocodiles.

3. In many states, you must be at least 16 years old to obtain a driver's license.

4. At least 350 students attended the dance Friday night.

5. You may not use a light bulb of more than 60 watts in this light fixture.

6. The Navy's flying team, the Blue Angels, makes more than 75 appearances each year.

7. a. *Group Activity* Write an inequality for the tiles shown.
   b. Add four positive tiles to each side. Write an inequality for the tiles.
   c. Use the original set of tiles. Subtract seven positive tiles from each side. Write an inequality to represent the tiles.
   d. Show how to use tiles to **verify** the inequality $-5 + 3 > -7 + 3$.
   e. *Open-ended* Write an inequality you can solve with tiles. Solve the inequality. Show all the steps.

Write four numbers that are solutions of each inequality.

8. $v \geq -5$ **9.** $0.5 > c$ **10.** $2 + q < -7$ **11.** $f - 10 \leq 16$ **12.** $5 > 4 - z$

Tell what you must do to the first inequality in order to get the second.

13. $36 \leq -4 + y$; $40 \leq y$ **14.** $9 + b > 24$; $b > 15$ **15.** $m - \frac{1}{2} < \frac{3}{8}$; $m < \frac{7}{8}$

Write each inequality in words.

16. $n < 5$ **17.** $b > 0$ **18.** $x \leq 7$ **19.** $m \leq -1$ **20.** $g - 2 < 7$ **21.** $z \geq -4$

22. Writing How is solving an addition or subtraction inequality similar to solving an addition or subtraction equation? How is it different?

23. To earn an A in Ms. Orlando's math class, students must score a total of at least 135 points on the three tests. On the first two tests, Amy's scores were 47 and 48. What is the minimum score she must get on the third test in order to meet the requirement?

24. Banking Suppose you must maintain a balance of at least $750 in your checking account in order to have free checking. The balance in your account is $814.22 before you write a check for $25. How much cash can you withdraw from the account and still have free checking?

Solve each inequality. Graph the solutions on a number line.

25. $x - 1 > 10$ **26.** $w + 4 \leq 9$ **27.** $h + \frac{3}{4} \geq \frac{1}{2}$ **28.** $-5 > b - 1$

29. $0 \leq x + 1.7$ **30.** $n - 2\frac{1}{2} > \frac{1}{3}$ **31.** $3.5 < m - 2$ **32.** $\frac{3}{2} + k \geq -45$

33. $y - 0.3 < 2.8$ **34.** $2 < s - 8$ **35.** $9.4 \leq t - 3.5$ **36.** $h - \frac{1}{2} \geq -1$

37. $-6 > n - \frac{1}{5}$ **38.** $8 + b < 1$ **39.** $-7.7 \neq x - 2$ **40.** $a + 3 \geq 2.7$

41. $c + \frac{1}{2} \neq 3\frac{2}{7}$ **42.** $f - 2.3 \leq -1.21$ **43.** $\frac{3}{2} + g \leq \frac{1}{3}$ **44.** $0 > k - 2\frac{3}{5}$

45. $7.5 + y < 13$ **46.** $-1.4 + s + 2.1 > 11$ **47.** $-7\frac{3}{4} + m + \frac{1}{2} \leq -2\frac{1}{4}$ **48.** $\frac{2}{3} + t - \frac{5}{6} \neq 0$

49. a. Open-ended Use the inequality symbols $<$, $\leq$, $>$, and $\geq$ to write four addition or subtraction inequalities.
b. Solve each of the inequalities in part (a) and graph the solutions on separate number lines.

50. Critical Thinking Sam says that he can solve $z - 8.6 \leq 5.2$ by replacing z with 13, 14, and 15. When $z = 13$, the inequality is false. When $z = 14$ and $z = 15$, the inequality is true. So Sam says that the solution is $z \geq 14$ Is his reasoning correct? **Justify** your answer.

51. Standardized Test Prep If $x - y > 0$, which expression(s) must equal $|x - y|$? Choose A, B, C, D, or E.
I. $x - y$ **II.** $-(x - y)$ **III.** $|y - x|$
A. I and II only   **B.** II and III only   **C.** III only   **D.** I, II, and III   **E.** I and III only

Statistics Use the bar graph about education.

52. Let w represent the average yearly income for women. For what education levels is $w > 22{,}000$ a true statement?

53. Write a single inequality that describes the average income for a man who does not graduate from high school.

54. On average, how much more do men who have at least a bachelor's degree earn than those who have a high school diploma?

55. On average, how much more do women earn per year if they graduate from high school instead of dropping out before 9th grade?

56. At what education level does a woman's average income exceed the average income for a man with no high school education?

57. Research Find the average salaries for men and women in a job of your choice. What level of education is necessary to get that job? Write inequalities to compare those salaries with the average salaries for that education level.

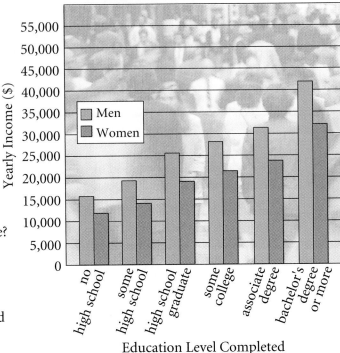

Average Yearly Income for Ages 25–34

Exercises   MIXED REVIEW

Find the sum or difference.

58. $\begin{bmatrix} 2 & 9 & 3 \\ 11 & 5 & 7 \end{bmatrix} + \begin{bmatrix} 18 & 0 & 15 \\ 6 & 12 & 4 \end{bmatrix}$

59. $\begin{bmatrix} -4 & 13 \\ 8 & 1 \end{bmatrix} - \begin{bmatrix} 4 & -5 \\ 10 & -14 \end{bmatrix}$

Solve.

60. $\frac{x}{3} = \frac{8}{24}$

61. $|m + 6| = 5$

62. $\frac{3}{4}k = 15$

63. $|p| - 2 = 10$

64. Law Enforcement In 1995, the 108-year-old California State Police became part of the California Highway Patrol. In what year was the California State Police founded?

Getting Ready for Lesson 4-6

65. State the multiplication property of equality and the division property of equality in your own words.

Solve and check each equation.

66. $8 = \frac{1}{2}t$

67. $14 = -21x$

68. $\frac{x}{6} = -1$

69. $5d = 32$

70. $0.5w = 4.5$

What You'll Learn

- Using multiplication and division to solve one-step inequalities
- Using inequalities to model real-world problems

...And Why

To solve inequalities that model real-world situations such as fundraising

What You'll Need

- calculator

4-6

Solving Inequalities Using Multiplication and Division

1 What is the solution of $|n + 3| - 5 = 7$?
(1) 9   (3) −15, 9
(2) −9   (4) −9, 9

2 The Wilson family has $800 for gas, motel, and food while on vacation. They estimate that they will spend $200 for gas and $250 for the motel. Write and solve an inequality to show what they can spend for food.

WORK TOGETHER

Work with a partner to explore what happens to an inequality when you multiply each side by the same number. Consider the inequality $4 > 1$.

1. Complete each statement by replacing each ▦ with $<, >$, or $=$.

2. What happens to the inequality when you multiply it by a positive number? by zero? by a negative number?

$4 \cdot 3$ ▦	$1 \cdot 3$
$4 \cdot 2$ ▦	$1 \cdot 2$
$4 \cdot 1$ ▦	$1 \cdot 1$
$4 \cdot 0$ ▦	$1 \cdot 0$
$4 \cdot -1$ ▦	$1 \cdot -1$
$4 \cdot -2$ ▦	$1 \cdot -2$
$4 \cdot -3$ ▦	$1 \cdot -3$

THINK AND DISCUSS

Solving Inequalities Using Multiplication

You can find an equivalent inequality by multiplying or dividing each side of an inequality by the same number. If the number is positive, the order remains the same. If the number is negative, you *reverse* the order.

Multiplication Property of Inequality

For all real numbers a and b, and for $c > 0$:

     If $a > b$, then $ac > bc$.   If $a < b$, then $ac < bc$.

Examples: $4 > -1$, so $4(5) > -1(5)$
              $-6 < 3$, so $-6(5) < 3(5)$

For all real numbers a and b, and for $c < 0$:

     If $a > b$, then $ac < bc$.   If $a < b$, then $ac > bc$.

Examples: $4 > -1$, so $4(-2) < -1(-2)$
              $-6 < 3$, so $-6(-2) > 3(-2)$

---

3. Consider the inequality $-2 \geq -5$.
   a. What inequality do you get when you multiply each side by 3?
   b. What inequality do you get when you multiply each side by -3?
   c. Explain why the Multiplication Property of Inequality applies to inequalities involving $\geq$ and $\leq$.

You can use the Multiplication Property of Inequality to write a simpler, equivalent inequality.

Example 1

Solve $\frac{x}{2} < -1$. Graph the solutions on a number line.

$$\frac{x}{2} < -1$$

$$2\left(\frac{x}{2}\right) < 2(-1) \quad \longleftarrow \text{ Multiply each side by 2.}$$

$$x < -2 \quad \longleftarrow \text{ Simplify each side.}$$

The solutions are all numbers less than –2.

$$\overset{\longleftarrow \;+\;+\;+\;\oplus\;+\;+\;+\;+\;+\;+\;+\;\longrightarrow}{\quad -5\;-4\;-3\;-2\;-1\;\;0\;\;1\;\;2\;\;3\;\;4\;\;5}$$

4. Describe the solutions for the inequality $\frac{x}{2} \leq -1$.

5. Jamal solved the inequality $-2 > \frac{y}{3}$ and got $-6 > y$. Erica solved the same inequality and got $y < -6$. Are they both correct? Explain.

Example 2

Solve $-\frac{2}{3}x \geq 2$. Graph the solutions on a number line.

$$-\frac{2}{3}x \geq 2$$

$$\left(-\frac{3}{2}\right)\left(-\frac{2}{3}x\right) \leq \left(-\frac{3}{2}\right)(2) \quad \longleftarrow \begin{array}{l}\text{Multiply each side by } -\frac{3}{2}.\text{ Reverse the}\\ \text{order of the inequality.}\end{array}$$

$$x \leq -3 \quad \longleftarrow \text{Simplify each side.}$$

The solutions are all numbers less than or equal to –3.

$$\overset{\longleftarrow \;+\;+\;+\;\bullet\;+\;+\;+\;+\;+\;+\;+\;\longrightarrow}{\quad -6\;-5\;-4\;-3\;-2\;-1\;\;0\;\;1\;\;2\;\;3\;\;4}$$

PROBLEM SOLVING

Look Back How would the solution be different if the inequality were $\frac{2}{3}x \geq -2$?

6. How can you use substitution to explain to a classmate why the solution to Example 2 cannot be $x \geq -3$?

7. a. **Try This** Solve the inequality $-t < \frac{1}{2}$.
   b. Graph the solution on a number line.
   c. Name four integers that are solutions of the inequality.

Solving Inequalities Using Division

You can use division to simplify and solve inequalities.

8. Consider the inequality $12 > 6$. Make a table to show what happens when you divide each side by the same number.

9. What happens when an inequality is divided by a positive number? by a negative number?

The pattern you see in your table can help you understand the Division Property of Inequality.

Division Property of Inequality

For all real numbers a and b, and for $c > 0$:

$$\text{If } a > b, \text{ then } \frac{a}{c} > \frac{b}{c}. \qquad \text{If } a < b, \text{ then } \frac{a}{c} < \frac{b}{c}.$$

Examples: $6 > -4$, so $\frac{6}{2} > \frac{-4}{2}$ $\qquad -2 < 8$, so $\frac{-2}{2} < \frac{8}{2}$

For all real numbers a and b, and for $c < 0$:

$$\text{If } a > b, \text{ then } \frac{a}{c} < \frac{b}{c}. \qquad \text{If } a < b, \text{ then } \frac{a}{c} > \frac{b}{c}.$$

Examples: $6 > -4$, so $\frac{6}{-2} < \frac{-4}{-2}$ $\qquad -2 < 8$, so $\frac{-2}{-2} > \frac{8}{-2}$

---

10. Critical Thinking Why can't $c = 0$ in the Multiplication and Division Properties of Inequality?

Example 3 Relating to the Real World

Community Service The student council is sponsoring a recycling drive to raise money to buy food for a food bank. A case of 12 jars of spaghetti sauce costs $13.50. What is the greatest number of cases of sauce the student council can buy if they collect $216?

Define $c =$ the number of cases of spaghetti sauce

Relate	13.5	times	the number of cases	is less than or equal to	216
Write	13.5	·	c	≤	216

$$13.5c \le 216$$

$$\frac{13.5c}{13.5} \le \frac{216}{13.5} \quad \leftarrow \text{Divide each side by 13.5.}$$

$$c \le 16 \quad \leftarrow \text{Use a calculator.}$$

The council can buy at most 16 cases of sauce for the food bank.

11. Explain why you use the symbol ≤ in the inequality in Example 3.

1. a. By what number can you divide each side of the inequality
$-t \le 7$ to get $t \ge -7$?

   b. By what number can you multiply each side of the inequality
$-m > -3$ to get $m < 3$?

Tell what you must do to the first inequality in order to get the second.

2. $5z > -25;\ z > -5$

3. $-b \ge 3.4;\ b \le -3.4$

4. $-\frac{7}{8}m > \frac{3}{4};\ m < -\frac{6}{7}$

Write four numbers that are solutions of each inequality.

5. $v \ge -5$

6. $0.5 > \frac{1}{2}c$

7. $2q < -7$

8. $-3f \le 16$

9. $\frac{r}{3} \ge -4$

10. $-3.5 < -m$

Replace each ▨ with the number that makes the inequalities equivalent.

11. $▨s > 14;\ s < -7$

12. $x + ▨ \ge 25;\ x \ge -12$

13. $8u \le ▨;\ u \le \frac{1}{2}$

14. $▨ > -17 + a;\ a < -9$

15. $36 < ▨r;\ r < -3.6$

16. $-k \le ▨;\ k \ge -7.5$

Solve each inequality. Check your solutions. Graph the solutions on a number line.

17. $-4x \le -16$ **18.** $6 < -9g$ **19.** $\frac{5}{6}x > -5$ **20.** $-1 \ge \frac{t}{3}$ **21.** $-1.5d < -8$ **22.** $-\frac{5}{3}u > 1$

23. Jobs Suppose you earn $5.85 per hour working part time at a dry cleaner. You need to earn at least $100. How many full hours must you work to earn the money?

24. Fund-raising The science club is sponsoring a car wash. At $2.50 per car, how many cars do they have to wash to earn at least $300?

25. Standardized Test Prep The number line shows the graph of all the solutions of an inequality. Which could *not* be that inequality?

A. $-2x > 4$ **B.** $-4 > 2x$ **C.** $-x < 2$
D. $8 < -4x$ **E.** $-2 > x$

Estimation **Estimate the solution of each inequality.**

26. $-2.099r < 4$

27. $3.87j > -24$

28. $20.95 \ge \frac{1}{2}p$

29. $\frac{20}{39}s \le -14$

30. Construction Swivel desks that each need 20 in. of space are being installed side by side in a new lecture hall. Each row of desks can be no longer than 25 ft. Find the maximum number of desks that will fit in each row.

31. a. Kia solved $-15q \le 135$ by adding 15 to each side of the inequality. What mistake did she make?

b. *Critical Thinking* Kia's solution was $q \le 150$. She checked her work by substituting 150 for q in the original problem. Why didn't her check let her know she'd made a mistake?

c. What substitution would have let her know she'd made a mistake? **Justify** your answer.

Solve each inequality. Graph the solutions on a number line.

32. $4d \le -28$

33. $\frac{u}{7} > 5$

34. $2 < -8s$

35. $\frac{3}{2}k \ge -45$

36. $0.3y < 2.7$

37. $9.4 \le -4t$

38. $-h \ge 4$

39. $24 < -3x$

40. $\frac{5}{2}x > 5$

41. $0 < -7b$

42. $\frac{5}{6} > -\frac{1}{3}p$

43. $-0.2m \ge 9.4$

44. *Writing* Write a paragraph explaining the Multiplication and Division Properties of Inequality to a classmate.

45. *Remodeling* The Sumaris' den floor measures 18 ft by 15 ft. They want to cover the floor with tiles that cover $\frac{9}{16}$ ft^2.

a. What is the least number of tiles they need to cover the floor?

b. Why might they need more tiles than the answer to part (a)?

46. *Open-ended* Write four different inequalities that you can solve using multiplication or division. Choose your inequalities so that the solution of each inequality is all numbers greater than 3.

Exercises   MIXED REVIEW

Solve for y in terms of x.

47. $2x + 3y = 6$

48. $5x - y + 8 = 4$

49. $-5y + 4x = 15$

50. $2x + 3y = -20$

51. a. *Biology* There are approximately 20 million bats in Bracken Cave, Texas. They eat about 250 tons of insects every night. How many tons do they eat in a week?

b. About how much does a single bat eat each night?

Getting Ready for Lesson 4-7

Solve and check each equation.

52. $3(c + 4) = 5$

53. $2x - 7 + 3x + 4 = -25$

54. $5p + 9 = 2p - 1$

55. $7x + 2(8 - x) = 4$

56. $\frac{1}{2}k - \frac{2}{3} + k = \frac{7}{6}$

57. $2t - 32 = \frac{15}{4}t + 1$

What You'll Learn

4-7 **S**olving Multi-Step Inequalities

- Solving multi-step inequalities and graphing the solutions on a number line
- Using multi-step inequalities to model and solve real-world problems

...And Why

To solve inequalities that model real-world situations such as designing

THINK AND DISCUSS

Solving with Variables on One Side

When you solve equations, sometimes you need to use more than one step. The same is true when you solve inequalities.

Example 1   Relating to the Real World

PROBLEM SOLVING HINT

Draw a diagram.

length   *width*

Design A school group needs a banner to carry in a parade. The narrowest street the parade is marching down measures 36 ft across, but some space is taken up by parked cars. The students have decided the length of the banner should be 18 ft. There are 45 ft of trim available to sew around the border of the banner. What is the greatest possible width for the banner?

Define w = width of the banner

Relate   Since the border goes around the edges of the banner, you can use the perimeter formula: $P = 2l + 2w$.

twice the length	plus	twice the width	can be no more than	the border

Write   2(18)   +   2w   ≤   45

$$2(18) + 2w \leq 45$$
$$36 + 2w \leq 45 \quad \longleftarrow \text{Simplify the left side.}$$
$$36 + 2w - 36 \leq 45 - 36 \quad \longleftarrow \text{Subtract 36 from each side.}$$
$$2w \leq 9$$
$$\frac{2w}{2} \leq \frac{9}{2} \quad \longleftarrow \text{Divide each side by 2.}$$
$$w \leq 4.5$$

The greatest possible width for the banner is 4.5 ft.

1. What could the model $2l + 2w > 45$ mean in the situation described in Example 1?

Sometimes solving an inequality involves the distributive property.

Example 2

Solve $2(w + 2) - 3w \geq -1$. Graph the solutions on a number line.

$$2(w + 2) - 3w \geq -1$$

$2w + 4 - 3w \geq -1$ ← Use the distributive property.

$-1w + 4 \geq -1$ ← Combine like terms.

$-1w + 4 - 4 \geq -1 - 4$ ← Subtract 4 from each side.

$-w \geq -5$ ← Simplify.

$\dfrac{-w}{-1} \leq \dfrac{-5}{-1}$ ← Divide each side by −1. Reverse the order of the inequality.

$w \leq 5$

PROBLEM SOLVING

Look Back What happens if you multiply each side of $-1w \geq -5$ by -1?

All numbers less than or equal to 5 are solutions.

2. You can check the solutions to Example 2 by substituting values into the inequality $2(w + 2) - 3w \geq -1$.
   a. Use the values 4, 5, and 6. Which values make the inequality true?
   b. Explain how part (a) serves as a check on Example 2.

Solving with Variables on Both Sides

Example 3

Solve $8z - 6 < 3z + 12$. Graph the solutions on a number line.

$$8z - 6 < 3z + 12$$

$8z - 6 - 3z < 3z + 12 - 3z$ ← Subtract 3z from each side.

$5z - 6 < 12$ ← Combine like terms.

$5z - 6 + 6 < 12 + 6$ ← Add 6 to each side.

$5z < 18$

$\dfrac{5z}{5} < \dfrac{18}{5}$ ← Divide each side by 5.

$z < 3.6$

GRAPHING CALCULATOR HINT

You can check your solutions to Example 3 by using the TEST feature.

All numbers less than 3.6 are solutions.

3. What happens when you replace z with 3.6 in $8z - 6 < 3z + 12$?

4. a. **Try This** Solve $3b + 12 > 21 - 2b$.
   b. Graph the solutions on a number line.

QUICK REVIEW

Equations such as
$1 + 3a = 3a + 1$ are *identities*.
Equations such as
$2 + a = a - 2$ have *no solution*.

Like equations, some inequalities are true for all values of the variable, and some inequalities are false for all values of the variable. When an inequality is false for all values of the variable, it has no solution.

5. **Critical Thinking** Without writing the steps of a solution, tell whether the inequality is *true* or *false* for all values of the variable. **Justify** your response.

a. $4s - 5 < 4s - 7$ b. $4s - 5 < 3 + 4s$

c. $4s + 6 \geq 6 + 4s$ d. $4s + 6 > 6 + 4s$

e. $4s - 9 < 4s$ f. $4s \leq 4s$

Exercises   ON YOUR OWN

Tell what you must do to the first inequality in order to get the second. Be sure to list *all* the steps.

1. $4j + 5 \geq 23; j \geq 4.5$

2. $2(q - 3) < 8; q < 7$

3. $8 - 4s > 16; -4s > 8$

4. $-8 > \frac{z}{-5} - 2; 30 < z$

5. $2y - 5 > 9 + y; y > 14$

6. $\frac{2}{3}g + 7 \geq 9; \frac{2}{3}g \geq 2$

7. $6 < 12 - s; s < 6$

8. $3 + 5t \geq 6(t - 1) - t; 3 \geq -6$

9. $6.2 < -r; -6.2 > r$

Match each inequality with its graph below.

10. $2x - 2 > 4$

11. $2 - 2x > 4$

12. $2x + 2 > 4$

13. $2x + 2 > 4x$

14. $-2x - 2 > 4$

15. $-2(x - 2) > 4$

A.

B.

C.

D.

E.

F.

16. **Recreation** The sophomore class is planning a picnic. The cost of a permit to use the park is $250. To pay for the permit, there is a fee of $.75 for each sophomore and $1.25 for each guest who is not a sophomore. Two hundred sophomores plan to attend. How many guests must attend in order to pay for the permit?

Solve each inequality. Graph the solutions on a number line.

17. $5 \leq 11 + 3h$

18. $3(y - 5) > 6$

19. $-4x - 2 < 8$

20. $r + 6 + 3r \geq 15 - 2r$

21. $5 - 2n \leq 3 - n$

22. $3(2v - 4) \leq 2(3v - 6)$

23. $2(m - 8) - 3m < -8$

24. $-(6b - 2) > 0$

25. $7a - (9a + 1) > 5$

26. **Writing** Suppose a friend is having difficulty solving the inequality $2.5(p - 4) > 3(p + 2)$. Explain how to solve the inequality, showing all necessary steps and identifying the properties you would use.

27. Freight Handling The freight elevator of a building can safely carry a load of at most 4000 lb. A worker needs to move supplies in 50-lb boxes from the loading dock to the fourth floor of the building. The worker weighs 160 lb. The cart she uses weighs 95 lb.
  a. What is the greatest number of boxes she can move in one trip?
  b. The worker must deliver 310 boxes to the fourth floor. How many trips must she make?

28. Critical Thinking Find a value of a such that the number line below shows all the solutions of $ax + 4 \leq -12$.

$$-5 \ -4 \ -3 \ -2 \ -1 \ \ 0 \ \ 1 \ \ 2 \ \ 3 \ \ 4 \ \ 5$$

Choose Use a calculator or paper and pencil. Solve and check each inequality.

29. $2 - 3k < 4 + 5k$

30. $\frac{1}{2}n - \frac{1}{8} \geq \frac{3}{4} + \frac{5}{6}n$

31. $-3(v - 3) \geq 5 - 3v$

32. $8 \leq 5 - m + 1$

33. $0.5(3 - 8t) > 20(1 - 0.2t)$

34. $\frac{2}{3}d - 4 > d + \frac{1}{8} - \frac{1}{3}d$

35. $38 - k \leq 5 - 2k$

36. $\frac{4}{3}r - 3 < r + \frac{2}{3} - \frac{1}{3}r$

37. $-2(0.5 - 4s) \geq -3(4 + 3.5s)$

38. Standardized Test Prep Which value of n is a solution of both $2(n + 5) \geq 4$ and $3(n - 1) < 3$?
  A. -7 **B.** -3 **C.** 2
  D. 4   **E.** none of these

39. Open-ended Write two different inequalities that you can solve by adding 5 and multiplying by -3. Show how to solve each inequality.

40. a. Generalize Solve $ax + b > c$ for x, where a is positive.
  b. Solve $ax + b > c$ for x, where a is negative.

41. Jobs JoLeen is a sales associate in a clothing store. Each week she earns $250 plus a commission equal to 3% of her sales. This week she would like to earn no less than $460. What dollar amount of clothes must she sell?

42. Geometry Artists often use the *golden rectangle* because it is considered to be pleasing to the eye. The length of a golden rectangle is about 1.62 times its width. Suppose you are making a picture frame in the shape of a golden rectangle. You have a 46-in. piece of wood. What are the length and width of the largest frame you can make? (Round your answers to the nearest tenth of an inch.)

Greece

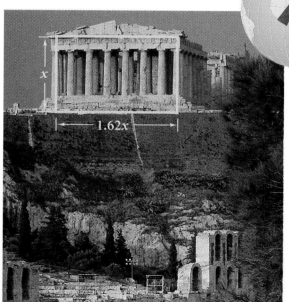

The Parthenon, an ancient Greek temple, was designed so that its dimensions form a golden rectangle.

193

43. **Business** Carlos plans to start a part-time word processing business out of his home. He is thinking of charging his customers $15 per hour. The table shows his expected monthly business expenses. Write an inequality to find the least number of hours he must work in a month to make a profit of at least $1200.

Monthly Expenses	
Expense	**Cost**
Equipment Rental	$490
Materials	$45
Business Phone	$65

Chapter Project ····· **Find Out by Researching**

Systolic blood pressure, the higher number in a blood pressure reading, is measured as your heart muscle contracts. The formula $P \leq \frac{1}{2}a + 110$ gives the normal systolic blood pressure P based on age a.

• Find your normal systolic blood pressure.

• At age 20, does 120 represent a maximum or a minimum systolic pressure? Explain.

• A blood pressure reading higher than the normal value indicates a possible need for a change in lifestyle or for special medication. Research some lifestyle changes that can help reduce high blood pressure.

Exercises   **MIXED REVIEW**

Write an inequality to model each situation.

44. An octopus can be up to 10 ft long.

45. A hummingbird migrates more than 1850 mi.

To which family of functions does each graph belong? Explain your reasoning.

46. $y = x^2 - 3x$

47. $y = |x| - 2$

48. $y = 5x + 1$

49. $y = 9 - x^2$

50. It takes 4.5 million jasmine petals to make 450 g of jasmine oil. How many petals are needed to make 1 kg of jasmine oil?

51. **Recycling** Each year, 9.5 million vehicles are recycled.
   a. About 75% of each vehicle's mass is reused. The average vehicle weighs 1.5 tons. About how many tons of materials can be reused from one vehicle?
   b. How many tons of materials can be reused from all the recycled vehicles each year?

FOR YOUR JOURNAL

Summarize what you have learned about the similarities and differences between equations and inequalities, using specific examples.

Getting Ready for Lesson 4-8

Graph each pair of inequalities on one number line.

52. $c < 8; c \geq 10$

53. $t \geq -2; t \leq -5$

54. $m \leq 7; m > 12$

55. $h > 1; h < 0$

What You'll Learn

4-8

Compound Inequalities

• Solving compound inequalities and graphing the solutions on a number line

• Solving absolute value inequalities and graphing the solutions on a number line

...And Why

To solve problems involving the chemistry of a swimming pool

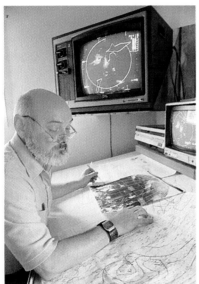

Meterologists use a variety of equipment to predict temperatures.

What? You can search the Internet for more than one topic at once. If you join two topics with *or,* you get all the references for either topic. If you join the topics with *and,* you get only those that relate to both topics.

Source: America Online

THINK AND DISCUSS

Solving Compound Inequalities Containing "And"

Today's temperatures will be above 32°F, but not as high as 40°F.

You can write this prediction as $32 < t$ and $t < 40$. Then you can combine the two inequalities into one, which you can read in two ways.

$$32 < t < 40$$

t is greater than 32, and less than 40.   *t is between 32 and 40.*

The graph of $32 < t < 40$ is an *interval* on a number line.

30 31 32 33 34 35 36 37 38 39 40 41 42

In the same way, you can write an inequality with $>$, $\le$, or $\ge$.

$$32 \le t \le 40$$

t is greater than or equal to 32, and less than or equal to 40.   *t is between 32 and 40 inclusive.*

1. Graph $32 \le t \le 40$ on a number line.

Two inequalities that are joined by the word *and* or the word *or* form a **compound inequality.** A solution of a compound inequality joined by *and* is any number that makes both inequalities true.

Example 1

Solve $-4 < r - 5 \le -1$. Graph the solutions on a number line.

Write the compound inequality as two inequalities joined by *and.*

$$\begin{array}{lcl} -4 < r - 5 & \text{and} & r - 5 \le -1 \\ -4 + 5 < r - 5 + 5 & | & r - 5 + 5 \le -1 + 5 \quad \leftarrow \text{Add 5.} \\ 1 < r & \text{and} & r \le 4 \quad \leftarrow \text{Simplify.} \end{array}$$

The solutions are all numbers greater than 1 *and* less than or equal to 4.

−5 −4 −3 −2 −1 0 1 2 3 4 5

2. In Example 1, why is there an open circle at 1 and a closed circle at 4?

3. To check the solution to Example 1, choose a value in the interval shown in the graph. Substitute your value in the original inequality to **verify** that the statement is true.

A second way to solve a compound inequality involving *and* is to work on all three parts of the inequality at the same time. You work to get the variable alone between the inequality symbols.

Example 2   **Relating to the Real World**

Chemistry The acidity of the water in a pool is considered normal if the average of three pH readings is between 7.2 and 7.8, inclusive. The first two readings for a pool are 7.4 and 7.9. What possible values for the third reading will make the pH normal?

Define p = value of third reading

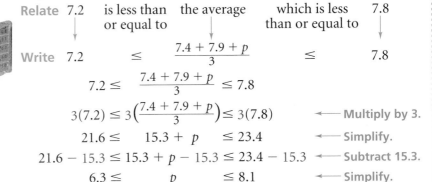

| Relate | 7.2 | is less than or equal to | the average | which is less than or equal to | 7.8 |

$$\text{Write} \quad 7.2 \quad \leq \quad \frac{7.4 + 7.9 + p}{3} \quad \leq \quad 7.8$$

$$7.2 \leq \frac{7.4 + 7.9 + p}{3} \leq 7.8$$

$$3(7.2) \leq 3\left(\frac{7.4 + 7.9 + p}{3}\right) \leq 3(7.8) \qquad \longleftarrow \text{Multiply by 3.}$$

$$21.6 \leq 15.3 + p \leq 23.4 \qquad \longleftarrow \text{Simplify.}$$

$$21.6 - 15.3 \leq 15.3 + p - 15.3 \leq 23.4 - 15.3 \qquad \longleftarrow \text{Subtract 15.3.}$$

$$6.3 \leq p \leq 8.1 \qquad \longleftarrow \text{Simplify.}$$

The value for the third reading must be between 6.3 and 8.1, inclusive.

4. Check the solution to Example 2 to **verify** that the solution gives an average pH in the normal range.

Solving Compound Inequalities Containing "Or"

A solution of a compound inequality containing *or* is any number that makes *either* inequality true.

Example 3

Solve $4v + 3 < -5$ or $-2v + 7 < 1$. Graph the solutions.

$$
\begin{array}{ccc}
4v + 3 < -5 & \text{or} & -2v + 7 < 1 \\
4v + 3 - 3 < -5 - 3 & & -2v + 7 - 7 < 1 - 7 \\
4v < -8 & & -2v < -6 \\
\tfrac{1}{4}(4v) < \tfrac{1}{4}(-8) & & -\tfrac{1}{2}(-2v) > -\tfrac{1}{2}(-6) \\
v < -2 & \text{or} & v > 3
\end{array}
$$

The solutions are all numbers that are less than –2 *or* are greater than 3.

5. Try This Graph each compound inequality on a separate line.

    a. $r < -1$ or $r > 3$ **b.** $r > -1$ and $r < 3$

6. Compare and contrast your graphs in Question 5.

Solving Absolute Value Inequalities

$|n| < 3$

$|n| > 3$

You can express the absolute value inequality $|n| < 3$ as the compound inequality $-3 < n < 3$. In a similar way, you can express the absolute value inequality $|n| > 3$ as the compound inequality $n > 3$ or $n < -3$. The graphs are at the left.

7. Complete each statement with *less than* or *greater than*.

    a. For $|n| < 3$, the graph includes all points whose distance from zero is ___?___ 3 units.

    b. For $|n| > 3$, the graph includes all points whose distance from zero is ___?___ 3 units.

8. Write an absolute value inequality to describe each graph.

    a.   **b.**

You can use absolute value inequalities to describe distances from numbers other than zero. The inequality $|n - 1| < 3$ represents all numbers whose distance from 1 is less than three units.

9. What does the inequality $|n - 1| > 3$ represent?

You can also solve an absolute value inequality by first writing it as a compound inequality.

Example 4

Solve $|v - 3| \geq 4$. Graph the solutions on a number line.

Write $|v - 3| \geq 4$ as two inequalities joined by *or*.

$$v - 3 \leq -4 \quad\quad \text{or} \quad\quad v - 3 \geq 4$$
$$v - 3 + 3 \leq -4 + 3 \mid v - 3 + 3 \geq 4 + 3 \quad \longleftarrow \text{Add 3.}$$
$$v \leq -1 \quad\quad \text{or} \quad\quad v \geq 7$$

The solutions are all numbers less than or equal to -1 *or* greater than or equal to 7.

PROBLEM SOLVING

Look Back How would the solution be different if the inequality were $|v - 3| > 4$?

QUICK REVIEW

$|x| = 6$ means
$x = 6$ or $x = -6$

10. How could you solve $|v - 3| \geq 4$ using only a graph?

11. a. Try This Solve $|v - 3| \leq 4$. Graph the solutions on a number line.
  b. Compare your solutions with the solutions in Example 4.

For each situation, define a variable and write a compound inequality.

1. The highest elevation in North America is 20,320 ft above sea level, at Mount McKinley, Alaska. The lowest elevation is 282 ft below sea level at Death Valley, California.

2. Wind speeds of a *tropical storm* are at least 40 mi/h but no more than 74 mi/h.

Write a compound inequality that each graph could represent.

3.
```
←--+--+--⊕--+--+--+--⊕--+--→
 −4 −3 −2 −1  0  1  2  3  4
```

4.
```
←--+--⊕--+--+--+--+--●--+--+--→
 −4 −3 −2 −1  0  1  2  3  4
```

5.
```
←--●--+--+--+--+--+--●--+--+--→
 −4 −3 −2 −1  0  1  2  3  4
```

6.
```
←--+--+--+--+--●--+--⊕--+--+--→
 −4 −3 −2 −1  0  1  2  3  4
```

7.
```
←--+--+--+--+--+--+--+--+--+--→
 −4 −3 −2 −1  0  1  2  3  4
```

8.
```
←--+--+--+--+--+--+--+--+--+--→
 −4 −3 −2 −1  0  1  2  3  4
```

Choose a variable and write an absolute value inequality that represents each set of numbers on a number line.

9. all numbers less than 3 units from 0

10. all numbers no less than 7.5 units from 0

11. all numbers more than 2 units from 6

12. all numbers at least 3 units from −1

Solve each inequality and graph the solutions.

13. $-3 < j + 2 < 7$

14. $12 > -3q$ and $-2q > -12$

15. $4 + k > 3$ or $6k < -30$

16. $x - 5 \leq 0$ or $x + 1 > -2$

17. $3 \geq 4r - 5 \geq -1$

18. $-1 \leq 3t - 2$ and $\frac{1}{2}t < -3$

19. $-2.8 \geq 2r + 0.2 > -3.8$

20. $6 - a < 1$ or $3a \leq 12$

21. $6.5 > w + 3 > 1.5$

22. $3a > -6$ and $7a < 14$

23. $0.25t \leq 3.5$ and $t \geq 4$

24. $25g < 400$ or $100 < 4g$

25. Open-ended Describe a real-life situation that you could represent with the inequality $-2 < x < 8$.

26. Sports A *welterweight* wrestler weighs at least 74 kg but no more than 82 kg. You can use the formula $k = 0.45p$ to find pounds p or kilograms k when one of the quantities is known. Write a compound inequality to describe the weight of a welterweight in pounds.

27. Manufacturing An electronics manufacturer needs a conveyer belt for its assembly plant. The completed conveyer belt may be 15 cm longer or shorter than shown. Find the possible lengths of the conveyer belt.

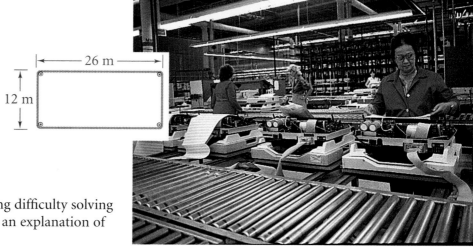

← 26 m →

12 m

28. Writing Suppose a friend is having difficulty solving absolute value inequalities. Write an explanation of the process, with examples.

Express each absolute value inequality as a compound inequality. Solve and graph the solutions on a number line.

29. $|f| > 2.5$ **30.** $|x + 3| < 5$ **31.** $|n + 8| \geq 5$ **32.** $|2y - 3| \geq 7$

33. $|w| > 2$ **34.** $|n| \leq 5$ **35.** $|6.5x| < 39$ **36.** $|3d| \geq 6$

37. $|y - 2| \geq 1$ **38.** $|2c - 3| < 9$ **39.** $|5t - 4| \geq 16$ **40.** $|p - 3| < 5$

41. $|3t + 1| > 8$ **42.** $|\frac{3}{4}x| - 3 < -5$ **43.** $4.5 + |3m - 2| > 2$ **44.** $0 \leq |3d - 1|$

Geometry **The sum of the lengths of any two sides of a triangle must be greater than the third side. The lengths of two sides of a triangle are given. Find the range of values for the possible lengths of the third side.**

Sample   3 cm, 7 cm

3 cm   7 cm

x

$x + 3 > 7$ and $x + 7 > 3$ and $3 + 7 > x$ ← Write inequalities.
    $x > 4$ and $x > -4$ and $10 > x$ ← Solve each inequality.
        $4 < x < 10$ ← Express as a compound inequality.

The length of the third side is greater than 4 cm and less than 10 cm.

45. 2.5 cm, 5 cm **46.** 1 in., 4 in. **47.** 28 mm, 21 mm **48.** 12 ft, 18 ft

Meteorology **The *high–low graph* shows the average monthly high and low temperatures for Detroit, Michigan, and Charlotte, North Carolina.**

49. Write a compound inequality to represent the average temperature in Charlotte in June.

50. Write a compound inequality to represent the average temperature in Detroit in January.

51. Use a compound inequality to describe the yearly temperature range for each city.

Monthly Average High and Low Temperatures

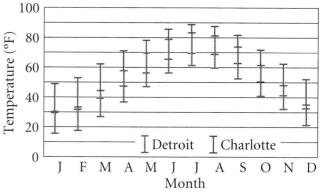

Temperature (°F)

J F M A M J J A S O N D
Month

I Detroit   I Charlotte

Source: *Statistical Abstract of the United States*

Find Out by Writing

When you exercise, your pulse rate rises. Recommended pulse rates vary with age and physical condition. For vigorous exercise, such as jogging, the inequality $0.7(220 - a) \leq R \leq 0.85(220 - a)$ gives a target range for pulse rate R (in beats per minute), based on age a (in years).

• In what range should your pulse rate be when you are jogging?

• What is the target range for a person 25 years old?

• Why should you see a doctor before starting an exercise program?

Exercises   M I X E D   R E V I E W

Solve and check. State if the equation is an *identity* or has *no solution*.

52. $3y + 1 = 2.5$　　　　**53.** $-6m - 1 = 2m$　　　　**54.** $4(w + 8) = 10$　　　　**55.** $-2 = 7c - 5c$

56. $8p - 4 = 4(2p - 1)$　　**57.** $3.8 = |4x| + 0.2$　　**58.** $-5k + 5 = 5(-1 - k)$　　**59.** $\left|t - \frac{1}{2}\right| = \frac{3}{4}$

60. Biology Plasma makes up 55% of blood by volume. A 155-lb man has about 1.3 gal of blood. How much plasma does his blood contain?

Getting Ready for Lesson 4-9

Which of $-3, -2, -1, 0, 1, 2, 3$ are solutions of each inequality?

61. $m + 2 \leq 3$　　　　**62.** $-4q > 0$　　　　**63.** $\frac{1}{2}z - 1 \leq 0$　　　　**64.** $3t + 5 < -4$

Exercises   C H E C K P O I N T

Solve each inequality. Graph the solutions.

1. $8 < c + 2$　　　　　**2.** $3x \leq -24$　　　　　**3.** $-9m \geq 36$　　　　　**4.** $7 - c \leq 12$

5. $5 < 6b + 3$　　　　**6.** $12n \leq 3n + 27$　　　**7.** $2 + 4r \geq 5(r - 1)$　　　**8.** $8w + 3w \leq -22$

9. $6 + h \geq 2$　　　　**10.** $0 \leq 2t - 10t \leq 4$　**11.** $\frac{x}{-3} > 9 \ or \ 3x > 12$　　**12.** $|g - 3| > 2$

Solve each absolute value inequality. Graph the solutions.

13. $|5d| \geq 15$　　　**14.** $|x + 3| < 7$　　　**15.** $|2x - 3| < 5$　　　**16.** $|4y - 2| \geq 18$　　**17.** $\frac{4}{5} \geq \left|\frac{1}{2}x - 2\right|$

18. Medicine Normal body temperature is within 0.6°C of 36.6°C. Write a compound inequality for the range of normal body temperature.

19. Open-ended Write a compound inequality to **predict** the temperature range for tomorrow.

20. Writing Explain the difference between the words *and* and *or* in a compound inequality.

Using a Venn Diagram

After Lesson 4-8

You can use a Venn diagram to illustrate relationships between sets and solve problems. First draw overlapping circles to represent the sets. Then draw a box around the circles to include any other information. Finally, fill in the diagram with information from the problem.

Example

An English teacher surveyed 48 ninth-grade students and found that 18 had read *Treasure Island*, 20 had read *Anne of Green Gables*, and 11 had read both books. How many students had not read either book?

After completing Steps 1 through 5, you can see that 21 students had not read either *Treasure Island* or *Anne of Green Gables*.

Step 1
number who read both books

Step 2
number who read only *Treasure Island*
$18 - 11 = 7$

Step 3
number who read only *Anne of Green Gables*
$20 - 11 = 9$

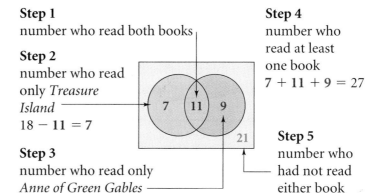

Step 4
number who read at least one book
$7 + 11 + 9 = 27$

Step 5
number who had not read either book
$48 - 27 = 21$

Use a Venn diagram to illustrate and solve each problem.

1. Between 1933 and 1995 there were 11 presidents of the United States and 14 vice presidents. If 9 of the vice presidents were never president, how many of the presidents were never vice president?

2. Recently there were 118,519 female physicians in the United States. Of these, 16,573 were pediatricians, 40,431 were under the age of 35, and 6761 of the pediatricians were under the age of 35.
   a. How many female pediatricians were age 35 or older?
   b. How many female physicians were 35 or older and not pediatricians?

3. In the 1994 Winter Olympics, 67 countries participated. The table shows how many countries won each possible medal.
   a. How many countries won gold, but not silver or bronze?
   b. How many countries won gold and silver, but not bronze?
   c. How many countries did not win any medals?

4. Writing   Write a problem that you could solve using a Venn diagram. Then give your solution to the problem.

PROBLEM SOLVING HINT

For each exercise, first decide how many circles you need to draw.

1994 Winter Olympics
14 won gold.
12 won gold and silver.
11 won gold and bronze.
17 won silver.
14 won bronze and silver.
18 won bronze.
10 won gold, silver, and bronze.

Source: *The Guinness Book of Records*

What You'll Learn

4-9 **I**nterpreting Solutions

- Solving inequalities given a specific replacement set
- Checking the reasonableness of solutions

...And Why

To model real-world situations, like car inspection problems

What You'll Need

- calculator

T H I N K   A N D   D I S C U S S

Solving Inequalities Given a Replacement Set

When you solve inequalities, the set of possible values for the variable, or **replacement set,** often is any real number, There are times, however, when the replacement set is limited to the set of integers or some other set. Your solution depends on the replacement set for the variable.

Example 1

Solve $-4 < 2k \le 5$. Then graph the solutions on a separate number line for each replacement set.

  a. the real numbers **b.** the integers **c.** $\{-5, -3, -2, 0, 3\}$

$$-4 < 2k \le 5$$
$$\tfrac{1}{2}(-4) < \tfrac{1}{2}(2k) \le \tfrac{1}{2}(5) \quad \longleftarrow \text{Multiply by } \tfrac{1}{2}.$$
$$-2 < k \le 2\tfrac{1}{2} \quad \longleftarrow \text{Simplify.}$$

a. All real numbers greater than -2 and less than or equal to $2\frac{1}{2}$ satisfy the inequality.

b. The integers that satisfy the inequality are $-1, 0, 1,$ and 2.

c. The value from $\{-5, -3, -2, 0, 3\}$ that satisfies the inequality is 0.

1. Try This Match each replacement set with its graph of $|y| < 4$.

  A. the real numbers

  B. the integers

  C. the positive integers

  D. the positive real numbers

2. Open-ended Write an inequality whose solutions are graphed on the number line below. Identify the replacement set for the variable.

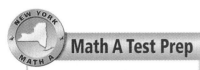

1 Choose the inequality whose solutions are shown on the number line.

$$-12\ -8\ -4\ \ 0\ \ 4\ \ 8\ \ 12$$

(1) $|w - 2| > 6$
(2) $|w - 2| \le -6$
(3) $|w - 2| \ge 6$
(4) $|w - 2| < 6$

2 When Jamie exercises, her heart rate goal is at least 160 beats per minute.
  a Write an inequality to show the number of beats Jamie should count in 10 seconds.
  b What is the replacement set for the variable in the inequality?
  c What is the minimum number of beats Jamie should count in 10 seconds?

Determining a Reasonable Answer

In many problems, you are given restrictions that indicate the replacement set for the variable. Other restrictions arise from common sense.

Example 2   **Relating to the Real World**

Car Service Felix Ramiro's Garage has just purchased special equipment for the state emission inspection. The equipment cost $1500. Each inspection costs the garage $2.60 for labor and supplies. The garage gets to keep $8.20 of each vehicle's inspection fee. How many inspections must the garage perform in order to make a profit?

Define x = number of inspections

Relate	income from inspections	is greater than	cost of equipment	plus	expense of inspections
Write	$8.2x$	$>$	1500	$+$	$2.6x$

$$8.2x > 1500 + 2.6x$$
$$8.2x - 2.6x > 1500 + 2.6x - 2.6x \quad \longleftarrow \text{Subtract } 2.6x \text{ from each side.}$$
$$5.6x > 1500$$
$$\frac{5.6x}{5.6} > \frac{1500}{5.6} \quad \longleftarrow \text{Divide each side by 5.6.}$$
$$x > 267.8571429$$

Since x represents the number of inspections, it makes sense to consider integer values only. So, the solutions are $x \ge 268$, where x is an integer. The garage must perform at least 268 inspections to make a profit.

$$266\ \ 267\ \ 268\ \ 269\ \ 270\ \ 271$$

3. Show how you would check Example 2. Be sure you check the words of the original problem, not simply the math of the inequality.

4. a. **Car Service** Felix's garage is open six days a week. It has enough mechanics to do 11 inspections a day. What is the minimum number of weeks it will take to make a profit on inspections? Explain.

   b. What is the maximum number of weeks it will take to make a profit on inspections? Explain.

A set of data that involves measurements, such as length, weight, or temperature, is usually *continuous*.

A set of data that involves a count, such as numbers of people or objects, is *discrete*.

It is important to consider replacement sets when you use an inequality to model a real-world situation. For instance, consider this situation:

The temperature t ranges from 25°F to 35°F, inclusive.

A set of temperatures is a continuous set of data. You graph $25 \leq t \leq 35$ as an interval, with the real numbers as the replacement set for t.

Now suppose you want to model this situation:

The number n of students in a homeroom is between 25 and 35, inclusive.

The numbers of students is a discrete set of data. You graph $25 \leq n \leq 35$ as a set of points, with the positive integers as the replacement set for n.

Exercises   ON YOUR OWN

Graph each inequality on a number line. Use the positive integers as a replacement set. If there are no solutions, write *no solutions*.

1. $p \leq 6$

2. $|c - 2| > 3$

3. $w \leq 0$

4. $-g > -8$

5. $-3 \leq a < 1$

6. $r < 3$ or $r \geq 5$

7. $-4 < k + 1 < 7$

8. $3(d + 2) < 6$

9. $-y < -4.2$

10. $|3 - r| > 2$

11. $2 > u$ or $u \geq 3$

12. $w \geq 0$

13. $-4 \leq q < 2.25$

14. $3(d - 1) \leq 4.5$

15. $4 < 2 - 2m \leq 8$

16. $|2a + 1| < 9$

Write an inequality that represents each situation. Graph the solutions on a number line.

17. If you are 12 to 64 years old, you pay full price for admission to the Science Museum.

18. A market researcher surveyed women who were at least 19 but less than 25 years old.

19. The circumference of a baseball is between 23 cm and 23.5 cm.

20. A box can hold from 15 to 20 books, inclusive.

21. Nursing In nursing school, students learn temperature ranges for bath water. Tepid water is approximately 80°F to 93°F, warm water is approximately 94°F to 98°F, and hot water is approximately 110°F to 115°F. Model these ranges on one number line. Label each interval.

22. Open-ended Create a problem for which the solution is any number between two positive numbers a and b.

23. a. Jobs A summer employee at a store can work at most 8 h/day. How many hours must Nadine work on Friday to meet her goal of earning at least $175 for the week?

b. Summarize the steps you would use to find the number of hours each employee must work on Friday in order to meet that goal.

Employee	Hourly Wage	Mon.	Tues.	Wed.	Thurs.
Radam	$5.25	7	7	8	8
Nadine	$5.30	8	6	7	7

24. Veterinary Science The table lists respiratory rates for certain birds.

a. Model the respiratory rate for a parrot on a number line.

b. Draw two other number lines and align the 0 marks on them with the 0 mark on the number line in part (a). Model the respiratory rates for canaries and cockatiels on the number lines.

At-Rest Respiratory Rates

Bird	Breaths/min
Canary	60–100
Cockatiel	100–125
Parrot	25–40

25. Writing Explain what a replacement set is and why you need to think about it when you are using an inequality to solve a problem.

Graph each inequality for the given replacement set.

26. $-8 < 2(c + 5) < 14$, for the set of negative integers **27.** $-3 \leq 9v + 6 \leq 24$, for $\{-4, -2, 0, 2, 4\}$

28. $12 \geq |6y - 3|$, for the set of positive real numbers **29.** $|2n + 6| < 12$, for the set of integers

Chapter Project ***Find Out by Interviewing***

How much exercise is enough? What kind of exercise is best for you?

• Interview a coach, a trainer, or a health professional to find out what type and amount of exercise they recommend for a teenager like you.

• Design your own exercise plan. Consider goals (muscle tone, heart workout) and amount and type of exercise.

Exercises   MIXED REVIEW

Find each statistic for the data 1, 3, 4, 4, 5, 5, 7, 9, 9, 9, 13.

30. mean   **31.** median   **32.** mode

Find the percent of change.

33. $24 to $36   **34.** 20 lb to 15 lb **35.** 300 to 750

36. Write an equation and solve.

a. Weather In August 1995, a storm in Stillwater, Oklahoma, dropped 5 in. of rain in 3 h. What was the hourly rate?

b. Suppose it rained all day at this rate. How many inches of rain would fall in a 24-h period?

PORTFOLIO

Select one or two items from your work for this chapter. Consider

• corrected work
• work based on manipulatives
• open-ended questions

Explain why you have included each selection you make.

NO SWEAT!

Questions on pages 162, 178, 194, 200, and 205 should help you to complete your project. Present all your information for the project in a notebook. Is your exercise plan realistic for your available time and resources? How close is it to what you already do? (If it is very different, you should begin only with an adult's guidance.) Be sure to include what you have learned about blood pressure and about personal exercise.

Reflect and Revise

Organize your notebook around your use of equations and inequalities (one section for each). Share your notebook with an adult. Check your work for accuracy and look for any items that are not clear. Make any changes necessary in your work.

Follow Up

Find out about cross-training techniques or the training programs used in an Olympic sport.

For More Information

Kettelkamp, Larry. *Modern Sport Science.* New York: William Morrow, 1986.

"Physical Fitness." *Marshall Cavendish Encyclopedia of Health* (Vol. 10: 568–574). North Bellmore, New York: Marshall Cavendish, 1991.

Schwarzenegger, Arnold. *Arnold's Fitness for Kids Ages 11–14.* New York: Doubleday, 1993.

Virtue, Doreen. "What's Your Fitness Personality? Find an Exercise Plan that Really Fits." *Vegetarian Times* (January 1995): 55.

Key Terms

compound inequalities (p. 195)
cross products (p. 159)
equivalent inequalities (p. 180)
identity (p. 166)
no solution (p. 165)
literal equation (p. 176)
proportion (p. 158)

ratio (p. 158)
replacement set (p. 202)
scale (p. 158)
similar figures (p. 159)
solution of the inequality
(p. 179)

How am I doing?

- State three ideas from this chapter that you think are important. Explain your choices.
- Describe several important rules that you must apply in order to solve inequalities.

Using Proportions   4-1

A **ratio** is a comparison of two numbers by division. A **proportion** is a statement that two ratios are equal. You can solve a proportion with a variable by using the **cross products.**

Solve each proportion.

1. $\frac{4}{12} = \frac{c}{6}$ 2. $\frac{t}{5} = \frac{23}{50}$ 3. $-\frac{9}{m} = \frac{3}{2}$ 4. $\frac{5}{4} = \frac{12.5}{z}$ 5. $\frac{x}{4} = -\frac{1}{10}$ 6. $\frac{8}{b} = \frac{16}{3}$

7. **Hobbies** A model airplane can be built to $\frac{1}{48}$ of actual size. Suppose a wing of the model airplane is $\frac{3}{4}$ ft long. How long is the wing of the full-size airplane?

Equations with Variables on Both Sides   4-2

You can use the properties of equality to solve an equation. An equation has no solution if no value of the variable makes the equation true. An equation is an **identity** if every value of the variable makes the equation true.

Write an equation for each model and solve.

8.

9.

Solve and check. If the equation is an identity or if it has no solution, write *identity* or *no solution*.

10. $5w = 6w + 11$ 11. $3(2t - 6) = 2(3t - 9)$ 12. $4n - 6n = 2n$ 13. $9c + 4 = 3c - 8$

Solving Absolute Value Equations 4-3

You can solve an **absolute value equation** by getting the absolute value by itself on one side of the equation. When the expression within the absolute value symbol contains more than one term, you must write and solve two equations.

Solve and check each equation. If there is no solution, explain.

14. $|y| = 5$ **15.** $|p + 3| = 9.5$ **16.** $|6 - b| = -1$ **17.** $|k - 8| = 0$

18. *Open-ended* Write an absolute value equation that has no solution and another that has one solution. Solve the one that has one solution.

Transforming Formulas 4-4

A formula shows the relationship between two or more variables. When you express one variable in terms of the others, you are solving the equation for that variable.

Solve each equation for the given variable.

19. $m = \dfrac{a + b + c}{3}$; c **20.** $C = \pi d$; d **21.** $y = mx + b$; x **22.** $A = \frac{1}{2}bh$; h

23. *Science* Ohm's Law states that in an electrical circuit $E = IR$, where E represents the potential (in volts), I represents the current (in amperes), and R represents the resistance (in ohms).
   a. Solve this formula for I.
   b. Find I if $E = 6$ volts and $R = 0.15$ ohms of resistance.

Solving Inequalities 4-5, 4-6, 4-7

You can add or subtract a number from both sides of an inequality to find a simpler **equivalent inequality.** You can multiply or divide both sides of an inequality by the same number to find a simpler equivalent inequality. If you multiply or divide by a positive number, the order of the inequality stays the same. If the number is negative, the order is *reversed*.

Solve each inequality. Graph the solutions on a number line.

24. $h + 3 > 2$ **25.** $4k - 1 \le -3$ **26.** $\frac{5}{8}b < 25$ **27.** $-\frac{2}{7}y - 6 \ge 42$

28. $6(c - 1) \le -18$ **29.** $3m > 5m + 12$ **30.** $t - 4 < -9$ **31.** $5x - 2 \ge 4x + 7$

32. *Critical Thinking* Without writing the steps of the solution, describe the solutions of the inequality $-2x + \frac{3}{4} \le -2x + \frac{1}{4}$. **Justify** your answer.

Compound inequalities are two inequalities that are joined by the word *and* or the word *or*. A solution of a compound inequality joined by *and* makes *both* inequalities true. A solution of a compound inequality joined by *or* makes *either* inequality true.

Solve each inequality and graph the solutions.

33. $|n + 2| \geq 4$ **34.** $-3 \leq z - 1 < 6$ **35.** $7t \geq 49$ or $2t \leq -4$ **36.** $0 < -8b \leq 12$

37. $-2 \leq 3a - 8 < 4$ **38.** $-6 < d + \frac{1}{2} < 4\frac{1}{2}$ **39.** $-1 \leq a - 3 < 2$ **40.** $|3x + 5| > -2$

41. Standardized Test Prep Which number is *not* a solution of the compound inequality $5w - 2 > 8$ or $-3w + 1 \geq 10$?

     A. -3 **B.** 5   **C.** 2   **D.** 3   **E.** -5

When you solve an inequality, the set of possible values for the variable is called the **replacement set**.

Graph each inequality on a number line. Use all integers as the replacement set. If there are no solutions, write *no solution*.

42. $|4h - 1| \geq 7$ **43.** $3t \leq 10$ **44.** $2 < y + 1 < 3$ **45.** $-3 \leq m < 0$ **46.** $-2q > -q$

Write and graph an inequality for each statement.

47. Meteorology Cumulus clouds form $\frac{1}{4}$ mi to 4 mi above the Earth's surface.

48. Languages There are more than 1000 different languages spoken on the continent of Africa.

49. Writing Suppose you use an inequality to model a real-world situation. Explain why you may need to specify a replacement set.

Getting Ready for ....▶ CHAPTER 5

Graph each set of points on a coordinate plane.

50. $(1, 2), (0, 1), (-2, -1), (4, 5)$ **51.** $(4, -2), (2, 1), (-6, 3), (2, -1)$ **52.** $(3, 1), (3, 4), (3, -2), (3, 3)$

Write a function rule for each table.

53.

x	$f(x)$
0	-5
1	-4
2	-3
3	-2

54.

x	$f(x)$
-2	7
5	14
12	21
19	28

55.

x	$f(x)$
4	2
10	5
16	8
22	11

56.

x	$f(x)$
-2	-6
1	3
4	12
7	21

Solve. If the equation is an identity or if it has no solution, write *identity* or *no solution*.

1. $\frac{3}{4} = \frac{c}{20}$ 2. $\frac{8}{15} = \frac{4}{w}$

3. $\frac{w}{6} = \frac{6}{15}$ 4. $\frac{5}{t} = \frac{21}{100}$

5. $9j + 3 = 3(3j + 1)$ 6. $8n = 5 + 3n$

7. $4v - 9 = 6v + 7$ 8. $|8b - 3| = -21$

9. $|t - 6| = 4$ 10. $|m + 1| = 11$

11. Find the value of each variable in the matrices.
$$\begin{bmatrix} w + 5 & 3x - 1 \\ 2y & z + 6 \end{bmatrix} = \begin{bmatrix} 2w - 6 & 8x \\ 2 - 4y & 12 \end{bmatrix}$$

12. The ratio of the length of a side of one square to that of another square is 3 : 4. A side of the smaller square is 9 cm. Find the length of a side of the larger square.

13. **Writing** Are $|x + 4| = 7$ and $|x| + 4 = 7$ equivalent equations? Explain.

14. Suppose you score 9.1, 9.6, 9.7, 9.3, and 9.4 in a diving competition. The diver who is in first place has a final score of 56.4. What is the lowest score you can get on your last dive to win the competition?

15. A taxicab company charges a flat fee of $1.85 plus an additional $.40 per quarter-mile.
    a. Write a formula to find the total cost for each fare.
    b. Use this formula to find the total cost for traveling 8 mi.

Solve each equation for the given variable.

16. $t = \frac{v + m}{3}$; m 17. $8b - 5c = 2$; c

18. $A = \frac{1}{2}bh$; b 19. $V = 2\pi r^2 h$; h

20. **Standardized Test Prep** If $6m + 3t = 8w$, then $m = \blacksquare$.

    A. $\frac{4}{3}w - 3t$ B. $\frac{8w - 3t}{6}$ C. $(8 - 3t) \div 6$

    D. $\frac{8w + 3t}{6}$ E. $\frac{1}{2}t + 8w$

21. **Open-ended** Write two different inequalities that you can solve by first subtracting 7, then multiplying by –6. Solve each inequality.

Define a variable and write an inequality to model each situation.

22. A student can take at most 7 classes.

23. The school needs at least 5 runners.

24. Elephants can drink up to 40 gal at a time.

25. The paper route has more than 32 homes.

Write a compound inequality that each graph could represent.

26.

27.

Solve each inequality. Graph the solutions on a number line.

28. $8 + u > 4$ 29. $-5 + 4t \le 3$

30. $5w \ge -6w + 11$ 31. $-\frac{7}{2}m < 13$

32. $|x - 5| \ge 10$ 33. $|2h + 1| < 5$

34. $9 \le 6 - b < 12$ 35. $-10 < 4q < 12$

36. $4 + 3n \ge 1$ or $-5n > 25$

37. $10k < 75$ and $4 - k \ge 0$

38. **Jobs** A clerk at the Radio Barn makes $300 a week plus 4% commission. How much does she have to sell to make at least $500 this week?

39. Solve $-13 \le 5g + 7 < 20$ for each replacement set.
    a. positive integers   b. all integers

40. Solve the equation modeled by tiles.

Part I

1 Which equation does not have the same solution as $\frac{7}{y} = \frac{31}{36}$?

(1) $\frac{7}{31} = \frac{y}{36}$

(3) $\frac{36}{31} = \frac{7}{y}$

(2) $\frac{y}{36} = \frac{7}{31}$

(4) $\frac{y}{7} = \frac{36}{31}$

2 A blueprint scale is 0.5 in. : 4 ft. On the plan, a living room measures 2.25 in. by 2.5 in. What are the actual dimensions of the living room?

(1) 18 ft by 20 ft   (3) 9 ft by 10 ft

(2) 11.25 ft by 12.5 ft   (4) 16 ft by 20 ft

3 Which equation is an example of an identity?

(1) $8x + 5 = -2(4x - 1) + 3$

(2) $8x - 5 = 2(4x - 1) - 3$

(3) $8x + 5 = 2(4x - 3) - 1$

(4) $8x - 5 = -3 - 2(4x + 1)$

4 What is the solution of $|a - 5| = 12$?

(1) 18   (3) -7

(2) 17, -7 (4) $-17, 17$

5 Which inequality is equivalent to $-6x > 12$?

(1) $x > -2$ (3) $3x < -6$

(2) $-2x < -4$ (4) $x < 2$

6 What is the solution of the inequality $4x + 2 < x - 5$?

(1) $x \le -\frac{1}{7}$

(3) $x \ge -\frac{7}{3}$

(2) $x > \frac{7}{3}$

(4) $x < -\frac{7}{3}$

7 Which inequality is represented by this graph?

(1) $|s| \le 3$

(3) $|s| \ge 3$

(2) $|s| > 3$

(4) $|s| < 3$

8 A spinner numbered from 1 to 6 is spun. Each outcome is equally likely. What is the probability of getting an odd number?

(1) $\frac{1}{6}$ (2) 0.16   (3) $\frac{2}{3}$ (4) 50%

Part II

9 Solve $w + 6 < -2$. Graph the solutions on a number line.

10 Suppose you want to save at least $200 for new speakers. You save $15 each week from your part-time job. How many full weeks of saving will it take you? Write an inequality to model this problem. Then solve it.

11 The number of subscribers to a magazine fell from 210,000 to 190,000. To the nearest whole number, find the percent of decrease this drop represents.

Part III

12 The formula $P = 2\ell + 2w$ gives the perimeter P of a rectangle with length ℓ and width w.
  a Solve this formula for ℓ.
  b Suppose you have 80 ft of fencing to enclose a garden. If you make the enclosure 25 ft long, how wide can you make it?

13 Graph the solutions of the inequality $-5 < 4(k + 6) \le 28$ for the set of negative integers.

Part IV

14 A car traveling for 6 hours covers the same distance as a truck traveling for 7.2 hours. The car is traveling 10 mi/h faster than the truck.
  a Write an equation to model this problem.
  b What is the car's speed?
  c What is the truck's speed?

15 A pair of jeans that normally costs $36 are on sale for $24.99.
  a To the nearest whole percent, how much are the jeans discounted?
  b What is the percent of decrease in price, to the nearest whole percent?
  c How are the two percents you have found related?

5

Graphing and Writing Linear Equations

Relating to the Real World

Algebra provides a shorthand way to look at a whole class of relationships. Many cause-and-effect relationships in everyday life, especially those involving time and money, use linear equations and graphs as models. By understanding properties of linear models, both economists and home budget makers can plan wisely.

	Slope	Rates of Change	Direct Variation	Slope-Intercept Form	Writing the Equation of a Line
Lessons	5-1	5-2	5-3	5-4	5-5

EXIT

Taking
THE
PLUNGE

Do you have a job? If not, what will your first job be? What expenses will you have? How much money will you actually earn? How can you compare earnings between two jobs? Linear equations can help to answer all these questions.

As you work through the chapter, you will make graphs and write equations that model different jobs. You will use these models to predict income. After interviewing someone about their first job, you will choose a job that you might like to have and explain why.

APPLICATION FOR EMPLOYMENT

Name _Lim_
Please print   Last
Address _357 Oak St._
         Street and Number   Sc
Home Phone (_919_) _555-2287_   B

Are you at least 18 years of age?
Are you legally eligible to work in the U.S.?
Do you have relatives working for Viacom I
If so, name

Position Objective
Type of Employment   Total numbe
☐ Full-Time   per week
☐ Part-Time   desired:
☐ Temporary
☒ Seasonal

Please describe the type of positio

Salary required $

Were you considered at an
employed with Viacom Inc

If yes, please provide app

These inquiries are
subsequent dismissa
national origin, sex

To help you complete the project:

▼ **p. 224**   *Find Out by Graphing*
▼ **p. 239**   *Find Out by Modeling*
▼ **p. 255**   *Find Out by Interviewing*
▼ **p. 260**   *Finishing the Project*

Scatter Plots and Equations of Lines	*Ax + By = C Form*	*Parallel and Perpendicular Lines*	*Using the x-intercept*
5-6	5-7	5-8	5-9

213

What You'll Learn

- Calculating the slope of a line
- Drawing a line through a point with a given slope

...And Why

To find slope in real-world situations, such as the landing of an airplane, and interpret its meaning

What You'll Need

- graph paper

5-1 Slope

WORK TOGETHER

Carpentry Carpenters use the terms rise and run to describe the steepness of a stairway or a roof line. You can use rise and run to describe the steepness of a hill.

$$\text{steepness} = \frac{\text{rise}}{\text{run}}$$

1. Which hill appears to be steeper in the photos?

A.   B.

2. **a.** Find a ratio for the steepness of each hill.
   b. For which hill is the ratio greater?

THINK AND DISCUSS

Counting Units to Find Slope

The mathematical term to describe steepness is slope.

$$\textbf{slope} = \frac{\text{vertical change (rise)}}{\text{hortizontal change (run)}}$$

Example 1 ········

Find the slope of each line.

a.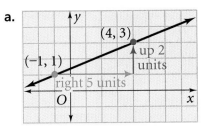

$$\text{slope} = \frac{\text{vertical change}}{\text{horizontal change}}$$
$$= \frac{2}{5}$$

The slope of the line is $\frac{2}{5}$.

b.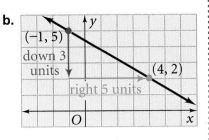

$$\text{slope} = \frac{\text{vertical change}}{\text{horizontal change}}$$
$$= -\frac{3}{5}$$

The slope of the line is $-\frac{3}{5}$.

3. Complete each statement with *upward* or *downward*.
   a. A line with positive slope goes ▨ from left to right.
   b. A line with negative slope goes ▨ from left to right.

You use the units associated with the axes to explain the meaning of the slope in a real-world situation.

Example 2   **Relating to the Real World**

Airplanes The graph models the altitude of an airplane from the time the wheels are lowered (time = 0 s) to when the plane lands. Find the slope of the line. Explain what the slope means in this situation.

Find any two points on the graph. Use the points to find the slope.

Airplane Landing

$$\text{slope} = \frac{\text{vertical change}}{\text{horizontal change}}$$

$$= \frac{-1000}{120}$$

$$= -8\frac{1}{3}$$

The slope of the line is $-8\frac{1}{3}$. The plane is descending $8\frac{1}{3}$ ft/s.

4. **Critical Thinking** Suppose a graph of a line with slope 12 indicates the relationship between altitude and time for another airplane. What would the slope mean in this situation?

Using Coordinates to Find Slope

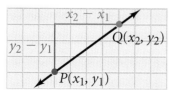

You read the coordinates (x_1, y_1) as "x sub 1, y sub 1."

You can use any two points on a line to find its slope. To find the slope of a line PQ (written $\overleftrightarrow{PQ}$), you can use this formula:

$$\text{slope} = \frac{\text{vertical change}}{\text{horizontal change}} = \frac{y_2 - y_1}{x_2 - x_1}, \text{ where } x_2 - x_1 \neq 0$$

5. **Critical Thinking** Why does the formula for the slope include the statement "where $x_2 - x_1 \neq 0$"?

Example 3

Find the slope of a line through $A(-2, 1)$ and $B(5, 7)$.

$$\text{slope} = \frac{y_2 - y_1}{x_2 - x_1}$$

$$= \frac{7 - 1}{5 - (-2)} \longleftarrow \text{Substitute (5, 7) for } (x_2, y_2) \text{ and } (-2, 1) \text{ for } (x_1, y_1).$$

$$= \frac{6}{7}$$

The slope of $\overleftrightarrow{AB}$ is $\frac{6}{7}$.

6. Try This Find the slope of the line through $C(4, 0)$ and $D(-1, 5)$.

Example 4

Using the points shown, find the slope and equation of each line.

a.

$$\text{slope} = \frac{y_2 - y_1}{x_2 - x_1}$$

$$= \frac{2 - 2}{4 - 1}$$

$$= \frac{0}{3}$$

$$= 0$$

b.

$$\text{slope} = \frac{y_2 - y_1}{x_2 - x_1}$$

$$= \frac{2 - (-1)}{4 - 4}$$

$$= \frac{3}{0},$$

$$\text{undefined}$$

The slope of a horizontal line is 0. All points on the graph have a y-coordinate of 2. The equation of the line is $y = 2$.

The slope of a vertical line is undefined. All points on the graph have an x-coordinate of 4. The equation of the line is $x = 4$.

7. Try This Describe the graph of $x = -5$ and the graph of $y = \frac{1}{2}$.

Graphing a Line Given Its Slope and a Point

Example 5

Draw a line through the point $(1, 2)$ with the slope $-\frac{3}{2}$.

  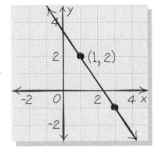

Plot $(1, 2)$.

Find another point using the slope $-\frac{3}{2}$.

Draw a line through the points.

8. Try This Graph the line through the point $(2, -3)$ with slope $\frac{5}{4}$.

Slope of Lines

A line with positive slope goes upward from left to right.

A line with negative slope goes downward from left to right.

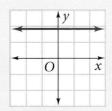

The slope of a horizontal line is 0. The equation of this line is $y = 1.8$.

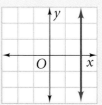

The slope of a vertical line is undefined. The equation of this line is $x = 2$.

Exercises   ON YOUR OWN

Use the diagram at the right for Exercises 1 and 2.

1. What is the slope of line q? of line z?

2. *Open-ended* What is the slope of a line through the origin that is in the red region? the yellow region? the green region? the blue region?

Find the slope of the line passing through each pair of points.

3. $(-8, 0), (1, 5)$ 4. $(8, 3), (-4, 3)$ 5. $(-4, -5), (-9, 1)$

6. $(\frac{1}{2}, 8), (1, -2)$ 7. $(4, -1), (4, 7)$ 8. $(9, -2), (3, 4)$

Through the given point, graph a line with the given slope.

9. $(3, 4)$; slope $= \frac{1}{2}$ 10. $(-2, 1)$; slope $= -2$ 11. $(0, 3)$; slope $= 0$ 12. $(-5, -2)$; slope $= \frac{3}{4}$

13. $(1, -3)$; slope $= -\frac{2}{3}$ 14. $(2, 5)$; slope $= -\frac{4}{3}$ 15. $(-1, 5)$; undefined slope   16. $(-2, 3)$; slope $= -\frac{5}{3}$

17. Write equations for the lines described in Exercises 4, 7, 11, and 15.

Critical Thinking **Tell whether each statement is *true* or *false*. Explain.**

18. All horizontal lines have the same slope.   19. A line with slope 1 passes through the origin.

20. Two lines may have the same slope.   21. The slope of a line in Quadrant III must be negative.

Carpentry **Tell whether the slope would *increase*, *decrease*, or *remain the same*.**

22. The rise of each step *increases* 1 in.

23. The run of each step *decreases* 1 in.

24. The rise and run both *increase* 1 in.

Geometry Find the slope of the sides of each figure.

25.

26.

27.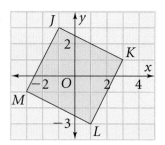

Do the points lie on the same line?

Sample $A(1, 3)$, $B(4, 2)$, $C(-2, 4)$

$$\text{slope of } \overleftrightarrow{AB} = \frac{2 - 3}{4 - 1} \qquad \text{slope of } \overleftrightarrow{BC} = \frac{4 - 2}{-2 - 4}$$

$$= -\frac{1}{3} \qquad\qquad\qquad = \frac{2}{-6} = -\frac{1}{3}$$

$\overleftrightarrow{AB}$ and $\overleftrightarrow{BC}$ have the same slope. So the points lie on the same line.

28. $A(3, 5)$, $B(-1, 3)$, $C(7, 7)$ 29. $P(4, 1)$, $Q(-1, 5)$, $R(1, 2)$ 30. $L(6, 4)$, $M(3, 2)$, $N(0, 0)$

31. **Fairs** The graph shows how much it costs to rent carousel equipment for a fair. Rental includes the cost of an operator.
    a. Estimate the slope of the line. What does that number mean?
    b. Customers pay $2 for a ride. What is the number of customers needed per hour to cover the rental cost?

Rent for a Carousel

32. **Writing** A friend says the slope of the line passing through $(1, 7)$ and $(3, 9)$ is equal to the ratio $\frac{1 - 9}{7 - 3}$. Is this correct? Explain.

33. **Standardized Test Prep** A line has a slope of $\frac{4}{3}$. Through which two points could this line pass?
    A. $(-4, 10)$, $(8, 19)$ **B.** $(8, 10)$, $(0, 16)$ **C.** $(-8, 10)$, $(-2, 2)$
    D. $(4, -4)$, $(10, 2)$ **E.** none of the above

Exercises   **M I X E D   R E V I E W**

Find each probability based on one roll of a number cube.

34. $P(1)$ 35. $P(\text{even number})$ 36. $P(3 \text{ or } 5)$ 37. $P(\text{integer})$ 38. $P(10)$

39. **Environment** In 1994, biologists released 200,000 salmon into Alaska's Ninilchik River. In 1995, they released only 50,000 because the native salmon population had grown. Find the percent of change.

Getting Ready for Lesson 5-2

Identify the independent and dependent variable for each function.

40. distance an airplane flies and the time a flight takes

41. the amount of home heating fuel used and the outside temperature

Dimensional Analysis

Before Lesson 5-2

You can use conversion factors to change from one unit of measure to another. The process of analyzing units to decide which conversion factors to use is called **dimensional analysis.**

Since 60 min = 1 h, $\frac{60 \text{ min}}{1 \text{ h}}$ equals 1. You can use $\frac{60 \text{ min}}{1 \text{ h}}$ to convert hours to minutes.

$$7 \text{ h} \cdot \frac{60 \text{ min}}{1 \text{ h}} = 420 \text{ min}$$

The hour units cancel, and the result is minutes.

Sometimes you need to use more than one conversion factor.

Example

Animals A cheetah ran 300 ft in 2.92 s. What was the cheetah's speed in miles per hour?

You need to convert feet to miles and seconds to hours.

$$\frac{300 \text{ ft}}{2.92 \text{ s}} \cdot \frac{1 \text{ mi}}{5280 \text{ ft}} \cdot \frac{60 \text{ s}}{1 \text{ min}} \cdot \frac{60 \text{ min}}{1 \text{ h}} = \frac{300 \text{ ft}}{2.92 \text{ s}} \cdot \frac{1 \text{ mi}}{5280 \text{ ft}} \cdot \frac{60 \text{ s}}{1 \text{ min}} \cdot \frac{60 \text{ min}}{1 \text{ h}}$$

← The feet, seconds, and minutes cancel. The result is miles per hour.

$$= \frac{(300 \cdot 1 \cdot 60 \cdot 60) \text{mi}}{(2.92 \cdot 5280 \cdot 1 \cdot 1) \text{h}}$$ ← Use a calculator.

$$\approx 70 \text{ mi/h}$$

The cheetah's speed was about 70 mi/h.

Choose A or B for the correct conversion factor for changing the units.

1. quarts to gallons

    A. $\frac{1 \text{ gal}}{4 \text{ qt}}$ B. $\frac{4 \text{ qt}}{1 \text{ gal}}$

2. ounces to pounds

    A. $\frac{1 \text{ lb}}{16 \text{ oz}}$ B. $\frac{16 \text{ oz}}{1 \text{ lb}}$

3. inches to yards

    A. $\frac{36 \text{ in.}}{1 \text{ yd}}$ B. $\frac{1 \text{ yd}}{36 \text{ in.}}$

Write each in the given unit or units.

4. 8 h = ▓ s

5. 120 in. = ▓ yd

6. $1.85/3.25 lb = ▓ ¢/oz

7. 18 qt/s = ▓ gal/min

Express each in miles per hour.

8. 300 yd in 10.9 min

9. 1 mi in 3.79 min

10. 120 ft in 30 s

11. 250 mi in 45 sec

12. Writing Explain how you determine which conversion factors to use when changing 3 in./s to feet per minute.

What You'll Learn

- Finding rates of change from tables and graphs

...And Why

To find rates of change in real-world situations, such as the rate of descent for a parachute or the cost of renting a computer

What You'll Need

- graph paper

QUICK REVIEW

A *rate* is a ratio that compares two quantities measured in different units.

5-2 Rates of Change

THINK AND DISCUSS

Finding Rate of Change

Suppose you type 140 words in 4 minutes. What is your typing rate?

$$\frac{140 \text{ words}}{4 \text{ min}} \quad \text{or} \quad \frac{35 \text{ words}}{1 \text{ min}} \quad \longleftarrow \quad \text{dependent variable} \atop \longleftarrow \quad \text{independent variable}$$

The number of words depends on the number of minutes you type. So, the number of words is the dependent variable.

1. Write each as a rate.
   a. You buy 5 yards of fabric for $19.95.
   b. You travel 268.8 mi on 12 gal of gasoline.

You use a rate to find the amount of one quantity per one unit of another, such as typing 35 words in 1 min. The **rate of change** allows you to see the relationship between two quantities that are changing.

$$\text{rate of change} = \frac{\text{change in the dependent variable}}{\text{change in the independent variable}}$$

On a graph, you show the dependent variable on the vertical axis and the independent variable on the horizontal axis. The slope of a line is the rate of change relating the variables.

$$\text{slope} = \frac{\text{vertical change}}{\text{horizontal change}} = \frac{\text{change in the dependent variable}}{\text{change in the independent variable}}$$

Example 1   Relating to the Real World

Parachuting Find the rate of change for data graphed on the line. Then explain what the rate of change means in this situation.

Height of Parachute

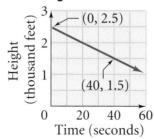

Find two points on the graph. Use the points to find the slope, which is also the rate of change.

$$\text{slope} = \frac{\text{vertical change}}{\text{horizontal change}}$$

$$= \frac{1.5 - 2.5}{40 - 0}$$

$$= -\frac{1}{40}$$

The rate of change is $-\frac{1}{40}$, which means that the parachute descends 1000 ft every 40 seconds.

2. In Example 1, why is height the dependent variable?

3. How many feet does the parachute descend in a second?

Using a Table

Cost of Renting a Computer	
Number of Days	Hraibe's Rental Company
1	$60
2	$75
3	$90
4	$105
5	$120

Example 2   **Relating to the Real World**

Rental Business You can rent a computer from Hraibe's Rental Company. The first day's rent is $60. Find the rate of change for renting a computer after the first day.

$$\text{rate of change} = \frac{\text{change in the dependent variable}}{\text{change in the independent variable}}$$

$$= \frac{\text{change in cost}}{\text{change in number of days}} \quad \longleftarrow \text{Cost depends on the number of days.}$$

$$= \frac{105 - 60}{4 - 1} \quad \longleftarrow \text{Use any two pairs of data.}$$

$$= \frac{45}{3}$$

$$= \frac{15}{1}$$

The rate of change is $\frac{15}{1}$, which means that it costs $15 for each day a computer is rented after the first day. ∎

4. Will the rate of change for the data in the table be the same for any pair of data items? Explain.

Linear Functions

The graph of a **linear function** is a line. You can also use a table to tell whether the relationship between sets of data is linear.

Graph	Table	Rate of Change
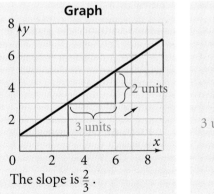 The slope is $\frac{2}{3}$.	3 units → 2 units	(0, 1) to (3, 3) $\frac{2}{3}$ (3, 3) to (6, 5) $\frac{2}{3}$ (6, 5) to (9, 7) $\frac{2}{3}$

As you can see from the table for the graph, the rate of change between consecutive pairs of data is constant. So, the relationship between the x-values and the y-values is linear.

Example 3 **Relating to the Real World**

Science Tell whether the relationship shown by the data is linear.

Boiling Temperature of Water

Altitude	Temperature	
0 ft	212° F	
4,000 ft	204.6° F	−7.4
8,000 ft	197.2° F	−7.4
12,000 ft	189.8° F	−7.4

(4000 between each altitude)

Each rise of 4000 ft in altitude results in a 7.4° decline in the boiling temperature of water. So the relationship is linear.

5. *Critical Thinking* How much does the boiling temperature of water change for each 1000-ft rise in altitude?

6. *Critical Thinking* How could you find the boiling temperature of water in Denver, which has an altitude of 5300 ft?

7. **Try This** Is the relationship shown by the data linear?

x	0	1	3	5	7	9
y	0	1	4	9	16	25

Exercises   O N   Y O U R   O W N

Find the rate of change for each situation.

1. A baby is 18 in. long at birth and 27 in. at ten months.

2. The cost of group tickets for a museum is $48 for four people and $78 for ten people.

3. You drive 30 mi in one hour and 120 mi in four hours.

Find the rate of change.

4.   **A Tank of Gas**

5.   **Price of Oregano**

6.   **Emissions: Generating Electricity for TV Use**

7. a. At colder temperatures, people burn more calories. Is the relationship between the two quantities linear? Explain.
   b. Critical Thinking How can you find the number of calories burned at 20°F?

Temperature	Calories Burned Per Day
68°F	3030
62°F	3130
56°F	3230
50°F	3330

Critical Thinking **Tell whether each statement is *true* or *false*. If true, explain why. If false, give an example.**

8. Rates of change are always constant.

9. The rate of change for a linear function is constant.

10. Two linear functions with positive slope are graphed on the same coordinate plane. The function with the greater rate of change will be steeper.

11. A rate of change must be either positive or zero.

Is the relationship shown by the data in each table linear?

12.

x	y
3	1
4	−2
5	−5
6	−8

13.

x	y
2	0
4	1
6	4
8	9

14.

x	y
0	3
1	6
2	9
3	12

15.

x	y
−3	5
−1	8
1	12
3	17

16.

x	y
1	0
8	1
15	2
22	3

17.

x	y
9	−4
5	1
1	6
−3	11

18. a. Critical Thinking Find the rate of change between consecutive pairs of data.

x	1	3	4	7
y	3	7	9	15

   b. Is the relationship shown by the data linear? Explain.

19. Video Recording The graph shows the lengths of videotape used in 30 min at three different settings of a VCR.
   a. At which setting does the tape move fastest? slowest? Explain.
   b. Critical Thinking At which setting can you record for the longest time? Explain.

Video Recording

20. Writing How can you tell if the relationship between two sets of data is linear?

21. a. Patterns Draw the next two figures for the pattern at the right.
   b. Make a table for the relationship between the number of squares and the perimeter of each figure.
   c. Is the relationship between the number of squares and the perimeter linear? Explain.

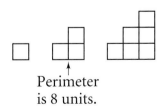

Perimeter is 8 units.

22. a. Biology Which line in the graph at the right is the steepest?

b. During the 5-week period, which plant had the greatest rate of change? the least rate of change? How do you know?

23. Open-ended Lanai is hiking up a mountain. She monitors and records her distance every half hour. Do you think the rates of change for every half hour are constant? Explain.

Plant Growth

24. a. Find the rate of change for the line.

b. Writing What situation could be modeled by the graph?

c. Critical Thinking What do you think is true about the rate of change for a horizontal line? Explain.

Chapter Project **Find Out by Graphing**

Find the starting hourly wage for two jobs that interest you.

• Make a graph that shows the income for each job. Show hours worked (0 to 10) on the horizontal axis and income on the vertical axis.

• Suppose you work eight hours. Explain how your graph shows the difference in income from the two jobs.

Exercises   M I X E D   R E V I E W

Solve.

25. $x + 3 = 2x - 1$ **26.** $3(2t + 5) = -9$ **27.** $2.8m - 1.3m = 4.5$ **28.** $\frac{6s + 4}{8} = \frac{1}{2}$

29. Food In the United States, people eat about 340 million pounds of cranberries per year. About 73 million pounds are eaten during Thanksgiving week alone. About what percent of the cranberries is consumed during the week of Thanksgiving?

Getting Ready for Lesson 5-3

Model each rule with a table of values and a graph.

30. $y = 3x$ **31.** $y = 0.8x$ **32.** $y = \frac{3}{4}x$ **33.** $y = 7.2x$

What You'll Learn

- Relating slope to constant of variation
- Using constant of variation to solve problems

...And Why

To solve real-world problems, such as finding the force needed to lift a given weight

Movie projectors run at 24 frames/s. Video cameras project at 30 frames/s.

5-3 Direct Variation

THINK AND DISCUSS

Direct Variation

Movies As you watch a movie, 24 individual pictures, or frames, flash on the screen each second. Here are three ways you can model the relationship between the number of frames and the number of seconds.

Table

x number of seconds	y number of frames
1	24
2	48
3	72
4	96
5	120

Graph

Number of Frames vs. Time (seconds)

Function Rule

$y = 24x$

1. **a.** What is the rate of change for the data in the table?
   b. What is the slope of the line shown in the graph?
   c. What is the relationship between the rate of change, the slope, and the coefficient of x in the function rule?

The number of frames *varies directly* with the number of seconds the movie has been shown. This relationship is called a direct variation.

> ### Direct Variation
> ....
> A **direct variation** is a linear function that can be written in the form $y = kx$, where $k \neq 0$.
>
> ↑
> constant of variation

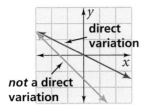

direct variation

not a direct variation

The function rule for a linear function is called a **linear equation.** Since a direct variation can be written as the linear equation $y = kx$, then when $x = 0$, $y = 0$. So the graph of a direct variation will pass through the origin, $(0, 0)$.

You can write the linear equation $y = kx$ as $k = \frac{y}{x}$, where $x \neq 0$. The **constant of variation** k equals the rate of change for data that describe the variation. The value of k also equals the slope of the line that graphs the equation.

2. The direct variation graphed at the left includes the point $(2, -1)$. What is its constant of variation?

To tell if a linear equation is a direct variation, you can transform the equation by solving for y.

Example 1

Is each equation a direct variation? If it is, find the constant of variation.

a. $5x + 2y = 0$

$2y = -5x$ ← Solve for y. →

$y = -\frac{5}{2}x$

Yes, $y = -\frac{5}{2}x$ is in the form $y = kx$. The constant of variation is $-\frac{5}{2}$.

b. $5x + 2y = 9$

$2y = -5x + 9$

$y = -\frac{5}{2}x + \frac{9}{2}$

No, the equation is *not* in the form $y = kx$.

3. **Critical Thinking** Diane tries substituting $(0, 0)$ for (x, y) to see if an equation is a direct variation. Does her method work? Explain.

4. **Try This** Is each equation a direct variation? If it is, find the constant of variation.
   a. $7y = 2x$ **b.** $3y + 4x = 8$ **c.** $y - 7.5x = 0$

Using the Constant of Variation to Write Equations

Example 2   Relating to the Real World

Weather The time it takes you to hear thunder varies directly with your distance from the lightning. If you are 2 mi from where lightning strikes, you will hear thunder about 10 s after you see the lightning. Write an equation for the relationship between time and distance.

Define $x =$ your distance in miles from the lightning

         $y =$ the number of seconds between seeing lightning and hearing thunder

Relate The time varies directly with the distance.
       When $x = 2, y = 10$.

Write $y = kx$ ← Use the general form of a direct variation.

        $10 = k(2)$ ← Substitute 2 for x and 10 for y.

        $\frac{10}{2} = \frac{2k}{2}$ ← Solve for k.

        $5 = k$

        $y = 5x$ ← Substitute 5 for k to write an equation.

The equation $y = 5x$ relates the distance x in miles you are from lightning to the time y in seconds it takes you to hear the thunder.

5. Use the equation in Example 2 to find about how far you are from lightning if you hear thunder 7 s after you see lightning.

What? A bolt of lightning that you see during a thunderstorm has a speed that varies from 100 to 1000 mi/s.

Source: *The Guinness Book of Records*

You can use the ratio $\frac{y}{x}$ to tell if two sets of data vary directly.

Example 3

For each table, tell whether y varies directly with x. If it does, write a function rule for the relationship shown by the data.

Find the ratio $\frac{y}{x}$ for each pair of data.

a.

x	y	$\frac{y}{x}$
-3	2.25	$\frac{2.25}{-3} = -0.75$
1	-0.75	$\frac{-0.75}{1} = -0.75$
4	-3	$\frac{-3}{4} = -0.75$

Yes, the constant of variation is -0.75. The function is $y = -0.75x$.

b.

x	y	$\frac{y}{x}$
2	-1	$\frac{-1}{2}$
4	1	$\frac{1}{4}$
6	3	$\frac{3}{6} = \frac{1}{2}$

No, the ratio $\frac{y}{x}$ is not the same for each pair of data.

6. **a.** Find the rate of change for the data in each table in Example 3.
   b. Is the relationship shown by the data in each table linear? Explain.
   c. *Critical Thinking* A direct variation is a linear function. Are all linear functions direct variations? Explain.

Using Proportions

In a direct variation, the ratio $\frac{y}{x}$ is the same for any pair of data where $x \neq 0$. So the proportion $\frac{y_1}{x_1} = \frac{y_2}{x_2}$ is true for the ordered pairs (x_1, y_1) and (x_2, y_2) where $x_1 \neq 0$ and $x_2 \neq 0$.

Example 4   Relating to the Real World

Physics The force you must apply to lift an object varies directly with the object's weight. You need to apply 0.625 lb of force to the windlass to lift a 28-lb weight. How much force would you need to lift 100 lb?

Relate   The force of 0.625 lb lifts 28 lb. The force of n lb lifts 100 lb.

Define   force$_1$ = 0.625 lb   force$_2$ = n
         weight$_1$ = 28 lb   weight$_2$ = 100 lb

Write $\dfrac{\text{force}_1}{\text{weight}_1} = \dfrac{\text{force}_2}{\text{weight}_2}$ ← Use a proportion.

$\dfrac{0.625}{28} = \dfrac{n}{100}$ ← Substitute.

$100(0.625) = 28n$ ← Cross-multiply.

$\dfrac{100(0.625)}{28} = n$ ← Divide each side by 28.

$n \approx 2.232142857$ ← Use a calculator.

You need about 2.2 lb of force to lift a 100-lb object.

7. Write an equation for the direct variation in Example 4.

8. a. Try This Use your equation in Question 7 or proportions to find how much weight you can lift with a force of 4.3 lb.

 b. Why did you choose the method you used for part (a)?

Exercises   ON YOUR OWN

1. Which of the lines at the right are graphs of direct variations? Explain.

Is each equation a direct variation? If it is, what is the constant of variation?

2. $y = \frac{5}{3}x$ **3.** $y = 2x + 4$ **4.** $y^2 = 2x$

5. $y = \frac{x}{4}$ **6.** $3y = 8x$ **7.** $x + 5y = 10$

8. Critical Thinking Can the points $(2, 3)$ and $(4, 6)$ be on the graph of the same direct variation? Explain.

For each table, tell whether y varies directly with x. If it does, write a function rule for the relationship shown by the data.

9.
x	y
3	5.4
7	12.6
12	21.6

10.
x	y
−2	1
3	6
8	11

11.
x	y
−6	9
1	−1.5
8	−12

12.
x	y
−5	−13
3	7.8
9	21.6

Draw the graph of a direct variation that includes the given point. Write an equation of the line.

13. $(2, 5)$ **14.** $(-2, 5)$ **15.** $(2, -5)$ **16.** $(-2, -5)$

17. Physics The maximum weight you can lift with the lever in the diagram varies directly with the amount of force you apply. What force do you need to lift a friend who weighs 130 lb?

18. Critical Thinking For what value of c is $ax - by = c$ a direct variation?

Critical Thinking Is each statement true? Explain.

19. The graph of a direct variation may pass through $(0, 3)$.

20. If you double an x-value of a direct variation, the y-value also doubles.

21. The graph of a direct variation can be a vertical line.

22. a. Writing How can you tell whether two sets of data vary directly?

 b. How can you tell if a line is the graph of a direct variation?

23. Biology The amount of blood in a person's body varies directly with body weight. Someone weighing 160 lb has about 5 qt of blood.

   a. Find the constant of variation and write an equation relating quarts of blood to weight.

   b. Graph your equation.

   c. Open-ended Estimate the number of quarts of blood in your body.

24. Bicycling A bicyclist traveled at a constant speed during a timed practice period. Use an equation or proportions to find the distance the cyclist will travel in 30 min.

Bicyclist's Practice

Elapsed Time	Distance
10 min	3 mi
25 min	7.5 mi

Suppose the ordered pairs in each exercise are for the same direct variation. Find each missing value.

25. $(3, 4)$ and $(9, y)$ **26.** $(-1, 2)$ and $(4, y)$ **27.** $(-5, 3)$ and $(x, -4.8)$ **28.** $(1, y)$ and $(\frac{3}{2}, -9)$

29. $(2, 5)$ and $(x, 12.5)$ **30.** $(-2, 5)$ and $(x, -5)$ **31.** $(-6, -3)$ and $(-4, y)$ **32.** $(x, -4)$ and $(-9, -12)$

33. a. Write an equation relating the data in the cartoon.

   b. How many dog years are 12 human years?

from the cartoon *Mother Goose and Grimm*

Exercises   MIXED REVIEW

Solve each equation. Graph the solutions on a number line.

34. $4m + 3 < 2$ **35.** $9 > 5 - 3t$ **36.** $-z + 8 \geq 5$

37. Jeans are on sale at four different stores. The original price of the jeans at each store is $35. Which of the following sales will give you the best price on the jeans?

   A. 25% off the original price   **B.** $\frac{1}{3}$ off the original price

   C. pay 70% of the original price   **D.** $10 off the original price

SELF ASSESSMENT

FOR YOUR JOURNAL

Explain how rate of change, slope, and constant of variation are related.

Getting Ready for Lesson 5-4

Draw a line with the given slope that passes through the given point.

38. slope $= 3$, passes through $(0, -5)$ **39.** slope $= -\frac{7}{8}$, passes through $(0, 4)$

What You'll Learn

• Using the slope and y-intercept to draw graphs and write equations

...And Why

To investigate flag designs and real-world situations, such as salary plus commission

What You'll Need

• graphing calculator

5-4 Slope-Intercept Form

WORK TOGETHER

1. a. *Graphing Calculator* Graph these equations on the same screen.
$$y = \frac{1}{2}x \qquad\qquad y = x \qquad\qquad y = 5x$$

 b. Generalize How does the coefficient of x affect the graph of an equation?

2. a. *Graphing Calculator* Many national flags include designs formed from straight lines. You can use equations to model these designs. Choose values for k in the equation $y = kx$ to create a display like the one for the flag of Jamaica. Use the standard settings.

Jamaica

 b. What do you notice about the values of k for the lines you graphed?

3. a. *Graphing Calculator* Graph these equations on the same screen.
$$y = 2x \qquad\qquad y = 2x + 3 \qquad\qquad y = 2x - 4$$
 b. Where does each line cross the y-axis?

Tanzania

4. Choose values for b in the equation $y = 1.1x + b$. Create a display that resembles the Tanzanian flag. Write the equations you used for your display.

5. Generalize What effect does the value of b have on the graph of an equation?

6. *Open-ended* Make a flag design of your own. Write the equations you use for your design.

THINK AND DISCUSS

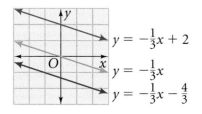

$$y = -\tfrac{1}{3}x + 2$$
$$y = -\tfrac{1}{3}x$$
$$y = -\tfrac{1}{3}x - \tfrac{4}{3}$$

Defining Slope-Intercept Form

The point where a line crosses the y-axis is the **y-intercept.**

7. a. What is the y-intercept of each line at the left?
 b. Generalize What is the connection between a line's equation and its y-intercept?

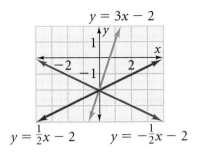

$y = 3x - 2$

$y = \frac{1}{2}x - 2$ $y = -\frac{1}{2}x - 2$

8. **a.** What is the slope of each line at the left?
   b. Generalize What is the connection between a line's equation and its slope?

In the last lesson you learned that the letter k indicates the constant of variation of a direct variation. For linear equations in general, the letter m indicates the slope and the letter b indicates the y-intercept.

Slope-Intercept Form of a Linear Equation

The **slope-intercept form** of a linear equation is $y = mx + b$.

slope y-intercept

9. **Try This** What are the slope and y-intercept of the line for each equation?
   a. $y = 3x - 5$ **b.** $y = \frac{7}{6}x + \frac{3}{4}$ **c.** $y = -\frac{4}{5}x$

10. **Try This** Write an equation of a line with the given slope and y-intercept.
    a. $m = \frac{2}{3}, b = -5$ **b.** $m = -\frac{1}{2}, b = 0$ **c.** $m = 0, b = -2$

You can use the slope and y-intercept to graph an equation.

Example 1

Graph the equation $y = 3x - 1$.

The y-intercept is -1, so plot a point at $(0, -1)$.

The slope is 3, or $\frac{3}{1}$. Use the slope to plot a second point.

Draw a line through the points.

11. **Critical Thinking** Could you find a second point by going down 3 and to the left 1? Explain.

12. **Try This** Graph $y = -\frac{3}{2}x + 2$.

You may need to rewrite a linear equation to express it in slope-intercept form.

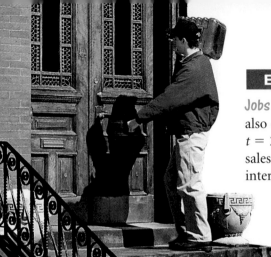

Example 2   **Relating to the Real World**

Jobs The base pay of a water delivery person is $210 per week. He can also earn 20% commission on any sales he makes. The equation $t = 210 + 0.2s$ relates total earnings t to sales s. Rewrite the equation in slope-intercept form. Then graph the equation.

$$t = 210 + 0.2s$$

↑ intercept   ↑ slope

$$t = 0.2s + 210 \quad \longleftarrow \text{slope-intercept form}$$

Weekly Earnings for a Water Delivery Person

13. Try This Rewrite $y + 5 = 4x$ in slope-intercept form.

You can use the equation of a line to determine if a point lies on the line.

Example 3

Does the point $(8, 4)$ lie on the line with equation $y = \frac{3}{4}x - 2$?
Test the coordinates of the point in the equation of the line.

$$y = \frac{3}{4}x - 2$$

$$4 \stackrel{?}{=} \frac{3}{4}(8) - 2 \quad \longleftarrow \text{Substitute 8 for } x \text{ and 4 for } y.$$

$$4 \stackrel{?}{=} 6 - 2 \quad \longleftarrow \text{Simplify.}$$

$$4 = 4 \ \checkmark \quad \longleftarrow \text{The values of } x \text{ and } y \text{ satisfy the equation.}$$

The point $(8, 4)$ lies on the line with equation $y = \frac{3}{4}x - 2$.

14. Try This **Verify** the result of Example 3 by graphing.

Writing Equations

Example 4

Write an equation for the line at the left.

Step 1 Find the y-intercept and another point.

The y-intercept is 2; $(0, 2)$ and $(4, -1)$ lie on the line.

Step 2 Find the slope.
Use $(0, 2)$ and $(4, -1)$.

$$\text{slope} = \frac{-1 - 2}{4 - 0}$$

$$= -\frac{3}{4}$$

Step 3 Write an equation in slope-intercept form.

Substitute $-\frac{3}{4}$ for m and 2 for b.

$$y = mx + b$$

$$y = -\frac{3}{4}x + 2$$

Find the slope and *y*-intercept of each equation.

1. $y = -\frac{3}{4}x - 5$ **2.** $y = \frac{1}{2}x$ **3.** $3x - 9 = y$ **4.** $2x = y + 7$ **5.** $y = 3$

6. Standardized Test Prep A music store sells CDs for $12 each. Customers may use one coupon good for $4 off the total purchase. Suppose a customer buys *n* number of CDs using a coupon. Which equation models the relationship between the total cost *t* and the number of CDs a customer buys?
     A. $t = 12n - 4$ **B.** $t = 4n - 12$ **C.** $4t = 12n$ **D.** $t = 12 - 4n$ **E.** $t = 4 - 12n$

Match the graph with the correct equation.

7. $y = x + 5$ **8.** $y = -\frac{5}{2}x + 5$ **9.** $y = -\frac{1}{2}x + 5$

I.   **II.**   **III.**

10. Graphing Calculator Suppose you want to graph the equation $y = \frac{5}{4}x - 3$. Enter each key sequence and display the graphs.

    a. `Y=` 5 `÷` 4 `X,T,θ` `−` 3   **b.** `Y=` `(` 5 `÷` 4 `)` `X,T,θ` `−` 3

    c. Which key sequence gives you the graph of $y = \frac{5}{4}x - 3$? Explain.

Graph each equation.

11. $y = -x + 3$ **12.** $y = 2x - 1$ **13.** $y = 5 + 2x$ **14.** $y - 4 = x$

15. $y + \frac{3}{4}x = 0$ **16.** $y = 7$ **17.** $y = -\frac{1}{2}x + \frac{3}{2}$ **18.** $y = -\frac{2}{3}x$

19. Does the point $(-3, 4)$ lie on the graph of $y = -2x + 1$? Explain.

20. Does the point $(2, 4)$ lie on the graph of $y = 3x - 2$? Explain.

Find the slope and *y*-intercept. Write an equation of each line.

21.   **22.**   **23.**

24. Recreation A group of mountain climbers begins an expedition with 265 lb of food. They plan to eat a total of 15 lb of food per day. The equation $r = 265 - 15d$ relates the remaining food supply r to the number of days d.
  a. Write the equation in slope-intercept form.
  b. Graph your equation.
  c. The group plans to eat the last of their food the day their expedition ends. Use your graph to find how many days the expedition will last.

25. Open-Ended Write an equation of your own. Identify the slope and y-intercept. Graph your equation.

26. Writing Explain how you would graph the line $y = \frac{3}{4}x + 5$.

Write an equation of a line with the given slope and y-intercept.

27. $m = \frac{2}{9}, b = 3$ **28.** $m = 5, b = -\frac{2}{3}$ **29.** $m = -\frac{5}{4}, b = 0$ **30.** $m = 0, b = 1$

Exercises   MIXED REVIEW

Find the slope of the line through each set of points.

31. $(-2, 8), (5, -1)$ **32.** $(4, 6), (2, -1)$ **33.** $(1, 2), (6, 1)$

34. The United States Postal Service delivers 177 billion pieces of mail each year. This number represents 40% of the world's mail. How many pieces are sent world-wide each year?

Getting Ready for Lesson 5-5

Through the given point, graph a line with the given slope. Then identify the y-intercept.

35. $(2, 0); m = -1$ **36.** $(2, 3); m = \frac{3}{2}$ **37.** $(3, 2); m = \frac{1}{3}$ **38.** $(-2, 1); m = -\frac{5}{2}$

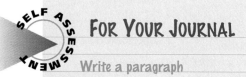

FOR YOUR JOURNAL
Write a paragraph explaining how to use the slope and y-intercept to write an equation and to draw a graph.

Exercises   CHECKPOINT

Is a line through the given point with the given slope a direct variation? Explain.

1. $(4, 2); m = \frac{1}{2}$ **2.** $(-2, -2); m = -1$ **3.** $(6, 9); m$ is undefined   **4.** $(-3, 5); m = -\frac{5}{3}$

5. Money In 1990, people charged $534 billion on the two most used types of credit cards. In 1994, people charged $1.021 trillion on these same two credit cards. What was the rate of change?

6. Writing How are the graphs of $y = 3x + 5$, $y = \frac{2}{3}x + 5$, and $y = \frac{3}{5}x + 5$ alike? How are they different?

Exploring Range and Scale

After Lesson 5-4

The minimum and maximum values for an axis determine the range of values shown on that axis. Screens A and B show the graph of $y = 4x$.

Screen A

Scale 1 means 1 unit between tic marks.

Xmin=–10   Ymin=–10
Xmax=10   Ymax=10
X s cl=1   Y s cl=1

Screen B

Scale 20 means 20 units between tic marks.

Xmin=–10   Ymin=–100
Xmax=10   Ymax=100
X s cl=1   Y s cl=20

Screen A shows standard settings for a graphing calculator screen.

The range on the y-axis is 10 times greater for Screen B than Screen A. So the line in Screen B appears flatter than the line in Screen A.

1. a. Explain how you would find the Xscl and Yscl for the screen at the right.
   b. Write an equation for the line shown on the screen.

To change the range, use the `WINDOW` feature. Then change the values of Xmin, Xmax, Ymin, or Ymax. For a negative number, use the `(-)` key. You can return to standard settings by pressing `ZOOM` `6`.

Xmin=–10   Ymin=–10
Xmax=10   Ymax=10
X s cl=▨   Y s cl=▨

2. a. *Open-ended* Graph the line $y = 2x + 30$ using standard settings. Then change the Ymin or Ymax value so that the y-intercept is on your screen. What Ymin or Ymax value did you choose?
   b. *Open-ended* Change the Xmin or Xmax value until you see where the line crosses the x-axis. Sketch your graph. State the minimum and maximum values you used for each axis.

Find Xmin, Xmax, Ymin, and Ymax values that allow you to see where each line crosses both axes. Sketch the graph of each equation.

3. $y = 3x + 20$ **4.** $y = -x + 100$ **5** $y = \frac{1}{5}x - 30$ **6.** $y = -\frac{1}{50}x + \frac{1}{10}$

7. $y = \frac{2}{3}x + 1500$ **8.** $y = -0.3x - 60$ **9.** $y = 55x + 55$ **10.** $y = -25x - \frac{1}{25}$

11. *Writing* How does changing the range affect how a graph looks?

What You'll Learn

5-5 **W**riting the Equation of a Line

- Writing an equation given the slope and a point
- Writing an equation given two points from a graph or a table

...And Why

To write equations to investigate real-world situations, such as carbon monoxide emissions

THINK AND DISCUSS

In some real-world situations you can identify the rate of change, or slope, and an ordered pair. Then you can use the slope and ordered pair to model the situation with a linear equation.

Example 1 **Relating to the Real World** ·················

Environment World-wide carbon monoxide emissions are decreasing about 2.6 million metric tons each year. In 1991, carbon monoxide emissions were 79 million metric tons. Use a linear equation to model the relationship between carbon monoxide emissions and time. Let $x = 91$ correspond to 1991.

Step 1 Use the data to write the slope and an ordered pair.

slope: -2.6; ordered pair: $(91, 79)$

Step 2 Find the y-intercept using the slope and the ordered pair.

$$y = mx + b$$
$$79 = -2.6(91) + b \quad \longleftarrow \text{Substitute (91, 76) for}$$
$$79 = -236.6 + b \qquad (x, y) \text{ and } -2.6 \text{ for } m.$$
$$315.6 = b$$

Step 3 Substitute values for m and b to write an equation.

$$y = mx + b$$
$$y = -2.6x + 315.6 \quad \longleftarrow \begin{array}{l}\text{Substitute } -2.6 \text{ for } m \\ \text{and } 315.6 \text{ for } b.\end{array}$$

The equation $y = -2.6x + 315.6$ models the relationship between carbon monoxide emissions and time.

1. a. Using the equation in Example 1, estimate the emissions for 1990.
   b. According to this model, what will the emissions be for 2000?

2. Try This Write an equation of a line with slope $\frac{2}{5}$ through the point $(4, -3)$.

You can use two points on a line to find an equation for the line. First find the slope of the line through the points. Then use the slope and one point to find the y-intercept and to write an equation of the line.

Example 2

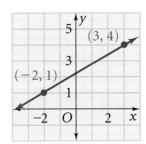

Find an equation of the line at the left.

Step 1 Use the coordinates of two points to find the slope of the line.

$$\text{slope} = \frac{y_2 - y_1}{x_2 - x_1}$$

$$= \frac{4 - 1}{3 - (-2)} \quad \longleftarrow \text{Substitute (3, 4) for } (x_2, y_2) \text{ and } (-2, 1) \text{ for } (x_1, y_1).$$

$$= \frac{3}{5}$$

Step 2 Find the y-intercept.

$$y = mx + b$$

$$4 = \frac{3}{5}(3) + b \quad \longleftarrow \text{Substitute (3, 4) for } (x, y) \text{ and } \frac{3}{5} \text{ for } m.$$
$$\phantom{4 = \frac{3}{5}(3) + b \quad \longleftarrow} \text{Solve for } b.$$

$$4 = \frac{9}{5} + b$$

$$2\frac{1}{5} = b$$

Step 3 Substitute values in $y = mx + b$.

$$y = \frac{3}{5}x + 2\frac{1}{5} \quad \longleftarrow \text{Substitute } \frac{3}{5} \text{ for } m \text{ and } 2\frac{1}{5} \text{ for } b.$$

3. Try This Find an equation of the line through $(-5, 3)$ and $(-2, -4)$.

You can also write a linear equation for data in tables. Two sets of data have a linear relationship if the rate of change between consecutive pairs of data is the same.

Example 3

x	y
-1	4
3	6
5	7
9	9

Is the relationship shown by the data linear? If it is, write an equation.

Step 1 Find the rate of change for consecutive ordered pairs.

$(-1, 4)$ to $(3, 6)$ $\qquad$ $(3, 6)$ to $(5, 7)$ $\qquad$ $(5, 7)$ to $(9, 9)$

$$\frac{6 - 4}{3 - (-1)} = \frac{2}{4} = \frac{1}{2} \qquad \frac{7 - 6}{5 - 3} = \frac{1}{2} \qquad \frac{9 - 7}{9 - 5} = \frac{2}{4} = \frac{1}{2}$$

The relationship is linear. The rate of change equals the slope. The slope is $\frac{1}{2}$.

Step 2 Find the y-intercept and write an equation.

$$y = mx + b$$

$$4 = \frac{1}{2}(-1) + b \quad \longleftarrow \text{Substitute } (-1, 4) \text{ for } (x, y) \text{ and } \frac{1}{2} \text{ for } m.$$

$$4 = -\frac{1}{2} + b$$

$$4\frac{1}{2} = b \quad \longleftarrow \text{Add } \frac{1}{2} \text{ to each side of the equation.}$$

$$y = \frac{1}{2}x + 4\frac{1}{2} \quad \longleftarrow \text{Substitute } \frac{1}{2} \text{ for } m \text{ and } 4\frac{1}{2} \text{ for } b \text{ in } y = mx + b.$$

PROBLEM SOLVING

Look Back Could you use a graph to find whether the relationship is linear? Explain.

4. Critical Thinking Is $(-1, 4)$ the only ordered pair that you could use to find the y-intercept in Example 3? Explain.

Write an equation of a line through the given point with the given slope.

1. $(3, -5); m = 2$ **2.** $(1, 2); m = -3$ **3.** $(2, 6); m = \frac{4}{3}$ **4.** $(-1, 5); m = -\frac{3}{5}$

5. $(0, 3); m = 1$ **6.** $(3, 0); m = -1$ **7.** $(-5, 2); m = 0$ **8.** $(6, 7); m$ undefined

9. $(3, 3); m = -\frac{1}{4}$ **10.** $(5, -2); m = \frac{7}{2}$ **11.** $(-6, 1); m = -\frac{3}{4}$ **12.** $(2.8, 10.5); m = 0.25$

13. a. Physics   Each gram of mass stretches the spring 0.025 cm. Use $m = 0.025$ and the ordered pair $(50, 8.5)$ to write a linear equation that models the relationship between the length of the spring and the mass.

     b. Critical Thinking   What does the y-intercept mean in this situation?

     c. What is the length of the spring for a mass of 70 g?

8.5 cm

50 g

Write an equation of a line through the given points.

14. $(3, -3), (-3, 1)$ **15.** $(7, 3), (2, 2)$ **16.** $(3, 5), (5, 3)$

17. $(-8, 2), (1, 3)$ **18.** $(-0.5, 2), (-2, 1.5)$ **19.** $(25, 100), (15, 120)$

Write an equation of each line.

20.   **21.**   **22.**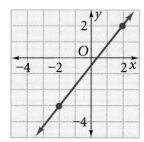

23. Entertainment   Total receipts for motion picture theaters were $3.9 billion in 1986. Receipts were $6.9 billion in 1992.

     a. Write an equation to model the relationship between receipts and time in years. Let 86 correspond to 1986.

     b. Use your equation to **predict** motion picture theater receipts in the year 2010. (*Hint:* Think about the number you will use for 2010.)

Tell whether the relationship shown by the data is linear. If it is, write an equation for the relationship.

24.

x	y
-10	-7
0	-3
5	-1
20	5

25.

x	y
-4	9
2	-3
5	-9
9	-17

26.

x	y
1	7
2	8
3	10
4	13

27.

x	y
-10	-5
-2	19
5	40
11	58

28.

x	y
3	1
6	4
9	13
15	49

29. a. Business A taxicab ride that is 2 mi long costs $7. One that is 9 mi long costs $24.50. Write an equation relating cost to length of ride.

   b. What do the slope and y-intercept mean in this situation?

30. National Parks The number of recreational visits to National Parks in the United States increases by about 9.3 million visits each year. In 1990 there were about 263 million visits.

   a. Write an equation to model the relationship between the number of visits and time in years. Let 90 correspond to 1990.

   b. Open-ended Suppose the number of recreational visits to National Parks continues to increase at the same rate. How many visits will there be this year?

Chapter Project   ***Find Out by Modeling***

> Suppose you earn $5.50/h at a bakery. From your first paycheck you discover that $1.15/h is withheld for taxes and benefits. You work x hours during a five-day week and you spend $3.75 each day for lunch.
>
> • Write an equation for your earnings for a week after taxes and expenses.
>
> • In this situation what does the slope represent? the y-intercept?
>
> • How many hours must you work to earn $120 after taxes and expenses?

Exercises MIXED REVIEW

Solve.

31. $4c < 24 + c$ **32.** $\frac{t}{2} + \frac{t}{3} = 5$ **33.** $-4m \geq 7$

34. $|5c| < 16$ **35.** $4(3h + 2) = 5h - 3$ **36.** $|2n + 5| \geq 9$

FOR YOUR JOURNAL

Explain how to use two points to find the equation of a line.

37. Real Estate In 1995, a new development was built near the home of Mary Davenport in Lawrence, Kansas. The appraised value of her property went from $41,500 to $426,870. What was the percent of change in the property's appraised value?

Getting Ready for Lesson 5-6

Determine whether each scatter plot shows *positive*, *negative*, or *no* correlation.

38.   **39.**   **40.**   **41.**

Displaying Data

Before Lesson 5-6

The data in the table are displayed on the two graphing calculator screens.

Data

Year	Profit (in thousands of dollars)
1990 ↔ 90	125
91	205
92	296
93	510
94	620
95	904
96	1040

List Display

L₁	L₂	L₃
90	125	-----
91	205	
92	296	
93	510	
94	620	
95	904	
96	1040	

L2 (7) = 1040

Scatter Plot Display

List Display To enter data into a list, press STAT 1 . Clear old data in column L1, by pressing ▲ CLEAR ENTER . Enter the year data in the first list. After each data item press ENTER . Press ▶ to move to column L2. Then clear any old data. Enter the second set of data.

Scatter Plot Display You can make a scatter plot of data that are in lists.

```
SET UP CALCS
1-Var Stats
Xlist: L1 L2 L3 L4 L5 L6
Freq:1 L1 L2 L3 L4 L5 L6
2-Var Stats
Xlist: L1 L2 L3 L4 L5 L6
Ylist: L1 L2 L3 L4 L5 L6
Freq:1 L1 L2 L3 L4 L5 L6
```

```
WINDOW FORMAT
Xmin=90
Xmax=100
Xscl=10
Ymin=0
Ymax=1100
Yscl=100
```

```
Plot1
On Off
Type: ▨ ⊾ ◻ ⊞
Xlist: L1 L2 L3 L4 L5 L6
Ylist: L1 L2 L3 L4 L5 L6
Mark: ◻ + ·
```

Step 1 Set Up Variables
Press STAT ▶ 3. Under 2-Var Stats, use the arrow keys to highlight L1 in the Xlist. Press ENTER .
Highlight L2 in the Ylist.

Step 2 Choose Range
The range for each variable should include the least and greatest number in the corresponding list.

Step 3 Make Graph Press 2nd Y= 1 ENTER .
Move the cursor and press ENTER to select the options shown. Then press GRAPH .

Display the data in a scatter plot. For each exercise, tell whether the data have a *positive correlation*, *negative correlation*, or *no correlation*.

1.

x	105	95	73	120	74	147	55	62
y	1.3	0.9	0.5	1.7	0.6	1.6	0.3	0.4

2.

x	10.1	10.6	11.1	12.3	9.3	13.1	10.6
y	47	35	64	22	55	27	9

3. **Writing** To view data to find correlations, do you prefer using a graphing calculator or graphing the data on graph paper? Why?

5-6 Scatter Plots and Equations of Lines

What You'll Learn

- Finding the equation of a trend line
- Using a calculator to find an equation for a line of best fit

...And Why

To analyze and make predictions based on real-world data

What You'll Need

- graphing calculator
- graph paper
- clock or watch with second hand

Ticket Sales for Forrest Gump

Week	Sales (in millions)
1	$39.9
2	$39.2
3	$35.3
4	$28.6
5	$22.9
6	$21.5

Source: *Variety*

THINK AND DISCUSS

Trend Line

Sometimes you can describe data that show a positive or negative correlation with a trend line. Then you can use the trend line to make predictions.

Example 1 **Relating to the Real World**

Entertainment A film usually makes the most money in ticket sales during the first few weeks after its release. Find the equation of a trend line for the data about ticket sales for *Forrest Gump*.

Step 1 Draw a scatter plot. Then use a straightedge to draw a trend line. There should be about the same number of points above and below the trend line. Estimate two points on your trend line.

Step 2 Find the slope and y intercept.

$$\text{slope} = \frac{22 - 40}{6 - 1} \qquad \leftarrow \frac{y_2 - y_1}{x_2 - x_1}$$

$$= -\frac{18}{5} = -3.6$$

$$y = mx + b \qquad \leftarrow \text{Use slope-intercept form to find the } y\text{-intercept.}$$

$$22 = -3.6(6) + b \qquad \leftarrow \text{Substitute } -3.6 \text{ for } m \text{ and } (6, 22) \text{ for } (x, y). \text{ Then solve for } b.$$

$$22 = -21.6 + b$$

$$43.6 = b \qquad \leftarrow \text{the } y\text{-intercept}$$

Step 3 Write an equation of the line.

$$y = -3.6x + 43.6 \qquad \leftarrow \text{Substitute } -3.6 \text{ for } m \text{ and } 43.6 \text{ for } b.$$

The equation $y = -3.6x + 43.6$ models the ticket sales.

1. Predict the ticket sales in the tenth week after the film's release.

Line of Best Fit

GRAPHING CALCULATOR HINT

The equation of the line of best fit will be in one of these forms:

$$y = ax + b$$

↑   ↑
slope *y*-intercept

$$y = a + bx$$

↑   ↑
y-intercept **slope**

The most accurate trend line showing the relationship between two sets of data is called the **line of best fit.** A graphing calculator computes the equation of a line of best fit using a method called linear regression.

The graphing calculator also gives you the **correlation coefficient** r, which will tell you how closely the equation models the data.

-1   0   1

negative   no   positive
correlation   correlation   correlation

When the data points cluster around a line, there is a strong correlation between the line and the data. The nearer r is to -1 or 1, the more closely the data cluster around the line of best fit.

Greeting Card Sales

Year	Sales (in billions)
1980	$2.05
1981	$2.30
1982	$2.45
1983	$2.70
1984	$3.20
1985	$3.45
1986	$3.65
1987	$3.75
1988	$3.90
1989	$4.20
1990	$4.60
1991	$5.00
1992	$5.35
1993	$5.60

Source: Greeting Card Association

Example 2   **Relating to the Real World**

Business Use a graphing calculator to find the equation of the line of best fit for the data at the left. Is there a strong correlation shown by the data?

Step 1 Let 80 correspond to 1980. Enter the data for years and then the data for sales in your graphing calculator.

Step 2 Find the equation for the line of best fit.

slope

y-intercept

correlation coefficient

```
LinReg
y=ax+b
a=.269010989
b=-19.54087912
r=.9936796698
```

The equation for the line of best fit is $y = 0.269010989x - 19.54087912$. Since r is very close to 1, there is a strong correlation shown by the data.

2. **Critical Thinking** What is the meaning of the slope for the data in Example 2?

3. Use the equation in Example 2 to **predict** sales of greeting cards in the year 2010.

4. **Try This** Find the equation of the line of best fit. Tell whether there is a strong correlation between the data.

a.

x	1	2	3	4	5
y	2	-3	8	9	-25

b.

x	1	2	3	4	5
y	21	15	12	9	7

Music   When you sing a song, your inner clock helps you keep the rhythm. Work with a partner or two to see if you keep a steady beat.

5. Data Collection   Choose a song. While you hum your song to yourself, tap out the beats. Have someone in your group count the number of beats you tap in 10 s, 20 s, 30 s, and 40 s.

6. Graph the data and find the equation of a trend line or use a graphing calculator to find the equation of the line of best fit.

7. Repeat Questions 5 and 6 for each person in your group.

8. Which song had the fastest beat? the slowest? How do you know?

9. Which of you kept a steady beat the best? How do you know?

Exercises   O N   Y O U R   O W N

Decide if the data in each scatter plot follow a linear pattern. If they do, find the equation of a trend line.

1. **Calories and Fat for Fast Food Meals**

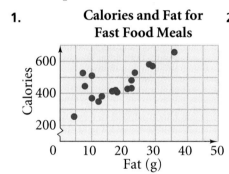

2. **Deer Population Bridger Mountains, Montana**

3. **Effect of Air Temperature on Speed of Sound**

4. **Olympic 5000 Meter Men's Speed Skating**

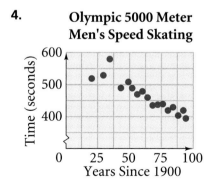

5. **Animal Longevity and Gestation**

6. **Public College Enrollment**

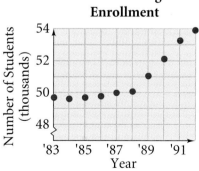

7. a. Data Collection   Measure the wrist and neck sizes of five different people. Make a scatter plot with the data you collected.

   b. Write an equation for your data. Then **predict** the neck size of someone whose wrist measures 6.5 in.

Critical Thinking **Match each graph with its correlation coefficient.**

8.   **9.**   **10.**

A. $r = -0.95$

B. $r = 0.13$

C. $r = 0.77$

For Exercises 11–14, follow these instructions.

a. Make a scatter plot of the data.

b. *Choose* Use paper and pencil to find the equation of a trend line, or use a graphing calculator to find the equation of the line of best fit.

c. Use your equation to make a prediction for the year 2005.

11.
Households with Television sets (in millions)

Year	Number
1986	158
1987	163
1988	168
1989	176
1990	193
1991	193
1992	192
1993	201

Source: *Statistical Abstract of the United States*

12.
Gallons of Ethanol Fuel Produced Annually (in millions)

Year	Amount
1987	820
1988	830
1989	850
1990	900
1991	960
1992	1080
1993	1200

Source: National Corn Growers Association; Renewable Fuels Association

Ethanol is a renewable fuel made from plants. In the United States, it is usually made from corn. In Brazil, the largest producer of ethanol, it is made from sugar cane.

13.
Hispanic Population Growth in the United States (percent of total population)

Year	Percent
1970	4.5
1980	6.4
1988	7.1
1990	9.0
1991	9.3
1992	9.5
1993	9.8

Source: United States Census Bureau

14.
Fast Food Sales (in billions)

Year	Sales
1985	$46.4
1986	$49.4
1987	$57.6
1988	$65.0
1989	$68.3
1990	$74.2
1991	$77.0

Source: United States Department of Agriculture

15. a. *Open-ended* Make a table of data for a linear function. Use a graphing calculator to find the equation of the line of best fit.

b. What is the correlation coefficient for your linear data?

16. a. Business Make a scatter plot of the data at the right. Find the equation of a trend line, or use a graphing calculator to find the equation of the line of best fit.
  b. Use your equation to **predict** the percent of refillable bottles used in 1950 and the percent that will be used in the year 2000.
  c. Are your answers to part(b) reasonable in the real-world situation? Explain.

17. Writing Decide whether the following statement is *true* or *false*. Then explain your answer: A trend line is a line that connects as many points in a set of data as possible.

18. a. Research Choose a topic below or one of your own. You can find data in an almanac or the *Statistical Abstract of the United States.*
  • population density of a state and its crime rate
  • population of a state and the number of physicians who practice there
  b. Find the equation of a trend line or use a graphing calculator to find the line of best fit for the data.
  c. Is there a strong correlation shown by the data? Explain.
  d. If the correlation is strong, use your equation to make a prediction.

19. a. Make a scatter plot of the data in the table below.
  b. Use a graphing calculator to find the equation of the line of best fit.
  c. Does the data show a strong correlation? Explain.
  d. Critical Thinking Do you think that the correlation would be similar for other school choruses? Why or why not?

Refillable Soft-Drink Containers

Year	Percent of Total Sold
1960	96
1965	84
1970	65
1975	57
1980	34
1985	23
1990	7

Members of the School Chorus

Age (in years)	13	15	17	16	16	13	14	15	17	17	16	14	14
Height (in inches)	62	70	65	62	71	59	64	63	68	60	67	60	61

Exercises   MIXED REVIEW

20. Health The spreadsheet shows the breathing rates for people of different ages.
  a. Write a formula for cell D2.
  b. Find the values of cells D2 through D7.

Solve each equation.

21. $3x + 4 = 73$ **22.** $-2.5 - 5z = -3z$

23. $\frac{4}{x} = \frac{2}{3 + x}$ **24.** $0.2t + 1.3 = -9.1$

25. $4(3y - 5) = 16$ **26.** $\frac{1}{2}x - \frac{3}{4} = \frac{3}{2} + x$

	A	B	C	D
1	Age	Breaths/min	Liters of oxygen/min	Liters of oxygen/breath
2	30–39	14.7	146.7	▦
3	40–49	14.6	139.1	▦
4	50–59	14.6	127.8	▦
5	60–69	14.2	117.3	▦
6	70–79	14.4	106.2	▦
7	80–89	13.2	75.5	▦

Source: *Prevention's Giant Book of Health Facts*

Getting Ready for Lesson 5-7

Find the value of *x* when *y* = 0.

27. $y = 3x + 8$ **28.** $4x - 5y = 7$ **29.** $y = \frac{1}{2}x - 10$ **30.** $y = 2x$

What You'll Learn

What You'll Learn

- Graphing equations using x- and y-intercepts
- Writing equations in $Ax + By = C$ form
- Modeling situations with equations in the form $Ax + By = C$

...And Why

To investigate real-world situations, such as burning calories when running and jogging

What You'll Need

- graph paper
- graphing calculator

5-7 $Ax + By = C$ Form

THINK AND DISCUSS

Graphing Equations

The slope-intercept form is just one form of a linear equation. Another form is $Ax + By = C$, which is useful in making quick graphs.

$Ax + By = C$ Form of a Linear Equation

$Ax + By = C$ is a linear equation, where A and B cannot both be zero.

$$3x + 4y = 8$$

To make a quick graph, you can use the x- and y-intercepts. The **x-intercept** is the x-coordinate of the point where a line crosses the x-axis.

Example 1

Graph $3x + 4y = 8$.

Step 1 To find the x-intercept, substitute 0 for y and solve for x.

$$3x + 4y = 8$$
$$3x + 4(0) = 8$$
$$3x = 8$$
$$x = \frac{8}{3}, \text{ or } 2\frac{2}{3}$$

The x-intercept is $2\frac{2}{3}$.

Step 2 To find the y-intercept, substitute 0 for x and solve for y.

$$3x + 4y = 8$$
$$3(0) + 4y = 8$$
$$4y = 8$$
$$y = 2$$

The y-intercept is 2.

Step 3 Plot $(2\frac{2}{3}, 0)$ and $(0, 2)$. Draw a line through the points.

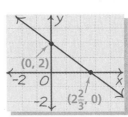

1. **Mental Math** Find the x- and y-intercept of each equation.

   a. $3x + 4y = 12$ **b.** $5x + 2y = -10$ **c.** $2x - y = 4$

To graph an equation on a graphing calculator, you must transform the equation to slope-intercept form. You can use the x- and y-intercepts to find an appropriate range for each axis.

1 Which equation represents a direct variation?
(1) $y = 2x$
(2) $y = x + 2$
(3) $y = x^2$
(4) $x + 2y = 2$

2 The equation of a line is $x - 3y = 6$. Find the slope of the line and the y-intercept.

Example 2

Graphing Calculator   Graph $5x - 3y = 120$.

Step 1 Write the equation in slope-intercept form.
$$5x - 3y = 120 \qquad \longleftarrow \text{Solve for } y.$$
$$-3y = -5x + 120 \qquad \longleftarrow \text{Subtract } 5x \text{ from each side.}$$
$$y = \frac{5}{3}x - 40 \qquad \longleftarrow \text{Divide each side by } -3.$$

Step 2 Find the x- and y-intercepts.
$$5x - 3y = 120$$
$$5x - 3(0) = 120$$
$$5x = 120$$
$$x = 24 \qquad \longleftarrow x\text{-intercept}$$

From Step 1, the y-intercept is –40.

Step 3 Set the ranges to include the x- and y-axes and the intercepts. Then graph $y = \frac{5}{3}x - 40$.

Xmin=–10   Ymin=–50
Xmax=30   Ymax=10
Xscl=5   Yscl=5

2. *Critical Thinking*   What advantage is there in making Xmin less than 0 and Xmax greater than 24 for the graph on the calculator?

3. Graphing Calculator   Graph $4x - 12y = 54$. Sketch your graph. Include Xmin, Xmax, Ymin, Ymax, and the x- and y-intercepts.

Writing Equations

You can write equations for real-world situations using the $Ax + By = C$ form.

Example 3   Relating to the Real World

Fitness   When you jog, you burn 7.3 calories/min. When you run, you burn 11.3 calories/min. Write an equation to find the times you would need to run and jog in order to burn 500 calories.

Define x = minutes spent jogging y = minutes spent running

Relate   7.3 × minutes jogging + 11.3 × minutes running = 500

Write $7.3x + 11.3y = 500$

4. **a.** Use the intercepts to graph the equation in Example 3, or graph the equation on a graphing calculator.
   b. *Open-ended*   Use your graph to estimate three different running and jogging times needed to burn 500 calories.

You can write an equation in $Ax + By = C$ form if you know the slope and one point. For a line with slope m through point (x_1, y_1), begin with the **point-slope form:**

$$\frac{y - y_1}{x - x_1} = m$$

Example 4

Write an equation of the line with slope $-\frac{1}{2}$ through the point $(-1, 7)$.

$\dfrac{y - y_1}{x - x_1} = m$ ⟵ Use the point-slope form.

$\dfrac{y - 7}{x - (-1)} = -\dfrac{1}{2}$ ⟵ Substitute $(-1, 7)$ for (x_1, y_1) and $-\frac{1}{2}$ for m.

$2(y - 7) = -1(x + 1)$ ⟵ Simplify $x - (-1)$ and cross multiply.

$2y - 14 = -x - 1$ ⟵ Use the distributive property.

$x + 2y = 13$ ⟵ Add x and 14 to each side in order to write $Ax + By = C$ form.

5. Critical Thinking How is $\dfrac{y - y_1}{x - x_1}$ related to the ratio for finding the slope of a line through two points?

Exercises   ON YOUR OWN

Match the equation with its graph.

1. $2x + 5y = 10$ **2.** $2x - 5y = 10$ **3.** $-2x + 5y = 10$

A.   **B.**   **C.**

Graph each equation.

4. $x + y = 2$ **5.** $5x - 12y = 30$ **6.** $-3x + y = 6$ **7.** $x - y = -7$

8. $-4x + y = -6$ **9.** $2x + 5y = 10$ **10.** $2x - y = 8$ **11.** $-3x + 4y = 12$

12. a. Fund Raising Suppose your school is having a dinner to raise money for new music and art supplies. You estimate that 200 children and 150 adults will attend. Write an equation to find what ticket prices you should set to raise $900.

    b. Open-ended Graph your equation. Choose three possible prices you could set for children's and adults' tickets. Explain which you think is the best choice.

13. **Writing** Two forms of a linear equation are the slope-intercept form and the $Ax + By = C$ form. Explain when each is most useful.

14. An equation is in standard form when A, B, and C are integers for $Ax + By = C$. Write each equation in standard form.

> **Sample:** $Ax + By = C$ Form   Standard Form
> $3.5x + 7.2y = 12$ ⟶ $35x + 72y = 120$ ⟵ Multiply each side by 10.

    a. $3.8x + 7.2y = 5.4$ **b.** $0.5x - 0.75y = 1.25$ **c.** $\frac{2}{3}x + \frac{1}{6}y = 4$

⊞ **Graphing Calculator** **Graph each equation. Make a sketch of the graph. Include the x- and y-intercepts.**

15. $12x + 15y = -60$ **16.** $8x - 10y = 100$ **17.** $-5x + 11y = 120$ **18.** $4x - 9y = -72$

19. $-3x + 7y = -42$ **20.** $12x - 9y = 144$ **21.** $9x + 7y = 210$ **22.** $3x - 8y = 72$

23. **Standardized Test Prep**
    a. Write $Ax + By = C$ in slope-intercept form by solving for y.
    b. Which expression equals the slope m?
        A. $-\frac{B}{A}$ **B.** $\frac{C}{A}$ **C.** $-\frac{A}{B}$ **D.** A **E.** $\frac{C}{B}$
    c. Which expression equals the y-intercept b?
        A. $-\frac{B}{A}$ **B.** $\frac{C}{A}$ **C.** $-\frac{A}{B}$ **D.** A **E.** $\frac{C}{B}$

Write an equation in $Ax + By = C$ form for the line through the given point with the given slope.

24. $(3, -4)$; $m = 6$ **25.** $(4, 2)$; $m = -\frac{5}{3}$ **26.** $(0, 2)$; $m = \frac{4}{5}$ **27.** $(-2, -7)$; $m = -\frac{3}{2}$

28. $(4, 0)$; $m = 1$ **29.** $(5, -8)$; $m = -3$ **30.** $(-5, 2)$; $m = 0$ **31.** $(1, -8)$; $m = -\frac{1}{5}$

32. **Nutrition** Suppose you are preparing a snack mix. You want the total protein from peanuts and granola to equal 28 g.
    a. Write an equation for the protein content of your mix.
    b. Graph your equation. Use your graph to find how many ounces of granola you should use if you use one ounce of peanuts.

Granola
Protein: 3 g/oz   Peanuts
Protein: 7 g/oz

Exercises   MIXED REVIEW

Probability **Find each probability.**

33. P(rolling a 2, then a 4 on a number cube)   **34.** P(getting heads on both coins when you toss two coins)

Getting Ready for Lesson 5-8
Graph each pair of lines on one set of axes.

35. $y = 4x + 1$
    $y = 4x - 3$

36. $y = 3x - 8$
    $y = -\frac{1}{3}x - 2$

37. $3y = 2x + 6$
    $y = \frac{2}{3}x + 4$

38. $4y = x - 8$
    $y = -4x - 1$

What You'll Learn

- Writing equations for parallel and perpendicular lines
- Using slope to determine if lines are parallel, perpendicular, or neither

...And Why

To investigate real-world situations, such as urban planning

5-8 Parallel and Perpendicular Lines

WORK TOGETHER

Work in pairs.

1. Match the story with its graph. Explain your choices.
   a. Elena gives her younger sister Rosa a head start in a race. Elena runs faster than her sister.
   b. Elena gives her younger sister Rosa a head start in a race. Elena is surprised that she and her sister run at the same rate.

A.

B.

2. a. In graph A, how far apart are the two runners at 0 s? 1 s? 2 s? 3 s?
   b. Suppose the race were longer and the pattern for the distance between runners remained the same as in part (a). Would the lines intersect? Explain.

3. What is the slope of each line in graph A?

THINK AND DISCUSS

Parallel Lines

In the Work Together activity, the lines in graph A are parallel. Two **parallel lines** are always the same distance apart. They do not intersect.

Slopes of Parallel Lines

Nonvertical lines are parallel if they have the same slope and different y-intercepts. Vertical lines are parallel.

Example The slope of $y = 2x + 3$ and $y = 2x - 5$ is 2. The graphs of these two equations are parallel.

---

4. Are horizontal lines parallel? Explain.

5. **Try This** What is the slope of a line parallel to $y = \frac{3}{5}x - 4$?

You can use slope to write an equation of a line parallel to a given line.

Example 1

Write an equation for a line that contains $(-2, 3)$ and is parallel to the graph of $5x - 2y = 8$.

Find the slope of $5x - 2y = 8$.

$5x - 2y = 8$
$-2y = -5x + 8$
$y = \frac{5}{2}x - 4$ ← The slope is $\frac{5}{2}$.

Use the slope-intercept form to find the y-intercept.

$y = mx + b$
$3 = \frac{5}{2}(-2) + b$ ← Substitute the coordinates $(-2, 3)$ for (x, y) and $\frac{5}{2}$ for m.
$3 = -5 + b$
$8 = b$ ← The y-intercept is 8.

The equation is $y = \frac{5}{2}x + 8$.

6. Why was the equation $5x - 2y = 8$ changed to slope-intercept form?

7. Graph $5x - 2y = 8$ and $y = \frac{5}{2}x + 8$. Do the lines appear parallel?

8. **Try This** Write an equation for the line that is parallel to $5x - 2y = 8$ and passes through the point $(4, 9)$.

9. Critical Thinking Is the line graphed by the equation $3x - 4y = 9$ parallel to the line graphed by the equation $y = -\frac{3}{4}x + 5$? Explain.

Perpendicular Lines

Perpendicular lines are lines that form right angles. The slopes of perpendicular lines also have a special relationship.

10. Find the slopes of the lines in each graph.

a.

b.

c.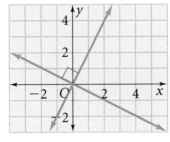

11. **a.** For each pair of lines, find the product of the slopes.
    b. What do you notice about the products of the slopes of the perpendicular lines?

Slopes of Perpendicular Lines

Two lines are perpendicular if the product of their slopes is -1.
A vertical and a horizontal line are perpendicular.

Example The slope of $y = -4x + 7$ is -4. The slope of $y = \frac{1}{4}x + 2$ is $\frac{1}{4}$. Since $-4 \cdot \frac{1}{4} = -1$, the graphs of the equations are perpendicular.

The product of two numbers is -1 if one number is the opposite of the reciprocal of the other. These numbers are called **opposite reciprocals**.

$$\text{fraction: } -\frac{3}{5} \qquad \text{reciprocal: } -\frac{5}{3} \qquad \text{opposite reciprocal: } \frac{5}{3}$$

12. Is $-\frac{2}{3}$ the opposite reciprocal of $\frac{3}{2}$? Explain.

13. Try This Find the slope of a line perpendicular to a line with this slope.

     a. -2 **b.** $\frac{2}{7}$ **c.** $\frac{1}{5}$ **d.** 0

You can use slope to write an equation of a line perpendicular to a given line.

Example 2   Relating to the Real World

Urban Planning A bike path for a new city park will connect the park entrance to Park Road. The path will be perpendicular to Park Road. Write an equation for the line representing the bike path.

 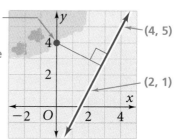

Find the slope m of Park Road.

$$m = \frac{y_2 - y_1}{x_2 - x_1} = \frac{5 - 1}{4 - 2} \quad \longleftarrow \text{Points (2, 1) and (4, 5) are on Park Road.}$$
$$= \frac{4}{2} = 2$$

The opposite of the reciprocal of 2 is $-\frac{1}{2}$. So the slope of the bike path is $-\frac{1}{2}$. The y-intercept is 4.

$$y = mx + b \quad \longleftarrow \text{Use the } y\text{-intercept form.}$$
$$y = -\frac{1}{2}x + 4 \quad \longleftarrow \text{Substitute } -\frac{1}{2} \text{ for } m \text{ and 4 for } b.$$

The equation for the bike path is $y = -\frac{1}{2}x + 4$.

14. Critical Thinking How can you use slope to tell if two lines are parallel, perpendicular, or neither?

Find the slope of a line parallel to the graph of each equation.

1. $y = \frac{1}{2}x + 2.3$ **2.** $y = -\frac{2}{3}x - 1$ **3.** $3x + 4y = 12$ **4.** $2x - 3y = -2$

5. $y = 6$ **6.** $x = 5$ **7.** $2x - y = 0$ **8.** $x = 0$

9. $y = -3x + 2.3$ **10.** $7x + 2y = 12$ **11.** $15x - 12y = 7$ **12.** $y = 0.5x - 8$

Find the slope of a line perpendicular to the graph of each equation.

13. $y = 2x$ **14.** $y = -3x$ **15.** $y = \frac{7}{5}x - 2$ **16.** $y = x$

17. $2x + 3y = 5$ **18.** $y = \frac{x}{-5} - 7$ **19.** $y = -8$ **20.** $x = 3$

21. $4x - 2y = 9$ **22.** $3x + 5y = 7$ **23.** $y = \frac{9}{2}x + 5$ **24.** $y = 0.25x$

Tell whether the lines for the pair of equations are *parallel, perpendicular,* or *neither.*

25. $y = 4x + \frac{3}{4}, y = -\frac{1}{4}x + 4$ **26.** $y = \frac{x}{3} - 4, y = \frac{1}{3}x + 2$ **27.** $y = -x + 5, y = x + 5$

28. $5x + y = 3, -5x + y = 8$ **29.** $x = 2, y = 9$ **30.** $y = x, y = x + 2$

31. **Graphing Calculator** The graphs of $y = x$ and $y = -x$ are shown on the standard screen at the right. The product of the slopes is -1. Explain why the lines do not appear to be perpendicular.

32. a. Open-ended Write an equation for a line parallel to the graph of $y = 4x - 1$.
   b. Can you write more than one equation for part (a)? Explain.

33. a. Are the lines $3x + 5y = 6$ and $3x + 5y = 2$ parallel? Explain.
   b. Explain how you can tell that the lines $7x - 3y = 5$ and $7x - 3y = 8$ are parallel without finding slopes.

34. Writing Suppose a friend missed class today. Explain what you would tell your friend about using slope to find each equation.
   a. the equation of a line parallel to a given line
   b. the equation of a line perpendicular to a given line

35. Geometry Are the points $(3, 8)$, $(5, 4)$ and $(-3, 3)$ the vertices of a right triangle? Explain.

36. a. Maps What is the slope of New Hampshire Avenue?
   b. Show that parts of Pennsylvania Avenue and Massachusetts Avenue near New Hampshire Avenue are parallel.
   c. Show that New Hampshire Avenue is not perpendicular to Pennsylvania Avenue.

Geometry A quadrilateral with both pairs of opposite sides parallel is a parallelogram. Use slopes to show if each figure is a parallelogram.

37.

38.

39.
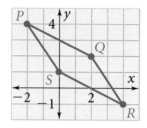

40. Standardized Test Prep Which of the following statements is true for the graphs of equations I and II?

    I: $2x + y = 15$ **II:** $3y = -6x + 30$

  A. The graphs of I and II are parallel.
  B. The graphs of I and II are perpendicular.
  C. The graphs of I and II are the same line.
  D. The graphs of I and II are neither parallel nor perpendicular.
  E. none of the above

Write an equation that satisfies the given conditions.

41. parallel to $y = 6x - 2$, through $(0, 0)$

42. perpendicular to $y = 2x + 7$, through $(0, 0)$

43. perpendicular to $y = x - 3$, through $(4, 6)$

44. parallel to $y = -3x$, through $(3, 0)$

45. parallel to $y = -\frac{2}{3}x + 12$, through $(5, -3)$

46. perpendicular to $y = -4x - \frac{5}{2}$, through $(1, 6)$

Tell whether each statement is *true* or *false*. Explain your choice.

47. In a coordinate plane, every horizontal line is perpendicular to every vertical line.

48. Two lines with positive slopes can be perpendicular.

49. Two lines with positive slopes must be parallel.

50. The graphs of two direct variations can be parallel.

Geometry A quadrilateral with four right angles is a rectangle. Use slopes to show whether each figure is a rectangle.

51.

52.

53.
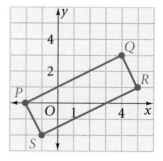

Chapter Project

Find Out by Interviewing

Interview an adult about a job he or she had as a teenager. Ask about positive and negative aspects of the job, salary, and expenses. Set up an equation that describes the person's earnings after expenses for a week.

Exercises   MIXED REVIEW

Solve.

54. $\frac{x}{2} + \frac{x}{3} = 6$

55. $3m - 4m > 2$

56. $-\frac{x}{4} > 3$

57. $9y - 3 > 5y + 1$

58. Social Studies There were 132,300 African Americans among the troops serving in the Gulf War, or 24.5% of the total. How many troops served in the Gulf War?

FOR YOUR JOURNAL

How can you identify parallel and perpendicular lines from their slopes?

Getting Ready for Lesson 5-9

Find the value of x when $y = 0$.

59. $y = 3x + 8$

60. $4x - 5y = 7$

61. $y = \frac{1}{2}x - 10$

62. $2x + 3y = 6$

Exercises   CHECKPOINT

Change each equation to $Ax + By = C$ form.

1. $3y = 2x + 6$

2. $y = 4x - 7$

3. $y = \frac{1}{3}x + 5$

4. $15y = 9x - 12$

Write an equation for a line that contains the given points.

5. $(3, 4)$ and $(-1, 5)$

6. $(0, -3)$ and $(\frac{1}{2}, 6)$

7. $(-7, -5)$ and $(7, 5)$

8. $(5, 9)$ and $(5, 10)$

Find the equation of a trend line or the line of best fit.

9.

x	1	2	3	4	5	6	7
y	7	12	19	20	28	33	40

10.

x	1	2	3	4	5	6	7
y	54	52	45	40	33	27	18

Open-ended Write an equation of a line that is parallel to each line and an equation of a line that is perpendicular to each line.

11. $y = 3x - 2$

12. $4x + 5y = 10$

13. $y = \frac{2}{3}x + \frac{1}{6}$

14. $y = 1.6x - 0.4$

15. Standardized Test Prep Which equation represents a line with the same y-intercept as $y = 4x - 3$?
  A. $y - 3 = x$ **B.** $y = 8x + 3$ **C.** $2y = 8x - 3$ **D.** $5x + 6y = -18$ **E.** $x = 3$

What You'll Learn

5-9 **U**sing the *x*-intercept

- Using the *x*-intercept of a linear equation to solve the related one-variable equation

...And Why

To use graphs to solve and check equations and to investigate business situations

What You'll Need

- graph paper
- graphing calculator

WORK TOGETHER

Work with a partner.

1. Solve the equation $\frac{2}{3}x + 4 = 0$.

2. **a.** Graph the function $y = \frac{2}{3}x + 4$.
   b. What is the value of *x* when the line crosses the *x*-axis?
   c. What is the value of *y* when the line crosses the *x*-axis?

3. Compare the results of Questions 1 and 2. What do you notice?

THINK AND DISCUSS

There is a special relationship between a one-variable equation and the related linear function. The solution of a one-variable equation equals the *x*-intercept of the graph of the related linear function.

One-Variable Equation   Related Linear Function

$$\frac{2}{3}x + 4 = 0 \qquad\qquad y = \frac{2}{3}x + 4$$

Notice that one side of the one-variable equation is 0. You replace 0 with *y* to write the related linear function.

QUICK REVIEW

The *x-intercept* is the *x*-coordinate of the point where a line crosses the *x*-axis.

Math A Test Prep

1 A line parallel to $y = \frac{2}{3}x - 5$ passes through the point (6, 8). Which other point lies on the line?
(1) (15, 2)   (3) (2, 14)
(2) (−3, 2)   (4) (−3, 14)

2 You are setting ticket prices for the fair, estimating that 350 students and 200 adults will attend.
a Write an equation for ticket prices that result in sales of $1300.
b Graph the equation.
c Choose two possible pairs of ticket prices that you could set. Explain.

Example 1

Solve $\frac{3}{4}x - 2 = -5$ by graphing.

Step 1 Write the equation so that one side is 0.

$$\frac{3}{4}x - 2 = -5$$

$$\frac{3}{4}x + 3 = 0 \quad \longleftarrow \text{Add 5 to both sides.}$$

Step 2 Replace 0 with *y* to write a function.

$$y = \frac{3}{4}x + 3$$

Step 3 Graph the function. Then find the *x*-intercept.

The solution of $\frac{3}{4}x - 2 = -5$ is −4.

x-intercept is −4.

Check $\quad \frac{3}{4}x - 2 = -5$

$$\frac{3}{4}(-4) - 2 \stackrel{?}{=} -5 \quad \longleftarrow \text{Substitute } -4 \text{ for } x.$$

$$-3 - 2 \stackrel{?}{=} -5$$

$$-5 = -5 ✔$$

4. Try This Solve each equation by graphing. Check each solution.

a. $2x + 4 = 0$ **b.** $6x + 7 = 10$ **c.** $\frac{1}{2}x - 3 = 0$

You can use a graphing calculator to solve a one-variable equation. Graph the related linear function. Next graph the equation for the *x*-axis, $y = 0$. To find the *x*-intercept, find the intersection point of the two lines.

Example 2

 Graphing Calculator   Find the solution of $5x - 12 = 0$.

PROBLEM SOLVING

Look Back **Describe how to check the solution of Example 2. Then check that the solution is 2.4.**

Graph $y = 5x - 12$ and $y = 0$.
The solution is 2.4.

Use the CALC feature to find the coordinates of the intersection point.

When starting a business, people want to know the **break-even point,** the point at which their income equals their expenses.

Example 3   Relating to the Real World

Business Suppose you invested \$140 to start a business selling painted T-shirts. You sell each shirt for \$7.50. Find the break-even point.

Relate   income = expenses

Define x = the number of shirts you sell

Write $7.50x = 140$

Rewrite the equation as $7.50x - 140 = 0$. The related function is $y = 7.5x - 140$.

Graph $y = 7.5x - 140$ and $y = 0$.

Select a range that includes the *x*-intercept.

Find the intersection point of the lines.

The break-even point is about 18.7.
You must sell 19 shirts to make a profit.

5. Graphing Calculator Use the TABLE feature on your calculator to find values for *y* close to 0 in Example 3. How can the TABLE feature help you choose range values for the *x*-axis?

Exercises   O N   Y O U R   O W N

Write the function you would graph to find the solution of each one-variable equation.

1. $3x - 8 = 0$

2. $7 = \frac{1}{2}x + 4$

3. $-x + 5 = 9$

Match each equation with its related graph.

4. $5 - 3x = 0$ **A.**

5. $\frac{x}{3} - 2 = 0$

6. $x + 5 = 0$

B.

C.

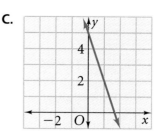

Solve each equation using a graph. Check each answer.

7. $0 = 2x + 3$

8. $3x + 4 = 13$

9. $4x - 3 = 9$

10. $-x + 7 = 13$

Choose **Solve each equation using a graphing calculator or with paper and pencil. Check each answer.**

11. $3x - 5 = 12$

12. $\frac{2x}{5} = -4$

13. $3x = 75$

14. $5(x + 2) = 18$

15. $27 = \frac{x}{3} + 15$

16. $\frac{3}{4}x + 6 = -20$

17. $4(x - 6) = 5$

18. $25x - 18 = 72$

19. Money Suppose you build birdhouses. An investment of $100 allows you to build ten houses. You sell each house for $15.
  a. Write an equation relating the income to the expenses.
  b. Graph a related linear function to find the break-even point.
  c. Suppose you sell all the houses. How much profit will you make?

20. Physical Science In 1787, the French scientist Jacques Charles discovered that as a gas cooled at a constant pressure, the relationship between volume and temperature was linear. Suppose that at 60°C the volume of the gas is 555 cm³ and at 30°C the volume is 505 cm³.
  a. Write a linear function relating volume of gas to temperature.
  b. Jacques Charles used a linear function to find *absolute zero*, the temperature at which a gas theoretically will have no volume. Graph your function to find absolute zero in degrees Celsius.

21. Open-ended Write a one-variable equation. Solve your equation using a graph.

Jacques Charles

22. Writing What advantages and disadvantages do you see in using a calculator to solve equations?

 Graphing Calculator **Solve each equation using a graphing calculator.**

23. $\frac{2x}{7} + 5 = 0$ **24.** $2x + 10 = -15$ **25.** $-8(x - 6) = 18$ **26.** $\frac{4}{5}x - 18 = 15$

Critical Thinking **Is each statement** *true* **or** *false*? **Explain.**

27. A vertical line has no x-intercept.

28. The x-intercept of a direct variation is 0.

29. The x-intercept of $y = mx + b$ is the solution to $mx + b = 0$.

Exercises   M I X E D   R E V I E W

Evaluate each function for $x = -3.2$.

30. $f(x) = |5 - x|$ **31.** $f(x) = 3x - 2$

32. $f(x) = 4x^2 - 8$ **33.** $f(x) = (x + 1)^2$

34. Zoology In July 1995, three Siberian tigers were born in Garden City, Kansas. There were already about 100 Siberian tigers in the United States. By what percent did the population increase?

A Point in Time

Judith A. Resnik

On August 30, 1984, Astronaut Judith A. Resnik became the second American woman to fly in space, on the shuttle *Discovery's* first voyage. Resnik was an electrical engineer with a Ph.D. from the University of Maryland. On the ground she helped to design and develop a remote manipulator system, a task that required skill in linear equations. Her job during *Discovery's* six-day voyage was to manipulate a robotic arm and to extend and retract the shuttle's solar power array. Resnik died tragically in the shuttle *Challenger* disaster in 1986.

Taking
THE
PLUNGE

Questions on pages 224, 239, and 255 should help you complete your project. Work with several classmates. Share what you have learned about jobs for a teenager. List positive and negative features about income and expenses for several jobs. On your own, assemble your graphs, equations, and job information in a notebook. Write a final paragraph that explains what job you would like and why.

Reflect and Revise

Your notebook should present job comparison information in a well-organized format. Are your graphs easy to understand? Have you explained clearly how your equations fit each job? Make any revisions necessary to improve your project.

Follow Up

Sometimes employers will hire only people with experience. You can get experience by creating your own job. Find out how to start your own business from the resources below.

For More Information

Bernstein, Daryl. *Better Than a Lemonade Stand: Small Business Ideas for Kids.* Hillsboro, Oregon: Beyond Words Publications, 1992.

Menzies, Linda. *A Teen's Guide to Business: The Secrets to a Successful Enterprise.* New York: MasterMedia, 1992.

Key Terms

$Ax + By = C$ form (p. 246)
break-even point (p. 257)
constant of variation (p. 225)
correlation coefficient (p. 242)
dimensional analysis (p. 219)
direct variation (p. 225)
linear equation (p. 225)
linear function (p. 221)
line of best fit (p. 242)

parallel lines (p. 250)
perpendicular lines (p. 251)
rate of change (p. 220)
slope (p. 214)
slope-intercept form
  (p. 231)
x-intercept (p. 246)
y-intercept (p. 230)

How am I doing?

- State three ideas from this chapter that you think are important. Explain your choices.
- Describe two ways that you can write an equation of a line.

Slope and Rates of Change

5-1, 5-2

Rate of change allows you to look at how two quantities change relative to each other. **Slope** is the ratio of the vertical change to the horizontal change. The rate of change is also called slope.

$$\text{slope} = \frac{\text{vertical change}}{\text{horizontal change}} = \frac{\text{rise}}{\text{run}}$$

$$\text{rate of change} = \frac{\text{change in the dependent variable}}{\text{change in the independent variable}}$$

Find two points on each graph. Then find the slope.

1.

2.

3.

Find the rate of change for each situation.

4. reading 5 pages in 6 min and 22 pages in 40 min

5. walking 1.5 mi in 25 min and 4 mi in 80 min

6. scoring 3 goals in 5 games and 9 goals in 7 games

7. copying 4 pages in 1 min and 52 pages in 5 min

Direct Variation

5-3

A function is a **direct variation** if it has the form $y = kx$, where $k \neq 0$. The coefficient k is the **constant of variation**.

Each set of ordered pairs is for a direct variation. Find each missing value.

8. $(4, 8)$ and $(3, y)$

9. $(-3, 9)$ and $(x, -12)$

10. $(16, y)$ and $(4, -1)$

Slope-Intercept Form

The **y-intercept** of a line is the y-coordinate of the point where the line crosses the y-axis. The **slope-intercept form** of a linear equation is $y = mx + b$, where m is the slope and b is the y-intercept.

Write an equation of a line with the given slope and y-intercept. Then graph each equation.

11. $m = \frac{3}{4}, b = 8$ **12.** $m = -7, b = \frac{1}{2}$ **13.** $m = \frac{2}{5}, b = 0$ **14.** $m = 0, b = -3$

Writing the Equation of a Line

When you know the slope of a line and a point on it, solve for the y-intercept. Then use the slope and the y-intercept to write an equation.

When you know two points on a line, first find the slope of the line through the points. Then find the y-intercept and write an equation.

Write an equation of a line through the given points.

15. $(4, 3), (-2, 1)$ **16.** $(5, -4), (0, 2)$ **17.** $(-1, 0), (-3, -1)$ **18.** $(2, 7), (-8, 4)$

Write an equation for each line.

19.   **20.**   **21.**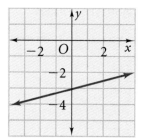

Scatter Plots and Equations of Lines

The **line of best fit** of a scatter plot is the most accurate trend line showing the relationship between the sets of data. You can find the equation of the line of best fit using a graphing calculator. The **correlation coefficient** tells how closely the equation models the data.

22. The table shows the average person's consumption of poultry from 1970 to 1993.

   a. Find the equation of a trend line or use a graphing calculator to find the equation of the line of best fit.

   b. Use your equation to **predict** how much poultry the average person will eat in 2005.

Average Poultry Consumption (pounds/person)

Year	Pounds
1970	33.8
1975	32.9
1980	40.6
1985	45.2
1990	56.0
1993	61.1

Ax + By = C Form

The **x-intercept** of a line is the x-coordinate of the point where the line crosses the x-axis. When a line is in **Ax + By = C form,** you can use the x- and y-intercepts to make a graph of the equation.

Find the x- and y- intercepts. Then graph each equation.

23. $5x + 2y = 10$ **24.** $6.5x - 4y = 52$ **25.** $-x + 3y = -15$ **26.** $8x - y = 104$

Parallel and Perpendicular Lines

Parallel lines have the same slope. Two lines are **perpendicular** if the product of their slopes is -1.

Write an equation that satisfies the given conditions.

27. parallel to $y = 5x - 2$, through $(2, -1)$ **28.** perpendicular to $y = -3x + 7$, through $(3, 5)$

29. parallel to $y = 9x$, through $(0, -5)$ **30.** perpendicular to $y = 8x - 1$, through $(4, 10)$

31. Open-ended Write the equations of four lines that form a rectangle.

Using the x-intercept

You can use a linear function to solve the related one-variable equation. Graph the linear function. The x-intercept is the solution of the related one-variable equation.

32. You start a lawn-mowing business. You buy a used power mower for $175. You plan to charge $30 per lawn.
  a. Write an equation relating your income to expenses.
  b. Graph the related linear function to find your break-even point.

33. Writing How is the break-even point related to profit?

34. Standardized Test Prep What is the x-intercept of $3x - 2y = 6$?
  A. -3 **B.** -2 **C.** 2 **D.** 3 **E.** -5

Getting Ready for.. ▶ CHAPTER

6

Graph each pair of equations on the same set of axes.

35. $y = 3x - 6$
     $y = -x + 2$

36. $y = -2x - 4$
     $y = 0.5x + 9$

37. $y = 6x + 1$
     $y = 6x - 4$

38. $y = x + 5$
     $y = -3x + 5$

39. $y = x^2$
     $y = 4x + 9$

40. $y = -4$
     $y = 2x^2 + 1$

Tell if each statement is *true* or *false*. Explain.

1. A rate of change must be positive.

2. The rate of change for a vertical line is 0.

Find the slope of the line passing through each pair of points.

3. $(4, 3), (3, 8)$

4. $(-2, 1), (6, -1)$

Draw the graph of a direct variation that includes the given point.

5. $(2, 2)$ 6. $(-8, -4)$ 7. $(3, -1)$ 8. $(-5, 3)$

Write each equation in $y = mx + b$ form.

9. $-7y = 8x - 3$

10. $x - 3y = -18$

11. $5x + 4y = 100$

12. $9x = 2y + 13$

Find the x- and y-intercepts of each line.

13. $3x + 4y = -24$

14. $2y = 3x - 8$

15. $y = 0.3x + 6$

16. $y = -x + 1$

17. **Writing** Explain why the x- and y-intercepts of a direct variation are always zero.

Write an equation of the line with the given slope that contains the given point.

18. slope $= 3, (4, -8)$

19. slope $= \frac{8}{3}, (-2, -7)$

20. slope $= -\frac{1}{2}, (0, 3)$

21. slope $= -5, (9, 0)$

Write an equation of the line that contains the given points.

22. $(4, 9), (-2, -6)$

23. $(-1, 0), (3, 10)$

24. $(5, -8), (-9, -8)$

25. $(0, 7), (1, 5)$

26. Which of the following lines is *not* perpendicular to $y = -2.5x + 13$?
    A. $y = 0.4x - 7$
    B. $-2x + 5y = 8$
    C. $y = \frac{2}{5}x + 4$
    D. $2y = 5x + 1.5$

Write an equation of a line that satisfies the given conditions.

27. parallel to $y = 5x$, through $(2, -1)$

28. perpendicular to $y = -2x$, through $(4, 0)$

29. parallel to $y = 5$, through $(-3, 6)$

30. perpendicular to $x = -7$, through $(0, 2)$

31. **Open-ended** Write the equation of a line parallel to $y = 0.5x - 10$.

32. You start a pet-washing service. You spend $30 on supplies. You charge $5 to wash each pet.
    a. Write an equation to relate your income y to the number of pets x you wash.
    b. Graph the equation. What are the x- and y-intercepts?
    c. How many pets do you need to wash to break even?

Use the data below for Exercises 33 and 34.

**Local Governments in the United States
(in thousands)**

Year	Municipalities	School Districts
1962	18.0	34.7
1967	18.0	21.8
1972	18.5	15.8
1977	18.9	15.2
1982	19.1	14.9
1987	19.2	14.7
1992	19.3	14.6

33. a. **Graphing Calculator** Find the equation of a trend line or the line of best fit for the number of municipalities and the year.
    b. **Predict** the number of municipalities in 2005.

34. a. **Graphing Calculator** Find the equation of a trend line or the line of best fit for the number of school districts and the year.
    b. Do the data show a strong correlation? Explain.

Part I

1 A horizontal line passes through $(5, -2)$. Which other point does it also pass through?
(1) $(5, 2)$ (3) $(-5, 2)$
(2) $(-5, -2)$ (4) $(5, 0)$

2 During the 6-week period, which kitten's weight showed the greatest rate of change?

(1) Kitten A   (3) Kitten C
(2) Kitten B   (4) Kitten D

3 Which equation represents a direct variation?
(1) $5y = 2x$ (3) $x + 5y = 2$
(2) $y^2 = 5x$ (4) $y = \frac{2}{5}x + 2$

4 Which equation is represented by this graph?
(1) $y = 2x + 3$
(2) $y = -2x + 3$
(3) $y = 2x - 3$
(4) $y = -2x - 3$

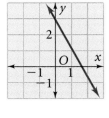

5 Which equation describes the line that passes through $(4, -8)$ and has a slope of $\frac{1}{4}$?
(1) $y = 4x - 8$ (3) $y = -\frac{1}{2}x + \frac{1}{4}$
(2) $y = \frac{1}{4}x + 6$ (4) $y = \frac{1}{4}x - 9$

6 A line perpendicular to $y = 3x - 2$ passes through the point $(0, 6)$. Which other point lies on the line?
(1) $(9, 3)$ (3) $(-9, -3)$
(2) $(-9, 3)$ (4) $(9, -3)$

7 Which inequality describes the numbers for which the following statement is true? The sum of a number and 15 is more than 27 but less than 32.
(1) $27 < n < 32$ (3) $n + 27 < 32$
(2) $n + 15 > 27$ (4) $12 < n < 17$

8 If $3x + 2 = 11$, then $5x + 1 = \blacksquare$.
(1) 3   (2) 21   (3) 16   (4) 15

Part II

9 Each gram of fat in a certain food contains 9 calories. Find the constant of variation and write an equation relating calories c to grams of fat g.

10 Write an equation for the line that passes through the points $(2, 3)$ and $(-4, 1)$.

Part III

11 Mariko runs 800 ft in one minute. What is the rate of change in her position, in miles per hour? Round to the nearest unit.

12 Find the x- and y- intercepts of the line described by the equation $5x + 3y = 15$. Then graph the line.

Part IV

13 Graph the data shown in the table. Draw a trend line and write its equation.

x	1	1	2	3	4	4	5	6
y	0	−1	1	6	8	7	12	15

14 The base charge for cab fare is $1.20. There is an additional charge of $.40 for each $\frac{1}{5}$ mile the cab travels.
a Write an equation in slope-intercept form that relates total cab fare to length of trip.
b Graph your equation.
c Use your graph to find the cost of taking a cab 1.8 miles from the train station to the museum.

Relating to the Real World

Often real-world problems contain more than one unknown quantity and more than one simple relationship. By writing two or more equations and solving the system, environmental and industrial planners can find the best way of assigning and using resources.

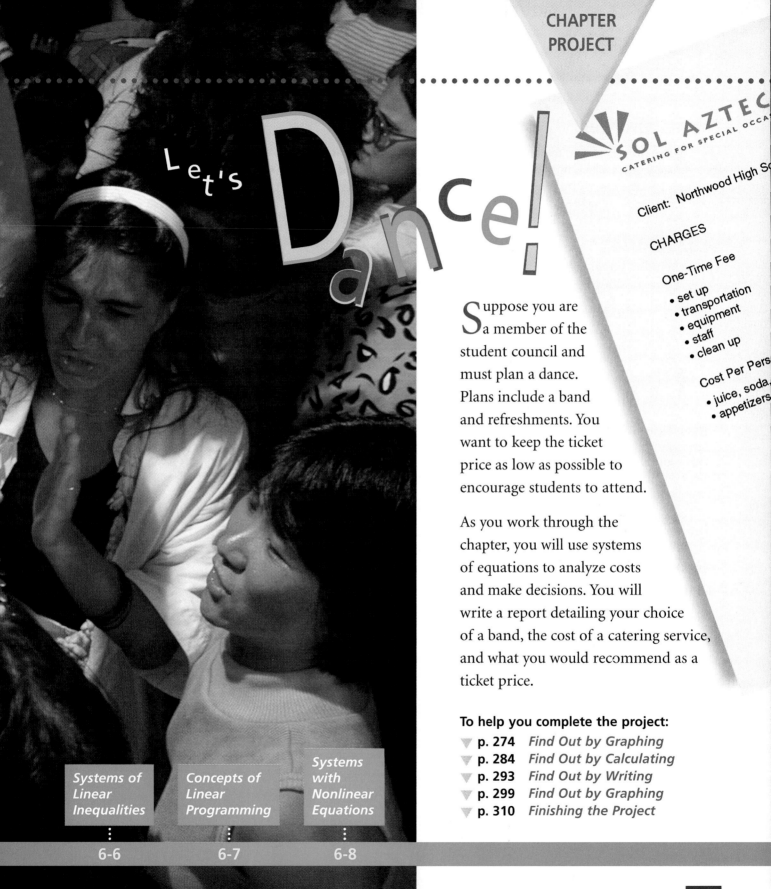

Let's Dance!

SOL AZTEC
CATERING FOR SPECIAL OCCA...

Client: Northwood High S...

CHARGES

One-Time Fee
- set up
- transportation
- equipment
- staff
- clean up

Cost Per Pers...
- juice, soda,
- appetizers

Suppose you are a member of the student council and must plan a dance. Plans include a band and refreshments. You want to keep the ticket price as low as possible to encourage students to attend.

As you work through the chapter, you will use systems of equations to analyze costs and make decisions. You will write a report detailing your choice of a band, the cost of a catering service, and what you would recommend as a ticket price.

To help you complete the project:

Systems of Linear Inequalities

Concepts of Linear Programming

Systems with Nonlinear Equations

6-6   6-7   6-8

Guess and Test

Before Lesson 6-1

You can use the *Guess and Test* strategy to solve many types of problems. First, make a guess. Then test your guess against the conditions of the problem. Use the results from your first guess to make a more accurate guess. Continue to guess and test until you find the correct answer.

Example

The ratio of boys to girls in a ninth-grade class at a high school is about 3 to 2. There are about 600 ninth-graders. How many are boys? girls?

Guess the number of boys.　　Subtract your guess from 600.　　Write the ratio and compare.

	Number of Boys	Number of Girls	$\dfrac{\text{boys}}{\text{girls}} \overset{?}{=} \dfrac{3}{2} = 1.5$
First guess	400	$600 - 400 = 200$	$\dfrac{400}{200} = 2$
Second guess	350	$600 - 350 = 250$	$\dfrac{350}{250} = 1.4$
Third guess	375	$600 - 375 = 225$	$\dfrac{375}{225} = 1.\overline{6}$
Fourth guess	360	$600 - 360 = 240$	$\dfrac{360}{240} = 1.5$

← too high, so try a lower number of boys

← too low, so try a number between 350 and 400

← too high, so try a number between 350 and 375

← correct

There are about 360 ninth-grade boys and 240 ninth-grade girls.

Solve each problem.

1. Find a pair of integers with a product of 32 and a sum of 12.

2. Find a pair of integers with a sum of 114 and a difference of 2.

3. Livingston is 25 mi east of Bozeman, Montana. Lisa left Bozeman at 2:00 P.M., driving east on I-90 at 65 mi/h. Jerome left Livingston at 2:00 P.M., driving west on I-90 at 55 mi/h.
   a. At what time will Lisa pass Jerome?
   b. How far will Lisa be from Bozeman when she passes Jerome?

4. Shigechiyo Izumi of Japan lived to be one of the oldest people in the world. Carrie White was the oldest known person in the United States. Carrie lived 4 years fewer than Izumi. The sum of their ages is 236 years. How many years did each person live?

5. **Writing** Describe some advantages and disadvantages of using *Guess and Test* to solve a problem.

6-1 Solving Systems by Graphing

What You'll Learn

• Solving systems of linear equations by graphing

...And Why

To solve problems by comparing costs for services like television

What You'll Need

• graph paper
• graphing calculator

QUICK REVIEW

The slope-intercept form of a linear equation is $y = mx + b$, with m = slope and b = y-intercept.

THINK AND DISCUSS

Solving Systems with One Solution

How can you show all the solutions of the linear equation $y = 2x - 3$? Graph the line, of course! Each point on the line is a solution.

Linear Equation
$y = 2x - 3$

1. **Open-ended** Use the graph to write three different solutions of the equation $y = 2x - 3$. Then show that each ordered pair makes the equation true.

Two or more linear equations together form a **system of linear equations.** One way to solve a system of linear equations is by graphing. Any point common to all the lines is a **solution of the system.** So, any ordered pair that makes *all* the equations true is a solution of the system.

Example 1

Solve the system of linear equations by graphing.
$$y = 2x - 3$$
$$y = x - 1$$

Graph both equations on the same coordinate grid.

$y = 2x - 3$: slope is 2,
     y-intercept is -3.
$y = x - 1$: slope is 1,
     y-intercept is -1.

Find the point of intersection.

The lines intersect at $(2, 1)$, so $(2, 1)$ is the solution of the system.

Check See if $(2, 1)$ makes both equations true.

$$y = 2x - 3 \qquad\qquad\qquad\qquad\qquad y = x - 1$$
$$1 \stackrel{?}{=} 2(2) - 3 \quad\longleftarrow\text{ Substitute (2, 1) }\longrightarrow\quad 1 \stackrel{?}{=} 2 - 1$$
$$1 \stackrel{?}{=} 4 - 3 \qquad\qquad \text{for } (x, y). \qquad\qquad 1 = 1 \checkmark$$
$$1 = 1 \checkmark$$

It checks, so $(2, 1)$ is the solution of the system of linear equations.

2. Try This Solve the system $y = x + 5$. Check your solution.
$$y = -4x$$

3. *Critical Thinking* Do you think a system of linear equations always has exactly one solution? Draw diagrams to support your answer.

You can use the graph of a system of linear equations to solve problems.

| Example 2 | Relating to the Real World |

Entertainment A cable company offers a "pay-per-view" club. Let c = the annual cost and n = the number of movies you watch in a year. Graph the system of equations below to decide whether to join the club.

Members: $c = 4n + 24$
Non-members: $c = 5.50n$

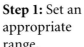

Watch Pay-Per-View!
Great Rates for Members Only:
Pay only $24/year . . .
Watch all your favorites
for ONLY $4 each!
(Non-members pay $5.50!)

Step 1: Set an appropriate range.

WINDOW FORMAT
Xmin=0
Xmax=30
Xscl=2
Ymin=0
Ymax=120
Yscl=10■

Step 3: Use the CALC key to find the coordinates of the intersection point.

Y₁⬛4X+24
Y₂⬛5.5X
Y₃=
Y₄=
Y₅=
Y₆=
Y₇=
Y₈=

Step 2: Input the equations. Let $n = x$ and $c = y$.

Intersection
X=16   Y=88

 GRAPHING CALCULATOR HINT

You can also use the TABLE feature to find the intersection point. The ZOOM and TRACE keys will only estimate the intersection point.

The solution of the system is $(16, 88)$ where $(x, y) = (n, c)$.

Check See if $(16, 88)$ makes both equations true.

$$c = 4n + 24 \qquad\qquad\qquad\qquad c = 5.50n$$
$$88 \stackrel{?}{=} 4(16) + 24 \quad\longleftarrow \text{Substitute 16 for } n \qquad 88 \stackrel{?}{=} 5.50(16)$$
$$88 \stackrel{?}{=} 64 + 24 \qquad \text{and 88 for } c. \longrightarrow \qquad 88 = 88 \checkmark$$
$$88 = 88 \checkmark$$

You find that 16 movies in a year cost $88 for both members and nonmembers. If you plan to watch more than 16 movies in a year, join the club. If you plan to watch fewer than 16, do not join the club.

 PROBLEM SOLVING HINT

For Question 4, you can use *Guess and Test* or *Draw a Graph.*

4. Suppose the annual fee is $15 instead of $24. What advice would you give a friend on whether or not to join the club?

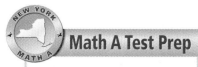
1 Find the solution of this system.

$x = -1$
$x - y = -2$

(1) $(-1, -1)$
(2) $(1, -1)$
(3) $(-1, 1)$
(4) $(1, 1)$

2 Corey said that if a point is not a solution of a system of two equations, then it is not a solution of either equation in the system. Is he correct? Explain.

Solving Special Types of Systems

A system of linear equations has **no solution** when the graphs of the equations are parallel. There are no points of intersection, so there is no solution.

$y = -x + 1$
$y = -x - 1$

$y = 3x - 2$
$y = 3x$

5. *Critical Thinking* Without graphing, how can you tell that a system has no solution? Give an example.

A system of linear equations has **infinitely many solutions** when the graphs of the equations are the same line. All points on the line are solutions of the system.

Example 3

Solve the system by graphing. $-4y = 4 + x$

$\frac{1}{4}x + y = -1$

First, write each equation in slope-intercept form.

$-4y = 4 + x$ $\frac{1}{4}x + y = -1$

$y = -\frac{1}{4}x - 1$ $y = -\frac{1}{4}x - 1$

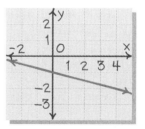

Then graph each equation on the same coordinate plane.

Since the graphs are the same line, the system has infinitely many solutions.

6. What do you notice about the slope-intercept form of each equation in Example 3? How could this help you solve a linear system?

7. **Try This** Solve each system by graphing.

   a. $y = x$ **b.** $2x + 2y = 1$ **c.** $x = 1$

   $y = x + 6$ $y = -x + \frac{1}{2}$ $x = -2$

PROBLEM SOLVING HINT

Start with the known information and use the strategy *Work Backward* to write an appropriate system.

Work with a partner to copy and complete the table. Your goal is to create a system of equations that satisfies the conditions given.

	System of Equations	Description of Graph	One Solution of the System	Number of Solutions
8.	■	2 intersecting lines	$(1, -5)$	■
9.	■	2 non-intersecting lines	■	■
10.	■	■	■	infinitely many

Graphing Calculator **Solve each system of linear equations by graphing. Sketch the graph on your paper.**

1. $y = \frac{1}{3}x + 3$
$y = \frac{1}{3}x - 3$

2. $y = x$
$y = 5x$

3. $y = 1$
$y = x$

4. $2x + y = 3$
$x - 2y = 4$

5. $3x - y = 7$
$y = 3x - 7$

6. Number Theory You can represent the set of nonnegative even numbers by the expression $2n$, for $n = 0, 1, 2, \ldots$. You can represent the set of nonnegative odd numbers by $2n + 1$, for $n = 0, 1, 2, \ldots$.
 a. Copy and complete the table at the right.
 b. Graph the system. $y = 2n$ $y = 2n + 1$
 c. Writing Why does it makes sense that this system has no solution?

n	Even Numbers $2n$	Odd Numbers $2n + 1$
0	$2(0) = 0$	$2(0) + 1 = 1$
1	■	■
2	■	■
3	■	■
4	■	■
5	■	■

Is $(-1, 5)$ a solution of each system? Verify your answer.

7. $x + y = 4$
$x = -1$

8. $y = -x + 4$
$y = -\frac{1}{5}x$

9. $y = 5$
$x = y - 6$

10. $y = 2x + 7$
$y = x + 6$

11. Below is a retelling of an Aesop fable. Use the story to answer the questions below.

One Day, the tortoise challenged the hare to a race. The hare laughed, while bragging about how fast a runner he was. On the day of the race, the hare was so confident that he took a nap during the race. When he awoke, he ran as hard as he could, but he could not beat the slow-but-sure tortoise across the finish line.

 a. The graph shows the race of the tortoise and the hare. What labels should be on each axis?
 b. Which color indicates the tortoise? Which indicates the hare?
 c. What does the point of intersection mean?

12. Math in the Media Suppose you see the two summer jobs advertised at the right. Let $x =$ the amount of sales and $y =$ money earned in a week.

Cellular Phone Sales: $y = 150 + 0.2x$
Stereo Sales: $y = 200 + 0.1x$

   a. To earn the same amount of money at both jobs, how much will you need to sell in a week?
   b. After talking with salespeople, you estimate weekly sales of about $600 with either job. At which job will you earn more money?

> **Sales Position**
> Salesperson Wanted
> Knowledge of Cellular Phones
> On-Site Sales
> $150/week + 20% commission

> **CAREER OPPORTUNITY**
> Sell Stereo Equipment in
> National Electronics Retail Chain!
> $200/week + 10% commission

Solve each system by graphing. Write *no solution* or *infinitely many solutions* where appropriate.

13. $y = -x + 4$
$y = 2x + 1$

14. $x = 10$
$y = -7$

15. $y = 3x$
$y = 5x$

16. $y = 3x + 4$
$4y = 12x + 16$

17. $3x + y = 5$
$x - y = 7$

18. $2x - 2y = 4$
$y - x = 6$

19. $x + y = -1$
$x + y = 1$

20. $y = 1$
$3y + x = 9$

21. $y = \frac{1}{2}x - 1$
$y = -\frac{1}{2}x - 1$

22. $x + 2y = 3$
$-x = 2y - 3$

23. $y = 4x - 3$
$y = 4x + 2$

24. $y = \frac{3}{4}x - 5$
$x = 4$

Critical Thinking **Is each statement *true* or *false*? Explain your reasoning.**

25. A system of linear equations can have one solution, no solution, or infinitely many solutions.

26. If a point is a solution of a system of linear equations, it is also a solution of each linear equation in the system.

27. If a point is a solution of a linear equation, it is also a solution of any system containing that linear equation.

28. If a system of linear equations has no solution, the graphs of the lines are parallel.

> **PROBLEM SOLVING HINT**
> For Exercises 25–28, you can *Draw a Graph.*

Without graphing, decide whether the lines in each system *intersect, are parallel,* or *are the same line*. Then write the number of solutions.

29. $y = 2x$
$y = 2x - 5$

30. $x + y = 4$
$2x + 2y = 8$

31. $y = -3x + 1$
$y = 3x + 7$

32. $3x - 5y = 0$
$y = \frac{3}{5}x$

33. $2y - 10x = 2$
$y = 5x + 1$

34. $y = -4x + 4$
$y = -4x + 8$

35. $y = x + 1$
$y = \frac{1}{2}x$

36. $y = 2x + 3$
$y - 2x = 5$

Open-ended **Write a system of two linear equations with the given characteristics.**

37. one solution; perpendicular lines

38. no solutions; one equation is $y = 2x + 5$

39. one solution; $(0, -4)$

40. infinitely many solutions; one equation is $y = 4x$

41. Music Suppose you and your friends form a band, and you want to record a demo tape. Studio A rents for $100 plus $50/h. Studio B rents for $50 plus $75/h. Let t = the number of hours and c = the cost.

$$\text{Studio A:} \qquad c = 100 + 50t$$
$$\text{Studio B:} \qquad c = 50 + 75t$$

   a. Solve the system by graphing.
   b. Explain what the solution of the system means in terms of your band renting a studio.

42. Writing When equivalent equations form a system, there are infinitely many solutions. Explain in your own words why this is true.

Chapter Project ▽ **Find Out by Graphing**

Band A charges $600 to play for the evening. Band B charges $350 plus $1.25 for each ticket sold. Write a linear equation for the cost of each band. Graph each equation and find the number of tickets for which the cost of the two bands will be equal.

Estimation Estimate the solution of each system. Use the equations to test your estimate. Adjust your estimate until you find the exact solution.

43. $y = 6.5$
   $y = x + 2$

44. $y = -4x - 10$
   $y = -6$

45. $y = -0.75x - 3$
   $y = 0.25x - 7$

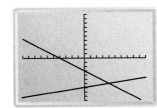

46. $y = -x - 1$
   $y = x + 8$

Exercises   MIXED REVIEW

Probability Find each probability for two rolls of a number cube.

47. $P(3, \text{ then } 4)$

48. $P(1, \text{ then even})$

49. $P(\text{two integers})$

50. $P(\text{at least one } 1)$

Write an inequality to model each situation.

51. Polar bears can swim as fast as 6 mi/h.

52. Each eyelash is shed every 3 to 5 months.

53. a. Geography Cairo, Egypt, has about 18 million residents. The average population density is 130,000 people/mi². What is Cairo's area?
   b. Cairo has $\frac{1}{4}$ of Egypt's population. What is the population of Egypt?

Egypt

Getting Ready for Lesson 6-2

Solve each equation for the given variable.

54. $x - y = 3; y$

55. $\frac{1}{2}x = 4y; x$

56. $\frac{x}{2} = \frac{y}{4}; y$

57. $2x - 3y = 5; x$

What You'll Learn

6-2 Solving Systems Using Substitution

- Solving systems of linear equations by substitution

...And Why

To solve problems involving transportation

What You'll Need

- graph paper
- graphing calculator

System:
$y = x + 6.1$
$y = -2x - 1.4$

W O R K   T O G E T H E R

Work with a partner.

1. **Estimation** Use the graph at the left to estimate the solution of the system.

2. **a.** *Graphing Calculator* Graph the system at the left.
   b. Use the **CALC** or **TABLE** features to find the intersection point.

3. Compare your estimate to your answer in Question 2(b).

4. **Choose** Use paper and pencil or a calculator to solve each system.
   a. $y = 3x - 6$
   $y = -6x$
   b. $y = x + 2.5$
   $y = 2x - 0.5$
   c. $2y - x = 3$
   $y = x - 2$

5. Explain why you chose the method(s) you used in Question 4.

T H I N K   A N D   D I S C U S S

Solving Systems with One Solution

Sometimes you won't have a graphing calculator to use. Another way to solve a system is to use substitution. **Substitution** allows you to create a one-variable equation.

Example 1

Solve the system $y = x + 6.1$ using substitution.
$$y = -2x - 1.4$$

$y = -2x - 1.4$ ⟵ Start with one equation.
$x + 6.1 = -2x - 1.4$ ⟵ Substitute $x + 6.1$ for y in that equation.
$3x = -7.5$ ⟵ Solve for x.
$x = -2.5$

Substitute -2.5 for x in either equation and solve for y.

$y = (-2.5) + 6.1$
$y = 3.6$

Since $x = -2.5$ and $y = 3.6$, the solution is $(-2.5, 3.6)$.

Check See if $(-2.5, 3.6)$ satisfies the other equation.

$3.6 \overset{?}{=} -2(-2.5) - 1.4$
$3.6 \overset{?}{=} 5 - 1.4$
$3.6 = 3.6$ ✔

PROBLEM SOLVING

Look Back Does the solution agree with the graph of the system in the Work Together?

6. Try This Solve each system using substitution. Check your solution.

a. $y = 2x + 1$
$y = x + 3$

b. $y = 2x$
$7x - y = 15$

c. $x + y = 6$
$x = -3y$

There is more than one way to solve a system using substitution. Solving for a variable with a coefficient of 1 or −1 is a good place to start. No matter what variable you solve for first, you should always get the same answer.

Example 2   **Relating to the Real World**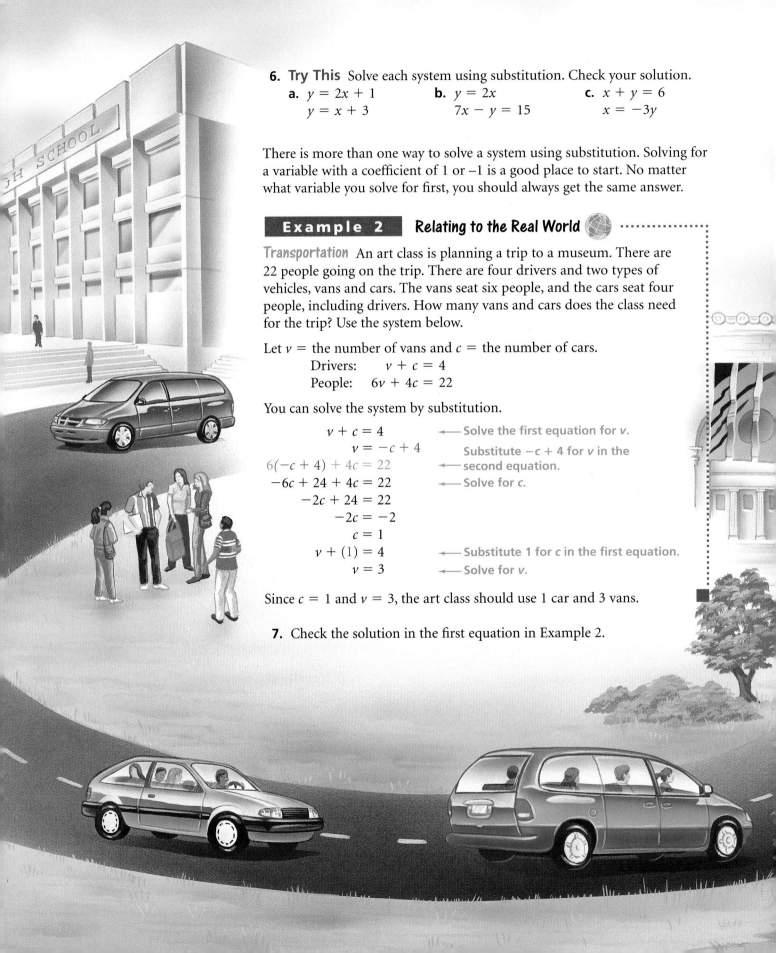

Transportation An art class is planning a trip to a museum. There are 22 people going on the trip. There are four drivers and two types of vehicles, vans and cars. The vans seat six people, and the cars seat four people, including drivers. How many vans and cars does the class need for the trip? Use the system below.

Let v = the number of vans and c = the number of cars.

Drivers: $v + c = 4$
People: $6v + 4c = 22$

You can solve the system by substitution.

$v + c = 4$ ←— Solve the first equation for v.
$v = -c + 4$ Substitute $-c + 4$ for v in the
$6(-c + 4) + 4c = 22$ ←— second equation.
$-6c + 24 + 4c = 22$ ←— Solve for c.
$-2c + 24 = 22$
$-2c = -2$
$c = 1$
$v + (1) = 4$ ←— Substitute 1 for c in the first equation.
$v = 3$ ←— Solve for v.

Since $c = 1$ and $v = 3$, the art class should use 1 car and 3 vans.

7. Check the solution in the first equation in Example 2.

8. a. Solve the system in Example 2 again. This time, start by solving the second equation for *c*.

    b. *Critical Thinking* Why is this procedure more difficult?

9. Describe a possible first step for solving each system by substitution.

    a. $3x - y = 17$
       $2x + y = 8$

    b. $x + 3y = 5$
       $2x - 4y = -5$

    c. $y = -2x - 3$
       $y = x$

Solving Special Types of Systems

You can use substitution to learn that systems have *no solution* or *infinitely many solutions.*

Example 3

Solve the system using substitution. $x + y = 6$
                                $5x + 5y = 10$

$$x + y = 6 \quad\longleftarrow \text{ Solve the first equation for } x.$$
$$x = 6 - y$$
$$5(6 - y) + 5y = 10 \quad\longleftarrow \begin{array}{l}\text{Substitute } 6 - y \text{ for } x\\ \text{in the second equation.}\end{array}$$
$$30 - 5y + 5y = 10 \quad\longleftarrow \text{ Solve for } y.$$
$$30 = 10 \quad\longleftarrow \text{ False!}$$

Since $30 = 10$ is a false statement, the system has no solution.

10. Describe the graph of the system in Example 3. Graph the system to **verify** your answer.

11. *Critical Thinking* How many solutions does a system of linear equations have if you get each result?

    a. a true statement, such as $2 = 2$

    b. a false statement, such as $10 = 1$

    c. a statement such as $x = 4$

12. Graphs of systems with no solution are parallel lines. What do you know about the equations of parallel lines?

13. Graphs of systems with infinitely many solutions are the same line. What do you know about the equations?

14. Without using substitution, decide whether each system has *no solution* or *infinitely many solutions.* (*Hint:* Write each equation in slope-intercept form and compare.)

    a. $3x - y = -2$
       $y = 3x + 2$

    b. $y = 4x$
       $2x - 0.5y = 0$

    c. $3x + y = 5$
       $6x + 2y = 1$

Critical Thinking **Suppose you try to solve a system of linear equations and get the following result. How many solutions does each system have?**

1. $x = 0$ **2.** $5 = 5$ **3.** $-3 = 2$ **4.** $n = 10$

5. $0 = 0$ **6.** $-8 = k$ **7.** $y = 6$ **8.** $0 = -9$

9. Geometry A rectangle is 4 times longer than it is wide ($l = 4w$). The perimeter of the rectangle is 30 cm ($2l + 2w = 30$). Find the dimensions of the rectangle.

10. Internet Suppose you want access to the Internet. With a subscription to *Access*, you pay $7.95 per month plus $2.95 per on-line hour. With a subscription to *Network*, you pay $12.95 per month plus $1.95 per on-line hour. The system below models this situation. Let c = the monthly cost and h = the number of on-line hours.

     Access: $c = 7.95 + 2.95h$
     Network: $c = 12.95 + 1.95h$

   a. Use substitution to solve the system.
   b. Explain how to decide which subscription to buy.

Solve each system using substitution. Write *no solution* or *infinitely many solutions* where appropriate.

11. $y = 2x$ **12.** $2x + y = 5$ **13.** $y = 3x + 1$ **14.** $x - 3y = 14$
     $6x - y = 8$ $2y = 10 - 4x$ $x = 3y + 1$ $x - 2 = 0$

15. $2x + 2y = 5$ **16.** $y = -3x$ **17.** $4x + y = -2$ **18.** $3x + 5y = 2$
     $y = \frac{1}{4}x$ $y + 3x = 2$ $-2x - 3y = 1$ $x + 4y = -4$

19. $y = x + 2$ **20.** $y = 3$ **21.** $x + 4y = -3$ **22.** $2y = 0.2x + 7$
     $y = 2x - 1$ $y = \frac{4}{3}x + 2$ $2x + 8y = -6$ $3y - 2x = 2$

Estimation **Graph each system to estimate the solution. Then use substitution to find the exact solution of the system.**

23. $y = 2x$ **24.** $y = \frac{1}{2}x + 4$ **25.** $x + y = 0$ **26.** $y = 0.7x + 3$ **27.** $y = 3x + 1$
     $y = -6x + 4$ $y = -4x - 5$ $5x + 2y = -3$ $y = -1.5x - 7$ $y = 3x - 2.5$

28. Writing Describe the advantages of using substitution to solve a system. **Justify** your answer with an example.

29. Standardized Test Prep Which system has no solution?
   A. $y = x + 3$ **B.** $2x + 2y = 1$ **C.** $y = \frac{1}{2}x + 1$
      $y + 4x = -2$ $y = -x + \frac{1}{2}$ $6y - 3x = 6$

   D. $y = x + 6$ **E.** $y = 2x - 1$
      $2y - 2x = 3$ $y = -2x$

Match each system with its solution at the right.

30. $y = x + 1$
$y = 2x - 1$

31. $2y - 8 = x$
$2y + 2x = 2$

32. $2y = x + 3$
$x = y$

33. $x - y = 1$
$x = \frac{1}{2}y + 2$

A. $(3, 2)$

B. $(3, 3)$

C. $(-2, 3)$

D. $(2, 3)$

How many solutions does each system have?

34. $3y + x = -1$
$x = -3y$

35. $2x + 4y = 0$
$y = -\frac{1}{2}x$

36. $y = 6x$
$y = 3x$

37. $5x - y = 1$
$5x - y = 7$

38. If two linear equations have the same slope and different y-intercepts, their graphs are __?__ lines. Such a system has __?__ solution(s).

39. Agriculture A farmer grows only soybeans and corn on his 240-acre farm ($s + c = 240$). This year he wants to plant 80 more acres of soybeans than of corn ($s = c + 80$). How many acres does the farmer need to plant of each crop?

40. Open-ended Write a system of linear equations with exactly one solution. Use substitution to solve your system.

Choose **Solve each system by graphing or using substitution.**

41. $y = -2x + 3$
$y = x - 6$

42. $y = \frac{1}{4}x$
$x + 2y = 12$

43. $y = 0$
$4x - y = 1$

44. $x - 3y = 1$
$2x - 6y = 2$

45. $x - y = 20$
$2x + 3y = 0$

46. $y = -x$
$x + y = 5$

47. $x = -2$
$3x - 2y = 4$

48. $0.4x + 0.5y = 1$
$x - y = 7$

Exercises   M I X E D   R E V I E W

Find the slope and y-intercept of each line.

49. $y = 7x - 4$ **50.** $3x + 8y = 16$ **51.** $y = 9x$ **52.** $5y = 6x - 25$

53. Write a linear function that passes through the points $(2, 3)$ and $(4, 6)$.

54. Human Biology The largest bone in the body is the femur. In a 5-ft tall woman, the femur is about 1.3 ft long. The smallest bone in the body, the stapes, is in the ear. It is only about 0.1 in. long. The femur is about how many times as long as the stapes?

stapes

femur

Getting Ready for Lesson 6-3
Simplify each expression.

55. $(x + 4) - 4(2x + 1)$ **56.** $5(2x - 3) + (7x + 15)$ **57.** $3(x - 2) + 6(2x + 1)$

What You'll Learn

- Solving systems of linear equations using elimination

...And Why

To investigate real-world situations, such as sales

What You'll Need

- graph paper

QUICK REVIEW

If $a = b$ and $c = d$, then
$a + c = b + d$ and
$a - c = b - d$.

PROBLEM SOLVING

Look Back Why was y eliminated?

6-3   Solving Systems Using Elimination

THINK AND DISCUSS

Adding or Subtracting Equations

When both linear equations of a system are in the form $Ax + By = C$, you can solve the system using **elimination.** You can add or subtract the equations to eliminate a variable.

Example 1

Solve the system using elimination. Check your solution.

$$5x - 6y = -32$$
$$3x + 6y = 48$$

First, eliminate one variable.

$$
\begin{array}{r}
5x - 6y = -32 \\
3x + 6y = 48 \\
\hline
8x + 0 = 16 \\
x = 2
\end{array}
$$

         ←—Add the equations to eliminate y.
         ←—Solve for x.

Then, find the value of the eliminated variable.

$$
\begin{aligned}
3x + 6y &= 48 &&\text{←—Pick one equation.}\\
3(2) + 6y &= 48 &&\text{←—Substitute 2 for } x.\\
6 + 6y &= 48 &&\text{←—Solve for } y.\\
6y &= 42 \\
y &= 7
\end{aligned}
$$

Since $x = 2$ and $y = 7$, the solution is $(2, 7)$.

Check   See if $(2, 7)$ makes the other equation true.

$$
\begin{aligned}
5(2) - 6(7) &\overset{?}{=} -32 \\
10 - 42 &\overset{?}{=} -32 \\
-32 &= -32 \;\checkmark
\end{aligned}
$$

Example 2   Relating to the Real World

Basketball Altogether 292 tickets were sold for a high school basketball game. An adult ticket costs $3. A student ticket costs $1. Ticket sales were $470. Use the system to find the number of each type of ticket sold.

number of tickets sold: $a + s = 292$
money collected: $3a + s = 470$

First, eliminate one variable.

$$
\begin{array}{r}
a + s = 292 \\
3a + s = 470 \\
\hline
-2a + 0 = -178 \\
a = 89
\end{array}
$$

         ←—Subtract the equations to eliminate s.
         ←—Solve for a.

Then, find the value of the eliminated variable.

$$89 + s = 292 \quad \longleftarrow \text{Substitute 89 for } a \text{ in the first equation.}$$
$$s = 203 \quad \longleftarrow \text{Solve for } s.$$

There were 89 adult tickets sold and 203 student tickets sold.

1. Check the solution to Example 2.

2. Would you *add* or *subtract* the equations to eliminate a variable?

   a. $a - b = 8$ b. $-3x + 2y = 1$ c. $m + t = 6$
      $a + 2b = 5$ $4x - 2y = -3$ $5m + t = 14$

3. **Try This** Use elimination to solve the system in Question 2(a).

Multiplying First

To eliminate a variable, you may need to multiply one or both equations in a system by a nonzero number. Then add or subtract the equations.

> **Example 3** **Relating to the Real World**

Sales Suppose your class receives $1084 for selling 205 packages of greeting cards and gift wrap. Let $w =$ the number of packages of gift wrap sold and $c =$ the number of packages of greeting cards sold. Use the system to find the number of each type of package sold.

total number of packages: $w + c = 205$
total amount of sales: $4w + 10c = 1084$

In the first equation, the coefficient of w is 1. In the second equation, the coefficient of w is 4. So multiply the first equation by 4. Then subtract to eliminate w.

$$w + c = 205: \quad 4w + 4c = 820 \quad \longleftarrow \begin{array}{l}\text{Multiply each}\\ \text{side of the first}\\ \text{equation by 4.}\end{array}$$
$$\underline{4w + 10c = 1084}$$
$$-6c = -264 \quad \longleftarrow \begin{array}{l}\text{Subtract the}\\ \text{two equations.}\end{array}$$
$$c = 44 \quad \longleftarrow \text{Solve for } c.$$

Find w.
$$w + c = 205 \quad \longleftarrow \text{Use the first equation.}$$
$$w + 44 = 205 \quad \longleftarrow \text{Substitute 44 for } c.$$
$$w = 161 \quad \longleftarrow \text{Solve for } w.$$

The class sold 161 packages of gift wrap and 44 packages of greeting cards.

4. Could you have multiplied the first equation by 10 rather than 4 and then solved the system? Why or why not?

For systems with no solution or infinitely many solutions, look for the same results as you did when you used substitution.

When you solve systems using elimination, plan a strategy. A flowchart like this one may help you to decide how to eliminate a variable.

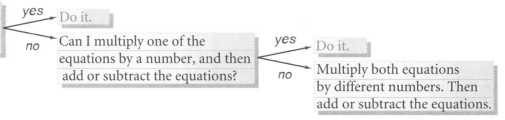

Can I eliminate a variable by adding or subtracting the given equations? *yes* → Do it.

no → Can I multiply one of the equations by a number, and then add or subtract the equations? *yes* → Do it.

no → Multiply both equations by different numbers. Then add or subtract the equations.

WORK TOGETHER

Work in groups.

5. Suppose you want to solve this system using elimination.
$$3x - 2y = 6$$
$$5x + 7y = 41$$
 a. What would you multiply each equation by to eliminate x?
 b. What would you multiply each equation by to eliminate y?
 c. Solve the system using elimination. Be sure to check your solution.

Decide which method makes solving each system easier: graphing, substitution, or elimination. Then solve the system and explain the method you chose.

6. $-5a + 14b = 13$
   $9a = 72b$

7. $3p - 8q = 4$
   $9p - 4q = 5$

8. $y = \frac{2}{3}x - 1$
   $y = -x + 4$

9. Describe how to solve this system using elimination.
   $x - 2y = 8$
   $y = x + 4$

Exercises   ON YOUR OWN

Describe a first step for solving each system using elimination. Then solve each system.

1. $3x - y = 21$
   $2x + y = 4$

2. $3x + 4y = -10$
   $5x - 2y = 18$

3. $2x - y = 6$
   $-3x + 4y = 1$

4. $x - y = 12$
   $x + y = 22$

5. $2r - 3n = 13$
   $8r + 3n = 7$

6. $5a + 6b = 54$
   $3a - 3b = 17$

7. $x + y = 6$
   $x + 3y = 10$

8. $2p - 5q = 6$
   $4p + 3q = -1$

9. **Business** A company orders two types of parts, brass b and steel s. One shipment contains 3 brass and 10 steel parts and costs $48. A second shipment contains 7 brass and 4 steel parts and costs $54. Solve the system to find the cost of each type of part.
   $3b + 10s = 48$
   $7b + 4s = 54$

Solve each system using elimination. Check your solution.

10. $x + y = 12$
    $x - y = 2$

11. $-a + 2b = -1$
    $a = 3b - 1$

12. $3u + 4w = 9$
    $-3u - 2w = -3$

13. $3x + 2y = 9$
    $-x + 3y = 8$

14. $r - 3p = 1$
    $6r - p = 6$

15. $5x + 3y = 1.5$
    $-8x - 2y = 20$

16. $-2z + y = 3$
    $z + 4y = 3$

17. $m - n = 0$
    $m + n = 28$

18. $2k - 3c = 6$
    $6k - 9c = 9$

19. $3b + 4e = 6$
    $-6b + e = 6$

20. $4x = -2y + 1$
    $2x + y = 4$

21. $2p - 3t = 4$
    $3p + 2t = 6$

22. $3x + y = 8$
    $x - y = -12$

23. $x + 4y = 1$
    $3x + 12y = 3$

24. $h = 2s - 1$
    $2s - h = 1$

25. $4x - 2y = 3$
    $5x - 3y = 2$

26. Writing Explain how to solve a system using elimination. Give examples of when you use addition, subtraction, and multiplication.

27. Electricity Two batteries produce a total voltage of 4.5 volts $(B_1 + B_2 = 4.5)$. The difference in their voltages is 1.5 volts $(B_1 - B_2 = 1.5)$. Determine the voltages of the two batteries.

Critical Thinking **Do you *agree* or *disagree* with each statement? Explain.**

28. A system of linear equations written in the form $Ax + By = C$ is solved most easily by elimination.

29. A system of linear equations written in slope-intercept form, $y = mx + b$, is solved most easily by substitution.

Choose **Choose any method to solve each system.**

30. $y = x + 5$
    $x + y = 1$

31. $4x - 2y = 6$
    $-2x + y = -3$

32. $y = 0.25x$
    $y = -4$

33. $-5x + 2y = 14$
    $-3x + y = -2$

34. $y = -2x + 7$
    $y = 4x - 5$

35. $y = 4$
    $3x - y = 5$

36. $2x - 3y = 4$
    $2x + y = -4$

37. $5x + 3y = 6$
    $2x - 4y = 5$

38. Open-ended Write a system of linear equations that you would solve using elimination. Solve the system.

39. Vacation A weekend at the Beach Bay Hotel in Florida includes two nights and four meals. A week includes seven nights and ten meals. The system of linear equations below models this situation. Let $n =$ the cost of one night and $m =$ the cost of one meal.

Weekend: $2n + 4m = 195$
Week: $7n + 10m = 650$

a. Use elimination to solve the system.
b. What does the solution mean in terms of the prices of the room and meals?

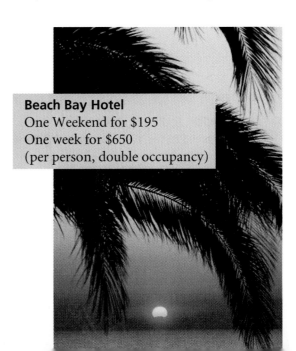

Beach Bay Hotel
One Weekend for $195
One week for $650
(per person, double occupancy)

Chapter Project

Find Out by Calculating

A caterer charges a fixed cost for preparing dinner plus a cost for each person served. You know that the cost for 100 people will be $750 and the cost for 150 people will be $1050. Find the caterer's fixed cost and the cost per person served.

Exercises   MIXED REVIEW

Write an equation of the line passing through the given points.

40. $(3, -7)$ and $(-4, 1)$ **41.** $(0, 4)$ and $(0, -7)$ **42.** $(5, -8)$ and $(9, 0)$ **43.** $(10, 2)$ and $(10, -2)$

44. Health In 1980, there were 400,000 cases of polio reported worldwide. From 1980 to 1993, the number of cases declined 75%. How many cases of polio were reported in 1993?

Getting Ready for Lesson 6-4

Write an equation to model each situation.

45. Two sandwiches and a drink cost $6.50.

46. A stack of ten paperbacks and three hardcover books is 18 in. high.

47. Five pieces of plywood and two bags of nails weigh 32 lb.

FOR YOUR JOURNAL

Make an outline or table titled "Methods for Solving Systems of Equations." Provide descriptions of procedures, helpful hints, and examples for each method.

Exercises   CHECKPOINT

Solve each system of equations.

1. $x + 2y = 5$
$-4x + y = 8$

2. $5x - 3y = 27$
$5x + 4y = -1$

3. $x + y = 19$
$10x - 7y = 20$

4. $6x - \frac{3}{4}y = 16$
$y = -\frac{8}{3}x$

5. Open-ended Write a system of equations where the solution is $x = 5$ and $y = 7$.

6. Photography A photographer offers two options for portraits. You can pay $25 for 12 pictures and $.40 for each extra print, or $30 for 12 pictures and $.15 for each extra print. Let c = the total cost and p = the number of extra prints.

first option: $c = 25 + 0.4p$
second option: $c = 30 + 0.15p$

a. Solve the system.
b. Writing Which option would you recommend to a friend? Explain.

What You'll Learn

- Writing and solving systems of linear equations
- Using systems to find the break-even point

...And Why

To model real-world situations, such as publishing a newsletter

6-4 **W**riting Systems

THINK AND DISCUSS

In the Math Toolbox before Lesson 6-1, the following problem was solved using the strategy *Guess and Test*.

The ratio of boys to girls in a ninth-grade class at a high school is about 3 to 2. There are about 600 ninth-graders. How many are boys? How many are girls?

You can also solve this problem using a system of linear equations.

Example 1 **Relating to the Real World**

Schools Use a system of linear equations to solve the problem stated above.

Define b = the number of boys
g = the number of girls

Relate The total number of ninth-graders is 600. The ratio of boys to girls is 3 to 2.

Write $b + g = 600$ $\dfrac{b}{g} = \dfrac{3}{2}$

You can solve the system by substitution.

$\dfrac{b}{g} = \dfrac{3}{2}$ ⟵ Solve the second equation for b.

$b = \dfrac{3}{2}g$

$b + g = 600$ ⟵ Use the first equation.

$\dfrac{3}{2}g + g = 600$ ⟵ Substitute $\dfrac{3}{2}g$ for b.

$\dfrac{5}{2}g = 600$ ⟵ Combine like terms.

$g = 240$ ⟵ Multiply both sides by $\dfrac{2}{5}$.

$\dfrac{b}{g} = \dfrac{3}{2}$ ⟵ Use the second equation.

$\dfrac{b}{240} = \dfrac{3}{2}$ ⟵ Substitute 240 for g.

$b = 360$ ⟵ Multiply both sides by 240.

There are about 360 ninth-grade boys and 240 ninth-grade girls.

PROBLEM SOLVING

Look Back Which method would you prefer to solve the system: substitution, graphing, or elimination? Why?

1. Graphing Calculator Rewrite the system $b + g = 600$ and $\dfrac{b}{g} = \dfrac{3}{2}$ so that you could use a graphing calculator to find its solution.

In Chapter 5, you found the break-even point for a business using one equation and the *x*-intercept of its graph. The graph shows the break-even point of two equations.

☐ Lose money   ▨ Make money

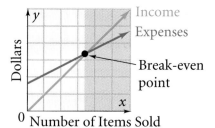

Income
Expenses
Break-even point

Dollars

0 Number of Items Sold

Example 2   **Relating to the Real World**

Publishing Suppose a paper manufacturer publishes a newsletter. Expenses are \$.90 for printing and mailing each copy, plus \$600 for research and writing. The price of the newsletter is \$1.50 per copy. How many copies of the newsletter must the company sell to break even?

Define x = the number of copies
y = the money for expenses or income

Relate   Expenses   Income
\$.90 × copies printed + \$600   \$1.50 × copies sold

Write $y = 0.9x + 600$ $y = 1.50x$

Choose a method to solve the system. Use substitution, since it is easy to substitute for *y* using these equations.

$$y = 0.9x + 600$$
$$y = 1.5x$$

$$1.5x = 0.9x + 600$$ ⟵ Substitute 1.5x for *y* in the first equation.
$$0.6x = 600$$ ⟵ Subtract 0.9x from each side.
$$x = 1000$$ ⟵ Divide each side by 0.6.

To break even, the manufacturer must sell 1000 copies. ■

2. What are the expenses for 1000 copies? the income?

3. Critical Thinking Can the company print more than it sells, but still earn a profit? If so, give an example. If not, explain why not.

4. Try This Suppose printing and mailing expenses increase to \$1.00 for each copy. How many copies of the newsletter must the company sell at \$1.50 per copy to break even?

1. **Geometry** The difference of the measures of two supplementary angles is 35°. Find both angle measures.

2. Suppose you have just enough coins to pay for a loaf of bread priced at $1.95. You have a total of 12 coins, with only quarters and dimes.
   a. Let q = the number of quarters and d = the number of dimes. Complete: ▧ + ▧ = 12
   b. Complete: 0.25▧ + 0.10▧ = ▧
   c. Use the equations you wrote for parts (a) and (b) to find how many of each coin you have.

3. Suppose you have 10 coins that total $.85. Some coins are dimes and some are nickels. How many of each coin do you have?

4. **Open-ended** Write a problem for the total of two types of coins. Then give your problem to a classmate to solve.

Choose **Solve each linear system using any method. Tell why you chose the method you used.**

5. $y = x + 2$
   $y = -2x + 3$

6. $3x + 4y = -10$
   $5x = 2y + 18$

7. $5y = x$
   $2x - 3y = 7$

8. $3x - 2y = -12$
   $5x + 4y = 2$

9. $4x = 5y$
   $8x = 10y + 15$

10. $x = y - 3$
    $x + 2y = 3$

11. $y = 3x$
    $y = -\frac{1}{2}x$

12. $y = 2x$
    $7x - y = 35$

13. **School Musical** Suppose you are the treasurer of the drama club. The cost for scripts for the spring musical is $254. The cost of props and costumes is $400. You must also pay royalty charges of $1.20 per ticket to the play's publisher. You charge $4.00 per ticket and expect to make $150 on refreshments.
    a. Write an equation for the expenses.
    b. Write an equation for the expected income.
    c. How many tickets must the drama club sell to break even?
    d. What method did you use to solve part (c)? Why?

14. **Pets** The ratio of cats to dogs at your local animal shelter is about 5 to 2. The shelter accepts 40 cats and dogs. From about how many dogs would you have to choose?

15. **Business** Suppose you invest $10,000 in equipment to manufacture a new board game. Each game costs $2.65 to manufacture and sells for $20. How many games must you make and sell before your business breaks even?

16. **Writing** Explain to a friend how to decide whether to rent a car from Auto-Rent or from Cars, Inc.

AUTO–RENT:
$10/day
+ 50¢/mile

Cars, Inc.:
$20/day
+ 25¢/mile

17. Chemistry A piece of glass with an initial temperature of 99°C is cooled at a rate of 3.5°C/min. At the same time, a piece of copper with an initial temperature of 0°C is heated at a rate of 2.5°C/min. Let m = the number of minutes and t = the temperature in °C. Which system models the given information?

A. $t = 99 + 3.5m$
$t = 0 + 2.5m$

B. $t = 99 - 3.5m$
$t = 0 - 2.5m$

C. $t = 99 - 3.5m$
$t = 0 + 2.5m$

D. $t = 99 + 3.5m$
$t = 0 - 2.5m$

18. Solve the system that models the situation in Exercise 17. Explain what the solution means in this situation.

Glass can be drawn into optical fibers 16 km long. One fiber can carry 20 times as many phone calls as 500 copper wires.

Without solving, what method would you choose to solve each system: *graphing, substitution,* or *elimination*? Explain your reasoning.

19. $4s - 3t = 8$
$t = -2s - 1$

20. $y = 3x - 1$
$y = 4x$

21. $3m - 4n = 1$
$3m - 2n = -1$

22. $y = -2x$
$y = -\frac{1}{2}x + 3$

23. $2x - y = 4$
$x + 3y = 16$

24. $u = 4v$
$3u - 2v = 7$

25. Geometry The perimeter of an isosceles triangle is 12 cm. The two sides s are each three times the length of the third side t.
a. Write an equation for the perimeter of the triangle.
b. Write an equation that describes the relationship between one side s and side t.
c. Find the length of each side.

26. Number Theory Find two integers with a sum of 1244 and a difference of 90.

Solve each equation.

27. $7t + 4 = -10$

28. $j + 9 = -j - 1$

29. $|c - 4| = 21$

30. $m - 5 = -6$

31. In 1995, about $\frac{2}{3}$ of United States currency in circulation was outside the United States. There was $390 billion in circulation. How much was in use within the United States?

Getting Ready for Lesson 6-5
Graph each equation.

32. $y = 2x + 1$

33. $y - 4 = 0$

34. $y = -\frac{2}{3}x + 1$

35. $y + 2x = -5$

Linear Inequalities

What You'll Learn

• Graphing linear inequalities

...And Why

To solve budget problems using linear inequalities

What You'll Need

• graph paper

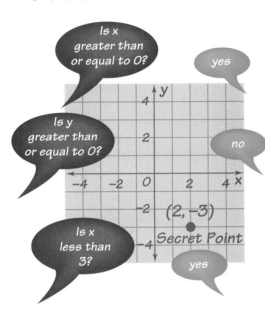

WORK TOGETHER

1. Play the game "What's the Point?" with a partner.

Object of the Game: To locate a secret point on the coordinate plane by asking as few questions as possible.

How to Play:
• Player A chooses a secret point on the coordinate plane. Each coordinate must be an integer from −10 to 10.

• Player B asks questions that contain the words *less than* or *greater than*. Player A answers each question with only *yes* or *no*. Count the number of questions asked until Player B names the secret point.

• The players switch roles to complete one round of the game.

How to Win: The player who names the point by asking fewer questions wins the round. The first player to win 3 rounds wins the game.

2. How many questions did you need to ask to locate the secret point?

3. If you were as lucky as possible, how many questions would you need to ask to locate the secret point? Explain with an example.

4. How do inequalities help you locate the secret point?

5. Describe a strategy for winning the game.

QUICK REVIEW

< "less than"

≤ "less than or equal to"

> "greater than"

≥ "greater than or equal to"

THINK AND DISCUSS

Just as you have used inequalities to describe graphs on a number line, you can use inequalities to describe regions of a coordinate plane.

Number line
x < 1

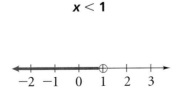

Coordinate plane
x < 1

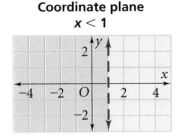

6. What do you think the graph of $y > 2$ looks like on a coordinate grid?

A **linear inequality** describes a region of the coordinate plane that has a boundary line. Every point in the region is a **solution of the inequality.**

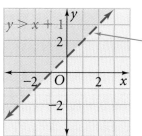
$y > x + 1$

Each point on a *dashed* boundary line is not a solution.

Each point on a *solid* boundary line is a solution.

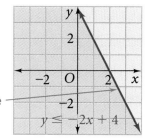
$y \leq -2x + 4$

7. Is $(1, 2)$ a solution for either inequality shown above? Explain.

8. *Open-ended* For each inequality above, name three solutions.

Example 1

Graph $y < 2x + 3$.

First, graph the boundary line $y = 2x + 3$.

Points on the boundary line do *not* make the inequality true. Use a dashed line.

Next, test a point. Use $(0, 0)$.

$y < 2x + 3$
$0 < 2(0) + 3$
$0 < 3$ True

The inequality is true for $(0, 0)$. Shade the region containing $(0, 0)$.

9. Try This Graph the inequality $y \geq 2x + 3$.

10. You can test any point on the graph. Why is $(0, 0)$ a good choice?

Sometimes it helps to rewrite the inequality to find its solution.

Example 2

Graph $2x - 5y \leq 10$.

Write the inequality in slope-intercept form.
$2x - 5y \leq 10$
$\quad -5y \leq -2x + 10$
$\quad\quad y \geq \frac{2}{5}x - 2$ Reverse the ← inequality symbol.

Graph $y = \frac{2}{5}x - 2$.

Test $(0, 0)$ in $y \geq \frac{2}{5}x - 2$.
$\quad 0 \geq (0)x - 2$
$\quad 0 \geq -2$ True

Shade the region containing $(0, 0)$.

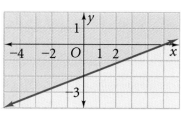

QUICK REVIEW

Use the slope m and the y-intercept b to graph an equation in the form $y = mx + b$.

PROBLEM SOLVING

Look Back Why did you test a point? Could you test the point $(0, 3)$ to make your graph?

11. a. When you graphed $y \geq \frac{2}{5}x - 2$ in Example 2, did you shade *above* or *below* the line?

b. When you graphed $y < 2x + 3$ in Example 1, did you shade *above* or *below* the line?

c. Critical Thinking Both inequalities are in slope-intercept form. Make a **conjecture** about the inequality symbol and the region shaded.

d. Does your **conjecture** stay true for inequalities in $Ax + By < C$ form? Explain.

You can graph inequalities to solve real-world problems.

Example 3   **Relating to the Real World**

Food Shopping Suppose you intend to spend no more than $12 on peanuts and cashews for a party. How many pounds of each can you buy?

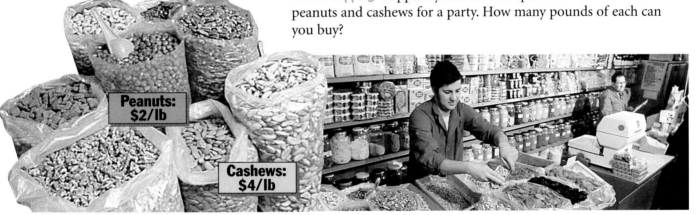

Peanuts: $2/lb

Cashews: $4/lb

Define x = the number of pounds of peanuts
y = the number of pounds of cashews

Relate   cost of peanuts + cost of cashews ≤ maximum total cost

Write $2x$ + $4y$ ≤   12

QUICK REVIEW

Use the intercepts to graph an equation in the form $Ax + By = C$.

Graph the boundary line $2x + 4y = 12$ using a solid line. Use only Quadrant I, since you cannot buy a negative amount of nuts.

Test $(0, 0)$: $2(0) + 4(0) \leq 12$
                              $0 \leq 12$

Party Snacks

Shade the region containing $(0, 0)$.

The graph shows all the possible solutions of the problem. For example, if you buy 2 lb of peanuts you can buy no more than 2 lb of cashews. ■

12. Which are solutions to Example 3?
   A. 2 lb peanuts and 1 lb cashews   **B.** 6 lb peanuts and no cashews
   C. 1 lb peanuts and 3 lb cashews   **D.** 1.5 lb peanuts and 2 lb cashews

Choose the linear inequality that describes each graph.

1.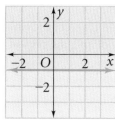

    A. $y \geq -1$

    B. $y \leq -1$

2.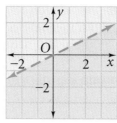

    A. $y > \frac{1}{2}x$

    B. $y < \frac{1}{2}x$

3.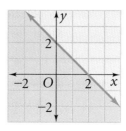

    A. $x + y \geq 2$

    B. $x + y \leq 2$

4.

    A. $x > -2$

    B. $x < -2$

5. For which of the graphs in Exercises 1–4 is $(-2, -1)$ a solution?

6. **Manufacturing** A company makes backpacks. How many backpacks must the company sell to make a profit of more than $250?
    a. Write a linear inequality that describes the situation.
    b. Graph the linear inequality.
    c. Write three possible solutions to the problem.
    d. Why is "10 nylon packs and 22 canvas packs" *not* a solution?

7. **Writing** Explain why a linear inequality is useful when there are many solutions to a problem.

Graph each linear inequality.

8. $x < -2$

9. $y \geq 1$

10. $y < \frac{1}{4}x - 1$

11. $6y - 4x > 0$

12. $y < 5x - 5$

13. $y \leq 4x - 1$

14. $y > -3x + 4$

15. $y > -3x$

16. $x + y \geq 2$

17. $x + 3y \leq 6$

18. $\frac{1}{2}x + \frac{3}{2}y \geq \frac{3}{4}$

19. $y \geq \frac{1}{2}x$

20. $4y > 6x + 2$

21. $2x + 3y \leq 6$

22. $4x - 4y \geq 8$

23. $y - 2x < 2$

24. **Standardized Test Prep** Which statement describes the graph?
    A. $y > x + 1$ **B.** $y < x + 1$ **C.** $y \leq x + 1$
    D. $y \geq x + 1$ **E.** $y = x + 1$

25. Write an inequality that describes the part of the coordinate plane *not* included in the graph of $y \geq x + 2$.

26. **Probability** Suppose you play a carnival game. You toss a blue and a red number cube. If the number on the blue cube is greater than the number on the red cube, you win a prize. The graph shows all the possible outcomes for tossing the cubes.
    a. Copy the graph and shade the region $b > r$.
    b. Does the shaded region include all of the winning outcomes?
    c. What is the probability that you will win a prize?

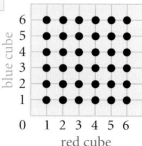

Comparing Cubes

Write the inequality shown in each graph.

27.

28.

29.

30.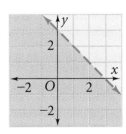

Write the linear inequality described. Then graph the inequality.

31. x is positive. **32.** y is negative. **33.** y is not negative. **34.** x is less than y.

35. Geometry Suppose you have 50 ft of fencing. You want to fence a rectangular area of your yard for a garden.
  a. Use the formula for the perimeter of a rectangle to write a linear inequality that describes this situation.
  b. Graph the inequality.
  c. Open-ended Give two possible sizes for a square garden.
  d. Can you make the garden 12 ft by 15 ft? **Justify** your answer, using both your graph and the inequality you wrote in part (a).

Is point *P* a solution of the linear inequality?

36. $y \leq -2x + 1; P(2, 2)$ **37.** $x < 2; P(1, 0)$

38. $y \geq 3x - 2; P(0, 0)$ **39.** $y > x - 1; P(0, 1)$

40. Consumer Suppose you are shopping for crepe paper to decorate the gym for a school dance. Gold crepe paper costs $5 per roll, and blue crepe paper costs $3 per roll. You have at most $48 to spend. How much gold and blue crepe paper can you buy? Explain your solution.

> **Chapter Project** ▼ ***Find Out by Writing***
>
> Use your information from the Find Out questions on pages 274 and 284. Assume that 200 people will come to the dance. Write a report listing which band you would choose and the cost per ticket that you need to charge to cover expenses. Then repeat the process assuming that 300 people will come.

Exercises   M I X E D   R E V I E W

Find the slope of each line.

41. $y = 5x - 9$ **42.** $7x + 4y = 20$ **43.** $3y = 8x - 12$ **44.** $y = 8x + 1$

45. Automobiles The average car is parked 95% of the time. How many hours is the average car on the road each day?

Getting Ready for Lesson 6-6
Solve each system of equations.

46. $y = 2x - 3$
$y = -4x$

47. $4y = 3x + 11$
$y = 2x - 1$

48. $y = 5x + 2$
$y = 4x - 6$

49. $y = 8x$
$y = 2x + 28$

Graphing Inequalities

After Lesson 6-5

You can use the DRAW feature of a graphing calculator to graph inequalities. The order you enter data depends on whether you are shading above or below a line. When shading below Y_1, use Shade $(Ymin, Y_1)$. When shading above Y_1, use Shade $(Y_1, Ymax)$. You do not have to use a close parenthesis before pressing ENTER.

Example

Graph each inequality.

a. $y < 2x + 3$

Shade below Y_1 for *less than*.

b. $y > 0.5x - 1$

Shade above Y_1 for *greater than*.

You can vary the darkness of the shading by entering an integer from 1 (dark) to 8 (light). Add a comma and the integer before pressing ENTER. The graph at the right has a darkness level of 2.

The graphing calculator does not make a distinction between a boundary line that is dotted (like *less than*) and a boundary line that is solid (like *less than or equal to*). You must decide if a boundary line should be solid or dotted when you sketch the inequality on your paper.

Shade$(Y_1,Ymax,2)$

Use a graphing calculator to graph each inequality. Sketch your graph.

1. $y < x$

2. $y > 2x + 1$

3. $y \geq -x + 3$

4. $y \leq 5$

5. $x - y \geq 4$

6. $2x + 3y \leq 12$

7. $6x - 30y < 45$

8. $x - 2y \geq 50$

9. Writing What instructions would you need to change in Example (b) to graph $y > 0.5x - 1$ using Y_2 instead of Y_1?

What You'll Learn

6-6

Systems of Linear Inequalities

• Solving systems of linear inequalities by graphing

...And Why

To solve real-world problems that have many possible solutions, such as those in agriculture

What You'll Need

• graph paper
• graphing calculator

WORK TOGETHER

Work in pairs. Explore what happens when you graph lines or linear inequalities on the same coordinate plane.

1. Can two lines be drawn with the given intersection? Support each answer with a diagram or an explanation.
   a. a point   **b.** a line   **c.** a region   **d.** no intersection

2. Can the graphs of two linear inequalities be drawn with the given intersection? Support each answer with a diagram or an explanation.
   a. a point   **b.** a line   **c.** a region   **d.** no intersection

3. **Summarize** your findings in Questions 1 and 2. Compare the possible intersections of two lines with the possible intersections of the graphs of two linear inequalities. What do you notice?

4. Find the possible intersections for more than two lines.

5. Find the possible intersections for the graphs of more than two linear inequalities.

THINK AND DISCUSS

Two or more linear inequalities together form a **system of linear inequalities.** Here is an example of a system that describes the shaded region of the graph. Notice that there are two boundary lines.

System of Linear Inequalities

$$x \geq 2$$
$$y < -1$$

6. You can describe all the points of a quadrant with a system of linear inequalities. Match each system with a quadrant.

   A. $x > 0$ **B.** $x > 0$ **C.** $x < 0$ **D.** $x < 0$
       $y > 0$ $y < 0$ $y > 0$ $y < 0$

A **solution of a system of linear inequalities** makes each inequality in the system true. The graph of a system shows all of its solutions.

1 Which inequality is graphed below?

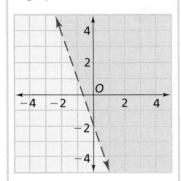

(1) $y \geq -3x - 2$
(2) $y = -3x - 2$
(3) $y \leq -3x - 2$
(4) $y > -3x - 2$

2 Solve this system.
$x + 2y = 6$
$2x - 3y = 5$

Example 1 **Relating to the Real World**

Animal Studies A zoo keeper wants to fence a rectangular pen for goats. The length of the pen should be at least 80 ft, and the distance around it should be no more than 310 ft. What are the possible dimensions of the pen?

Define $x = $ width of the pen
$y = $ length of the pen

Relate	The length	is at least	80 ft.	The perimeter	is no more than	310 ft.
Write	y	$\geq$	80	$2x + 2y$	$\leq$	310

Use slope-intercept form to graph.

$y \geq 80$
$m = 0$
$b = 80$

Test $(0, 1)$.
$y \geq 80$
$(1) \geq 80$ **False**

Shade above.

Use intercepts to graph.

$2x + 2y \leq 310$
$(155, 0)$
$(0, 155)$

Test $(0, 0)$.
$2(0) + 2(0) \leq 310$
$0 \leq 310$ **True**

Shade below.

The solutions are all the points in the shaded region above $y = 80$ but below $2x + 2y \leq 310$. ■

7. Give three possible dimensions (length and width) for the pen. How many solutions does this system have?

8. Why is the solution region shown only in Quadrant I?

9. *Graphing Calculator* Use the *Shade* feature to graph the system of linear inequalities in Example 1.

10. Try This Solve each system by graphing.
  a. $y \leq 2x + 3$ **b.** $y > x$
     $y \geq x - 1$ $x \leq 3$
  c. $x + y > -2$
     $x - y > 2$

11. *Critical Thinking* How can you decide whether or not points on boundary lines of a solution region are part of the solution of a system?

Some systems of linear inequalities do not have a solution region. The graphs of the inequalities might intersect in a line or not at all.

Example 2

Solve the system by graphing. $4y \geq 6x$
$$-3x + 2y \leq -6$$

Use slope-intercept form to graph.   Use intercepts to graph.

$4y \geq 6x$ $-3x + 2y \leq -6$

$y \geq \dfrac{3}{2}x$ $(0, -3)$
                                                                   $(2, 0)$

Test $(0, 1)$.   Test $(0, 0)$.
Shade above.   Shade below.

Since the shaded regions do not overlap, the system has no solution.

12. Explain why $(0, 0)$ was not tested when $4y \geq 6x$ was graphed.

13. How are the boundary lines in Example 2 related?

PROBLEM SOLVING HINT

For Questions 14 and 15, first draw a diagram. Then write the inequalities.

14. **a.** *Open-ended* Write another system of two linear inequalities that has no solution.
     b. Must the boundary lines be parallel? Explain.

15. *Critical Thinking* Write a system of linear inequalities in which the solution is a line.

Exercises   ON YOUR OWN

1. *Standardized Test Prep* Which of these points is a solution of the system $y \leq x + 5$ and $y + x > 3$?
    A. $(0, 0)$ **B.** $(-1, 4)$ **C.** $(3, 3)$ **D.** $(-2, 6)$ **E.** $(2, 0)$

2. Which system is represented in the graph at the right?
    A. $x + y \leq 3$ **B.** $x + y > 3$
         $y > x - 3$ $y \leq x - 3$
    C. $x + y \geq 3$ **D.** $x + y < 3$
         $y < x - 3$ $y \geq x - 3$

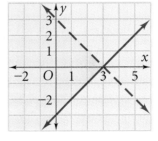

3. *Critical Thinking* Without graphing, explain why the point where the boundary lines intersect in the system $2x + y > 2$ and $x - y \geq 3$ is *not* a solution of the system.

4. *Writing* Write a problem that can be solved using the system of inequalities at the right.

$2l + 2w \leq 100$
$l \leq 30$

Solve each system of linear inequalities by graphing.

5. $x \geq 2$
$y < 4$

6. $y > 3$
$x < -1$

7. $y \leq x$
$y \geq x + 1$

8. $y > 4x + 2$
$y \leq 4$

9. $y \leq 2x + 2$
$y < -x + 1$

10. $y \geq -2x + 1$
$y < x + 2$

11. $x + y \leq 6$
$x - y < 1$

12. $y - 3x < 6$
$y > 3x + 9$

13. $x > y$
$y > 0$

14. $x + y \leq 5$
$x \geq 1$

15. $y < \frac{1}{2}x$
$y > \frac{1}{2}x - 3$

16. $-x - y \leq 2$
$y - 2x > 1$

17. Construction A contractor has at most $33 to spend on nails for a project. The contractor needs at least 9 lb of finish nails and at least 12 lb of common nails. How many pounds of each type of nail should the contractor buy?
  a. Write a system of three inequalities that describes this situation.
  b. Graph the system to show all possible solutions.
  c. Name a point that is a solution of the system.
  d. Name a point that is *not* a solution of the system.

Common Nails
$.55/lb

Finish Nails
$.60/lb

Open-ended **Write a system of linear inequalities with the given characteristics.**

18. $(0, 0)$ is a solution.

19. Solutions are only in Quadrant II.

20. There is no solution.

21. The solution region is triangular.

22. a. Solve the system of three inequalities at the right by graphing.
   b. **Verify** your solution by testing a point from the overlapping region in all three inequalities.

$x \leq 4$
$y < x + 2$
$x + 2y \geq -2$

Geometry **For the solution region of each system of linear inequalities, (a) describe the shape, (b) find the vertices, and (c) find the area.**

23. $y \geq \frac{1}{2}x + 1$
$y \leq 2$
$x \geq -4$

24. $x \geq 1$
$x \leq 5$
$y \geq -1$
$y \leq 3$

25. $x \geq 0$
$x \leq 2$
$y \geq -4$
$y \leq -x + 2$

26. $x \geq 2$
$y \geq -3$
$x + y \leq 4$

27. Shopping Suppose you receive a $50 gift certificate to the Music and Books store. You want to buy some books and at least one CD. How can you spend your gift certificate on x paperbacks and y CDs?
  a. Write a system of linear inequalities that describes this situation.
  b. Graph the system to show possible solutions to this problem.
  c. What purchase does the ordered pair $(2, 6)$ represent? Is it a solution to your system? Explain.
  d. Find a solution in which you spend almost all of the gift certificate.
  e. What is the greatest number of paperbacks you can buy and still buy one CD?

Cityside Music and Books
All CDs $9.99
All books $5.99

Find Out by Graphing

In the Find Out question on page 293, you found two ticket prices. Each price covers the cost of the dance under certain conditions. Decide what the ticket price should be. Plan for between 200 and 300 people. Graph a system of linear inequalities to show the total amount received from tickets.

Exercises   M I X E D   R E V I E W

Solve each equation.

28. $5m + 4 = 8m - 2$ **29.** $5(t + 1) = 10$ **30.** $4x = 2x + 5$ **31.** $6h - 11 = 13$

32. $3p = -\frac{3}{4}p + 5$ **33.** $-k - 7 = -3k + 1$ **34.** $\frac{3c - 1}{4} = \frac{5}{2}$ **35.** $\frac{1}{2}(t - 8) = 7$

36. a. Identify the independent and dependent variables.
b. Graph the data.
c. What scales did you use and why?

Price	Sales Tax
$1.00	$.05
$3.00	$.15
$4.00	$.20
$7.00	$.35

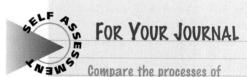

FOR YOUR JOURNAL

Compare the processes of graphing a system of linear inequalities and graphing a system of linear equations. How are they similar? How are they different?

Getting Ready for Lesson 6-7

Evaluate each formula for the given point.

37. $B = 2x + 5y$; $(6, 10)$ **38.** $C = x + 6y$; $(100, 550)$

39. $P = 6x + 2y$; $(200, 75)$ **40.** $P = 2l + 2w$; $(30, 18)$

Exercises   C H E C K P O I N T

Solve each system of linear inequalities.

1. $y < -2x + 5$
$y > 3x - 1$

2. $y \geq 2x - 1$
$x \geq -5$

3. $y < 0.5x + 3$
$y \geq -x + 2.5$

4. $3x + 2y \leq 12$
$x - y < 10$

5. Standardized Test Prep Which of these points is a solution of the system $y \geq 4x - 1$ and $2x + 3y < 6$?
A. $(3, 0)$ **B.** $(0, 4)$ **C.** $(4, 1)$ **D.** $(-3, 1)$ **E.** $(3, -4)$

6. You are going out for pizza!
a. Write a system of equations for the cost of a large pizza at each restaurant.
b. Solve the system of equations. Interpret your solution.
c. Open-ended Where will you go for pizza? Explain your reasons.

Tony's Pizza:
Large cheese $7
each topping $.75

Maria's Pizza:
Large cheese $8
each topping $.50

What You'll Learn

- Solving linear programming problems

...And Why

To investigate real-world situations, such as time management

6-7 Concepts of Linear Programming

WORK TOGETHER

Suppose you are offered a part-time job. You wonder how much time you have available to work. You can use mathematics to help you organize your thoughts and make a good decision.

Work with a partner.

1. **a.** Write the different ways you spend your time during a week.
   b. Organize your list into no more than ten categories.

2. Make a personal calendar for the last week.
   a. Assign time to the categories from Question 1.
   b. How much time do you have available to work at a part-time job?
   c. Discuss what you could or could not give up in your schedule.

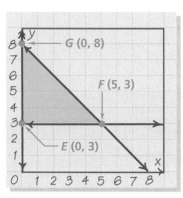

THINK AND DISCUSS

You can answer questions like those above by using a process called linear programming. **Linear programming** identifies conditions that make a quantity as large as or as small as possible. The variables used in the equation for the quantity have restrictions. The maximum and minimum values of the quantity occur at vertices of the graph of the restrictions.

Example 1

Step 1
Graph the restrictions.

Use linear programming. Find the values of x and y that maximize the quantity.

Restrictions $\begin{cases} x + y \leq 8 \\ x \geq 0 \\ y \geq 3 \end{cases}$

Equation $Q = 3x + 2y$

Step 2
Find coordinates of each vertex.

Step 3
Evaluate Q at each vertex.

Vertex	$Q = 3x + 2y$	
$E(0, 3)$	$Q = 3(0) + 2(3) = 6$	
$F(5, 3)$	$Q = 3(5) + 2(3) = 21$	← maximum value of Q
$G(0, 8)$	$Q = 3(0) + 2(8) = 16$	

The maximum value 21 occurs when $x = 5$ and $y = 3$.

3. Find the values of x and y that minimize the quantity in Example 1.

4. Find the value of the equation in Example 1 at each point.
  a. (1, 3)   **b.** (4, 3)   **c.** (4, 4)   **d.** (1, 7)   **e.** (3, 4)

In the Work Together activity, you listed some restrictions you have on your time in relation to a part-time job. In the next example one student finds the best way to use her time.

| **Example 2** | **Relating to the Real World** |

Time Management Marta plans to start a part-time job. Here are the restrictions she has found on her time for homework hours *x* and job hours *y*.

Restriction	Inequality
She has no more than 24 h/wk for homework and a job.	$x + y \leq 24$
The boss wants her to work at least 6 h/wk.	$y \geq 6$
She spends 10–15 h/wk on homework.	$x \geq 10$
	$x \leq 15$

She decides that homework hours are twice as valuable as work hours. Find the best way *B* for Marta to split her time between homework and the job using the equation $B = 2x + y$.

Step 1
Graph the restrictions.

Step 2
Find the coordinates of each vertex.

Vertex
E (10, 6)
F (15, 6)
G (15, 9)
H (10, 14)

Step 3
Evaluate *B* at each vertex.

B = 2x + y
$B = 2(10) + 6 = 26$
$B = 2(15) + 6 = 36$
$B = 2(15) + 9 = 39$ ◄—— **maximum value of B**
$B = 2(10) + 14 = 34$

The best way for Marta to split her time each week is to spend 15 h on homework and 9 h at her job.

5. What does the point (10, 14) mean in terms of homework and job time?

6. Critical Thinking For each situation, would the best solution be a *maximum value* or a *minimum value*? Explain.
  a. You are selling tomatoes and beans from your garden. You want to determine how much of each to grow for the most profit.
  b. Suppose you manage a grocery store. You can buy tomatoes from two different farmers. You consider the price of the tomatoes and transportation costs. You must decide which supplier to use.

To solve linear programming problems, you must be able to write the inequalities for the restrictions and write the equation.

Example 3 **Relating to the Real World**

Business A seafood restaurant owner orders at least 50 fish. He cannot use more than 30 halibut or more than 35 flounder. How many of each fish should he use to minimize his cost?

Step 1 Write inequalities to describe the restrictions.

Define x = number of halibut used
             y = number of flounder used

Relate		Write
He needs at least 50 fish.		$x + y \geq 50$
He cannot use more than 30 halibut.		$x \leq 30$
He cannot use more than 35 flounder.		$y \leq 35$

Step 2 Write the equation.

Define C = cost of fish

Relate   cost is $4 for each halibut and $3 for each flounder

Write $C = 4x + 3y$

Halibut $4 each

Flounder $3 each

Step 3
Graph the restrictions.

Step 4
Find the coordinates of each vertex.

Vertex
E (15, 35)
F (30, 35)
G (30, 20)

Step 5
Evaluate C at each vertex.

$C = 4x + 3y$
$C = 4(15) + 3(35) = 165$ ⟵ minimum value of C
$C = 4(30) + 3(35) = 225$
$C = 4(30) + 3(20) = 180$

The seafood restaurant owner should buy 15 halibut and 35 flounder to minimize his cost.

7. Try This Suppose the restaurant owner changes his order to at least 40 fish. How many of each kind should he use to minimize his cost?

Evaluate each equation at the points given. Which point gives the maximum value? the minimum value?

1. $Q = 3x + 5y$
(8, 0), (4, 4), (3, 5), (0, 6)

2. $B = 40x + 20y$
(0, 0), (0, 40), (15, 10), (25, 0)

3. $A = 35x + 10y$
(0, 0), (0, 10), (0, 40), (20, 10)

Find the values of x and y that maximize or minimize each quantity for each graph.

4. Maximum for
$P = x + y$

5. Maximum for
$P = 3x + 2y$

6. Minimum for
$C = 2x + 5y$

7. Minimum for
$C = \frac{1}{2}x + y$

   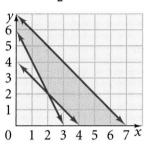

Evaluate the equation to find minimum and maximum values.

8. $x \geq 2$
$x \leq 5$
$y \geq 3$
$y \leq 6$
$A = 5x + 4y$

9. $x \geq 0$
$y \geq 0$
$x + y \leq 12$
$D = 3x + y$

10. $y \geq -x + 4$
$y \leq -2x + 10$
$x \geq 0$
$y \geq 0$
$P = 2x + 3y$

11. $y \leq -x + 8$
$y \geq 2x - 2$
$x \geq 0$
$y \geq 0$
$Q = x + y$

12. Open-ended Write a system of restrictions that form a trapezoid.

13. Environment A town is trying to find the best mix of sand and salt for treating icy roads. One consideration is cost, which they want to minimize. Sand costs $8 per ton, and salt costs $20 per ton. Write the equation for minimizing cost.

14. Manufacturing A toy manufacturer wants to minimize her cost for producing two lines of toy airplanes. Because of the supply of materials, no more than 40 Flying Bats can be built each day, and no more than 60 Flying Falcons can be built each day. There are enough workers to build at least 70 toy airplanes each day.
a. Write the inequalities for the restrictions.
b. It costs $12 to manufacture a Flying Bat and $8 to build a Flying Falcon. Write an equation for the cost of manufacturing the toy airplanes.
c. Use linear programming to find how many of each toy airplane should be produced each day to minimize cost.
d. Critical Thinking What else should the manufacturer consider before deciding how many of each toy to manufacture each day?

15. Business A computer company has budgeted $6000 to rent display space at two locations for a new line of computers. Each location requires a minimum of 100 ft².

a. Writing Explain what each inequality represents.

Restrictions: $10x + 20y \le 6000$, $x \ge 100$, $y \ge 100$

b. Write an equation for the potential number of customers.

c. Use linear programming to find the amount of space to rent at each location to maximize the number of potential customers.

Rental Locations

Location	Cost	Potential
A	$10/ft²	30 customers/ft²
B	$20/ft²	40 customers/ft²

Exercises   MIXED REVIEW

Write each linear equation in slope-intercept form.

16. $5y = 6x - 3$ **17.** $4x + 8y = 20$ **18.** $y = 3(x - 2)$ **19.** $9y = 24x$

20. Probability You roll a number cube and toss a coin at the same time. Find each probability.

a. $P(3$ and T$)$ **b.** $P($odd number and H$)$ **c.** $P($prime and T$)$ **d.** $P(6)$

Getting Ready for Lesson 6-8

To which family of functions does each function belong?

21. $y = 3x^2 - x + 6$ **22.** $y = |5x - 2|$ **23.** $y = 4x - 9$ **24.** $y = -7x^2 - 1$

Algebra at Work

Businessperson

Some of the goals of a business are to minimize costs and maximize profits. People in business use linear programming to analyze data in order to achieve these goals. The illustration lists some of the variables involved in operating a small manufacturing company. To solve a problem, a businessperson must identify the variables and restrictions and then search for the best possible solutions.

Mini Project: Work with a partner. Decide on a small business you could start. Identify the variables connected with your business and the restrictions on the variables.

Restriction Polygon

■ = Advertising
□ = Raw Materials
■ = Transportation
■ = Packaging
■ = Equipment
■ = Labor

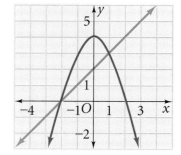
What You'll Learn

6-8   **Systems with Nonlinear Equations**

- Solving systems with linear, quadratic, and absolute value equations by graphing

...And Why

To solve problems involving engineering and architecture

What You'll Need

- graphing calculator
- graph paper

THINK AND DISCUSS

A system of equations can include equations that are not linear. The system shown consists of a linear equation and a quadratic equation.

$$y = x + 2$$
$$y = -x^2 + 4$$

Notice that the graphs intersect at $(-2, 0)$ and $(1, 3)$. These two points are solutions of the system.

1. Check $(-2, 0)$ and $(1, 3)$ in both equations to **verify** that they are solutions of the system.

You can solve a system with a nonlinear equation by graphing.

Example 1

Solve the system of equations. $y = \frac{1}{2}x + 1$
$$y = |x - 1|$$

Graph each equation.

$y = \frac{1}{2}x + 1 \qquad y = |x - 1|$

Use $y = mx + b$.   Make a table of values.

$m = \frac{1}{2}$
$b = 1$

x	y
-2	3
-1	2
0	1
1	0
2	1
3	2

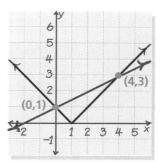

The graphs intersect at $(0, 1)$ and $(4, 3)$.

Check (0, 1):

$y = \frac{1}{2}x + 1 \qquad\qquad y = |x - 1|$

$1 \stackrel{?}{=} \frac{1}{2}(0) + 1 \qquad\quad 1 \stackrel{?}{=} |0 - 1|$

$1 \stackrel{?}{=} 0 + 1 \qquad\qquad\quad 1 \stackrel{?}{=} |-1|$

$1 = 1 \checkmark \qquad\qquad\qquad 1 = 1 \checkmark$

Check (4, 3):

$y = \frac{1}{2}x + 1 \qquad\qquad y = |x - 1|$

$3 \stackrel{?}{=} \frac{1}{2}(4) + 1 \qquad\quad 3 \stackrel{?}{=} |4 - 1|$

$3 \stackrel{?}{=} 2 + 1 \qquad\qquad\quad 3 \stackrel{?}{=} |3|$

$3 = 3 \checkmark \qquad\qquad\qquad 3 = 3 \checkmark$

1 What is the maximum value for $R = 2x - y$ given the following restrictions?

$x \geq 0$ $y \geq 2x + 1$
$y \geq 0$ $y \leq -x + 7$

(1) −9 (3) 0
(2) −1 (4) 14

2 A mix contains nuts that cost \$2.89 per pound and cereal that costs \$3.79 per pound. There are at least 3 pounds of nuts, and the total cost is not more than \$15.00.
a Write a system of linear inequalities that describes this situation.
b Name three possible combinations of nuts and cereal.

2. **Critical Thinking** Do systems made up of one linear equation and one absolute-value equation always have two solutions? If not, what are the other possibilities? Give examples.

Some systems of nonlinear equations have no solution.

Example 2

Solve the system of equations. $y = x^2 + 3$
 $y = x$

Graph each equation.

$y = x^2 + 3$
Make a table of values.

x	y
−2	7
−1	4
0	3
1	4
2	7

$y = x$
Use $y = mx + b$.
$m = 1$ $b = 0$

The graphs do not intersect, so the system has no solution.

3. **Try This** Solve each system.

a. $y = |x| + 2$
 $y = 4x - 1$

b. $y = -x^2$
 $y = x^2 - 8$

c. $y = |x - 2|$
 $y = -\frac{1}{3}x + 2$

You can use a graphing calculator to solve systems with nonlinear equations.

Example 3   **Relating to the Real World**

Engineering Use the bridge diagram to find the coordinates of the points where the top arch intersects the road. Round answer to the nearest unit.

Arch
$y = -\frac{1}{600}x^2 + 100$

Road $y = 40$

You can use the TABLE feature or the ZOOM and TRACE keys to estimate the intersection points.

Set an appropriate range.

Input the equations.

Use the CALC key to find the coordinates of the intersection points.

The solutions, rounded to the nearest unit, are $(190, 40)$ and $(-190, 40)$. ∎

4. Each unit in Example 3 equals 1 ft. Find the length of the bridge.

Exercises   ON YOUR OWN

Write the solution(s) of each system of equations. Check that each solution makes both equations of the system true.

1. $y = 2x$
$y = x^2$

2. $y = 3$
$y = |x|$

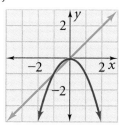

3. $y = -0.4x^2$
$y = -4x^2$

4. $y = |x|$
$y = -x + 5$

5. $y = -|x|$
$y = x^2 - 6$

6. $y = x$
$y = -x^2$

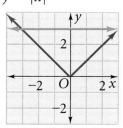

7. $y = |0.5x|$
$y = |3x| - 5$

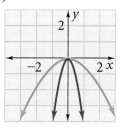

8. $y = x^2 + 2$
$y = -x^2 + 2$

 9. Communications Satellite dishes are used to receive television and radio signals. Use a graphing calculator to find the coordinates of S and T, the points at which the horn supports meet the dish. Round your answers to the nearest hundredth.

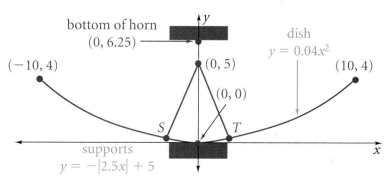

bottom of horn
$(0, 6.25)$

dish
$y = 0.04x^2$

$(-10, 4)$ $(0, 5)$ $(10, 4)$

$(0, 0)$

S T

supports
$y = -|2.5x| + 5$

Match each system of equations with its graph. Write the solution(s) of the system.

10. $y = |x + 2|$
$y = |x - 2|$

11. $y = -2$
$y = x^2 - 3$

12. $y = 2.5x + 5$
$y = -|x - 2|$

13. $y = x^2 + 2$
$y = -\frac{1}{2}x^2$

A.

B.

C.

D.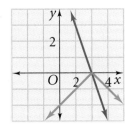

14. Native American Art This design was created by the Crow. The Crow are a people of the northern Great Plains of the United States. Patterns in the design can be described with a system of nonlinear equations. Find the coordinates of the points A and B.

15. Standardized Test Prep How many solutions does this system of equations have?

$$y = \frac{1}{2}x^2$$
$$y = -|x + 3|$$

A. one   **B.** two   **C.** three
D. none   **E.** infinitely many

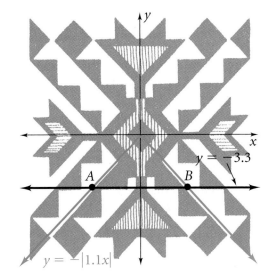

Open-ended **Sketch the graph of a system of two equations with the given characteristics.**

16. two quadratic equations, no solution

17. two absolute-value equations, two solutions

18. linear equation and absolute-value equation, one solution

19. linear equation and quadratic equation, no solution

▦ Choose **Use paper and pencil or a graphing calculator to solve each system of equations.**

20. $y = 3x - 4$
$y = -|x|$

21. $y = |x + 3|$
$y = \frac{1}{2}x$

22. $y = \frac{3}{2}x + 1$
$y = |x| + 1$

23. $y = x^2 - 1$
$y = -x + 1$

24. $y = |x|$
$y = -|x|$

25. $y = -x^2 + 2$
$y = x + 3$

26. $y = 2x$
$y = |x| + 3$

27. $y = -2x^2$
$y = |3x| - 5$

28. $y = -3$
$y = |x - 2|$

29. $y = x^2$
$y = x^2 - 2$

30. $y = |2x| - 3$
$y = |x|$

31. $y = \frac{1}{4}x^2$
$y = \frac{1}{2}x + 2$

$y = -\dfrac{3}{2000}x^2 + 104$

$y = -\dfrac{1}{900}x^3$

32. a. Architecture The University of Illinois Assembly Hall in Urbana can be described by a system with nonlinear equations. Use a graphing calculator to find the coordinates of points S and E.
   b. Find the length of $\overline{SE}$.

33. Writing How can you tell if a system with nonlinear equations has any solutions?

Exercises   MIXED REVIEW

34. What is 15% of 96?   **35.** 34 is what percent of 32?   **36.** What percent of 40 is 27?

37. 6 is what percent of 92?   **38.** What percent of 6 is 2?   **39.** What is 85% of 108,000?

Find each sum or difference.

40. $\begin{bmatrix} -4 & a & 5 \\ 0 & b & 4c \end{bmatrix} + \begin{bmatrix} -12 & -a & 0 \\ d & 3b & -2c \end{bmatrix}$

41. $\begin{bmatrix} 7 & x \\ 0 & -2y \\ 4z & -x \end{bmatrix} - \begin{bmatrix} x & 5 \\ 3x & -y \\ -4z & -x \end{bmatrix}$

42. Writing Explain the difference between the solution of an equation and the solution of a system of two equations.

43. a. Medicine Write a formula for cell D2 in the spreadsheet.
   b. Find the values in cells D2 and D3.

44. What is the rate of change in the total number of doctors from 1900 to 1995?

	A	B	C	D
1	Year	Number of Doctors	Population	Number of Doctors per Million People
2	1900	119,749	75,994,575	▪
3	1995	638,200	263,434,000	▪

Finishing the Chapter Project

L e t ' s

Dance!

Questions on pages 274, 284, 293, and 299 should help you complete your project. Your report should include your analysis of the cost for refreshments and each band, depending on how many people buy tickets. Include your recommended ticket price and note any conditions under which this ticket price leads to a loss for the event. Illustrate your reasoning with graphs of linear equations and inequalities.

Client: Northwood High School

CHARGES

One-Time Fee
- set up
- transportation
- equipment
- staff
- clean up

Cost Per Person
- juice, soda, seltzer
- appetizers

Reflect and Revise

Present your analysis of this dance to a small group of classmates. After you have heard their analyses and presented your own, decide if your work is complete, clear, and convincing. If necessary, make changes to improve your presentation.

Follow Up

Are there other expenses you could expect to have in planning and holding this dance? Estimate them and change your recommended ticket price if necessary.

For More Information

Splaver, Bernard R. *Successful Catering*. New York: Van Nostrand Reinhold, 1991.

Watkins, Andrea and Patricia Clarkson. *Dancing Longer, Dancing Stronger: A Dancer's Guide to Improving Technique and Preventing Injury*. Princeton, New Jersey: Princeton Book Company, 1990.

Key Terms

elimination (p. 280)
infinitely many solutions (p. 271)
linear inequality (p. 290)
linear progamming (p. 300)
no solution (p. 271)
solution of a system of linear inequalities (p. 295)
solution of the inequality (p. 290)

solution of the system (p. 269)
substitution (p. 275)
system of linear equations (p. 269)
system of linear inequalities (p. 295)

How am I doing?

- State three ideas from this chapter that you think are important. Explain your choices.
- Describe the different ways you can solve systems of equations and inequalities.

Solving Systems by Graphing   6-1

Two or more linear equations form a **system of linear equations.** You can solve a system of linear equations by graphing. Any point where all the lines intersect is the **solution of the system.**

For each graph, write the system of linear equations and its solution.

1.   **2.**   **3.**   **4.**

Solve each system by graphing.

5. $y = 3x - 1$
$y = -x + 3$

6. $x - y = -3$
$3x + y = -1$

7. $-x + 2y = -2$
$y = \frac{1}{2}x + 3$

8. $y = -2x + 1$
$y = 2x - 3$

Solving Systems Using Substitution   6-2

You can also solve a system of linear equations using **substitution.** First, solve for one variable in terms of the other. Then substitute this result in either equation and solve.

Solve each system using substitution.

9. $y = 3x + 11$
$y = -2x + 1$

10. $4x - y = -12$
$-6x + 5y = -3$

11. $y = 5x - 8$
$5y = 2x + 6$

12. $8x = -2y - 10$
$2x = 4y$

13. Writing Explain how you determine if a system has no solution or infinitely many solutions when you solve a system using substitution.

You can solve a system of linear equations using **elimination.** You add or subtract the equations to eliminate one variable. You can multiply one or both of the equations by a nonzero number before adding or subtracting.

Solve each system using elimination. Check your solution.

14. $y = -3x + 5$
$y = -4x - 1$

15. $2x - 3y = 5$
$x + 2y = -1$

16. $x + y = 10$
$x - y = 2$

17. $-x + 4y = 12$
$2x - 3y = 6$

You can use systems of linear equations to solve word problems. First, define variables. Then model the situation with a system of linear equations.

Solve using any method. Check your solution.

18. A furniture finish consists of turpentine and linseed oil. It contains twice as much turpentine as linseed oil. If you need 16 fl oz of furniture finish, how much turpentine do you need?

19. Geometry The difference between the measures of two complementary angles is 36°. Find both angle measures. (*Hint:* Two angles are complementary if the sum of their measures is 90°.)

A **linear inequality** describes a region of the coordinate plane. To graph the **solution of the inequality,** first graph the boundary line. Then test a point to shade the region that makes the inequality true.

Graph each linear inequality.

20. $y < -3x + 8$

21. $y \geq 2x - 1$

22. $y \leq 0.5x + 6$

23. $y > -\frac{1}{4}x - 2$

Two or more linear inequalities form a **system of linear inequalities.** To find the **solution of a system of linear inequalities,** graph each linear inequality. The solution region is where all the inequalities are true.

Solve each system of linear inequalities by graphing.

24. $y \geq -4x + 1$
$y \leq 3x - 5$

25. $x - y < 10$
$x + y \leq 8$

26. $y \leq x - 3$
$y > x - 7$

27. $y < 5x$
$y \geq 0$

28. Open-ended Write a system of linear inequalities for which the solution region is a pentagon.

Concepts of Linear Programming

6-7

You can use **linear programming** to minimize or maximize quantities. The variables used in the equation for the quantity have restrictions. The maximum and minimum values of the equation occur at the vertices of the graph of the restrictions.

Evaluate the equation to find minimum and maximum values.

29. $x + y \le 7$
$x + 2y \le 8$
$x \ge 0$
$y \ge 0$
$P = 3x + y$

30. $x + 2y \le 5$
$x \ge 0$
$y \ge 1$

$P = 2x + 3y$

31. $x + y \le 6$
$2x + y \le 10$
$x \ge 0$
$y \ge 0$
$P = 4x + y$

32. $x \ge 1$
$x \le 4$
$y \ge 3$
$y \le 6$
$P = x + 2y$

33. *Standardized Test Prep* Which point minimizes the equation
$C = 5x + 2y$?
  A. $(4, 1)$ **B.** $(5, 0)$ **C.** $(2, 6)$ **D.** $(3, 2)$ **E.** $(1, 5)$

Systems with Nonlinear Equations

6-8

You can solve systems that have linear, absolute value, and quadratic equations. Graph the equations on the same coordinate plane. Any point where the graphs intersect is a solution.

Solve each system of equations.

34. $y = x^2 - 4$
$y = -x + 2$

35. $y = |2x| - 3$
$y = x - 1$

36. $y = -x + 3$
$y = |2x - 3|$

37. $y = 2x + 6$
$y = x^2 + 3$

38. *Critical Thinking* How many solutions can a system with an absolute-value equation and a quadratic equation have? Explain.

Getting Ready for...► CHAPTER

7

Find the square of each number.

39. 3   **40.** -7 **41.** 4.5   **42.** $\frac{1}{2}$ **43.** 11   **44.** -8.2

Make a table of values to graph each function.

45. $y = x^2 - 4x + 3$ **46.** $y = x^2 + x - 2$ **47.** $y = -x^2 + 4x + 5$

Evaluate the expression $b^2 - 4ac$ for the given values.

48. $a = 2, b = -5, c = 3$ **49.** $a = -7, b = 9, c = 1$ **50.** $a = 4.5, b = 8, c = 0$

51. $a = 1, b = 3, c = -2$ **52.** $a = 0.5, b = 4, c = 2.5$ **53.** $a = -8, b = -3.2, c = 5$

Solve each system of linear equations by graphing.

1. $y = 3x - 7$
$\quad y = -x + 1$

2. $4x + 3y = 12$
$\quad 2x - 5y = -20$

Critical Thinking **Suppose you try to solve a system of linear equations using substitution and get this result. How many solutions does each system have?**

3. $x = 8$

4. $5 = y$

5. $-7 = 4$

6. $x = -1$

7. $2 = y$

8. $9 = 9$

Solve each system using substitution.

9. $y = 4x - 7$
$\quad y = 2x + 9$

10. $y = -2x - 1$
$\quad y = 3x - 16$

Solve each system using elimination.

11. $4x + y = 8$
$\quad -3x - y = 0$

12. $2x + 5y = 20$
$\quad 3x - 10y = 37$

13. $x + y = 10$
$\quad -x - 2y = -14$

14. $3x + 2y = -19$
$\quad x - 12y = 19$

Write a system of equations to model each situation. Then use your system to solve.

15. *Cable Service* Your local cable television company offers two plans: basic service with one movie channel for $35 per month, or basic service with two movie channels for $45 per month. What is the charge for the basic service and the charge for each movie channel?

16. *Education* A writing workshop enrolls novelists and poets in a ratio of 5 to 3. There are 24 people at the workshop. How many novelists are there? How many poets?

17. You have 15 coins in your pocket that are either quarters or nickels. They total $2.75. How many of each coin do you have?

18. *Writing* Compare solving a linear equation with solving a linear inequality. What are the similarities? What are the differences?

19. *Standardized Test Prep* Which point is *not* a solution of $y < 3x - 1$?
A. $(2, -4)$ **B.** $(5, 7)$ **C.** $(0, -1)$
D. $(-3, -13)$ **E.** $(4, -8)$

Solve each system by graphing.

20. $y > 4x - 1$
$\quad y \leq -x + 4$

21. $y \geq 3x + 5$
$\quad y > x - 2$

22. $y = x^2 + x + 1$
$\quad y = -3x + 6$

23. $y = 4x - 5$
$\quad y = |3x + 1|$

Open-ended **Write a system of equations with the given characteristics.**

24. two linear equations with no solution

25. a linear equation and a quadratic equation with two solutions

26. three linear inequalities with a triangular solution region

27. *Fund Raising* You are making bread to sell at a holiday fair. A loaf of oatmeal bread takes 2 cups of flour and 2 eggs. A loaf of banana bread takes 3 cups of flour and 1 egg. You have 12 cups of flour and 8 eggs.

$\quad x$ = number of loaves of oatmeal bread
$\quad y$ = number of loaves of banana bread
$\quad$ Restrictions: $2x + 3y \leq 12$
$\quad\quad\quad\quad\quad\quad\quad 2x + y \leq 8$
$\quad\quad\quad\quad\quad\quad\quad x \geq 0, y \geq 0$

a. Explain each restriction.
b. You will make $1 profit for each loaf of oatmeal bread and $2 profit for each loaf of banana bread. Write the equation.
c. Use linear programming to find how many loaves of each type you should make to maximize profits.

Part I

1 The graph of which of the following equations is a vertical line through $(-7, -4)$?
(1) $x = -7$ (3) $y = 7$
(2) $x = -4$ (4) $y = -4$

2 What is true of the graphs of $3y - 8 = -5x$ and $3x = 2y - 18$?
(1) no intersection   (3) intersect at $(-2, 6)$
(2) intersect at $(2, -6)$ (4) are identical

3 Which system has no solutions?
(1) $y = 3x + 1$ (3) $2x - 5y = -15$
     $3y = x - 12$ $y = \frac{2}{5}x + 3$

(2) $x + y = 4$ (4) $y = 2x + 3$
     $y = x + 4$ $2x - y = 6$

4 Which inequality is shown in the graph?
(1) $y \le 2x + 1$
(2) $y \ge 2x + 1$
(3) $y < 2x + 1$
(4) $y > 2x + 1$

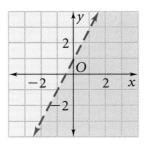

5 Which statement is true for every solution of the following system?

$2y > x + 4$
$3y + 3x > 13$

(1) $x \le -3$ (3) $x > 4$
(2) $y > 2$ (4) $y < 5$

6 Which system of equations has only one solution?
(1) $y = |x + 3|$ (3) $y = x^2 + 3$
     $y = x^2$ $y = 2x + 4$
(2) $y = |x - 3|$ (4) $y = -3$
     $y = 3x - 4$ $y = 2x^2 - 4$

7 Which x and y values minimize the quantity $Q = 3x - 4y$?

(1) $(1, -1)$
(3) $(5, 6)$
(2) $(3, 6)$
(4) $(1, 6)$

Part II

8 Solve this system using substitution.

$y = x + 10$
$y = 2x + 8$

9 Solve this system using elimination.

$5x - y = 5$
$3x + y = 11$

Part III

10 Plumber A charges \$40 for a house call plus \$30 per hour for labor. Plumber B charges \$20 for a house call plus \$35 per hour for labor. How long must a job take before plumber A is the less expensive choice for the homeowner?

11 The drama club sold 700 tickets to the school play and received \$3400. Adult tickets cost \$6 each, and student tickets cost \$4 each. How many of each type ticket did the club sell?

Part IV

12 Suppose you want to spend less than \$30 for the meat for subs at a party. Turkey costs \$4.00 per pound, and ham costs \$6.00 per pound. You want to buy at least 2 pounds of turkey as well as some ham.
  a Write a system of linear inequalities that describes this situation.
  b Graph the system of inequalities.
  c Name three possible solutions.

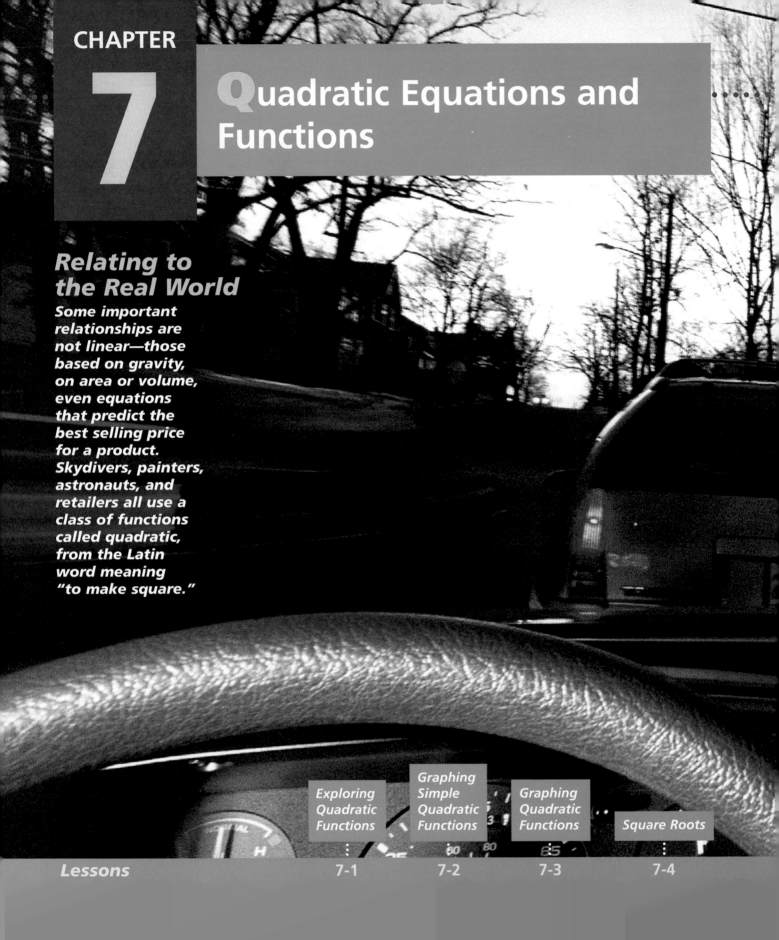

Relating to the Real World

Some important relationships are not linear—those based on gravity, on area or volume, even equations that predict the best selling price for a product. Skydivers, painters, astronauts, and retailers all use a class of functions called quadratic, from the Latin word meaning "to make square."

Full STOP Ahead

What is a safe stopping distance for cars traveling on the highway? How do accident investigators determine whether cars involved in an accident were traveling at safe speeds? There are many variables that affect how quickly a car can stop. These include the car's speed, the driver's reaction time, the type of road, and the weather conditions.

As you work through the chapter, you will use formulas to estimate safe speeds under various conditions. You will make graphs to illustrate the relationships between speed, reaction time, and stopping distance. Then, with your classmates, you will plan a skit to present what you have learned about safe highway driving.

To help you complete the project:

Solving Quadratic Equations

Using the Quadratic Formula

Using the Discriminant

7-5   7-6   7-7

317

What You'll Learn

• Graphing quadratic functions of the form $y = ax^2$

...And Why

To understand how changing a affects the graph of a quadratic function

What You'll Need

• graphing calculator

7-1 Exploring Quadratic Functions

Work with a partner. Complete a table of values and plot points, or use a graphing calculator set at the standard scale.

1. **a.** Graph the equations $y = x^2$ and $y = 3x^2$.
   b. How are the graphs in part (a) alike? different?

2. **a.** Graph the equations $y = -x^2$ and $y = -3x^2$.
   b. How are the graphs in part (a) different from the graphs in Question 1? How are they like the graphs in Question 1?

x	y
−2	■
−1	■
0	■
1	■
2	■

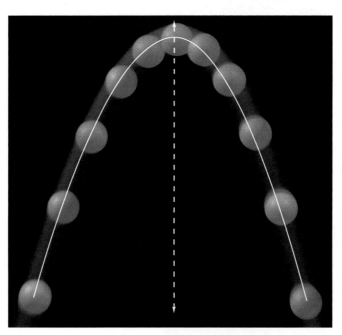

Quadratic Functions

The graphs you analyzed in the Work Together are all examples of **parabolas.** If you draw a parabola on a piece of paper, you can fold the paper down the middle of the parabola and the two sides will match exactly. The line down the middle of the parabola is the **axis of symmetry.**

3. **Try This** Trace each parabola on a sheet of paper and draw its axis of symmetry.

   a.

   b.

1 How does the graph of
$y = \frac{2}{3}x^2$ differ from the
graph of $y = -\frac{2}{3}x^2$?

(1) $y = \frac{2}{3}x^2$ is wider.

(2) $y = \frac{2}{3}x^2$ is narrower.

(3) $y = \frac{2}{3}x^2$ opens
upward rather than
downward.

(4) $y = \frac{2}{3}x^2$ opens
downward rather
than upward.

2 Tonya said that the
graph of $y = -2x^2$ is
wider than the graph of
$y = 3x^2$. Is she correct?
How do you know?

Each parabola that you have seen is the graph of a *quadratic function.*

> **Quadratic Function**
>
> For $a \neq 0$, the function $y = ax^2 + bx + c$ is a **quadratic function.**
>
> Examples: $y = 2x^2$, $y = x^2 + 2$, $y = -x^2 - x - 3$

When a quadratic function is written in the form $y = ax^2 + bx + c$, it is in
standard form.

4. Name the values of *a*, *b*, and *c* for each quadratic function.
   a. $y = 3x^2 - 2x + 5$ **b.** $y = 3x^2$ **c.** $y = -0.5x^2 + 2x$

5. Write each quadratic function in standard form.
   a. $y = 7x + 9x^2 - 4$ **b.** $y = 3 - x^2$

The Role of "a"

When you graph a quadratic function, if the value of *a* is positive, the
parabola opens upward. If the value of *a* is negative, the parabola opens
downward.

Example 1

Make a table of values and graph the quadratic functions
$y = 2x^2$ and $y = -2x^2$.

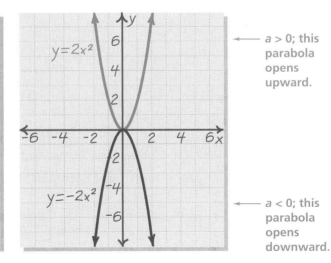

x	y=2x²	y=-2x²
-3	18	-18
-2	8	-8
-1	2	-2
0	0	0
1	2	-2
2	8	-8
3	18	-18

a > 0; this parabola opens upward.

a < 0; this parabola opens downward.

6. What is the axis of symmetry for the graphs in Example 1?

7. What would happen to the graph of $y = 2x^2$ if you could fold the
   graph over the *x*-axis? Explain.

The highest or lowest point on a parabola is called the **vertex** of the parabola.

When a parabola opens upward, the y-coordinate of the vertex is the **minimum value** of the function.

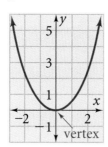

When a parabola opens downward, the y-coordinate of the vertex is the **maximum value** of the function.

8. Answer these questions for $y = -3x^2$ and $y = 4x^2$.
   a. What is the value of a?
   b. In which direction does each graph open?
   c. Is the y-coordinate of the vertex a minimum or a maximum value of the function?

9. **Summarize** what you know so far about how the value of a affects the parabola.

The value of a also affects the width of a parabola.

Example 2

Graph $-4x^2$, $y = \frac{1}{4}x^2$, and $y = x^2$. Compare the widths of the graphs.

$y = -4x^2$

$y = \frac{1}{4}x^2$

$y = x^2$

Of the three graphs, $y = \frac{1}{4}x^2$ is the widest, $y = x^2$ is narrower, and $y = -4x^2$ is the narrowest.

10. *Critical Thinking* What does the absolute value of a tell you about the width of a parabola? Use the graphs in Example 2 to explain your answer.

11. **Try This** Order each group of quadratic functions from widest to narrowest graph.
    a. $y = 2x^2, y = 3x^2, y = -5x^2$
    b. $y = \frac{3}{2}x^2, y = \frac{2}{3}x^2, y = \frac{1}{2}x^2$

Find the values of *a*, *b*, and *c* for each quadratic function.

1. $y = x^2 + 2x + 4$ **2.** $y = 2x^2$ **3.** $y = -x^2 - 3x - 9$ **4.** $y = -2x^2 + 5$

Tell whether each parabola opens *upward* or *downward* and whether the *y*-coordinate of the vertex is a *maximum* or a *minimum*.

5. $y = x^2$ **6.** $y = 9x^2$ **7.** $y = -\frac{2}{5}x^2$ **8.** $y = -6x^2$

Choose **Graph each quadratic function. Use either a table of values or a graphing calculator.**

9. $y = \frac{1}{2}x^2$ **10.** $y = 1.5x^2$ **11.** $y = -4x^2$ **12.** $y = -\frac{1}{3}x^2$

13. $y = 4x^2$ **14.** $y = \frac{1}{3}x^2$ **15.** $y = -1.5x^2$ **16.** $y = -\frac{1}{2}x^2$

Order each group of quadratic functions from widest to narrowest graph.

17. $y = 3x^2,\ y = x^2,\ y = 7x^2$ **18.** $y = 4x^2,\ y = \frac{1}{3}x^2,\ y = x^2$

19. $y = -2x^2,\ y = -\frac{2}{3}x^2,\ y = -4x^2$ **20.** $y = -\frac{1}{2}x^2,\ y = 5x^2,\ y = -\frac{1}{4}x^2$

Give the letter or letters of the graph(s) that make each statement true.

21. $a > 0$

22. $a < 0$

23. $|a|$ has the greatest value.

24. $|a|$ has the least value.

Trace each parabola on a sheet of paper and draw its axis of symmetry.

25.

26.

27.

28.

Writing Without graphing, describe how each graph differs from the graph of $y = x^2$.

29. $y = 2x^2$ **30.** $y = -x^2$ **31.** $y = 1.5x^2$ **32.** $y = \frac{1}{2}x^2$

33. Open-ended Give an example of a quadratic function for each description.
   a. Its graph opens upward.
   b. Its graph has the same shape as the graph in part (a), but the graph opens downward.
   c. Its graph is wider than the graph in part (b).

Match each function with its graph.

A. $y = x^2$ **B.** $y = -x^2$ **C.** $y = 3.5x^2$ **D.** $y = -3.5x^2$ **E.** $y = \frac{1}{4}x^2$ **F.** $y = -\frac{1}{4}x^2$

34.   **35.**   **36.**

37.   **38.**   **39.**

Exercises   M I X E D   R E V I E W

Find each percent of change.

40. 12 lb to 14 lb **41.** 5 ft to 7 ft **42.** $4.50 to $2.25

43. A type of spring toy begins as 80 ft of wire. In 50 years of production, 3,030,000 mi of wire weighing 50,000 tons have been used.
   a. How many of these toys have been made?
   b. How much does 1 mi of wire weigh?
   c. The 3,030,000 mi of wire could go around the equator 126 times. What is the length of the equator? What is the diameter of Earth?

SELF ASSESSMENT

FOR YOUR JOURNAL

Describe a quadratic function and its graph. Explain how the value of "a" affects the graph. Give examples of quadratic functions to support your statements.

Getting Ready for Lesson 7-2
Graph each linear equation.

44. $y = 2x$ **45.** $y = 2x - 3$ **46.** $y = 2x + 1$

What You'll Learn
- Graphing quadratic functions of the form $y = ax^2 + c$
- Graphing quadratic functions that represent real-life situations

...And Why
To understand how changing c affects the graph of a quadratic function

What You'll Need
- graphing calculator

7-2 Graphing Simple Quadratic Functions

WORK TOGETHER

Work with a partner. Use a table of values or a graphing calculator set at the standard scale.

1. a. Graph the quadratic functions $y = x^2$, $y = x^2 - 5$, and $y = x^2 + 1$.
   b. How are the graphs in part (a) alike? How are they different?

2. a. Graph the quadratic functions $y = -\frac{1}{2}x^2$, $y = -\frac{1}{2}x^2 + 4$, and $y = -\frac{1}{2}x^2 - 2$
   b. How are the graphs in part (a) alike? How are they different?

THINK AND DISCUSS

You have seen that changing the value of a in the function $y = ax^2$ affects whether the parabola opens upward or downward and how wide or narrow the parabola is. Changing the value of c in the function $y = ax^2 + c$ changes the position of the parabola.

Example 1

Graph the quadratic functions $y = -x^2 + 3$ and $y = -x^2 - 1$. Compare them to the graph of $y = -x^2$ at the left.

Make a table of values.

x	$y=-x^2+3$	$y=-x^2-1$
-3	-6	-10
-2	-1	-5
-1	2	-2
0	3	-1
1	2	-2
2	-1	-5
3	-6	-10

Plot the points. Connect the points to form smooth curves.

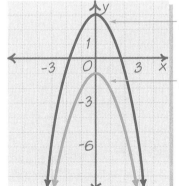

$y = -x^2 + 3$ shifts the parabola $y = -x^2$ *up* 3 units.

$y = -x^2 - 1$ shifts the parabola $y = -x^2$ *down* 1 unit.

3. Try This Graph $y = 2x^2$ and $y = 2x^2 - 4$. Compare the graphs.

4. Summarize how the graphs of $y = ax^2$ and $y = ax^2 + c$ are different and how they are alike.

5. Since the parabolas in Example 1 open downward, the y-coordinate of each vertex is a maximum value. Find the maximum value of each function.

When you graph a quadratic function that represents a real-life situation, you should limit the domain and range of your graph to x- and y-values that make sense in the situation.

<table>
<tr><td>**Example 2**</td><td>**Relating to the Real World** </td></tr>
</table>

Nature Suppose you see an eagle flying over a canyon. The eagle is 30 ft above the level of the canyon's edge when it drops a stick from its claws. The function $d = -16t^2 + 30$ gives the height of the stick in feet after t seconds. Graph this quadratic function.

Graph t on the horizontal or x-axis. Graph d on the vertical or y-axis.

Choose nonnegative values of t that represent the first few seconds of the stick's fall.

Choose values for d that show the height of the stick as it falls.

Xmin=0   Ymin=–40
Xmax=5   Ymax=40
Xscl=1   Yscl=10

6. In Example 2, why is the domain limited to nonnegative values of t?

7. Explain why the range does not include any values greater than 30.

8. The height of the stick is represented by d. From what level is the height measured?

1. **Writing** Describe how the graphs of the functions $y = 5x^2$, $y = 5x^2 + 50$, and $y = 5x^2 - 90$ are alike and how they are different.

Describe whether each quadratic function has a *maximum* or *minimum*.

2. $y = x^2 - 2$ 3. $y = -x^2 + 6$ 4. $y = 3x^2 + 1$ 5. $y = -\frac{1}{2}x^2 - 9$

Choose **Graph each quadratic function. Use either a table of values or a graphing calculator.**

6. $y = x^2 + 2$ 7. $y = x^2 - 3$ 8. $y = -x^2 + 4$ 9. $y = -x^2 - 1$

10. $y = -2x^2 + 2$ 11. $y = -2x^2 - 2$ 12. $y = -\frac{1}{4}x^2$ 13. $y = -\frac{1}{4}x^2 + 3$

14. $y = 4x^2$ 15. $y = 4x^2 - 7$ 16. $y = -1.5x^2 + 5$ 17. $y = -1.5x^2 - 1$

Open-ended **Give an example of a quadratic function for each description.**

18. It opens upward and its vertex is below the origin.

19. It opens downward and its vertex is above the origin.

20. **Geometry** Suppose that a pizza must fit into a box with a base that is 12 in. long and 12 in. wide. You can use the quadratic function $A = \pi r^2$ to find the area of a pizza in terms of its radius.
    a. What values of r make sense in the function?
    b. What values of A make sense in the function?
    c. Graph the function. Use $\pi \approx 3.14$.

12 in.

Match each function with its graph.
     A. $y = x^2 - 1$ B. $y = x^2 + 4$ C. $y = -x^2 + 2$
     D. $y = 3x^2 - 5$ E. $y = -3x^2 + 8$ F. $y = -0.2x^2 + 5$

21.

22.

23.

24.

25.

26.

Give the letter of the parabola(s) that make each statement true.

27. $c > 0$　　　　　　　　　　**28.** $c < 0$

29. $a > 0$　　　　　　　　　　**30.** $a < 0$

31. The function has a maximum.　**32.** The function has a minimum.

33. a. Landscaping The plan for a rectangular patio has a square garden centered in the patio with sides parallel to the sides of the patio. The patio is 20 ft long by 12 ft wide. If each side of the garden is x ft, the function $y = 240 - x^2$ gives the area of the patio in ft^2. Graph this function.
　b. What values make sense for the domain? Explain why.
　c. What is the range of the function? Explain why.

34. Architecture An architect wants to design an archway with these requirements.
　　　　• The archway is 6 ft wide and has vertical sides 7 ft high.
　　　　• The top of the archway is modeled by the function $y = -\frac{1}{3}x^2 + 10$.

Italy

　a. Sketch the architect's design by drawing vertical lines 7 units high at $x = -3$ and $x = 3$ and graphing the portion of the quadratic function that lies between $x = -3$ and $x = 3$.
　b. The plan for the archway is changed so that the top is modeled by the function $y = -0.5x^2 + 11.5$. Make a revised sketch of the archway.
　c. Research Find out how arches were used by the architects of ancient Rome or during the Middle Ages.

Exercises　　MIXED REVIEW

Write an equation of the line perpendicular to the given line through the given point.

35. $y = 5x - 2;\ (7, 0)$　　**36.** $y = -2x + 9;\ (3, 5)$　　**37.** $y = 0.5x;\ (-8, -2)$

38. $x + y = 6;\ (3, 1)$　　**39.** $y - 4x = 2;\ (0, 3)$　　**40.** $y = -6x - 2;\ (0, 0)$

41. Real Estate Fox Island is a 4.5-acre island in Rhode Island. It has an assessed value of \$290,400. Use a proportion to find out how much a similar 2-acre island nearby might be worth.

Getting Ready for Lesson 7-3

Find $\frac{-b}{2a}$ for each quadratic function.

42. $y = x^2 + 4x - 2$　　　**43.** $y = -8x^2 + x + 13$　　　**44.** $y = 6x^2 + x + 7$

What You'll Learn

- Graphing quadratic functions of the form $y = ax^2 + bx + c$
- Finding the axis of symmetry and vertex
- Graphing quadratic inequalities

...And Why

To solve problems involving weather and road safety

What You'll Need

- graph paper

7-3 | **G**raphing Quadratic Functions

WORK TOGETHER

To find the reflection of the point $(-1, 2)$ over the line $x = 2$, fold your paper on the line. Then mark the image of the original point.

Work with a partner to find the image of each point.

1. Find the reflection over the line $x = -2$.
    a. $(-4, 5)$ **b.** $(-6, 1)$ **c.** $(2, -2)$ **d.** $(-1, 0)$ **e.** $(0, 4)$

THINK AND DISCUSS

Graphing $y = ax^2 + bx + c$

In the quadratic functions you have graphed so far, $b = 0$. When $b \neq 0$, the parabola shifts right or left. The axis of symmetry is no longer the y-axis.

axis of symmetry
$x = \frac{-b}{2a}$

vertex
$\left(\frac{-b}{2a}, y\right)$

> #### Graph of a Quadratic Function
>
> The graph of $y = ax^2 + bx + c$, where $a \neq 0$, has the line $x = \frac{-b}{2a}$ as its axis of symmetry. The x-coordinate of the vertex is $\frac{-b}{2a}$.

The y-intercept of the graph of a quadratic function is c. This is because substituting $x = 0$ gives you the function value c. You can use the axis of symmetry and the y-intercept to help you graph the function.

7-3 Graphing Quadratic Functions   **327**

Example 1 ··

Graph the quadratic function $f(x) = 5 - 4x - x^2$.

Step 1 Find the y-intercept.

The value of c is 5, so the y-intercept of the graph is 5.

Step 2 Find the equation of the axis of symmetry and the coordinates of the vertex.

$f(x) = -x^2 - 4x + 5$ ⟵ Write the function in standard form.

$x = -\dfrac{b}{2a} = -\dfrac{-4}{2(-1)} = -2$ ⟵ Find the equation of the axis of symmetry.

The x-coordinate of the vertex is -2.

$f(x) = -(-2)^2 - 4(-2) + 5$ ⟵ To find the y-coordinate of the vertex, substitute –2 for x.
$f(x) = 9$

The vertex is at $(-2, 9)$.

Step 3 Make a table of values and graph the function.

Pair each point on one side of the axis of symmetry with a point on the other side that will have the same $f(x)$ value.

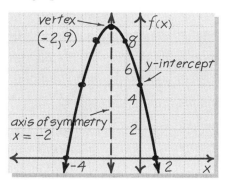

2. Try This Graph $y = x^2 - 6x + 9$. Find the equation of the axis of symmetry, the coordinates of the vertex, and the y-intercept.

You can use what you know about quadratic functions to find maximum or minimum values in real-world problems.

Example 2   **Relating to the Real World** ·····················

Weather Meteorologists use equations to model weather patterns. This function predicts atmospheric pressure over a certain 24-hour period.

$$y = 0.005x^2 - 0.113x + 30.22$$

In the equation, x represents the number of hours after 12:00 midnight and y represents the atmospheric pressure in inches of mercury. At what time will the pressure be lowest? What will the lowest pressure be?

Weather balloons measure conditions in the atmosphere. About 1600 balloons a day are launched in the world.

Look Back Use the graph of the function to check your solution.

Xmin=0   Ymin=28
Xmax=24   Ymax=31
X s c l=4   Y s c l=1

Since the coefficient of x^2 is positive, the curve opens upward and the y-coordinate of the vertex is a minimum.

$$-\frac{b}{2a} = -\frac{-0.113}{2(0.005)} = 11.3 \quad \longleftarrow \text{Find the } x\text{-coordinate of the vertex.}$$

After 11.3 hours (at 11:18 A.M.), the pressure will be at its lowest.

$$y = 0.005(11.3)^2 - 0.113(11.3) + 30.22 \quad \longleftarrow \text{Substitute 11.3 for } x.$$

$$y = 29.58$$

The minimum pressure will be 29.58 in. of mercury.

3. Why is it important to check the coefficient of the squared term when solving a real-world maximum or minimum problem?

Quadratic Inequalities

Graphing a quadratic inequality is similar to graphing a linear inequality. The curve is dashed if the inequality involves $<$ or $>$. The curve is solid if the inequality involves $\leq$ or $\geq$.

Example 3   **Relating to the Real World**

Road Safety An archway over a road is cut out of rock. Its shape is modeled by the quadratic function $y = -0.1x^2 + 12$. Can a camper 6 ft wide and 7 ft high fit under the arch without crossing the median line?

The camper will fit if each point on it satisfies $y < -0.1x^2 + 12$. Graph the inequality $y < -0.1x^2 + 12$.

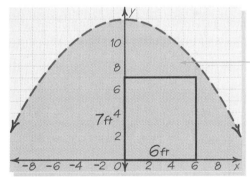

Shade the region under the parabola.

The camper should be able to fit since each point that represents the camper is in the shaded region.

4. Check the solution by showing that the values $x = 6$ and $y = 7$ satisfy the inequality $y < -0.1x^2 + 12$.

5. How does the graph of $y > -0.1x^2 + 12$ differ from the graph above?

6. Try This Graph $y \geq x^2 + 2x + 1$.

Find the equation of the axis of symmetry and the coordinates of the vertex of the graph of each function.

1. $y = 0.2x^2 + 4$
2. $y = x^2 - 8x - 9$
3. $y = 2x^2 + 4x - 5$

4. $y = 3x^2 - 9x + 5$
5. $f(x) = 4x^2 - 3$
6. $y = 3x^2 - 9$

7. $f(x) = x^2 + 4x + 3$
8. $y = 2x^2 - 6x$
9. $y = 12 + x^2$

Match each graph with its function.

A. $y = x^2 - 6x$ **B.** $y = x^2 + 6x$ **C.** $y = -x^2 - 6x$
D. $y = -x^2 + 6x$ **E.** $y = -x^2 + 6$ **F.** $y = x^2 - 6$

10.

11.

12.

13.

14.

15.

Choose Graph each function. Use a graphing calculator or a table of values. Label the axis of symmetry, the vertex, and the *y*-intercept.

16. $f(x) = x^2 - 6x + 8$
17. $y = -x^2 + 4x - 4$

18. $y = x^2 + 1$
19. $y = -x^2 + 4x$

20. $y = -2x^2 + 6$
21. $f(x) = 3x^2 + 6x$

22. $y = x^2 - 4x + 3$
23. $f(x) = -x^2 - 4x - 6$

24. $y = x^2 - 2x + 1$
25. $f(x) = 2x^2 + x - 3$

26. $y = x^2 + 3x + 2$
27. $y = -x^2 + 4x - 7$

28. Fireworks A skyrocket is shot into the air. Its altitude *h* in feet after *t* seconds is given by the function $h = -16t^2 + 128t$.
  a. In how many seconds does the skyrocket reach maximum altitude?
  b. What is the skyrocket's maximum altitude?

29. Gardening Suppose you have 80 ft of fence to enclose a rectangular garden. The function $A = 40x - x^2$ gives you the area of the garden in square feet where *x* is the width in feet. What width gives you the maximum gardening area? What is the maximum area?

30. Writing Explain how changing the values of a, b, and c in a quadratic function affects the graph of the function.

Graph each quadratic inequality.

31. $y > x^2$

32. $y < -x^2$

33. $y \leq x^2 + 3$

34. $y < -x^2 + 4$

35. $y \geq -2x^2 + 6$

36. $y > -x^2 + 4x - 4$

37. $y \leq x^2 + 5x + 6$

38. $y < x^2 - x - 6$

39. $y \geq 3x^2 + 6x$

Open-ended **Give a quadratic function for each description.**

40. Its axis of symmetry is to the right of the y-axis.

41. Its graph opens downward and has vertex at $(0, 0)$.

42. Its graph lies entirely above the x-axis.

Chapter Project .... **Find Out by Graphing**

To avoid skidding, you want to know what a safe stopping distance is. Assume you are traveling on a dry road and have an average reaction time. The formula $f(x) = 0.044x^2 + 1.1x$ gives you a safe stopping distance in feet, where x is your speed in miles per hour. Make a table of values for speeds of 10, 20, 30, 40, 50, and 60 mi/h. Then graph the function.

Exercises   M I X E D   R E V I E W

Find each probability for two rolls of a number cube.

43. P(even and odd)

44. P(7 and 5)

45. P(two odd numbers)

46. P(6 and 2)

47. a. Rowing The-Head-of-the-Charles Regatta is a 3 mi rowing race held annually in Cambridge, Massachusetts. In 1994, Xeno Muller won the men's singles title in 17 min, 47 s. What was his pace in mi/h? Round your answer to the nearest tenth.

   b. Muller rowed at 32 strokes/min. How many strokes did he row over the course of the race?

FOR YOUR JOURNAL

Summarize what you have learned about graphing quadratic functions. Include examples to support your statements.

Getting Ready for Lesson 7-4

Evaluate for $a = -1$, $b = 2$, $c = 3$, **and** $d = -4$.

48. a^2

49. $-a^2$

50. $-b^2$

51. dc^2

52. $(dc)^2$

What You'll Learn

7-4 **S**quare Roots

- Finding square roots
- Using square roots

...And Why

To use square roots in real-world situations, such as finding the distance from a satellite to the horizon

What You'll Need

- calculator

THINK AND DISCUSS

Finding Square Roots

The diagram shows the relationship between squares and square roots. Every positive number has *two* square roots.

$$4^2 \qquad (-4)^2$$
$$\searrow \quad 16 \quad \swarrow$$
$$\text{square root of } 16$$
$$\swarrow \qquad \searrow$$
$$4 \qquad -4$$

Square Root
....

If $a^2 = b$, then a is a **square root** of b.

Example: $4^2 = 16$ and $(-4)^2 = 16$, so 4 and -4 are square roots of 16.

A radical symbol $\sqrt{}$ indicates a square root. The expression $\sqrt{16}$ means the **principal** (or positive) **square root** of 16. The expression $-\sqrt{16}$ means the **negative square root** of 16. You can use the symbol $\pm$, read "plus or minus," to indicate both square roots.

Example 1

Simplify each expression.

a. $\sqrt{64} = 8$ ⟵ positive square root

b. $-\sqrt{100} = -10$ ⟵ negative square root

c. $\pm\sqrt{\frac{9}{16}} = \pm\frac{3}{4}$ ⟵ The square roots are $\frac{3}{4}$ and $-\frac{3}{4}$.

d. $\pm\sqrt{0} = 0$ ⟵ There is only one square root of 0.

e. $\sqrt{-16}$ is undefined ⟵ For real numbers, the square root of a negative number is undefined.

1. Try This Simplify each expression.

a. $\sqrt{49}$ b. $\pm\sqrt{36}$ c. $-\sqrt{121}$ d. $\sqrt{\frac{1}{25}}$

QUICK REVIEW

Rational and irrational numbers make up the set of *real numbers.* In decimal form, *rational* numbers terminate or repeat. *Irrational* numbers continue without repeating number patterns.

Some square roots are rational numbers and some are irrational numbers.

Rational: $\pm\sqrt{81} = \pm 9$, $-\sqrt{1.44} = -1.2$, $\sqrt{\frac{4}{9}} = \frac{2}{3} = 0.\overline{6}$

Irrational: $-\sqrt{5} = -2.23606797\ldots$, $\sqrt{\frac{1}{3}} = 0.57735026\ldots$

2. Try This Classify each expression as *rational* or *irrational*.

a. $\sqrt{8}$ b. $\pm\sqrt{225}$ c. $-\sqrt{75}$ d. $\sqrt{\frac{1}{4}}$

Math A Test Prep

Estimating and Using Square Roots

The squares of integers are called **perfect squares.**

consecutive integers:	1	2	3	4	5	6	7
	↓	↓	↓	↓	↓	↓	↓
consecutive perfect squares:	1	4	9	16	25	36	49

You can estimate square roots by using perfect squares and by using a calculator.

Example 2

Estimation Between what two consecutive integers is $\sqrt{14.52}$?

$\sqrt{9} < \sqrt{14.52} < \sqrt{16}$ ◄—— 14.52 is between the two consecutive square numbers 9 and 16.

$3 < \sqrt{14.52} < 4$

$\sqrt{14.52}$ is between 3 and 4.

3. Try This Between what two consecutive integers is $-\sqrt{105}$?

Example 3

Calculator Find $\sqrt{14.52}$ to the nearest hundredth.

$\boxed{\sqrt{}}$ 14.52 $\boxed{\text{ENTER}}$ *3.8105111777* ◄—— Use a calculator.

$\sqrt{14.52} \approx 3.81$

4. Critical Thinking How can you use consecutive perfect squares to mentally check calculator answers for square roots?

Example 4   Relating to the Real World

Towers A tower is supported with a wire. The formula $d = \sqrt{x^2 + (2x)^2}$ gives the length d of the wire for the tower at the left. Find the length of the wire if $x = 12$ ft.

$d = \sqrt{x^2 + (2x)^2}$

$d = \sqrt{12^2 + (2 \cdot 12)^2}$ ◄—— Substitute 12 for x.

$d = \sqrt{144 + 576}$ ◄—— Simplify.

$d = \sqrt{720}$

$d = $ *26.83281573* ◄—— Use a calculator.

$d \approx 26.8$

The wire is about 26.8 ft long.

5. Try This Suppose the tower is 140 ft tall. How long is the supporting wire?

Find both the principal and negative square root of each number.

1. 169   **2.** 1.96   **3.** $\frac{1}{9}$ **4.** 900

5. 0.25   **6.** $\frac{36}{49}$ **7.** 1.21   **8.** 1681

Tell whether each expression is *rational* or *irrational*.

9. $\sqrt{37}$ **10.** $-\sqrt{0.04}$ **11.** $\pm\sqrt{\frac{1}{5}}$ **12.** $-\sqrt{\frac{16}{121}}$

Between what two consecutive integers is each square root?

13. $\sqrt{35}$ **14.** $\sqrt{27}$ **15.** $-\sqrt{245}$ **16.** $\sqrt{880}$

Calculator **Use a calculator to simplify each expression. Round to the nearest hundredth.**

17. $\sqrt{12}$ **18.** $-\sqrt{203}$ **19.** $\sqrt{11,550}$ **20.** $-\sqrt{150}$

21. Sports The elasticity coefficient e of a ball relates the height r of its rebound to the height h from which it is dropped. You can find the elasticity coefficient using the function $e = \sqrt{\frac{r}{h}}$.
   a. What is the elasticity coefficient for a tennis ball that rebounds 3 ft after it is dropped from a height of 3.5 ft?
   b. Critical Thinking Suppose that the elasticity coefficient of a basketball is 0.88. How high is its rebound if it is dropped 6 ft?

22. Critical Thinking What number other than 0 is its own square root?

Find the square roots of each number.

23. 0.36   **24.** 144   **25.** $\frac{25}{16}$ **26.** 0.01

27. 400   **28.** 0   **29.** 625   **30.** $\frac{9}{49}$

31. $\frac{1}{81}$ **32.** 1.69   **33.** 729   **34.** 2.25

35. a. Space Find the distance to the horizon from a satellite 4200 km above Earth. The formula $d = \sqrt{12{,}800h + h^2}$ tells you the distance d in kilometers to the horizon from a satellite h kilometers above Earth.
   b. Find the distance to the horizon from a satellite 3600 km above Earth.

36. Standardized Test Prep If $x^2 = 16$ and $y^2 = 25$, choose the least possible value for the expression $y - x$.
   A. -1 **B.** 0   **C.** 1
   D. -9 **E.** -4

37. In the cartoon, to what number is the golfer referring?

©1995 Tribune Media Services, Inc.
All Rights Reserved.

METRO MATHEMATICS CLUB OPEN

$\sqrt{16}$

6-1

from cartoon *Bound and Gagged*

🖩 *Choose* **Use a calculator, paper and pencil, or mental math. Find the value of each expression. If the value is irrational, round to the nearest hundredth.**

38. $\sqrt{441}$

39. $-\sqrt{\dfrac{4}{25}}$

40. $\sqrt{2}$

41. $\sqrt{\dfrac{1}{36}}$

42. $-\sqrt{1.6}$

43. $-\sqrt{157}$

44. $\sqrt{200}$

45. $-\sqrt{13}$

46. $\sqrt{30}$

47. $\sqrt{1089}$

48. $-\sqrt{0.64}$

49. $\sqrt{41}$

50. *Writing* Explain the difference between $-\sqrt{1}$ and $\sqrt{-1}$.

51. *Open-ended* Find two integers a and b, both between 1 and 25, such that $a^2 + b^2$ is a perfect square.

Tell whether each expression is *rational, irrational,* or *undefined.*

52. $-\sqrt{3600}$

53. $\sqrt{8}$

54. $\sqrt{-25}$

55. $\sqrt{6.25}$

56. $\sqrt{12.96}$

57. $\sqrt{129.6}$

58. $-\sqrt{12.96}$

59. $\sqrt{-12.96}$

60. *Physics* If you drop an object, the time t in seconds that it takes to fall d feet is given by $t = \sqrt{\dfrac{d}{16}}$.

  a. Find the time it takes an object to fall 400 ft.
  b. Find the time it takes an object to fall 1600 ft.
  c. *Critical Thinking* In part (b), the object falls four times as far as in part (a). Does it take four times as long to fall? Explain.

Tell whether each statement is *true* or *false*. If the statement is false, rewrite it as a true statement.

61. $6 < \sqrt{38} < 7$

62. $-7 < -\sqrt{56} < -6$

63. $-4 < -\sqrt{17} < -5$

64. $3.3 \le \sqrt{10.25} < 3.4$

65. $-16 < -\sqrt{280} < -15$

66. $21 < \sqrt{436} < 22$

67. $-38 < -\sqrt{1300} < -37$

68. $-9 \le -\sqrt{72} < -8$

69. $0.1 < \sqrt{0.03} < 0.2$

Chapter Project

Find Out by Calculating

Suppose a car left a skid mark d feet long. The formulas shown will estimate the speed s in miles per hour at which the car was traveling when the brakes were applied. Use the formulas to complete the table of estimated speeds.

- Why do you think the estimates of speed do not double when the skid marks double in length?

- Based on these results, what conclusions can you make about safe following distances?

Traveling Speed	
Dry Road	$s = \sqrt{27d}$
Wet Road	$s = \sqrt{13.5d}$

Skid Mark Length (d)	Estimated Speed (s)	
	Dry Road	Wet Road
60 ft	▪	▪
120 ft	▪	▪

Exercises   MIXED REVIEW

Solve each inequality. Graph the solution on a number line.

70. $2x > 8$
71. $14 < -7s$
72. $z - 1 \geq -1$
73. $-2 - b > 4$

74. $5b + 4 < -6$
75. $-2c \geq 5c - 1$
76. $8(m - 3) \leq 4$
77. $2 > 7 - 3t$

78. One in four residents of the United States has myopia, or nearsightedness. What is the probability that two people chosen at random are both nearsighted?

Getting Ready for Lesson 7-5

Solve each equation.

79. $3x - 14 = 27$
80. $4(y - 5) = 20$
81. $-6b + 12 = 12$
82. $3 - 9m = 0$

Exercises   CHECKPOINT

Graph each quadratic function. Find the vertex of each parabola.

1. $y = 4x^2$
2. $y = 2x^2 + 7$
3. $y = -x^2 - 2x + 10$

Choose Use a calculator, paper and pencil, or mental math to find the value of each square root. Round to the nearest hundredth.

4. $\sqrt{7}$
5. $-\sqrt{100}$
6. $\sqrt{23}$
7. $\sqrt{144}$
8. $-\sqrt{150}$
9. $-\sqrt{\frac{1}{9}}$

10. Writing What does the rule for a quadratic function tell you about how the graph of the function will look?

11. Open-ended Give an example of a quadratic function for each of the following descriptions.
   a. Its graph opens downward.
   b. Its graph is wider than the graph of $y = \frac{1}{2}x^2 - 3$.

7-5 Solving Quadratic Equations

What You'll Learn

- Solving quadratic equations in $ax^2 = c$ form
- Finding if a quadratic equation has two solutions, one solution, or no solution

...And Why

To solve real-world problems, such as finding the radius of a pond

What You'll Need

- calculator

WORK TOGETHER

1. Work with a partner. Find the x-intercepts of each graph.

   a. $y = 2x - 3$

   b. $y = -x^2 - 2x + 3$

2. Use the graph in Question 1(a) to find the solution of $2x - 3 = 0$.

3. Are the x-intercepts that you found in Question 1(b) solutions of $-x^2 - 2x + 3 = 0$? Explain.

4. Graph $y = x^2 + x - 6 = 0$.

5. **a.** Where does the graph of $y = x^2 + x - 6$ cross the x-axis?

   b. Do the values you found in part (a) satisfy the equation $x^2 + x - 6 = 0$?

THINK AND DISCUSS

Using Square Roots to Solve Equations

In the Work Together, you investigated a quadratic equation and its related quadratic function. Any values that make the equation true are solutions.

> **Standard Form of a Quadratic Equation**
> ....
> A **quadratic equation** is an equation that can be written in **standard form**:
> $$ax^2 + bx + c = 0, \text{ where } a \neq 0$$

6. Write $6x^2 = 5x - 12$ in standard form.

7. Is $5x - 3 = 0$ a quadratic equation? Why or why not?

There are two square roots for numbers greater than 0. So there are two solutions for an equation like $x^2 = 36$. You can solve equations in the form $x^2 = a$ by finding the square roots of each side.

$$x^2 = 36 \longrightarrow x = \pm 6$$

Example 1 ....

Solve $2x^2 - 98 = 0$.

$2x^2 - 98 = 0 + 98$ ⟵ **Add 98 to each side.**
$ 2x^2 = 98$
$ x^2 = 49$ ⟵ **Divide each side by 2.**
$ \sqrt{x^2} = \pm\sqrt{49}$ ⟵ **Find the square roots.**
$ x = \pm 7$

8. Try This Use a calculator to solve $x^2 - 7 = 0$. Round your solutions to the nearest tenth.

9. Critical Thinking Find a value for c so that the equation $x^2 - c = 0$ has 11 and -11 as solutions.

You can solve many geometric problems by finding square roots.

Example 2 **Relating to the Real World** ·················

City Planning A city is planning a circular duck pond for a new park. The depth of the pond will be 4 ft. Because of water resources, the maximum volume will be 20,000 ft³. Find the radius of the pond. Use the equation $V = \pi r^2 h$, where V is the volume, r is the radius, and h is the depth.

$ V = \pi r^2 h$
$ 20{,}000 = \pi r^2(4)$ ⟵ **Substitute 20,000 for V and 4 for h.**
$ \dfrac{20{,}000}{\pi(4)} = r^2$ ⟵ **Put in calculator-ready form.**
$ \sqrt{\dfrac{20{,}000}{\pi(4)}} = r$ ⟵ **Find the principal square root.**
$ 39.89422804 = r$ ⟵ **Use a calculator.**

The pond will have a radius of about 39.9 ft.

10. *Critical Thinking* Why is the principal square root the only root that makes sense in Example 2?

11. **Justify** this step in Example 2:
    If $20{,}000 = \pi r^2(4)$, then $\frac{20{,}000}{\pi(4)} = r^2$.

12. *Calculator* Which keystrokes can you use to find r in Example 2?
    A. ☐√ ☐(20000 ☐÷ ☐(☐π ☐× 4 ☐) ☐) |ENTER|
    B. ☐√ 20000 ☐÷ ☐π ☐× 4 |ENTER|

13. **a.** **Try This** Suppose the pond could have a volume of 40,000 ft³. What will be the radius of the pond if the depth is not changed?
    b. *Critical Thinking* Does the radius of the pond double when the volume doubles? Explain.

Finding the Number of Solutions

You have seen quadratic equations that have two real numbers as solutions. For real numbers, a quadratic equation can have two solutions, one solution, or no solution.

You can use a graph to find the solution(s) of a quadratic equation by finding the x-intercepts of the related quadratic function.

Example 3

Solve each equation by graphing the related function.
    a. $x^2 - 4 = 0$ **b.** $x^2 = 0$ **c.** $x^2 + 4 = 0$

    Graph $y = x^2 - 4$.   Graph $y = x^2$.   Graph $y = x^2 + 4$.

      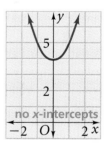

    There are two   There is one   There is no
    solutions, $x = \pm 2$.   solution, $x = 0$.   solution.

14. **a.** *Critical Thinking* For what values of c will $x^2 = c$ have two solutions?
    b. For what value of c will $x^2 = c$ have one solution?
    c. For what values of c will $x^2 = c$ have no solution?

15. *Mental Math* Tell the number of solutions for each equation.
    a. $x^2 = -36$ **b.** $x^2 - 12 = 6$ **c.** $x^2 - 15 = -15$

Choose **Solve each equation by graphing, using mental math, or using paper and pencil. If the equation has no solution, write *no solution*.**

1. $x^2 = 4$

2. $x^2 = 49$

3. $3x^2 + 27 = 0$

4. $x^2 + 25 = 25$

5. $3x^2 - 7 = -34$

6. $x^2 - 225 = 0$

7. $49x^2 - 16 = -7$

8. $x^2 - 9 = 16$

9. $4x^2 = 25$

10. $x^2 + 36 = 0$

11. $4x^2 - 100 = -100$

12. $x^2 - 63 = 81$

13. *Critical Thinking* Michael solved $x^2 + 25 = 0$ and found the solutions -5 and 5. Explain the mistake that Michael made.

Solve each equation. Round solutions to the nearest tenth.

14. $b^2 = 3$

15. $8x^2 = 64$

16. $n^2 - 5 = 16$

17. $3m^2 + 7 = 13$

18. $2x^2 - 179 = 0$

19. $b^2 - 1 = 20$

Model each problem with a quadratic equation. Then solve.

20. *Photography* Find the dimensions of the square picture that make the area of the picture equal to 75% of the total area enclosed by the frame.

21. *Geometry* Find the radius of a sphere with surface area 160 in.^{2}. Use the formula $A = 4\pi r^2$, where A is the surface area and r is the radius of the sphere. Round your answer to the nearest tenth of an inch.

x 12 in.

Susan La Flesche Picotte (1865–1915) was a physician and the leader of the Omaha people.

For each equation, you are given a statement about the number of solutions of each equation. If the claim is true, verify it by solving the equation. If the claim is false, write a correct statement.

22. $n^2 + 2 = 11$; there are two solutions.

23. $g^2 = -49$; there are two solutions.

24. $x^2 + 9 = 25$; there is one solution.

25. $4x^2 - 96 = 0$; there is one solution.

26. $-4r^2 = -64$; there are two solutions.

27. $4n^2 - 256 = 0$; there are two solutions.

28. $4b^2 + 9 = 9$; there are two solutions.

29. $-x^2 - 15 = 0$; there is no solution.

30. *Open-ended* Suppose you have 225 square tiles, all the same size. You can tile one surface using all the tiles. How could you tile more than one square surface using all the tiles? No surface can have only one tile.

31. *Painting* Suppose you have a can of paint that will cover 400 ft^2. Find the radius of the largest circle you can paint. Round your answer to the nearest tenth of a foot. (*Hint:* Use the formula $A = \pi r^2$.)

Physics **Use this information for Exercises 32–35.** The time t it takes a pendulum to make a complete swing back and forth depends on the length of the pendulum. This formula relates the length of a pendulum ℓ in meters to the time t in seconds.

$$\ell = \frac{2.45t^2}{\pi^2}$$

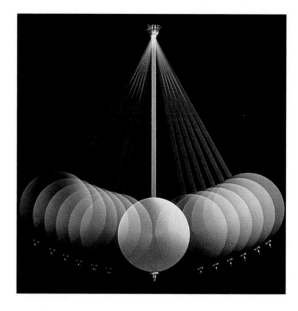

32. Find the length of the pendulum if $t = 1\ s$. Round to the nearest tenth.

33. Find t if $\ell = 1.6$ m. Round to the nearest tenth.

34. Find t if $\ell = 2.2$ m. Round to the nearest tenth.

35. **Writing** You can adjust a clock with a pendulum by making the pendulum longer or shorter. If a clock is running slowly, would you lengthen or shorten the pendulum to make the clock run faster? Explain.

36. **Standardized Test Prep** Suppose that $2x^2 - 36 = x^2 - 49$. Which statement is correct?
   A. The equation has two real solutions.
   B. The equation has no real solutions.
   C. The equation has exactly one real solution.
   D. You cannot determine the number of real solutions.

Solve each equation. If the equation has no solution, write *no solution*.

37. $5x^2 + 9 = 40$

38. $2x^2 + 8x^2 + 16 = 16$

39. $8x^2 - 4 - 3x^2 + 6 = 30$

40. $x^2 + 3 - 2x^2 - 9 = 30$

41. $3x^2 - 10 + 5x^2 + 3 = 25$

42. $6x^2 + 22 + 2x^2 + 50 = 60$

Exercises   MIXED REVIEW

Solve each system of equations.

43. $3x + 2y = 12$
$\quad\ x - 2y = -4$

44. $-x + 4y = 18$
$\quad\ 3x + y = -2$

45. $0.4x - 1.2y = 24$
$\quad\ 1.6x + 0.6y = 15$

46. a. **Space** NASA astronauts must be between 4 ft $10\frac{1}{2}$ in. and 6 ft 4 in. tall. Russian cosmonauts must be between 5 ft $4\frac{1}{2}$ in. and 6 ft. Change these values to inches. Use a number line to graph an inequality that models each situation.

b. Use a number line to graph the heights that are acceptable for an astronaut but not acceptable for a cosmonaut.

Getting Ready for Lesson 7-6

Evaluate each expression. Round to the nearest hundredth, where necessary.

47. $\sqrt{5^2 - 15}$

48. $\sqrt{36 + 64}$

49. $\sqrt{(-4)^2 - (2)(-3)}$

50. $-3 - \sqrt{36}$

Finding Roots

After Lesson 7-5

The solutions of a quadratic equation are the x-intercepts of the related quadratic function. The solutions of a quadratic equation and the related x-intercepts are often called *roots of the equation* or *roots of the function*.

Example

Use a graphing calculator to solve $x^2 - 6x + 3 = 0$.

Step 1	Step 2	Step 3	Step 4
Enter $y = x^2 - 6x + 3$. Use the CALC feature. Select 2:ROOT. The calculator will plot the graph.	Move the cursor to the left of the first x-intercept. Press ENTER to set the lower bound.	Move the cursor slightly to the right of the intercept. Press ENTER to set the upper bound.	Press ENTER to display the first root, which is about 0.55.

Repeating the steps near the second intercept, you find the second root is about 5.45. So, the solutions are about 0.55 and 5.45.

Suppose you cannot see both of the x-intercepts on your graph. You can find the range for the x-axis by using the TABLE feature. The calculator screen at the right shows part of the table for $y = 2x^2 - 48x + 285$.

The graph crosses the x-axis when the values for y change signs. So the range of values of x should include 10.5 and 13.5.

1. Find the x-intercepts of $y = 2x^2 - 48x + 285$.

Use a graph to solve each equation.

2. $x^2 - 6x - 16 = 0$

3. $2x^2 + x - 6 = 0$

4. $\frac{1}{3}x^2 + 8x - 3 = 0$

5. $x^2 - 18x + 5 = 0$

6. $0.25x^2 - 8x - 45 = 0$

7. $0.5x^2 + 3x - 36 = 0$

8. Writing Solve $3x^2 = 48$ using a calculator or paper and pencil. Explain why you chose the method you used.

What You'll Learn

7-6

Using the Quadratic Formula

- Using the quadratic formula to solve quadratic equations

...And Why

To investigate real-world situations, such as the vertical motion of model rockets

What You'll Need

- calculator

THINK AND DISCUSS

In Lesson 7-5, you solved some simple quadratic equations by finding square roots and by graphing. In this lesson, you will learn to solve any quadratic equation by using the **quadratic formula.** In Chapter 10 you will learn additional ways to solve a quadratic equation.

Quadratic Formula

If $ax^2 + bx + c = 0$ and $a \neq 0$, then $x = \dfrac{-b \pm \sqrt{b^2 - 4ac}}{2a}$.

Example 1

Solve $x^2 + 5x + 6 = 0$ by using the quadratic formula.

$x = \dfrac{-b \pm \sqrt{b^2 - 4ac}}{2a}$ ◄—— Use the quadratic formula.

$x = \dfrac{-(5) \pm \sqrt{5^2 - (4)(1)(6)}}{2(1)}$ ◄—— Substitute 1 for a, 5 for b, and 6 for c.

$x = \dfrac{-5 \pm \sqrt{1}}{2}$

$x = \dfrac{-5 + 1}{2}$ or $x = \dfrac{-5 - 1}{2}$ ◄—— Write two solutions.

$x = -2$ or $x = -3$

The solutions are -2 and -3.

PROBLEM SOLVING

Look Back Could you check the solutions by graphing? Explain.

Check   for $x = -2$ for $x = -3$

$(-2)^2 + 5(-2) + 6 \overset{?}{=} 0$ $(-3)^2 + 5(-3) + 6 \overset{?}{=} 0$

$4 - 10 + 6 \overset{?}{=} 0$ $9 - 15 + 6 \overset{?}{=} 0$

$0 = 0$ ✔ $0 = 0$ ✔

1. Try This Use the quadratic formula to solve $x^2 - 2x - 8 = 0$.

2. What values would you use for a, b, and c in the quadratic formula to solve $2x^2 = 140$?

3. How many solutions does $9x^2 - 24x + 16 = 0$ have? Explain.

When the quantity under the radical sign in the quadratic formula is not a perfect square, you can use a calculator to approximate the solutions of an equation.

Example 2 ....

Solve $2x^2 + 4x - 7 = 0$. Round the solutions to the nearest hundredth.

$$x = \frac{-b \pm \sqrt{b^2 - 4ac}}{2a}$$ ⟵ Use the quadratic formula.

$$x = \frac{-4 \pm \sqrt{4^2 - (4)(2)(-7)}}{2(2)}$$ ⟵ Substitute 2 for a, 4 for b, and -7 for c.

$$x = \frac{-4 \pm \sqrt{72}}{4}$$

$$x = \frac{-4 + \sqrt{72}}{4} \text{ or } x = \frac{-4 - \sqrt{72}}{4}$$ ⟵ Write two solutions.

$$x \approx \frac{-4 + 8.485281374}{4} \text{ or } x \approx \frac{-4 - 8.485281374}{4}$$ ⟵ Use a calculator.

$$x \approx 1.12 \text{ or } x \approx -3.12$$

The solutions are approximately 1.12 and -3.12.

Check Graph the related function $y = 2x^2 + 4x - 7$. Use the ROOT option to find the x-intercept.

Root
X=-3.121320 Y=0

Root
X=-1.1213203 Y=0

4. Do the graphing calculator screens indicate that the solutions in Example 2 check? Explain.

5. Try This Find the solutions of $-3x^2 + 5x - 2 = 0$. Round to the nearest hundredth.

The quadratic formula is important in physics when finding vertical motion. When an object is dropped, thrown, or launched either straight up or down, you can use the **vertical motion formula** to find the height of the object.

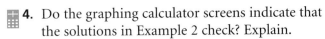

Vertical motion formula: $h = -16t^2 + vt + s$

h is the height of the object in feet.

t is the time it takes an object to rise or fall to a given height.

v is the starting velocity in feet per second.

s is the starting height in feet.

Example 3   Relating to the Real World

Model Rockets   Members of the science club launch a model rocket from ground level with starting velocity of 96 ft/s. After how many seconds will the rocket have an altitude of 128 ft?

$h = -16t^2 + vt + s$ ⟵ Use the vertical motion formula.

$128 = -16t^2 + 96t + 0$ ⟵ Substitute 128 for h, 96 for v, and 0 for s.

$0 = -16t^2 + 96t - 128$ ⟵ Subtract 128 from each side.

$x = \dfrac{-b \pm \sqrt{b^2 - 4ac}}{2a}$ ⟵ Use the quadratic formula.

$t = \dfrac{-(96) \pm \sqrt{(96)^2 - (4)(-16)(-128)}}{2(-16)}$ ⟵ Substitute -16 for a, 96 for b, and -128 for c.

$t = \dfrac{-96 \pm \sqrt{9216 - 8192}}{-32}$ ⟵ Simplify.

$t = \dfrac{-96 \pm \sqrt{1024}}{-32}$

$t = \dfrac{-96 + 32}{-32}$ or $t = \dfrac{-96 - 32}{-32}$ ⟵ Write two solutions and simplify.

$t = 2$ or $t = 4$

s = 0 because the rocket is launched from the ground.

The rocket is 128 ft above the ground after 2 s and after 4 s.

6. Critical Thinking Use a diagram to explain how the rocket could have an altitude of 128 ft at two different times.

7. a. Try This In Example 3, after how many seconds of flight does the rocket have an altitude of 80 ft?

 b. Critical Thinking Estimate the number of seconds it will take the rocket to reach its maximum height. Explain how you made your estimate.

Exercises   ON YOUR OWN

Write each equation in standard form.

1. $3x^2 - 10 = -13x$

2. $4x^2 = 144x$

3. $x^2 - 3x = 2x + 7$

4. $5x^2 = -7x - 8$

5. $-12x^2 + 25x = 84$

6. $-x^2 + 9x = 4x - 12$

Use the quadratic formula to solve each equation. Round solutions to the nearest hundredth when necessary.

7. $6x^2 + 7x - 5 = 0$

8. $3x^2 - 3x - 1 = 0$

9. $6x^2 - 130 = 0$

10. $x^2 + 6x + 8 = -1$

11. $5x^2 - 4x = 33$

12. $3x^2 = 6x + 4$

13. $9x^2 - 5x = 0$

14. $7x^2 = 13$

15. $2x^2 + 3x - 1 = 0$

16. $2x^2 - 12 = 11x$

17. $2x^2 + 5x + 3 = 0$

18. $4x^2 = 12x - 9$

19. Population The function below models the United States population P in millions since 1900, where t is the number of years after 1900.

$$P = 0.0089t^2 + 1.1149t + 78.4491$$

a. Open-ended Use the function to estimate the United States population the year you graduate from high school.

b. Estimate the United States population in 2025.

c. Use the function to **predict** the year in which the population reaches 300 million.

20. Recreation Suppose you throw a ball in the air with a starting velocity of 30 ft/s. The ball is 5 ft high when it leaves your hand. After how many seconds will it hit the ground? Use the vertical motion formula $h = -16t^2 + vt + s$.

Choose Use any method you choose to solve each equation.

21. $2t^2 = 72$

22. $3x^2 + 2x - 4 = 0$

23. $5b^2 - 10 = 0$

24. $3x^2 + 4x = 10$

25. $x^2 = -5x - 6$

26. $m^2 - 4m = -4$

27. $d^2 - d - 6 = 0$

28. $13n^2 - 117 = 0$

29. $3s^2 - 4s = 2$

30. $5b^2 - 2b - 7 = 0$

31. $15x^2 - 12x - 48 = 0$

32. $4t^2 = 81$

33. Writing Compare how you solve the linear equation $mx + b = 0$ with how you solve the quadratic equation $ax^2 + bx + c = 0$.

34. Open-ended Give an example of a quadratic equation that is easier to solve by finding the square roots of each side than by using the quadratic formula or by graphing. Explain your choice.

35. Math in the Media Use the data at the right. Suppose that a cleaner at the top of the Gateway Arch drops a cleaning brush. Use the vertical motion formula $h = -16t^2 + vt + s$.

a. What is the value of s, the starting height?

b. What is the value of h when the brush hits the ground?

c. The starting velocity is 0. Find how many seconds it takes the brush to hit the ground.

GATEWAY TO THE WEST

ST. LOUIS, MISSOURI

The Gateway Arch was completed in 1965.

The arch spans 630 feet at its base and is 630 feet tall.

More than 5100 tons of steel and 38,100 tons of concrete were used in its construction.

Chapter Project — *Find Out by Reasoning*

The formula $d = 0.044s^2 + 1.1s$ relates the maximum speed s in miles per hour that you should travel in order to be able to stop in d feet. Suppose you have 150 ft (about 10 car lengths) between your car and the car in front of you. Find the maximum speed you should travel.

Exercises   MIXED REVIEW

Find each probability for two rolls of a number cube.

36. P(a 2 and a 6)   **37.** P(two odds)

38. P(two 5's)   **39.** P(two fractions)

40. a. Transportation A commuter train has a 150-ton locomotive and 70-ton double-decker passenger cars. Write a linear function for the weight of a train with c passenger cars.

  b. How much does a train with 7 passenger cars weigh?

FOR YOUR JOURNAL

Write and answer three questions that review what you learned about quadratic equations in this chapter.

Getting Ready for Lesson 7-7

For each equation, find the value of $b^2 - 4ac$.

41. $2x^2 + 3x - 4 = 0$ **42.** $3x^2 + 2x + 1 = 0$ **43.** $x^2 + 2x - 5 = 0$

44. $3x^2 - 6x = 5$ **45.** $2x^2 - 5x = 3$ **46.** $2x^2 + 3 = 7x$

Exercises   CHECKPOINT

Solve each equation.

1. $x^2 - 16 = 49$ **2.** $8x^2 + 1 = 33$ **3.** $x^2 - 120 = 1$

Use the quadratic formula to solve each equation.

4. $x^2 - 4x + 3 = 0$ **5.** $5x^2 + 3x - 2 = 0$ **6.** $4x^2 = 14x - 3$

7. Standardized Test Prep Which expression could you use to solve $2x^2 + 5 = 3x$?

  A. $\dfrac{-5 \pm \sqrt{5^2 - (4)(2)(3)}}{4}$ **B.** $\dfrac{-3 \pm \sqrt{3^2 - (4)(2)(5)}}{4}$

  C. $\dfrac{-(-3) \pm \sqrt{(-3)^2 - (4)(2)(-3)}}{4}$ **D.** $\dfrac{-(-3) \pm \sqrt{(-3)^2 - (4)(2)(5)}}{4}$

Work Backward

After Lesson 7-6

Sometimes you can solve a problem by working backward. To write
a quadratic function from its graph, you need to find the x- and y-intercepts.

Example

Work backward to write the equation of the quadratic
function shown in the graph.

A quadratic function is in the form $y = ax^2 + bx + c$
($a \neq 0$). Since the y-intercept of the graph is -3, you know
that $c = -3$. Notice that the graph has x-intercepts at -1
and 3. Substitute the points $(-1, 0)$ and $(3, 0)$ into
$y = ax^2 + bx - 3$. The result is a system of equations.

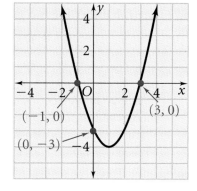

$$y = ax^2 + bx - 3 \qquad\qquad y = ax^2 + bx - 3$$
$$0 = a(-1)^2 + b(-1) - 3 \qquad 0 = a(3)^2 + b(3) - 3$$
$$0 = a - b - 3 \qquad\qquad\qquad 0 = 9a + 3b - 3$$
$$a - b = 3 \qquad\qquad\qquad\quad 9a + 3b = 3$$
$$\qquad\qquad\qquad\qquad\qquad\qquad 3a + b = 1$$

When you solve the system of equations, $\quad a - b = 3$
you find that $a = 1$ and $b = -2$. $\qquad\quad 3a + b = 1$

The equation of the graph above is $y = x^2 - 2x - 3$.

Work backward to find the equation of each graph.

1.

2.

3.
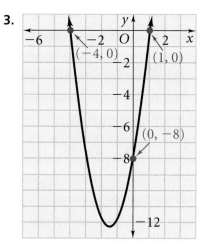

4. **Writing** Explain why this method would not be ideal for all graphs.

What You'll Learn

- Using the discriminant to find the number of solutions of a quadratic equation

...And Why

To solve physics and home improvement problems

What You'll Need

- graphing calculator

7-7 **U**sing the Discriminant

Work with a partner.

1. Each equation is in the form of $ax^2 + bx + c = 0$. Find the value of the expression $b^2 - 4ac$ for each equation.
   a. $x^2 + 2x + 5 = 0$ b. $-3x^2 + 2x - 1 = 0$ c. $\frac{1}{2}x^2 + x + 4 = 0$

2. a. **Graphing Calculator** Graph the related function for each equation in Question 1.
   b. How many x-intercepts do these graphs have?
   c. How many solutions do the equations in Question 1 have?

3. **Generalize** Based on Questions 1 and 2, complete this statement: For an equation in which $b^2 - 4ac$ ▓ 0, the equation has ▓ solutions.

Math A Test Prep

1 Which equation has exactly one solution?
(1) $2x^2 - 5x + 5 = 0$
(2) $2x^2 - 4x + 2 = 0$
(3) $2x^2 - 5x + 2 = 0$
(4) $2x^2 - 4x - 2 = 0$

2 A model rocket is launched from the ground. Its height h in feet after t seconds is given by the function $h = -16t^2 + 84t$. Solve each problem to the nearest tenth.
a In how many seconds will the rocket be at a height of 100 ft?
b In how many seconds will the rocket reach its maximum height?

In the Work Together activity, you investigated the discriminant of three quadratic equations. The quantity $b^2 - 4ac$ is called the **discriminant** of a quadratic equation. The discriminant is part of the quadratic formula.

$$x = \frac{-b \pm \sqrt{b^2 - 4ac}}{2a} \longleftarrow \text{the discriminant}$$

The graph of the related function of a quadratic equation gives you a picture of what happens when a discriminant is positive, 0, or negative.

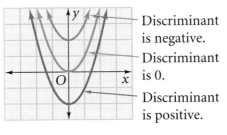
Discriminant is negative.
Discriminant is 0.
Discriminant is positive.

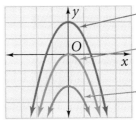
Discriminant is positive.
Discriminant is 0.
Discriminant is negative.

4. How many solutions will an equation have if the discriminant is positive? Explain.

5. How many solutions will an equation have if the discriminant is 0? Explain.

6. How many solutions will an equation have if the discriminant is negative? Explain.

7. Does the direction a graph opens affect the number of solutions found by using the discriminant?

Property of the Discriminant

For the quadratic equation $ax^2 + bx + c = 0$ where $a \neq 0$, the value of the discriminant tells you the number of solutions.

Discriminant	Number of Solutions
$b^2 - 4ac > 0$	two solutions
$b^2 - 4ac = 0$	one solution
$b^2 - 4ac < 0$	no solution

Example 1

Find the number of solutions of $3x^2 - 5x = 1$.

$3x^2 - 5x - 1 = 0$ ← Write in standard form.

$b^2 - 4ac = (-5)^2 - (4)(3)(-1)$ ← Substitute for a, b, and c.

$\qquad\qquad\quad = 25 - (-12)$

$\qquad\qquad\quad = 37$

Since $37 > 0$, the equation has two solutions. ■

8. Graphing Calculator Check the result in Example 1 by graphing the related function $y = 3x^2 - 5x - 1$.

9. Try This Find the number of solutions of $x^2 = 2x - 3$.

10. Critical Thinking Kenji claimed that the discriminant of $2x^2 + 5x - 1 = 0$ had the value 17. What error did he make?

Example 2   Relating to the Real World

Physics A construction worker throws an apple toward a fellow worker who is 25 ft above ground. The starting height of the apple is 5 ft. Its starting velocity is 30 ft/s. Will the apple reach the second worker?

$h = -16t^2 + vt + s$ ← Use the vertical motion formula.

$25 = -16t^2 + 30t + 5$ ← Substitute 25 for h, 30 for v, and 5 for s.

$0 = -16t^2 + 30t - 20$ ← Write in standard form.

$b^2 - 4ac = (30)^2 - 4(-16)(-20)$ ← Evaluate the discriminant.

$\qquad\qquad\quad = 900 - 1280$

$\qquad\qquad\quad = -380$

The discriminant is negative. The apple will not reach the second worker. ■

11. **Try This** Suppose the first construction worker in Example 2 goes up to the next floor. He then throws the apple at a starting height of 17 ft and starting velocity of 30 ft/s. Will the apple reach the second worker?

For which discriminant is each graph possible?

1.

2.

3.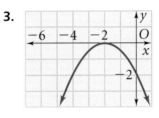

A. $b^2 - 4ac = 0$

B. $b^2 - 4ac = -2$

C. $b^2 - 4ac = 5$

Mental Math **Find the number of solutions of each equation.**

4. $x^2 - 3x + 4 = 0$ 5. $x^2 - 6x + 9 = 0$ 6. $x^2 + 4x - 2 = 0$ 7. $x^2 - 1 = 0$

8. $x^2 - 2x - 3 = 0$ 9. $x^2 + x = 0$ 10. $2x^2 - 3x + 4 = 0$ 11. $2x^2 + 4x = -15$

12. $x^2 - 7x + 6 = 0$ 13. $x^2 + 2x + 1 = 0$ 14. $4x^2 + 5x = -2$ 15. $x^2 - 8x = -12$

16. Open-ended   Write a quadratic equation that has no solution.

17. Home Improvements   The Reeves family garden is 18 ft long and 15 ft wide. They want to modify it according to the diagram at the right. The new area is modeled by the equation $A = -x^2 + 3x + 270$.
    a. What value of x, if any, will give a new area of 280 ft²?
    b. Is there any value of x for which the garden has an area of 266 ft²? Explain.

18. Writing   How can you use the discriminant to write a quadratic equation that has two solutions?

19. Physics   Suppose the equation $h = -16t^2 + 35t$ models the altitude a football will reach t seconds after it is kicked. Which of the following altitudes are possible?
    A. $h = 16$ ft   B. $h = 25$ ft
    C. $h = 30$ ft   D. $h = 35$ ft

20. Find the value of the discriminant and the solutions of each equation.
    a. $x^2 - 6x + 5 = 0$ b. $x^2 + x - 20 = 0$ c. $2x^2 - 7x - 3 = 0$

21. Critical Thinking   Use your results to Question 20. When the discriminant is a perfect square, are the solutions rational or irrational? Explain.

Find the number of x-intercepts of each function.

22. $y = x^2 - 6x + 5$ **23.** $y = 2x^2 + 4x - 3$ **24.** $y = x^2 + 2x + 9$

25. $y = -x^2 - 2x$ **26.** $y = x^2$ **27.** $y = 3x^2 - 2x + 5$

28. $y = 8x^2 - 2x - 45$ **29.** $y = -x^2 - 2$ **30.** $y = -x^2$

31. Standardized Test Prep Compare the quantities in Column A and Column B.

Column A	Column B
the number of solutions of	the number of solutions of
$35 = 20x^2 - 15x + 47$	$15x + 7 = 0$

   A. The quantity in Column A is greater.
   B. The quantity in Column B is greater.
   C. The quantities are equal.
   D. The relationship cannot be determined from the information given.

For each function, decide if its graph crosses the x-axis. For those that do, find the coordinates of the points at which they cross.

32. $y = x^2 - 2x + 5$ **33.** $y = 2x^2 - 4x + 3$ **34.** $y = 4x^2 + x - 5$

35. $y = -3x^2 - x + 2$ **36.** $y = x^2 - 5x + 7$ **37.** $y = 2x^2 - 3x - 5$

38. For the equation $x^2 + 4x + k = 0$, find all values of k such that the equation has each number of solutions.
   a. none   **b.** one   **c.** two

39. Electrical Engineering The function $P = 3i^2 - 2i + 450$ models the power P in an electric circuit with a current i. Can the power in this circuit ever be zero? If so, at what value of i?

40. Business An apartment rental agency uses the formula $I = 5400 + 300n - 50n^2$ to find its monthly income I based on renting n number of apartments. Will the agency's monthly income ever be $7000? Explain.

41. Computer You can use a spreadsheet like the one at the right to find the discriminant for each value of b shown in column A.
   a. What spreadsheet formula would you use to find the value in cell B2? in cell C2?
   b. Describe the integer values of b for which $x^2 + bx + 1 = 0$ has solutions.
   c. Describe the integer values of b for which $x^2 + bx + 2 = 0$ has no solution.

	A	B	C
1	b	x^2 + bx + 1 = 0	x^2 + bx + 2 = 0
2	-3		
3	-2		
4	-1		
5	0		
6	1		
7	2		
8	3		

Chapter Project

Find Out by Communicating

Work with a group of your classmates to plan a skit that will present what you have learned about safe distances in driving. Illustrate the relationships among reaction time, road conditions, speed, and stopping distances.

Exercises MIXED REVIEW

Solve each system by graphing.

42. $4x + y \leq 5$
$3x - 2y > 10$

43. $-6x - 3y \geq 8$
$y > -9$

44. $x < 7$
$-3x + 7y \geq 0$

45. $y = 3x - 2$
$y = -x + 6$

Evaluate each function for $x = 3$.

46. $f(x) = \frac{1}{2}x + 3$

47. $g(x) = \frac{x + 3}{2}$

48. $h(x) = 3 - x$

49. $f(x) = -x - 1$

50. Geology Mount Shishalding is a 9372-ft tall volcano on Unimak Island, Alaska. In 1995 it erupted and sent up a 35,000-ft plume of ash. How far above sea level did the ash reach?

PORTFOLIO

Select one or two items from your work for this chapter. Consider:
• cooperative work
• work you found challenging
• diagrams, graphs, or charts
Explain why you have included each selection that you make.

A Point in Time

1500 1600 1700 1800 1900 2000

Juan de la Cierva

In 1923, Juan de la Cierva (1895–1936) designed the first successful autogyro, a rotor-based aircraft. The autogyro had rotating blades to give the aircraft lift, a propeller for forward thrust, and short, stubby wings for balance. Autogyros needed only short runways for takeoff and could descend almost vertically.

By hinging the rotor blades at the hub, de la Cierva allowed each blade to respond to aerodynamic forces. This was a significant contribution in the development of the modern helicopter.

De la Cierva's work on problems of lift and gravity, like the work of aeronautical engineers of today, involved quadratic functions.

Questions on pages 331, 336, 347, and 353 should help you to complete your project. Gather together all the data you compiled as you worked on the project. Include the equations you analyzed and your graphs. Discuss your conclusions about safe driving, stopping distance, road conditions, and so on with your classmates. Then, as a group, plan and rehearse your skit.

Reflect and Revise

Present your skit to a small group of classmates. After you have heard their comments, decide if your presentation is clear and convincing. If needed, make changes to improve your skit for the rest of the class.

Follow Up

If you have access to a commercial online service or the Internet, explore some of the forums and user groups that are related to driving and motor vehicles.

You may also want to contact highway patrol officers or registry of motor vehicle officials you know for information about the habits of drivers. Ask them what errors or violations are most common.

For More Information:

Highway Safety: Motorcycle helmet laws save lives and reduce costs to society. A Report to Congressional Requesters. Washington, D.C.: U.S. General Accounting Office, 1991.

Hewett, Joan. *Motorcycle on Patrol.* New York: Clarion Books, 1986.

Ross, Daniel Charles. "Ford F150." *Car and Driver* (January 1996): 134.

Saperstein, Robert. *Surviving an Auto Accident.* Ventura, California: Pathfinder Publishers, 1994.

Key Terms

axis of symmetry (p. 318)
discriminant (p. 349)
maximum value (p. 320)
minimum value (p. 320)
negative square root (p. 332)
parabola (p. 318)
perfect squares (p. 333)
principal square root (p. 332)
quadratic equation (p. 337)
quadratic formula (p. 343)
quadratic function (p. 319)

square root (p. 332)
standard form of a
    quadratic equation
    (p. 337)
standard form of a
    quadratic function
    (p. 319)
vertex (p. 320)
vertical motion
    formula (p. 344)

How am I doing?

- State three ideas from this chapter that you think are important. Explain your choices.
- Describe the different ways you can solve quadratic equations.

Exploring Quadratic Functions   7-1

A function of the form $y = ax^2 + bx + c$ is a **quadratic function**. The shape of its graph is a **parabola.** The **axis of symmetry** of a parabola divides the parabola into two congruent halves.

The **vertex** of a parabola is where the axis of symmetry intersects the parabola. When a parabola opens downward, the y-coordinate of the vertex is a **maximum value** of the function. When a parabola opens upward, the y-coordinate of the vertex is a **minimum value** of the function.

The value of a determines whether the parabola opens upward or downward and how wide or narrow it is.

Open-ended **Give an example of a quadratic function for each of the following descriptions.**

1. Its graph opens downward.

2. Its graph opens upward.

3. Its vertex is at the origin.

4. Its graph is wider than $y = x^2$.

Graphing Simple Quadratic Functions   7-2

Changing the value of c in a quadratic function $y = ax^2 + c$ shifts the parabola up or down. The value of c is the y-intercept of the graph.

Graph each quadratic equation.

5. $y = \frac{2}{3}x^2$

6. $y = -x^2 + 1$

7. $y = x^2 - 4$

8. $y = 5x^2 + 8$

State whether each function has a *maximum* or *minimum* value.

9. $y = 4x^2 + 1$

10. $y = -3x^2 - 7$

11. $y = \frac{1}{2}x^2 + 9$

12. $y = -x^2 + 6$

Graphing Quadratic Functions

The graph of $y = ax^2 + bx + c$, where $a \neq 0$, has the line $x = \frac{-b}{2a}$ as its axis of symmetry. The x-coordinate of the vertex is $\frac{-b}{2a}$.

Graph each function. Label the axis of symmetry and the vertex.

13. $y = -\frac{1}{2}x^2 + 4x + 1$ **14.** $y = -2x^2 - 3x + 10$ **15.** $y = x^2 + 6x - 2$

Graph each quadratic inequality.

16. $y \leq 3x^2 + x - 5$ **17.** $y > 2x^2 + 6x - 3$ **18.** $y \geq -x^2 - x - 8$

Square Roots

If $a^2 = b$, then a is a **square root** of b. The **principal** (or positive) **square root** of b is indicated by $\sqrt{b}$. The **negative square root** is indicated by $-\sqrt{b}$. The squares of integers are called **perfect squares.**

Tell whether each expression is *rational* or *irrational*.

19. $\sqrt{86}$ **20.** $-\sqrt{1.21}$ **21.** $\pm\sqrt{\frac{1}{2}}$ **22.** $\sqrt{64}$ **23.** $\sqrt{2.55}$ **24.** $-\sqrt{\frac{4}{25}}$

Find the value of each expression. If the value is irrational, round your answer to the nearest hundredth.

25. $\sqrt{9}$ **26.** $-\sqrt{47}$ **27.** $\sqrt{0.36}$ **28.** $\sqrt{140}$ **29.** $-\sqrt{1}$ **30.** $\sqrt{196}$

31. *Standardized Test Prep* What is the principal square root of 2.25?

     A. 15   **B.** 1.5   **C.** -15 **D.** -1.5 **E.** 0.15

Solving Quadratic Equations

A **quadratic equation** can be written in the **standard form** $ax^2 + bx + c = 0$, where $a \neq 0$. Quadratic equations can have two, one, or no real solutions. You can solve some quadratic equations by taking the square root of each side, or by finding the x-intercepts of the related quadratic function.

If the statement is true, verify it by solving the equation. If it is false, write a true statement.

32. $x^2 - 10 = 3$; there is one solution.   **33.** $3x^2 = 27$; there are two solutions.

Solve each equation. If the equation has no solution, write *no solution*.

34. $6(x^2 - 2) = 12$ **35.** $-5m^2 = -125$ **36.** $9(w^2 + 1) = 9$ **37.** $3r^2 + 27 = 0$

38. *Geometry* The area of a circle is given by the formula $A = \pi r^2$. Find the radius of a circle with area 16 in.^{2} to the nearest tenth of an inch.

You can solve a quadratic equation using the **quadratic formula**.

If $ax^2 + bx + c = 0$ and $a \neq 0$, then $x = \dfrac{-b \pm \sqrt{b^2 - 4ac}}{2a}$.

Use the quadratic formula to solve each equation. Round solutions to the nearest hundredth when necessary.

39. $4x^2 + 3x - 8 = 0$ **40.** $2x^2 - 7x = -3$ **41.** $-x^2 + 8x + 4 = 5$ **42.** $9x^2 - 270 = 0$

43. Vertical Motion   Suppose you throw a ball in the air. The ball is 6 ft high when it leaves your hand. Use the equation $0 = -16t^2 + 20t + 6$ to find the number of seconds t that the ball is in the air.

You can use the **discriminant** to find the number of real solutions of a quadratic equation. When a quadratic equation is in the form $ax^2 + bx + c = 0$ $(a \neq 0)$, the discriminant is $b^2 - 4ac$.

If $b^2 - 4ac > 0$, there are two solutions.
If $b^2 - 4ac = 0$, there is one solution.
If $b^2 - 4ac < 0$, there is no solution.

Evaluate the discriminant. Determine the number of real solutions of each equation.

44. $x^2 + 5x - 6 = 0$ **45.** $-3x^2 - 4x + 8 = 0$ **46.** $2x^2 + 7x + 11 = 0$

47. Writing   Explain why a quadratic equation has one real solution if its discriminant equals zero.

Getting Ready for..▶ CHAPTER 8

Use exponents to write each expression.

48. $3 \cdot 3 \cdot 5 \cdot 5 \cdot 5$ **49.** $8 \cdot 8 \cdot 8 \cdot x \cdot x \cdot x \cdot x$ **50.** $h \cdot h \cdot h \cdot h \cdot h \cdot w \cdot w$

Simplify each expression.

51. $5 \cdot 10^3$ **52.** $-4^3 - (-4)^3$ **53.** $8 \cdot 10^4$

54. $\dfrac{3^4}{3^2}$ **55.** $10(3^2 - 3^4)$ **56.** $7 \cdot 10^2 \div 10^3$

Evaluate each expression.

57. $d^2 \cdot g^2$ for $d = -2$ and $g = 3$ **58.** $7n^8 - 5n^3$ for $n = -1$ **59.** $\dfrac{m^3}{m^4}$ for $m = 3$

Match each function with its graph.

1. $y = 3x^2$

2. $y = -3x^2 + 1$

3. $y = -2x^2$

4. $y = x^2 - 3$

A.

B.

C.

D.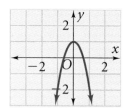

Find the coordinates of the vertex of the graph and an equation for the axis of symmetry.

5. $y = 3x^2 - 7$

6. $y = x^2 - 3x + 2$

7. $y = -2x^2 + 10x - 1$

8. $y = \frac{1}{2}x^2 + 6x$

Make a table of values and graph each function.

9. $y = x^2 - 4$

10. $y = -x^2 + 1$

11. $y = 5x^2$

12. $y = \frac{1}{2}x^2 - 2$

13. Writing Explain what you can determine about the shape of a parabola from its equation without graphing.

Find the number of x-intercepts of each function.

14. $y = 5x^2$

15. $y = 3x^2 + 10$

16. $y = -2x^2 + x + 7$

17. $y = x^2 - 4x$

Graph each quadratic function.

18. $y = -3x^2 - x + 10$

19. $y = \frac{1}{2}x^2 + 2x + 4$

20. $y = x^2 - 3x + 5$

Find both the principal and negative square roots of each number.

21. 1.44

22. 1600

23. $\frac{4}{9}$

Between what two consecutive integers is each square root?

24. $\sqrt{28}$

25. $\sqrt{136}$

26. $\sqrt{332}$

Use any method to solve each quadratic equation. Round solutions to the nearest hundredth.

27. $2x^2 = 50$

28. $-3x^2 + 7x = -10$

29. $x^2 + 6x + 9 = 25$

30. $-x^2 - x + 2 = 0$

31. Open-ended Write the equation of a parabola that has two x-intercepts and a maximum value. Include a graph of your parabola.

Model each problem with a quadratic equation. Then solve the problem.

32. Geometry The volume of a cylinder is given by the formula $V = \pi r^2 h$, where r is the radius of the cylinder and h is the height. A cylinder with height of 10 ft has volume 140 ft^3. What is the radius to the nearest tenth of a foot?

33. Landscaping The area of a rectangular patio is 800 ft^2. The length of the patio is twice the width. Find the dimensions of the patio. (*Hint*: use the formula $A = l \cdot w$.)

Evaluate the discriminant. Determine the number of real solutions of each equation.

34. $x^2 + 4x = 5$

35. $x^2 - 8 = 0$

36. $2x^2 + x = 0$

37. $3x^2 - 9x = -5$

38. Standardized Test Prep Find the value of k for which the equation $kx^2 - 10x + 25k = 0$ has one real root.

A. −1   **B.** 2   **C.** 3   **D.** 5   **E.** 10

Part I

1 The graph of $y = -3x^2 + 1$
(1) opens upward.
(2) is narrower than the graph of $y = 4x^2$.
(3) has its vertex at the origin.
(4) is narrower than the graph of $y = -\frac{1}{3}x^2$.

2 What is the equation of the axis of symmetry of $y = 5x^2 - 2x + 3$?

(1) $x = -\frac{1}{5}$ (3) $x = \frac{1}{5}$

(2) $y = \frac{4}{5}$ (4) $y = -\frac{4}{5}$

3 What is the maximum value of y in $y = -3x^2 - 6x - 1$?
(1) 2   (3) -1
(2) -2 (4) 0

4 Between what two consecutive integers is $\sqrt{52}$?
(1) 5 and 6   (3) 7 and 8
(2) 6 and 7   (4) 8 and 9

5 How many solutions are there for the equation $2x^2 + 7 = 20$?
(1) 0   (3) 2
(2) 1   (4) 3

6 Which is the best approximation of the solutions of $3x^2 - 5x + 1 = 0$?
(1) 2 and -3 (3) 1.5 and 1.75
(2) 1.5 and 0.25   (4) 1.5 and -0.5

7 What is the value of the discriminant of $0 = 3x^2 - 4x - 3$?
(1) -20 (3) 25
(2) 52   (4) 4

8 How many solutions are there for the system $y = x^2$ and $6y - x = 24$?
(1) 0   (3) 2
(2) 1   (4) 3

9 What is the solution of the system $-2x - 3y = -15$ and $3x + 2y = 0$?
(1) $(-6, 9)$ (3) $(6, -9)$
(2) $(4, -6)$ (4) $(-6, 6)$

10 How many solutions are there for the system $x - y = -4$ and $x = -2$?
(1) one   (3) infinitely many
(2) two   (4) none

Part II

11 Graph $y = -\frac{1}{2}x^2 + 2$.

12 Find the vertex and the axis of symmetry of the graph of the equation $y = 4x^2 - 3x$.

13 Solve $x^2 - 6x + 8 = 0$.

Part III

14 Graph the inequality $y < 2x^2 - 8x + 1$.

15 A square photograph with sides of 15 in. must be reduced to an area 40% of its original size to fit in a book. Find the length of a side of the reduced photograph by modeling the problem with a quadratic equation and solving it.

Part IV

16 The plan for a square garden has a circular fountain centered in it. The garden has sides 20 ft long. If the radius of the fountain is x ft, the function $y = \pi x^2$ gives the area of the fountain in square feet.
a What values make sense for the domain?
b What values make sense for the range?

17 Suppose you throw a ball upward at 40 ft/sec. The ball is 4 ft high when it leaves your hand. Use the vertical motion formula
$$h = -16t^2 + vt + s.$$
a What is the height h when the ball hits the ground?
b What is the value of v, the starting velocity?
c What is the starting height s?
d How many seconds does it take the ball to hit the ground?

8

Exponents and Exponential Functions

Relating to the Real World

What do money in a savings account, the population of the world, and radioactive waste all have in common? You can use exponential functions to describe them and predict the future. Exponential relationships are widely used by scientists, business people, and even politicians trying to predict budget surpluses and deficits.

Exploring Exponential Functions	Exponential Growth	Exponential Decay	Zero and Negative Exponents	Scientific Notation
Lessons 8-1	8-2	8-3	8-4	8-5

MoLDY
OLDIES

You take a piece of bread from the bread bag and find that there is green mold on it. The bread was fine two days ago! You open the refrigerator to look for a snack only to see that the cheese is covered with a fuzzy white mold. So, just how fast does mold grow, anyway?

As you work through the chapter, you will grow your own mold. You will gather data, create graphs, and make predictions. As part of your research, you will plan and complete an experiment to monitor growth.

To help you complete the project:

▼ p. 366 *Find Out by Doing*
▼ p. 372 *Find Out by Recording*
▼ p. 389 *Find Out by Graphing*
▼ p. 395 *Find Out by Analyzing*
▼ p. 400 *Find Out by Interpreting*
▼ p. 406 *Finishing the Project*

A Multiplication Property of Exponents

More Multiplication Properties of Exponents

Division Properties of Exponents

8-6   8-7   8-8

What You'll Learn

- Examining patterns in exponential functions

...And Why

To model different patterns

What You'll Need

- notebook paper
- calculator

8-1 Exploring Exponential Functions

Work with a partner.

1. Fold a sheet of notebook paper in half. Notice that the fold line divides the paper into 2 rectangles.

2. Fold the paper in half again. Now how many rectangles are there?

3. Continue folding the paper in half until you cannot make another fold. Keep track of your results in a table like the one at the right.

4. **Patterns** What pattern do you notice in the number of rectangles as the number of folds increases? Explain.

5. Suppose you could continue to fold the paper. Extend your table to include 10 folds. How many rectangles would there be?

Number of Folds	Number of Rectangles
0	1
1	2
2	4
3	■
4	■
5	■

Exploring Exponential Patterns

The pattern that you explored in the Work Together involves repeated multiplication by 2. The table below uses exponents to show the pattern.

QUICK REVIEW

base $\longrightarrow b^x \longleftarrow$ exponent

Number of Folds	Number of Rectangles	Pattern	Written with Exponents
0	1		
1	2	$= 2$	$= 2^1$
2	4	$= 2 \cdot 2$	$= 2^2$
3	8	$= 2 \cdot 2 \cdot 2$	$= 2^3$
4	16	$= 2 \cdot 2 \cdot 2 \cdot 2$	$= 2^4$
5	32	$= 2 \cdot 2 \cdot 2 \cdot 2 \cdot 2$	$= 2^5$

6. Use an exponent to write each number.
   a. $3 \cdot 3 \cdot 3 \cdot 3$ b. $(-2)(-2)(-2)$ c. 125

Example 1   **Relating to the Real World**

Biology Suppose there are 20 rabbits on an island and that the rabbit population can triple every half-year. How many rabbits would there be after 2 years?

Time	Number of Rabbits
Initial	20
$\frac{1}{2}$ year	$20 \cdot 3 = 60$
1 year	$60 \cdot 3 = 180$
$1\frac{1}{2}$ years	$180 \cdot 3 = 540$
2 years	$540 \cdot 3 = 1620$

Use the problem-solving strategy *Make a Table*.

To triple the amount, multiply the previous half-year's total by 3.

After two years, there would be 1620 rabbits.

Rabbits were brought from Europe to Australia around 1860. The number of rabbits increased exponentially, and by 1870 there were millions of rabbits.

Evaluating Exponential Functions

CALCULATOR HINT

To evaluate 2^n for $n = 10$, press 2 y^x 10 $=$ or press 2 $\wedge$ 10 ENTER .

You can write the pattern you found in the Work Together as a function with a variable as an exponent. To find the number of rectangles r created by n folds, use the function $r = 2^n$. You read the expression 2^n as "2 to the nth power." The number of rectangles increases *exponentially* as the paper-folding continues.

7. a. Substitute 10 for n in the function $r = 2^n$. Use your calculator to find the value for r.
　　b. How does your answer compare to your answer to Question 5?

The function $r = 2^n$ is an *exponential function*.

Exponential Function

For all numbers a and for $b > 0$ and $b \neq 1$, the function $y = a \cdot b^x$ is an **exponential function**.

Examples: $y = 0.5 \cdot 2^x$; $f(x) = -2 \cdot 0.5^x$

Example 2

Evaluate each exponential function.

a. $y = 5^x$ for $x = 2, 3, 4$

x	$y = 5^x$	y
2	$5^2 = 25$	25
3	$5^3 = 125$	125
4	$5^4 = 625$	625

b. $t(n) = 4(3^n)$ for the domain $\{3, 6\}$

n	$t(n) = 4(3^n)$	$t(n)$
3	$4 \cdot 3^3 = 4 \cdot 27 = 108$	108
6	$4 \cdot 3^6 = 4 \cdot 729 = 2916$	2916

8. Try This Evaluate the functions $y = 6^x$ and $y = 3(2^x)$ for $x = 1, 2,$ and 3. Which function increases more quickly? Why?

Graphing Exponential Functions

The graphs of many exponential functions look alike.

Example 3 · Relating to the Real World

Technology Some photocopiers allow you to choose how large you want an image to be. The function $f(x) = 1.5^x$ models the increase in size of a picture being copied over and over at 150%. Graph the function.

Make a table of values.

x	$f(x) = 1.5^x$	$f(x)$
1	$1.5^1 = 1.5$	1.5
2	$1.5^2 = 2.25$	2.25
3	$1.5^3 = 3.375 \approx 3.4$	3.4
4	$1.5^4 = 5.0625 \approx 5.1$	5.1
5	$1.5^5 = 7.59375 \approx 7.6$	7.6

Plot the points. Connect the points with a smooth curve.

Growth of the Picture

Percent of Original (Decimal)

Number of Enlargements

GRAPHING CALCULATOR HINT

These range values will give you a clear picture of $y = 2^x$.

Xmin = 0   Ymin = 0
Xmax = 10   Ymax = 100
 Xscl = 1   Yscl = 10

9. a. Graphing Calculator Use your graphing calculator to graph the function $y = 2^x$.

b. How is the graph of $y = 2^x$ similar to the graph of $f(x) = 1.5^x$? How is it different?

1. **Patterns** Bacteria in a laboratory culture can double in number every 20 min. Suppose a culture starts with 75 cells. Copy, complete, and extend the table to find when there will be more than 30,000 bacteria cells.

Time	Number of 20-min Time Periods	Pattern	Number of Bacteria Cells
Initial	0	75	75
20 min	1	$75 \cdot 2$	$75 \cdot 2^{\blacksquare} = 150$
40 min	▨	$75 \cdot 2 \cdot 2$	$75 \cdot 2^{\blacksquare} = 300$
▨	▨	▨	$75 \cdot 2^{\blacksquare} = 600$
▨	▨	▨	$75 \cdot 2^{\blacksquare} = \blacksquare$

2. **Finance** An investment of $10,000 doubles in value every 13 years. How much is the investment worth after 52 years? after 65 years?

Which function is greater at the given value?

3. $y = 5^x$ and $y = x^5$ at $x = 5$

4. $f = 10 \cdot 2^t$ and $f = 200 \cdot t^2$ at $t = 7$

5. $f(x) = 2^x$ and $f(x) = 100x^2$ at $x = 10$

6. $y = 3^x$ and $y = x^3$ at $x = 4$

Evaluate each function for the domain {1, 2, 3, 4, 5}. Is the function *increasing*, *decreasing*, or *neither*?

7. $f(x) = 4^x$

8. $c = a^3$

9. $h(x) = 1^x$

10. $f(x) = 5 \cdot 4^x$

11. $y = 0.5^x$

12. $y = \left(\frac{2}{3}\right)^x$

13. $g(x) = 4 \cdot 10^x$

14. $d = 100 \cdot 0.3^t$

15. **Standardized Test Prep** A population of 6000 doubles in size every 10 years. Which equation relates the size of the population y to the number of 10-year periods x?
   A. $y = 6000 \cdot 10^x$ **B.** $y = 6000 \cdot 2^x$ **C.** $y = 10 \cdot 2^x$ **D.** $y = 2 \cdot 10^x$ **E.** $y = 2 \cdot 6000^x$

16. **Graphing Calculator** Graph the functions $y = x^2$ and $y = 2^x$ on the same set of axes.
   a. What happens to the graphs between $x = 1$ and $x = 3$?
   b. **Critical Thinking** How do you think the graph of $y = 6^x$ would compare to the graphs of $y = x^2$ and $y = 2^x$?

17. **Writing** **Analyze** the range for the function $f(x) = 500 \cdot 1^x$ using the domain {1, 2, 3, 4, 5}. Explain why the restriction $b \neq 1$ is included in the definition of an exponential function.

18. **Ecology** In 50 days, a water hyacinth can generate 1000 offspring (the number of plants is multiplied by 1000). How many hyacinth plants could there be after 150 days?

Evaluate each expression.

19. $50 \cdot x^5$ for $x = 0.5$

20. $50{,}000 \cdot m^3$ for $m = 1.1$

21. $0.0125 \cdot c^4$ for $c = 2$

22. Open-ended Select one of the exponential functions from this lesson.
   a. What number is multiplied repeatedly in your example?
   b. As the exponent increases, tell whether the outputs of your function increase, decrease, or do neither.

23. Match each table with the function that models the data.

Table I	
x	*y*
1	3
2	6
3	9
4	12

Table II	
x	*y*
1	3
2	9
3	27
4	81

Table III	
x	*y*
1	1
2	8
3	27
4	64

Functions:
A. $y = 3x$
B. $y = x^3$
C. $y = 3^x$

24. Critical Thinking Why don't two 150% enlargements on a photocopier produce the same size picture as one 300% enlargement?

25. Patterns The base in the function $y = (-2)^x$ is a negative number.
   a. Make a table of values for the domain $\{1, 2, 3, 4, 5, 6\}$.
   b. What pattern do you see in the outputs?
   c. Critical Thinking Is $y = (-2)^x$ an exponential function? **Justify** your answer.

Graph each function.

26. $y = 3^x$

27. $y = 3\left(\dfrac{3}{2}\right)^x$

28. $y = 1.5^x$

29. $y = \dfrac{1}{4} \cdot 2^x$

30. $y = 0.1 \cdot 2^x$

31. $y = 10^x$

> **Chapter Project** *Find Out by Doing*
>
> Gather the materials for your project: $\frac{1}{16}$ in. or 1 mm graph paper, a packet of unflavored gelatin, a flat dish or plate, a small piece of unprocessed cheese, and plastic wrap.
>
> • Decide where you will keep your dish. A warm, humid place is best for growing mold.
>
> • Cut the graph paper to cover the bottom of the dish. Follow the directions on the gelatin packet. Cover the graph paper with about $\frac{1}{8}$ in. of gelatin. Add the cheese to the gelatin. Leave the dish uncovered overnight; then cover tightly with the plastic wrap.

Exercises   M I X E D   R E V I E W

Solve each equation.

32. $5(g - 1) = \dfrac{1}{2}$

33. $t^2 + 3t - 4 = 0$

34. $|m - 7| = 9$

35. $x^2 - 5x + 6 = 0$

36. Books The smallest book in the Library of Congress is *Old King Cole*. Each square page has area $\frac{1}{25}$ in.^{2}. How wide is one page?

Getting Ready for Lesson 8-2

Find the range of each function for the domain $\{1, 2, 3, 4, 5\}$.

37. $y = 2^x$

38. $y = 4 \cdot 2^x$

39. $y = 0.5 \cdot 2^x$

40. $y = \dfrac{3}{2} \cdot 2^x$

41. $y = 3 \cdot 2^x$

42. How are the functions in Exercises 37–41 alike? How are they different?

What You'll Learn

- Modeling exponential growth
- Calculating compound interest

...And Why

To solve problems involving medical costs and finance

What You'll Need

- calculator

QUICK REVIEW

A 10% increase in an amount means you have 110% of the original amount. To find 110%, multiply by 1.1.

Time	Job A	Job B
Start	$5.00	$4.80
6 mo	▢	▢
1 yr	▢	▢

8-2   Exponential Growth

WORK TOGETHER

Jobs Suppose you are offered a choice of two jobs. Job A has a starting wage of $5.00/h, with a $.50 raise every 6 months. Job B starts at $4.80/h, with a 10% raise every 6 months. Work with a partner.

1. How do you find the new wage after each raise for Job A?

2. In Job B, each new wage is 110% of the previous wage. How do you find each new wage for Job B?

3. Organize the wages for each job in a table like the one at the left. Show wages from the start of the job through the raise at three years. Round each wage to the nearest cent.

4. a. Patterns Which wage pattern involves repeated multiplication?
   b. Which wage pattern results in a linear function?

5. Which graph represents the wages for Job A? for Job B?

6. When would you prefer to have Job A? Job B? Explain.

THINK AND DISCUSS

Modeling Exponential Growth

You can use an exponential function to show how the wages for Job B grow.

beginning wage

new wage ⟶ $y = 4.8 \cdot 1.1^x$ ⟵ number of wage increases

110% as a decimal

Because multiplying over and over by 1.1 causes the wage to increase, this kind of exponential function is an example of *exponential growth*.

When you use exponential functions to model real-world situations, you must identify the initial amount a and the growth factor b. To show growth, b must be greater than 1.

7. Suppose the population of a city is 50,000 and is growing 3% each year.
   a. The initial amount a is ▦.
   b. The growth factor b is 100% + 3%, which is $1 + ▦ = ▦$.
   c. To find the population after one year, you multiply ▦ · 1.03.
   d. Complete the equation to find the population after x years.
      $$y = ▦ \cdot ▦^{▦}$$
   e. Use your equation to find the population after 25 years.

Example 1   Relating to the Real World

Medical Care Since 1985, the daily cost of patient care in community hospitals in the United States has increased about 8.6% per year. In 1985, hospital costs were an average of $460 per day.
a. Write an equation to model the cost of hospital care.
b. Use your equation to find the approximate cost per day in 1995.

a. Use an exponential function to model repeated percent increases.

   Relate $y = a \cdot b^x$

   Define $x =$ the number of years since 1985
            $y =$ the cost of hospital care at various times
            $b = 100\%$ plus 8.6% of the cost $= 108.6\% = 1.086$
            $a =$ initial cost in 1985 $= \$460$

   Write $y = 460 \cdot 1.086^x$ ← Substitute values for the initial amount a and the growth factor b.

b. 1995 is 10 years after 1985, so solve the equation for $x = 10$.
   $$y = 460 \cdot 1.086^{10}$$ ← Substitute.
   $$= 1049.677974$$

The average cost per day in 1995 was about $1050.

8. **Try This** **Predict** the cost per day for the year 2000.

9. Find the first year in which the predicted cost per day will be greater than $2000.

10. The cost per day more than doubled between 1985 and 1995. Using the function from Example 1, about how long will it take to double the 1995 cost per day?

Finding Compound Interest

When a bank pays interest on both the principal *and* the interest an account has already earned, the bank is paying **compound interest.** An **interest period** is the length of time over which interest is calculated. Compound interest is an exponential growth situation.

Example 2   Relating to the Real World

Savings Suppose your parents deposited $500 in an account paying 6.5% interest, compounded annually (once a year), when you were born. Find the account balance after 18 years.

Relate $y = a \cdot b^x$ ← Use an exponential function.

Define $x =$ the number of interest periods
$y =$ the balance at various times
$a = 500$ ← initial deposit
$b = 1.065$ ← 100% + 6.5% = 106.5% = 1.065

Write $y = 500 \cdot 1.065^x$ Once a year for 18 years is
$ = 500 \cdot 1.065^{18}$ ← 18 interest periods. Substitute 18 for *x*.
$ = 1553.32719$

The balance after 18 years will be $1553.33.

11. **Try This** Suppose the interest rate on the account was 8%. How much would be in the account after 18 years?

1 Which equation represents a population of 26,000 growing at a rate of 2% per year?
(1) $y = 26{,}000 \cdot 1.02^x$
(2) $y = 26{,}000 \cdot 0.02^x$
(3) $y = 0.02 \cdot 26{,}000^x$
(4) $y = 26{,}000 \cdot x^{1.02}$

2 Certain bacteria in a lab culture double in number every 15 minutes. If a culture originally contains 50 cells, how many cells will it contain at the end of 1 hour?

Banks sometimes pay compound interest more than once a year. When they use shorter interest periods, the interest rate for each period is also reduced.

Annual Interest Rate of 8%

Compounded	Periods per Year	Rate per Period
annually	1	8% every year
semi-annually	2	$\frac{8\%}{2} = 4\%$ every 6 months
quarterly	4	$\frac{8\%}{4} = 2\%$ every 3 months
monthly	12	$\frac{8\%}{12} = 0.\overline{6}\%$ every month

12. In an account that pays 6.5% interest, what is the interest rate if the interest is compounded quarterly? monthly?

Example 3

Suppose the account in Example 2 paid interest compounded quarterly instead of annually. Find the account balance after 18 years.

Relate $y = a \cdot b^x$ ⟵ Use an exponential function.

Define $x =$ the number of interest periods (quarters)
   $y =$ the balance at various times
   $a = 500$ ⟵ initial deposit
   $b = 1 + \frac{0.065}{4}$ ⟵ There are 4 interest periods in 1 year,
      $= 1.01625$ so divide the interest into four parts.

Write $y = 500 \cdot 1.01625^x$
      $= 500 \cdot 1.01625^{72}$ ⟵ $18 \cdot 4 = 72$ interest periods in 18 years
      $= 1595.916716$ ⟵ Use a calculator.

The balance after 18 years will be $1595.92.

13. a. How many interest periods per year are there for an account with interest compounded daily?
   b. Try This Suppose the account above paid interest compounded daily. How much money would be in the account after 18 years?

Exercises   ON YOUR OWN

Identify the initial amount a and the growth factor b in each exponential function.

1. $g(x) = 20 \cdot 2^x$ **2.** $y = 200 \cdot 1.0875^x$ **3.** $y = 10{,}000 \cdot 1.01^x$ **4.** $f(t) = 1.5^t$

What repeated percent of increase is modeled in each function?

5. $r = 70 \cdot 1.5^n$ **6.** $f(t) = 30 \cdot 1.095^t$ **7.** $y = 1000 \cdot 1.04^x$ **8.** $y = 2^x$

Write the growth factor used to model each percent of increase in an exponential function.

9. 4%   **10.** 5%   **11.** 3.7%   **12.** 8.75%   **13.** 0.5%   **14.** 15%

Write an exponential function to model each situation. Tell what each variable you use represents.

15. A population of 130,000 grows 1% per year

16. A price of $50 increases 6% each year

17. A deposit of $3000 earns 5% annual interest compounded monthly.

18. Writing Would you rather have $500 in an account paying 6% interest compounded quarterly or $750 in an account paying 5.5% compounded annually? **Summarize** your reasoning.

19. Education The function $y = 355 \cdot 1.08^x$ models the average annual cost y (in dollars) for tuition and fees at public two-year colleges. The variable x represents the number of years since 1980.
   a. What was the average annual cost in 1980?
   b. What is the average percent increase in the annual cost?
   c. Find the average annual cost for 1990.
   d. Open-ended **Predict** the average annual cost for the year you plan to graduate from high school.

20. History The Dutch bought Manhattan Island in 1626 for $24 worth of merchandise. Suppose the $24 had been invested in 1626 in an account paying 4.5% interest compounded annually. Find the balance today.

21. Standardized Test Prep An investment of $100 earns 5% interest compounded annually. Which expression represents the value of the investment after 10 years?
   A. $10 \cdot 100^5$ **B.** $100 \cdot 0.05^{10}$ **C.** $100 \cdot 100^{0.05}$
   D. $10 \cdot 100^{1.05}$ **E.** $100 \cdot 1.05^{10}$

Workstations Replace Supercomputers

Workstations—sophisticated computers that sit on a desktop—are replacing larger mainframe computers in industry. Since 1987, sales of workstation computers in industry have increased about 30% per year. In 1987, sales totaled about $3 billion.

22. a. Math in the Media Write an equation to model the sales of workstation computers since 1987.
   b. Use your model to find the total sales in 1995.

Graph the function represented in each table. Then tell whether the table represents a *linear function* or an *exponential function*.

23.

x	y
1	20
2	40
3	60
4	80

24.

x	y
1	3
2	9
3	27
4	81

25.

x	y
1	6
2	12
3	24
4	48

26.

x	y
1	3
2	9
3	15
4	21

Tell whether each graph is a *linear function,* an *exponential function,* or *neither.* Justify your reasoning.

27.

28.

29.

30. Statistics Since 1970, the population of Virginia has grown at an average annual rate of about 1.015%. In 1970, the population was about 4,651,000.
  a. Graphing Calculator Write and graph a function to model population growth in Virginia since 1970.
  b. Estimate the population of Virginia in 1980 and 1990.
  c. Predict the population of Virginia in the years 2000 and 2025.

Write an exponential function to model each situation. Find each amount after the specified time.

31. $20,000 principal
  3.5% compounded
  quarterly10 years

32. $30 principal
  4.5% compounded daily
  2 years

33. $2400 principal
  7% compounded annually
  10 years

34. $2400 principal
  7% compounded monthly
  10 years

Chapter Project

Find Out by Recording

Count the number of graph paper squares covered by mold once a day for 10 days. Record the mold growth. (Don't worry if you don't see any mold for the first few days.)

Exercises   M I X E D   R E V I E W

Find the vertex of each parabola. Identify it as a *maximum* or a *minimum.*

35. $y = 3x^2 + 2x - 8$

36. $y = \frac{1}{2}x^2 - 5x + 1$

37. $y = 4x^2 - 11$

38. a. History The boardwalk in Atlantic City was 1 mi long and 12 ft wide when it was built in 1870. What was its area in square feet?
  b. In 1995, the boardwalk was 4.5 mi long and up to 60 ft wide. What could be its maximum area in square feet?
  c. About how many times larger was the boardwalk in 1995 than in 1870?

Getting Ready for Lesson 8-3
Simplify each expression.

39. $\left(\frac{1}{2}\right)^2$

40. 0.5^4

41. $\left(\frac{3}{4}\right)^1$

42. 0.9^3

43. 0.98^2

44. $\left(\frac{5}{6}\right)^2$

- Modeling exponential decay
- Using half-life models

...And Why

To solve problems involving population and radioactive decay

What You'll Need

- calculator

8-3 **Exponential Decay**

In Lesson 8-2 you used the exponential function $y = a \cdot b^x$ to model growth. You can also use it to model decay. The difference between growth and decay is the value of b, the base. With growth, b is greater than 1. With decay, b is between 0 and 1 and is called the **decay factor.**

Exponential Decay
....

For $a > 0$ and $0 < b < 1$, the function $y = a \cdot b^x$ models **exponential decay.**

Example: $y = 5 \cdot \left(\frac{1}{2}\right)^x$

Exponential Decay
y-values decrease because of repeated multiplication by a number between 0 and 1.

$y = 5 \cdot 2^x$

$y = 5 \cdot \frac{1}{2}^x$

Xmin=0	Ymin=0
Xmax=4	Ymax=15
Xscl=0.5	Yscl=1

Exponential Growth
y-values increase because of repeated multiplication by a number greater than 1.

You can use an exponential function to model the decay of a radioactive substance.

Example 1   **Relating to the Real World**   · · · · · · · · · · · · · ·

Medicine To treat some forms of cancer, doctors use radioactive iodine. Use the graph to find how much iodine-131 is left in a patient eight days after the patient receives a dose of 20 mCi (millicuries).

Iodine-131 Decay

The x-value 8 represents eight days.
The y-value 10 represents the amount of iodine-131 remaining.

After eight days, there are 10 mCi of iodine-131 left.

1. **Try This** Use the graph in Example 1 to find the amount of iodine-131 left after 24 days.

The *half-life* of a radioactive substance is the length of time it takes for one half of the substance to decay.

2. **a.** How long does it take for half of the 20 mCi dose in Example 1 to decay? How much is left?
   b. Use your answer to part (a). How long does it take for half of that amount to decay? How much is left?
   c. What is the half-life of iodine-131?
   d. How many half-lives of iodine-131 occur in 32 days?
   e. *Critical Thinking* Suppose you start with a 50 mCi sample of iodine-131. What is its half-life? How much iodine-131 is left after one half-life? after two half-lives?

You can use exponential decay to model other real-world situations.

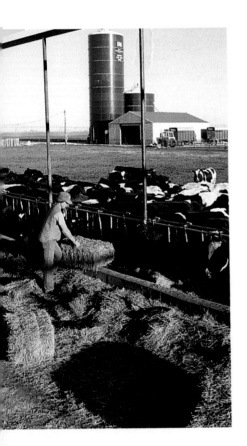

> **Example 2**   Relating to the Real World

Consumer Trends An exponential function models the amount of whole milk each person in the United States drinks in a year. Graph the function $y = 21.5 \cdot 0.955^x$, where y is the number of gallons of whole milk and x is the number of years since 1975.

Make a table of values.

Graph the points. Draw a smooth curve through the points.

$y = 21.5 \cdot 0.955^x$

x	y
0	21.5
5	17.1
10	13.6
15	10.8
20	8.6
25	6.8

Annual Whole Milk Consumption

3. Which x-value corresponds to the year 1995?

4. In which year did whole milk consumption fall to about 10.8 gal/person?

5. **a.** Use the function $y = 21.5 \cdot 0.955^x$ and your calculator to **predict** whole milk consumption for the year 2010.
   b. *Open-ended* Use the function to **predict** whole milk consumption 10 years from now.

Example 3 ·

Consumer Trends Use the equation $y = 21.5 \cdot 0.955^x$ to find the annual percent of decrease in whole milk consumption in the United States.

$$0.955 = 95.5\% \quad \longleftarrow \text{Change the decay factor to a percent.}$$

$$100\% - 95.5\% = 4.5\% \quad \longleftarrow \text{Subtract.}$$

Whole milk consumption is decreasing by 4.5% per year.

6. **Try This** What percent of decrease does each decay factor model?
   a. 0.75   **b.** 0.4   **c.** 0.135   **d.** 0.0074

7. By what number would you multiply 15 to decrease it
   a. by 6%?   **b.** by 12%?   **c.** by 3.5%?   **d.** by 53.9%?

8. Suppose an initial population of 10,000 people decreases by 2.4% each year. Write an exponential function in the form $y = \blacksquare \cdot \blacksquare^x$ to model the population y after x years have passed.

Exercises   ON YOUR OWN

Identify each function as *exponential growth* or *exponential decay*.

1. $y = 0.68 \cdot 2^x$ 2. $y = 2 \cdot 0.68^x$ 3. $y = 68 \cdot 2^x$ 4. $y = 68 \cdot 0.2^x$

Identify the decay factor in each function.

5. $y = 5 \cdot 0.5^x$ 6. $f(x) = 10 \cdot 0.1^x$ 7. $g(x) = 100 \cdot \left(\dfrac{2}{3}\right)^x$ 8. $y = 0.1 \cdot 0.9^x$

Find the percent of decrease for each function.

9. $r = 70 \cdot 0.9^n$ 10. $f(t) = 45 \cdot 0.998^t$ 11. $r = 50 \cdot \left(\dfrac{1}{2}\right)^n$ 12. $y = 1000 \cdot 0.75^x$

Use the graph to estimate the half-life of each radioactive substance.

13.

14.

15.

Choose Use a graphing calculator or make a table of values to graph each function. Label each graph as *exponential growth* or *exponential decay*.

16. $f(x) = 100 \cdot 0.9^x$

17. $s = 64 \cdot \left(\frac{1}{2}\right)^n$

18. $g = 8 \cdot 1.5^x$

19. $y = 3.5 \cdot 0.01^x$

20. $y = 2 \cdot 10^x$

21. $g(x) = \left(\frac{1}{10}\right) \cdot 0.1^x$

22. $f = 10 \cdot 0.1^x$

23. $y = \frac{2}{5} \cdot \left(\frac{1}{2}\right)^x$

24. $y = 0.5 \cdot 2^x$

25. Writing Describe a situation that can be modeled by the equation $y = 100 \cdot 0.9^x$.

Write an exponential function to model each situation. Find each amount after the specified time.

26. 3,000,000 initial population
1.5% annual decrease
10 years

27. $900 purchase
20% loss in value each year
6 years

28. $10,000 investment
12.5% loss each year
7 years

29. Statistics In 1980, the population of Warren, Michigan, was about 161,000. Since then the population has decreased about 1% per year.
  a. Write an equation to model the population of Warren since 1980.
  b. Estimation Estimate the population of Warren in 1990.
  c. Suppose the current trend continues. **Predict** the population of Warren in 2010.

30. a. Open-ended Write two exponential decay functions, one with a base near 0 and one with a base near 1.
  b. Find the range of each function using the domain {1, 2, 3, 4}.
  c. Graph each function.

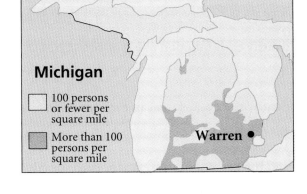

Michigan

100 persons or fewer per square mile

More than 100 persons per square mile

Warren •

Calculate the decay factor for each percent of decrease.

31. 3%   **32.** 70%   **33.** 2.6%   **34.** 4.75%   **35.** 0.7%   **36.** 23.4%

37. Graphing Calculator The function $y = 15 \cdot 0.84^x$ models the amount y of a 15-mg dose of antibiotic remaining in the bloodstream after x hours.
  a. Estimation Study the graphing calculator screen to estimate the half-life of this antibiotic in the bloodstream.
  b. Use your estimate to **predict** the fraction of the dose that will remain in the bloodstream after 8 hours.
  c. Verify your prediction by using the function to find the amount of antibiotic remaining after 8 hours.

Antibiotic Decay in the Bloodstream

X=4.0106383   Y=7.4542313

Xmin=0   Ymin=0
Xmax=13   Ymax=15

How many half-lives occur in each length of time?

38. 2 days (1 half-life = 8 h)

39. 300 years (1 half-life = 75 yr)

Exercises   MIXED REVIEW

Solve.

40. $3 = |x - 7|$

41. $2 - x > 5$

42. $\frac{t}{3} - \frac{t}{6} = 15$

43. $j^2 + 3 = 12$

44. Biology A mouse's heart beats 600 times/min. The average mouse lives about 3 yr. About how many times does the average mouse's heart beat in its lifetime?

FOR YOUR JOURNAL

Explain the differences and similarities between exponential growth and exponential decay. Give an example of each.

Getting Ready for Lesson 8-4

Complete each expression.

45. $\frac{1}{2^2} = \frac{1}{\blacksquare}$

46. $\frac{8}{27} = \frac{2^{\blacksquare}}{3^{\blacksquare}}$

47. $\frac{2^2}{4^2} = \frac{\blacksquare}{\blacksquare} = \blacksquare$

Exercises   CHECKPOINT

Write an exponential function to model each situation. Find each amount after the specified time.

1. $65,000 initial market value
3.2% annual increase
15 years

2. 200,000 initial population
5% loss each year
20 years

3. $300 initial value
doubles every 10 years
50 years

4. Standardized Test Prep From 1790 to 1860, the population of the United States grew slowly but steadily from 4 million. Which exponential function is the most likely model for the population p in the years after 1790?

A. $p = 4 \cdot 2.6^x$ **B.** $p = 4 \cdot 1.03^x$ **C.** $p = 4 \cdot 0.98^x$ **D.** $p = 4 \cdot 3^x$ **E.** $p = 0.98 \cdot 4^x$

Graph each function. Label each graph as *exponential growth* or *exponential decay*.

5. $y = \left(\frac{9}{10}\right) \cdot 2^x$

6. $f(x) = 5 \cdot 0.5^x$

7. $y = 2 \cdot \left(\frac{3}{2}\right)^x$

8. Open-ended Suppose you have $1000 to deposit into a savings account for your education. One account pays 6.7% compounded annually. Another account pays 5% compounded monthly.
a. Which account would you choose? Consider the length of time you would leave the money in the account. **Summarize** your reasoning.
b. Calculate how much will be in the account if you close it when you are 18.

Fitting Exponential Curves to Data

After Lesson 8-3

In Chapter 5, you learned how to find a line of best fit for a set of data. Some data sets are better modeled by exponential functions. A graphing calculator makes it easy to graph exponential functions for a set of data.

U.S. Sales of Compact Discs

Year	Millions of CDs
1987 ↔ 7	102.1
8	149.7
9	207.2
10	286.5
11	333.3
12	407.5
13	495.4
1994 ↔ 14	662.1

Example

Use a graphing calculator to graph the data and find the best-fitting exponential function $y = a \cdot b^x$.

Step 1: Use the STAT feature to enter the data. Let 1980 correspond to $x = 0$.

Step 2: Use the STAT PLOT feature to graph the data in a scatter plot.

Step 3: Find the equation for the best-fitting exponential function. Press STAT ▶ ALPHA A ENTER to get the ExpReg equation.

```
ExpReg
y=a*b^x
a=19.82510651
b=1.287856937
r=.9908425236
```

Step 4: Graph the function. Press Y= CLEAR VARS 5 ▶ ▶ 7 to enter the ExpReg results. Press GRAPH to display the data and the function together.

Xmin=0   Ymin=0
Xmax=15   Ymax=700
Xscl=5   Yscl=100

Use a graphing calculator to write the exponential function that fits each set of data. Sketch the graph of the function and show the data points.

1. **U.S. Movie Earnings.** Let 1980 correspond to $x = 0$.

Year	1986	1987	1988	1989	1990	1991	1992
Billions of Dollars	23.8	27.8	31.2	35.0	38.1	41.1	43.8

2. **U.S. Homes Heated by Coal.** Let 1950 correspond to $x = 0$.

Year	1950	1960	1970	1980	1991
Percent of Homes	33.8	12.2	2.9	0.4	0.3

3. **a.** The table gives the population of New Mexico at various times. Use the best-fitting exponential function to **predict** the population of New Mexico in 2010.
   b. Writing Explain how the r-value affects your answer to part (a).

Population of New Mexico (millions)

1970	1.017
1980	1.303
1985	1.438
1990	1.515
1994	1.654

8-4 Zero and Negative Exponents

What You'll Learn

- Evaluating and simplifying expressions in which zero and negative numbers are used as exponents

...And Why

To analyze exponential functions over a broader domain

What You'll Need

- graphing calculator

```
Xmin=-3
Xmax=3
Xscl=1
Ymin=0
Ymax=100
Yscl=10
```

WORK TOGETHER

Work with a partner to copy and complete the table. Replace each box with a whole number or a fraction in lowest terms.

$y = 2^x$	$y = 5^x$	$y = 10^x$
$2^2 = 4$	$5^2 = 25$	$10^2 = 100$
$2^1 = 2$	$5^1 = 5$	$10^1 = 10$
$2^0 = \blacksquare$	$5^0 = \blacksquare$	$10^0 = \blacksquare$
$2^{-1} = \blacksquare$	$5^{-1} = \blacksquare$	$10^{-1} = \blacksquare$
$2^{-2} = \blacksquare$	$5^{-2} = \blacksquare$	$10^{-2} = \blacksquare$

1. You can describe what happens in the first column of the table as division by 2. What happens in the other columns of the table?

2. a. Graph the three functions on your calculator. Use the range values at the left. Sketch the graphs.
   b. At what point do the three graphs intersect?

3. a. What pattern do you notice in the row containing 0 as an exponent?
   b. Use your calculator to calculate other numbers to the zero power. What do you notice?

4. Copy and complete each expression.
   a. $2^{-1} = \frac{1}{\blacksquare} = \frac{1}{2^{\blacksquare}}$ b. $2^{-2} = \frac{1}{\blacksquare} = \frac{1}{2^{\blacksquare}}$ c. $2^{-3} = \frac{1}{\blacksquare} = \frac{1}{2^{\blacksquare}}$

5. Critical Thinking Look for a pattern in your answers to Question 4. Does this pattern hold true for the other columns? Explain.

THINK AND DISCUSS

Using Zero and Negative Integers as Exponents

The pattern you saw in Question 3 is an important property of exponents.

> **Zero as an Exponent**
>
> For any nonzero number a, $a^0 = 1$.
> **Examples:** $5^0 = 1$; $(-2)^0 = 1$; $\left(\frac{3}{8}\right)^0 = 1$; $1.02^0 = 1$

Notice that 0 is excluded as a base. The expression 0^0 is undefined, just as the expressions $\frac{2}{0}$ and $\frac{0}{0}$ are undefined.

Example 1 **Relating to the Real World**

Population Growth The function $f(t) = 1000 \cdot 2^t$ models an initial population of 1000 insects that doubles every time period t. Evaluate the function for $t = 0$. Then describe what $f(0)$ represents in the situation.

$$f(0) = 1000 \cdot 2^0 \quad \longleftarrow \text{Substitute 0 for } t.$$
$$= 1000 \cdot 1 \quad \longleftarrow 2^0 = 1$$
$$= 1000$$

The value of $f(0)$ represents the initial population of insects. This makes sense because when $t = 0$, no time has passed.

A large aphid population can destroy an apple orchard's produce. One way of controlling the aphids is to release ladybugs into the orchard, where they feed on the apple aphid colonies.

The pattern from Questions 4 and 5 illustrates another important property.

Negative Exponents

For any nonzero number a and any integer n, $a^{-n} = \frac{1}{a^n}$.

Examples: $6^{-4} = \frac{1}{6^4}$ and $7^{-1} = \frac{1}{7^1}$

Example 2

QUICK REVIEW

Unless grouping symbols are used, exponents operate on only one factor.

$-4^2 = -(4 \cdot 4) = -16$

$(-4)^2 = -4 \cdot -4 = 16$

$2x^3 = 2 \cdot x \cdot x \cdot x$

$(2x)^3 = 2x \cdot 2x \cdot 2x$

Write each expression as a simple fraction.

a. 4^{-3}

$$4^{-3} = \frac{1}{4^3} \quad \longleftarrow \begin{array}{c}\text{definition of a} \\ \text{negative exponent}\end{array}$$
$$= \frac{1}{64}$$

b. $(-3)^{-2}$

$$(-3)^{-2} = \frac{1}{(-3)^2}$$
$$= \frac{1}{9}$$

6. Try This Write each expression as a simple fraction.

a. 3^{-4} **b.** $(-7)^0$ **c.** $(-4)^{-3}$ **d.** 7^{-3} **e.** -3^{-2}

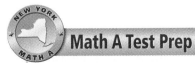

1 Which expression does not equal $\frac{1}{27}$?

(1) $\frac{3^0}{3^3}$ (3) -3^3

(2) $\left(\frac{1}{3}\right)^3$ (4) 3^{-3}

2 Use x, y, 0.74, and 38 to write an exponential decay function. Explain what each value and variable in the function represents.

You can use what you know about rewriting the expression a^{-n} to see how the values of a^n and a^{-n} are related.

$$a^n \cdot a^{-n} = a^n \cdot \frac{1}{a^n}$$
$$= \frac{a^n}{1} \cdot \frac{1}{a^n} = 1$$

Therefore, a^n and a^{-n} are *reciprocals*.

7. **Verify** that a^n and a^{-n} are reciprocals by evaluating each product.
   a. $3^2 \cdot 3^{-2}$ **b.** $2^4 \cdot 2^{-4}$ **c.** $5^3 \cdot 5^{-3}$

8. Write the reciprocal of each number in two ways: as a simple fraction and using a negative exponent.
   a. 10^1 **b.** 10^2 **c.** 1000   **d.** 10,000

9. Write each expression as a decimal.
   a. 10^{-3} **b.** $3 \cdot 10^{-2}$ **c.** $-5 \cdot 10^{-4}$ **d.** 10^{-6}

Example 3

Rewrite each expression so that all exponents are positive.

a. $4yx^{-3} = 4y\left(\frac{1}{x^3}\right)$ ⟵ definition of negative exponent

$$= \frac{4y}{x^3}$$

b. $\frac{1}{w^{-4}} = 1 \div w^{-4}$ ⟵ rewrite using a division symbol

$$= 1 \div \frac{1}{w^4}$$
$$= 1 \cdot w^4$$ ⟵ multiply by the reciprocal
$$= w^4$$

10. **Try This** Complete each expression using only positive exponents.
   a. $\frac{1}{x^{-3}} = x^{\blacksquare}$ **b.** $\frac{1}{v^{-2}} = v^{\blacksquare}$ **c.** $w^{-3} = \frac{1}{w^{\blacksquare}}$ **d.** $\frac{w^{-3}}{v^{-2}} = \frac{\blacksquare^{\blacksquare}}{\blacksquare^{\blacksquare}}$

Relating the Properties to Exponential Functions

Zero and negative integer exponents allow you to understand the graph of an exponential function more completely.

Example 4

Graphing Calculator Graph the functions $y = 2^x$ and $y = \left(\frac{1}{2}\right)^x$ on the same set of axes. Show the functions over the domain $\{-3 \le x \le 3\}$.

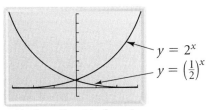

Xmin=-3   Ymin=-1
Xmax=3   Ymax=8

GRAPHING CALCULATOR HINT

You can generate values for a function with the TABLE key on some graphing calculators.

11. **a.** Is the value of 2^x always positive? Explain.

    b. In what quadrants do the graphs of $y = 2^x$ and $y = \left(\frac{1}{2}\right)^x$ appear? Explain.

12. *Critical Thinking* The graph of $y = 2^{-x}$ is identical to one of the two graphs shown in Example 4. Use the definition of negative exponents to help decide which one. Explain.

Exercises   ON YOUR OWN

Write each expression as an integer or simple fraction.

1. -2.57^0 **2.** 4^{-2} **3.** $(-5)^{-1}$ **4.** $\left(\frac{2}{3}\right)^{-1}$ **5.** $\frac{1}{2^{-3}}$ **6.** 5^{-3}

7. $\left(\frac{1}{3}\right)^{-2}$ **8.** -3^{-4} **9.** 2^{-6} **10.** $(-12)^{-1}$ **11.** $45 \cdot (0.5)^0$ **12.** $\left(\frac{2}{5}\right)^{-2}$

13. $54 \cdot 3^{-2}$ **14.** $\left(-\frac{1}{4}\right)^{-3}$ **15.** $5 \cdot 10^{-2}$ **16.** $\frac{5^{-2}}{7^{-3}}$ **17.** $\frac{4^{-1}}{9^0}$ **18.** $\frac{(-3)^{-1}}{-2^{-1}}$

19. **a.** *Patterns* Complete the pattern.

$$\frac{1}{5^2} = \blacksquare \qquad \frac{1}{5^1} = \blacksquare \qquad \frac{1}{5^0} = \blacksquare \qquad \frac{1}{5^{-1}} = \blacksquare \qquad \frac{1}{5^{-2}} = \blacksquare$$

    b. Write $\frac{1}{5^{-4}}$ using a positive exponent.

    c. *Generalize* Rewrite $\frac{1}{a^{-n}}$ so that the power of a is in the numerator.

Write each expression so that it contains only positive exponents.

20. $\frac{1}{c^{-1}}$ **21.** $\frac{1}{x^{-7}}$ **22.** $3ab^0$ **23.** $(5x)^{-4}$ **24.** $\frac{5^{-2}}{p}$ **25.** $a^{-4}b^0$

26. $\frac{3x^{-2}}{y}$ **27.** $12xy^{-3}$ **28.** $\frac{7ab^{-2}}{3w}$ **29.** $5ac^{-5}$ **30.** $x^{-5}y^{-7}$ **31.** $\frac{8a^{-5}}{c^{-3}d^3}$

32. $x^{-5}y^7$ **33.** $\frac{7s^{-5}}{5t^{-3}}$ **34.** $\frac{6a^{-1}c^{-3}}{b^0}$ **35.** $\frac{1}{a^{-3}b^3}$ **36.** $\frac{c^4}{x^2y^{-1}}$ **37.** $\frac{mn^{-4}}{p^0q^{-2}}$

Evaluate each expression for $a = 3$, $b = 2$, and $c = -4$.

38. c^b **39.** $a^{-b}b$ **40.** b^{-a} **41.** b^c **42.** $c^{-a}b^{ab}$ **43.** c^a

Graph each function over the domain $\{-3 \le x \le 3\}$.

44. $y = 2^x$ **45.** $f(x) = (2)^{-x}$ **46.** $g(x) = 0.5 \cdot 3^x$ **47.** $y = 1.5 \cdot (1.5)^{-x}$

Match each graphing calculator screen with the functions it displays.

48.   **49.**

I. $y = \left(\frac{5}{4}\right)^x$; $y = \left(\frac{4}{5}\right)^x$

II. $y = 3^x$; $y = \left(\frac{1}{3}\right)^x$

III. $y = 15^x$; $y = \left(\frac{1}{15}\right)^x$

50. Writing Explain why the value of -3^0 is negative and the value of $(-3)^0$ is positive.

51. Copy and complete the table.

a	4	0.2	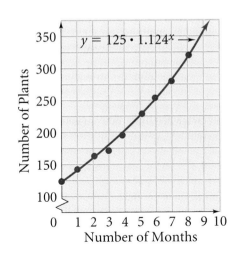		$\frac{7}{8}$	
a^{-1}			3	$\frac{1}{6}$		0.5

Determine whether the value of each expression is *positive* or *negative*.

52. -2^2 **53.** $(-2)^2$ **54.** 2^{-2} **55.** $(-2)^3$ **56.** $(-2)^{-3}$ **57.** 4^{-1}

Copy and complete each equation.

58. $2^{\blacksquare} = 0.5$ **59.** $3xy^{\blacksquare} = \dfrac{3x}{y^3}$ **60.** $\dfrac{x^{\blacksquare}}{2y^{\blacksquare}} = \dfrac{1}{2x^{-3}y^4}$ **61.** $\dfrac{a^{\blacksquare}}{3b^{\blacksquare}} = \dfrac{b^3}{3}$

62. $(-5)^{\blacksquare} = -\dfrac{1}{125}$ **63.** $\dfrac{4n^{\blacksquare}}{m^{\blacksquare}} = \dfrac{4m^2}{n^3}$ **64.** $\dfrac{5x^{\blacksquare}}{y^{\blacksquare}} = \dfrac{5}{xy^2}$ **65.** $\dfrac{x^{\blacksquare}}{y^{\blacksquare}} = x^{-2}y^3$

66. Standardized Test Prep Compare the quantities in Column A and Column B.
   A. The quantity in Column A is greater.
   B. The quantity in Column B is greater.
   C. The quantities are equal.
   D. The relationship cannot be determined from the information given.

Column A	Column B
3^x	3^{-x}

67. Which expressions equal $\frac{1}{4}$?
   A. 4^{-1} **B.** 2^{-2} **C.** -4^1
   D. $\dfrac{1}{2^2}$ **E.** 1^4 **F.** -2^{-2}

68. Open-ended Choose a fraction to use as a value for the variable a. Find the values of a^{-1}, a^2, and a^{-2}.

69. Research Certain small units of length have special names. For each unit, give its length in the form $10^{\blacksquare}$ meters.
   a. fermi   **b.** micron   **c.** angstrom

70. Botany A botanist studying plant life on a remote island in the Pacific Ocean discovers that the number of plants of a particular species is increasing at a high rate. Each month for the next eight months, she counts the number of these plants in an acre plot of land. She then fits an exponential function to the data.
   a. By what percent is the number of plants increasing each month?
   b. If $x = 0$ represents the time of her initial count of the plants, what does $x = -3$ represent?
   c. Graphing Calculator Graph the function on a graphing calculator. Use the |TRACE| feature to estimate when the plant was first introduced to the island. (*Hint:* Find the value of x when $y = 1$.)

71. Communications Suppose you are the only person in your class who knows a story. After a minute you tell a classmate. Each minute after that, every student who knows the news tells another student (sometimes the person being told will already have heard it). In a class of 30 students, the formula $N = \dfrac{30}{1 + 29 \cdot 2^{-t}}$ predicts the number of people N who will have heard the news after t minutes. Find how many students will have heard your news after 2 minutes, 5 minutes, and 10 minutes.

72. Critical Thinking Are $3x^{-2}$ and $3x^2$ reciprocals? Explain.

Graph each pair of functions on the same set of axes over the domain $\{-3 \le x \le 3\}$.

73. $y = 10 \cdot 2^x$; $y = 20 \cdot 2^x$ **74.** $y = 1.2^x$; $y = 1.8^x$

75. a. Geometry What fraction of each figure is shaded?
  b. Rewrite each fraction from part (a) in the form $2^{\blacksquare}$.
  c. Patterns Look for a pattern in your answers to part (b). Write a function that relates the figure number n to the shaded rectangle r.
  d. What portion of the square would be shaded in Figure 10?

Figure 1   Figure 2

Figure 3   Figure 4

Exercises   MIXED REVIEW

Solve each system.

76. $2x + 2y = 3$
    $4x + 3y = 5$

77. $4x + y < 8$
    $2x \ge 3$

78. $3y = \frac{1}{3}|x| - 2$
    $|x| + 9y = 6$

79. Each person in Colorado spends an average of $31.17/yr on books.
  a. Write a function to represent the amount b a group of p people spend on books in a year.
  b. On average, how much does a family of four living in Denver spend on books in a year?
  c. Writing Does this mean every person in Colorado spends exactly $31.17 on books? Explain.

Getting Ready for Lesson 8-5

Simplify each expression.

80. $3.4 \cdot 10^1$ **81.** $7 \cdot 10^{-2}$ **82.** $8.2 \cdot 10^5$ **83.** $3 \cdot 10^{-3}$ **84.** $6 \cdot 10^4$

85. Write $3 \times 10^3 + 6 \times 10^1 + 7 \times 10^0 + 8 \times 10^{-1} + 5 \times 10^{-2}$ as a standard decimal number.

What You'll Learn

- Writing numbers in scientific notation
- Using scientific notation

...And Why

To calculate with very large or very small numbers

What You'll Need

- calculator

8-5 **S**cientific Notation

T H I N K   A N D   D I S C U S S

Writing Numbers in Scientific Notation

Jupiter has an average radius of 69,075 km. What is Jupiter's volume?

To answer this question, you probably want to find the formula for the volume of a sphere and use a calculator.

$$V = \frac{4}{3}\pi r^3 \qquad \longleftarrow \text{formula for the volume of a sphere}$$

$$= \frac{4}{3}\pi(69{,}075)^3 \qquad \longleftarrow \text{Substitute 69,075 for } r.$$

When you use a calculator to find the answer, the display looks something like *1.380547297E 15*.

The calculator displays the answer in this form, called *scientific notation*, because the answer contains more digits than the calculator can display. Scientific notation is a kind of shorthand for very large or very small numbers.

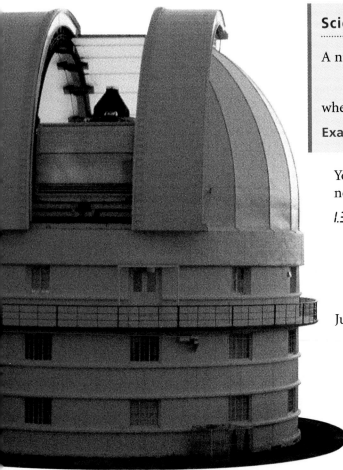

Scientific Notation

....

A number is in **scientific notation** if it is written in the form

$$a \times 10^n,$$

where n is an integer and $1 \le |a| < 10$.

Examples: $3.4 \times 10^6, 5.43 \times 10^{13}, 9 \times 10^{-10}$

You can change a number from scientific notation into standard notation.

1.380547297E 15

$$\approx 1.38 \times 10^{15} \qquad \longleftarrow \text{scientific notation}$$

$$= 1.38 \times 1{,}000{,}000{,}000{,}000{,}000 \qquad \longleftarrow 10^{15} \text{ has 15 zeros.}$$

$$= 1{,}380{,}000{,}000{,}000{,}000 \qquad \longleftarrow \text{standard notation}$$

Jupiter has a volume slightly greater than 1 quintillion km³.

1. a. Try This Evaluate the expression $\frac{4}{3}\pi(6000)^3$ on your calculator. What does your calculator display?

   b. Write the number in standard notation.

To write a number in scientific notation, you use a *power of 10*.
A **power of 10** is an expression in the form $10^{\blacksquare}$.

2. a. Copy and complete the table.

Power of 10	$10^{\blacksquare}$	10^3	$10^{\blacksquare}$	$10^{\blacksquare}$	$10^{\blacksquare}$
Standard Notation	1,000,000	$\blacksquare$	1	0.001	$\blacksquare$
Unit Name	millions	$\blacksquare$	ones	$\blacksquare$	millionths

b. Patterns What pattern did you notice in part (a)?

3. a. Order the data in the table from least to greatest mass.

Masses of Planets (kg)

Jupiter	Saturn	Uranus	Neptune
1.9×10^{27}	5.7×10^{26}	8.7×10^{25}	1.0×10^{26}

b. Summarize the reasoning you used and the steps you took to order the data.

4. Physical Science Write each number in scientific notation.
  a. mass of Earth's atmosphere: 5,700,000,000,000,000 tons
  b. mass of the smallest insect, a parasitic wasp: 0.000 004 92 g

computer-generated image of the solar system

You can use what you know about place value and multiplication by 10 to convert from scientific notation to standard notation.

Example 1   **Relating to the Real World** ....

Physical Science Write each number in standard notation.
  a. temperature at the Sun's core: 1.55×10^6 K
  b. lowest temperature ever in a lab: 2×10^{-11} K

What? One kelvin (1 K) is equal to 1°C, but the kelvin temperature scale starts at absolute zero (−273.15°C). Because nothing can be colder than absolute zero, there are no negative temperatures on the kelvin scale.

a. $1.55 \times 10^6 = 1.550000.$

        $= 1,550,000$

A positive exponent indicates a large number. Move the decimal point 6 places to the right.

b. $2 \times 10^{-11} = 0.00000000002.$

        $= 0.000\ 000\ 000\ 02$

A negative exponent indicates a small number. Move the decimal point 11 places to the left.

5. Try This Write each number in standard notation.
  a. distance light travels in one year (one light-year): 5.88×10^{12} mi
  b. highest elevation in Florida: 6.53×10^{-2} mi

6. Which numbers are *not* in scientific notation? Explain. Write each number in scientific notation.
  a. 11.24×10^4 **b.** 2.004×10^{-23} **c.** -12×10^{-2}

Calculating with Scientific Notation

Standard Notation	Scientific Notation
0.0617	$6.17 \times 10^{\blacksquare}$
0.617	$6.17 \times 10^{\blacksquare}$
6.17	$6.17 \times 10^{\blacksquare}$
61.7	$6.17 \times 10^{\blacksquare}$
617	$6.17 \times 10^{\blacksquare}$
6170	$6.17 \times 10^{\blacksquare}$

7. a. Copy and complete the table at the left.
  b. Patterns Look for a pattern in the exponents as you scan down the table. As you multiply a number by 10 repeatedly, the exponent in the power of 10 __?__ by ▒ repeatedly.

8. Write each expression as a single power of ten.
  a. $10^{12} \times 10$ **b.** 10×10^{-8} **c.** $10^{-7} \times 10$

Example 2

Mental Math Simplify $7 \times (4 \times 10^5)$. Give your answer in scientific notation.

$$7 \times (4 \times 10^5) = 28 \times 10^5 \qquad \longleftarrow \text{Multiply whole numbers.}$$
$$= 2.8 \times 10 \times 10^5 \quad \longleftarrow \text{Write 28 as } 2.8 \times 10.$$
$$= 2.8 \times 10^6 \qquad \longleftarrow \text{Combine powers of 10.}$$

9. Try This Simplify. Give each answer in scientific notation.
  a. $2.5 \times (6 \times 10^3)$ **b.** $1.5 \times (3 \times 10^4)$ **c.** $9 \times (7 \times 10^{-9})$

10. Mental Math Double each number. Give your answers in scientific notation.
  a. 4×10^5 **b.** $6.3 million   **c.** 1.2×10^{-3}

11. You express 1 billion as 10^9. Explain why you express 436 billion as 4.36×10^{11}.

Most calculators have a key labeled [EE] or [EXP] that allows you to enter a number in scientific notation.

Example 3   Relating to the Real World

Telecommunications In 1993, 436 billion telephone calls were placed by 130 million United States telephone subscribers. What was the average number of calls placed per subscriber?

$$\frac{436 \text{ billion calls}}{130 \text{ million subscribers}} = \frac{4.36 \times 10^{11}}{1.3 \times 10^8} \qquad \longleftarrow \text{Write in scientific notation.}$$
$$= 4.36 \text{ [EE] } 11 \text{ [÷] } 1.3 \text{ [EE] } 8 \text{ [ENTER]}$$
$$= 3353.846154$$

Each subscriber made an average of 3354 calls in 1993.

12. Try This The closest star to Earth (other than the sun) is Alpha Centauri, 4.35 light-years from Earth. How many miles from Earth is Alpha Centauri? (*Hint:* See Question 5(a).)

Order each set of numbers from least to greatest.

1. $10^5, 10^{-3}, 10^0, 10^{-1}, 10^1$

2. $6.2 \times 10^7, 5.1 \times 10^7, 8 \times 10^7, 1.02 \times 10^7$

3. $4.02 \times 10^5, 4.1 \times 10^4, 4.1 \times 10^5, 4 \times 10^5$

4. $5.1 \times 10^{-3}, 4.8 \times 10^{-1}, 5.2 \times 10^{-3}, 5.6 \times 10^{-2}$

Determine whether each number is in scientific notation. If it is not, write it in scientific notation.

5. 23×10^7 **6.** 385×10^{-6} **7.** 0.0027×10^{-4} **8.** 9.37×10^{-8} **9.** 25.79×10^{-5}

Write each number in scientific notation.

10. 0.00325   **11.** 9,040,000,000   **12.** 13,030,000   **13.** 0.00092   **14.** 0.001 002

15. 370 billion   **16.** 9.3 million   **17.** 41.8 billion   **18.** 60.7×10^{22} **19.** 62.9×10^{15}

20. 2 thousandths   **21.** 33 billionths   **22.** 950 millionths   **23.** 83.5×10^{-6} **24.** 350×10^{-9}

25. lightest blue whale: 418,000 lb   **26.** thinnest glass: 0.00098 in.

27. lightest bird egg: 0.0128 oz   **28.** diameter of thinnest copper wire: 0.000 5 in.

29. diameter of smallest bacteria cells: 4 millionths in.   **30.** closest star (other than the Sun): 25.6 trillion mi

31. Writing Explain how to convert numbers like 350 billion, 7.2 trillion, or 48 millionths quickly to scientific notation.

Write each number in standard notation.

32. 7.042×10^9 **33.** 4.69×10^{-6} **34.** 1.7×10^{-13} **35.** 5×10^{10} **36.** 1.097×10^8

Mental Math **Calculate each product or quotient. Give your answers in scientific notation.**

37. $8 \times (7 \times 10^{-3})$ **38.** $8 \times (3 \times 10^{14})$ **39.** $2 \times (3 \times 10^2)$

40. $(28 \times 10^5) \div 7$ **41.** $(8 \times 10^{-8}) \div 4$ **42.** $(8 \times 10^{12}) \div 4$

43. Probability In 1990, there were approximately 249 million residents of the United States. The census counted 37,306 centenarians (age 100 or greater). What is the probability that a randomly selected U.S. resident is a centenarian? Give your answer in scientific notation.

44. Precious Metals Earth's crust contains approximately 120 trillion metric tons of gold. One metric ton of gold is worth about $11.5 million. What is the approximate value of the gold in Earth's crust?

45. Astronomy Light travels through space at a constant speed of about 3×10^5 km/s. Earth is about 1.5×10^8 km from the Sun. How long does it take for light from the sun to reach Earth?

Marie Rinne, 101, is a retired teacher. Ezekiel Gibbs, 102, is a folk artist.

FOX TROT by Bill Amend

46. a. Write 500 trillion in scientific notation.
   b. Since the 10-second length of the movie is off by a factor of 500 trillion, what time span does the movie actually represent?
   c. Open-ended Find out the length of one of your favorite movies. Calculate how many frames it has, and express the number of frames in scientific notation.

Mental Math **Double each number. Give your answers in scientific notation.**

47. 3.5×10^{-3} **48.** $75 million   **49.** 450×10^{-1}

50. 3550   **51.** 250×10^{5} **52.** 790

53. Health Care The total amount spent for health care in the United States in 1993 was $884.2 billion. The U.S. population in 1993 was 258.1 million. What was the average amount spent per person on health care?

> **Chapter Project** **Find Out by Graphing**
>
> Make a scatter plot of the growth data. Compare your graph with graphs made by other students in your group. Do the data plots look exponential? Are there differences that seem to be related to where and how long the dish was exposed?

Exercises   M I X E D   R E V I E W

Find each sum or difference.

54. $\begin{bmatrix} 2 & 9 & 5 \\ 3 & 6 & 1 \end{bmatrix} + \begin{bmatrix} 5 & 2 & 9 \\ 3 & 4 & 7 \end{bmatrix}$ **55.** $\begin{bmatrix} 2.6 & 4 \\ 8.1 & 6.7 \end{bmatrix} - \begin{bmatrix} 5.8 & 1.6 \\ 4 & 7.9 \end{bmatrix}$

Hockey Standings Central Division

Goals	FOR	OPP	DIF
Detroit	356	275	+81
Toronto	280	243	−37
Dallas	286	265	+21
St. Louis	270	283	−13
Chicago	254	240	−14
Winnipeg	245	344	+99

56. Sports In the hockey statistics, the FOR column tells the number of goals made by each team. The OPP column tells the number of goals made by a team's opponents. The DIF column reports the difference. Find the errors in the DIF column.

Getting Ready for Lesson 8-6

Rewrite each expression using exponents.

57. $t \cdot t \cdot t \cdot t \cdot t \cdot t \cdot t \cdot t$ **58.** $(6 - m)(6 - m)(6 - m)$ **59.** $5 \cdot 5 \cdot 5 \cdot s \cdot s \cdot s$

Significant Digits

After Lesson 8-5

Significant digits tell scientists how precise a measurement is. The more significant digits there are, the more precise the measurement is. Scientists consider all the significant digits in a measurement to be exact except for the final digit, which is considered to be rounded.

Example 1

Express the length of the computer chip in centimeters to (a) one significant digit and (b) two significant digits.

a. The length of the chip is 5 cm.
b. The length of the chip is 5.2 cm.

Example 2

The moon can come within 221,463 mi of Earth. Express this distance in scientific notation to three significant digits.

$$221{,}463 = 2.21463 \times 10^5 \quad \longleftarrow \text{Write in scientific notation.}$$
$$\approx 2.21 \times 10^5 \quad \longleftarrow \begin{array}{l}\text{Round 2.21463 to the}\\ \text{hundredths' place.}\end{array}$$

To three significant digits, the distance is 2.21×10^5 mi.

Tell how many significant digits are in each measurement.

1. Mercury's period of revolution: 87.9686 da

2. largest known galaxy: 3.3×10^{19} mi in diameter

3. tallest sand castle: 19.5 ft high

Express each number in scientific notation to three significant digits.

4. the surface area of Earth: 196,949,970 mi^2

5. smallest diamond: 0.000 102 2 carat

6. thinnest commercial glass: 0.000 984 in.

7. the farthest the moon can be from Earth: 252,710 mi

8. average weight of the smallest bone in the inner ear: 0.010 853 75 oz

9. 1991 U.S. deaths from heart disease: 725,010

10. Writing When would it be important to measure something to three or more significant digits? Explain.

8-6 A Multiplication Property of Exponents

What You'll Learn
• Multiplying powers with the same base

...And Why
To solve problems that involve the multiplication of numbers in scientific notation

What You'll Need
• calculator

WORK TOGETHER

To evaluate $5^3 \cdot 5^5$, you could multiply the value of 5^3 by the value of 5^5. But is there a shortcut for finding the value of expressions like this? Work in your group to find one.

1. **Calculator** Find the value of each expression.
   a. $5^3 \cdot 5^5$ b. $5^6 \cdot 5^2$ c. $5^1 \cdot 5^7$ d. $5^4 \cdot 5^4$

2. **Patterns** What pattern do you notice in your answers to Question 1?

3. Write each expression from Question 1 in the form shown below.
$$5^3 \cdot 5^5 = (5 \cdot 5 \cdot 5) \cdot (5 \cdot 5 \cdot 5 \cdot 5 \cdot 5) = 5^8$$

4. Look for a pattern in the expressions you wrote in Question 3. Write a shortcut for finding the value of expressions such as $5^3 \cdot 5^5$.

5. Use your shortcut to find the missing value in each expression. **Verify** your answers by using a calculator.
   a. $5^3 \cdot 5^4 = 5^{\blacksquare}$ b. $3^2 \cdot 3^5 = 3^{\blacksquare}$
   c. $1.2^3 \cdot 1.2^3 = 1.2^{\blacksquare}$ d. $7^3 \cdot 7^2 = 7^{\blacksquare}$

CALCULATOR HINT

Use the $\boxed{y^x}$ or $\boxed{\wedge}$ key to evaluate expressions with exponents.

THINK AND DISCUSS

Multiplying Powers

QUICK REVIEW

Read 5^4 as "5 to the 4th power."

Any expression in the form a^n, such as 5^4, is called a **power.** In the Work Together, you discovered a shortcut for multiplying powers with the same base. This shortcut works because the factors of a power such as 8^6 can be combined in different ways. Here are two examples:

$$8^6 = \underbrace{8 \cdot 8 \cdot 8 \cdot 8} \cdot \underbrace{8 \cdot 8} \qquad 8^6 = \underbrace{8 \cdot 8 \cdot 8} \cdot \underbrace{8 \cdot 8 \cdot 8}$$
$$= \qquad 8^4 \quad \cdot \quad 8^2 \qquad\qquad = \qquad 8^3 \quad \cdot \quad 8^3$$

Notice that $8^4 \cdot 8^2 = 8^3 \cdot 8^3 = 8^6$. When you multiply powers with the same base, you add the exponents.

Multiplying Powers with the Same Base

For any nonzero number a and any integers m and n, $a^m \cdot a^n = a^{m+n}$.

Example: $3^5 \cdot 3^4 = 3^{5+4} = 3^9$

---

6. Write 5^7 as a product of powers in three different ways.

7. Does $3^2 \cdot 3^5 \cdot 3^1 = 3^{2+5+1} = 3^8$? Explain.

8. Does $3^4 \cdot 2^2 = 6^{4+2}$? Explain.

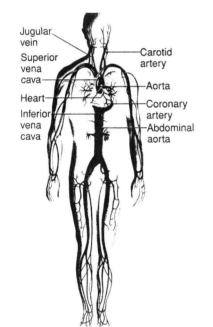

Jugular vein
Superior vena cava
Carotid artery
Aorta
Heart
Coronary artery
Inferior vena cava
Abdominal aorta

Example 1

Simplify each expression.

a. $c^4 \cdot d^3 \cdot c^2$

$= c^4 \cdot c^2 \cdot d^3$ ←—— Rearrange factors.

$= c^{4+2} \cdot d^3$ ←—— Add exponents of powers with the same base.

$= c^6 d^3$

b. $5x \cdot 2y^4 \cdot 3x^8$

$= (5 \cdot 2 \cdot 3)(x \cdot x^8)(y^4)$

Multiply coefficients. —→ $= (30)(x^1 \cdot x^8)(y^4)$

$= (30)(x^{1+8})(y^4)$

$= 30x^9 y^4$

9. **Try This** Simplify each expression.
   a. $a \cdot b^2 \cdot a^5$
   b. $6x^2 \cdot 3y^3 \cdot 2y^4$
   c. $m^2 \cdot n^2 \cdot 7m$

Working with Scientific Notation

Example 2   Relating to the Real World

Biology A human body contains about 3.2×10^4 μL (microliters) of blood for each pound of body weight. Each microliter of blood contains about 5×10^6 red blood cells. Find the approximate number of red blood cells in the body of a 125-lb person.

$\text{pounds} \cdot \dfrac{\text{microliters}}{\text{pound}} \cdot \dfrac{\text{cells}}{\text{microliter}} = \text{cells}$ ←—— Use dimensional analysis.

$125 \text{ lb} \cdot (3.2 \times 10^4)\dfrac{\mu L}{lb} \cdot (5 \times 10^6)\dfrac{\text{cells}}{\mu L}$

$= (125 \cdot 3.2 \cdot 5) \cdot (10^4 \cdot 10^6)$ ←—— Rearrange factors.

$= (125 \cdot 3.2 \cdot 5) \cdot 10^{10}$ ←—— Add exponents.

$= 2000 \cdot 10^{10}$ ←—— Simplify.

$= 2 \times 10^3 \cdot 10^{10}$ ←—— Write 2000 as 2×10^3.

$= 2 \times 10^{13}$ ←—— Use scientific notation.

There are about 2×10^{13} (20 trillion!) red blood cells in a 125-lb person.

10. **Try This** About how many red blood cells are in your body?

The average blood donation is 1 pint, which contains about 2.4×10^{12} red blood cells.

The property of multiplying powers with the same base works with negative exponents, also.

Example 3

Simplify $(0.2 \times 10^5)(4 \times 10^{-12})$. Give the answer in scientific notation.

$(0.2 \times 10^5)(4 \times 10^{-12})$

$= (0.2 \times 4)(10^5 \times 10^{-12})$ ← Rearrange factors.

$= 0.8 \times 10^{5+(-12)}$ ← Multiply.

$= 0.8 \times 10^{-7}$ ← Add exponents.

$= 8 \times 10^{-1} \times 10^{-7}$ ← Write 0.8 as 8×10^{-1}.

$= 8 \times 10^{-8}$ ← Add exponents.

11. **Try This** Simplify each expression. Give your answers in scientific notation.
   a. $(0.5 \times 10^{13})(0.3 \times 10^{-4})$ **b.** $(0.7 \times 10^{-9})(0.03 \times 10^8)$

12. **Verify** that $2^5 \cdot 2^{-2} = 2^3$ by writing 2^5 as an integer and 2^{-2} as a fraction, then multiplying.

Exercises   **ON YOUR OWN**

Write each expression as a product of powers, then simplify.

1. $(x \cdot x \cdot x \cdot x)(x \cdot x \cdot x)$ 2. $(x \cdot x)\left(\dfrac{1}{x \cdot x \cdot x}\right)$ 3. $\left(\dfrac{1}{x \cdot x}\right)\left(\dfrac{1}{x \cdot x \cdot x \cdot x \cdot x}\right)$

Complete each equation.

4. $5^2 \cdot 5^{\blacksquare} = 5^{11}$ 5. $5^7 \cdot 5^{\blacksquare} = 5^3$ 6. $a^{12} \cdot a^{\blacksquare} = a^{12}$ 7. $a \cdot a \cdot a^3 = a^{\blacksquare}$

8. $2^{\blacksquare} \cdot 2^4 = 2^1$ 9. $a^{\blacksquare} \cdot a^4 = 1$ 10. $c^{-5} \cdot c^{\blacksquare} = c^6$ 11. $x^3 y^{\blacksquare} \cdot x^{\blacksquare} = y^2$

Multiply. Give your answers in scientific notation.

12. $(9 \times 10^7)(3 \times 10^{-16})$ 13. $(8 \times 10^{-3})(0.1 \times 10^9)$ 14. $(0.7 \times 10^{-12})(0.3 \times 10^8)$

15. $(2 \times 10^6)(3 \times 10^3)$ 16. $1 \times 10^3 \cdot 10^{-8}$ 17. $(4 \times 10^6) \times 10^{-3}$

18. **Standardized Test Prep** Simplify $p^8 \cdot 9q^2 \cdot q^4 \cdot p^3 \cdot 2q$.
   A. $-11p^{11}q^7$ **B.** $11p^{14}q^8$ **C.** $18p^{11}q^6$ **D.** $18p^{11}q^7$ **E.** $18pq^{17}$

19. **a.** *Open-ended* Write y^8 in four different ways as the product of two powers with the same base. Use only positive exponents.
   b. Write y^8 in four different ways as the product of two powers with the same base, using negative or zero exponents in each.
   c. How many ways are there to write y^8 as the product of two powers? **Summarize** your reasoning.

Simplify each expression. Use only positive exponents.

20. $(0.99^2)(0.99^4)$

21. $(1.025)^3(1.025)^{-3}$

22. $c^{-2}c^7$

23. $3r \cdot r^4$

24. $5t^{-2} \cdot 2t^{-5}$

25. $(a^2b^3)(a^6)$

26. $(x^5y^2)(x^{-6}y)$

27. $3x^2 \cdot x^2$

28. $(1.03^8)(1.03^4)$

29. $-(0.99^3)(0.99^0)$

30. $a \cdot a^{-7}$

31. $b^{-2} \cdot b^4 \cdot b$

32. $10^{-13} \cdot 10^5$

33. $(-2m^3)(3.5m^{-3})$

34. $(7x^5)(8x)$

35. $(15a^3)(-3a)$

36. $(-2.4n^4)(2n^{-1})$

37. $bc^{-6} \cdot b$

38. $(5x^5)(3y^6)(3x^2)$

39. $(4c^4)(ac^3)(3a^5c)$

40. $x^6 \cdot y^2 \cdot x^4$

41. $a^6b^3 \cdot a^2b^{-2}$

42. $\dfrac{1}{x^2 \cdot x^{-5}}$

43. $\dfrac{1}{a^3 \cdot a^{-2}}$

44. $\dfrac{5}{c \cdot c^{-4}}$

45. $2a^2(3a + 5)$

46. $8m^3(m^2 + 7)$

47. $-4x^3(2x^2 - 9x)$

48. Chemistry The term *mole* is used in chemistry to refer to a specific number of atoms or molecules. One mole is equal to 6.02×10^{23}. The mass of a single hydrogen atom is approximately 1.67×10^{-24} gram. What is the mass of 1 mole of hydrogen atoms?

49. a. Jerome wrote $a^3b^2b^4 = (a \cdot a \cdot a)(b \cdot b)(b \cdot b \cdot b \cdot b)$. Jeremy wrote $a^3b^2b^4 = ab^9$. Whose work is correct? Explain.
   b. Use the correct work to simplify $a^3b^2b^4$.

50. Writing Explain why $x^3 \cdot y^5$ cannot be simplified.

Geometry Find the area of each figure.

51.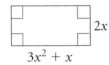
$3x^2 + x$, $2x$

52.
$4c$, $2c^3$

53.
$4y^2$, $y^3 + 2$

54.
$2x^2$

Critical Thinking Find and correct the errors in Exercises 55–57.

55. $(3x^2)(-2x^4) = 3(-2)x^{2 \cdot 4}$
$= -6x^8$

56. $4a^2 \cdot 3a^5 = (4 + 3)a^{2+5}$
$= 7a^7$

57. $x^6 \cdot x \cdot x^3 = x^{6+3}$
$= x^9$

58. Technology A CD-ROM stores about 600 megabytes (6×10^8 bytes) of information along a spiral track. Each byte uses about 9 micrometers (9×10^{-6} m) of space along the track. Find the length of the track.

59. Medicine Medical X-rays, with a wavelength of about 10^{-10} m, can penetrate the flesh (but not the bones) of your body.
   a. Ultraviolet rays, which cause sunburn by penetrating only the top layers of skin, have a wavelength about 1000 times as long as X-rays. Find the wavelength of ultraviolet rays.
   b. Critical Thinking The wavelengths of visible light are between 4×10^{-7}m and 7.5×10^{-7}m. Are these wavelengths longer or shorter than those of ultraviolet rays?

The music on a compact disc comes from a series of notches that can be read by a laser. The disc is enclosed in two layers of plastic. The plastic surface of this CD is cracked to show the notched layer underneath.

Find Out by Analyzing

- Starting with the first day you see at least one square of mold, find the percent of growth from each day to the next.
- Use the average of these percents as an estimate for the base of an exponential function.
- Write an exponential function to fit the data. Graph it on your data plot.

Exercises   MIXED REVIEW

Identify each square root as *rational* or *irrational*. Simplify if possible.

60. $\sqrt{121}$ **61.** $\sqrt{67}$ **62.** $-\sqrt{49}$ **63.** $\sqrt{\frac{1}{4}}$ **64.** $-\sqrt{13}$ **65.** $\sqrt{\frac{9}{16}}$

66. Sports   In 1989, United States sales of in-line skates were $21 million. In 1994, sales were $369 million. Find the percent of increase.

Getting Ready for Lesson 8-7
Rewrite each expression with one exponent.

67. $3^2 \cdot 3^2 \cdot 3^2$ **68.** $2^3 \cdot 2^3 \cdot 2^3 \cdot 2^3$ **69.** $5^7 \cdot 5^7 \cdot 5^7 \cdot 5^7$ **70.** $7 \cdot 7 \cdot 7$

Exercises   CHECKPOINT

Write each expression as an integer or simple fraction.

1. $(-7.3)^0$ **2.** 3^{-2} **3.** -8^{-1} **4.** $\left(\frac{1}{5}\right)^{-3}$ **5.** -4^2 **6.** $(-2)^{-3}$

Simplify each expression. Use only positive exponents.

7. $s^{-2} \cdot s^4 \cdot s$ **8.** $a^7 b^2 \cdot 21 a^{-6}$ **9.** $(2a^3)(-3a^{-3})(\frac{1}{6}a^0)$ **10.** $g^3 h^{-4}$ **11.** $\frac{x^{-5}}{y^2 y^{-8}}$

Mental Math   **Simplify. Give your answers in scientific notation.**

12. $(5 \times 10^6) \times 3$ **13.** $0.4 \times (2 \times 10^{-7})$ **14.** $(9 \times 10^{11}) \div 3$ **15.** $6 \times (4 \times 10^3)$

16. a. Biology   Georg Frey collected beetles. When he died, his collection contained 3 million beetles of 90,000 different species. Write each number in scientific notation.
   b. About how many beetles fit into each of his 6500 packing cases?

17. Writing   LaWanda wrote $a^5 + a^5 = 2a^5$. Amanda wrote $a^5 + a^5 = a^{10}$. Whose work is correct? Explain.

Graph each function over the domain $\{-3 \leq x \leq 3\}$.

18. $f(x) = 0.8 \cdot 2^x$ **19.** $y = 0.5 \cdot 1.5^x$ **20.** $g(x) = 2 \cdot 3^x$

What You'll Learn

• Using two more multiplication properties of exponents

...And Why

To solve problems that involve raising numbers in scientific notation to a power

What You'll Need

• calculator

8-7 **M**ore Multiplication Properties of Exponents

T H I N K   A N D   D I S C U S S

Raising a Power to a Power

In Lesson 8-6, you used patterns to discover how to multiply powers with the same base. You can use what you discovered there to find a shortcut for simplifying expressions such as $(8^6)^3$.

1. Copy and complete each statement.
   a. $(a^3)^2 = a^3 \cdot a^3 = a^{\blacksquare + \blacksquare} = a^{3 \cdot \blacksquare} = a^{\blacksquare}$
   b. $(4^5)^3 = 4^5 \cdot 4^5 \cdot 4^5 = 4^{\blacksquare + \blacksquare + \blacksquare} = 4^{5 \cdot \blacksquare} = 4^{\blacksquare}$
   c. $(2^7)^4 = 2^7 \cdot 2^7 \cdot 2^7 \cdot 2^7 = 2^{7 \cdot \blacksquare} = 2^{\blacksquare}$
   d. $(8^6)^2 = 8^6 \cdot 8^6 = 8^{6 \cdot \blacksquare} = 8^{\blacksquare}$
   e. $(g^4)^3 = g^4 \cdot g^4 \cdot g^4 = g^{4 \cdot \blacksquare} = g^{\blacksquare}$

2. **Patterns** Look for a pattern in your answers to Question 1. Write a shortcut for simplifying an expression such as $(8^6)^3$.

You can use the property below to simplify some exponential expressions.

> ### Raising a Power to a Power
> For any nonzero number a and any integers m and n, $(a^m)^n = a^{mn}$.
> **Example:** $(5^4)^2 = 5^{4 \cdot 2} = 5^8$

3. The work you did in Question 1 involves repeated multiplication. Simplify each expression below by using repeated multiplication. Then check your work by using the property.
   a. $(2^3)^2$ b. $(h^2)^4$ c. $(3^3)^4$

4. Simplify each expression. What do you notice?
   a. $(5^2)^4 = 25^4 = \blacksquare$ b. $(5^2)^4 = 5^8 = \blacksquare$

CALCULATOR HINT

When evaluating an expression such as $(3^4)^2$, you do not need to use parentheses because the calculator evaluates powers from left to right. Pressing 3 ∧ 4 ∧ 2 ENTER will give you 6561.

5. Use the property to find each missing value. Then use a calculator to evaluate each expression and verify your answers.
   a. $(3^{\blacksquare})^4 = 9^4$ b. $(5^2)^{\blacksquare} = 5^8$ c. $(2^{\blacksquare})^{\blacksquare} = 4^2$
   d. $(3^4)^2 = 3^{\blacksquare}$ e. $(1.1^5)^7 = 1.1^{\blacksquare}$ f. $(123^0)^{87} = 123^{\blacksquare}$

Example 1

Simplify each expression.
   a. $(x^3)^6 = x^{3 \cdot 6}$ ←—Multiply exponents when raising a power to a power.
        $= x^{18}$ ←—Simplify.

b. $c^5(c^3)^2 = c^5 \cdot c^{3 \cdot 2}$ ⟵ Multiply exponents in $(c^3)^2$.

$\qquad = c^5 \cdot c^6$ ⟵ Simplify.

$\qquad = c^{5+6}$ ⟵ Add exponents when multiplying powers with the same base.

$\qquad = c^{11}$

6. Try This Simplify $(a^4)^2 \cdot (a^2)^5$.

Raising a Product to a Power

You can use repeated multiplication to simplify expressions like $(5y)^3$.

$$(5y)^3 = 5y \cdot 5y \cdot 5y$$
$$= 5 \cdot 5 \cdot 5 \cdot y \cdot y \cdot y$$
$$= 5^3 \cdot y^3$$
$$= 125y^3$$

Notice from the steps above that $(5y)^3 = 5^3 y^3$. This illustrates another property of exponents.

Raising a Product to a Power

For any nonzero numbers a and b and any integer n, $(ab)^n = a^n b^n$.

Example: $(3x)^4 = 3^4 x^4 = 81x^4$

7. Calculator Verify each equation for two values of the variable (other than 0 and 1).

a. $(5y)^3 = 125y^3$ **b.** $(3x)^4 = 3^4 x^4$ **c.** $(7c)^2 = 49c^2$

Example 2

Simplify each expression.

a. $(2x^2)^4 = 2^4(x^2)^4$ ⟵ Raise each factor to the 4th power.

$\qquad = 2^4 x^8$ ⟵ Multiply exponents.

$\qquad = 16x^8$ ⟵ Simplify.

b. $(x^{-2})^2(3xy^2)^4 = (x^{-2})^2 \cdot 3^4 x^4 (y^2)^4$ ⟵ Raise three factors to the 4th power.

$\qquad = x^{-4} \cdot 3^4 x^4 y^8$ ⟵ Multiply exponents.

$\qquad = 3^4 \cdot x^{-4} \cdot x^4 \cdot y^8$ ⟵ Rearrange factors.

$\qquad = 3^4 x^0 y^8$ ⟵ Add exponents.

$\qquad = 81y^8$ ⟵ Simplify.

8. Try This Simplify each expression.

a. $(15z)^3$ **b.** $(4g^5)^2$ **c.** $(6mn)^3(5m^{-3})^4$

You can use the properties of exponents to solve real-world problems.

Example 3   **Relating to the Real World**

Physical Science All objects, even resting ones, contain energy. The expression $10^{-3} \cdot (3 \times 10^8)^2$ describes the amount of resting energy a raisin contains, where 10^{-3} kg is the mass of the raisin. Simplify the expression.

$10^{-3} \cdot (3 \times 10^8)^2$
$= 10^{-3} \cdot 3^2 \cdot (10^8)^2$ ← Raise two factors to the 2nd power.
$= 10^{-3} \cdot 3^2 \cdot 10^{16}$ ← Multiply exponents.
$= 3^2 \cdot 10^{-3} \cdot 10^{16}$ ← Rearrange factors.
$= 3^2 \cdot 10^{-3 + 16}$ ← Add exponents.
$= 9 \times 10^{13}$ ← Simplify.

One raisin contains about 9×10^{13} joules of resting energy. ■

9. Multiply. Give your answers in scientific notation.
   a. $(4 \times 10^5)^2$
   b. $(2 \times 10^{-10})^3$
   c. $(10^3)^4(4.3 \times 10^{-8})$

Who? Albert Einstein is famous for discovering the relationship $e = mc^2$, where e is energy (in joules), m is mass (in kg), and c is the speed of light (about 3×10^8 meters per second).

10. *Energy* An hour of television use consumes 1.45×10^{-1} kWh of electricity. Each kilowatt-hour (kWh) of electric use is equivalent to 3.6×10^6 joules of energy.
    a. How many joules does a television use in 1 h? (Hint: Use a proportion.)
    b. Suppose you could release the resting energy in a raisin. About how many hours of television use could be powered by that energy?

Exercises   ON YOUR OWN

Simplify each expression. Use positive exponents.

1. $(xy)^9$
2. $(c^5)^2$
3. $(a^2b^4)^3$
4. $(3m^3)^4$

5. $(g^{10})^{-4}$
6. $g^{10} \cdot g^{-4}$
7. $(x^3y)^4$
8. $(x^{-2})^3x^{-12}$

9. $(0.5^2)^{-2}$
10. $(2xy)^3x^2$
11. $(g \cdot g^4)^2$
12. $(c^2)^{-2}(c^3)^4$

13. $s^3(s^2)^4$
14. $(mg^4)^{-1}$
15. $m(g^4)^{-1}$
16. $(7cd^4)^2$

17. $(2p^6)^0$
18. $(5ac^3)^{-2}$
19. $(4a^2b)^3(ab)^3$
20. $(4xy^2)^4(2y)^{-3}$

21. $3^7 \cdot \left(\frac{1}{3}\right)^7$
22. $(5x)^2 + 5x^2$
23. $2^4 \cdot 5^4$
24. $(64.1^{-3})^0$

25. $(b^n)^3b^2$
26. $15^2 \cdot (0.2)^2$
27. $(4.1)^5 \cdot (4.1)^{-5}$
28. $3^2 \cdot (3x)^3$

29. a. Geography Earth has a radius of about 6.4×10^6 m. Approximate the surface area of Earth by using the formula for the surface area of a sphere, $S = 4\pi r^2$.

b. Earth's surface is about 70% water, almost all of it in oceans. About how many square meters of Earth's surface are covered with water?

c. The oceans have an average depth of 3795 m. What is the approximate volume of water on Earth?

Multiply. Give your answers in scientific notation.

30. $(3 \times 10^5)^2$

31. $(2 \times 10^{-3})^3$

32. $(7 \times 10^4)^2$

33. $(6 \times 10^{12})^2$

34. $(3 \times 10^{-4})^3$

35. $(4 \times 10^8)^{-2}$

36. Which expression or expressions do *not* equal 64?
   A. $2^5 \cdot 2$ **B.** 2^6 **C.** $2^2 \cdot 2^3$ **D.** $(2^3)^2$ **E.** $(2^2)(2^2)^2$

37. Writing Explain how the properties of exponents help you simplify algebraic expressions.

38. a. Geometry Write an expression for the surface area of each cube.
   b. How many times greater than the surface area of the small cube is the surface area of the large cube?
   c. Write an expression for the volume of each cube.
   d. How many times greater than the volume of the small cube is the volume of the large cube?

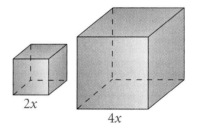

$2x$

$4x$

39. Open-ended Write a^{24} as a product of the form $(a^m)^n$ in four different ways. Use only positive exponents.

40. Technology In computer memory chips currently being developed, a square piece of chip is one thousandth of an inch (10^{-3} in.) on each side. It will hold 3000 bits of data. Find the area of the piece of chip.

Complete each equation.

41. $(x^2)^{\blacksquare} = x^6$

42. $(x^{\blacksquare})^3 = x^{-12}$

43. $(ab^2)^{\blacksquare} = a^4b^8$

44. $(5x^{\blacksquare})^2 = 25x^4$

45. $(3x^3y^{\blacksquare})^3 = 27x^6$

46. $(m^2n^3)^{\blacksquare} = \dfrac{1}{m^6n^9}$

Solve each equation. Use the sample below.

Sample:
$$25^3 = 5^x$$
$$(5^2)^3 = 5^x \longleftarrow \text{Write 25 as a power of 5.}$$
$$5^6 = 5^x \longleftarrow \text{Multiply exponents.}$$
$$x = 6$$

The solution is 6.

47. $8^2 = 2^x$

48. $3^x = 27^4$

49. $4^x = 2^6$

50. $5^6 = 25^x$

51. Biology There are an estimated 200 million insects for each person on Earth. The world population is about 5.5 billion. About how many insects are there on Earth?

Write each expression with only one exponent. Use parentheses.

52. $m^4 \cdot n^4$

53. $(a^5)(b^5)(a^0)$

54. $49x^2y^2z^2$

55. $\dfrac{12x^{-2}}{3y^2}$

Chapter Project

Find Out by Interpreting

Use your exponential function to predict the growth of your mold at two weeks. Compare your predictions to the actual growth of the mold. Discuss any factors that may influence the accuracy of your exponential model.

Exercises   M I X E D   R E V I E W

56. Solve $3x^2 - 5x - 2 = 0$.

57. Solve $x^2 + 2x + 1 = 0$.

58. Textiles To make felt, thin layers of cotton are built up $\frac{1}{32}$ in. at a time. How many layers does it take to make felt $\frac{1}{4}$ in. thick?

Getting Ready for Lesson 8-8

Simplify each expression.

59. $x^2 \cdot x^{-3}$

60. $u^8 \cdot u^{-4}$

61. $t^{-6} \cdot t$

62. $h^{-3} \cdot h^0$

FOR YOUR JOURNAL

Summarize the three multiplication properties of exponents that you have learned in the last two lessons. Give an example of each.

A Point in Time

1500   1600   1700   1800   1900   2000

Dr. Jewel Plummer Cobb

Dr. Jewel Plummer Cobb was born in 1924 and obtained her master's and doctorate degrees in cell physiology from New York University. Dr. Cobb has concentrated on the study of normal and malignant skin cells and has published nearly fifty books, articles, and reports.

Because the number of cancer cells grows exponentially, cell biologists often write cancer cell data in scientific notation.

What You'll Learn

8-8

Division Properties of Exponents

- Applying division properties of exponents

...And Why

To solve problems that involve dividing numbers in scientific notation

What You'll Need

- calculator

Dividing Powers with the Same Base

In Lessons 8-6 and 8-7 you studied patterns that occur when you multiply powers with the same base. You can see a similar pattern when you divide powers with the same base.

You can use repeated multiplication to simplify fractions. Expand the numerator and denominator using repeated multiplication. Then cancel like terms.

$$\frac{5^6}{5^2} = \frac{\cancel{5} \cdot \cancel{5} \cdot 5 \cdot 5 \cdot 5 \cdot 5}{\cancel{5} \cdot \cancel{5}} = 5^4$$

1. Simplify each expression by expanding the numerator and the denominator and then canceling. Describe any patterns you see.

    a. $\dfrac{5^7}{5^3}$ **b.** $\dfrac{5^{12}}{5^8}$ **c.** $\dfrac{5^8}{5^4}$ **d.** $\dfrac{5^5}{5^1}$ **e.** $\dfrac{5^5}{5^8}$

Dividing Powers with the Same Base

For any nonzero number a and any integers m and n, $\dfrac{a^m}{a^n} = a^{m-n}$.

Example: $\dfrac{3^7}{3^2} = 3^{7-2} = 3^5$

---

 2. Calculator Find each missing value. Use a calculator to check.

    a. $\dfrac{5^9}{5^2} = 5^{\blacksquare}$ **b.** $\dfrac{2^4}{2^3} = 2^{\blacksquare}$ **c.** $\dfrac{3^2}{3^5} = 3^{\blacksquare}$ **d.** $\dfrac{5^3}{5^2} = 5^{\blacksquare}$

Example 1

Simplify each expression. Use only positive exponents.

a. $\dfrac{a^6}{a^{14}} = a^{6-14}$ ⟵ Subtract exponents when dividing powers with the same base.

        $= a^{-8}$

        $= \dfrac{1}{a^8}$ ⟵ Rewrite using positive exponents.

b. $\dfrac{c^{-1}d^3}{c^5d^{-4}} = c^{-1-5} \cdot d^{3-(-4)}$ ⟵ Subtract exponents.

        $= c^{-6}d^7$

        $= \dfrac{d^7}{c^6}$ ⟵ Use positive exponents.

3. **Try This** Simplify each expression. Use positive exponents.

    a. $\dfrac{b^4}{b^9}$ **b.** $\dfrac{z^{10}}{z^5}$ **c.** $\dfrac{a^2b}{a^4b^3}$ **d.** $\dfrac{m^{-1}n^2}{m^3n}$ **e.** $\dfrac{x^2yz^4}{xy^4z^{-3}}$

Example 2 **Relating to the Real World**

Environment In 1993 the total amount of waste paper and cardboard recycled in the United States was 77.8 million tons. The population in 1993 was 258.1 million. How much paper was recycled per person?

$$\frac{77.8 \text{ million tons}}{258.1 \text{ million people}} = \frac{77.8 \times 10^7 \text{ tons}}{2.581 \times 10^8 \text{ people}}$$ ⟵ Write in scientific notation.

$$= \frac{7.78}{2.581} \times 10^{7-8}$$ ⟵ Subtract exponents when dividing powers with the same base.

$$= \frac{7.78}{2.581} \times 10^{-1}$$

$$\approx 3.01 \times 10^{-1}$$ ⟵ Simplify.

$$\approx 0.3$$

In 1993, 0.3 ton (600 lb!) of waste paper was recycled per person.

4. Only 34% of the waste paper generated in 1993 was recycled. How many pounds of waste paper were generated per person in 1993?

5. Try This Find each quotient. Give your answer in scientific notation.

a. $\dfrac{2 \times 10^3}{8 \times 10^8}$

b. $\dfrac{7.5 \times 10^{12}}{2.5 \times 10^{-4}}$

c. $\dfrac{4.2 \times 10^5}{12.6 \times 10^2}$

Raising a Quotient to a Power

You can use repeated multiplication to simplify the expression $\left(\frac{x}{y}\right)^3$.

$$\left(\frac{x}{y}\right)^3 = \frac{x}{y} \cdot \frac{x}{y} \cdot \frac{x}{y}$$

$$= \frac{x \cdot x \cdot x}{y \cdot y \cdot y}$$

$$= \frac{x^3}{y^3}$$

6. **Calculator** **Verify** that $\left(\frac{x}{y}\right)^3 = \frac{x^3}{y^3}$ for three values of x and y.

Raising a Quotient to a Power

For any nonzero numbers a and b, and any integer n, $\left(\frac{a}{b}\right)^n = \frac{a^n}{b^n}$.

Example: $\left(\frac{4}{5}\right)^3 = \frac{4^3}{5^3} = \frac{64}{125}$

---

1 What is the simplest form of $\left(\frac{3c^{-5}d}{c^{-3}}\right)^4$?

(1) $81c^{-8}d^4$

(2) $81cd^4$

(3) $\frac{12d^4}{c^4}$

(4) $\frac{81d^4}{c^8}$

2 A cubic inch is approximately 0.0000214 cubic yards.
   a How is this measure expressed in scientific notation?
   b The volume of a wooden puzzle cube is 9 cubic inches. Express the volume in cubic yards using scientific notation.

Example 3

Simplify each expression.

a. $\left(\frac{4}{x^2}\right)^3 = \frac{4^3}{(x^2)^3}$ ← Raise the numerator and denominator to the 3rd power.

$= \frac{4^3}{x^6}$ ← Multiply exponents.

$= \frac{64}{x^6}$ ← Simplify.

b. $\left(-\frac{3}{5}\right)^{-2} = \left(\frac{-3}{5}\right)^{-2}$ ← Write the fraction with a negative numerator.

$= \frac{(-3)^{-2}}{5^{-2}}$ ← Raise the numerator and denominator to the -2 power.

$= \frac{5^2}{(-3)^2}$ ← Apply the definition of negative exponents.

$= \frac{25}{9}$ ← Simplify.

7. In Example 3, part (b), the first step could have been to rewrite the fraction as $\left(\frac{3}{-5}\right)^{-2}$. Explain how this step would affect the rest of your work.

8. *Open-ended* Suppose you wanted to simplify $\left(\frac{5}{3}\right)^3$. What would be your first step?

When you have reduced an expression as far as possible, and when all your exponents are positive, the expression is in **simplest form.**

9. Is each expression in simplest form? If not, simplify it.

   a. $\frac{(x^3)^2}{y^7}$ **b.** $x^{-3}y^2$ **c.** $\frac{a^5}{ab}$ **d.** $\frac{(2x)^2}{2x^2}$

Sometimes you can combine steps to shorten your work.

10. Copy and complete each statement.

   a. $\left(\frac{4a^3}{b}\right)^2 = \frac{\blacksquare a^{\blacksquare}}{b^{\blacksquare}}$ ← Raising products, quotients, and powers to a power.

   b. $\frac{x^{-3}x^8}{x^2} = x^{\blacksquare + \blacksquare - \blacksquare} = x^{\blacksquare}$ ← Multiplying and dividing powers with the same base.

11. Try This Simplify each expression.

   a. $\left(\frac{2m^5}{m^2}\right)^4$ **b.** $\left(\frac{2n^3t}{t^2}\right)^2$ **c.** $\left(\frac{5x^7y^4}{x^{-2}}\right)^2$

Exercises   ON YOUR OWN

Simplify each expression. Use only positive exponents.

1. $\frac{2^5}{2^7}$ **2.** $\left(\frac{2^2}{5}\right)^2$ **3.** $\left(\frac{3}{4}\right)^2$ **4.** $\left(\frac{2}{3}\right)^{-2}$ **5.** $\left(\frac{3^3}{3^4}\right)^2$ **6.** $\frac{c^{12}}{c^{15}}$

7. $\frac{x^{13}y^2}{x^{13}y}$ **8.** $\frac{m^{-2}}{m^{-5}}$ **9.** $\frac{(2a^7)(3a^2)}{6a^3}$ **10.** $\left(\frac{3b^2}{5}\right)^0$ **11.** $\left(\frac{-2}{3}\right)^{-3}$ **12.** $\frac{3^2 \cdot 5^0}{2^3}$

Explain why each expression is *not* in simplest form.

13. $5^3 m^3$ **14.** $x^5 y^{-2}$ **15.** $(2c)^4$ **16.** $\dfrac{d^7}{d}$ **17.** $x^0 y$ **18.** $(3z^2)^3$

⊞ Choose **Use a calculator, paper and pencil, or mental math to simplify each quotient. Give your answers in scientific notation.**

19. $\dfrac{6.5 \times 10^{15}}{1.3 \times 10^8}$ **20.** $\dfrac{2.7 \times 10^8}{0.9 \times 10^3}$ **21.** $\dfrac{2.7 \times 10^8}{3 \times 10^5}$ **22.** $\dfrac{8.4 \times 10^{-5}}{2 \times 10^{-8}}$ **23.** $\dfrac{4.7 \times 10^{-4}}{3.1 \times 10^2}$

24. a. Writing While simplifying the expression $\dfrac{c^4}{c^6}$, Kneale said, "I've found a property of exponents that's not in my algebra book!" Write an explanation of why Kneale's method works.

b. Open-ended Apply Kneale's method to an example you create.

Kneale

$$\dfrac{c^4}{c^6} = \dfrac{1}{c^{6-4}} = \dfrac{1}{c^2}$$

25. a. Television In 1999 people in the United States will watch television a total of 450 billion hours, according to industry projections. The population will be about 274 million people. Find the number of hours of TV viewing per person for 1999.

b. According to these projections, about how many hours per day will people watch television in 1999?

26. Lena and Jared used different methods to simplify $\left(\dfrac{b^7}{b^3}\right)^2$. Are both methods correct? Explain.

Lena
$$\left(\dfrac{b^7}{b^3}\right)^2 = \dfrac{b^{14}}{b^6}$$
$$= b^8$$

Jared
$$\left(\dfrac{b^7}{b^3}\right)^2 = (b^4)^2$$
$$= b^8$$

Simplify each expression. Use only positive exponents.

27. $\dfrac{2^7}{2^5}$ **28.** $2^5 \cdot 2^{-7}$ **29.** $\left(\dfrac{3^5}{3^2}\right)^2$ **30.** $\dfrac{a^7}{a^9}$ **31.** $\dfrac{6c^7}{3c}$ **32.** $\dfrac{5x^5}{15x^3}$

33. $\dfrac{a^7 b^3 c^2}{a^2 b^6 c^2}$ **34.** $\dfrac{a^{-21} a^{15}}{a^3}$ **35.** $\dfrac{c^3 d^7}{c^8 d^{-1}}$ **36.** $\dfrac{p^7 q r^{-1}}{p q^{-2} r^5}$ **37.** $\dfrac{5x^3}{(5x)^3}$ **38.** $\left(\dfrac{5x^3}{20x}\right)^3$

39. $\left(\dfrac{c^5}{c^9}\right)^3$ **40.** $\left(\dfrac{7a}{b^3}\right)^2$ **41.** $\left(\dfrac{3b^0}{5}\right)^2$ **42.** $\dfrac{(3a^3)^2}{10a^{-1}}$ **43.** $\left(\dfrac{5m^3 n}{m^5}\right)^3$ **44.** $\left(\dfrac{x^4 x}{x^{-2}}\right)^{-4}$

Write each expression with only one exponent. You may need to use parentheses.

45. $\dfrac{3^5}{5^5}$ **46.** $\dfrac{m^7}{n^7}$ **47.** $\dfrac{d^8}{d^5}$ **48.** $\dfrac{10^7 \cdot 10^0}{10^{-3}}$ **49.** $\dfrac{27x^3}{8y^3}$ **50.** $\dfrac{4m^2}{169m^4}$

51. a. Finance In 1980, the U.S. Government owed $909 billion to its creditors. The population of the United States was 226.5 million people. How much did the government owe per person in 1980?

b. In 1994 the debt had grown to $4.64 trillion, with a population of 260 million. How much did the government owe per person?

c. What was the percent of increase in the amount owed per person from 1980 to 1994?

PROBLEM SOLVING HINT

Use a proportion.

Which property(ies) of exponents would you use to simplify each expression?

52. 2^{-3}
53. $\dfrac{2^2}{2^5}$
54. $\left(\dfrac{1}{2}\right)^3$
55. $\dfrac{1}{2^{-4} \cdot 2^7}$
56. $\dfrac{(2^4)^3}{2^{15}}$

57. Astronomy The ratio of a planet's maximum to minimum distance from the Sun is a measure of how circular its orbit is.
  a. Copy and complete the table below.
  b. Which planet has the least circular orbit? the most circular orbit? Explain your reasoning.

Distances from the Sun (km)

Planet	Maximum	Minimum	Maximum : Minimum
Mercury	6.97×10^7	4.59×10^7	$\blacksquare : \blacksquare = \dfrac{6.97 \times 10^7}{4.59 \times 10^7} = \dfrac{6.97}{4.59} \approx 1.52$
Venus	1.089×10^8	1.075×10^8	$1.089 \times 10^8 : \blacksquare \approx \blacksquare$
Earth	1.521×10^8	1.471×10^8	$\blacksquare : 1.471 \times 10^8 \approx \blacksquare$
Mars	2.491×10^8	2.067×10^8	$\blacksquare : \blacksquare \approx \blacksquare$
Jupiter	8.157×10^8	7.409×10^8	$\blacksquare : \blacksquare \approx \blacksquare$
Saturn	1.507×10^9	1.347×10^9	$\blacksquare : \blacksquare \approx \blacksquare$
Uranus	3.004×10^9	2.735×10^9	$\blacksquare : \blacksquare \approx \blacksquare$
Neptune	4.537×10^9	4.457×10^9	$\blacksquare : \blacksquare \approx \blacksquare$
Pluto	7.375×10^9	4.425×10^9	$\blacksquare : \blacksquare \approx \blacksquare$

min.

max.

58. Medicine If you donate blood regularly, the American Red Cross recommends a 56-day waiting period between donations. One pint of blood contains about 2.4×10^{12} red blood cells. Your body normally produces about 2×10^6 red blood cells per second.
  a. At its normal rate, in how many seconds will your body replace the red blood cells lost by giving one pint of blood?
  b. Convert your answer from part (a) to days.

Exercises   MIXED REVIEW

Solve each equation.

59. $x^2 = 0.36$
60. $t^2 - 13 = 0$
61. $m + 4 = -2$

Graph each inequality.

62. $y \le 3x - 4$
63. $y > -2x$
64. $y \ge -x + 1$

65. The Folsom Dam in California holds 1 million acre-feet of water in a reservoir. An acre-foot of water is the amount of water that covers an acre to the depth of one foot, or 326,000 gal. How many gallons are in the reservoir?

SELF ASSESSMENT

PORTFOLIO

For your portfolio, select one or two items from your work for this chapter. Here are some possibilities:
• best work
• work you found challenging
• part of your project
Explain why you have included each selection that you make.

Finishing the Chapter Project

MOLDY
OLDIES

Questions on pages 366, 372, 389, 395, and 400 should help you to complete your project. Record all your information for the project in a notebook. Be sure to include your data and calculations. Include a picture or illustration of the mold as it appeared when it began to grow and at the end of your experiment. Add any additional information you feel is necessary.

Reflect and Revise

Share your notebook with others in your group. Check that your presentation is clear and accurate. Make any changes necessary in your work.

Follow Up

What difference in the rate of growth of the mold might have occurred if you had placed the cheese in a cooler environment? in a drier environment? Investigate other sources of mold and fungus in the natural environment.

For More Information

Dashevsky, H. Steve. *Microbiology: 49 Science Fair Projects.* Blue Ridge Summit, Pennsylvania: TAB Books, 1994.

Hershey, David R. *Plant Biology Science Projects.* New York: John Wiley & Sons, 1995.

VanCleave, Janice Pratt. *Janice VanCleave's A+ Projects in Biology: Winning Experiments for Science Fairs and Extra Credit.* New York: John Wiley & Sons, 1993.

Key Terms

compound interest (p. 369)
decay factor (p. 373)
exponential decay (p. 373)
exponential function (p. 363)
exponential growth (p. 368)
growth factor (p. 368)

interest period (p. 369)
power (p. 391)
power of ten (p. 386)
scientific notation (p. 385)
simplest form (p. 403)

How am I doing?

SELF ASSESSMENT

- State three ideas from this chapter that you think are important. Explain your choices.
- Describe several rules that you can use to simplify expressions with exponents.

Exploring Exponential Functions 8-1

You can use exponents to show repeated multiplication. An **exponential function** repeatedly multiplies an amount by the same positive number.

Evaluate each function for the given values.

1. $f(x) = 3 \cdot 2^x$ for the domain {1, 2, 3, 4}

2. $y = 10 \cdot (0.75)^x$ for the domain {1, 2, 3}

3. a. One kind of bacterium in a laboratory culture triples in number every 30 minutes. Suppose a culture is started with 30 bacteria cells. How many bacteria will there be after 2 hours?
   b. After how many minutes will there be more than 20,000 bacteria?

Exponential Growth and Decay 8-2, 8-3

The general form of an exponential function is $y = a \cdot b^x$.

When $b > 1$, the function increases, and the function shows **exponential growth.** The base, b, of the exponent is called the **growth factor.** An example of exponential growth is **compound interest.**

When $0 < b < 1$, the function decreases, and the function shows **exponential decay.** Then b is called the **decay factor.** An example of exponential decay is half-life.

Identify each exponential function as *exponential growth* **or** *exponential decay.* **Then identify the growth or decay factor.**

4. $y = 5.2 \cdot 3^x$

5. $y = 0.15 \cdot \left(\frac{3}{2}\right)^x$

6. $y = 7 \cdot 0.32^x$

7. $y = 1.3 \cdot \left(\frac{1}{4}\right)^x$

Graph each function.

8. $f(x) = 2.5^x$

9. $y = 0.5 \cdot (0.5)^x$

10. $f(x) = \left(\frac{1}{2}\right) \cdot 3^x$

11. $y = 0.1^x$

What percent increase or decrease is modeled in each function?

12. $y = 100 \cdot 1.025^x$

13. $y = 32 \cdot 0.75^x$

14. $y = 0.4 \cdot 2^x$

15. $y = 1.01 \cdot 0.9^x$

16. The population of a city is 100,000 and is growing 7% each year.
  a. Write an equation to model the population of the city after any number of years.
  b. Use your equation to find the population after 25 years.

17. a. Finance Suppose you earned $1200 last summer and you put it into a savings account that pays 5.5% interest compounded quarterly. Find the balance after 9 months and after 12 months.
  b. Writing Would you rather have an account that pays 5.5% interest compounded quarterly or 6% interest compounded annually? Explain.

18. Chemistry The half-life of radioactive carbon-11 is 20 min. You start an experiment with 160 mCi of carbon-11. After 2 h, how much radioactivity remains?

You can use zero and negative numbers as exponents. For any nonzero number a, $a^0 = 1$. For any nonzero number a and any integer n, $a^{-n} = \frac{1}{a^n}$.

Write each expression so that all exponents are positive.

19. $b^{-4}c^0d^6$ **20.** $\dfrac{x^{-2}}{y^{-8}}$ **21.** $7k^{-8}h^3$ **22.** $\dfrac{1}{p^2q^{-4}r^0}$ **23.** $\left(\dfrac{2}{3}\right)^{-4}$

24. Critical Thinking Is $(-3b)^4 = -12b^4$? Why or why not?

25. Standardized Test Prep If $a = 4$, $b = -3$, and $c = 0$, which expression has the greatest value?
  A. a^b **B.** b^c **C.** $\dfrac{1}{b^{-a}}$ **D.** $\dfrac{a^c}{b^c}$ **E.** $\dfrac{c}{a^{-b}}$

You can use **scientific notation** to express very large or very small numbers. A number is in scientific notation if it is in the form $a \times 10^n$, where $1 \le |a| < 10$ and n is an integer.

Determine whether each number is in scientific notation. If it is not, write it in scientific notation.

26. 950×10^5 **27.** 72.35×10^8 **28.** 1.6×10^{-6} **29.** 84×10^{-5} **30.** 0.26×10^{-3}

Write each number in scientific notation.

31. The space probe *Voyager 2* traveled 2,793,000 miles.

32. There are 189 million passenger cars and trucks in use in the United States.

Double each number. Give your answers in scientific notation.

33. 8.03×10^7 **34.** 2.3×10^{-9} **35.** 7.084×10^6 **36.** 5×10^{-13}

Multiplication Properties of Exponents

To multiply powers with the same base, add the exponents.	To raise a power to a power, multiply the exponents.	To raise a product to a power, raise each factor in the product to the power.
$a^m \cdot a^n = a^{m+n}$	$(a^m)^n = a^{mn}$	$(ab)^n = a^n b^n$

Simplify each expression. Use only positive exponents.

37. $2d^2 d^3$ **38.** $(q^3 r)^4$ **39.** $(5c^{-4})(-4m^2 c^8)$ **40.** $(1.34^2)^5 (1.34)^{-8}$ **41.** $(12x^2 y^{-2})^5 (4xy^{-3})^{-8}$

42. Estimation Each square inch of your body has about 6.5×10^2 pores. The back of your hand has area about 0.12×10^2 in.^{2}. About how many pores are on the back of one hand?

43. Open-ended Write and solve a problem that involves multiplying exponents.

Division Properties of Exponents

To divide powers with the same base, subtract the exponents.	$\dfrac{a^m}{a^n} = a^{m-n}$	To raise a quotient to a power, raise the dividend and the divisor to the power.	$\left(\dfrac{a}{b}\right)^n = \dfrac{a^n}{b^n}$

Determine whether each expression is in simplest form. If it is not, simplify it.

44. $\dfrac{w^2}{w^5}$ **45.** $(8^3) \cdot 8^{-5}$ **46.** $\left(\dfrac{21x^3}{5y^2}\right)$ **47.** $\left(\dfrac{n^5}{v^3}\right)^7$ **48.** $\dfrac{e^{-6} c^3}{e^5}$ **49.** $\left(\dfrac{x^9}{s^{-3}}\right)^5$

Find each quotient. Give your answer in scientific notation.

50. $\dfrac{4.2 \times 10^8}{2.1 \times 10^{11}}$ **51.** $\dfrac{3.1 \times 10^4}{12.4 \times 10^2}$ **52.** $\dfrac{4.5 \times 10^3}{9 \times 10^7}$ **53.** $\dfrac{5.1 \times 10^5}{1.7 \times 10^2}$

54. Writing List the steps that you would follow to simplify $\left(\dfrac{5a^8}{10a^6}\right)^{-3}$.

Getting Ready for...► CHAPTER 9

Find the distance between the numbers on a number line.

55. 5 and 3   **56.** −7 and 4   **57.** −5 and −11

Simplify each expression.

58. $7r(11 + 4x)$ **59.** $8m(3 - 2t)$ **60.** $b(8 + 2b)$

61. $8p + 6d - 3p$ **62.** $-5n - 4n + 10n$ **63.** $5^2 + 6^2$

64. $9^2 - 4^2$ **65.** $(3t)^2 + (2t)^2$ **66.** $20y^2 - (4y)^2$

Find the range and mean of each set of data.

67. $40, $58, $44, $47, $39, $58, $56   **68.** 4 kg, 3 kg, 6 kg, 3 kg, 5 kg, 8 kg, 4 kg, 3 kg

69. 1.3 min, 1.4 min, 1.1 min, 1.0 min, 1.4 min

Evaluate each function for $x = 1, 2,$ and 3.

1. $y = 3 \cdot 5^x$

2. $f(x) = \frac{1}{2} \cdot 4^x$

3. $f(x) = 4 \cdot (0.95)^x$

4. $g(x) = 5 \cdot \left(\frac{3}{4}\right)^x$

5. The function $y = 10 \cdot 1.08^x$ models the cost of annual tuition (in thousands of dollars) at a local college in the years since 1987.
   a. Graph the function.
   b. What is the annual percent increase?
   c. How much was tuition in 1987? in 1992?
   d. How much will tuition be the year you plan to graduate from high school?

6. The function $y = 1.3 \cdot (1.07)^n$ models a city's annual electrical consumption for the n years since 1965, where y is billions of kilowatt-hours.
   a. Determine whether the function models exponential growth or decay, and find the growth or decay factor.
   b. What value of n should be substituted to find the value of y now? Use this value for n to find y.
   c. What will be the annual electrical usage in 10 years?
   d. What was the annual electrical usage 10 years ago?

7. Open-ended Write and solve a problem involving exponential decay.

8. Writing Explain when the function $y = a \cdot b^x$ shows exponential growth and when it shows exponential decay.

9. Standardized Test Prep If $a = -3$, which expression has the least value?
   A. $a^2 a^0$ **B.** a^a **C.** $a^8 a^{-5}$
   D. $-a^a a^{-4}$ **E.** $(a^3 a^{-4})^2$

Graph each function.

10. $y = \frac{1}{2} \cdot 2^x$ **11.** $y = 2 \cdot \left(\frac{1}{2}\right)^x$ **12.** $f(x) = 3^x$

13. Critical Thinking Is there a solution to the equation $3^x = 5^x$? Explain.

Write each number in scientific notation.

14. There were 44,909,000 votes cast for Bill Clinton in the 1992 presidential election.

15. More than 450,000 households in the United States have reptiles as pets.

Determine whether each number is in scientific notation. If it is not, write it in scientific notation.

16. 76×10^{-9} **17.** 7.3×10^5

18. $4.05 \times 10 \times 10^{-8}$ **19.** 32.5×10^{13}

Simplify each expression. Use positive exponents.

20. $\dfrac{r^3 t^{-7}}{t^5}$ **21.** $\left(\dfrac{a^3}{m}\right)^{-4}$ **22.** $\dfrac{t^{-8} m^2}{m^{-3}}$

23. $c^3 v^9 c^{-1} c^0$ **24.** $h^2 k^{-5} d^3 k^2$ **25.** $9y^4 j^2 y^{-9}$

26. $(w^2 k^0 p^{-5})^{-7}$ **27.** $2y^{-9} h^2 (2y^0 h^{-4})^{-6}$

28. $(1.2)^5 (1.2)^{-2}$ **29.** $(-3q^{-1})^3 q^2$

30. a. Astronomy The speed of light in a vacuum is 186,300 mi/s. Use scientific notation to express how far light travels in one hour.
   b. How long does light take to travel to Saturn, about 2.3×10^9 mi away from Earth?

31. Banking A customer deposits $1000 in a savings account that pays 4% interest compounded quarterly. How much money will the customer have in the account after 2 years? after 5 years?

32. Automobiles Suppose a new car is worth $14,000. Its value decreases by one fifth each year. The function $y = 14,000(0.8)^x$ models the car's value after x years.
   a. Find the value of the car after one year.
   b. Find the value of the car after four years.

Preparing for the Math A Exam

Part I

1 Which function models exponential decay?
(1) $y = 0.25 \cdot 5^x$
(2) $y = 5 \cdot 0.25^x$
(3) $y = 0.5 \cdot 2.5^x$
(4) $y = 2.5 \cdot 5^x$

2 What percent of increase or decrease is modeled in the function $y = 45 \cdot 1.6^x$?
(1) 40% decrease
(2) 160% increase
(3) 60% increase
(4) 60% decrease

3 Which expression is equivalent to $\frac{4m^{-2}}{xy^{-4}}$?
(1) $\frac{4xy^4}{m^2}$
(3) $\frac{4y^4}{m^2x}$
(2) $\frac{xy^4}{4m^2}$
(4) $\frac{4y^{-4}}{m^{-2}x}$

4 Which expression has the least value when $b = 3$ and $c = -2$?
(1) c^b
(3) $b^0 c^0$
(2) b^c
(4) $(b^c)^b$

5 Which number is expressed in scientific notation as 4.278×10^{-6}?
(1) 0.0000004278
(3) 0.427800
(2) 0.004278
(4) 0.000004278

6 Which expression is in simplest form and equivalent to $(3s^3)(2t^2)(4s^4)$?
(1) $24st^9$
(3) $24s^7t^2$
(2) $24s^{12}t^2$
(4) $(12s^7)(2t^2)$

7 Which expression is equivalent to $\frac{a^2}{b^3}$?
(1) $\frac{a^6b^3}{a^3b^9}$
(3) $\frac{a^6b^2}{a^4b^5}$
(2) $\frac{a^2a}{b^{-1}b^4}$
(4) $\frac{a^8b^{-1}}{a^4b^{-2}}$

8 If a is positive and b is negative, which of the following is negative?
(1) $|ab|$
(3) $a|b|$
(2) $a + |b|$
(4) $|a|b$

9 You flip a coin and roll a number cube. Find the probability of getting a head and a multiple of 3.
(1) $\frac{1}{4}$
(3) $\frac{1}{12}$
(2) $\frac{1}{6}$
(4) $\frac{5}{6}$

Part II

10 An investment of $5000 doubles every 6 years. How much is this investment worth after 30 years?

11 Write an exponential function to model an initial population of 60,000 that has a steady annual loss of 1.75%.

12 Simplify: $(m^{-4})^2(4n)^3$. Use positive exponents.

Part III

13 Evaluate $f(x) = 0.8^x$ for the domain $\{1, 2, 3, 4\}$. Tell whether this function is increasing, decreasing, or neither.

14 Write a simplified binomial for the area of this parallelogram.

Part IV

15 Write a simplified binomial for the surface area of this rectangular prism.

16 Light travels at 186,000 mi/sec. Sound travels at 1080 ft/sec. (5280 ft = 1 mi)
a Write the speed of light in ft/sec. Use scientific notation.
b Write the speed of sound in scientific notation.
c How much faster does light travel than sound?

Right Triangles and Radical Expressions

Relating to the Real World

Right triangles have been important in surveying and construction since early civilization. Since then, special relationships in right triangles have led to improved navigation for ships and planes, to formulas for a pendulum and for distance, and to other areas of mathematics that use radical expressions.

On a *CLEAR Day...*

Suppose it's a clear day and you have a view with no obstructions — maybe not as clear as from an air traffic control tower, but fairly clear. How far would you be able to see to the horizon? You can use the Pythagorean theorem and other concepts in this chapter to find this distance.

h = your height (ft)
r = radius of the
    planet (mi)
d = distance you
    can see (mi)

As you work through the chapter, you will determine and compare the distances you would be able to see to the horizon if you could stand on any planet, including Earth. Your project should include diagrams of the planets, formulas for the distances visible, and graphs of these formulas.

To help you complete the project:
▼ **p. 418** *Find Out by Writing*
▼ **p. 424** *Find Out by Calculating*
▼ **p. 429** *Find Out by Researching*
▼ **p. 444** *Find Out by Communicating*
▼ **p. 449** *Find Out by Organizing*
▼ **p. 456** *Finishing the Project*

Solving
Radical
Equations

Graphing
Square Root
Functions

Analyzing
Data Using
Standard
Deviation

9-6   9-7   9-8

What You'll Learn

- Finding lengths of sides of a right triangle
- Deciding if a triangle is a right triangle

...And Why

To calculate distances that cannot be measured directly

What You'll Need

- rectangular objects
- ruler
- graph paper

9-1 The Pythagorean Theorem

WORK TOGETHER

Work with a partner.

1. Measure the length l and width w of the cover of your mathematics textbook. Be as precise in your measurements as you can.

2. Use a calculator to find the value of the expression $l^2 + w^2$.

3. Measure the length d of one of the diagonals of the cover of your book. Calculate the value of d^2.

4. What can you say about the values of $l^2 + w^2$ and d^2?

5. Choose rectangular objects or draw rectangles on graph paper. Repeat the same steps. What can you say about the length of a diagonal?

THINK AND DISCUSS

Solving Equations Using the Pythagorean Theorem

When you draw a diagonal of a rectangle, you separate the rectangle into two right triangles. In a right triangle, the side opposite the right angle is the longest. It is called the **hypotenuse.** The other two sides are called **legs.** There is a relationship among the lengths of the sides of a right triangle.

QUICK REVIEW

A *right triangle* is a triangle with one right angle.

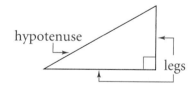

diagonal

hypotenuse

legs

The Pythagorean Theorem

In a right triangle, the sum of the squares of the lengths of the legs is equal to the square of the length of the hypotenuse.

$$a^2 + b^2 = c^2$$

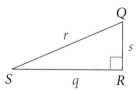

6. Restate the Pythagorean theorem for $\triangle QRS$ to the left.

7. A right triangle has legs of length 5 in. and 12 in. The length of the hypotenuse is 13 in. **Verify** that the Pythagorean theorem is true for this triangle.

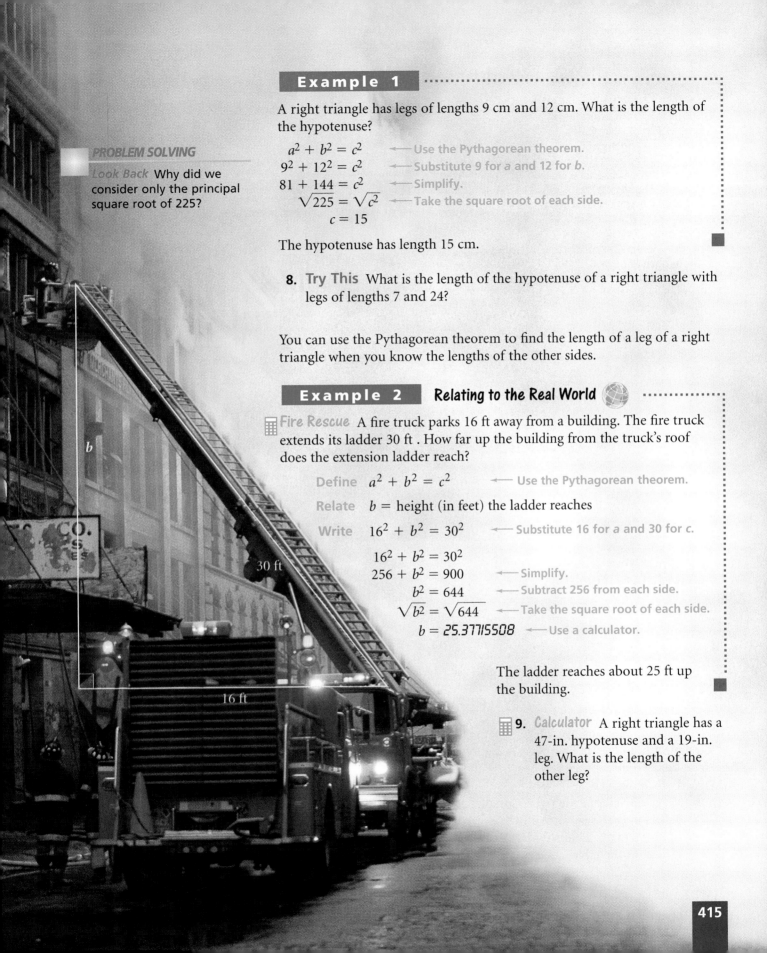

Example 1

A right triangle has legs of lengths 9 cm and 12 cm. What is the length of the hypotenuse?

PROBLEM SOLVING

Look Back Why did we consider only the principal square root of 225?

$$a^2 + b^2 = c^2 \quad \longleftarrow \text{Use the Pythagorean theorem.}$$
$$9^2 + 12^2 = c^2 \quad \longleftarrow \text{Substitute 9 for } a \text{ and 12 for } b.$$
$$81 + 144 = c^2 \quad \longleftarrow \text{Simplify.}$$
$$\sqrt{225} = \sqrt{c^2} \quad \longleftarrow \text{Take the square root of each side.}$$
$$c = 15$$

The hypotenuse has length 15 cm.

8. **Try This** What is the length of the hypotenuse of a right triangle with legs of lengths 7 and 24?

You can use the Pythagorean theorem to find the length of a leg of a right triangle when you know the lengths of the other sides.

Example 2   *Relating to the Real World* 🌐

Fire Rescue A fire truck parks 16 ft away from a building. The fire truck extends its ladder 30 ft . How far up the building from the truck's roof does the extension ladder reach?

Define $a^2 + b^2 = c^2$ $\quad \longleftarrow$ Use the Pythagorean theorem.

Relate $b =$ height (in feet) the ladder reaches

Write $16^2 + b^2 = 30^2$ $\quad \longleftarrow$ Substitute 16 for a and 30 for c.

$$16^2 + b^2 = 30^2$$
$$256 + b^2 = 900 \quad \longleftarrow \text{Simplify.}$$
$$b^2 = 644 \quad \longleftarrow \text{Subtract 256 from each side.}$$
$$\sqrt{b^2} = \sqrt{644} \quad \longleftarrow \text{Take the square root of each side.}$$
$$b = 25.37715508 \quad \longleftarrow \text{Use a calculator.}$$

The ladder reaches about 25 ft up the building.

9. *Calculator* A right triangle has a 47-in. hypotenuse and a 19-in. leg. What is the length of the other leg?

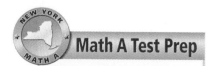

1 City A is 12 miles due east of City B. City C is 8 miles due north of City B. To the nearest mile, what is the straight-line distance from City A to City C?
(1) 20 mi (3) 14 mi
(2) 15 mi (4) 12 mi

2 The lengths of two sides of a right triangle are 4 and 6. Find all possible lengths of the third side. Round to the nearest tenth.

Using the Converse

You can find out whether a triangle is a right triangle by using the converse of the Pythagorean theorem.

The Converse of the Pythagorean Theorem

If a triangle has sides of lengths a, b, and c, and $a^2 + b^2 = c^2$, then the triangle is a right triangle with hypotenuse of length c.

Example 3 ·

A triangle has sides of lengths 7, 9, and 12. Is it a right triangle?

Apply the converse of the Pythagorean theorem.

$$a^2 + b^2 \stackrel{?}{=} c^2$$
$$7^2 + 9^2 \stackrel{?}{=} 12^2 \quad \longleftarrow \text{Substitute 12 for } c \text{, since 12 is the length of the}$$
$$49 + 81 \stackrel{?}{=} 144 \qquad \text{longest side. Substitute 7 and 9 for } a \text{ and } b.$$
$$130 \neq 144$$

The triangle is not a right triangle.

10. Try This A triangle has sides of lengths 10, 24, and 26. Is the triangle a right triangle? Explain.

Exercises   ON YOUR OWN

Calculator Use the triangle at the right.
Find the length of the missing side
to the nearest tenth.

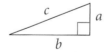

1. $a = 6, b = 8, c = \blacksquare$ **2.** $a = 8, b = 24, c = \blacksquare$ **3.** $a = 1, b = 2, c = \blacksquare$

4. $a = 3, b = \blacksquare, c = 5$ **5.** $a = \blacksquare, b = 7, c = 10$ **6.** $a = \blacksquare, b = 12, c = 13$

7. $a = 4, b = 4, c = \blacksquare$ **8.** $a = 13, b = 2, c = \blacksquare$ **9.** $a = 15, b = \blacksquare, c = 25$

10. $a = \blacksquare, b = 10, c = 15$ **11.** $a = 75, b = \blacksquare, c = 100$ **12.** $a = \blacksquare, b = 12, c = 18$

13. Any set of three positive integers that satisfies the relationship $a^2 + b^2 = c^2$ is called a *Pythagorean triple*.
  a. Verify that the numbers 6, 8, and 10 form a Pythagorean triple.
  b. Copy the table at the right. Complete the table so that the values in each row form a Pythagorean triple.
  c. Group Activity Find a Pythagorean triple that does not appear in the table.

a	b	c
3	4	$\blacksquare$
5	$\blacksquare$	13
$\blacksquare$	24	25
9	40	$\blacksquare$

Find the missing length to the nearest tenth.

14.
20
x
12

15.
10   y
2.5

16.
x
9   12.7

17.
252
z
500
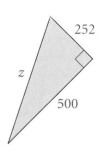

18. Birds A pigeon leaves its nest and flies 5 km due east. The pigeon then flies 3 km due north. How far is the pigeon from its nest?

19. You know that two sides of a right triangle measure 10 in. and 8 in.
   a. Writing Why is this not enough information to be sure of finding the length of the third side?
   b. Give two different possible values for the length of the third side. Explain how you found your answers.

20. Geometry The yellow, green, and blue figures are squares. Use the Pythagorean theorem and your knowledge of lengths to find the length of one side of the blue square.

6
4

Can each set of three numbers represent the lengths of the sides of a right triangle? Explain your answers.

21. 9, 12, 15

22. 1, 2, 3

23. 2, 4, 5

24. 34, 16, 30

25. 4, 4, 8

26. 5000, 4000, 3000

27. 1.25, 3, 3.25

28. 19, 21, 23

29. 14, 48, 50

30. $\frac{1}{3}, \frac{1}{4}, \frac{1}{5}$

31. 2, 1.5, 1

32. 10, 24, 26

33. 4, 5, 6

34. 15, 20, 25

35. 18, 80, 82

36. $\frac{3}{4}, 1, 1\frac{1}{4}$

37. a. Sightseeing A gondola travels between two elevations along a cable. What is the distance the gondola travels from the bottom of the hill to the top?
   b. The gondola travels from the bottom of the hill to the top of the hill in 20 min. What is the average speed of the gondola in feet per minute? in miles per hour?

upper elevation
7761 ft
lower elevation
6421 ft
3350 ft

38. Solar Heating Technician Find the length of the glass insert for the solar heating panel shown. Round your answer to the nearest inch.

15 in.

21 in.

24 in.

x

39. What is the diameter of the smallest circular opening that the rectangular rod shown will fit through? Round your answer to the nearest tenth.

3 cm

10 cm

3 cm

Chapter Project

Find Out by Writing

- How many feet are in a mile?
- How would you convert 15 ft into miles?
- How would you represent the quantity *h* feet in miles?
- In the diagram on page 413, replace *h* with the expression that represents *h* feet in miles. Use the Pythagorean theorem to write an equation relating *r*, *d*, and *h*. Do not simplify the equation.

Exercises   M I X E D   R E V I E W

Solve each system of equations by substitution.

40. $y = 3x + 5$, $x + y = 4$

41. $y = -3x + 2$, $x - y = 0$

42. Architecture A model of a house is $\frac{1}{25}$ of its actual size. One side of the model house is 48 in. long. How long is the corresponding side in the actual house?

Getting Ready for Lesson 9-2

Let $c = \sqrt{a^2 + b^2}$. For each set of values, calculate c to the nearest tenth.

43. $a = 3$, $b = 4$ **44.** $a = -2$, $b = 5$ **45.** $a = -3$, $b = 8$ **46.** $a = 7, b = -5$

Testing for a Right Triangle

After Lesson 9-1

With a graphing calculator, you can create a program and save it to use in the future. This program tests three numbers to see if they can be the lengths of the sides of a right triangle.

To input the program, choose PRGM, then *NEW*. To name the program, press **1**, type PYTHAG, and then press ENTER.

To enter the program you will find commands in the PRGM feature under *CTL* and *I/O*. After each line press ENTER to go to the next line.

To type the variables *A*, *B*, and *C*, use ALPHA before typing each letter. You can use *A-LOCK* to type a string of letters such as the information in quotes. The equal sign is in the TEST feature.

After entering your program, press 2nd QUIT. To run your program, press PRGM, select PYTHAG, and choose *EXEC*.

```
PROGRAM:PYTHAG
:Prompt A,B,C
:If A²+B²=C²
:Goto 1
:Disp "NOT A RIGHT
TRIANGLE"
:Goto 2
:Lbl 1
:Disp "RIGHT TRIANGLE"
:Lbl 2
```

Use the program to tell if each set of numbers can represent the sides of a right triangle. Always input the longest side as *c*.

1. {3, 4, 5}   **2.** {7, 9, 12}   **3.** {9, 12, 15}   **4.** {10, 11, 12}

5. {8, 15, 17}   **6.** {17, 17, 17}   **7.** {1.4, 4.8, 5}   **8.** {6, 8, 10}

9. {3, 7, 8}   **10.** {7, 24, 25 }   **11.** {20, 21, 29}   **12.** {12, 13, 20}

Use the program to see if each triangle is a right triangle.

13.

14.

15.
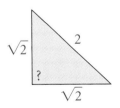

16. Any three integers *a*, *b*, and *c* form a Pythagorean triple if $a^2 + b^2 = c^2$. The following formulas generate Pythagorean triples using positive integers *x* and *y* where $x > y$.

$a = x^2 - y^2$
$b = 2xy$
$c = x^2 + y^2$

   a. Find the Pythagorean triple that is generated by the values $x = 3$ and $y = 2$.
   b. Find the values of *x* and *y* that generate the set {9, 40, 41}.

17. Writing The set {−3, −4, 5} could not represent the sides of a right triangle because the sides of triangles cannot have negative lengths. Explain why the calculator display indicates a right triangle when you input the values −3, −4, and 5.

```
prgmPYTHAG
A=?–3
B=?–4
C=?5
RIGHT TRIANGLE
               Done
```

9-2 The Distance Formula

What You'll Learn

- Finding the distance between two points in a coordinate plane
- Finding the coordinates of the midpoint of two points

...And Why

To find the distance between two groups of hikers

What You'll Need

- graph paper
- ruler

QUICK REVIEW

AB is the distance between points A and B and the length of $\overline{AB}$.

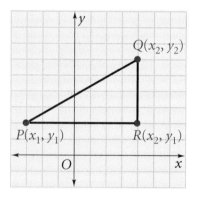

WORK TOGETHER

Work with a partner as you apply the Pythagorean theorem to find the distance between two points.

1. On graph paper, graph points $A(-3, 4)$, $B(1, 1)$, and $C(-3, 1)$. Then connect the points.

2. Find AC and BC.

3. $\triangle ABC$ is a right triangle. Use the Pythagorean theorem to write an equation relating AC, BC, and AB.

4. Substitute values for AC and BC in the equation you wrote in Question 3. Solve the equation to find AB.

THINK AND DISCUSS

Finding the Distance

In the Work Together activity, you found the distance between two particular points. If you have any two points $P(x_1, y_1)$ and $Q(x_2, y_2)$, you can graph them and form a right triangle as shown in the diagram. You can then use the Pythagorean theorem to find the distance between the points.

$(PQ)^2 = (PR)^2 + (RQ)^2$ ⟵ Use the Pythagorean theorem.

$(PQ)^2 = (x_2 - x_1)^2 + (y_2 - y_1)^2$ ⟵ Substitute the lengths you know.

$PQ = \sqrt{(x_2 - x_1)^2 + (y_2 - y_1)^2}$ ⟵ Take the principal square root of each side.

This method for finding the distance between two points is summarized in the *distance formula*.

The Distance Formula
....

The distance d between any two points (x_1, y_1) and (x_2, y_2) is

$$d = \sqrt{(x_2 - x_1)^2 + (y_2 - y_1)^2}.$$

Example 1   Relating to the Real World

Hiking The Gato and Wilson families are staying at a campground. The Gatos leave camp and hike 2 km west and 5 km south. The Wilsons leave camp and hike 1 km east and 4 km north. How far apart are the families?

Let the campground be $(0, 0)$. Then the Gato family's location is $(-2, -5)$ and the Wilson family's location is $(1, 4)$.

$d = \sqrt{(x_2 - x_1)^2 + (y_2 - y_1)^2}$ ⟵ Use the distance formula.

$d = \sqrt{(1 - (-2))^2 + (4 - (-5))^2}$ ⟵ Substitute $(1, 4)$ for (x_2, y_2) and $(-2, -5)$ for (x_1, y_1).

$d = \sqrt{3^2 + 9^2}$ ⟵ Simplify.

$d = \sqrt{90}$

$d = 9.486832981$ ⟵ Use a calculator.

The two families are about 9.5 km apart.

PROBLEM SOLVING

Look Back Would the result in Example 1 be different if you used $(1, 4)$ for (x_1, y_1) and $(-2, -5)$ for (x_2, y_2)? Explain your answer.

5. **Try This** One hiker is 4 mi west and 3 mi north of the campground. Another is 6 mi east and 3 mi south of the campground. How far apart are the hikers?

You can also use the distance formula to determine if lengths of opposite sides in a figure are equal.

Example 2

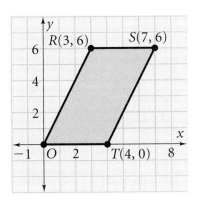

Geometry Quadrilateral *ORST* is shown here in a coordinate plane. Use the distance formula to show that $\overline{OR}$ and $\overline{ST}$ are equal in length.

$OR = \sqrt{(3 - 0)^2 + (6 - 0)^2}$ $ST = \sqrt{(7 - 4)^2 + (6 - 0)^2}$

$OR = \sqrt{3^2 + 6^2}$ $ST = \sqrt{3^2 + 6^2}$

$OR = \sqrt{45}$ $ST = \sqrt{45}$

$OR = ST$. So, $\overline{OR}$ and $\overline{ST}$ are equal in length.

6. Use slopes to show that $\overline{OR}$ and $\overline{ST}$ are parallel.

7. a. Try This Quadrilateral *KLMN* has vertices with coordinates
$K(-3, -2)$, $L(-5, 6)$, $M(2, 6)$, and $N(4, -2)$. Show that $LK = MN$.
b. Use slopes to show that $\overline{LK}$ and $\overline{MN}$ are parallel.
c. Critical Thinking Describe quadrilateral *KLMN* in as much detail as you can. **Justify** your descriptions and conclusions.

Using the Midpoint Formula

The **midpoint** of a segment $\overline{AB}$ is the point *M* halfway between *A* and *B* where $AM = MB$. The coordinates of the midpoint of a line segment are the averages of the coordinates of the endpoints.

The Midpoint Formula

The midpoint *M* of a line segment with endpoints $A(x_1, y_1)$ and $B(x_2, y_2)$ is
$\left(\dfrac{x_1 + x_2}{2}, \dfrac{y_1 + y_2}{2}\right)$.

Example 3

Geometry Find the midpoint of the segment from $A(-1, 6)$ to $B(5, 0)$.

$$\left(\frac{x_1 + x_2}{2}, \frac{y_1 + y_2}{2}\right) = \left(\frac{-1 + 5}{2}, \frac{6 + 0}{2}\right)$$

$$= \left(\frac{4}{2}, \frac{6}{2}\right)$$

$$= (2, 3)$$

The midpoint of $\overline{AB}$ is $M(2, 3)$.

8. In Example 3, use the distance formula to **verify** that $AM = MB$.

9. Try This Find the coordinates of the midpoint of the line segment with endpoints $X(-7.2, 2)$ and $Y(4.5, 7.5)$.

Exercises   ON YOUR OWN

Calculator **Approximate *AB* to the nearest tenth of a unit.**

1.

2.

3.

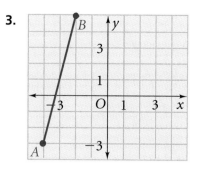

Find the distance between each pair of points to the nearest tenth.

4. $(3, -2), (-1, 5)$

5. $(-4, -4), (4, 4)$

6. $(0, 3), (13, -6)$

7. $(4, 0), (2, -1)$

8. $(7, -2), (-8, -2)$

9. $(5, 9), (10, -1)$

10. $(0, 0), (6, -9)$

11. $(-3, 7), (-11, 9)$

12. $(11, 0), (-3, -7)$

13. $(-2, 7), (-2, -7)$

14. $(9, 10), (11, 12)$

15. $(-3.5, 4.5), (-4.5, 5.5)$

16. a. News Coverage Two news helicopters are on their way to a political rally, flying at the same altitude. One helicopter is 20 mi due west of the rally. The other is 15 mi south and 15 mi east of the rally. How far apart are they?

    b. How far from the rally are they?

    c. Each helicopter is flying at 80 mi/h. How many minutes will it take each of them to arrive at the scene?

17. a. Electrical Line Technician Graph Mr. Tanaka's and Ms. Elisa's locations on a coordinate grid with the substation at the origin.

    b. What are the coordinates of the point where they will meet?

    c. Describe their meeting point in miles north/south and east/west of the substation.

I am 4 mi south and 3 mi west of the substation.

Copy that. I am 3 mi north and 3 mi east of the substation. I will meet you halfway between our locations.

Ms. Elisa   Mr. Tanaka

Find the midpoint of $\overline{XY}$.

18. $X(2, 5)$ and $Y(0, 7)$

19. $X(-3, 14)$ and $Y(6, 1)$

20. $X(8, -5)$ and $Y(-4, 5.5)$

21. $X(4, 3)$ and $Y(-9, 3)$

22. $X(0, 6)$ and $Y(-5, -8)$

23. $X(-1, 8)$ and $Y(-7, 0)$

24. $X(4, 1)$ and $Y(1, 4)$

25. $X(5, -11)$ and $Y(12, -7)$

26. $X(2, 9)$ and $Y(-2, -9)$

27. $X(3, 11)$ and $Y(11, 3)$

28. $X\left(4\frac{1}{2}, -2\right)$ and $Y\left(-1\frac{1}{2}, 5\right)$

29. $X(9, 7)$ and $Y(-9, -7)$

30. a. Transportation On the map, each unit represents one mile. A van breaks down on its way to a factory. The driver calls a garage for a tow truck. There is a bridge halfway between the garage and the van. How far is the bridge from the van?

    b. The van is towed to the factory and then to the garage. How many miles does the tow truck tow the van?

Geometry Find the perimeter of each figure to the nearest tenth.

31.

32.

33.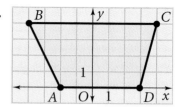

34. a. Open-ended Suppose the distance between two points on a coordinate plane is between 10 and 13 units. Identify two points A and B not directly above or across from one another that meet this requirement.

b. Plot your points on graph paper.

c. Verify that your points satisfy the requirement by finding AB.

35. Critical Thinking If the midpoint of a line segment is the origin, what must be true of the coordinates of the endpoints of the segment?

36. Writing Summarize the distance formula and the midpoint formula. Use examples of your own to show the use of each formula.

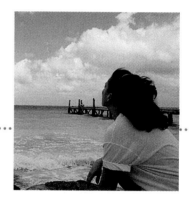

▼ **Chapter Project** **Find Out by Calculating**

The radius of Earth is about 3960 mi. The formula for the distance you can see to the horizon on Earth is $d = 1.225\sqrt{h}$ where d is the distance visible in miles and h is your height in feet. How far can you see on a clear day with no obstructions?

■ **Exercises** **M I X E D   R E V I E W**

Solve each equation for the given variable.

37. $2x + 7y = 4; x$ **38.** $3x - 5y = 7; y$ **39.** $V = \pi r^2 h; h$ **40.** $S = 2\pi r h; r$

41. Finance You deposit $3000 into a bank account paying 6% simple interest annually. How much interest will you receive after 4 years?

Getting Ready for Lesson 9-3

Let $c = \frac{A}{H}, s = \frac{O}{H}, t = \frac{O}{A}$. Calculate c, s, and t for each of the following.

42. $A = 3, O = 4, H = 5$ **43.** $A = 5, O = 12, H = 13$

Solve each equation.

44. $\frac{15}{x} = 0.75$ **45.** $\frac{x}{20} = 0.34$ **46.** $0.82x = 25$ **47.** $\frac{x}{0.52} = 14$

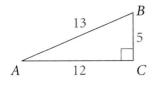
What You'll Learn

- Exploring and calculating trigonometric ratios
- Using sine, cosine, and tangent to solve problems

...And Why

To find distances indirectly

What You'll Need

- graph paper
- ruler

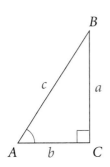

9-3 Trigonometric Ratios

WORK TOGETHER

Work with a partner.

1. On graph paper, draw a right triangle like the one at the left. Extend sides $\overline{AB}$ and $\overline{AC}$ to form a second triangle similar to the first triangle. One example is shown at the left.

2. **a.** Copy the table below. Measure and record the lengths of the legs of each triangle.

Triangle	a	b	c	$\frac{a}{b}$	$\frac{a}{c}$	$\frac{b}{c}$
first	▓	▓	▓	▓	▓	▓
second	▓	▓	▓	▓	▓	▓

   b. Calculate and record c, the length of each hypotenuse.

   c. Calculate and record the ratios $\frac{a}{b}$, $\frac{a}{c}$, and $\frac{b}{c}$ for each triangle.

3. How do corresponding ratios in the two triangles compare?

THINK AND DISCUSS

Finding Trigonometric Ratios

The ratios you explored in the Work Together are called **trigonometric ratios,** meaning triangle measurement ratios. In $\triangle ABC$, $\overline{BC}$ is the leg opposite $\angle A$ and $\overline{AC}$ is the leg adjacent to $\angle A$. The hypotenuse is $\overline{AB}$.

You can use these relationships to express trigonometric ratios.

sine of $\angle A = \dfrac{\text{length of leg opposite } \angle A}{\text{length of hypotenuse}}$ or $\sin A = \dfrac{a}{c}$

cosine of $\angle A = \dfrac{\text{length of leg adjacent to } \angle A}{\text{length of hypotenuse}}$ or $\cos A = \dfrac{b}{c}$

tangent of $\angle A = \dfrac{\text{length of leg opposite } \angle A}{\text{length of leg adjacent to } \angle A}$ or $\tan A = \dfrac{a}{b}$

Example 1

Use the diagram at the left. Find $\sin A$, $\cos A$, and $\tan A$.

$$\sin A = \frac{5}{13} \qquad \cos A = \frac{12}{13} \qquad \tan A = \frac{5}{12}$$

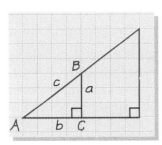

4. **Try This** Use the diagram to find $\sin B$, $\cos B$, and $\tan B$.

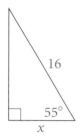

16

55°

x

You can use trigonometry to find missing lengths in a triangle.

Example 2

Find the value of x in the triangle at the left.

First, decide which trigonometric ratio to use. You know the angle and hypotenuse and are trying to find the adjacent side. So use cosine.

$$\cos 55° = \frac{\text{side adjacent}}{\text{hypotenuse}} \quad \longleftarrow \text{This is a short form of the definition.}$$

$$\cos 55° = \frac{x}{16}$$

$$0.573576436 = \frac{x}{16} \quad \longleftarrow \text{Use a calculator.}$$

$$16(0.573576436) = x \quad \longleftarrow \text{Cross multiply.}$$

$$9.177222982 = x \quad \longleftarrow \text{Use a calculator.}$$

The value of x is about 9.2.

CALCULATOR HINT

Use degree mode when finding trigonometric ratios. Use the key sequence COS 55 ENTER .

5. You know the lengths of two sides of the triangle in Example 2. You can use different methods to find the length of the third side.
  a. Use the Pythagorean theorem to find the length of the third side.
  b. Use either the sine or tangent ratio to find the length of the third side.
  c. Compare your answers to parts (a) and (b).

Solving Problems Using Trigonometric Ratios

You can use trigonometric ratios to measure distances indirectly when you know an angle of elevation. An **angle of elevation** is an angle from the horizontal up to a line of sight.

angle of elevation

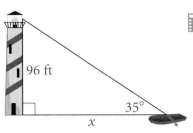

96 ft

35°

x

Example 3   **Relating to the Real World**

Navigation Suppose that an angle of elevation from a rowboat to a lighthouse is 35°. You know that the lighthouse is 96 ft tall. How far from the lighthouse is the rowboat?

Make a diagram.

Define x = the distance from the lighthouse to the boat

Relate   You know the angle and the opposite side and you are trying to find the adjacent side. So use tangent.

Write $\tan A = \dfrac{\text{side opposite}}{\text{side adjacent}}$

$\tan 35° = \dfrac{96}{x}$ ←——Substitute for the angle and sides.

$x(\tan 35°) = 96$ ←——Cross multiply.

$x = \dfrac{96}{\tan 35°}$ ←——Divide to put in calculator-ready form.

$x = \mathit{137.1022086}$ ←——Use a calculator.

$x \approx 137$

The rowboat is about 137 ft from the lighthouse.

6. Could you use the sine or cosine to solve Example 3? Explain.

Exercises   O N   Y O U R   O W N

1. Language Arts Write a nonmathematical sentence using the word *adjacent*.

Use △RST to evaluate each expression.

2. sin R **3.** cos R

4. tan R **5.** sin S

6. cos S **7.** tan S

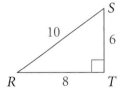

Calculator **Evaluate each expression. Round to four decimal places.**

8. sin 32°   **9.** cos 40°   **10.** tan 52°   **11.** sin 85°   **12.** tan 7°

For each figure, find sin A, cos A, and tan A.

13.

14.

15.

A

26

10

C   a   B

Find the value of *x* to the nearest tenth.

16.
14
67°
x

17.
14
x
48°

18.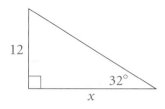
12
32°
x

19. Nature Suppose you look up from a cabin on the floor of a canyon to a cliff at the top of a vertical wall of rock. The angle of elevation from your location to the cliff is 32°. The cabin is 400 ft from the base of the canyon wall. How high is the canyon wall?

20. Recreation A Ferris wheel is shown at the right. Find the distance *x* that the seat is above the horizontal line through the center of the wheel. Then find the seat's height above the ground.

21. Aviation Suppose you live about 5 mi from a tower. From your home, you see a plane directly above the tower. Your angle of elevation to the plane is 21°. What is the plane's altitude?

22. Writing Suppose you know that a right triangle has a 30° angle and you know the length of the leg adjacent to the 30° angle. Describe how you would find the length of the leg opposite the 30° angle.

32.8 ft
x
53°
41.2 ft

Find the indicated length to the nearest tenth.

23.
59.2
n
49°

24.
5.65
m
53°

25.
12°
21°
p
792

26. Standardized Test Prep $\triangle KLM$ is a right triangle with a right angle at *M*. Which of the following is false?

A. $\sin K = \frac{LM}{KL}$ **B.** $\cos K = \frac{KL}{KM}$ **C.** $\tan K = \frac{LM}{KM}$ **D.** $\cos L = \frac{LM}{KL}$ **E.** $\sin L = \frac{KM}{KL}$

27. Open-ended Name some ways you might use a trigonometric ratio to calculate a distance instead of measuring it directly.

28. Nature Suppose you are lying on the ground looking up at a California redwood tree. Your angle of elevation to the top of the tree is 42°. You are 280 ft from the base of the tree.
a. How tall is the tree?
b. How far would a bird have to fly to get from the top of the tree to your location?

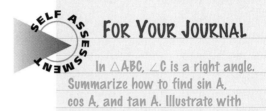

Exercises   MIXED REVIEW

Graph each equation.

29. $y = x + 2$

30. $y = |x| + 2$

31. $y = x^2 + 2$

32. $y = 2^x$

33. Transportation A car is traveling at a constant speed. After 3 h, the car has gone 150 mi. How many miles will the car have gone after 5 h?

> **SELF ASSESSMENT**
>
> **FOR YOUR JOURNAL**
>
> In △ABC, ∠C is a right angle. Summarize how to find sin A, cos A, and tan A. Illustrate with diagrams.

Getting Ready for Lesson 9-4

Find each value.

34. $\sqrt{4}$

35. $\sqrt{169}$

36. $3\sqrt{25}$

37. $-2\sqrt{9}$

38. $-3\sqrt{49}$

Exercises   CHECKPOINT

A right triangle has legs of lengths a and b and hypotenuse of length c. Find the missing value.

1. $a = 2, b = 4$

2. $a = 3, b = 5$

3. $a = 1, b = 7$

4. $a = 4, b = 3$

5. $a = 10, c = 26$

6. $b = 3, c = 9$

7. $a = 8, c = 12$

8. $b = 20, c = 25$

9. Writing Describe how to find the distance between points (x_1, y_1) and (x_2, y_2). Include examples.

10. The angle of elevation from a point on the ground 300 ft from a tower is 42°. How tall is the tower?

Approximate AB to the nearest tenth.

11. $A(1, 4), B(2, 7)$

12. $A(-2, -1), B(4, 2)$

13. $A(-3, 5), B(6, 1)$

14. $A(2, 3), B(5, 4)$

15. Open-ended Write the coordinates of a pair of points A and B. Then find the midpoint of $\overline{AB}$.

In $\triangle ABC$, $\angle C$ is a right angle. Find the length of the indicated side.

16. $m\angle B = 43°, AB = 4, AC = \blacksquare$

17. $m\angle A = 33°, AC = 7, BC = \blacksquare$

What You'll Learn

What You'll Learn

- Simplifying radicals involving products and quotients
- Solving problems involving radicals

...And Why

To solve distance problems

9-4 Simplifying Radicals

THINK AND DISCUSS

Multiplication with Radicals

A radical expression is in **simplest form** when *all three* statements are true.

- The expression under the radical sign has no perfect square factors other than 1.
- The expression under the radical sign does not contain a fraction.
- The denominator does not contain a radical expression.

1. Explain why each expression *is* or *is not* in simplest form.

     a. $\sqrt{20}$ **b.** $4\sqrt{5}$ **c.** $\dfrac{1}{\sqrt{3}}$ **d.** $\sqrt{\dfrac{2}{5}}$

Multiplication Property of Square Roots

For any numbers $a \geq 0$ and $b \geq 0$, $\sqrt{ab} = \sqrt{a} \cdot \sqrt{b}$.

Example: $\sqrt{54} = \sqrt{9} \cdot \sqrt{6} = 3 \cdot \sqrt{6} = 3\sqrt{6}$

You can simplify radical expressions that contain numbers and variables. Assume that all variables under radicals represent positive numbers.

Example 1

Simplify each radical expression.

a. $\sqrt{192} = \sqrt{64 \cdot 3}$ ⟵ 64 is a perfect square and a factor of 192.

         $= \sqrt{64} \cdot \sqrt{3}$ ⟵ Use the multiplication property.

         $= 8\sqrt{3}$ ⟵ Simplify $\sqrt{64}$.

b. $\sqrt{16a^3} = \sqrt{16} \cdot \sqrt{a^2} \cdot \sqrt{a}$ ⟵ Use the multiplication property.

         $= 4a\sqrt{a}$ ⟵ Simplify.

Example 2

Simplify the radical expression $\sqrt{6} \cdot \sqrt{15}$.

$\sqrt{6} \cdot \sqrt{15} = \sqrt{90}$ ⟵ Combine factors under one radical.

         $= \sqrt{9 \cdot 10}$ ⟵ 9 is a perfect square and a factor of 90.

         $= \sqrt{9} \cdot \sqrt{10}$ ⟵ Use the multiplication property.

         $= 3\sqrt{10}$ ⟵ Simplify $\sqrt{9}$.

2. **Try This** Simplify each expression.

     a. $5\sqrt{300}$ **b.** $\sqrt{13} \cdot \sqrt{52}$ **c.** $\sqrt{x^2 y^5}$ **d.** $(3\sqrt{5})^2$

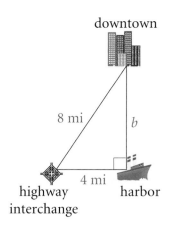

downtown

8 mi

b

4 mi

highway
interchange

harbor

PROBLEM SOLVING

Look Back Explain how you can use $\sqrt{49}$ to check the reasonableness of the answer in Example 3.

When you use radical expressions to solve real-world problems, you need to evaluate any radicals to get a numerical answer.

Example 3   Relating to the Real World

Commuting Use the figure at the left. About how many miles is it from downtown to the harbor? Round to the nearest tenth of a mile.

$$a^2 + b^2 = c^2 \quad \longleftarrow \text{Use the Pythagorean theorem.}$$
$$4^2 + b^2 = 8^2 \quad \longleftarrow \begin{array}{l}\text{Substitute. Remember that the}\\ \text{hypotenuse is the longest side.}\end{array}$$
$$b^2 = 8^2 - 4^2$$
$$b = \sqrt{8^2 - 4^2} \quad \longleftarrow \text{Solve for } b.$$
$$= \sqrt{48} \quad \longleftarrow \text{Use a calculator.}$$
$$= 6.92820323$$

It is about 6.9 miles from downtown to the harbor.

3. *Calculator* Suppose a classmate did Example 3 and got the answer $4\sqrt{3}$. Use a calculator to check if this answer is correct.

Division with Radicals

You can use the division property of square roots to simplify expressions.

> **Division Property of Square Roots**
>
> For any numbers $a \geq 0$ and $b > 0$, $\sqrt{\dfrac{a}{b}} = \dfrac{\sqrt{a}}{\sqrt{b}}$.
>
> Example: $\sqrt{\dfrac{4}{9}} = \dfrac{\sqrt{4}}{\sqrt{9}} = \dfrac{2}{3}$

4. Explain why there are the restrictions $a \geq 0$ and $b > 0$ in the properties of square roots.

When you simplify a radical expression involving division, sometimes it is easier to simplify the numerator and denominator separately.

Example 4

Simplify each radical expression.

a. $\sqrt{\dfrac{11}{49}} = \dfrac{\sqrt{11}}{\sqrt{49}}$ ←— Use the division property.

$\qquad\quad = \dfrac{\sqrt{11}}{7}$ ←— Simplify $\sqrt{49}$.

b. $\sqrt{\dfrac{25}{b^4}} = \dfrac{\sqrt{25}}{\sqrt{b^4}}$ ←— Use the division property.

$\qquad\quad = \dfrac{5}{b^2}$ ←— Simplify $\sqrt{25}$ and $\sqrt{b^4}$. ■

When you simplify a radical expression involving division, sometimes it is easier to divide first and then simplify the radical expression.

Example 5

Simplify the radical expression $\dfrac{\sqrt{96}}{\sqrt{12}}$.

$\dfrac{\sqrt{96}}{\sqrt{12}} = \sqrt{\dfrac{96}{12}}$ ←— Use the division property.

$\qquad = \sqrt{8}$ ←— Divide.

$\qquad = \sqrt{4 \cdot 2}$ ←— 4 is a perfect square and a factor of 8.

$\qquad = \sqrt{4} \cdot \sqrt{2}$ ←— Use the multiplication property.

$\qquad = 2\sqrt{2}$ ←— Simplify $\sqrt{4}$. ■

5. Try This Simplify each expression.

a. $\sqrt{\dfrac{144}{9}}$ **b.** $\dfrac{\sqrt{24}}{\sqrt{8}}$ **c.** $\sqrt{\dfrac{25c^3}{b^2}}$

When you have a square root in a denominator that is not a perfect square, you should **rationalize** the denominator. To do this, make the denominator a rational number without changing the value of the expression.

Example 6

Simplify $\dfrac{2}{\sqrt{5}}$.

$\dfrac{2}{\sqrt{5}} = \dfrac{2}{\sqrt{5}} \cdot \dfrac{\sqrt{5}}{\sqrt{5}}$ ←— Multiply by $\dfrac{\sqrt{5}}{\sqrt{5}} = 1$.

$\qquad = \dfrac{2\sqrt{5}}{\sqrt{25}}$ ←— Use the multiplication property.

$\qquad = \dfrac{2\sqrt{5}}{5}$ ←— Simplify. ■

PROBLEM SOLVING

Look Back Why did you choose to multiply by $\dfrac{\sqrt{5}}{\sqrt{5}}$ to rationalize the expression?

6. Try This Simplify each expression by rationalizing the denominator.

a. $\dfrac{3}{\sqrt{3}}$ **b.** $\dfrac{14}{\sqrt{7}}$ **c.** $\dfrac{9}{\sqrt{10}}$

Tell whether each expression is in simplest form.

1. $\dfrac{13}{\sqrt{4}}$ **2.** $2\sqrt{12}$ **3.** $\dfrac{3}{\sqrt{13}}$ **4.** $5\sqrt{30}$ **5.** $\sqrt{\dfrac{2}{5}}$

Simplify each radical expression.

6. $\sqrt{25} \cdot \sqrt{100}$ **7.** $\sqrt{8} \cdot \sqrt{32}$ **8.** $3\sqrt{81} \cdot \sqrt{81}$ **9.** $\sqrt{10} \cdot \sqrt{40}$ **10.** $\sqrt{10^4}$

11. $\sqrt{200}$ **12.** $5\sqrt{320}$ **13.** $(5\sqrt{7})^3$ **14.** $\sqrt{96}$ **15.** $(2\sqrt{18})^2$

16. $\sqrt{12} \cdot \sqrt{75}$ **17.** $\sqrt{3} \cdot \sqrt{51}$ **18.** $\sqrt{26} \cdot 2$ **19.** $2\sqrt{6} \cdot 4$ **20.** $\sqrt{8} \cdot \sqrt{26}$

Use the Pythagorean theorem to find s. Express s as a radical in simplest form.

21.

22.

23.

24. Diving Suppose you are standing at the top of a diving platform h feet tall. Looking down, you can see a raft on the water 8 feet from the bottom of the diving platform.
   a. Find the distance d from you to the raft if $h = 6$ ft.
   b. Find the distance d from you to the raft if $h = 12$ ft.
   c. Suppose you know the distance d from you to the raft is 16 ft. About how tall is the diving platform?
   d. Critical Thinking Could the distance d from you to the raft be 7 ft? Why or why not?

Simplify each radical expression.

25. $3\sqrt{\dfrac{1}{4}}$ **26.** $\sqrt{\dfrac{21}{49}}$ **27.** $\sqrt{\dfrac{625}{100}}$ **28.** $\dfrac{\sqrt{96}}{\sqrt{9}}$ **29.** $\sqrt{\dfrac{120}{121}}$

30. $\dfrac{\sqrt{15}}{\sqrt{5}}$ **31.** $\dfrac{\sqrt{72}}{\sqrt{64}}$ **32.** $\sqrt{\dfrac{48}{24}}$ **33.** $\dfrac{\sqrt{169}}{\sqrt{144}}$ **34.** $\dfrac{\sqrt{400}}{\sqrt{121}}$

35. Packaging Use the diagram at right. Find the width w that the box needs to be to fit the fishing rod.

36. Writing How do you know when to rationalize a radical expression?

37. Suppose a and b are positive integers.
   a. Verify that if $a = 18$ and $b = 10$, then $\sqrt{a} \cdot \sqrt{b} = 6\sqrt{5}$.
   b. Open-ended Find several other pairs of positive integers a and b such that $\sqrt{a} \cdot \sqrt{b} = 6\sqrt{5}$.

38. Sailing The diagram at the right shows a sailboat.

   a. Use the Pythagorean theorem to find the height of the sail in simplest radical form.

   b. Use the result of part (a) and the formula for the area of a triangle to find the area of the sail. Round your answer to the nearest tenth.

39. Standardized Test Prep Suppose that x and y are positive numbers. Which of the following is *not* equivalent to $\sqrt{24x^2y}$?

   A. $2x\sqrt{6y}$ **B.** $\sqrt{24x}\sqrt{xy}$ **C.** $\sqrt{4xy}\sqrt{6x}$

   D. $2x^2\sqrt{6y}$ **E.** $x\sqrt{24y}$

Simplify each radical expression. Assume that all variables represent positive numbers.

40. $\sqrt{v^6}$ **41.** $\dfrac{2}{\sqrt{a^3}}$ **42.** $\sqrt{20a^2b^3}$ **43.** $\sqrt{a^3b^5c^3}$

44. $\sqrt{12x^3y^2}$ **45.** $\sqrt{4y^4}$ **46.** $\dfrac{\sqrt{x^2}}{\sqrt{y^3}}$ **47.** $\sqrt{\dfrac{18x}{81}}$

Simplify each expression by rationalizing the denominator.

48. $\dfrac{3}{\sqrt{7}}$ **49.** $\dfrac{12}{\sqrt{12}}$ **50.** $\dfrac{2\sqrt{2}}{\sqrt{5}}$ **51.** $\dfrac{9}{\sqrt{8}}$

52. $\dfrac{3\sqrt{2}}{\sqrt{6}}$ **53.** $\dfrac{25}{\sqrt{5}}$ **54.** $\dfrac{2\sqrt{5}}{\sqrt{12}}$ **55.** $\dfrac{16}{\sqrt{6}}$

56. Hobbies Use the Pythagorean theorem to find the missing dimensions a, b, and c of each triangle in the quilt square.

6 in.

Find the x- and y-intercepts of each equation.

57. $2x + 3y = 6$ **58.** $4x + 2y = 8$ **59.** $-3x + 5y = 15$ **60.** $-2x - 4y = 12$

61. Consumer You are shopping for food to serve for a lunch party. Crab sandwiches cost \$5 per serving and turkey sandwiches cost \$3 per serving. You have \$30.00 total to spend on sandwiches. Write an inequality to model the situation. How many of each kind can you buy?

Getting Ready for Lesson 9-5

Simplify each square root. Then add or subtract.

62. $\sqrt{16} + \sqrt{36}$ **63.** $\sqrt{49} - \sqrt{64}$ **64.** $\sqrt{121} + \sqrt{81}$ **65.** $\sqrt{400} - \sqrt{100}$

Adding and Subtracting Radicals

What You'll Learn

- Simplifying radicals involving addition and subtraction
- Solving problems involving sums and differences of radicals

...And Why

To solve geometric problems involving art

W O R K   T O G E T H E R

Work in pairs.

1. Copy and complete the table.

a	b	$\sqrt{a}$	$\sqrt{b}$	$\sqrt{a}+\sqrt{b}$	$\sqrt{a+b}$	$\sqrt{a}-\sqrt{b}$	$\sqrt{a-b}$
9	16	▦	▦	▦	▦	▦	▦
25	100	▦	▦	▦	▦	▦	▦
64	36	▦	▦	▦	▦	▦	▦
4	121	▦	▦	▦	▦	▦	▦
49	1	▦	▦	▦	▦	▦	▦

2. a. Compare the values in the addition columns. What do you notice?
 b. In general, does $\sqrt{a} + \sqrt{b} = \sqrt{a + b}$? Explain.

3. a. Compare the values in the subtraction columns. What do you notice?
 b. Does $\sqrt{a} - \sqrt{b} = \sqrt{a - b}$? Explain.

4. Is there a rule for adding and subtracting radicals? **Justify** your reasoning.

T H I N K   A N D   D I S C U S S

Simplifying Sums and Differences

You can simplify radical expressions by combining like terms. Like terms have the same radical part.

like terms	unlike terms
$4\sqrt{7}$ and $-12\sqrt{7}$	$3\sqrt{11}$ and $2\sqrt{5}$

5. Identify each pair of expressions as like or unlike terms. **Justify** your answers.
 a. $\sqrt{8}$ and $2\sqrt{8}$ **b.** $2\sqrt{3}$ and $3\sqrt{2}$ **c.** $2\sqrt{7}$ and $-3\sqrt{7}$

Example 1

Simplify the expression $\sqrt{2} + 3\sqrt{2}$.

$$\sqrt{2} + 3\sqrt{2} = 1\sqrt{2} + 3\sqrt{2} \quad \longleftarrow \text{Both } 1\sqrt{2} \text{ and } 3\sqrt{2} \text{ have } \sqrt{2}.$$
$$= 4\sqrt{2} \quad \longleftarrow \text{Combine like terms.}$$

9-5 Adding and Subtracting Radicals **435**

Example 2 ··

Simplify the expression $4\sqrt{3} - \sqrt{12}$.

$4\sqrt{3} - \sqrt{12} = 4\sqrt{3} - \sqrt{4 \cdot 3}$ ←— 4 is a perfect square and a factor of 12.

$= 4\sqrt{3} - \sqrt{4} \cdot \sqrt{3}$ ←— Use the multiplication property.

$= 4\sqrt{3} - 2\sqrt{3}$ ←— Simplify $\sqrt{4}$.

$= 2\sqrt{3}$ ←— Combine like terms.

6. Try This Simplify each expression.

a. $2\sqrt{5} + \sqrt{5}$ **b.** $3\sqrt{45} + 2\sqrt{5}$ **c.** $3\sqrt{3} - 2\sqrt{12}$

Simplifying Products, Sums, and Differences

QUICK REVIEW

The distributive property says $a(b + c) = ab + ac$.

Sometimes you need to use the distributive property and what you have learned in lessons 9-4 and 9-5 to simplify expressions.

Example 3   **Relating to the Real World** ·············

Art The ratio length : width of this painting by Mondrian is approximately equal to the *golden ratio* $(1 + \sqrt{5}) : 2$. The width of the painting is 50 in. Find the length of the painting. Express your answer in simplest radical form. Then estimate the length in inches.

Define 50 = width of painting
            x = length of painting

Relate $(1 + \sqrt{5}) : 2 =$ length : width

Write $\dfrac{1 + \sqrt{5}}{2} = \dfrac{x}{50}$

      $50(1 + \sqrt{5}) = 2x$ ←— Cross multiply.

      $\dfrac{50(1 + \sqrt{5})}{2} = x$ ←— Solve for x.

      $25(1 + \sqrt{5}) = x$

      $25 + 25\sqrt{5} = x$ ←— Use the distributive property.

      $80.90169944 = x$ ←— Use a calculator.

           $81 \approx x$

The length of Mondrian's painting is about 81 in.

7. a. Calculator Write the golden ratio as a decimal to the nearest hundredth.

     b. Calculator Write $\dfrac{25 + 25\sqrt{5}}{50}$ as a decimal to the nearest hundredth.

     c. Compare your answers to parts (a) and (b). What do you notice about the two values?

Example 4

Simplify $\sqrt{2}(5 - \sqrt{8})$.

$\sqrt{2}(5 - \sqrt{8}) = \sqrt{2}(5) - \sqrt{2}(\sqrt{8})$ ◄── Use the distributive property.

$\qquad\qquad\qquad = 5\sqrt{2} - \sqrt{2 \cdot 8}$ ◄── Use the multiplication property.

$\qquad\qquad\qquad = 5\sqrt{2} - \sqrt{16}$ ◄── Multiply.

$\qquad\qquad\qquad = 5\sqrt{2} - 4$ ◄── Simplify.

8. Try This Simplify each expression.

    a. $2(2 + \sqrt{3})$

    b. $\sqrt{2}(1 - 2\sqrt{10})$

    c. $\sqrt{3}(5\sqrt{2} - 2\sqrt{6})$

9. Simplify $3\sqrt{2}(\sqrt{24} + 2\sqrt{6})$ by first simplifying $\sqrt{24}$.

Exercises   ON YOUR OWN

Simplify each expression.

1. $15\sqrt{9} - \sqrt{9}$

2. $3(\sqrt{27} + 1)$

3. $\sqrt{18} + \sqrt{3}$

4. $2\sqrt{12} - 7\sqrt{3}$

5. $2\sqrt{3}(\sqrt{3} - 1)$

6. $\sqrt{8} + 2\sqrt{2}$

7. $\sqrt{27} - \sqrt{18}$

8. $-3\sqrt{6} + 8\sqrt{6}$

9. $3\sqrt{7} - \sqrt{28}$

10. $16\sqrt{10} + 2\sqrt{10}$

11. $\sqrt{3}(\sqrt{15} + \sqrt{4})$

12. $\sqrt{5} - 3\sqrt{5}$

13. $\sqrt{12} + \sqrt{24} - \sqrt{36}$

14. $\sqrt{3}(\sqrt{2} + 2\sqrt{3})$

15. $\sqrt{2}(\sqrt{8} - 4)$

16. Recreation You can make a box kite in the shape of a rectangular solid. The opening at each end of the kite is a square.

    a. Suppose the sides of the square are 2 ft long. How long are the diagonal struts used for bracing?

    b. Suppose each side of the square has length *s*. Find the length of the diagonal struts in terms of *s*. Write your answer in simplest form.

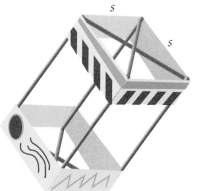

▦**Calculator** **Use a calculator to evaluate each expression. Round your answers to the nearest tenth.**

17. $\sqrt{2} + \sqrt{3}$

18. $4\sqrt{5} + \sqrt{10}$

19. $\sqrt{40} + \sqrt{90}$

20. $6\sqrt{8} - 8\sqrt{6}$

21. $\sqrt{3}(\sqrt{6} + 1)$

22. $\sqrt{18} + \sqrt{2}$

23. $5\sqrt{5} - \sqrt{7}$

24. $\sqrt{13} - 2\sqrt{2}$

25. $3\sqrt{2} - 3\sqrt{3}$

Simplify each expression.

26. $3\sqrt{3}(4\sqrt{27} - \sqrt{3})$

27. $\sqrt{12} + \sqrt{32}$

28. $\sqrt{5} + 2\sqrt{50}$

29. $2\sqrt{2}(-2\sqrt{32} + \sqrt{8})$

30. $3\sqrt{10}(\sqrt{10} + 4\sqrt{5})$

31. $3\sqrt{2}(2 + \sqrt{6})$

32. $\sqrt{18} - 2\sqrt{2}$

33. $\sqrt{68} + 17$

34. $-\sqrt{6}(\sqrt{6} - 5)$

35. Open-ended Make up three sums that are less than or equal to 50. Use the square roots of 2, 3, 5, or 7 and the whole numbers less than 10. For example, $8\sqrt{5} + 9\sqrt{7} \leq 50$.

36. Choose Use a calculator, paper and pencil, or estimation to find the value of the numerical expression in the cartoon.

from the cartoon *Bound & Gagged*

37. Bill wrote $\sqrt{24} + \sqrt{48} = 3\sqrt{24} = 6\sqrt{6}$.
 a. Simplify $\sqrt{24} + \sqrt{48}$.
 b. Critical Thinking What error did Bill make? Explain.

38. Writing Explain the errors in the work below.
 a. $\sqrt{5} + \sqrt{11} = \sqrt{16} = 4$
 b. $\sqrt{41} = \sqrt{16 + 25} = \sqrt{16} + \sqrt{25} = 9$

Geometry **Find the perimeter of each figure below.**

39.

40.

41.

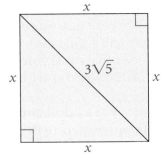

42. Architecture The ratio width : height of the front face of a building is equal to the *golden ratio* $(1 + \sqrt{5}) : 2$. The height of the front face of the building is 24 ft. Find the width of the building. Express your answer in simplest radical form. Then estimate in feet.

43. Standardized Test Prep Simplify $\dfrac{\sqrt{50} + \sqrt{32}}{\sqrt{2}}$.

   A. $\sqrt{41}$ **B.** $5 + 4\sqrt{2}$ **C.** $4 + 5\sqrt{2}$ **D.** $9\sqrt{2}$ **E.** 9

Exercises   MIXED REVIEW

44. a. Travel Aruba is changing $\frac{1}{4}$ of its 75 mi^2 into protected parkland. How many square miles will the protected area be?

   b. The island has 88,000 residents. What is its population density (people/mi^2) for the whole island?

   c. What is the population density excluding the protected parkland?

Aruba

Solve using the quadratic formula. Tell whether each solution is *rational* or *irrational*.

45. $x^2 - 2x - 15 = 0$ **46.** $x^2 + 6x + 2 = 0$

Getting Ready for Lesson 9-6

Evaluate each expression for the given value.

47. $\sqrt{x} - 3$ for $x = 16$ **48.** $\sqrt{x + 7}$ for $x = 9$ **49.** $2\sqrt{x + 3} - 4$ for $x = 1$

Algebra at Work

Auto Mechanic

An auto mechanic's job is to see that car engines get the most out of every gallon of gas. Formulas used by mechanics often involve radicals. For example, a car gets its power when gas and air in each cylinder are compressed and ignited by a spark plug. An engine's efficiency (e) is given by the formula $e = \dfrac{c - \sqrt{c}}{c}$, where c is the compression ratio.

Because of the complexity of such formulas and of modern high-performance engines, today's auto mechanic must be a highly trained and educated professional who understands algebra, graph reading, and the operation of computerized equipment.

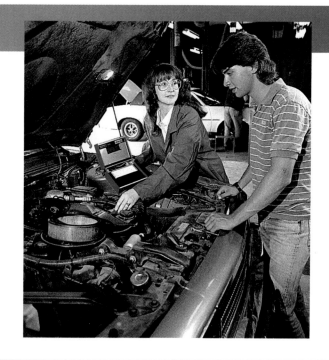

Mini Project: Evaluate the formula to find the engine efficiency for even-numbered compression ratios from 2 to 20.

What You'll Learn

9-6 **S**olving Radical Equations

- Solving equations that contain radicals
- Identifying extraneous solutions

...And Why

To design amusement park rides

Solving a Radical Equation

An equation that has a variable under a radical is a **radical equation.** You can often solve a radical equation by squaring both sides. To do this, first get the radical by itself on one side of the equation. Remember that the expression under the radical must be positive.

$$\text{When } x \geq 0, (\sqrt{x})^2 = x.$$

Example 1

Solve $\sqrt{x} - 3 = 4$. Check your solution.

$$\sqrt{x} - 3 = 4$$
$$\sqrt{x} - 3 + 3 = 4 + 3 \quad \longleftarrow \text{Add 3 to both sides.}$$
$$\sqrt{x} = 7 \quad \longleftarrow \text{Simplify.}$$
$$(\sqrt{x})^2 = 7^2 \quad \longleftarrow \text{Square both sides.}$$
$$x = 49$$

Check $\quad \sqrt{x} - 3 = 4$
$$\sqrt{49} - 3 \stackrel{?}{=} 4 \quad \longleftarrow \text{Substitute 49 for } x.$$
$$7 - 3 = 4 \checkmark$$

The solution of $\sqrt{x} - 3 = 4$ is 49.

1. **a.** Find the values of $\sqrt{36} - 3$ and $\sqrt{64} - 3$.
    b. *Critical Thinking* Do the results in part (a) suggest that $x = 49$ is a reasonable solution to $\sqrt{x} - 3 = 4$? Explain.
    c. Explain how parts (a) and (b) are a form of estimation.

2. **Try This** Solve and check.
    a. $\sqrt{x} + 5 = 12$ **b.** $2\sqrt{x} + 7 = 19$ **c.** $\sqrt{x} + 3 = 5$

3. **a.** Solve $x^2 - 3 = 4$.
    b. Compare and contrast how you solved the equation in part (a) with how you solved $\sqrt{x} - 3 = 4$.

4. **a.** *Graphing Calculator* Graph $y = \sqrt{x} - 3$ and $y = 4$ together. Use the range shown on the screen at the left.
    b. How many intersection points are there?
    c. What are the coordinates of the intersection point(s)?
    d. *Critical Thinking* How does your answer to part (c) confirm the solution of $\sqrt{x} - 3 = 4$ in Example 1?

WINDOW FORMAT
Xmin=0
Xmax=64
Xscl=1
Ymin=-10
Ymax=10
Yscl=1

Example 2 Relating to the Real World

Amusement Parks On a roller coaster ride, your speed in a loop depends on the height of the hill you have just come down and the radius of the loop in feet. The equation $v = 8\sqrt{h - 2r}$ gives the velocity v in feet per second of a car at the top of the loop. Suppose the loop has a radius of 18 ft. You want the car to have a velocity of 30 ft/s at the top of the loop. How high should the hill be?

Solve $v = 8\sqrt{h - 2r}$ for $v = 30$ and $r = 18$.

$$30 = 8\sqrt{h - 2(18)} \quad \longleftarrow \text{Substitute for } r \text{ and } v.$$
$$\frac{30}{8} = \sqrt{h - 2(18)} \quad \longleftarrow \text{Divide each side by 8}$$
$$\qquad\qquad\qquad\qquad\qquad \text{to get the radical alone.}$$
$$3.75 = \sqrt{h - 36}$$
$$(3.75)^2 = (\sqrt{h - 36})^2 \quad \longleftarrow \text{Square both sides.}$$
$$14.0625 = h - 36$$
$$50.0625 = h$$

The hill should be about 50 ft high.

5. **Try This** Find the height of the hill when the velocity at the top of the loop is 35 ft/s and radius of the loop is 24 ft.

6. **Try This** Find the radius of the loop when the hill is 150 ft high and the velocity of the car is 30 ft/s.

7. About how many miles per hour is 30 ft/s? (*Hint:* 1 mi = 5280 ft)

8. Critical Thinking Would you expect the velocity of the car to increase or decrease in each situation? Explain your reasoning.
   a. as the radius of the loop increases
   b. as the height of the hill decreases

Squaring both sides of an equation also works when each side of the equation is a radical expression.

Example 3

Solve $\sqrt{3x - 2} = \sqrt{x + 6}$.

$(\sqrt{3x - 2})^2 = (\sqrt{x + 6})^2$ ← Square both sides.

$$3x - 2 = x + 6$$
$$3x = x + 8$$
$$2x = 8$$
$$x = 4$$

The solution is 4.

PROBLEM SOLVING

Look Back Show how to check that 4 is the solution of $\sqrt{3x - 2} = \sqrt{x + 6}$.

9. *Graphing Calculator* Graph the equations $y = \sqrt{3x - 2}$ and $y = \sqrt{x + 6}$ together. How does the display confirm the solution of Example 3?

10. Try This Solve $\sqrt{5x - 6} = \sqrt{3x + 5}$. Check your solution.

Solving Equations with Extraneous Solutions

When you solve equations by squaring both sides, you sometimes find two possible solutions. You need to determine which solution actually satisfies the original equation.

Example 4

Solve $x = \sqrt{x + 6}$.

$(x)^2 = (\sqrt{x + 6})^2$ ← Square both sides.

$x^2 = x + 6$

$x^2 - x - 6 = 0$ ← Subtract x and 6 from both sides.

$x = \dfrac{-(-1) \pm \sqrt{(-1)^2 - 4(1)(-6)}}{2(1)}$ ← Use the quadratic formula to solve for x.

$x = \dfrac{1 \pm \sqrt{1 - (-24)}}{2}$

$x = \dfrac{1 \pm \sqrt{25}}{2}$

$x = \dfrac{1 \pm 5}{2}$ ← Simplify $\sqrt{25}$.

$x = \dfrac{1 + 5}{2}$ or $x = \dfrac{1 - 5}{2}$

$x = 3$ or $x = -2$

Check
$$x = \sqrt{x + 6}$$

$3 \overset{?}{=} \sqrt{3 + 6}$ $-2 \overset{?}{=} \sqrt{-2 + 6}$ ← $\sqrt{4} = 2$

$3 = 3$ ✔ $-2 \neq 2$

The only solution is 3.

QUICK REVIEW

The quadratic formula states that for an equation of the form $ax^2 + bx + c = 0$, if $a \neq 0$,

then $x = \dfrac{-b \pm \sqrt{b^2 - 4ac}}{2a}$.

The value -2 is called an **extraneous solution** of Example 4. It is a solution of the derived equation ($x^2 = x + 6$), but not of the original equation ($x = \sqrt{x + 6}$).

11. How could you have determined that -2 was not a solution of $x = \sqrt{x + 6}$ without going through all the steps of the check?

Exercises   ON YOUR OWN

Solve each radical equation. Check your solutions.

1. $\sqrt{5x + 10} = 5$

2. $7 = \sqrt{x + 5}$

3. $6 - \sqrt{3x} = -3$

4. $\sqrt{n} = \frac{7}{8}$

5. $20 = \sqrt{x} - 5$

6. $\sqrt{x} - 10 = 1$

7. Geometry In the right triangle $\triangle ABC$, the altitude $\overline{CD}$ is at a right angle to the hypotenuse. You can use $CD = \sqrt{(AD)(DB)}$ to find certain lengths.
   a. Find AD if $CD = 10$ and $DB = 4$.
   b. Find DB if $AD = 20$ and $CD = 15$.

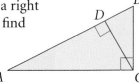

8. Physics The equation $T = \sqrt{\dfrac{2\pi^2 r}{F}}$ gives the time T in seconds it takes a body with mass 0.5 kg to complete one orbit of radius r meters. The force F in newtons pulls the body toward the center of the orbit.
   a. It takes 2 s for an object to make one revolution with a force of 10 N (newtons). Find the radius of the orbit.
   b. Find the radius of the orbit if the force is 160 N and $T = 2$.

Solve each radical equation. Check your solutions.

9. $\sqrt{3x + 1} = \sqrt{x}$

10. $\sqrt{x + 5} = \sqrt{3x + 6}$

11. $\sqrt{3x + 10} = \sqrt{9 - x}$

12. $\sqrt{7x + 5} = \sqrt{x - 3}$

13. $\frac{x}{2} = \sqrt{3x}$

14. $\sqrt{x + 12} = 3\sqrt{x}$

15. $\sqrt{5x - 4} = \sqrt{3x + 10}$

16. $\sqrt{2x} = \sqrt{9 - x}$

17. $x = \sqrt{2x + 3}$

18. Standardized Test Prep Which of the following radical equations has no *real* solution?
   A. $-\sqrt{x} = -25x$
   B. $\sqrt{2x + 1} = \sqrt{3x - 5}$
   C. $-3\sqrt{3x} = -5$
   D. $\sqrt{3x + 1} = -10$
   E. $\frac{x}{2} = \sqrt{x - 1}$

19. Packaging The volume V in cubic units of a cylindrical can is given by the formula $V = \pi r^2 h$, where r is the radius of the can and h is its height. The radius of a can is 2.5 in. and the height of the can is 5 in. Find the can's volume in cubic inches.

20. Writing Tell how you would solve the equation $\sqrt{2x} + \sqrt{x + 2} = 0$.

Storage tanks in Knoxville, Tennessee

Solve each radical equation. Check your solutions.

21. $x = \sqrt{x + 2}$

22. $2x = \sqrt{10x + 6}$

23. $\frac{x}{3} = \sqrt{x - 2}$

24. $\sqrt{x + 5} = 2x$

25. $2x = 2\sqrt{x - 5}$

26. $\sqrt{2x - 15} = \frac{x}{4}$

27. $\sqrt{x + 12} = x$

28. $\sqrt{2x - 1} = \frac{x + 8}{2}$

29. $x = \sqrt{7x - 6}$

30. Writing Explain in your own words what an extraneous solution is.

31. The diagram shows a piece of cardboard that makes a box when sections of it are folded and taped. The ends of the box are x in. long and the box is 10 in. long.
  a. Write the formula for the volume V of the box.
  b. Solve the equation in part (a) for x.
  c. Open-ended Find some integer values of x that make the box have a volume between 40 in.^{3} and 490 in.^{3}.

10 in.

x

x

Tell which solution(s), if any, are extraneous for the given equation.

32. $-x = \sqrt{-x + 6}$; $x = -3, x = 2$

33. $\sqrt{12 - x} = x$; $x = -4, x = 3$

34. $x = \sqrt{2x}$; $x = 0, x = 2$

35. $2x = \sqrt{4x + 3}$; $x = \frac{3}{2}, x = -\frac{1}{2}$

36. $x = \sqrt{28 - 3x}$; $x = 4, x = -7$

37. $-x = \sqrt{-6x - 5}$; $x = -5, x = -1$

Chapter Project · · · · **Find Out by Communicating**

• Solve the formula $d = 1.225\sqrt{h}$ for h where d is in miles and h is in feet. (*Hint:* See page 424.)

• How tall would a person on Earth have to be to see 7 mi to the horizon?

• Could a person possibly see such a distance? Why or why not?

Exercises   MIXED REVIEW

Simplify each expression. Assume that no denominator is equal to zero.

38. $\dfrac{x^2 y^7}{x^4 y^5}$

39. $\dfrac{a^2 b^5}{a^7 b^{10}}$

40. $\dfrac{15x^4 y^5}{45x^2 y^3}$

41. $\dfrac{14x^2 y^3}{7x^3 y^5}$

42. Business A salesperson earns $750 per month plus 8% commission on the amount she sells. Write an equation to show how her monthly income relates to her sales in dollars.

Getting Ready for Lesson 9-7

Find the value of y for the given value of x.

43. $y = \sqrt{x + 7} - 3$
    for $x = 2$

44. $y = 3\sqrt{x} + 2$
    for $x = 9$

45. $y = -2\sqrt{x - 1} + 2$
    for $x = 1$

What You'll Learn

- Graphing and exploring square root functions
- Solving real-world problems using square root functions

...And Why

To solve problems involving firefighting

What You'll Need

- graphing calculator

9-7   Graphing Square Root Functions

THINK AND DISCUSS

Firefighters When firefighters are trying to put out a fire, the rate at which they can spray water on the fire is very important to them. For a hose with a 2 in. nozzle diameter, the flow rate, f, in gal/min is given by this formula.

$$f = 120\sqrt{p}, \text{ where } p \text{ is the nozzle pressure in lb/in.}^2$$

The flow-rate function is an example of a square root function. The simplest **square root function** is $y = \sqrt{x}$.

x	y
0	0
1	1
4	2
9	3
16	4

Graph points: (0, 0), (1, 1), (4, 2), (9, 3), (16, 4), with curve labeled $y = \sqrt{x}$.

1. Why do you think the x-values in the table were chosen?

2. Find an approximate value of $\sqrt{3}$ and see if it seems to fit the graph.

3. Why is the graph not continued to the left of the y-axis?

Example 1

Compare the graph of $y = \sqrt{x} - 1$ to the graph of $y = \sqrt{x}$.

Method 1 Use a table.

x	$\sqrt{x}$	$\sqrt{x} - 1$
0	$\sqrt{0} = 0$	$\sqrt{0} - 1 = -1$
1	$\sqrt{1} = 1$	$\sqrt{1} - 1 = 0$
4	$\sqrt{4} = 2$	$\sqrt{4} - 1 = 1$
9	$\sqrt{9} = 3$	$\sqrt{9} - 1 = 2$
16	$\sqrt{16} = 4$	$\sqrt{16} - 1 = 3$

Method 2 Use a graphing calculator.

Xmin=–2   Ymin=–2
Xmax=16   Ymax=8
Xscl=1   Yscl=1

For each value of x, the value of $\sqrt{x} - 1$ is one less than the value of $\sqrt{x}$. The graph of $y = \sqrt{x} - 1$ is one unit lower than the graph of $y = \sqrt{x}$.

4. **Try This** **Analyze** the graph of $y = \sqrt{x} + 1$ by comparing it to the graph of $y = \sqrt{x}$.

5. a. **Predict** how the graph of $y = \sqrt{x} + k$ will compare to the graph of $y = \sqrt{x}$ when k is a negative number.
   b. *Graphing Calculator* Confirm your prediction by graphing $y = \sqrt{x} - 3$ and $y = \sqrt{x}$.

6. The calculator display at the left shows the graph of a square root function of the form $y = \sqrt{x} + k$. What is the value of k?

Xmin=–2   Ymin=–2
Xmax=15   Ymax=8
Xscl=1   Yscl=1

You can solve an inequality to find the domain of a square root function.

Example 2

Find the domain of $y = \sqrt{x + 3}$. Then graph the function.

The square root limits the domain because the expression under the radical cannot be negative. To find the domain, solve $x + 3 \geq 0$.

$$x + 3 \geq 0$$
$$x \geq -3$$

The domain is the set of all real numbers greater than or equal to –3.

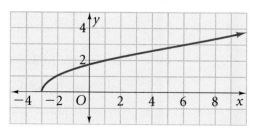

7. Compare the graph in Example 2 to the graph of $y = \sqrt{x}$.

8. **Try This** Find the domain of $y = \sqrt{x} - 3$. Then graph the function.

9. a. The diagram at the left shows the graphs of two functions of the form $y = \sqrt{x} + k$. Describe the domain of each function.
   b. Which graph is the graph of $y = \sqrt{x} + 1$? **Justify** your response.

10. **Summarize** how the graph of $y = \sqrt{x} + k$ compares to the graph of $y = \sqrt{x}$.

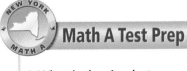

Xmin=–2   Ymin=–2
Xmax=16   Ymax=8
Xscl=1   Yscl=1

You can use square root functions to describe real-life situations.

Example 3   **Relating to the Real World**

Firefighting Graph the flow-rate function $f = 120\sqrt{p}$ introduced on page 445. Evaluate the function when the nozzle pressure is 40 lb/in.^{2}.

page 445

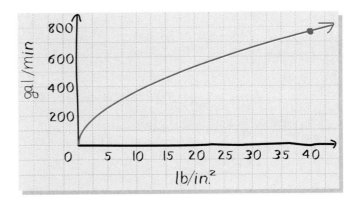

$f = 120\sqrt{40}$ ← Substitute 40 for p.
  $= 758.9466384$ ← Use a calculator.

The flow rate is about 759 gal/min when the nozzle pressure is 40 lb/in.^{2}. ■

11. In Example 3, why are there different scales on the axes?

12. Compare the graph in Example 3 to the graph of $y = \sqrt{x}$.

13. **Summarize** how the graph of $y = k\sqrt{x}$ compares to the graph of $y = \sqrt{x}$.

Math A Test Prep

1 What is the simplest form of the expression $\sqrt{12} \cdot \sqrt{48}$?

(1) $\sqrt{576}$ (3) 576
(2) $2\sqrt{36}$ (4) 24

2 Solve:
$\sqrt{2x + 1} = \sqrt{3x - 5}$.

Exercises   ON YOUR OWN

Find the domain of each function.

1. $y = \sqrt{x} - 2$

2. $f(x) = \sqrt{4x + 3}$

3. $y = \sqrt{1.5x}$

4. $y = \sqrt{3x + 5}$

5. $y = \sqrt{7 + x}$

6. $f(x) = \sqrt{2 + x}$

7. $f(x) = \sqrt{3 + x}$

8. $y = \sqrt{x + 3} - 1$

9. $y = \sqrt{x - 5} + 1$

10. **Business** Last year a store had an advertising campaign. Sales figures for disposable cameras are shown. The function $n = 27\sqrt{5t} + 53$ models sales volume n of the cameras as a function of time t, the number of months after the start of the campaign.

Disposable Camera Sales

   a. Evaluate the function to find how many disposable cameras the store sold in the seventh month.
   b. Solve an equation to find the month in which the number of disposable cameras sold was about 175.

Match each function with its graph.

11. $y = \sqrt{x} + 4$
   A.

12. $y = \sqrt{x} - 2$
   B.

13. $y = 3\sqrt{x}$
   C.

14. **Standardized Test Prep** In which of the following quadrants will your calculator display the graph of $y = \sqrt{x} + 7$?
   A. I, II, and III   **B.** I and IV   **C.** I   **D.** IV   **E.** I and II

Graph each function.

15. $y = \sqrt{x} + 2$
16. $y = \sqrt{x} - 2.5$
17. $f(x) = \sqrt{x} - 5$
18. $y = 4\sqrt{x}$
19. $f(x) = \sqrt{x} + 2$
20. $y = \sqrt{x} + 3$
21. $y = \sqrt{x - 6}$
22. $f(x) = 5\sqrt{x}$
23. $y = \sqrt{x - 2} + 3$
24. $f(x) = \sqrt{x - 3} - 1$
25. $y = \sqrt{x + 5} + 2$
26. $f(x) = \sqrt{x + 2} - 4$

Writing Using words like "shift up," "shift down," "shift left," and "shift right," describe to a friend how to use the graph of $y = \sqrt{x}$ to obtain the graph of each function.

27. $f(x) = \sqrt{x + 8}$
28. $y = \sqrt{x} - 10$
29. $y = \sqrt{x} + 12$
30. $f(x) = \sqrt{x - 9}$

31. a. **Open-ended** Give an example of a square root function in each form. Assume $k > 0$.
   $y = \sqrt{x + k},$
   $y = \sqrt{x} + k,$
   $y = k\sqrt{x}$
   b. Graph each function on the same coordinate grid.

Chapter Project · · · · · · · · Find Out by Organizing

- The formula for the distance you can see on any planet is $d = \sqrt{\dfrac{rh}{2640}}$, where h is your height in feet and r is the radius of the planet in miles. Use the planet radii you researched on page 429 to write a separate formula for each planet.
- Graph each formula.

Exercises   M I X E D   R E V I E W

Solve each system of equations by graphing.

32. $x + y = 5$
$2x - 3y = -5$

33. $3x - y = 4$
$4x + 2y = 2$

34. Finance You deposit $1000 into a bank account that pays 6% compounded annually. How much will be in the bank account at the end of 3 years?

Getting Ready for Lesson 9-8

Find the mean of each set of data.

35. 4, 6, 8, 10, 11

36. 3, 4, 5, 7, 9

37. $-8, -6, 0, 2, 3$

38. $-3, -2, 0, 2, 9$

> **SELF ASSESSMENT**
> ## FOR YOUR JOURNAL
> Explain how to find the domain of a square root function. Include an example.

Exercises   C H E C K P O I N T

Simplify each radical expression.

1. $\sqrt{3} \cdot \sqrt{27}$

2. $\sqrt{7} \cdot 28$

3. $\sqrt{64b^5}$

4. $\sqrt{18} - \sqrt{8}$

5. $\sqrt{3}(\sqrt{3} + 4)$

6. $\dfrac{\sqrt{24}}{\sqrt{3}}$

7. $\sqrt{\dfrac{x^3}{4}}$

8. $\dfrac{6}{\sqrt{3}}$

Solve each radical equation. Check your solutions.

9. $8 = \sqrt{x - 4}$

10. $\sqrt{x} = \sqrt{3x - 12}$

11. $\sqrt{2x - 5} = \sqrt{11}$

12. $7 - \sqrt{2x} = 1$

Graph each function.

13. $y = \sqrt{x} + 4$

14. $f(x) = \sqrt{x - 5}$

15. $f(x) = 2\sqrt{x}$

16. $y = \sqrt{x} - 3$

17. Writing How is combining like terms with radicals similar to combining like terms with variables?

18. Standardized Test Prep What is the perimeter of the figure?

A. $2\sqrt{7} + \sqrt{5}$ **B.** $\sqrt{5} + \sqrt{7}$ **C.** $\sqrt{35}$

D. $2\sqrt{7} + 2\sqrt{5}$ **E.** none of the above

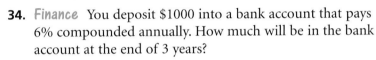

Box-and-Whisker Plots

Before Lesson 9-8

To show how data items are spread out, you can arrange a set of data in order from least to greatest. The maximum, minimum, and median give you some information about the data. You can better describe the data by dividing it into fourths. The **lower quartile** is the median of the lower half of the data. The **upper quartile** is the median of the upper half of the data.

The data below describes the highway gas mileage (mi/gal) for several brands of cars.

minimum   median = 38.5   maximum

$$17 \quad 19 \quad 27 \quad 37 \quad 40 \quad 42 \quad 52 \quad 58$$

lower quartile $\frac{19 + 27}{2} = 23$ upper quartile $\frac{42 + 52}{2} = 47$

A **box-and-whisker plot** is a visual representation of data. The box-and-whisker plot at the right displays the gas mileage information. The box represents the data from the lower quartile to the upper quartile. The vertical line segment represents the median. Horizontal line segments called whiskers show the spread of the data to the minimum and to the maximum.

Highway Gas Mileage (mi/gal)

15 20 25 30 35 40 45 50 55 60

box

whiskers

Create a box-and-whisker plot for each data set.

1. {3, 2, 3, 4, 6, 6, 7}

2. {1, 1.5, 1.7, 2, 6.1, 6.2, 7}

3. {1, 2, 5, 6, 9, 12, 7, 10}

4. {65, 66, 59, 61, 67, 70, 67, 66, 69, 70, 63}

5. {29, 32, 40, 31, 33, 39, 27, 42}

6. {3, 3, 5, 7, 1, 10, 10, 4, 4, 7, 9, 8, 6}

7. {1, 1.2, 1.3, 4, 4.1, 4.2, 7}

8. {1, 3.8, 3.9, 4, 4.3, 4.4, 7, 5}

9. Jobs Below are the number of hours a student worked each week at her summer job. When she applied for the job, she was told the typical work week was 29 hours.

29, 23, 21, 20, 17, 16, 15, 33, 33, 32, 15

a. Make a box-and-whisker plot for the data.

b. How many weeks are above the upper quartile? What are the number of hours worked?

c. What is the median number of hours she worked? What is the mean? Compare these to the typical work week.

10. Writing In what ways are histograms and box-and-whisker plots alike and in what ways are they different?

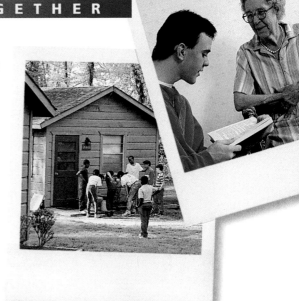

What You'll Learn

- Exploring standard deviation
- Calculating and using standard deviation

...And Why

To analyze job opportunities

9-8 Analyzing Data Using Standard Deviation

WORK TOGETHER

Jobs Work with a partner.

Four students had summer jobs at a camp last year. Four other students had jobs at a nursing home. Their weekly pay is listed below.

Salaries

Camp	Nursing Home
$150	$140
$160	$190
$220	$210
$270	$260

1. **a.** Calculate the mean for the pay in each location.
    b. What does the mean represent?

QUICK REVIEW

The *range* of a set of data is the difference between the greatest number and the least number in the set.

2. **a** What is the range of weekly pay for each location?
    b. Use the ranges to describe how the pay varies at the two locations.

3. Copy the table below.

Salary	Mean	Deviation from Mean	Square of Deviation
$150	$200	−50	2500
$160	$200	▪	▪
$220	$200	▪	▪
$270	$200	70	▪
sum of the squares of the deviations →			▪

4. You find deviation from the mean by subtracting the mean from each salary value. Fill in the missing values in column 3.

5. Complete column 4 by squaring each value in column 3.

6. Complete a table like the one above for the nursing home workers.

7. **a.** Compare the deviations from the mean at the two locations. At which location does the pay vary more from the mean?
    b. Compare the sum of the squares of the deviations for the two locations. How does this support your answer to part (a)?

A way to show how a set of data is spread out is the **standard deviation.** It reflects how all the data points in a set vary from the mean. The symbol for standard deviation is σ, pronounced "sigma."

small standard deviation ⟶ data cluster around the mean
large standard deviation ⟶ data spread out from the mean

You can calculate the standard deviation by following these six steps.

- Find the mean of the data set. The expression $\bar{x}$ represents the mean.

- Find the difference of each data value from the mean.

- Calculate the square of each difference.

- Find the sum of the squares of the differences.

- Divide the sum by the number of data values.

- Take the square root of the quotient just calculated.

Example 1

Find the standard deviation of the two data sets below.
a. Data Set 1 {83, 88, 75, 69, 70}   **b.** Data Set 2 {69, 75, 76, 77, 88}

a. Find the mean.

mean
$$= \frac{83 + 88 + 75 + 69 + 70}{5}$$
$$= \frac{385}{5}$$
$$= 77$$

Calculate the standard deviation.

x	$\bar{x}$	$x - \bar{x}$	$(x - \bar{x})^2$
83	77	6	36
88	77	11	121
75	77	-2	4
70	77	-7	49
69	77	-8	64
		Sum:	274

sum of squares = 274
$$\frac{\text{sum of squares}}{5} = \frac{274}{5}$$
$$= 54.8$$
$$\sqrt{54.8} = 7.402702209$$

The standard deviation is about 7.4.

b. Find the mean.

mean
$$= \frac{69 + 75 + 76 + 77 + 88}{5}$$
$$= \frac{385}{5}$$
$$= 77$$

Calculate the standard deviation.

x	$\bar{x}$	$x - \bar{x}$	$(x - \bar{x})^2$
69	77	-8	64
75	77	-2	4
76	77	-1	1
77	77	0	0
88	77	11	121
		Sum:	190

sum of squares = 190
$$\frac{\text{sum of squares}}{5} = \frac{190}{5}$$
$$= 38$$
$$\sqrt{38} = 6.164414003$$

The standard deviation is about 6.2.

8. In which data set do the values cluster closer to the mean?

You can use a calculator to find the standard deviation of a set of data.

Example 2   Relating to the Real World

Golf   Three friends play golf. Their scores on six holes of golf are below.
       Calculate the mean and standard deviation for Player 1's scores.

Player 1	5	4	2	4	10	5
Player 2	5	5	5	5	5	5
Player 3	3	10	4	4	7	2

You can use a calculator to calculate the mean and standard deviation.

- Choose $\boxed{STAT}$ and *EDIT* to enter your data.

- Choose $\boxed{STAT}$, *CALC*, and *1-VAR STATS* to calculate.

- The screen displays information about your data including the mean, $\overline{x}$, the standard deviation, σx, and the number of entries, n.

The mean of Player 1's scores is 5. The standard deviation is about 2.4. ■

9. a. **Predict** whether the standard deviations of Player 2's and Player 3's scores will be greater or less than the standard deviation of Player 1's scores.
   b. Explain how you made your predictions in part (a).

10. a. **Try This** Use a calculator to find the mean and standard deviation for Player 2's and Player 3's golf scores.
    b. What does a standard deviation of zero mean?
    c. Estimation Suppose a friend got the answer 27.5 when using a calculator to find the standard deviation of Player 3's golf scores. How do you know that your friend made an error?

◀ **At age 20, Tiger Woods was a three-time United States Amateur champion.**

▦ Calculator   **Make a table like the one in Example 1 to find the standard deviation for each data set. Use a calculator to find the square root.**

1. {5, 3, 2, 5, 10}

2. {10, 9, 10, 12, 11, 14}

3. {3.5, 4.5, 6.0, 4.0, 2.5, 2.5, 5.0}

4. {11, 11, 17, 17, 10, 11, 12, 19}

5. Tell what you know about the following data sets.
   a. Data Set 1: The mean is 25 and the standard deviation is 100.
   b. Data Set 2: The mean is 25 and the standard deviation is 2.

6. The table at the right records the outdoor temperatures (°F) reported to a local meteorologist by twelve weather watchers near Denver, Colorado, in January. Find the standard deviation of the temperature data.

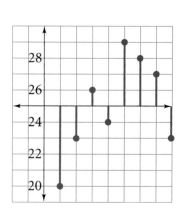

January Temperatures (°F)	
15.8°	16.3°
16.5°	17.0°
15.9°	16.1°
16.5°	16.2°
16.0°	16.4°
16.1°	16.6°

7. Writing   Explain the effects of a very large or very small data value on the mean and standard deviation of a data set.

8. Open-ended   Create data sets with at least 6 entries as follows.
   a. The mean is 12 and the standard deviation is 0.
   b. The mean is 7 and the range is 12.

9. Jobs   When Lyman interviewed for a summer job, he asked about the average salary of summer employees. He was excited that the average weekly wage was $400. When his employer offered him a job at $265 a week, he was confused. His employer stated: "Of my 20 summer employees, 17 make $265 per week."
   a. During the job interview, what other statistics should Lyman have asked about in order to find out more information about salaries? Explain your choice(s).
   b. The three highly-paid summer employees each earn the same amount. How much do they earn?
   c. Estimate   Do you expect the standard deviation for the company's summer salaries to be large or small? Why?
   d. Verify your prediction by calculating the standard deviation.

10. The graph at the right shows the differences from the mean in a set of data containing eight data values.
   a. Find the square of each difference from the mean.
   b. Find the sum of the squares calculated in part (a).
   c. Use the result of part (b) to find the standard deviation of the data set.

Graphing Calculator **Use a calculator to find the standard deviation of each set of data.**

11. {11.4, 10.1, 9.5, 9.9, 10.1, 11.2, 12.0, 12.3}

12. {102.4, 100.8, 99.5, 103.4, 105.6, 111.5, 120.5}

13. {13, 19, 23, 50, 43, 44, 50, 52, 74, 83, 88, 90}

14. {−3.2, 0, 1.3, −2.0, −3.5, 0, 3.2, 2.3, 1.1, 0.3}

15. **Math in the Media** You are writing a magazine article on ski resorts in the Sierras. The information at the right is part of your research.
    a. What is the range for the price of a lift ticket?
    b. Find the standard deviation of the ticket prices.
    c. To give your readers a feel for the variability of ticket prices, you include the following sentence in your article. Fill in the blanks.

    Lift ticket prices vary about $ ■ around an average of $ ■ for an all-day adult ticket.

    d. **Writing** Explain why your sentence in part (c) is more helpful than simply telling your readers the range, as in "The prices vary from $26 to $46."

16. **Research** Collect data on a topic of interest such as classmates' batting averages or students' curfew times. Gather at least 15 measurements and calculate the mean and standard deviation. Write a paragraph describing your data.

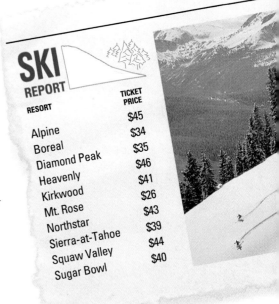

SKI REPORT	
RESORT	**TICKET PRICE**
Alpine	$45
Boreal	$34
Diamond Peak	$35
Heavenly	$46
Kirkwood	$41
Mt. Rose	$26
Northstar	$43
Sierra-at-Tahoe	$39
Squaw Valley	$44
Sugar Bowl	$40

Exercises   MIXED REVIEW

Write each number in scientific notation.

17. 0.00347

18. 3,112,200

19. 0.000825

20. 50,147,235

Solve each system of equations.

21. $3x + 2y = 7$
    $2x + 3y = 8$

22. $5x − 2y = 3$
    $4x + 2y = 6$

23. $x + y = 7$
    $2x − y = 8$

24. $3x − 4y = 5$
    $3x + 2y = 11$

Find the domain of each function.

25. $y = \sqrt{x − 5}$

26. $f(x) = 5 + \sqrt{6 + 3x}$

27. **Automobiles** A new car costs $20,000. It loses value at a rate of 7% per year. How much is the car worth in four years?

On a CLEAR Day...

Questions on pages 418, 424, 429, 444, and 449 should help you to complete your project. Prepare a visual display and a report of your results. You should include the formula and graph for each planet and the formula for height on Earth when sight distance is known.

Reflect and Revise

Your notebook should present a comparison of sight distances and graphs for each planet. Check that your formulas and graphs are clearly labeled and easy to understand. Be sure that you have included a separate category with your display for Earth giving the formula for height on Earth when sight distance is known.

Follow Up

Suppose you were in an airplane at 30,000 ft above your town. How far could you see? Write a description of what you would see. Include any points of interest, cities or towns, and geological features like rivers or mountains.

For More Information

Adler, David. *Hyperspace! Facts and Fun from All Over the Universe.* New York: Viking Children's Books, 1982.

"Living and Working in Space: The Countdown Has Begun." PBS Video, 1320 Braddock Place, Alexandria, Virginia 22314. (800) 344-3337.

Free videotapes, slides, books, pamphlets: National Aeronautics and Space Administration, Education Programs Officer, NASA Headquarters, Code XEE, Washington, D.C. 20546. (202) 453-8396.

Key Terms

angle of elevation (p. 426)
box-and-whisker plot (p. 450)
converse of the Pythagorean theorem (p. 416)
cosine (p. 425)
distance formula (p. 420)
division property of square roots (p. 431)
extraneous solution (p. 443)
hypotenuse (p. 414)
legs (p. 414)
like terms (p. 435)

lower quartile (p. 450)
midpoint (p. 422)
midpoint formula (p. 422)
multiplication property of square roots (p. 430)
Pythagorean theorem (p. 414)
radical equation (p. 440)
rationalize (p. 432)
simplest form (p. 430)
sine (p. 425)
square root function (p. 445)
standard deviation (p. 452)

tangent (p. 425)
trigonometric ratios (p. 425)
unlike terms (p. 435)
upper quartile (p. 450)

How am I doing?

- State three ideas from this chapter that you think are important. Explain your choices.
- Describe the method for finding the distance between two points A and B.

The Pythagorean Theorem 9-1

For a right triangle with **legs** a and b and **hypotenuse** c, the **Pythagorean theorem** states that $a^2 + b^2 = c^2$. The **converse of the Pythagorean theorem** states that if a triangle has sides of lengths a, b, and c, and if $a^2 + b^2 = c^2$, then it is a right triangle with hypotenuse of length c.

A rectangle has sides with lengths a and b. Find the length of the diagonal to the nearest hundredth.

1. $a = 3, b = 5$
2. $a = 11, b = 14$
3. $a = 7, b = 13$
4. $a = 4, b = 9$

5. Writing The hypotenuse of a right triangle is 26 cm. The length of one leg is 10 cm. Describe how to find the length of the other leg.

The Distance Formula 9-2

The **distance formula** $d = \sqrt{(x_2 - x_1)^2 + (y_2 - y_1)^2}$ gives the distance between two points (x_1, y_1) and (x_2, y_2). The **midpoint formula** $M = \left(\dfrac{x_1 + x_2}{2}, \dfrac{y_1 + y_2}{2}\right)$ gives the coordinates of their midpoint.

Find the midpoint of $\overline{AB}$.

6. $A(3, 7), B(-2, 4)$
7. $A(5, -2), B(6, 14)$
8. $A(3, -9), B(14, 16)$
9. $A(12, 17), B(-7, 9)$

10. Open-ended Find two points with integer coordinates $\sqrt{74}$ units apart.

Trigonometric Ratios

Trigonometric ratios are triangle measurement ratios. For a right triangle of a given shape, they do not change no matter how large or small the triangle is. Three trigonometric ratios are **sine** (sin), **cosine** (cos), and **tangent** (tan), shown at the right.

$$\sin A = \frac{\text{length of side of opposite } \angle A}{\text{length of hypotenuse}}$$

$$\cos A = \frac{\text{length of side of adjacent to } \angle A}{\text{length of hypotenuse}}$$

You can use trigonometric ratios to measure distances indirectly. You can use an **angle of elevation** to measure heights indirectly.

$$\tan A = \frac{\text{length of side opposite } \angle A}{\text{length of side adjacent to } \angle A}$$

In $\triangle ABC$, $\angle C$ is a right angle. Find the lengths of the missing sides.

11. $AB = 12, m\angle A = 34°$ **12.** $BC = 9, m\angle B = 72°$ **13.** $AC = 8, m\angle B = 52°$

14. *Standardized Test Prep* In $\triangle ABC$, $\angle C$ is a right angle. Which of the following is (are) true?

I. $\cos B = \frac{AC}{AB}$ **II.** $\tan B = \frac{BC}{AC}$ **III.** $\sin A = \frac{BC}{AB}$

A. I only   **B.** II only   **C.** III only   **D.** I and II   **E.** II and III

Simplifying Radicals

You can simplify some radical expressions by using products or quotients. The **multiplication property of square roots** states that for any two nonnegative numbers $\sqrt{ab} = \sqrt{a} \cdot \sqrt{b}$. The **division property of square roots** is at the right.

$$\sqrt{\frac{a}{b}} = \frac{\sqrt{a}}{\sqrt{b}}$$

$a \geq 0, b > 0$
division property

Simplify each radical expression.

15. $\sqrt{32} \cdot \sqrt{144}$ **16.** $\frac{\sqrt{84}}{\sqrt{121}}$ **17.** $\sqrt{96} \cdot \sqrt{25}$ **18.** $\sqrt{\frac{100}{169}}$

19. A rectangle is 7 times as long as it is wide. Its area is 1400 cm². Find the dimensions of the rectangle in simplified form.

Adding and Subtracting Radicals

You can use the distributive property to simplify expressions with sums and differences of radicals. First, simplify the radicals to have like terms.

Simplify each radical expression.

20. $6\sqrt{7} - 2\sqrt{28}$ **21.** $5(\sqrt{20} + \sqrt{80})$ **22.** $\sqrt{54} - 2\sqrt{6}$ **23.** $\sqrt{125} - 3\sqrt{5}$

24. $\sqrt{10}(\sqrt{10} - \sqrt{20})$ **25.** $7\sqrt{90} + \sqrt{160}$ **26.** $\sqrt{72} + 3\sqrt{32}$ **27.** $\sqrt{28} + 5\sqrt{63}$

28. A box is 2 in. long, 3 in. wide, and 4 in. tall. What is the length of the longest distance between corners of the box? Express your answer in simplified form.

Solving Radical Equations

A **radical equation** has a variable under a radical. You can often solve a radical equation by solving for the square root, then squaring both sides of the equation. Squaring each side of an equation also works when both sides are square roots. When you square both sides of a radical equation, you may produce an **extraneous solution**. It is not a solution of the original equation.

Solve each radical equation.

29. $\sqrt{x + 7} = 3$ **30.** $\sqrt{x} + 3\sqrt{x} = 16$ **31.** $\sqrt{x + 7} = \sqrt{2x - 1}$ **32.** $\sqrt{x - 5} = 4$

33. The volume V of a cylinder is given by $V = \pi r^2 h$, where r is the radius of the cylinder and h is its height. If the volume of a cylinder is 54 in.^{2}, and its height is 2 in., what is its radius to the nearest 0.01 in.?

Graphing Square Root Functions

The simplest **square root function** is $y = \sqrt{x}$. To find the domain of a square root function, solve the inequality where the expression under the radical is greater than or equal to zero.

Find the domain of each function. Then graph the function.

34. $y = \sqrt{x} + 5$ **35.** $y = \sqrt{x - 2}$ **36.** $y = \sqrt{x + 1}$ **37.** $y = 2\sqrt{x}$

Analyzing Data Using Standard Deviation

The **standard deviation** shows how spread out a set of data is from the mean. You can calculate the standard deviation by following these six steps. Find the mean, $\bar{x}$, of the data set. Find the difference of each data value from the mean. Square each difference. Find the sum of the squares of the differences. Divide the sum by the number of data values. The square root of the quotient just calculated is the standard deviation.

Find the standard deviation of each set of data.

38. 2, 7, 9, 15, 17   **39.** 5, 8, 11, 12, 19   **40.** 4, 10, 12, 13, 23   **41.** 7, 15, 20, 23, 29

Getting Ready for...▶ CHAPTER 10

Use the quadratic formula to solve these equations to the nearest hundredth. If the equation has no real solution, write *no solution.*

42. $2x^2 + 5x - 4 = 0$ **43.** $3x^2 - 2x - 7 = 0$ **44.** $x^2 - 3x - 8 = 0$

45. $2x^2 - 5x + 15 = 0$ **46.** $5x^2 - 4x - 12 = 0$ **47.** $7x^2 + 2x - 18 = 0$

Find whether the following sets of numbers determine a right triangle.

1. 6, 8, 10   **2.** 6, 7, 9

3. 4, 5, 11   **4.** 10, 24, 26

Approximate AB to the nearest hundredth.

5. $A(1, -2), B(5, 7)$ **6.** $A(3, 5), B(7, 4)$

7. $A(4, 7), B(-11, -6)$ **8.** $A(0, -5), B(3, 2)$

Find the coordinates of the midpoint of $\overline{AB}$.

9. $A(4, 9), B(1, -5)$ **10.** $A(-2, -7), B(3, 0)$

11. $A(3, -10), B(-4, 6)$ **12.** $A(0, 8), B(-1, 1)$

Find the lengths to the nearest hundredth.

13. AB

14. AC

15. The distance between consecutive bases in a baseball diamond is 90 ft. How far is it from first base to third base?

16. One house is 12 mi east of a school. Another house is 9 mi north of the school. How far apart from each other are the houses?

Simplify each radical expression.

17. $\sqrt{\dfrac{128}{64}}$ **18.** $\dfrac{\sqrt{27}}{\sqrt{75}}$

19. $\sqrt{48}$ **20.** $\sqrt{12} \cdot \sqrt{8}$

21. $3\sqrt{32} + 5\sqrt{2}$ **22.** $2\sqrt{27} + 5\sqrt{3}$

23. $7\sqrt{125} - 3\sqrt{175}$ **24.** $\sqrt{128} - \sqrt{192}$

25. Standardized Test Prep If x and y are positive, which expression(s) is (are) equivalent to

$\sqrt{24x^2y^3}$?

  I. $2xy\sqrt{12xy^2}$ **II.** $2xy\sqrt{6y}$ **III.** $xy\sqrt{24y}$
  A. I only   **B.** II only   **C.** III only
  D. I and II   **E.** II and III

26. Open-ended Write a problem involving addition of two like terms with radical expressions. Simplify the sum.

Solve each radical equation.

27. $3\sqrt{x} + 2\sqrt{x} = 10$ **28.** $8 = \sqrt{5x - 1}$

29. $5\sqrt{x} = \sqrt{15x + 60}$

30. $\sqrt{x} = \sqrt{2x - 7}$

31. $3\sqrt{x + 3} = 2\sqrt{x + 9}$

32. A rectangle is 5 times as long as it is wide. The area of the rectangle is 100 ft². How wide is the rectangle? Express your answer in simplified form.

Find the domain of each function. Then graph the function.

33. $y = 3\sqrt{x}$ **34.** $y = \sqrt{x} + 4$

35. $y = \sqrt{x - 4}$ **36.** $y = \sqrt{x + 9}$

37. A cube has 3-in. sides. Find the longest distance between a pair of corners. Express your answer in simplified form.

Find the standard deviation of each set of data.

38. 5, 7, 9, 11, 12   **39.** 2, 4, 7, 11, 15

40. 4, 12, 13, 15, 17   **41.** 1, 2, 4, 6, 7

42. Writing Explain how these two data sets differ based on the following information.
Set A: mean 20; range 10; standard deviation 4
Set B: mean 20; range 20; standard deviation 2

43. Geometry The formula for the volume V of a cylinder of height h and radius r is $V = \pi r^2 h$. Solve the formula for r in terms of V and h.

44. From the ground you can see a satellite dish on the roof of a building 60 feet high. The angle of elevation is 62°. How far away is the building from you?

Part I

1 Which could be the lengths of the sides of a right triangle?
  (1) 2, 5, 7   (3) 36, 6, 8
  (2) 24, 10, 26   (4) 4, 7, 65

2 What is the midpoint of the segment from $C(-2, 10)$ to $D(8, 3)$?
  (1) $(3, 6\frac{1}{2})$ (3) $(4, 5\frac{1}{2})$
  (2) $(5, 6\frac{1}{2})$ (4) $(5, 5\frac{1}{2})$

3 The two shorter sides of right triangle PQR are $\overline{QP}$ and $\overline{QR}$. Which is true?
  (1) $\sin P = \dfrac{QP}{PR}$ (3) $\cos R = \dfrac{QR}{PR}$
  (2) $\tan P = \dfrac{QR}{PR}$ (4) $\tan R = \dfrac{QR}{QP}$

4 Which expression is in simplest form?
  (1) $3\sqrt{20}$ (3) $\dfrac{2}{\sqrt{6}}$
  (2) $4\sqrt{35}$ (4) $\sqrt{\dfrac{3}{10}}$

5 The simplest form of the sum of $\sqrt{3}$ and $2\sqrt{27}$ is ■.
  (1) $3\sqrt{3}$ (3) $6\sqrt{6}$
  (2) $2\sqrt{30}$ (4) $7\sqrt{3}$

6 What is the solution of $\sqrt{x-8} = \sqrt{6x+2}$?
  (1) no solution   (3) -2
  (2) 2   (4) $-1\frac{1}{5}$

7 In which set of data is the data spread farthest apart?
  (1) The mean is 20; the standard deviation is 15.
  (2) The mean is 70; the standard deviation is 10.
  (3) The mean is 30; the standard deviation is 12.
  (4) The mean is 10; the standard deviation is 9.

8 The sum of four consecutive integers is 190. What is the third integer?
  (1) 45   (3) 47
  (2) 46   (4) 48

Part II

9 Suppose you live at the base of a mountain. The angle of elevation from your home to the top of the mountain is 27°. The distance along this line of elevation is 3 miles. Find the height of the mountain to the nearest tenth of a mile.

10 Graph the function $y = \sqrt{x} - 4$.

Part III

11 Find the missing length. Express it as a radical in simplest form.

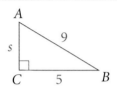

12 A square photo is placed in a frame 9 in. by 12 in. The area of the mat surrounding the photo is 65 in.^{2}. To the nearest tenth of an inch, what is the length of each side of the photo?

Part IV

13 The map shows the locations of Ms. Martin's house and the factory where she works. On the map, each unit represents one mile.

  a What is the length of the shortest route from Ms. Martin's house to the factory?
  b If Ms. Martin drives to work at an average speed of 40 mi/h, how long does it take her to drive the route found in (a)?

14 One city has five car rental agencies. The costs per day of renting an economy car with unlimited mileage in that city are: $25, $19, $30, $24, $32.
  a What is the range of the daily rates?
  b What is the mean of the daily rates?
  c Display the data in a box-and-whisker plot.

Relating to the Real World

Algebra is useful because it provides tools for describing and solving problems. You can use polynomials and their properties to solve problems in engineering, communications, and economics. Properties of polynomials make it possible to find the most efficient use of time and materials.

Trees are us.

Rings indicate age.

Wood splits as it dries.

Scar shows fire damage.

Many schools celebrate Arbor Day by planting young trees to replenish our ecosystem. Trees use the carbon dioxide that humans and animals exhale to make oxygen. Trees anchor the soil and prevent erosion. They also produce fruit. Wood from trees is used for the construction of everything from pencils to houses.

As you work through the chapter, you will learn more about the uses of trees. You will use formulas to analyze data and predict the production of wood and fruit. Then you will decide how to organize and display your results.

To help you complete the project:

Factoring Special Cases

Solving Equations by Factoring

Choosing an Appropriate Method for Solving

10-5   10-6   10-7

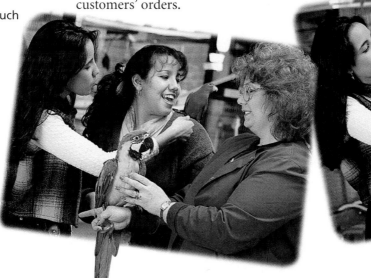

What You'll Learn

- Describing polynomials
- Adding and subtracting polynomials

...And Why

To use polynomials in real-world situations, such as working in a store

What You'll Need

- tiles

10-1 Adding and Subtracting Polynomials

WORK TOGETHER

Business Work in groups. Suppose you work at a pet store. The spreadsheet shows the contents of several customers' orders.

ROCKY'S FRIENDS
Bird Supplies

- bird seed (5 lb) $3.99
- cuttlebone (2 ct)   2.00
- spray millet (5 lb)   24.00
- gravel paper (1 pkg)   2.29
- perches (2 ct)   1.89

Tidbits

	A	B	C	D	E	F
1	Customer	Seed	Cuttlebone	Millet	G. Paper	Perches
2	Davis			✔		
3	Brooks	✔	✔			
4	Casic	✔		✔		
5	Martino	✔			✔	✔

The variables represent the number of each item ordered.
s = bags of birdseed m = bags of millet p = packages of perches
c = packages of cuttlebone g = packages of gravel paper

1. Which expression represents the cost of Casic's order?
   A. $27.99(s + m)$ **B.** $3.99s + 24m$ **C.** $27.99sm$

2. Write expressions to represent each of the other customers' orders.

3. Martino buys 10 bags of birdseed, 4 packages of gravel paper, and 2 packages of perches. What is the total cost of his order?

4. **Open-ended** Make up several orders and write expressions for these orders. Have other members of your group find the cost of your orders. Check each other's work.

Describing Polynomials

A **polynomial** is one term or the sum or difference of two or more terms. A polynomial has no variables in a denominator. For a term that has only one variable, the **degree of a term** is the exponent of the variable.

$$x^3 - 4x + 5x^2 + 7 \quad \longleftarrow \begin{array}{l}\text{The degree of a}\\ \text{constant is 0.}\end{array}$$

degree $\longrightarrow$ 3 1 2 0

The **degree of a polynomial** is the same as the degree of the term with the highest degree. You can name a polynomial by its degree or by the number of its terms.

Polynomial	Degree	Name Using Degree	Number of Terms	Name Using Number of Terms
$7x + 4$	1	linear	2	**binomial**
$3x^2 + 2x + 1$	2	quadratic	3	**trinomial**
$4x^3$	3	cubic	1	**monomial**
5	0	constant	1	monomial

The polynomials in the chart are in **standard form,** which means the terms decrease in degree from left to right and no terms have the same degree.

Example 1

Write each polynomial in standard form. Then name each polynomial by its degree and the number of its terms.

a. $5 - 2x$

$-2x + 5$
linear binomial

b. $3x^4 - 4 + 2x^2$

$3x^4 + 2x^2 - 4$
fourth degree
trinomial

c. $-2x + 5 - 4x^2 + x^3$

$x^3 - 4x^2 - 2x + 5$
cubic polynomial
with four terms

5. **Try This** Write each polynomial in standard form. Then name each polynomial by its degree and the number of its terms.

a. $6x^2 + 7 - 9x^4$
b. $3y - 9 - y^3$
c. $9 + 7v$

Adding Polynomials

You can use tiles to add and subtract polynomials.

Opposite terms $\longrightarrow$ form zero pairs.

x^2 $-x^2$ = 0 x $-x$ = 0   1 -1 = 0

6. What polynomial is shown using each set of tiles?

a.

b.

Example 2

Find $(2x^2 - 3x + 4) + (3x^2 + 2x - 3)$.

Method 1 Add using tiles.

$2x^2 - 3x + 4$

$3x^2 + 2x - 3$

Group like tiles together. Remove zero pairs. Write an expression for the remaining tiles.

$5x^2 - x + 1$

QUICK REVIEW

Like terms are terms that have exactly the same variable factors.

Method 2 Add vertically.

Line up like terms.
Then add the coefficients.
$$2x^2 - 3x + 4$$
$$\underline{3x^2 + 2x - 3}$$
$$5x^2 - \ x + 1$$

The sum is $5x^2 - x + 1$.

Method 3 Add horizontally.

Group like terms. Then add the coefficients.
$$(2x^2 - 3x + 4) + (3x^2 + 2x - 3)$$
$$= (2x^2 + 3x^2) + (-3x + 2x) + (4 - 3)$$
$$= 5x^2 - x + 1$$

7. a. Try This Find $(5x^2 + 4x - 7) + (-4x^2 + 8x - 1)$ using any method you choose.

b. Why did you choose the method you used?

Subtracting Polynomials

In Chapter 1, you learned that subtraction means to add the opposite. So when you subtract a polynomial, change each of its terms to the opposite. Then add the coefficients.

1 Which statement about the expression $5x^4 - 3x^2 + 1$ is true?
(1) It is a binomial.
(2) It is a monomial.
(3) It is a third degree polynomial.
(4) It is a fourth degree polynomial.

2 The perimeter of the triangle is $13c + 3$. Write a polynomial expression in standard form for the missing side length.

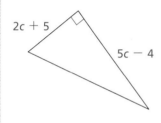

| **Example 3** |

Find $(7x^3 - 3x + 1) - (x^3 + 4x^2 - 2)$.

Method 1 Subtract vertically.

Line up like terms.   Add the opposite.

$$
\begin{array}{rr}
7x^3 \qquad -3x + 1 \\
-(x^3 + 4x^2 \qquad -2) \\
\hline
\end{array}
\longrightarrow
\begin{array}{rr}
7x^3 \qquad -3x + 1 \\
-x^3 - 4x^2 \qquad +2 \\
\hline
6x^3 - 4x^2 - 3x + 3
\end{array}
$$

Method 2 Subtract horizontally.

Write the opposite of each term in the polynomial being subtracted. Group like terms. Then add the coefficients of like terms.

$(7x^3 - 3x + 1) - (x^3 + 4x^2 - 2)$

$= 7x^3 - 3x + 1 - x^3 - 4x^2 + 2$

$= (7x^3 - x^3) - 4x^2 - 3x + (1 + 2)$ ← The coefficients of $7x^3$ and $-x^3$ are 7 and -1. $7x^3 - 1x^3 = 6x^3$.

$= 6x^3 - 4x^2 - 3x + 3$

The difference is $6x^3 - 4x^2 - 3x + 3$.

Check Substitute a value for x to check. Here 2 is substituted for x.

$(7x^3 - 3x + 1) - (x^3 + 4x^2 - 2) \overset{?}{=} 6x^3 - 4x^2 - 3x + 3$

$7(2^3) - 3(2) + 1 - [2^3 + 4(2^2) - 2] \overset{?}{=} 6(2^3) - 4(2^2) - 3(2) + 3$

$(56 - 6 + 1) - (8 + 16 - 2) \overset{?}{=} 48 - 16 - 6 + 3$

$51 - 22 \overset{?}{=} 29$

$29 = 29$ ✔

8. Try This Subtract $(3x^2 + 4x - 1) - (x^2 - x - 2)$.

9. Critical Thinking How are subtracting vertically and subtracting horizontally alike?

Exercises   ON   YOUR   OWN

Match each expression with its name.

1. $5x^2 - 2x + 3$ **A.** constant monomial

2. $\frac{3}{4}z + 5$ **B.** *not* a polynomial

3. $7a^3 + 4a - 12$ **C.** quadratic trinomial

4. $\frac{3}{x} + 5$ **D.** linear binomial

5. -15 **E.** cubic trinomial

Write each polynomial in standard form. Then name each polynomial by its degree and number of terms.

6. $4x - 3x^2$

7. $4x + 9$

8. $6 - 3x - 7x^2$

9. $9z^2 - 11z^3 + 5z - 5$

10. $y - 7y^3 + 15y^8$

11. $c^2 - 2 + 4c$

12. $7 + 5b^2$

13. $-10 + 4q^4 - 8q + 3q^2$

Find the sum of the two sets of tiles.

14.

15.

Find each sum or difference.

16. $(7y^2 - 3y + 4y) + (8y^2 + 3y^2 + 4y)$

17. $(2x^3 - 5x^2 + 3x - 1) - (8x^3 - 8x^2 + 4x + 3)$

18. $(-7z^3 + 3z - 1) - (-6z^2 + z + 4)$

19. $(7a^3 + 3a^2 - a + 2) + (8a^2 - 3a - 4)$

20. $(5y^3 + 7y) - (3y^3 + 9y^2) + (7y^3 + 2y)$

21. $(2x^2 - 4) + (3x^2 - 6) - (-x^2 + 2)$

22. Critical Thinking Kwan rewrote $(5x^2 - 3x + 1) - (2x^2 - 4x - 2)$ as $5x^2 - 3x + 1 - 2x^2 - 4x - 2$. What mistake did he make?

Language Arts **Use a dictionary if necessary.**

23. Writing Write the definition of each word.
  a. monogram **b.** binocular **c.** tricuspid **d.** polyglot

24. a. Open-ended Find other words that begin with *mono, bi, tri,* or *poly.*
  b. Do these prefixes have meanings similar to those in mathematics?

Geometry **Find the perimeter of each figure.**

25.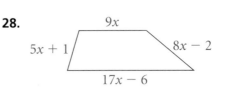

2y

26.
$5a + 7$
$2a - 1$
$4a + 6$

27.
$9c - 10$
$5c + 2$

28.
$9x$
$5x + 1$
$8x - 2$
$17x - 6$

29. Open-ended In his will, Mr. McAdoo is leaving equal shares of the land shown at the right to his two brothers. Write a polynomial expression for the land that each brother should inherit.

30. Critical Thinking Is it possible to write a binomial with degree 0? Explain.

Geometry Find each missing length.

31. Perimeter $= 25x + 8$

32. Perimeter $= 23a - 7$

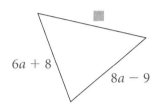

33. Perimeter $= 38y + 2$

Simplify. Write each answer in standard form.

34. $(3 - 2x + 3x^2) + (7 + 6x - 2x^2)$

35. $(4x^3 - 2x^2 - 13) + (-4x^3 + 2 - 7x)$

36. $(3x^3 - 3x^2 - x - 1) - (3x^2 - 6x)$

37. $(-2r^2 + r - 6) - (1 + 2r - 4r^2)$

38. $(9c^3 - c + 8 + 6c^2) - (3c^3 + 3c - 4)$

39. $(b^4 - 6 + 5b) + (8b^4 + 2b - 3b^2)$

40. Critical Thinking Why is $3x^2$ a monomial and $3x^{-2}$ *not* a monomial?

Exercises   MIXED REVIEW

Use exponential notation to write each expression.

41. $4 \cdot 4 \cdot 4 \cdot 4$

42. $(0.5)(0.5)(0.5)$

43. $\left(\frac{2}{3}\right)\left(\frac{2}{3}\right)\left(\frac{2}{3}\right)\left(\frac{2}{3}\right)$

44. $28 \cdot 28 \cdot 28$

Find the standard deviation of each set of numbers to the nearest tenth.

45. $10, 12, 16, 5, 2$

46. $11, 7, 10, 12$

47. $5, 3, 7, 8, 3, 4$

48. Science The surface area of a sphere is found using the formula $S = 4\pi r^2$. The approximate radius of Jupiter is 4.4×10^4 mi. Find the approximate surface area of Jupiter.

Getting Ready for Lesson 10-2
Multiply.

49. $2(x - 3)$

50. $-6(3x - 2)$

51. $(-3)(-5a + 7)$

52. $(-7)(c^2 - 8c)$

What You'll Learn

• Multiplying a polynomial by a monomial

• Factoring a monomial from a polynomial

...And Why

To explore formulas for area

What You'll Need

• tiles

10-2   Multiplying and Factoring

Multiplying by a Monomial

You can use the distributive property to multiply polynomials. You can also use tiles to multiply polynomials.

Example 1

Multiply $3x$ and $(2x + 1)$.

Method 1 Use tiles.

Method 2 Use the distributive property.

$$3x\,(2x + 1) = 3x(2x) + 3x(1)$$
$$= 6x^2 + 3x$$

1. **Try This** Use the distributive property to multiply $2x(x - 2)$. Then check your work by using tiles.

2. **a.** Use tiles to find each product: $2x(4x - 3)$ and $(4x - 3)(2x)$.
   b. Do both models represent the same area? Explain.

3. **a.** *Critical Thinking* Kevin said that $-2x(4x - 3) = -8x^2 - 6x$. Karla said that $-2x(4x - 3) = -8x^2 + 6x$. Who is correct?
   b. Explain the error that Kevin or Karla made.

Factoring Out a Monomial

Factoring a polynomial reverses the multiplication process. You can use tiles to make a rectangle to find the factors of a polynomial.

Example 2

Factor $2x^2 - 10x$.

Model using tiles.

Make a rectangle that is as close to square as possible.

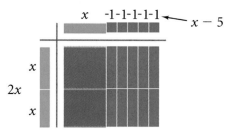

x -1-1-1-1-1 $x - 5$

$2x$ x x

Find the factors.

$$2x^2 - 10x = 2x(x - 5)$$

4. **Try This** Use tiles to factor each polynomial.
   a. $x^2 + 8x$ **b.** $3x^2 - 12x$ **c.** $-3x^2 + 6x$

QUICK REVIEW

The *greatest common factor* (GCF) is the greatest factor that divides evenly into each term.

For practice with greatest common factors, see Skills Handbook page 584.

To factor out a monomial using the distributive property, it is helpful to find the greatest common factor (GCF).

Example 3

Find the GCF of the terms of the polynomial $4x^3 + 12x^2 - 8x$.

List the factors of each term. Identify the factors common to all terms.

$$4x^3 = 2 \cdot 2 \cdot x \cdot x \cdot x$$
$$12x^2 = 2 \cdot 2 \cdot 3 \cdot x \cdot x$$
$$8x = 2 \cdot 2 \cdot 2 \cdot x$$

The GCF is $2 \cdot 2 \cdot x$ or $4x$.

5. **Try This** Find the GCF of the terms of each polynomial.
   a. $4x^3 - 2x^2 - 6x$ **b.** $5x^5 + 10x^3$ **c.** $3x^2 - 18$

Example 4 ·······························

Factor $3x^3 - 9x^2 + 15x$.

Step 1 Find the GCF.

$$3x^3 = 3 \cdot x \cdot x \cdot x$$
$$9x^2 = 3 \cdot 3 \cdot x \cdot x$$
$$15x = 3 \cdot 5 \cdot x$$

The GCF is $3 \cdot x$ or $3x$.

Step 2 Factor out the GCF.

$$3x^3 - 9x^2 + 15x$$
$$= 3x(x^2) - 3x(3x) + 3x(5)$$
$$= 3x(x^2 - 3x + 5)$$

6. Use the distributive property to check the factoring in Example 4.

7. **Try This** Use the GCF to factor each polynomial.
   a. $8x^2 - 12x$ b. $5x^3 + 10x$ c. $6x^3 - 12x^2 - 24x$

Example 5   **Relating to the Real World** ···············

Building Models Suppose you are building a model of the square castle shown. The moat of the model castle is made of silver paper. Find the area of the moat.

Define M = area of the moat
$2x$ = length of the side of the castle
$4x$ = radius of the moat
$A = \pi r^2$ ◄——— formula for the area of a circle

Relate   area of   is   area of   minus   area of
              moat   circle   square

Write M = $\pi(4x)^2$ – $(2x)^2$

$M = 16\pi x^2 - 4x^2$ ◄—— Simplify $(4x)^2$ and $(2x)^2$.
$= 4x^2(4\pi - 1)$ ◄—— The GCF is $4x^2$.

The area of the moat is $4x^2(4\pi - 1)$.

8. **Try This** Use the GCF to factor each polynomial.
   a. $2g^2 - 4$
   b. $2x^3 - 4x^2 + 6x$
   c. $6x^3 + 24x^2 + 6x$

Use tiles to find each product.

1. $3(x + 4)$ **2.** $x(x - 3)$ **3.** $2x(2x + 1)$ **4.** $4x(5x - 8)$ **5.** $4x(2x + 3)$

For each set of tiles, find the missing factors or product. Then write the factors and product as variable expressions.

6.

7.

8.

Find each product.

9. $4(2x + 7)$ **10.** $t(5t^2 + 6t)$ **11.** $6x(-9x^3 + 6x - 8)$ **12.** $2g^2(g^2 + 6g + 5)$

13. $-3a(4a^2 - 5a + 9)$ **14.** $7x^2(5x^2 - 3)$ **15.** $-3p^2(-2p^3 + 5p)$ **16.** $4n^2(2n^2 + 4n)$

17. $x(x + 3) - 5x(x - 2)$ **18.** $12c(-5c^2 + 3c - 4)$ **19.** $x^2(x + 1) - x(x^2 - 1)$ **20.** $-4j(3j^2 - 4j + 3)$

Find the greatest common factor (GCF) for each polynomial.

21. $15x + 21$ **22.** $6a^2 - 8a$ **23.** $36s + 24$ **24.** $x^3 + 7x^2 - 5x$

25. $5b^3 - 30$ **26.** $w^4 - 9w^2$ **27.** $9x^3 - 6x^2 + 12x$ **28.** $5r^5 - 3r^2 + 4r$

29. $25s^2 + 5s - 15s^3$ **30.** $8p^3 - 24p^2 + 16p$ **31.** $56x^4 - 32x^3 - 72x^2$ **32.** $2x + 3x^2$

33. a. Open-ended Draw two different tile diagrams to represent $6x^2 + 12x$ as a product. Place the x^2 tiles in the upper left area.
   b. Write the factored form of $6x^2 + 12x$ for each diagram in part (a).

34. a. Factor $n^2 - n$.
   b. Writing Suppose n is an integer. Is $n^2 - n$ *always*, *sometimes*, or *never* even? **Justify** your answer.

35. Manufacturing The diagram shows a solid block of metal with a cylinder cut out of it. The formula for the volume of a cylinder is $V = \pi r^2 h$, where r is the radius and h is the height.
   a. Write a formula for the volume of the cube in terms of s.
   b. Write a formula for the volume of the cylinder in terms of s.
   c. Write a formula in terms of s for the volume of the metal left after the cylinder has been removed.
   d. Factor your formula from part (c).
   e. What is the volume of the block of metal after the cylinder has been removed if $s = 15$ in?

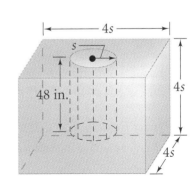

Factor each expression.

36. $6x - 4$

37. $s^4 + 4s^3 - 2s$

38. $10r^2 - 25r + 20$

39. $2x^2 - 4x^4$

40. $12p^3 + 4p^2 - 2p$

41. $7k^3 - 35k^2 + 70k$

42. $15n^3 + 3n^2 - 12n$

43. $9x + 12x^2$

44. $24n^3 - 12n^2 + 12n$

45. $6m^6 - 24m^4 + 6m^2$

46. $15k^3 + 3k^2 - 12k$

47. $5m^3 - 7m^2$

Factor by grouping like terms.

Sample $2x^3 + 2x + 3x^2 + 3$ ⟵ Group the terms with common factors together.

$2x(x^2 + 1) + 3(x^2 + 1)$ ⟵ Factor the GCF from each group.

$(2x + 3)(x^2 + 1)$ ⟵ Factor out the common polynomial.

48. $3v^3 + 18v^2 - 4v - 24$

49. $2x^3 + x^2 - 14x - 7$

50. $2x^3 + 3x^2 + 4x + 6$

51. a. Geometry How many sides does the polygon at the right have? How many diagonals does it have from one vertex?

b. Suppose a polygon, like the one at the right, has n sides. How many diagonals will it have from one vertex?

c. The number of diagonals that can be drawn from all the vertices is $\frac{n}{2}(n - 3)$. Multiply the two factors.

Chapter Project **Find Out by Researching**

A board foot is a linear measure of lumber equal to a square foot of wood 1 in. thick. What can you make from 10 board feet? 100 board feet? 1000 board feet? How is the size of a house related to the amount of wood used to build it? What different types of wood are needed for cabinets, floors, and roofs? What tools do carpenters use to make these items?

Exercises   M I X E D   R E V I E W

Use $\triangle ABC$ to find each trigonometric ratio.

52. $\sin A$ **53.** $\cos B$ **54.** $\tan A$ **55.** $\sin B$ **56.** $\cos A$ **57.** $\tan B$

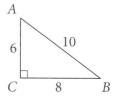

58. Geography Two buses are on their way to the same bus terminal. One bus is 1.5 mi due north of the terminal. The other bus is 2.0 mi due east of the terminal. How far from each other are the buses?

Getting Ready for Lesson 10-3

Simplify and write in standard form.

59. $(4x)(32) - (4x)(12x) + (4x)(7x^2)$

60. $(3y)(7) - (3y)(2y) + (3)(5y^2) - (7y)(6) - (7y)(8y)$

What You'll Learn

- Multiplying two binomials
- Multiplying a trinomial and a binomial

...And Why

To investigate real-world situations, such as savings accounts

What You'll Need

- tiles
- graphing calculator

10-3 Multiplying Polynomials

THINK AND DISCUSS

Multiplying Two Binomials

You can use tiles or the distributive property to multiply two binomials.

Example 1

Find the product $(2x + 1)(x - 5)$.

Method 1 Use tiles.

Step 1 Show the factors.   **Step 2** Find the product.

$(x - 5)$

$(2x + 1)$

$2x^2 - 10x + x - 5$ ← Add coefficients
$2x^2 - 9x - 5$ of like terms.

Method 2 Use the distributive property.

$(2x + 1)(x - 5)$ $= 2x(x) + 2x(-5) + 1(x) + 1(-5)$
$= 2x^2 - 10x + x - 5$
$= 2x^2 - 9x - 5$

The product is $2x^2 - 9x - 5$.

1. Rework Example 1 using tiles. Put $2x + 1$ on the horizontal line and $x - 5$ on the vertical line. Do you get the same result as in Example 1?

2. **Try This** Find the product $(3x + 1)(2x + 3)$ using tiles.

3. **Try This** Find the product $(6x - 7)(3x + 5)$ using the distributive property.

4. **a.** Graphing Calculator Graph $y = (2x + 1)(x - 5)$ and $y = 2x^2 - 9x - 5$ on the same calculator screen. What appears to be true of the two graphs?
   b. Use graphs to check your answers to Questions 2 and 3.

Multiplying Using FOIL

One way to organize how you multiply two binomials is to use *FOIL*, which stands for "First, Outer, Inner, Last." The term FOIL is a memory device for applying the distributive property.

Example 2

Find the product $(3x - 5)(2x + 7)$.

$$(3x - 5)(2x + 7) = \overset{\text{First}}{(3x)(2x)} + \overset{\text{Outer}}{(3x)(7)} - \overset{\text{Inner}}{(5)(2x)} - \overset{\text{Last}}{(5)(7)}$$
$$= 6x^2 + 21x - 10x - 35$$
$$= 6x^2 + 11x - 35$$

— middle term

The product is $6x^2 + 11x - 35$.

---

5. **Mental Math** What is the middle term of each product?
   a. $(2x + 3)(x + 1)$
   b. $(2x - 3)(x + 1)$
   c. $(2x + 3)(x - 1)$
   d. $(2x - 3)(x - 1)$

6. **Try This** Find each product.
   a. $(3x + 4)(2x + 5)$
   b. $(3x - 4)(2x + 5)$
   c. $(3x + 4)(2x - 5)$
   d. $(3x - 4)(2x - 5)$

7. **Graphing Calculator** Use a graphing calculator to check your answers in Question 6.

Example 3 **Relating to the Real World**

Savings Many students and their families start saving money early to pay for college. Suppose you deposit $500 at the beginning of each of two consecutive years. If your bank pays interest annually at the rate r, you can use the expression $(1 + r)(2 + r)500$ to find the amount in your account at the end of the two years. Write the expression in standard form.

$(1 + r)(2 + r)500$

$= (1 + r)(2 + r)500$ ⟵ Use FOIL to simplify $(1 + r)(2 + r)$.

$= (2 + r + 2r + r^2)(500)$

$= (2 + 3r + r^2)(500)$ ⟵ Add like terms.

$= 1000 + 1500r + 500r^2$ ⟵ Use the distributive property.

$= 500r^2 + 1500r + 1000$ ⟵ Write in standard form.

8. How much money is in your account if the interest rate in Example 3 is 4%? (*Hint:* Write the interest rate as a decimal.)

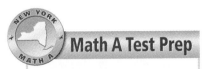
1 The area of a rectangle is described by the expression $6x^4 - 12x^3 + 9x^2$. The GCF of the terms of the polynomial describe the width of the rectangle. What is the length?
(1) $2x - 4x + 9x$
(2) $3x^2$
(3) $3x^2 - 9x + 6$
(4) $2x^2 - 4x + 3$

2 Simplify:
$(3x + 4)(2x - 1)$.

Multiplying a Trinomial and a Binomial

FOIL works when you multiply two binomials, but it is not helpful when multiplying a trinomial and a binomial. You can use the vertical method or the horizontal method to distribute each term in a factor.

Example 4

Find the product $(3x^2 + x - 6)(2x - 3)$.

Method 1 Multiply vertically.

$$
\begin{array}{r}
3x^2 + x - 6 \\
2x - 3 \\
\hline
-9x^2 - 3x + 18 \\
6x^3 + 2x^2 - 12x \\
\hline
6x^3 - 7x^2 - 15x + 18
\end{array}
$$

$\longleftarrow$ Multiply by -3.
$\longleftarrow$ Multiply by $2x$.
$\longleftarrow$ Add like terms.

Method 2 Multiply horizontally.

$$(2x - 3)(3x^2 + x - 6)$$

$$= 2x(3x^2) + 2x(x) + 2x(-6) - 3(3x^2) - 3(x) - 3(-6)$$

$$= 6x^3 + 2x^2 - 12x - 9x^2 - 3x + 18$$

$$= 6x^3 - 7x^2 - 15x + 18 \quad \longleftarrow \text{Add like terms.}$$

The product is $6x^3 - 7x^2 - 15x + 18$.

9. a. Try This Find the product $(3a + 4)(5a^2 + 2a - 3)$ using both methods shown in Example 4.
   b. Do you prefer the vertical or the horizontal method? Why?

Exercises   ON YOUR OWN

What are the factors shown with the tiles? What will be the product?

1.   **2.**   **3.**

Use tiles to find each product.

4. $(x + 2)(x + 5)$ **5.** $(x - 5)(x + 4)$ **6.** $(2x - 1)(x + 2)$

Copy and fill in each blank.

7. $(5a + 2)(6a - 1) = \blacksquare a^2 + 7a - 2$

8. $(3c - 7)(2c - 5) = 6c^2 - 29c + \blacksquare$

9. $(z - 4)(2z + 1) = 2z^2 - \blacksquare z - 4$

10. $(2x + 9)(x + 2) = 2x^2 + \blacksquare x + 18$

Choose **Use any method you choose to find each product.**

11. $(x + 7)(x - 6)$

12. $(a - 8)(a - 9)$

13. $(2y + 5)(y - 3)$

14. $(r + 6)(r - 4)$

15. $(y + 4)(5y - 8)$

16. $(x + 9)(x^2 - 4x + 1)$

17. $(a - 4)(a^2 - 2a + 1)$

18. $(x - 3)(2x^2 + 3x + 3)$

19. $(2t^2 - 6t + 3)(2t - 5)$

20. *Geometry* Use the formula $V = lwh$ to write a polynomial in standard form for the volume of the box shown at the right.

21. *Open-ended* Write a binomial and a trinomial. Find their product.

22. *Construction* You are planning a rectangular garden. Its length is 4 ft more than twice its width. You want a walkway 2 ft wide around the garden. Write an expression for the area of the garden and walk. (*Hint:* Draw a diagram.)

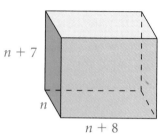

$n + 7$

n

$n + 8$

Find each product using FOIL.

23. $(x + 3)(x + 5)$

24. $(2y + 1)(3y + 4)$

25. $(a - 1)(a - 7)$

26. $(4x + 3)(4x - 3)$

27. $(5a - 2)(a + 3)$

28. $(6x + 1)(2x - 3)$

29. $(3y - 7)(-2y + 2)$

30. $(8 - 6x)(5 + 2x)$

31. *Writing* Which method do you prefer for multiplying two binomials? Why?

32. *Financial Planning* Suppose you deposit \$2000 in a savings account for college that has an annual interest rate r. At the end of three years, the value of your account will be $2000(1 + r)^3$ dollars.

a. Simplify $2000(1 + r)^3$ by finding the product of $2000(1 + r)(1 + r)(1 + r)$. Write your answer in standard form.

b. Find the amount of money in the account if the interest rate is 3%.

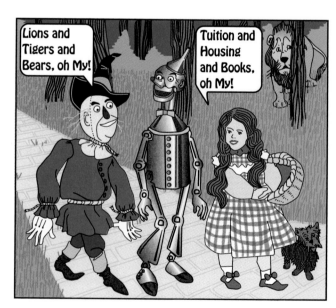

Lions and Tigers and Bears, oh My!

Tuition and Housing and Books, oh My!

Find each product. Is the product *rational* or *irrational*?

33. $(\sqrt{3} + \sqrt{2})(\sqrt{3} - \sqrt{2})$

34. $(\sqrt{3} + 2)^2(\sqrt{3} - 2)^2$

35. $(\sqrt{5} + 3)(\sqrt{5} + 7)$

36. **a.** Find $(x + 1)(x + 1)$.

b. Find $(x + 1)(x^2 + x + 1)$.

c. Find $(x + 1)(x^3 + x^2 + x + 1)$.

d. *Patterns* Use the pattern you see in parts (a) − (c) to **predict** the product of $(x + 1)(x^7 + x^6 + x^5 + x^4 + x^3 + x^2 + x + 1)$.

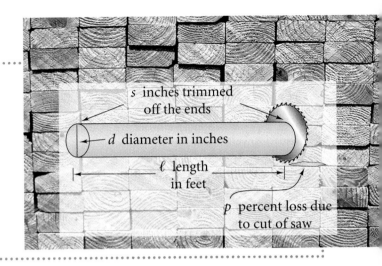

Chapter Project
Find Out by Calculating

You can use the expression $0.0655\ell(1 - p)(d - s)^2$ to find the number of usable board feet in a log.

- Estimate the usable board feet in a 35-ft log if its diameter is 20 in. Assume the log loses 10% (0.10) of its volume from the saw cuts and a total of 2 in. is trimmed off the log.

- The diameter of a log is 25 in. A total of 2 in. will be trimmed off the log. The estimated volume loss due to saw cuts is 10%. How long must the log be to yield 600 board feet of lumber?

Exercises   MIXED REVIEW

Solve each equation.

37. $6x^2 = 24$ **38.** $8x - 23 = 41$ **39.** $-x^2 + x + 2 = 0$

40. Language The *Oxford English Dictionary* defines 616,500 words. Write this number in scientific notation.

FOR YOUR JOURNAL

Describe the steps you would use to multiply $(3x - 4)$ by $(2x + 3)$.

Getting Ready for Lesson 10-4
Factor by grouping.

41. $2x(3x + 5) + 4(3x + 5)$ **42.** $5x(2x - 7) + 3(2x - 7)$ **43.** $-3x(4x + 1) + 5(4x + 1)$

Exercises   CHECKPOINT

Simplify.

1. $(x^2 + x - 3) + (2x^2 + 4x - 1)$

2. $(3a^3 + 2a^2 - 5) - (a^3 + a^2 + 2)$

3. $(m^2 - m + 7) - (3m^2 + 4m - 1)$

4. $(6x^2 - 2x - 5) + (3x^2 + x - 3)$

Find each product.

5. $(-w + 3)(w + 3)$ **6.** $2t(-3t^2 - 2t + 6)$ **7.** $(m + 4)(m - 3)$ **8.** $(b - 6)(b - 3)$

Factor each expression.

9. $-3c^3 + 15c^2 - 3c$ **10.** $10a^3 + 5a^2 + 5a$ **11.** $8p^3 - 20p^2 - 24p$ **12.** $x^3 + 4x^2 + 7x$

13. a. Open-ended Write two binomials using the variable z.
    b. Find the sum and product of the two binomials.

14. Writing How is distributing a number similar to distributing a term with a variable? Include examples.

Polynomial Division

To divide a polynomial by a monomial, divide each term of the polynomial by the monomial.

$$\frac{8x^4 + 4x^3 + 12x^2}{2x^2} = \frac{8x^4}{2x^2} + \frac{4x^3}{2x^2} + \frac{12x^2}{2x^2}$$
$$= 4x^2 + 2x^1 + 6x^0 \quad \longleftarrow \text{ Use the exponent rules for division.}$$
$$= 4x^2 + 2x + 6$$

To divide a polynomial by a binomial, use *polynomial long division*.

Example

Divide $x^3 + 3x^2 - 12$ by $x - 3$.

Step 1 Use a process similar to whole number long division.

$$\begin{array}{r} x^2 \qquad\qquad\qquad\qquad \\ x-3{\overline{\smash{\big)}\,x^3 + 3x^2 + 0x - 12}} \\ \underline{x^3 - 3x^2\qquad\qquad} \\ 6x^2 + 0x \end{array}$$

Express the dividend in descending powers of the variable, with a 0 coefficient for any missing power.

$\longleftarrow$ Divide: $\frac{x^3}{x} = x^2$

$\longleftarrow$ Multiply: $x^2(x - 3) = x^3 - 3x^2$

$\longleftarrow$ Subtract: $(x^3 + 3x^2) - (x^3 - 3x^2) = 6x^2$

Bring down 0x.

Step 2 Repeat the process: divide, multiply, subtract, bring down.

$$\begin{array}{r} x^2 + 6x\qquad\qquad\quad \\ x-3{\overline{\smash{\big)}\,x^3 + 3x^2 + 0x - 12}} \\ \underline{x^3 - 3x^2\qquad\qquad} \\ 6x^2 + 0x\quad \\ \underline{6x^2 - 18x\quad} \\ 18x - 12 \end{array} \qquad \begin{array}{r} x^2 + 6x + 18 \\ x-3{\overline{\smash{\big)}\,x^3 + 3x^2 + 0x - 12}} \\ \underline{x^3 - 3x^2\qquad\qquad} \\ 6x^2 + 0x\quad \\ \underline{6x^2 - 18x\quad} \\ 18x - 12 \\ \underline{18x - 54} \\ 42 \end{array}$$

The remainder is 42. $\longrightarrow$

Therefore, $\dfrac{x^3 + 3x^2 - 12}{x - 3} = x^2 + 6x + 18 + \dfrac{42}{x - 3}$ $\longleftarrow$ $\dfrac{\text{dividend}}{\text{divisor}} = \text{quotient} + \dfrac{\text{remainder}}{\text{divisor}}$

Divide.

1. $(x^6 - x^5 + x^4) \div x^2$

2. $(12x^8 - 8x^5) \div 4x^4$

3. $(9x^4 + 6x^3 - 3x^2) \div 3x^2$

4. $(x^2 - 5x + 3) \div (x - 2)$

5. $(x^2 - 9) \div (x + 4)$

6. $(x^3 + x^2 - x + 2) \div (x + 2)$

7. The volume of a rectangular prism is $m^3 + 8m^2 + 19m + 12$. The height of the prism is $m + 3$. Find the area of the base of the prism.

What You'll Learn

10-4 Factoring Trinomials

- Factoring quadratic expressions
- Identifying quadratic expressions that cannot be factored

...And Why

To solve civil engineering and landscaping problems

What You'll Need

- tiles
- graph paper

WORK TOGETHER

Construction A contractor has agreed to pour the concrete for the floor of a garage. He knows the area of the floor is 221 ft² but cannot remember its dimensions. He does remember that the dimensions are prime numbers.

Work with a partner to find the dimensions of the garage floor.

1. Explain how you know that 221 is not the product of two 1-digit numbers.

2. Explain how you could decide if 221 has a factor greater than 20 other than itself.

3. Use graph paper. Cut out several 10 × 10 squares, some 1 × 10 rectangles, and some 1 × 1 squares. Use these pieces to make a rectangle representing the garage floor. What are its dimensions?

4. Repeat this process to find a pair of prime numbers with each product.
   a. 133   **b.** 161   **c.** 209

$\leftarrow x + 2 \rightarrow$

$x + 8$

THINK AND DISCUSS

Using Tiles

Some quadratic trinomials are the product of two **binomial factors.**

quadratic trinomial	binomial factors
$x^2 + 10x + 16$ $\longrightarrow$	$(x + 2)(x + 8)$

The diagram at the left shows how $x^2 + 10x + 16$ can be displayed as a rectangle with sides of length $x + 2$ and $x + 8$.

You can use tiles to factor quadratic trinomials.

Example 1

Use tiles to factor $x^2 + 7x + 12$.

Choose one x^2-tile, seven x-tiles and twelve 1-tiles. Use the strategy *Guess and Test* to form a rectangle using all the tiles.

Write the correct factors as a product.

$x^2 + 7x + 12 = (x + 3)(x + 4)$

5. Try This Use tiles to factor these trinomials. **Verify** your answers using FOIL.

    a. $x^2 + 6x + 8$ **b.** $x^2 + 11x + 10$

Testing Possible Factors

To factor trinomials of the form $x^2 + bx + c$, you can use FOIL with the strategy *Guess and Test*.

The sum of the numbers you use here must equal *b*.

$$x^2 + bx + c = (x + \boxed{})(x + \boxed{})$$

The product of the numbers you use here must equal *c*.

Example 2

Factor $x^2 - 9x + 20$.

Choose numbers that are factors of 20. Look for a pair with sum -9.

Factors of 20	Sum of Factors
-1 and -20	$-1 + (-20) = -21$
-2 and -10	$-2 + (-10) = -12$
-4 and -5	$-4 + (-5) = -9$

List only negative factors because you are looking for a sum of -9. Two positive numbers cannot have a negative sum.

The numbers -4 and -5 have a product of 20 and a sum of -9.
The correct factors are $(x - 4)$ and $(x - 5)$.
So, $x^2 - 9x + 20 = (x - 4)(x - 5)$.

1 Which polynomial *cannot* be factored into two binomials?
(1) $x^2 + 5x - 3$
(2) $2x^2 - 7x + 6$
(3) $x^2 - 9x - 10$
(4) $3x^2 + 4x + 1$

2 Write a formula in factored form for the volume of the cylinder after the square hole has been drilled.

Check $x^2 - 9x + 20 \stackrel{?}{=} (x - 4)(x - 5)$ ← Find the product of the right side.
$x^2 - 9x + 20 \stackrel{?}{=} x^2 - 5x - 4x + 20$
$x^2 - 9x + 20 = x^2 - 9x + 20$ ✔

6. *Critical Thinking* Is $x^2 - 6x - 16 = (x - 8)(x + 2)$ factored correctly? Explain.

Example 3

Factor $x^2 - 2x - 8$.

Choose numbers that are factors of -8. Look for a pair with sum -2.

Factors of -8	Sum of Factors
-1 and 8	$-1 + 8 = 7$
-8 and 1	$-8 + 1 = -7$
-2 and 4	$-2 + 4 = 2$
-4 and 2	$-4 + 2 = -2$

← -4 and 2 have a sum of -2.

$x^2 - 2x - 8 = (x - 4)(x + 2)$

7. Try This Factor $x^2 - 4x - 12$.

Factoring $ax^2 + bx + c$

To factor quadratic trinomials where $a \neq 1$, list factors of a and c. Use these factors to write binomials. Test for the correct value for b.

Example 4

Factor $3x^2 - 7x - 6$.

List factors of 3: 1 and 3; -1 and -3.

List factors of -6: 1 and -6; -1 and 6; 2 and -3; -2 and 3.

Use the factors to write binomials. Look for -7 as the middle term.

$(\boxed{1}x + \boxed{1})(\boxed{3}x + \boxed{-6})$ $-6x + 3x = -3x$
$(\boxed{1}x + \boxed{-6})(\boxed{3}x + \boxed{1})$ $1x - 18x = -17x$
$(\boxed{1}x + \boxed{-1})(\boxed{3}x + \boxed{6})$ $6x - 3x = 3x$
$(\boxed{1}x + \boxed{6})(\boxed{3}x + \boxed{-1})$ $-1x + 18x = 17x$
$(\boxed{1}x + \boxed{2})(\boxed{3}x + \boxed{-3})$ $-3x + 6x = 3x$
$(\boxed{1}x + \boxed{-3})(\boxed{3}x + \boxed{2})$ $2x - 9x = -7x$ Correct!

$3x^2 - 7x - 6 = (x - 3)(3x + 2)$.

8. Try This Factor $2x^2 - 3x - 5$.

Write the length and width of each rectangle as a binomial. Then write an expression for the area of each rectangle.

1.

2.

3.

Can you form a rectangle using all the pieces in each set? Explain.

4. one x^2-tile, two x-tiles, and one 1-tile

5. one x^2-tile, five x-tiles, and eight 1-tiles

6. one x^2-tile, six x-tiles, and six 1-tiles

7. one x^2-tile, nine x-tiles, and eight 1-tiles

Use tiles or make drawings to represent each expression as a rectangle. Then write the area as the product of two binomials.

8. $x^2 + 4x + 3$ **9.** $x^2 - 3x + 2$ **10.** $x^2 + 3x - 4$ **11.** $x^2 - 2x - 8$

12. $x^2 + 5x + 6$ **13.** $x^2 - 3x - 4$ **14.** $x^2 + x - 6$ **15.** $x^2 - 2x + 1$

Complete.

16. $x^2 - 6x - 7 = (x + 1)(x + \blacksquare)$ **17.** $k^2 - 4k - 12 = (k - 6)(k + \blacksquare)$

18. $t^2 + 7t + 10 = (t + 2)(t + \blacksquare)$ **19.** $c^2 + c - 2 = (c + 2)(c + \blacksquare)$

20. $y^2 - 13y + 36 = (y - 4)(y + \blacksquare)$ **21.** $x^2 + 3x - 18 = (x + 6)(x + \blacksquare)$

22. Writing Suppose you can factor $x^2 + bx + c$ into the product of two binomials.
  a. Explain what you know about the factors if $c > 0$.
  b. Explain what you know about the factors if $c < 0$.

23. Community Gardening The diagram at the right shows 72 plots in a community garden.
  a. Write a quadratic expression that represents the area of the garden.
  b. Write the factors of the expression you wrote in part (a).

Factor each quadratic trinomial.

24. $x^2 + 6x + 8$ **25.** $a^2 - 5a + 6$ **26.** $d^2 - 7d + 12$ **27.** $k^2 + 9k + 8$

28. $y^2 - 4y - 45$ **29.** $r^2 - 10r - 11$ **30.** $c^2 + 2c + 1$ **31.** $x^2 + 2x - 15$

32. $t^2 + 7t - 18$ **33.** $x^2 + 12x + 35$ **34.** $y^2 - 10y + 16$ **35.** $a^2 - 9a + 14$

36. $r^2 + 6r - 16$ **37.** $y^2 + 13y - 48$ **38.** $x^2 + 10x + 25$ **39.** $w^2 - 2w - 24$

Open-ended Find three different values to complete each expression so that it can be factored into the product of two binomials. Show each factorization.

40. $x^2 - 3x - $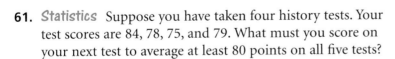

41. $x^2 + x - $ ■

42. $x^2 + $ ■$x + 12$

Factor each expression.

43. $2x^2 - 15x + 7$

44. $5x^2 - 2x - 7$

45. $2x^2 - x - 3$

46. $8x^2 - 14x + 3$

47. $2x^2 - 11x - 21$

48. $3x^2 + 13x - 10$

49. $2x^2 - 7x + 3$

50. $6t^2 + 13t - 5$

51. $7x^2 - 20x - 3$

52. $2x^2 + x - 3$

53. $3x^2 + 17x + 20$

54. $2x^2 + 3x - 20$

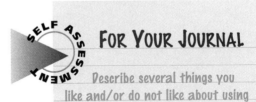

▽ **Chapter Project**   **Find Out by Calculating**

With aerial photography, you can study a forest of ponderosa pines without ever walking through it.

To find the diameter in inches of trees in the forest, use this expression:

$3.76 + (1.35 \times 10^{-2})hv - (2.45 \times 10^{-6})hv^2 + (2.44 \times 10^{-10})hv^3$

The variable h is the height of the tree in feet, and v is the crown diameter visible in feet (from a photograph).

• Determine the diameter of 100-ft trees that have a visible crown diameter of 20 ft.

■ **Exercises**   **M I X E D   R E V I E W**

Find the distance between the given points.

55. $(3, 5)$; $(6, 1)$

56. $(-2, 8)$; $(4, -1)$

57. $(-7, -2)$; $(-3, -9)$

58. $(8, 0)$; $(-3, -4)$

Graph each inequality.

59. $y \leq 4x - 9$

60. $y > x^2 + 3x + 1$

61. Statistics Suppose you have taken four history tests. Your test scores are 84, 78, 75, and 79. What must you score on your next test to average at least 80 points on all five tests?

SELF ASSESSMENT

FOR YOUR JOURNAL

Describe several things you like and/or do not like about using tiles.

Getting Ready for Lesson 10-5

Find each product.

62. $(x + 9)^2$

63. $(2x + 3)^2$

64. $(5x - 4)^2$

65. $(x + 8)(x - 8)$

66. $(x + 4)(x - 4)$

67. $(2x + 7)(2x - 7)$

68. $(3x + 5)(3x - 5)$

69. $(2x - 1)^2$

What You'll Learn

- Factoring the difference of two squares
- Factoring perfect square trinomials

...And Why

To solve problems related to geometry and construction

What You'll Need

- tiles
- graphing calculator

10-5 **F**actoring Special Cases

WORK TOGETHER

Work with a partner. Answer each question for Groups A, B, and C.

Group A	Group B	Group C
$(x + 7)(x - 7)$	$(x + 7)(x + 7)$	$(x - 7)(x - 7)$
$(k + 3)(k - 3)$	$(k + 3)(k + 3)$	$(k - 3)(k - 3)$
$(w + 5)(w - 5)$	$(w + 5)(w + 5)$	$(w - 5)(w - 5)$
$(3x + 1)(3x - 1)$	$(3x + 1)(3x + 1)$	$(3x - 1)(3x - 1)$

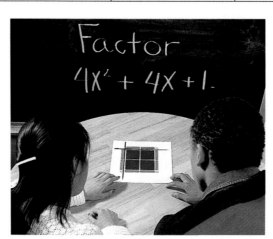

1. Describe the pattern in each of the pairs of factors.

2. Find each product.

3. How can you use mental math to quickly multiply binomials like those in each group? Explain using examples.

THINK AND DISCUSS

Factoring a Difference of Two Squares

As you saw in the Work Together activity, sometimes when you multiply two binomials, the *middle* term in the product is 0.

4. What polynomial is modeled by each set of tiles ? What are the factors of each polynomial?

a.

b.

When you factor a difference of two squares, the result is two binomial factors that are the same except for the signs between the terms.

Difference of Two Squares
....

For all real numbers a and b, $a^2 - b^2 = (a + b)(a - b)$.

Example: $x^2 - 16 = (x + 4)(x - 4)$

Example 1 ....

Factor $x^2 - 64$.

$x^2 - 64 = x^2 - 8^2$ ← Rewrite 64 as 8^2.

$= (x + 8)(x - 8)$ ← Factor.

Check   Use FOIL to multiply.

$(x + 8)(x - 8)$

$x^2 - 8x + 8x - 64$

$x^2 - 64$ ✔

5. Mental Math   Factor $x^2 - 36$.

Example 2 ....

Factor $4x^2 - 121$.

$4x^2 - 121 = 4x^2 - 11^2$ ← Rewrite 121 as 11^2.

$= (2x)^2 - (11)^2$ ← Rewrite $4x^2$ as $(2x)^2$.

$= (2x + 11)(2x - 11)$ ← Factor.

6. Critical Thinking   Suppose a classmate factored $4x^2 - 121$ and got $(4x + 11)(4x - 11)$. What mistake did this classmate make?

7. Mental Math   Factor $9x^2 - 25$.

Factoring a Perfect Square Trinomial

In the Work Together activity you multiplied a binomial by itself. This is called squaring a binomial. The result is a **perfect square trinomial.** When you factor a perfect square trinomial, the two binomial factors are the same.

Perfect Square Trinomial
....

For all real numbers a and b:

$a^2 + 2ab + b^2 = (a + b)(a + b) = (a + b)^2$

$a^2 - 2ab + b^2 = (a - b)(a - b) = (a - b)^2$

Examples: $x^2 + 10x + 25 = (x + 5)(x + 5) = (x + 5)^2$

$x^2 - 10x + 25 = (x - 5)(x - 5) = (x - 5)^2$

Example 3

Factor $x^2 - 8x + 16$.

$$x^2 - 8x + 16 = x^2 - 8x + 4^2 \quad \longleftarrow \text{Rewrite 16 as } 4^2.$$

$$= x^2 - 2(x)(4) + 4^2 \quad \longleftarrow \begin{array}{l}\text{Does the middle term equal} \\ 2ab? \ 8x = 2(x)(4) \ \checkmark\end{array}$$

$$= (x - 4)^2 \quad \longleftarrow \text{Factor as a squared binomial.}$$

So, $x^2 - 8x + 16 = (x - 4)^2$.

8. a. *Graphing Calculator* Graph $y = x^2 - 8x + 16$.
   b. Find the x-intercept(s) of the graph.
   c. *Critical Thinking* What information about the factorization does the x-intercept(s) give you?

9. The expression $(3x + 4)^2$ equals $9x^2 + \blacksquare + 16$. What is the middle term?

Example 4

Factor $9x^2 + 12x + 4$

$$9x^2 + 12x + 4$$

$$= (3x)^2 + 12x + 2^2 \quad \longleftarrow \text{Rewrite } 9x^2 \text{ as } (3x)^2 \text{ and 4 as } 2^2.$$

$$= (3x)^2 + 2(3x)(2) + 2^2 \quad \longleftarrow \begin{array}{l}\text{Does the middle term equal} \\ 2ab? \ 12x = 2(3x)(2) \checkmark\end{array}$$

$$= (3x+ 2)^2 \quad \longleftarrow \text{Factor as a square binomial.}$$

So, $9x^2 + 12x + 4 = (3x+ 2)^2$

PROBLEM SOLVING

Look Back Multiply the factors to check the factorization.

10. Try This Factor each trinomial.
   a. $x^2 - 14x + 49$ **b.** $x^2 + 18x + 81$ **c.** $4x^2 - 12x + 9$

11. a. *Open-ended* Write a quadratic expression of your own that is a perfect square trinomial.
   b. Explain how you know your trinomial is a perfect square trinomial.

Sometimes a quadratic expression looks like it can't be factored when actually it can. Take out any common factors. Then see if you can factor further.

Example 5

Factor $10x^2 - 40$.

$$10x^2 - 40 = 10(x^2 - 4) \quad \longleftarrow \text{Factor out the GCF: 10.}$$

$$= 10(x - 2)(x+ 2) \quad \longleftarrow \text{Factor } (x^2 - 4).$$

So, $10x^2 - 40 = 10(x - 2)(x+ 2)$.

12. Try This Factor $8x^2 - 50$.

488 **Chapter 10** Polynomials

What polynomial is modeled by each set of tiles and what are the factors of each polynomial?

1.

2.

3.

4. a. *Open-ended* Use a minimum of three x^2-tiles, one x-tile, and one 1-tile. Draw the model of the difference of two squares and a model of a perfect square trinomial.

    b. Represent each model from part (a) as a polynomial in both factored and unfactored form.

Factor each expression.

5. $x^2 + 2x + 1$

6. $t^2 - 144$

7. $x^2 - 18x + 81$

8. $15t^2 - 15$

9. $3x^2 - 6x + 3$

10. $9w^2 - 16$

11. $6x^2 - 150$

12. $k^2 - 6k + 9$

13. $x^2 - 49$

14. $a^2 + 12a + 36$

15. $4x^2 - 4x + 1$

16. $16n^2 - 56n + 49$

17. $9x^2 + 6x + 1$

18. $2g^2 + 24g + 72$

19. $x^2 - 400$

20. $2x^3 - 18x$

21. *Writing* **Summarize** the procedure for factoring a perfect square trinomial. Give at least two examples.

22. *Math in the Media* Use the brochure below.
    a. Show by factoring that this inequality is true.
      $(\pi d - \sqrt{15w})(\pi d + \sqrt{15w}) \geq 0$

    b. Show that $d \geq \dfrac{\sqrt{15w}}{\pi}$.

    c. *Calculator* Is a cable 3 in. in diameter sufficient to lift an object weighing 5 tons? **Justify** your response.

Load Requirements For Crane Operators

The weight of a load is limited by the diameter of the fiber cable. As the load gets heavier, the diameter of the cable must increase. To raise a load weighing w tons, a fiber cable having diameter d in inches must satisfy the inequality $(\pi d)^2 - (\sqrt{15w})^2 \geq 0$.

23. a. Geometry Write two expressions in terms of n and m for the area of the solid region at the right. One expression should be in factored form.

   b. Use either form of your answer to part (a). Find the area of the solid region if $n = 10$ in. and $m = 3$ in.

24. Standardized Test Prep Which of the following expressions is the factorization of $100x^2 + 220x + 121$?

   A. $(10x + 1)(10x - 1)$ **B.** $(10x - 11)(10x - 11)$
   C. $(10x + 11)(10x + 11)$ **D.** $(10x - 10)(11x + 11)$

Mental Math **Find each product using the difference of two squares.**

Sample: $(17)(23) = (20 - 3)(20 + 3)$ ⟵ Write the factors in the form $(a - b)(a + b)$.

$\qquad\qquad\quad = 400 - 9$ ⟵ Multiply.

$\qquad\qquad\quad = 391$ ⟵ Subtract.

25. $(27)(33)$ **26.** $(19)(21)$ **27.** $(43)(37)$ **28.** $(29)(31)$

29. $(16)(24)$ **30.** $(51)(49)$ **31.** $(18)(22)$ **32.** $(98)(102)$

Factor each expression using rational numbers in your factors.

33. $\frac{1}{4}m^2 - \frac{1}{9}$ **34.** $\frac{1}{4}p^2 - 2p + 4$ **35.** $\frac{1}{9}n^2 - \frac{1}{25}$ **36.** $\frac{1}{25}k^2 + \frac{6}{5}k + 9$

37. a. Critical Thinking The expression $(t - 3)^2 - 16$ is a difference of two squares. Using the expression $a^2 - b^2$, identify a and b.

   b. Factor $(t - 3)^2 - 16$.

38. a. Graphing Calculator Graph $y = 4x^2 - 12x + 9$.

   b. Use the x-intercept(s) of the graph to write $4x^2 - 12x + 9$ in factored form.

Exercises   MIXED REVIEW

Simplify each expression.

39. $\sqrt{25} + \sqrt{72}$ **40.** $8^2 - (4 + \sqrt{8})$ **41.** $\sqrt{5^2 + 4^2}$ **42.** $\sqrt{100} - \sqrt{4}$

43. Sales Suppose you buy a watch for $35 that regularly sells for $50. Find the percent of decrease in the price of the watch.

Getting Ready for Lesson 10-6

Solve each equation.

44. $2x + 3 = 0$ **45.** $-3x - 4 = 0$

46. $8x - 9 = 0$ **47.** $-3x + 5 = 0$

10-6 Solving Equations by Factoring

What You'll Learn

- Solving quadratic equations by factoring

...And Why

To find the dimensions of a box that can be manufactured from a given amount of material

What You'll Need

- graphing calculator

THINK AND DISCUSS

When you solve a quadratic equation by factoring, you use the zero-product property.

Zero-Product Property

For all real numbers a and b, if $ab = 0$, then $a = 0$ or $b = 0$.

Example: If $(x + 3)(x + 2) = 0$, then $x + 3 = 0$ or $x + 2 = 0$.

Example 1

Solve $(x + 5)(x + 6) = 0$.

$(x + 5)(x + 6) = 0$
$x + 5 = 0$ or $x + 6 = 0$ ⟵ Use the zero-product property.
$x = -5$ or $x = -6$ ⟵ Solve for x.

The solutions are -5 and -6.

PROBLEM SOLVING

Look Back How could you solve $(x + 5)(x + 6) = 0$ by graphing?

Check Substitute -5 for x.
$(-5 + 5)(-5 + 6) \stackrel{?}{=} 0$
$(0)(1) = 0$ ✔

Substitute -6 for x.
$(-6 + 5)(-6 + 6) \stackrel{?}{=} 0$
$(-1)(0) = 0$ ✔

1. **Try This** Solve each equation.
   a. $(x + 7)(x - 4) = 0$
   b. $(3y - 5)(y - 2) = 0$

You can sometimes solve a quadratic equation by factoring. Write the equation in standard form. Factor the quadratic expression. Then use the zero-product property.

Example 2

Solve $2x^2 - 5x = 88$ by factoring.

$2x^2 - 5x = 88$
$2x^2 - 5x - 88 = 0$ ⟵ Subtract 88 from each side.
$(2x + 11)(x - 8) = 0$ ⟵ Factor $2x^2 - 5x - 88$.

$2x + 11 = 0$ or $x - 8 = 0$ ⟵ Use the zero-product property.
$x = -5.5$ or $x = 8$ ⟵ Solve for x.

The solutions are -5.5 and 8.

2. a. *Graphing Calculator* Graph $y = 2x^2 - 5x - 88$.
  b. In the CALC feature, use *ROOT* to find the x-intercepts of the graph.
  c. Explain how your answers to part (b) are related to the solutions found in Example 2.

3. a. Solve $x^2 - 12x + 36 = 0$ by factoring.
  b. *Critical Thinking* Why does the equation in part (a) have only one solution?

You can solve some real-world problems by factoring and using the zero-product property.

waste material

Example 3 **Relating to the Real World**

Manufacturing The diagram shows a pattern for an open-top box. The total area of the sheet of material used to manufacture the box is 144 in.^{2}. The height of the box is 1 in. Therefore 1 in. × 1 in. squares are cut from each corner. Find the dimensions of the box.

Define   width $= x + 1 + 1 = x + 2$
        length $= x + 1 + 1 = x + 2$

Relate   length × width = area

Write $(x + 2)(x + 2) = 144$

$(x + 2)(x + 2) = 144$
$x^2 + 4x + 4 = 144$ ⟵ Find the product $(x + 2)(x + 2)$.
$x^2 + 4x - 140 = 0$ ⟵ Subtract 144 from each side.
$(x + 14)(x - 10) = 0$ ⟵ Factor $x^2 + 4x - 140$.
$x + 14 = 0$ or $x - 10 = 0$ ⟵ Use the zero-product property.
$x = -14$ or $x = 10$

Since the length must be positive, the solution is 10. The dimensions of the box are 10 in. × 10 in. × 1 in.

4. Suppose that a box with a square base has height 2 in. It is cut from a square sheet of material with area 121 in.^{2}. Find the dimensions of the box.

Mental Math **Use mental math to solve each equation.**

1. $(x - 3)(x - 7) = 0$

2. $(x + 4)(2x - 9) = 0$

3. $(7x + 2)(5x + 4) = 0$

Solve each equation by factoring.

4. $b^2 + 3b - 4 = 0$

5. $m^2 - 5m - 14 = 0$

6. $w^2 - 8w = 0$

7. $x^2 - 16x + 55 = 0$

8. $x^2 - 3x - 10 = 0$

9. $n^2 + n - 12 = 0$

10. $2x^2 - 7x + 5 = 0$

11. $x^2 - 10x = 0$

12. $4x^2 - 25 = 0$

13. $5q^2 + 18q = 8$

14. $z^2 - 5z = -6$

15. $10 = x^2 - 9x$

16. Writing **Summarize** the procedure for solving a quadratic equation by factoring. Include an example.

17. Geometry The sides of a square are each increased by 3 cm. The area of the new square is 64 cm². Find the length of a side of the original square.

Simplify each equation and write it in standard form. Then solve each equation.

18. $3a^2 + 4a = 2a^2 - 2a - 9$

19. $4x^2 + 20 = 10x + 3x^2 - 4$

20. $6y^2 + 12y + 13 = 2y^2 + 4$

21. $2q^2 + 22q = -60$

22. $3t^2 + 8t = t^2 - 3t - 12$

23. $4 = -5n + 6n^2$

24. $3x^2 = 9x + 30$

25. $20p^2 - 74 = 6$

26. $2x^2 + 5x^2 = 3x$

27. $7n^2 = 3n^2 + 100$

28. $12x^2 + 8x = -4x^2 + 8x$

29. $9c^2 = 36$

30. Standardized Test Prep If $a^2 + b^2 = 9$ and $ab = 6$, what does $(a + b)^2$ equal?

   A. 3   **B.** 15   **C.** 21   **D.** 30   **E.** 36

31. Geometry A rectangular box has volume 280 in.³. Its dimensions are 4 in. × $(x + 2)$ in. × $(x + 5)$ in. Find x. Use the formula $V = lwh$.

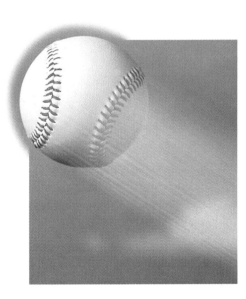

32. Baseball Suppose you throw a baseball into the air from a starting height s. You toss the ball with an upward starting velocity of v ft/s. You can use the equation $h = -16t^2 + vt + s$ to find the ball's height h in feet t seconds after it is thrown.

   a. Suppose you toss a baseball directly upward with an starting velocity of 46 ft/s from a starting height of 6 ft. When will the ball hit the ground?

   b. Graphing Calculator Graph the related function for the equation you wrote in part (a). Use your graph to estimate how high the ball is tossed.

33. Sailing The height of a right-triangular sail on a boat is 2 ft greater than twice the base of the sail. Suppose the area of the sail is 110 ft².
   a. Find the dimensions of the sail.
   b. Find the approximate length of the hypotenuse of the sail. (*Hint:* Use the Pythagorean theorem $(c^2 = a^2 + b^2)$.)

34. Construction You are building a rectangular wading pool. You want the area of the bottom to be 90 ft². You want the length of the pool to be 3 ft longer than twice its width. What will be the dimensions of the pool?

Solve each cubic equation.

Sample: $x^3 + 7x^2 + 12x = 0$ ⟵ The highest degree of a term is three. This is a cubic equation.

$$x^3 + 7x^2 + 12x = 0$$
$$x(x^2 + 7x + 12) = 0$$ ⟵ Factor out the GCF.
$$x(x + 3)(x + 4) = 0$$ ⟵ Factor the quadratic trinomial.
$$x = 0, \ x + 3 = 0, \ \text{or} \ x + 4 = 0$$ ⟵ Use the zero-product property.
$$x = 0, \quad x = -3, \quad \text{or} \quad x = -4$$ ⟵ Solve for x.

The solutions are 0, −3, and −4.

35. $x^3 - 10x^2 + 24x = 0$ **36.** $x^3 - 5x^2 + 4x = 0$ **37.** $3x^3 - 9x^2 = 0$

38. $x^3 + 3x^2 - 70x = 0$ **39.** $3x^3 - 30x^2 + 27x = 0$ **40.** $2x^3 = -2x^2 + 40x$

In each diagram, you are given a right triangle that has special characteristics. Use the Pythagorean theorem $(c^2 = a^2 + b^2)$ to find possible lengths of the sides of each right triangle.

41. three consecutive integers

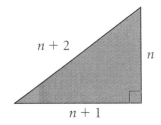

42. three consecutive even integers

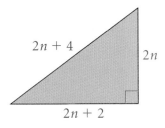

43. Critical Thinking A number plus its square equals zero. For which two numbers is this true?

44. Open-ended In the diagram at the right, x is a positive integer and a and b are integers. List several possible values for x, a, and b so that the large rectangle will have an area of 56 square units.

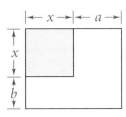

45. Manufacturing An open box with height 1 in. has a length that is 2 in. greater than its width. The box was made with minimum waste from an 80 in.² rectangular sheet of material. What were the dimensions of the sheet of material? (*Hint:* Draw a diagram.)

Chapter Project

Find Out by Graphing ....

You can use the function $b = -0.01t^2 + 0.8t$ to find the number of bushels b of walnuts produced on an acre of land. The variable t represents the number of trees per acre.

- Graph this function. What number of trees per acre gives the greatest yield?

- How many walnut trees would you advise a farmer to plant on 5 acres of land? Explain your reasoning.

Exercises   MIXED REVIEW

Simplify.

46. $(x^2)^4$ **47.** $(3y^3)^{-1}$ **48.** $4(n^3)^0$ **49.** $(x^3)(x^{-3})$

Solve each equation.

50. $\sqrt{a} = 5$ **51.** $\sqrt{3a} = 5$ **52.** $3\sqrt{a} = \sqrt{a} + 18$

FOR YOUR JOURNAL

Suppose you are to solve $2x^2 - 11x + 5 = 0$. Would you use the quadratic formula or factoring? Explain why.

53. Out of 100 students, 30 students play football, 25 students play baseball, and 15 play both sports. How many play neither sport?

Getting Ready for Lesson 10-7

Use the quadratic formula to solve each equation. If there is no real solution, write *no real solution*.

54. $x^2 + x - 12 = 0$ **55.** $10x^2 + 13x - 3 = 0$ **56.** $4x^2 + 4x + 3 = 0$

Exercises   CHECKPOINT

Factor.

1. $x^2 - 5x + 6$ **2.** $n^2 - 6n + 9$ **3.** $g^2 - 8g - 20$ **4.** $9x^2 - 49$

Mental Math Use mental math to solve each equation.

5. $(a + 3)(3a - 2) = 0$ **6.** $(m - 6)(2m + 3) = 0$ **7.** $(x + 7)(x + 2) = 0$

Solve each equation.

8. $25x^2 - 100 = 0$ **9.** $9x^2 + 24x = -16$ **10.** $10x^2 - 11x - 6 = 0$

11. Standardized Test Prep If $x^2 + 4x = -4$, what is the value of x^3?
   A. -8 **B.** 0 **C.** 8 **D.** 16
   E. It cannot be determined from the information given.

Skills Review

Completing the Square

After Lesson 10-6

In Chapter 7, you solved quadratic equations by taking the square root of each side of an equation. In Lesson 10-5 you factored perfect square trinomials. Completing the square allows you to combine these skills to solve any quadratic equation that has real solutions.

What is the value of c needed to create a perfect square trinomial?

1. $y^2 + 4y + c$ **2.** $a^2 - 10a + c$ **3.** $n^2 + 14n + c$ **4.** $x^2 - 20x + c$

5. Explain the steps you used to find c in Questions 1–4.

To solve an equation using completing the square, you create a perfect square trinomial on one side of the equation so that you can take the square root of both sides.

Example

Solve by completing the square: $x^2 + 6x + 4 = 0$.

$$x^2 + 6x + 4 = 0$$
$$x^2 + 6x = -4 \quad\longleftarrow \text{Subtract 4 from each side.}$$
$$x^2 + 6x + 3^2 = -4 + 3^2 \quad\longleftarrow \text{Find half of 6. Square it, and add the result to both sides.}$$
$$x^2 + 6x + 9 = 5 \quad\longleftarrow \text{Simplify.}$$
$$(x + 3)^2 = 5 \quad\longleftarrow \text{Write the left side in factored form.}$$
$$\sqrt{(x + 3)^2} = \pm\sqrt{5} \quad\longleftarrow \text{Take the square root of each side.}$$
$$x + 3 = \pm\sqrt{5} \quad\longleftarrow \text{Simplify.}$$
$$x = -3 + \sqrt{5} \text{ or } x = -3 - \sqrt{5} \quad\longleftarrow \text{Solve for } x.$$

The solutions are $-3 \pm \sqrt{5}$.

Solve each equation by completing the square.

6. $x^2 - 2x - 3 = 0$ **7.** $x^2 + 8x + 12 = 0$ **8.** $x^2 + 2x = 8$ **9.** $x^2 + 6x = 16$

10. $x^2 + 10x = 16$ **11.** $x^2 + 4x = 12$ **12.** $x^2 - 4x = 3$ **13.** $x^2 - 4x - 45 = 0$

14. $x^2 - 12x = 4$ **15.** $x^2 + 10x = 10$ **16.** $x^2 - 6x = 10$ **17.** $x^2 + 8x + 3 = 0$

18. Writing Solve one of the equations in Exercises 6–17 using the quadratic formula. Which method do you prefer, completing the square or the quadratic formula? Why?

What You'll Learn

• Choosing the best way to solve a quadratic equation

...And Why

To choose efficient ways to solve construction problems

What You'll Need

• graphing calculator

10-7 Choosing an Appropriate Method for Solving

THINK AND DISCUSS

In this chapter and in Chapter 7, you learned many methods for solving quadratic equations. You can always use the quadratic formula to solve a quadratic equation, but sometimes another method may be easier. Other methods include graphing and factoring.

Methods for Solving Quadratic Equations

Example: $2x^2 - 4x - 6 = 0$

Graphing	Quadratic Formula	Factoring

Graphing

Graph the related function.

$y = 2x^2 - 4x - 6$

The x-intercepts are -1 and 3.

Quadratic Formula

If $ax^2 + bx + c = 0$ and $a \neq 0$,

$x = \dfrac{-b \pm \sqrt{b^2 - 4ac}}{2a}$.

$x = \dfrac{-(-4) \pm \sqrt{(-4)^2 - (4)(2)(-6)}}{2(2)}$

$= \dfrac{4 \pm \sqrt{64}}{4}$

$= \dfrac{12}{4}$ or $\dfrac{-4}{4}$

$= 3$ or -1

Factoring

Factor the equation. Use the zero-product property.

$2x^2 - 4x - 6 = 0$
$(2x - 6)(x + 1) = 0$
$2x - 6 = 0$ or $x + 1 = 0$
$2x = 6$
$x = 3$ or $\quad x = -1$

When you have an equation to solve, first write it in standard form. Then decide which method to use.

Method	When to Use
Graphing	Use if you have a graphing calculator handy.
Square Roots	Use if the equation has only an x^2 term and a constant term.
Factoring	Use if you can factor the equation easily.
Quadratic Formula	Use if you cannot factor the equation or if you are using a scientific calculator.

1. *Open-ended* Which method(s) would you choose to solve each equation? **Justify** your reasoning.
  a. $2x^2 - 6 = 0$
  b. $9x^2 + 24x + 16 = 0$
  c. $25x^2 - 36 = 0$
  d. $6x^2 + 5x - 6 = 0$
  e. $2x^2 + 7x - 15 = 0$
  f. $16t^2 - 96t + 135 = 0$

4 ft

←☐

←—w—→

2w

Example 1   Relating to the Real World

City Parks A fountain has dimensions w and $2w$. The concrete walkway around it is 4 ft wide. Together, the fountain and walkway cover 1500 ft^2 of land. Find the dimensions of the fountain.

Define $w =$ width of fountain $2w =$ length of fountain
$w + 2(4) = w + 8 =$ width of fountain and walkway
$2w + 2(4) = 2w + 8 =$ length of fountain and walkway

Relate   width of   times   length of   =   area of
fountain and   fountain and   fountain and
walkway   walkway   walkway

Write $(w + 8)$ · $(2w + 8)$ =   1500

$$(w + 8)(2w + 8) = 1500$$
$$2w^2 + 24w + 64 = 1500 \quad \longleftarrow \text{Expand the product.}$$
$$2w^2 + 24w - 1436 = 0 \quad \longleftarrow \text{Write in standard form.}$$
$$w = \frac{-24 \pm \sqrt{24^2 - 4(2)(-1436)}}{2(2)} \quad \longleftarrow \text{Use the quadratic formula.}$$
$$w = \frac{-24 + 109.8}{4} \quad \longleftarrow \text{Take the positive square root.}$$
$$w \approx 21.5 \text{ and } 2w \approx 43$$

The fountain is about 21.5 ft wide and about 43 ft long.

2. **Critical Thinking** Why would using the negative square root have led to an unreasonable solution of Example 1?

3. Which of the methods for solving quadratic equations would *not* be appropriate for solving Example 1? Explain.

Example 2

Solve $7x^2 - 175 = 0$.

Because this equation has only an x^2 term and a constant, try taking the square root of both sides or factoring a difference of two squares.

QUICK REVIEW

Zero-Product Property

For all real numbers a and b, if $ab = 0$, then $a = 0$ or $b = 0$.

Method 1 Square roots

$7x^2 - 175 = 0$
$7x^2 = 175$
$x^2 = 25$
$x = \pm 5$
$x = 5 \text{ or } x = -5$

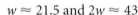 Both methods give the same solutions. →

Method 2 Factoring

$7x^2 - 175 = 0$
$7(x^2 - 25) = 0$
$7(x - 5)(x + 5) = 0$
$x - 5 = 0 \text{ or } x + 5 = 0$
$x = 5 \text{ or } x = -5$

4. Try This Solve each equation.

    a. $4x^2 = 256$ **b.** $y^2 - 12 = 0$ **c.** $3t^2 - 192 = 0$

Example 3

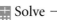 Solve $-x^2 - 6x - 14 = 0$.

The equation cannot be easily factored, so you can use a graphing calculator.

Graph the related quadratic function $y = -x^2 - 6x - 14$. The related function has no x-intercepts. Therefore, the equation $-x^2 - 6x - 14 = 0$ has no real solutions.

QUICK REVIEW

For a quadratic equation in standard form, the discriminant is $b^2 - 4ac$.

If $b^2 - 4ac < 0$, then there are no real number solutions.

5. Use the discriminant to show why the equation in Example 3 has no real number solutions.

6. Try This Solve each equation by graphing.

    a. $x^2 - 4x - 11 = 0$ **b.** $2x^2 + 7x - 15 = 0$

You can also use the discriminant to check if an equation can be factored. If the discriminant is a perfect square, then there are two rational solutions, and the equation can be factored.

Example 4

Solve $2x^2 - 7x - 4 = 0$.

First, find the discriminant to determine if the equation can be factored.

$$b^2 - 4ac = (-7)^2 - (4)(2)(-4)$$
$$= 49 - (-32)$$
$$= 81$$

Since the discriminant is a perfect square, you can factor.

    $(x - 4)(2x + 1) = 0$ ⟵ Use guess and test to factor.

$x - 4 = 0$ or $2x + 1 = 0$ ⟵ Use the zero-product property.

    $x = 4$ or $x = -0.5$ ⟵ Solve for x.

PROBLEM SOLVING

Look Back Check the solutions of Example 4.

7. *Critical Thinking* Explain why you should substitute your solutions in the original equation and not in the factored equation to check Example 4.

8. Try This Use the discriminant to check if each can be factored. If so, solve each by factoring. Otherwise, use the quadratic formula.

    a. $5x^2 + 14x - 3 = 0$ **b.** $3c^2 - 6c + 1 = 0$

    c. $2d^2 - d + 1 = 0$ **d.** $6y^2 - 5y - 4 = 0$

Calculator **Use the quadratic formula to solve each equation. Round solutions to the nearest hundredth.**

1. $13x^2 + 170x + 13 = 0$ **2.** $2.5w^2 + 10w - 2 = 0$ **3.** $12n^2 + n = 20$

4. $49x^2 - 64x = 25$ **5.** $6x^2 - 2x + 4 = 0$ **6.** $-x^2 - 5x + 9 = 0$

Solve each equation using square roots and then using factoring. Compare your solutions.

7. $9d^2 - 81 = 0$ **8.** $36e^2 = 121$ **9.** $2n^2 - 8 = 0$ **10.** $98 = 128x^2$

11. a. Find the x-intercepts of the parabola at the right.
   b. Use the graph to find the solutions of the equation $2x^2 - 5x - 3 = 0$.
   c. Verify your answer to part (b) by solving the equation using factoring.

12. Writing Explain how to solve $x^2 + 8 = 7x$ by graphing.

Graphing Calculator **Solve each quadratic equation by graphing the related quadratic function and finding the x-intercepts. If there are no real solutions, write *no real solutions*.**

13. $x^2 + 2x - 8 = 0$ **14.** $2x^2 + 3x = 6$ **15.** $x^2 - 2x + 5 = 0$

16. $8x^2 - 4x - 16 = 0$ **17.** $0.5x^2 + x = -2$ **18.** $x^2 = 2x$

Choose **Select a method to solve each quadratic equation. Explain why you chose each method. Then solve. If the equation has no real solutions, write *no real solutions*.**

19. $2k^2 = 16k - 32$ **20.** $4t^2 + 8t + 8 = 0$

21. $8n = 10n^2$ **22.** $-y^2 + y = -3$

23. $3k^2 - 9k - 27 = 0$ **24.** $36g^2 = 121$

25. $16k^2 - 56k + 49 = 0$ **26.** $1.5r^2 + 2r - 2.5 = 0$

27. $169 = 49b^2$ **28.** $5a^2 + 7a = 7a^2 + 5a - 2$

29. Standardized Test Prep Which quadratic equation has 2 and -7 as its solutions?
   A. $x^2 + 5x + 14 = 0$ **B.** $x^2 + 5x - 14 = 0$
   C. $x^2 - 5x + 14 = 0$ **D.** $x^2 - 5x - 14 = 0$

30. Show that the man in the cartoon is not a whiz at physics. Suppose he steps off the board. Use $0 = -16t^2 + 50$ to find the number of seconds before he hits the water. Use $v = -32t \cdot \frac{60}{88}$ to find his velocity in miles per hour when he hits the water.

CLOSE TO HOME by John McPherson

There are times when being a whiz at physics can be a definite drawback.

31. Surveying To find the distance across a marsh, a surveyor marked off a right triangle and measured two sides. Solve the equation $d^2 = 150^2 + 75^2$ to find this distance. Explain what solution method you used and why.

150 ft

d

75 ft

32. Geometry Find all values of x such that rectangle $ACDG$ at the right has an area of 70 square units *and* rectangle $ABEF$ has an area of 72 square units.

33. Open-ended Create an area situation and a question you can answer by solving a quadratic equation. Illustrate and solve your problem.

Exercises   MIXED REVIEW

Find the minimum and maximum of each equation.

34. $x \geq 0, y \geq 0$
$x \leq 5$
$y \leq 4$
$C = x + 2y$

35. $x + y \leq 10$
$x \geq 2$
$y \geq 3$
$C = 2x + 3y$

36. $2x + y \leq 7$
$x \geq 0$
$y \geq 0$
$C = 4x + y$

37. Describe the graph of $y = x^2 - 4x + 3$. Where is the axis of symmetry? What is the y-intercept? What are the roots?

38. Find the product of $3x$ and $4x^2 - 2x + 5$.

A Point in Time

1200   1400   1600   1800   2000

Chu Shih-Chieh

Very little is known about the life of Chu Shih-Chieh, the Chinese mathematician and teacher who had many pupils during the last two decades of the 1200s. In 1303 Chu wrote *Ssu-yüan-yü-chien*, "The Precious Mirror of the Four Elements." He described what is now known as Pascal's Triangle and how it could be used to solve polynomial equations. He also invented "the method of the celestial element" to write and solve polynomial equations and linear systems with up to four variables.

Finishing the Chapter Project

Trees are us.

Questions on pages 474, 479, 485, and 495 should help you to complete your project. Assemble all the parts of your project in a notebook. Add a summary telling what you have learned about the uses of trees.

Reflect and Revise

Ask a classmate to review your project notebook with you. Together, check that your graphs are clearly labeled and accurate. Check that you have used formulas correctly and that your calculations are accurate. Make any revisions necessary to improve your work.

Follow Up

Trees have many uses that you could investigate. You can do more research by contacting the United States Department of Agriculture Forest Service or a local, state, or national park. You can also get more information by using the Internet or one of the resources listed below.

For More Information

Hoadley, R. Bruce. *Identifying Wood: Accurate Results with Simple Tools.* Newtown, Connecticut: Taunton Press, 1990.

Miller, Cameron. *Woodlore.* New York: Ticknor & Fields Books for Young Readers, 1995.

The Encyclopedia of Wood. Alexandria, Virginia: Time-Life Books, 1993.

Warren, Jean. *Exploring Wood and the Forest.* Everett, Washington: Warren Publishing House, 1993.

Key Terms

binomial (p. 465)
binomial factors (p. 481)
degree of a polynomial (p. 465)
degree of a term (p. 465)
difference of two squares (p. 487)
monomial (p. 465)

perfect square trinomial
(p. 487)
polynomial (p. 465)
standard form (p. 465)
trinomial (p. 465)
zero-product property
(p. 491)

How am I doing?

- State three ideas from this chapter that you think are important. Explain your choices.
- Explain the different methods you can use to factor $2x^2 + 7x - 15$.

SELF ASSESSMENT

Adding and Subtracting Polynomials   10-1

The **degree of a term** with one variable is the exponent of the variable. A **polynomial** is one term or the sum or difference of two or more terms. The **degree of a polynomial** is the same as the degree of the term with the highest degree. A polynomial can be named by its degree or by the number of its terms. You can simplify polynomials by adding the coefficients of like terms.

Find each sum or difference.

1. $(3x^3 + 8x^2 + 2x + 9) - (-4x^3 + 5x - 3)$ **2.** $(3g^4 + 5g^2 + 5) + (5g^4 - 10g^2 + 11g)$

3. $(-4b^5 + 3b^3 - b + 10) + (3b^5 - b^3 + b - 4)$ **4.** $(2t^3 - 4t^2 + 9t - 7) - (t^3 + t^2 - 3t + 1)$

5. Open-ended Write a polynomial using the variable z. What is the degree of your polynomial?

Multiplying and Factoring   10-2

You can use the distributive property or tiles to multiply polynomials. You can factor a polynomial by finding the greatest common factor (GCF) of the terms of the polynomial, or by using tiles.

Find each product. Write it in standard form.

6. $8x(2 - 5x)$ **7.** $5g(3g + 7g^2 - 9)$ **8.** $8t^2(3t - 4 - 5t^2)$

9. $5m(3m + m^2)$ **10.** $-2w^2(4w - 10 + 3w^2)$ **11.** $b(10 + 5b - 3b^2)$

Find the greatest common factor (GCF) of the terms of each polynomial. Then factor the polynomial.

12. $9x^4 + 12x^3 + 6x$ **13.** $4t^5 - 12t^3 + 8t^2$ **14.** $40n^5 + 70n^4 - 30n^3$

Multiplying Polynomials

You can use tiles or the distributive property to multiply polynomials. You can use the FOIL method (First, Outer, Inner, Last) to multiply two binomials.

Find each product.

15. $(x + 3)(x + 5)$ 16. $(5x + 2)(3x - 7)$ 17. $(2x + 5)(3x - 2)$ 18. $(x - 1)(-x + 4)$

19. $(x + 2)(x^2 + x + 1)$ 20. $(4x - 1)(x - 5)$ 21. $(x - 4)(x^2 - 5x - 2)$ 22. $(3x + 4)(x + 2)$

23. **Geometry** A rectangle has dimensions $2x + 1$ and $x + 4$. Write an expression for the area of the rectangle as a product and as a polynomial in standard form.

Factoring Trinomials

Some quadratic trinomials are the product of two **binomial factors.** You can factor trinomials using tiles or by using FOIL with the strategy *Guess and Test.*

Factor each quadratic trinomial.

24. $x^2 + 3x + 2$ 25. $y^2 - 9y + 14$ 26. $x^2 - 2x - 15$ 27. $2w^2 - w - 3$

28. $-b^2 + 7b - 12$ 29. $2t^2 + 3t - 2$ 30. $x^2 + 5x - 6$ 31. $6x^2 + 10x + 4$

32. **Standardized Test Prep** What is $21x^2 - 22x - 8$ in factored form?
   A. $(7x + 2)(3x - 4)$ **B.** $(21x + 8)(x - 1)$ **C.** $(3x + 2)(7x - 4)$
   D. $(3x - 2)(7x + 4)$ **E.** $(x - 8)(21x + 1)$

Factoring Special Cases

When you factor a **difference of two squares,** the two binomial factors are the sum and difference of two terms.
$$a^2 - b^2 = (a + b)(a - b)$$

When you factor a **perfect square trinomial,** the two binomial factors are the same.
$$a^2 + 2ab + b^2 = (a + b)^2 \qquad a^2 - 2ab + b^2 = (a - b)^2$$

Factor each polynomial.

33. $q^2 + 2q + 1$ 34. $b^2 - 16$ 35. $x^2 - 4x + 4$ 36. $4t^2 - 121$

37. $4d^2 - 20d + 25$ 38. $9c^2 + 6c + 1$ 39. $9k^2 - 25$ 40. $x^2 + 6x + 9$

41. **Critical Thinking** Suppose you are using tiles to factor a quadratic trinomial. What do you know about the factors of the trinomial if the tiles form a square?

Solving Equations by Factoring

You can solve a quadratic equation by factoring and using the **zero-product property.** For all real numbers a and b, if $ab = 0$, then $a = 0$ or $b = 0$.

Simplify each equation if necessary. Then solve by factoring.

42. $x^2 + 7x + 12 = 0$

43. $5x^2 - 10x = 0$

44. $2x^2 - 9x = x^2 - 20$

45. $2x^2 + 5x = 3$

46. $3x^2 - 5x = -3x^2 + 6$

47. $x^2 - 5x + 4 = 0$

48. Gardening Alice is planting a garden. Its length is 3 feet less than twice its width. Its area is 170 ft^2. Find the dimensions of the garden.

Choosing an Appropriate Method for Solving

You can solve a quadratic equation four different ways. You can graph the related function and find the x-intercepts. For $x^2 = c$, you can take the square root of each side of the equation. You can factor the equation and use the zero-product property. You can use the quadratic formula.

If the discriminant is a perfect square, there are two rational solutions, and the equation can be factored.

Writing **Solve each quadratic equation. Explain why you chose the method you used.**

49. $5x^2 - 10 = x^2 + 90$

50. $9x^2 + 30x - 29 = 0$

51. $8x^2 - 6x = 4x^2 + 6x - 2$

52. A square pool has length p. The border of the pool is 1 ft wide. The combined area of the border and the pool is 400 ft^2. Find the area of the pool.

Getting Ready for..
CHAPTER 11

Rewrite each decimal as an improper fraction.

53. 5.7   **54.** -8.25 **55.** 3.14   **56.** 10.4   **57.** -1.849 **58.** 7.67

Evaluate each expression.

59. $\dfrac{3}{2x+1}$ for $x = 4$

60. $\dfrac{3x^2}{5x+2}$ for $x = -2$

61. $\dfrac{-3}{y^2+3}$ for $y = 2$

62. $\dfrac{2x}{3x-2}$ for $x = 5$

Solve each proportion.

63. $\dfrac{x}{3} = \dfrac{10}{4}$

64. $\dfrac{1}{y} = \dfrac{3}{7}$

65. $\dfrac{11}{3} = \dfrac{2r}{5}$

66. $\dfrac{6}{13} = \dfrac{12}{d}$

67. Probability Make a tree diagram to show all the possible outcomes of rolling two number cubes.

Simplify. Write each answer in standard form.

1. $(4x^2 + 2x + 5) + (7x^2 - 5x + 2)$

2. $(9a^2 - 4 - 5a) - (12a - 6a^2 + 3)$

3. $(-4m^2 + m - 10) + (3m + 12 - 7m^2)$

4. $(3c - 4c^2 + c^3) - (5c^2 + 8c^3 - 6c)$

5. Open-ended Write a trinomial with degree 6.

Write each product in standard form.

6. $8b(3b + 7 - b^2)$ 　　　 7. $-t(5t^2 + t)$

8. $3q(4 - q + 3q^3)$ 　　　 9. $2c(c^5 + 4c^3)$

10. $(x + 6)(x + 1)$ 　　　 11. $(x + 4)(x - 3)$

12. $(2x - 1)(x - 4)$ 　　　 13. $(2x + 5)(3x - 7)$

14. $(x + 2)(2x^2 - 5x + 4)$

15. $(x - 4)(6x^2 + 10x - 3)$

16. Writing Explain how to use the distributive property to multiply polynomials. Include an example.

Find the greatest common factor of the terms of each polynomial.

17. $21x^4 + 18x^2 + 36x^3$ 　 18. $3t^2 - 5t - 2t^4$

19. $-3a^{10} + 9a^5 - 6a^{15}$ 　 20. $9m^3 - 7m^4 + 8m^2$

Write an expression for each situation as a product and in standard form.

21. A plot of land has width x meters. The length of the plot of land is 5 m more than 3 times its width. What is the area of the land?

22. The height of a box is 2 in. less than its width w. The length of a box is 3 in. more than 4 times its width. What is the volume of the box in terms of w?

Factor each expression.

23. $x^2 - 5x - 14$ 　　　 24. $x^2 + 10x + 25$

25. $9x^2 + 24x + 16$ 　　 26. $x^2 - 100$

27. $x^2 - 4x + 4$ 　　　 28. $4x^2 - 49$

29. Standardized Test Prep Which of the following are perfect square trinomials?
   I. $x^2 + 14x + 49$
   II. $16x^2 + 25$
   III. $9x^2 - 30x + 25$
   IV. $4x^2 - 81$

   A. I only　　　　　　　 B. II only
   C. I and III　　　　　　 D. I, III, and IV
   E. I, II, III, and IV

Write each equation in standard form. Then solve the equation.

30. $4x^2 - 5x = -2x^2 + 2x + 3$

31. $2x^2 + 3x = x^2 + 28$

32. $3x^2 - 4 = x^2 - 5x + 12$

33. $x^2 - 5 = -x^2 + 9x$

34. Geometry The base of a triangle is 8 ft more than twice its height. The area of the triangle is 45 ft². Find the dimensions of the triangle.

Use the quadratic formula to solve each equation to the nearest hundredth. If there are no real solutions, write *no real solutions*.

35. $4x^2 + 4x + 9 = 0$

36. $x^2 + 10x + 11 = 0$

37. $-2x^2 - x + 8 = 0$

38. $x^2 - 7x + 10 = 0$

39. Writing Explain when you would use the different methods of solving quadratic equations. Give examples.

Part I

1 Which of the following is a monomial?

(1) $5x^2$ (3) $\frac{1}{x}$

(2) $17x^{-2}$ (4) $x + 1$

2 The polynomial $3x^2 + 4x - 5$ is a

(1) constant monomial. (3) linear binomial.

(2) cubic trinomial.   (4) quadratic trinomial.

3 The greatest common factor (GCF) of $18x^3 + 6x^2 - 4x$ is ■.

(1) $2x$ (3) $6x$

(2) x (4) 2

4 Find the product: $(3x - 1)(5x + 3)$.

(1) $15x^2 + 2x - 3$ (3) $15x^2 + 4x - 3$

(2) $15x^2 + 2x + 3$ (4) $15x^2 - 4x - 3$

5 Which of the following is a factor of $c^2 - 7c + 10$?

(1) $(c + 2)$ (3) $(c - 3)$

(2) $(c - 5)$ (4) $(c + 5)$

6 Which of the following equals the difference of two squares?

(1) $(x - 5)(x - 5)$ (3) $(x + 7)(x - 7)$

(2) $(x + 4) - (x + 4)$ (4) $(x + 6)(x + 6)$

7 Which relation(s) are functions?

(1) I   (3) III

(2) II   (4) II and III

I.

x	1	−1	2	1
y	3	4	5	7

II.

x	1	2	3	4
y	1	1	3	5

III.

x	0	1	2	3
y	0	1	3	2

8 A parachutist opens her parachute at 800 feet. Her rate of change in altitude is -30 ft/s. Which expression represents her altitude in feet t seconds after she opens her parachute?

(1) $30t$ (3) $800 - 30t$

(2) $-30t$ (4) $800 + 30t$

9 A and B are independent events. If $P(A) = \frac{5}{6}$ and $P(A \text{ and } B) = \frac{1}{8}$, what is $P(B)$?

(1) $\frac{1}{10}$ (3) $\frac{1}{5}$

(2) $\frac{3}{20}$ (4) $\frac{1}{4}$

10 One leg of a right isosceles triangle measures 8 cm. What is the length of the hypotenuse?

(1) 16 cm   (3) $8\sqrt{3}$ cm

(2) $16\sqrt{2}$ cm   (4) $8\sqrt{2}$ cm

Part II

11 Simplify: $(3x^2 - 4x + x^3 - 5) - (2x^2 + 6)$.

12 A rectangular prism is $3x + 1$ units long, x units wide, and 2 units high. Write the volume of the prism as a product and as a polynomial in standard form.

Part III

13 Solve: $x^2 - 7x - 18 = 0$.

14 The base of a triangle is $(2x + 2)$ units. Its height is $(x + 3)$ units, and its area is 24 square units. What is the value of x?

Part IV

15 Solve: $4x^2 + 4x - 15 = 0$.

16 The length of a rectangular swimming pool is 20 m longer than its width. The pool is surrounded by a walkway that is 2 m wide. Together, the pool and the walkway cover an area of 1836 m². Find the dimensions of the pool.

17 Suppose you are considering buying a season pass to the park pool for $55. Without a pass, you must pay $3 per visit to the pool. You decide to find the break-even point.

a Write an equation relating the cost of a pass to the cost of swimming without a pass.

b Graph the related linear function.

c How many times would you have to swim to pass the break-even point? Explain.

11

Rational Expressions and Functions

Relating to the Real World

Sixty dollars will buy you six $10 pizzas or four $15 pizzas. This simple relationship leads to fractions with variables in the denominators, called rational expressions. Rational expressions give social scientists and others who use statistics flexibility in applying formulas to their work.

Inverse Variation	Rational Functions	Rational Expressions	Operations with Rational Expressions

Lessons

11-1   11-2   11-3   11-4

GOOD VIBRATIONS

Sounds are caused by vibrations—for example, a string vibrating on a violin. When the string is shortened it vibrates faster, and a higher pitch results. Pitch is also affected by tension (an example is your vocal cords).

As you work through the chapter, you will investigate a variety of musical pitches. You will use inverse variation to find pitch. You will create simple musical instruments to compare ratios of lengths to different pitches. Finally, you will choose a musical instrument and explain how it produces sounds at different pitches.

To help you complete the project:

Solving
Rational
Equations

Counting
Outcomes
and
Permutations

Combinations

11-5

11-6

11-7

What You'll Learn

- Solving inverse variations

- Comparing direct and inverse variation

...And Why

To investigate real-world situations, such as those relating time and rate of work

11-1 Inverse Variation

WORK TOGETHER

Construction Suppose you are part of a volunteer crew constructing low-cost housing. Building a house requires a total of 160 workdays. For example, a crew of 20 people can complete a house in 8 days.

1. How long should it take a crew of 40 people?

2. Copy and complete the table.

Crew Size (x)	Construction Days (y)	Total Workdays
2	80	160
5	■	160
8	■	■
■	16	■
20	8	160
40	■	■

3. Graph the (x, y) data from the table.

4. Describe what happens to construction time as the crew size increases.

Who? Using volunteers, Habitat for Humanity has helped build thousands of homes for low-income families around the world.

Source: Habitat for Humanity

THINK AND DISCUSS

Solving Inverse Variations

When the product of two quantities remains constant, they form an **inverse variation.** As one quantity increases, the other decreases. The product of the quantities is called the **constant of variation** k. An inverse variation can be written $xy = k$, or $y = \frac{k}{x}$.

5. **a.** In the Work Together, what two quantities vary?
   b. What is the constant of variation?
   c. Write an equation that models this variation.

6. **a.** Complete the table for the inverse variation $xy = 100$.

x	1	2	4	5	10	20	50	100
y	100	■	■	■	■	■	■	■

   b. Describe how the values of y change as the values of x increase.

Inverse variations have graphs with the same general shape.

$xy = 12$
$xy = 6$
$xy = 2$

7. **a.** Name the constant of variation k for each graph shown above.
   b. Open-ended Name three points that lie on the graph of each inverse variation.

Suppose (x_1, y_1) and (x_2, y_2) are two ordered pairs in an inverse variation. Since each ordered pair has the same product, you can write the *product equation* $x_1 \cdot y_1 = x_2 \cdot y_2$. You can use this equation to solve problems involving inverse variation.

Example 1   Relating to the Real World

120 lb   **150 lb**

←—6 ft—→|←—x ft—→

fulcrum

Physics The weight needed to balance a lever varies inversely with the distance from the fulcrum to the weight. Where should Julio sit to balance the lever?

Relate A weight of 120 lb is 6 ft from the fulcrum. A weight of 150 lb is x ft from the fulcrum. Weight and distance vary inversely.

Define $\text{weight}_1 = 120$ lb
$\text{weight}_2 = 150$ lb
$\text{distance}_1 = 6$ ft
$\text{distance}_2 = x$ ft

Write $\text{weight}_1 \cdot \text{distance}_1 = \text{weight}_2 \cdot \text{distance}_2$ ←— Use a product equation.

$120 \quad \cdot \quad 6 \quad = \quad 150 \quad \cdot \quad x$ ←— Substitute.

$720 = 150x$

$x = \dfrac{720}{150}$

$x = 4.8$

Julio should sit 4.8 feet from the fulcrum to balance the lever.

8. **Try This** Solve each inverse variation.
   a. When $x = 75$, $y = 0.2$. Find x when $y = 3$.
   b. What weight placed on a lever 6 ft from the fulcrum will balance 80 lb placed 9 ft from the fulcrum?
   c. A trip takes 3 h at 50 mi/h. Find the time when the rate is 60 mi/h.

1 Which situation is *not* a direct variation?
(1) total cost and number of an item purchased
(2) lengths and areas of rectangles with same width
(3) lengths and widths of rectangles with same area
(4) amount of sales tax and total amount

2 $\left(8, \frac{1}{2}\right)$ and $\left(\frac{1}{16}, y\right)$ are points on the graph of a direct variation. What is the value of y?

Comparing Direct and Inverse Variation

This summary will help you recognize and use direct and inverse variations.

Direct Variation	Inverse Variation
y varies directly with x.	y varies inversely with x.
y is directly proportional to x.	y is inversely proportional to x.
The ratio $\frac{y}{x}$ is constant.	The product xy is constant.

Example 2

Do the data in each table represent a *direct variation* or an *inverse variation*? For each table, write an equation to model the data.

a.

x	2	4	10
y	5	10	25

The values of y seem to vary directly with the values of x. Check the ratio $\frac{y}{x}$.

$$\frac{y}{x} = \frac{5}{2} = 2.5$$

$$\frac{10}{4} = 2.5$$

$$\frac{25}{10} = 2.5$$

The ratio $\frac{y}{x}$ is the same for each pair of data. So, this is a direct variation and $k = 2.5$. The equation is $y = 2.5x$.

b.

x	5	10	25
y	20	10	4

The values of y seem to vary inversely with the values of x. Check the product xy.

$$xy = 5(20) = 100$$

$$10(10) = 100$$

$$25(4) = 100$$

The product xy is the same for each pair of data. So, this is an inverse variation and $k = 100$. The equation is $xy = 100$.

9. Match each situation with the equation that models it. Is the relationship between the data *direct* or *inverse*?
   a. The cost of $20 worth of gasoline is split among several people.
   b. You buy several markers for 20¢ each.
   c. You walk 5 miles each day. Your pace (speed) and time vary from day to day.
   d. Several people buy souvenirs for $5 apiece.

   I. $y = 5x$
   II. $xy = 5$
   III. $y = \frac{20}{x}$
   IV. $y = 20x$

1. **a.** Suppose you want to earn $80. How long will it take you if you are paid $5/h; $8/h; $10/h; $20/h?
    b. What are the two variable quantities in part (a)?
    c. Write an equation to represent this situation.

2. Critical Thinking The graphs p and q represent a direct variation and an inverse variation. Write the equation for each graph.

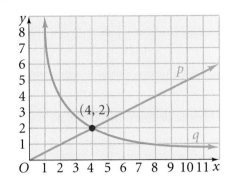

Each pair of points is from an inverse variation. Find the missing value.

3. $(6, 12)$ and $(9, y)$ 4. $(3, 5)$ and $(1, n)$ 5. $(x, 55)$ and $(5, 77)$ 6. $(9.4, b)$ and $(6, 4.7)$

7. $(24, 1.6)$ and $(c, 0.4)$ 8. $(\frac{1}{2}, 24)$ and $(6, y)$ 9. $(x, \frac{1}{2})$ and $(\frac{1}{3}, \frac{1}{4})$ 10. $(500, 25)$ and $(4, n)$

11. $(\frac{1}{2}, 5)$ and $(b, \frac{1}{8})$ 12. $(x, 11)$ and $(1, 66)$ 13. $(50, 13)$ and $(t, 5)$ 14. $(4, 3.6)$ and $(1.2, g)$

15. Standardized Test Prep Which proportion represents an inverse variation?

   A. $\frac{x_2}{y_2} = \frac{y_1}{x_1}$ **B.** $\frac{x_1}{y_2} = \frac{y_1}{x_2}$ **C.** $\frac{x_2}{y_2} = \frac{x_1}{y_1}$ **D.** $\frac{x_1}{x_2} = \frac{y_2}{y_1}$ **E.** $\frac{x_1}{y_1} = \frac{x_2}{y_2}$

Find the constant of variation k for each inverse variation.

16. $y = 8$ when $x = 4$ 17. $r = 3.3$ when $t = \frac{1}{3}$ 18. $a = 25$ when $b = 0.04$

19. $x = \frac{1}{2}$ when $y = 5$ 20. $p = 10.4$ when $q = 1.5$ 21. $x = 5$ when $y = 75$

22. According to the First Law of Air Travel, will the distance to your gate be *greater* or *less* for this trip than for your last trip?
    a. You have more luggage.
    b. You have less time to make your flight.
    c. You have less luggage.

23. Travel The time to travel a certain distance is inversely proportional to your speed. Suppose it takes you $2\frac{1}{2}$ h to drive from your house to the lake at a rate of 48 mi/h.
    a. What is the constant of variation? What does it represent?
    b. How long will your return trip take at 40 mi/h?

Solve each inverse variation.

24. Surveying Two rectangular building lots are each one-quarter acre in size. One plot measures 99 ft by 110 ft. Find the length of the other plot if its width is 90 ft.

25. Construction If 4 people can paint a house working 3 days each, how long will it take a crew of 5 people?

CLOSE TO HOME by John McPherson

The First Law of Air Travel: The distance to your connecting gate is directly proportional to the amount of luggage you are carrying and inversely proportional to the amount of time you have.

Do the data in each table represent a *direct* or an *inverse* variation? Write an equation to model the data. Then complete the table.

26.

x	y
5	6
2	15
10	■

27.

x	y
0.4	28
1.2	84
■	63

28.

x	y
10	4
20	■
8	3.2

29.

x	y
1.6	30
4.8	10
■	96

30.

x	y
3	1
1	3
9	■

Does each formula represent a *direct* or an *inverse* variation? Explain.

31. the perimeter of an equilateral triangle: $P = 3s$

32. a rectangle with area 24 square units: $lw = 24$

33. the time t to travel 150 mi at r mi/h: $t = \dfrac{150}{r}$

34. the circumference of a circle with radius r: $C = 2\pi r$

35. **Writing** Explain how the variable y changes in each situation.
   a. y varies directly with x. The value of x is doubled.
   b. y varies inversely with x. The value of x is doubled.

36. **Open-ended** Write and graph a direct variation and an inverse variation that use the same constant of variation.

Chapter Project

Find Out by Calculating

Under equal tension, the frequency of a vibrating string varies inversely with the string length. Violins and guitars use this principle to produce the different pitches of a musical scale. Find the string lengths for a C-Major scale.

C-Major Scale

Pitch	C	D	E	F	G	A	B	C
Frequency (cycles/s)	523	587	659	698	784	880	988	1046
String length (mm)	420	■	■	■	■	■	■	■

Exercises MIXED REVIEW

Factor each polynomial.

37. $x^2 + 10x + 25$ 38. $4t^2 - 9m^2$ 39. $x^2 - 6x + 9$

40. **Education** The number of high school students taking advanced placement exams increased from 177,406 in 1984 to 459,000 in 1994. What percent increase is this?

Getting Ready for Lesson 11-2

Find the reciprocal of each number.

41. 5   42. -4 43. $\dfrac{8}{3}$ 44. $3\frac{1}{7}$ 45. -1 46. $\dfrac{3}{4}$

FOR YOUR JOURNAL

Describe differences and similarities between direct variation and inverse variation. Include equations and graphs.

Graphing Rational Functions

Before Lesson 11-2

When you use a graphing calculator to graph a rational function, sometimes false connections appear on the screen. When this happens, you need to make adjustments to see the true shape of the graph.

False connection

For example, on your graphing calculator the graph of the function $y = \frac{1}{x + 2} - 4$ may look like the graph at the right. The highest point and lowest point on the graph are not supposed to connect. If you trace the graph, no point on the graph lies on this connecting line. So, this is a false connection.

Here's how you can graph a rational function and avoid false connections.

| First press the MODE key. Then scroll down and right to highlight the word "Dot." Then press ENTER . | Graph again. Now the false connection is gone! | Use the TRACE key or TABLE key to find points on the graph. Sketch the graph. |

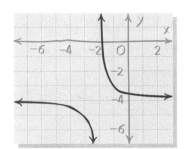

Graphing Calculator **Use a graphing calculator to graph each function. Then sketch the graph. (*Hint:* Use parentheses to enter binomials.)**

1. $y = \frac{1}{x - 3}$

2. $y = \frac{1}{x} + 3$

3. $y = \frac{5}{3x + 2}$

4. $y = \frac{4}{3x + 6}$

5. $y = \frac{x + 3}{x - 2}$

6. $y = \frac{1}{x - 2} + 1$

7. $y = \frac{6}{x^2 - x - 6}$

8. $y = \frac{1}{x - 4} + 2$

9. $y = \frac{8}{x}$

10. $y = \frac{4}{x + 1} - 3$

11. $y = \frac{3x}{x + 3}$

12. $y = \frac{2x + 1}{x - 4}$

13. a. Graphing Calculator Graph $y = \frac{1}{x}, y = \frac{1}{x - 3}$, and $y = \frac{1}{x + 4}$. What do you notice?

   b. Graphing Calculator Graph $y = \frac{1}{x}, y = \frac{1}{x} - 3$, and $y = \frac{1}{x} + 4$. What do you notice?

14. Writing Graph $y = \frac{1}{x}$.

   a. Examine both negative and positive values of x. Describe what happens to the y-values when x is near zero.

   b. Describe what happens to the y-values as $|x|$ increases.

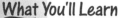

What You'll Learn

- Evaluating rational functions
- Graphing rational functions

...And Why

To solve problems using rational functions, such as those involving light intensity

What You'll Need

- graph paper
- graphing calculator
- index cards

QUICK REVIEW

Two numbers are *reciprocals* of each other if their product is 1.

11-2 Rational Functions

THINK AND DISCUSS

Exploring Rational Functions

Photography Automatic cameras calculate shutter speed based on the amount of available light. The relationship between shutter speed and the amount of light can be modeled with a rational function. A **rational function** is a function that can be written in the form

$$f(x) = \frac{\text{polynomial}}{\text{polynomial}}.$$

1. Evaluate each rational function for $x = 3$.

   a. $f(x) = \dfrac{1}{x - 4}$ **b.** $y = \dfrac{2}{x^2}$ **c.** $g(x) = \dfrac{x^2 - 3x + 2}{x + 2}$

The function $y = \frac{1}{x}$ is an example of a rational function. You can use the graph of $y = \frac{1}{x}$ to show the relationship between reciprocals.

Table

Number (x)	-1	$-\frac{1}{3}$	1	1.5	3
Reciprocal (y)	-1	-3	1	$\frac{2}{3}$	$\frac{1}{3}$

Graph

Since 3 and $\frac{1}{3}$ are reciprocals of each other, both $(3, \frac{1}{3})$ and $(\frac{1}{3}, 3)$ are on the graph.

Negative numbers have negative reciprocals.

For $x = 0$ and $y = 0$ the function is undefined. So the graph never intersects either axis.

2. Does each point lie on the graph of $y = \frac{1}{x}$? Why or why not?
   a. $(-100, -0.01)$ **b.** $(-5, 0.2)$ **c.** $(1{,}000{,}000, 0)$ **d.** $(0.04, 25)$

A line is an **asymptote** of a graph if the graph of the function gets closer and closer to the line, but does not cross it.

3. The y-axis is a vertical asymptote of the function $y = \frac{1}{x}$. Is there a horizontal asymptote of the graph? Explain.

Graphing Rational Functions

When you evaluate a rational function, some values of x may lead to division by zero. For the function $y = \frac{1}{x-3}$, the denominator is zero for $x = 3$. So, the function is undefined when $x = 3$, and the vertical line $x = 3$ is an asymptote of the graph of $y = \frac{1}{x-3}$.

Example 1

Graph $y = \frac{4}{x+3}$.

Step 1 Find the vertical asymptote.

$$x + 3 = 0$$
$$x = -3 \longleftarrow \text{vertical asymptote}$$

Step 2 Make a table using values of x near -3.

Step 3 Draw the graph.

Use a dashed line for the asymptote $x = -3$.

PROBLEM SOLVING

Look Back How does the graph of a rational function compare with the graph of an exponential function?

4. **a.** Copy the graph above and add the graph of the line $y = -x - 3$.
   b. *Critical Thinking* Fold the graph along the line you drew. What is true about the two parts of the graph of $y = \frac{4}{x+3}$?

5. **a.** Evaluate $y = \frac{4}{x+3}$ for $x = 1000$ and $x = -1000$.
   b. Is there a horizontal asymptote for the graph? Explain.

The graphs of many rational functions are related to each other.

$y = \frac{1}{x}$

$y = \frac{1}{x-2}$

vertical asymptote when $x = 0$
horizontal asymptote
along the x-axis

vertical asymptote when $x = 2$
horizontal asymptote
along the x-axis

The graphs are identical in shape, but the second graph is shifted two units to the right.

6. Where is the vertical asymptote of the graph of each function?

    a. $y = \dfrac{6}{x}$ **b.** $y = \dfrac{6}{x - 3}$ **c.** $y = \dfrac{6}{x + 1}$

7. **Try This** Graph each function in Question 6.

8. *Critical Thinking* Graph the functions $y = \frac{3}{x}$ and $y = \frac{3}{x} + 2$. Are the graphs identical in shape? What shift occurs?

You can use rational functions to describe relationships in the real world.

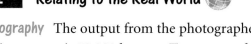 **Example 2**   **Relating to the Real World** ·············

Photography The output from the photographer's lighting system is 72,000 lumens. To get a good photo, the intensity of light at the circus performers must be at least 600 lumens. The light intensity y is related to their distance x in feet from the light by the function $y = \dfrac{72{,}000}{x^2}$. How far can the circus performers be from the light?

Relate   light intensity at performers is at least 600 lumens

Write $\dfrac{72{,}000}{x^2}$ $\geq$ 600

Use a graphing calculator. Enter $y = \dfrac{72{,}000}{x^2}$ and $y = 600$. Find the point of intersection.

Intersection
X=10.954451 Y=600

The curved graph shows that the light intensity y decreases as the distance x increases.

Xmin=0   Ymin=0
Xmax=20   Ymax=2000
Xscl=5   Yscl=100

The light intensity is about 600 lumens when $x \approx 11$. The circus performers should be within about 11 ft of the light.

 GRAPHING CALCULATOR HINT

Use a viewing window for Quadrant I, since distance and lumens are positive.

9. **a.** Use the function in Example 2 to find the light intensity at each distance in the table.

   b. Describe how the light intensity changes when the distance doubles.

Distance (x)	Intensity (y)
3 ft	▨
6 ft	▨
12 ft	▨

10. Graphing Calculator Graph $y = \frac{1}{x}$ and $y = \frac{1}{x^2}$.
  a. What is the vertical asymptote of the graph of each function?
  b. *Critical Thinking* What is the range of $y = \frac{1}{x}$? of $y = \frac{1}{x^2}$?

W O R K   T O G E T H E R

You have studied six families of functions this year. Their properties and graphs are shown in this summary.

Families of Functions

Linear function
$y = mx + b$

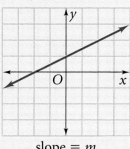

slope = m
y-intercept = b

Absolute value function
$y = |x - b|$

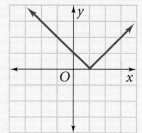

V-shape with vertex at $(b, 0)$

Quadratic function
$y = ax^2 + bx + c$

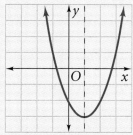

parabola with axis of
symmetry at $x = -\frac{b}{2a}$

Exponential function
$y = ab^x$

growth for $b > 1$
decay for $0 < b < 1$

Radical function
$y = \sqrt{x - b} + c$

shift horizontally b units
shift vertically c units

Rational function
$y = \frac{k}{x - b} + c$

vertical asymptote
at $x = b$

11. Work with a partner to prepare a note card for each family of functions. Include this information:

  ▪ one or more examples for that family

  ▪ a graph for each example

  ▪ notes about each function you have graphed (for instance, how to find the slope, the axis of symmetry, or an asymptote)

12. Make duplicate cards so that you and your partner each have a full set.

Evaluate each function for $x = -1$, $x = 2$, and $x = 4$.

1. $y = \dfrac{x - 2}{x}$ **2.** $f(x) = \dfrac{3}{x - 1}$ **3.** $y = \dfrac{2x}{x - 3}$ **4.** $g(x) = \dfrac{12}{x^2}$

What value of x makes the denominator of each function equal zero?

5. $f(x) = \dfrac{3}{x}$ **6.** $y = \dfrac{1}{x - 2}$ **7.** $y = \dfrac{x}{x + 2}$ **8.** $h(x) = \dfrac{3}{2x - 4}$

Describe the asymptotes in each graph.

9.   **10.**   **11.**   **12.**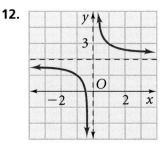

Graph each function. Include a dashed line for each asymptote.

13. $y = \dfrac{4}{x}$ **14.** $f(x) = \dfrac{4}{x - 5}$ **15.** $y = \dfrac{4}{x + 4}$ **16.** $g(x) = \dfrac{4}{x} + 2$

17. $g(x) = \dfrac{12}{x}$ **18.** $y = \dfrac{12}{x + 2}$ **19.** $f(x) = \dfrac{12}{x} - 3$ **20.** $h(x) = \dfrac{12}{x + 2} - 3$

21. $f(x) = \dfrac{-1}{x}$ **22.** $y = \dfrac{-4}{x}$ **23.** $g(x) = \dfrac{4}{x - 2} + 1$ **24.** $y = \dfrac{x + 2}{x - 2}$

25. Physics   As radio signals move away from a transmitter, they become weaker. The function $s = \dfrac{1600}{d^2}$ relates the strength s of a signal at a distance d miles from the transmitter.

   a. Graphing Calculator   Graph the function. For what distances is $s \le 1$?

   b. Use the function to find the signal strength at 10 mi, 1 mi, and 0.1 mi.

   c. Critical Thinking   Suppose you drive by the transmitter for one radio station while your car radio is tuned to a second station. The signal from the first station can interfere and come through your radio. Use your results from part (b) to explain why.

26. Open-ended   Write two rational functions whose graphs are identical except that one has been shifted vertically 3 units from the other.

27. Writing   Suppose a friend missed class. How would you explain how to graph $y = \dfrac{5}{x - 1} + 2$?

28. In the formula $I = \dfrac{445}{x^2}$, I is the intensity of light at a distance x feet from the light bulb. What is the intensity of light 5 ft from the light bulb? 15 ft from the light bulb?

Graph each function on a graphing calculator. Then sketch the graph. Include a dashed line for each asymptote.

29. $y = \frac{x + 4}{x}$
30. $y = \frac{x + 1}{x + 3}$
31. $y = \frac{4}{x^2 - 1}$
32. $y = \frac{6}{x^2 - x - 2}$

Graph each function.

33. $y = x^2 + 3$
34. $y = \sqrt{x + 3}$
35. $y = x + 3$
36. $y = |x - 3|$

37. $y = 3x$
38. $y = 3^x$
39. $y = \frac{3}{x}$
40. $y = \frac{1}{x + 3} + 3$

41. $y = x^2 + 3x + 2$
42. $y = \left(\frac{1}{3}\right)^x$
43. $y = \frac{3}{x - 3}$
44. $y = \frac{3}{x} + 3$

Exercises   MIXED REVIEW

Factor.

45. $g^2 - 12g + 35$
46. $9h^2 + 24h + 16$
47. $a^2 + 6a - 7$
48. $25x^2 - 4$

49. Delivery Services During the blizzard of 1996, a pizza delivery driver in Alexandria, Virginia, got tips that were 1000% of the usual $1 for each delivery. How much did the delivery driver receive in tips for a delivery during the blizzard?

Getting Ready for Lesson 11-3

Find the value(s) of x that makes each expression equal zero.

50. $10 - x$
51. $x^2 - 3x$
52. $x + 4$
53. $x^2 - 16$

Exercises   CHECKPOINT

Each pair of points is from an inverse variation. Find the missing value.

1. $(9, 2)$ and $(x, 6)$
2. $(8.2, 3)$ and $(12.3, y)$
3. $(0.5, 7.2)$ and $(0.9, y)$

Graph each function.

4. $y = \frac{5}{x}$
5. $y = \frac{8}{x - 4}$
6. $y = \frac{6}{x^2}$
7. $y = \frac{1}{x} + 4$

8. Writing Describe the similarities and differences between the graphs of $y = \frac{3}{x}$ and $y = \frac{-3}{x}$.

9. Physics What weight placed on a lever 9 ft from the fulcrum will balance 126 lb placed 6.5 ft from the fulcrum?

10. The graphs of a direct variation and an inverse variation both pass through the point $(3, 5)$. Write an equation for each graph.

What You'll Learn

- Simplifying rational expressions
- Multiplying and dividing rational expressions

...And Why

To solve real-world problems that involve ratios of unknown quantities

11-3 Rational Expressions

Work in groups to review how to simplify, multiply, and divide rational numbers.

1. a. Simplify each expression.

$$\frac{8}{2} \qquad -\frac{15}{24} \qquad \frac{25}{35}$$

b. Consider the steps you took to simplify each expression in part (a). Write the steps you use to simplify rational numbers.

2. a. Express each product in simplest form.

$$-\frac{8}{21} \cdot \frac{7}{4} \qquad \frac{3}{5} \cdot \frac{2}{7} \qquad -\frac{3}{4} \cdot (-2)$$

b. Consider the steps you took to find each product in part (a). Write the steps you use to multiply rational numbers.

3. a. Express each quotient in simplest form.

$$6 \div \frac{3}{8} \qquad \frac{2}{3} \div \left(-\frac{4}{5}\right) \qquad \frac{3}{4} \div 2$$

b. Consider the steps you took to find each quotient in part (a). Write the steps you use to divide rational numbers.

QUICK REVIEW

Rational numbers are numbers that can be represented as the ratio of two integers.

THINK AND DISCUSS

Simplifying Rational Expressions

A **rational expression** is an expression that can be written in the form $\frac{polynomial}{polynomial}$, where a variable is in the denominator.

4. Evaluate each rational expression for $x = 2$. What do you notice?

a. $\frac{1}{x-2}$ **b.** $\frac{3}{x^2-4}$ **c.** $\frac{2}{x^2+x-6}$

The **domain** of a rational expression is all real numbers excluding the values for which the denominator is zero. The values that are excluded are restricted from the domain. For the expression $\frac{1}{x-2}$, 2 is restricted from the domain.

5. What other values are restricted from the domain in parts (b) and (c) of Question 4? (*Hint:* Solve an equation to find the values for which the denominator equals zero.)

A rational expression is in *simplest form* if the numerator and denominator have no common factors except 1.

Example 1

Simplify $\frac{6x + 12}{x + 2}$ and state any values restricted from the domain.

$x + 2 = 0, x = -2$ ◄——— Find the values restricted from the domain.

$\frac{6x + 12}{x + 2} = \frac{6(x + 2)}{x + 2}$ ◄——— Factor the numerator. The denominator cannot be factored.

$= \frac{6}{1} \cdot \frac{x + 2}{x + 2}$ ◄——— Rewrite to show a fraction equal to 1.

$= 6$ ◄——— Simplify.

The solution is 6. The domain does not include $x = -2$.

6. Try This Simplify each expression and state any restrictions on the domain of the variable.

a. $\frac{15b}{25b^2}$ **b.** $\frac{12c^2}{3c + 6}$ **c.** $\frac{x + 3}{x^2 - 9}$

Example 2   **Relating to the Real World**

Baking The baking time for bread depends, in part, on its size and shape. A good approximation for the baking time, in minutes, of a cylindrical loaf is $\frac{60 \cdot \text{volume}}{\text{surface area}}$, where the radius r and height h of the baked loaf are in inches. Rewrite this expression in terms of r and h.

$\frac{60 \cdot \text{volume}}{\text{surface area}} = \frac{60\pi r^2 h}{2\pi r^2 + 2\pi rh}$ ◄——— Use formulas for the volume and surface area of a cylinder.

$= \frac{(2)(30)\pi rrh}{2\pi r(r + h)}$ ◄——— Factor the numerator and denominator.

$= \frac{2\pi r}{2\pi r} \cdot \frac{30rh}{r + h}$ ◄——— Rewrite to show a fraction equal to 1.

$= \frac{30rh}{r + h}$ ◄——— Simplify.

You can approximate the baking time using the expression $\frac{30rh}{r + h}$.

7. Check the answer to Example 2 by substituting values for r and h in both the original expression and the simplified expression.

8. Critical Thinking What values of r and h make sense in this situation? Would any values you would reasonably choose for r and h be restricted from the domain? Explain.

Multiplying and Dividing Rational Expressions

To multiply the rational expressions $\frac{a}{b}$ and $\frac{c}{d}$, where $b \neq 0$ and $d \neq 0$, you multiply the numerators and multiply the denominators. Then write the product in simplest form.

$$\frac{a}{b} \cdot \frac{c}{d} = \frac{ac}{bd}$$

Example 3

Multiply $\frac{2x + 1}{3} \cdot \frac{6x}{4x^2 - 1}$.

$= \frac{2x + 1}{3} \cdot \frac{6x}{(2x + 1)(2x - 1)}$ ⟵ Factor the denominator.

$= \frac{{}^1\cancel{2x + 1}}{\cancel{3}_1} \cdot \frac{{}^2\cancel{6x}}{\cancel{(2x + 1)}_1(2x - 1)}$ ⟵ Divide out the common factors 3 and $(2x + 1)$.

$= \frac{2x}{2x - 1}$ ⟵ Simplify.   ■

9. What values are restricted from the domain in Example 3?

10. Check the solution to Example 3 by substituting a value for x in the original expression and the simplified expression.

11. Robin's first step in finding the product $\frac{2}{w} \cdot w^5$ was to rewrite the expression as $\frac{2}{w} \cdot \frac{w^5}{1}$. Why do you think Robin did this?

To divide the rational expression $\frac{a}{b}$ by $\frac{c}{d}$, where $b \neq 0$, $c \neq 0$, and $d \neq 0$, you multiply by the reciprocal of $\frac{c}{d}$.

$$\frac{a}{b} \div \frac{c}{d} = \frac{a}{b} \cdot \frac{d}{c}$$

12. Find the reciprocal of each expression.

    a. $\frac{-6d^2}{5}$ **b.** $x^2 - 1$ **c.** $\frac{1}{s + 4}$

Example 4

Divide $\frac{3x^3}{2}$ by $(-15x^5)$.

$\frac{3x^3}{2} \div (-15x^5) = \frac{3x^3}{2} \cdot \frac{1}{-15x^5}$ ⟵ Multiply by the reciprocal of $-15x^5$.

$= \frac{{}^1\cancel{3x^3}}{2} \cdot \frac{1}{\underset{-5x^2}{\cancel{-15x^5}}}$ ⟵ Divide out the common factor $3x^3$.

$= -\frac{1}{10x^2}$ ⟵ Simplify.   ■

13. Try This Find each product or quotient.

    a. $\frac{8y^3}{3} \cdot \frac{9}{y^4}$ **b.** $\frac{m - 2}{3m + 9} \cdot (2m + 6)$ **c.** $\frac{y + 3}{y + 2} \div (y + 2)$

Simplify each expression and state any values restricted from the domain.

1. $\frac{5a^2}{20a}$

2. $\frac{3c}{12c^3}$

3. $\frac{4x - 8}{4x + 8}$

4. $\frac{24y + 18}{36}$

5. $\frac{6a + 9}{12}$

6. $\frac{5c - 15}{c - 3}$

7. $\frac{4x^3}{28x^4}$

8. $\frac{5 - 2m}{15 - 6m}$

9. $\frac{24 - 2p}{48 - 4p}$

10. $\frac{b - 4}{b^2 - 16}$

11. $\frac{2x^2 + 2x}{3x^2 + 3x}$

12. $\frac{2s^2 + s}{s^3}$

13. $\frac{3x^2 - 9x}{x - 3}$

14. $\frac{3x + 6}{3x^2}$

15. $\frac{w^2 + 7w}{w^2 - 49}$

16. $\frac{a^2 + 2a + 1}{a + 1}$

17. *Critical Thinking* Explain why $\frac{x^2 - 9}{x + 3}$ is not the same as $x - 3$.

18. *Baking* Use the expression $\frac{30rh}{r + h}$, where r is the radius and h is the height, to estimate the baking times in minutes for each type of bread shown.

a.

biscuit:
$r = 1$ in., $h = 0.75$ in.

b.

pita:
$r = 3.5$ in., $h = 0.5$ in.

c.

baguette:
$r = 1.25$ in., $h = 26$ in.

19. *Writing* Explain why the simplified form of $\frac{7 - x}{x - 7}$ is -1 when $x \neq 7$.

Find each product or quotient.

20. $\frac{7}{3} \cdot \frac{6}{21}$

21. $\frac{25}{4} \div \left(-\frac{4}{5}\right)$

22. $\frac{7b^2}{10} \div \frac{14b^3}{15}$

23. $\frac{6x^2}{5} \cdot \frac{10}{x^3}$

24. $15x^2 \div \frac{5x^4}{6}$

25. $\frac{-x^3}{8} \div \frac{-x^2}{16}$

26. $\frac{3}{a^2} \div 6a^4$

27. $\frac{5x^3}{x^2} \cdot \frac{3x^4}{10x}$

28. $\frac{x - 1}{x + 4} \div \frac{x + 3}{x + 4}$

29. $\frac{3t + 12}{5t} \div \frac{t + 4}{10t}$

30. $\frac{3x + 9}{x} \div (x + 3)$

31. $\frac{y - 4}{10} \div \frac{4 - y}{5}$

32. $\frac{4x + 1}{5x + 10} \cdot \frac{30x + 60}{2x - 2}$

33. $\frac{11k + 121}{7k - 15} \div (k + 11)$

34. *Open-ended* Write an expression that has 2 and -3 restricted from the domain.

35. *Geometry* Write and simplify the ratio for the $\frac{\text{volume of sphere}}{\text{surface area of sphere}}$.
The formula for the volume of a sphere is $\frac{4}{3}\pi r^3$, and the formula for the surface area of a sphere is $4\pi r^2$, where r is the radius of the sphere.

36. Standardized Test Prep Compare the quantities in Column A and Column B. Assume $x \neq -1, 0$.

Column A	Column B
$\dfrac{-(5x + 5)}{x + 1}$	$-10x \cdot \dfrac{2x}{4x^2}$

   A. The quantity in Column A is greater.
   B. The quantity in Column B is greater.
   C. The quantities are equal.
   D. The relationship cannot be determined from the information given.

Geometry Write an expression in simplest form for $\dfrac{\text{area of shaded figure}}{\text{area of larger figure}}$.

37.

38.

39.
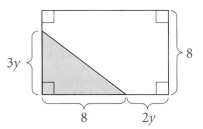

Chapter Project ····· **Find Out by Analyzing**

Pythagoras (540 B.C.) discovered that simple ratios of length produce pleasing combinations of musical pitches.

- Use the lengths you calculated in the Find Out question on page 514 to find pairs of pitches near each ratio.

      2 : 1   3 : 2   4 : 3   5 : 4   6 : 5

- A C-major chord consists of the pitches C, E, G, and C. What ratios are between the pitches of this chord?

Exercises   M I X E D   R E V I E W

Find each product.

40. $y^2(5 - y)$ **41.** $3^x \cdot 3^5$ **42.** $4x^7z^2 \cdot 9xz^{-6}$ **43.** $-6m(2m^3 + 3)$

44. Writing Explain why a vertical line cannot be the graph of a function.

Getting Ready for Lesson 11-4

Express each sum or difference in simplest form.

45. $\dfrac{1}{3} + \dfrac{1}{3}$ **46.** $\dfrac{1}{2} - \dfrac{2}{3}$ **47.** $\dfrac{4}{5} - \dfrac{1}{5}$ **48.** $\dfrac{4}{9} + \dfrac{1}{6}$

11-4 Operations with Rational Expressions

What You'll Learn

- Adding and subtracting rational expressions
- Finding the LCD of two rational expressions

...And Why

To investigate real-world situations, such as groundspeed for air travel

WORK TOGETHER

Work with a partner to complete the following.

1. Add.
   a. $\frac{4}{9} + \frac{2}{9}$
   b. $\frac{4x}{9} + \frac{2x}{9}$
   c. $\frac{4}{9x} + \frac{2}{9x}$

2. Subtract.
   a. $\frac{7}{12} - \frac{1}{12}$
   b. $\frac{7x}{12} - \frac{x}{12}$
   c. $\frac{7}{12x} - \frac{1}{12x}$

3. If $\frac{a}{b}$ and $\frac{c}{b}$ are rational expressions, where $b \neq 0$, write rules for adding and subtracting the two expressions.

THINK AND DISCUSS

In the Work Together activity, you added and subtracted rational expressions with the same monomial denominator. You use the same method when you have a denominator that is a polynomial.

Example 1

Simplify $\frac{2}{x + 3} + \frac{5}{x + 3}$.

$\frac{2}{x + 3} + \frac{5}{x + 3} = \frac{2 + 5}{x + 3}$ ⟵ Add the numerators.

$= \frac{7}{x + 3}$ ⟵ Simplify the numerator.

4. **Try This** Simplify each expression.
   a. $\frac{3}{x + 2} - \frac{2}{x + 2}$
   b. $\frac{y}{y - 5} + \frac{3y}{y - 5}$
   c. $\frac{2n + 5}{n + 1} - \frac{n - 1}{n + 1}$

To add or subtract rational expressions with different denominators, you must write the expressions with a common denominator. Your work will be simpler if you find the least common denominator (LCD), which is the least common multiple of the denominators.

5. Look at the table below. How is finding the LCD of $\frac{3}{4}$ and $\frac{1}{6}$ like finding the LCD of $\frac{3}{4x}$ and $\frac{1}{6x^2}$?

LCD of Numbers	*LCD of Variable Expressions*
$4 = 2 \cdot 2$	$4x = 2 \cdot 2 \cdot \quad x$
$6 = 2 \cdot \quad 3$	$6x^2 = 2 \cdot \quad 3 \cdot x \cdot x$
$LCD = 2 \cdot 2 \cdot 3 = 12$	$LCD = 2 \cdot 2 \cdot 3 \cdot x \cdot x = 12x^2$

Example 2

Simplify $\frac{2}{3x} + \frac{1}{6}$.

Step 1: Find the LCD of $\frac{2}{3x}$ and $\frac{1}{6}$.

$3x = 3 \cdot x$ and $6 = 2 \cdot 3$ ⟵ Factor each denominator.
The LCD is $3 \cdot x \cdot 2$ or $6x$.

Step 2: Rewrite the original expression and add.

$\frac{2}{3x} = \frac{2 \cdot 2}{3x \cdot 2} = \frac{4}{6x}$ ⟵ Multiply numerator and denominator by 2.

$\frac{1}{6} = \frac{1 \cdot x}{6 \cdot x} = \frac{x}{6x}$ ⟵ Multiply numerator and denominator by x.

Step 3: Rewrite the original expression and add.

$\frac{2}{3x} + \frac{1}{6} = \frac{4}{6x} + \frac{x}{6x}$ ⟵ Replace each expression with its equivalent.

$\phantom{\frac{2}{3x} + \frac{1}{6}} = \frac{4 + x}{6x}$ ⟵ Add the numerators.

6. Try This Simplify.

a. $\frac{5}{12b} + \frac{1}{36b^2}$ **b.** $\frac{3}{7y^4} + \frac{2}{3y^2}$ **c.** $\frac{4}{25x} - \frac{49}{100}$

You can factor to find the LCD when the denominators are polynomials.

Example 3

Simplify $\dfrac{1}{y^2 + 5y + 4} - \dfrac{3}{5y + 5}$.

Step 1: Find the LCD.

$y^2 + 5y + 4 = (y + 1)(y + 4)$ and $5y + 5 = 5(y + 1)$ ⟵ Factor each denominator.
The LCD is $5(y + 1)(y + 4)$.

Step 2: Write equivalent expressions with denominator $5(y + 1)(y + 4)$.

$\dfrac{1}{(y + 1)(y + 4)} = \dfrac{5}{5(y + 1)(y + 4)}$ ⟵ Multiply numerator and denominator by 5.

$\dfrac{3}{5(y + 1)} = \dfrac{3(y + 4)}{5(y + 1)(y + 4)}$ ⟵ Multiply numerator and denominator by $(y + 4)$.

Step 3: Subtract.

$\dfrac{5}{5(y + 1)(y + 4)} - \dfrac{3(y + 4)}{5(y + 1)(y + 4)} = \dfrac{5 - 3(y + 4)}{5(y + 1)(y + 4)}$

$ = \dfrac{5 - 3y - 12}{5(y + 1)(y + 4)}$

$ = \dfrac{-7 - 3y}{5(y + 1)(y + 4)}$

7. Explain why the LCD in Example 3 is not $5(y + 1)(y + 1)(y + 4)$.

PROBLEM SOLVING

Look Back Why is multiplying both the numerator and the denominator of a fraction by $2x$ equivalent to multiplying the fraction by 1?

Math A Test Prep

1 Which is the axis of symmetry of the graph of $y = x^2 + 10x + 10$?
(1) $x = -5$ (3) $x = 3$
(2) $y = 4$ (4) $y = -4$

2 Find the quotient: $\frac{2m + 6}{m + 3} \div m$. State any values restricted from the domain.

You can combine rational expressions to investigate real-world situations.

Example 4 **Relating to the Real World**

Air Travel The groundspeed for jet traffic from Los Angeles to New York City is about 15% faster than the groundspeed from New York City to Los Angeles. This difference is due to a strong westerly wind at high altitudes. If r is a jet's groundspeed from New York to Los Angeles, write an expression for the round-trip air time. The two cities are about 2500 mi apart.

NYC to LA time: $\dfrac{2500}{r}$ ◀—— time $= \dfrac{\text{distance}}{\text{rate}}$

LA to NYC time: $\dfrac{2500}{1.15r}$ ◀—— time $= \dfrac{\text{distance}}{\text{rate}}$

Write an expression for the total time.

$$\dfrac{2500}{r} + \dfrac{2500}{1.15r} = \dfrac{2875}{1.15r} + \dfrac{2500}{1.15r}$$ ◀—— Rewrite using the LCD.

$$= \dfrac{5375}{1.15r}$$ ◀—— Add.

$$\approx \dfrac{4674}{r}$$ ◀—— Simplify.

The expression $\dfrac{4674}{r}$ approximates the total time for the trip, where r is the speed of the jet.

8. Suppose a jet flies from Los Angeles to New York City at 420 mi/h. How long will the round-trip take?

Simplify the following expressions.

1. $\frac{4}{5} + \frac{3}{5}$

2. $\frac{6}{x} + \frac{1}{x}$

3. $-\frac{2}{3b} - \frac{4}{3b}$

4. $\frac{5}{h} - \frac{3}{h}$

5. $\frac{7}{11g} - \frac{3}{11g}$

6. $\frac{3x}{7} + \frac{6x}{7}$

7. $\frac{5}{6d} + \frac{7}{6d}$

8. $\frac{5x}{9} - \frac{x}{9}$

9. $\frac{3n}{7} + \frac{2n}{7}$

10. $\frac{6}{17p} - \frac{9}{17p}$

11. $\frac{12r}{5} + \frac{14r}{5}$

12. $-\frac{8}{7k} - \frac{9}{7k}$

Find the LCD.

13. $\frac{1}{2x}; \frac{1}{4x^2}$

14. $\frac{b}{6}; \frac{2b}{9}$

15. $\frac{6}{2m^2}; \frac{1}{m}$

16. $\frac{1}{z}; \frac{3}{7z}$

17. $\frac{-5}{6t^5}; \frac{3}{2t^2}$

18. $\frac{3}{7s^5}; \frac{-4}{5s^2}$

19. $\frac{24}{23d^3}; \frac{25}{2d^4}$

20. $-\frac{3y^2}{15}; \frac{11y^5}{6}$

21. $\frac{6a}{5}; \frac{-5}{a}$

22. $\frac{7}{2k^4}; \frac{7}{9k^{11}}$

23. $\frac{8}{5b}; \frac{12}{7b^3}$

24. $\frac{6}{h^7}; \frac{1}{k^3}$

Simplify.

25. $\frac{7}{3a} + \frac{2}{5a^4}$

26. $\frac{4}{x} - \frac{2}{3x^5}$

27 $\frac{6}{5x^8} + \frac{4}{3x^6}$

28. $\frac{12}{k} - \frac{5}{k^2}$

29. $\frac{3}{6b} - \frac{4}{2b^4}$

30. $\frac{2}{y} + \frac{3}{5y}$

31. $\frac{3}{8m^3} + \frac{1}{12m^2}$

32. $\frac{1}{5x^3} + \frac{3}{20x^2}$

33. $-\frac{5}{4k} - \frac{8}{9k}$

34. $\frac{27}{n^3} - \frac{9}{7n^2}$

35. $\frac{9}{4x^2} + \frac{9}{5}$

36. $\frac{5}{12m^3} + \frac{7}{6m^8}$

37. a. Exercise Suppose Jane walks one mile from her house to her grandparents' house. Then she returns home walking with her grandfather. Her return rate is 70% of her normal walking rate. Let r represent her normal walking rate. Write an expression for the amount of time Jane spends walking.

    b. Suppose Jane's normal walking rate is 3 mi/h. How much time does she spend walking?

Simplify.

38. $\frac{10}{x-1} - \frac{5}{x-1}$

39. $\frac{7}{m+1} + \frac{3}{m+1}$

40. $\frac{4}{6m-1} + \frac{3}{6m-1}$

41. $\frac{m}{m+3} + \frac{2}{m+3}$

42. $\frac{3n+2}{n+4} - \frac{n-6}{n+4}$

43. $\frac{5}{t^2+1} - \frac{3}{t^2+1}$

44. $\frac{2y+1}{y-1} - \frac{y+2}{y-1}$

45. $\frac{s^2+3}{4s^2+2} + \frac{s^2-1}{4s^2+2}$

46. $\frac{1}{2-b} - \frac{4}{2-b}$

47. $\frac{1}{m+2} + \frac{1}{m^2+3m+2}$

48. $\frac{4}{x-5} - \frac{3}{x+5}$

49. $\frac{5}{y+2} + \frac{4}{y^2-y-6}$

50. Writing When adding or subtracting rational expressions, will the answer be in simplest form if you use the LCD? Explain.

51. Open-ended Write two rational expressions with different denominators. Find the LCD and add the two expressions.

Chapter Project

Find Out by Creating

How does a flute or a pipe organ create different pitches? Get two cardboard tubes used to hold wrapping paper or to mail posters. Cut one tube into two lengths *A* and *B* whose ratio is 2:1. Hold your hand tightly over the longer piece (*A*) and blow over the open end until you get a pitch. Now try the shorter piece. What do you hear?

Cut two more pieces from the other tube by measuring them against piece *A*. Make one $\frac{2}{3}$ of *A* and the other $\frac{4}{5}$ of *A*. (You should have a small piece left over.) Get some friends together and play the first phrase of "The Star Spangled Banner."

Exercises   M I X E D   R E V I E W

Find the hypotenuse of a right triangle with the given legs.

52. $a = 9, b = 12$ **53.** $a = 10, b = 7$ **54.** $a = 12, b = 5$ **55.** $a = 6, b = 9$

56. Population Surveys The 1990 census may have missed 4 million people out of about 250 million people living in the United States. What percent of the people may have been missed?

Getting Ready for Lesson 11-5

Mental Math **Find the value of each variable.**

57. $\frac{1}{2} + \frac{1}{m} = \frac{3}{4}$ **58.** $\frac{3}{x} + \frac{1}{x} = 1$ **59.** $\frac{2}{n} + \frac{1}{n} = \frac{1}{2}$ **60.** $\frac{4}{3} - \frac{2}{x} = \frac{2}{3}$

Algebra at Work

Electrician

More than half a million men and women make their livings as electricians. All are highly skilled technicians licensed by the states in which they work. Electricians use formulas containing rational expressions. For example, when a circuit connected "in parallel" contains two resistors with resistances r_1 and r_2 ohms, the total resistance *R* (in ohms) of the circuit can be found using the formula $\frac{1}{R} = \frac{1}{r_1} + \frac{1}{r_2}$.

Mini Project: Research the difference between circuits connected *in parallel* and *in series*. Write a brief report of your findings. Include diagrams with your report.

11-5 Solving Rational Equations

THINK AND DISCUSS

A **rational equation** contains rational expressions. A method for solving rational equations is similar to the method you learned in Chapter 3 for solving equations with rational numbers.

Solving Equations with Rational Numbers

$$\frac{1}{2}x + \frac{3}{4} = \frac{1}{5}$$ ⟵ The denominators are 2, 4, and 5. The LCD is 20.

$$20\left(\frac{1}{2}x + \frac{3}{4}\right) = 20\left(\frac{1}{5}\right)$$ ⟵ Multiply each side by 20.

$$\overset{10}{20}\left(\frac{1}{2}x\right) + \overset{5}{20}\left(\frac{3}{4}\right) = \overset{4}{20}\left(\frac{1}{5}\right)$$ ⟵ Use the distributive property.

$$10x + 15 = 4$$ ⟵ No fractions! This equation is much easier to solve.

Solving Equations with Rational Expressions

$$\frac{1}{2x} + \frac{3}{4} = \frac{1}{5x}$$ ⟵ The denominators are 2x, 4, and 5x. The LCD is 20x.

$$20x\left(\frac{1}{2x} + \frac{3}{4}\right) = 20x\left(\frac{1}{5x}\right)$$ ⟵ Multiply each side by 20x.

$$\overset{10}{20}x\left(\frac{1}{2x}\right) + \overset{5}{20}x\left(\frac{3}{4}\right) = \overset{4}{20}x\left(\frac{1}{5x}\right)$$ ⟵ Use the distributive property.

$$10 + 15x = 4$$ ⟵ No rational expressions! Now you can solve.

1. Find the LCD of each equation.

  a. $\frac{3}{4n} - \frac{1}{2} = \frac{2}{n}$ **b.** $\frac{1}{3x} + \frac{2}{5} = \frac{4}{3x}$ **c.** $\frac{1}{8y} = \frac{5}{6} - \frac{1}{y}$

There are often values that are excluded from the domain of a rational expression. When you solve rational equations, check your solutions to be sure that your answer satisfies the original equation.

Example 1

Solve $\frac{5}{x^2} = \frac{6}{x} - 1$.

$$x^2\left(\frac{5}{x^2}\right) = x^2\left(\frac{6}{x} - 1\right)$$ ⟵ Multiply each side by the LCD, x^2.

$$\overset{1}{x^2}\left(\frac{5}{x^2}\right) = \overset{x}{x^2}\left(\frac{6}{x}\right) - x^2(1)$$ ⟵ Use the distributive property.

$$5 = 6x - x^2$$ ⟵ Simplify.

$$x^2 - 6x + 5 = 0$$ ⟵ Collect terms on one side.

$$(x - 5)(x - 1) = 0$$ ⟵ Factor the quadratic expression.

$(x - 5) = 0 \text{ or } (x - 1) = 0$ ← Use the zero-product property.
$\qquad x = 5 \qquad\qquad x = 1$ ← Solve.

Check $\dfrac{5}{5^2} \overset{?}{=} \dfrac{6}{5} - 1 \qquad\qquad \dfrac{5}{1^2} \overset{?}{=} \dfrac{6}{1} - 1$

$\qquad\qquad \dfrac{1}{5} = \dfrac{1}{5} \checkmark \qquad\qquad\qquad 5 = 5 \checkmark$

Since 5 and 1 check in the original equation, they are the solutions.

Example 2 **Relating to the Real World**

Business The Fresia Company owns two electronic mail processors. The newer machine works three times as fast as the older one. Together the two machines process 1000 pieces of mail in 25 min. How long does it take each machine, working alone, to process 1000 pieces of mail?

Define

	Time to process 1000 pieces (min)	Processing rate (pieces/min)
New machine	n	$\dfrac{1000}{n}$
Old machine	$3n$	$\dfrac{1000}{3n}$
Both machines	25	$\dfrac{1000}{25} = 40$

Relate Processing rate of $+$ Processing rate of $=$ Processing rate of
new machine $\qquad$ old machine $\qquad$ both machines

Write $\qquad \dfrac{1000}{n} \qquad + \qquad \dfrac{1000}{3n} \qquad = \qquad 40$

$3n\left(\dfrac{1000}{n} + \dfrac{1000}{3n}\right) = 3n(40)$ ← Multiply each side by the LCD, $3n$.

$3\overset{3}{n}\left(\dfrac{1000}{\cancel{n}_1}\right) + \overset{1}{3n}\left(\dfrac{1000}{\cancel{3n}_1}\right) = 3n(40)$ ← Use the distributive property.

$\qquad\qquad 3000 + 1000 = 120n$ ← Simplify.

$\qquad\qquad\qquad\quad 4000 = 120n$

$\qquad\qquad\qquad\quad 33.3 \approx n$ ← Divide each side by 120.

The new machine can process 1000 pieces of mail in about 33 min. The old machine takes $3 \cdot 33.3$, or 100 min, to process 1000 pieces of mail.

1 What is the LCD of $\frac{3}{2x + 1}$ and $\frac{6}{2x^2 - 5x - 3}$?
(1) $2x + 1$
(2) 3
(3) $2x^2 - 5x - 3$
(4) $x - 3$

2 Tom can rake all the leaves in his yard in half the time it takes his brother. Together it took the boys 4 hours to rake the yard. They filled 50 bags. How long would it have taken each brother working alone?

2. Try This Solve each equation.

a. $\frac{1}{3} + \frac{1}{3x} = \frac{1}{7}$

b. $\frac{2}{3x} = \frac{1}{5} - \frac{3}{x}$

The process of multiplying by the LCD can sometimes lead to a solution that does not check in the original equation.

Example 3

Solve $\frac{-1}{x - 2} = \frac{x - 4}{2(x - 2)} + \frac{1}{3}$.

The LCD is $6(x - 2)$. Multiply each side by the LCD, then solve.

$$6(x - 2)\left(\frac{-1}{x - 2}\right) = 6(x - 2)\left(\frac{x - 4}{2(x - 2)} + \frac{1}{3}\right)$$

$$6(x - 2)\left(\frac{-1}{x - 2}\right) = 6(x - 2)\left(\frac{x - 4}{2(x - 2)}\right) + 6(x - 2)\left(\frac{1}{3}\right)$$

$$-6 = 3(x - 4) + 2(x - 2) \quad \longleftarrow \text{ Simplify.}$$
$$-6 = 3x - 12 + 2x - 4 \quad \longleftarrow \text{ distributive property}$$
$$-6 = 5x - 16 \quad \longleftarrow \text{ Combine like terms.}$$
$$10 = 5x \quad \longleftarrow \text{ Add 16 to each side.}$$
$$2 = x \quad \longleftarrow \text{ Divide each side by 5.}$$

Check

$$\frac{-1}{2 - 2} \stackrel{?}{=} \frac{2 - 4}{2(2 - 2)} + \frac{1}{3}$$

$$\frac{-1}{0} = \frac{-2}{0} + \frac{1}{3} \quad \longleftarrow \text{ Undefined!}$$

The equation has *no* solution because 2 makes a denominator equal 0. ■

3. Try This Solve each equation. Be sure to check your answers!

a. $\frac{2}{x} - \frac{8}{x^2} = -1$

b. $\frac{1}{w + 1} = 1 - \frac{1}{w(w + 1)}$

Exercises   O N   Y O U R   O W N

1. Carlos studied the problem at the right and said, "I'll start by finding the LCD." Ingrid studied the problem and said, "I'll start by cross-multiplying."
   a. Solve the equation using Carlos's method, and then using Ingrid's method.
   b. **Writing** Which method do you prefer? Why?
   c. **Critical Thinking** Will Ingrid's method work for all rational equations? Explain.

Solve $\frac{40}{x} = \frac{15}{x - 20}$.

Solve each equation. Be sure to check your answers!

2. $\frac{1}{2} + \frac{2}{x} = \frac{1}{x}$

3. $\frac{1}{20} + \frac{1}{30} = \frac{1}{x}$

4. $5 + \frac{2}{p} = \frac{17}{p}$

5. $\frac{3}{a} - \frac{5}{a} = 2$

6. $\frac{5}{n} - \frac{1}{2} = 2$

7. $\frac{1}{x + 2} = \frac{1}{2x}$

8. $y - \dfrac{6}{y} = 5$

9. $\dfrac{30}{x + 3} = \dfrac{30}{x - 3}$

10. $\dfrac{4}{a + 1} = \dfrac{8}{2 - a}$

11. $\dfrac{5}{y} + \dfrac{3}{2} = \dfrac{1}{3y}$

12. $\dfrac{2}{3b} - \dfrac{3}{4} = \dfrac{1}{6b}$

13. $\dfrac{5}{2s} + \dfrac{3}{4} = \dfrac{9}{4s}$

14. Business The PRX Company owns one scanning machine that scans 10,000 documents in 25 min. The company then buys a newer scanner, and together, the two machines scan 10,000 documents in 10 min. How long would it take the newer machine, working alone, to scan 10,000 documents?

15. Plumbing You can fill a 30-gallon tub in 15 min with both faucets running. If the cold water faucet runs twice as fast as the hot water faucet, how long will it take to fill the tub with only cold water?

 16. Graphing Calculator Write two functions using the expressions on each side of the equation $\dfrac{6}{x^2} + 1 = \dfrac{(x + 7)^2}{6}$. Graph the functions. Find the coordinates of the points of intersection. Are the x-values solutions to the equation? Explain.

Geometry Find each value of x if the area of each shaded region is 64 square units. Assume that each quadrilateral shown is a rectangle.

17.

18.

19.

Solve each equation. Be sure to check your answers!

20. $\dfrac{1}{2} = -\dfrac{1}{3(x - 3)}$

21. $\dfrac{1}{t - 2} = \dfrac{t}{8}$

22. $\dfrac{x - 11}{3x} = \dfrac{x - 19}{5x}$

23. $\dfrac{4}{3(c + 4)} + 1 = \dfrac{2c}{c + 4}$

24. $\dfrac{8}{x + 3} = \dfrac{1}{x} + 1$

25. $\dfrac{x + 2}{x + 4} = \dfrac{x - 2}{x - 1}$

26. $\dfrac{2}{c - 2} = 2 - \dfrac{4}{c}$

27. $\dfrac{5}{3p} + \dfrac{2}{3} = \dfrac{5 + p}{2p}$

28. $\dfrac{3}{s - 1} + 1 = \dfrac{12}{s^2 - 1}$

29. Standardized Test Prep Which inequality contains both of the solutions of the equation $5x = \dfrac{7}{2} + \dfrac{6}{x}$?

A. $-1 < x < 3$

B. $0 < x < \dfrac{3}{2}$

C. $-2 \le x < 0$

D. $-3 \le x \le -1$

E. none of the above

30. A plane flies 450 mi/h. It can travel 980 mi with a wind in the same amount of time as it travels 820 mi against the wind. Solve the equation $\dfrac{980}{450 + s} = \dfrac{820}{450 - s}$ to find the speed s of the wind.

31. Find the value of each variable.
$$\begin{bmatrix} \dfrac{5a}{3} & \dfrac{7}{3b} \\ \dfrac{2c-15}{35c} & \dfrac{5}{2d} + \dfrac{3}{4} \end{bmatrix} = \begin{bmatrix} 2 + \dfrac{7a}{6} & 9 \\ \dfrac{1}{5c} & \dfrac{9}{4d} \end{bmatrix}$$

Chapter Project **Find Out by Interviewing**

The pitch produced by a vibrating string is affected by how tightly it is stretched, or its tension. Find out how a violin, guitar, or other stringed instrument is tuned by talking with someone who plays it.

Exercises   MIXED REVIEW

Solve each equation. Round to the nearest hundredth, where necessary.

32. $x^2 = 3x + 8$ **33.** $x^2 - 4 = 0$ **34.** $2x^2 + 6 = 4x$ **35.** $7x = 5x - 11$

36. Open-ended Give an example of two quantities that vary inversely. Write an equation to go with your example.

Getting Ready for Lesson 11-6

List the possible outcomes of each action.

37. rolling a number cube once   **38.** tossing a coin twice   **39.** tossing a coin and rolling a number cube

Exercises   CHECKPOINT

Simplify each expresssion and state any restrictions on the variable.

1. $\dfrac{8m^2}{2m^3}$ **2.** $\dfrac{6x^2 - 24}{x + 2}$ **3.** $\dfrac{3c + 9}{3c - 9}$ **4.** $\dfrac{3z^2 + 12z}{z^4}$

5. Open-ended Write an expression where the variable cannot equal 3.

Solve each equation.

6. $\dfrac{9}{t} + \dfrac{3}{2} = 12$ **7.** $\dfrac{10}{z+4} = \dfrac{30}{2z+3}$ **8.** $\dfrac{1}{m-2} = \dfrac{5}{m}$ **9.** $c - \dfrac{8}{c} = 10$

Find each sum or difference.

10. $\dfrac{5}{c} + \dfrac{4}{c}$ **11.** $\dfrac{9}{x-3} - \dfrac{4}{x-3}$ **12.** $\dfrac{8}{m+2} - \dfrac{6}{3-m}$ **13.** $\dfrac{6}{t} + \dfrac{3}{t^2}$

14. Standardized Test Prep What is the LCD of $\dfrac{8}{n}, \dfrac{5}{3-n}$, and $\dfrac{1}{n^2}$?

A. $n^2 + 3n$ **B.** $3n^2 - n^3$ **C.** $n^2 + 3$ **D.** $3n^3 - n^4$ **E.** $n^3 - 3n^2$

Algebraic Reasoning

After Lesson 11-5

You can use the properties you have studied and the three below to prove algebraic relationships and to justify steps in the solution of an equation.

Properties of Equality

For all real numbers a, b, and c:

Reflexive Property: $a = a$ Example: $5x = 5x$

Symmetric Property: If $a = b$, then $b = a$.   Example: If $15 = 3t$, then $3t = 15$.

Transitive Property: If $a = b$ and $b = c$, then $a = c$.   Example: If $d = 3y$ and $3y = 6$, then $d = 6$.

Example 1

Prove that if $a = b$, then $ac = bc$.

Statements	Reasons
$a = b$	⟵ Given
$ac = ac$	⟵ Reflexive prop.
$ac = bc$	⟵ Substitute b for a.

Example 2

Solve $-32 = 4(y - 3)$. Justify each step.

Steps	Reasons
$-32 = 4(y - 3)$	⟵ Given
$-32 = 4y - 12$	⟵ Distributive prop.
$-20 = 4y$	⟵ Addition prop. of equality
$-5 = y$	⟵ Division prop. of equality
$y = -5$	⟵ Symmetric prop. of equality

Name the property that each exercise illustrates.

1. If $3.8 = z$, then $z = 3.8$.

2. If $x = \frac{1}{2}y$, and $\frac{1}{2}y = -2$, then $x = -2$.

3. $-4r = -4r$

Supply the missing reasons.

4. Solve $-5 = 1 + 3d$. Justify each step.

Steps	Reasons
$-5 = 1 + 3d$	⟵ Given
$-6 = 3d$	⟵ **a.** __?__
$-2 = d$	⟵ **b.** __?__
$d = -2$	⟵ **c.** __?__

5. Prove that if $ax^2 + bx = 0$, then $x = 0$ or $-\frac{b}{a}$.

Statements	Reasons
$ax^2 + bx = 0$	⟵ Given
$x^2 + \frac{b}{a}x = 0$	⟵ **a.** __?__
$x(x + \frac{b}{a}) = 0$	⟵ **b.** __?__
$x = 0$ or $x + \frac{b}{a} = 0$	⟵ Zero-product prop.
$x = 0$ or $x = -\frac{b}{a}$	⟵ **c.** __?__

6. Writing If Cal is Mia's cousin, then Mia is Cal's cousin. This relationship is symmetric. Describe a relationship that is transitive.

11-6 Counting Outcomes and Permutations

What You'll Learn
- Using the multiplication counting principle to count outcomes
- Using permutations to count outcomes
- Finding probability

...And Why

To investigate the number of arrangements in situations such as the arrangement of players on a team

What You'll Need

- calculator

WORK TOGETHER

Entertainment Suppose you play the following CDs:

- *cracked rear view* by Hootie and the Blowfish
- *Design of a Decade* by Janet Jackson
- *Destiny* by Gloria Estefan

1. In how many different orders can you play the CDs?

2. Describe how you determined the number of different ways to order the CDs.

3. What is the probability that the CDs will be played in alphabetical order?

THINK AND DISCUSS

Using the Multiplication Counting Principle

One way you could find outcomes is to make an organized list or a tree diagram. Both help you to see if you have thought of all possibilities.

Suppose you have three shirts and two pair of pants that coordinate well together. You can use a tree diagram to find the number of possible outfits you have.

Shirts	Pants	Outfits
Shirt 1	Pants 1	Shirt 1, Pants 1
	Pants 2	Shirt 1, Pants 2
Shirt 2	Pants 1	Shirt 2, Pants 1
	Pants 2	Shirt 2, Pants 2
Shirt 3	Pants 1	Shirt 3, Pants 1
	Pants 2	Shirt 3, Pants 2

There are six possible outfits.

4. Would you want to use a tree diagram to find the number of outfits for five shirts and eight pairs of pants? Explain.

QUICK REVIEW

When one event does not affect the result of a second event, they are *independent events*.

When events are independent, you can find the number of outcomes by using the multiplication counting principle.

Multiplication Counting Principle

If there are m ways to make a first selection and n ways to make a second selection, there are $m \times n$ ways to make the two selections.

Example: For 3 shirts and 2 pairs of pants, the number of possible outfits is $3 \cdot 2 = 6$.

Example 1 **Relating to the Real World**

Travel Suppose there are two routes you can choose to get from Austin, Texas, to Dallas, Texas, and four routes from Dallas to Tulsa, Oklahoma. How many routes are there from Austin to Tulsa through Dallas?

$2 \cdot 4 = 8$ ← routes from Austin to Tulsa through Dallas

routes from ⌐ └ routes from Dallas to Tulsa
Austin to Dallas

There are eight possible routes from Austin to Tulsa.

TONIGHT'S TOPPINGS
vegetable: mushrooms
broccoli
onions
peppers
eggplant

meat: chicken
ground beef
pepperoni

5. **Try This** At the neighborhood pizza shop, there are five vegetable toppings and three meat toppings for a pizza. How many possible pizzas can you order with one meat and one vegetable topping?

Finding Permutations

ABC ACB
BAC BCA
CAB CBA

A common kind of counting problem is to find the number of arrangements of a set of objects. The list at the left shows the possible arrangements for the letters A, B, and C without repeating any letters in an arrangement.

Each of the arrangements is called a permutation. A **permutation** is an arrangement of some or all of a set of objects in a specific order.

Example 2 **Relating to the Real World**

Sports In how many ways can nine baseball players be listed for batting order?

There are 9 choices for the first batter, 8 for the second, 7 for the third, and so on.

$9 \cdot 8 \cdot 7 \cdot 6 \cdot 5 \cdot 4 \cdot 3 \cdot 2 \cdot 1 = 362880$ ← Use a calculator.

There are 362,880 possible arrangements of the batters.

CALCULATOR HINT

The notation 9!, read as *nine factorial*, means the product of the integers from 9 to 1. Use this sequence to find 9!:

9 **PRB!**

6. *Critical Thinking* Why are there only 8 choices for the second batter and 7 choices for the third batter?

In how many ways can you select a right, center, and left fielder from eight people? This means finding the number of permutations of 8 objects (players) arranged 3 at a time. You can use $_nP_r$ to express the number of permutations where n equals the number of objects and r equals the number of selections to make. Eight players arranged three at a time is $_8P_3$.

You can use the multiplication counting principle to evaluate permutations.

$_8P_3 = 8 \cdot 7 \cdot 6$, or 336 arrangements of 8 players arranged 3 at a time.
$_nP_r = n(n-1)(n-2) \ldots$ **Stop when you have r factors.**

first factor ⌐ └ **number of factors**

7. a. Use $_nP_r$ to express the number of permutations of twelve players for five positions on a baseball team.
   b. *Calculator* Evaluate the number of permutations for part (a).

Example 3 **Relating to the Real World** · · · · · · · · · · · ·

Computers Suppose you use six different letters to make a computer password. Find the number of possible six-letter passwords.

There are 26 letters in the alphabet. You are finding the number of permutations of 26 letters arranged 6 at a time.

$_{26}P_6 = 26 \cdot 25 \cdot 24 \cdot 23 \cdot 22 \cdot 21 = 165,765,600$ ◀—Use a calculator.

There are 165,765,600 six-letter passwords in which letters do not repeat. ■

8. What would $_{26}P_8$ mean if you were making a password?

9. a. *Probability* Lena wants a password that uses the four letters of her name. How many permutations are possible using each letter in her name only once?
   b. Suppose a four-letter password with no repeated letters is assigned randomly. What is the probability that it uses the letters L, E, N, and A?
   c. *Critical Thinking* Is creating a password based on your name a good idea? Explain.

1. **Jobs** James must wear a shirt and tie for a job interview. He has two dress shirts and five ties. How many shirt-tie choices does he have?

2. **Telephones** A seven-digit telephone number can begin with any digit except 0 and 1.
   a. How many possible choices are there for the first digit? the second digit? the third digit? the seventh digit?
   b. How many different seven-digit telephone numbers are possible?

3. On a bookshelf there are five novels, two volumes of short stories, and three biographies. In how many ways can you select one of each?

4. A student council has 24 members. A 3-person committee is to arrange a car wash. Each person on the committee will have a task: One person will find a location, another will organize publicity, and the third will schedule workers. In how many different ways can three students be selected and assigned a job?

5. **a.** How many different 3-digit numbers are possible using 2, 3, 5, and 7 if you do *not* repeat any digits?
   b. **Critical Thinking** How many of the 3-digit numbers are even?
   c. **Writing** Explain how you found how many numbers are even in part (b).
   d. What is the probability that a number selected at random is even?

Calculator **Use a calculator to evaluate.**

6. $_8P_3$ 7. $_7P_3$ 8. $_6P_3$ 9. $_5P_3$ 10. $_4P_3$ 11. $_3P_3$

12. $_7P_7$ 13. $_7P_6$ 14. $_7P_5$ 15. $_7P_4$ 16. $_7P_2$ 17. $_7P_1$

18. **School Paper** For an article in the school newspaper, Cora took a poll in which she asked students to rank the top four basketball players on the high school team. There are fifteen members on the team. How many possible outcomes are there?

19. **Writing** Write a problem for which $_{24}P_3$ would be the solution.

20. **a.** **Open-ended** Use the letters of your last name. If any letters are repeated, use only one of them. For example, for the last name Bell, use the letters BEL. In how many ways can the resulting letters be arranged?
    b. In how many ways can two different letters be selected and arranged from your last name?

21. **Sports** In ice skating competitions, the order in which competitors skate is determined by a draw. If there are eight skaters in the finals, how many different orders are possible for the final program?

Which is greater?

22. $_8P_6$ or $_6P_2$

23. $_9P_7$ or $_9P_2$

24. $_{10}P_3$ or $_8P_4$

25. Standardized Test Prep For $r = 3$ and $_nP_r = 210$, find n.
   A. 3   **B.** 6   **C.** 7   **D.** 8   **E.** 70

Use the tiles at the right for Exercises 26 and 27.

26. a. What is the number of possible arrangements in which you can select four letters?
   b. Find the probability that you select C, A, R, and then E.

27. a. What is the number of possible arrangements in which you can select five letters?
   b. Find the probability that you select B, R, A, I, and then N.

28. Safety A lock, such as the ones used on many bikes and school lockers, uses permutations. This is because the order of the numbers *is* important. Suppose you have a lock with the digits 0–9. A three-digit sequence opens the lock, and no numbers are repeated.
   a. How many different sequences are possible?
   b. How many sequences use a 7 as the first digit?
   c. What is the probability that the sequence of numbers that opens your lock uses a 7 as the first digit?
   d. Critical Thinking What is the probability that the sequence of numbers that opens your lock includes a 7?

Exercises   MIXED REVIEW

Graph each function.

29. $y = 6x$ **30.** $y = \sqrt{x}$

31. $y = \dfrac{5}{x}$ **32.** $y = |x| + 3$

33. Camping Your family is planning a camping trip. The state park has two camping plans available. The first costs $95 for four nights at a campsite with family trail passes for three days. The second costs $70 for three nights at a campsite with family trail passes for two days. There is one daily charge for the campsite and one daily charge for the trail pass. Find each daily charge.

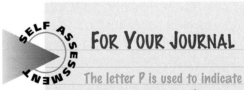

FOR YOUR JOURNAL

The letter *P* is used to indicate permutations and probability. Explain how you can tell what *P* means in a given problem.

Getting Ready for Lesson 11-7

A and B are independent events. Find $P(A$ and $B)$ for the given probabilities.

34. $P(A) = \dfrac{1}{3}, P(B) = \dfrac{3}{4}$

35. $P(A) = \dfrac{1}{8}, P(B) = \dfrac{5}{9}$

36. $P(A) = \dfrac{9}{10}, P(B) = \dfrac{5}{6}$

What You'll Learn

11-7 **Combinations**

- Finding combinations
- Solving probability problems involving combinations

...And Why

To investigate situations like selecting a jury

What You'll Need

- calculator

Food Suppose you are making a sandwich with three of these ingredients: turkey, cheese, tomato, and lettuce. Below are the permutations of the four ingredients taken three at a time.

- turkey, cheese, lettuce
- turkey, lettuce, cheese
- cheese, turkey, turkey
- cheese, lettuce, lettuce
- lettuce, cheese, turkey
- lettuce, cheese, turkey

- turkey, tomato, lettuce
- turkey, lettuce, tomato
- tomato, lettuce, turkey
- tomato, turkey, lettuce
- lettuce, turkey, tomato
- lettuce, tomato, turkey

- cheese, tomato, lettuce
- cheese, lettuce, tomato
- tomato, lettuce, cheese
- tomato, cheese, lettuce
- lettuce, cheese, tomato
- lettuce, tomato, cheese

- turkey, cheese, tomato
- turkey, tomato, cheese
- cheese, tomato, turkey
- cheese, turkey, tomato
- tomato, turkey, cheese
- tomato, cheese, turkey

For sandwiches the *order* of the ingredients does not matter. So there are only four types of sandwiches. Each sandwich type is a **combination,** a collection of objects without regard to order.

The number of combinations of sandwiches equals the number of permutations divided by the number of times each type of sandwich is repeated.

$$\text{number of combinations} = \frac{\text{total number of permutations}}{\text{number of times the objects in each group are repeated}}$$

You can use the notation $_nC_r$ to write the number of combinations of n objects chosen r at time. The number of times each group of objects is repeated depends on r.

$$_4C_3 = \frac{_4P_3}{_3P_3} = \frac{4 \cdot 3 \cdot 2}{3 \cdot 2 \cdot 1}$$

$$_nC_r = \frac{_nP_r}{_rP_r} = \frac{n(n-1)(n-2)\ldots}{r(r-1)(r-2)\ldots} \quad \begin{array}{l}\longleftarrow r \text{ factors starting with } n \\ \longleftarrow r \text{ factors starting with } r\end{array}$$

CALCULATOR HINT

You can use the following calculator steps to find $_4C_3$:

   `4` `MATH` PRB $_NC_R$ `3` `ENTER`

1. **Calculator** Evaluate each expression.
   - **a.** $_4C_2$
   - **b.** $_8C_5$
   - **c.** $_7C_3$
   - **d.** $_{10}C_4$

2. **a.** **Try This** For your history report, you can choose to write about two of five Presidents of the United States. Use $_nC_r$ notation to write the number of combinations possible for your report.
   - **b.** Calculate the number of combinations of presidents on whom you could report.

| Example 1 | Relating to the Real World |

Juries Twenty people report for jury duty. How many different twelve-person juries can be chosen?

The order in which jury members are listed does not distinguish one jury from another. You need the number of combinations of 20 objects chosen 12 at a time.

$$_{20}C_{12} = \frac{20 \cdot 19 \cdot 18 \cdot 17 \cdot 16 \cdot 15 \cdot 14 \cdot 13 \cdot 12 \cdot 11 \cdot 10 \cdot 9}{12 \cdot 11 \cdot 10 \cdot 9 \cdot 8 \cdot 7 \cdot 6 \cdot 5 \cdot 4 \cdot 3 \cdot 2 \cdot 1}$$

$$= 125970 \quad \longleftarrow \text{Use a calculator.}$$

There are 125,970 different twelve-person juries possible.

3. For some civil cases, at least nine of twelve jurors must agree on a verdict. How many combinations of nine jurors are possible on a twelve-person jury?

You can use combinations to solve probability problems. When finding the number of favorable outcomes, use the total number of objects that may give you a favorable outcome as the n value in $_nC_r$.

| Example 2 | Relating to the Real World |

Restaurants You and four friends visit a Thai restaurant. There are twelve different items on the menu. Seven are mild and the rest are spicy. You each order a different item at random. What is the probability that your group orders only mild items?

number of favorable outcomes $= _7C_5 \longleftarrow$ number of ways to choose 5 mild items from 7 mild items

number of possible outcomes $= _{12}C_5 \longleftarrow$ number of ways to choose 5 items from 12 items

$$P(5 \text{ mild menu items}) = \frac{\text{number of favorable outcomes}}{\text{total number of outcomes}}$$

$$= \frac{_7C_5}{_{12}C_5}$$

$$= \frac{7}{264}$$

The probability your group orders only mild items is $\frac{7}{264}$, or about 3%.

4. Suppose you and your friends like spicy food. What is the probability that you choose five different spicy items at random?

1. a. Spelling Bee Every spring the National Spelling Bee Championships are held in Washington, D.C. Prizes are awarded to the top three spellers. In 1995, 247 students competed. How many different arrangements of winners were possible?

   b. Many students in the competition hoped to make it to the final round of 10 students. How many combinations of 10 students were possible?

2. Sports A basketball team has 11 players. Five players are on the court at a time. Your little brother doesn't know much about basketball and randomly names 5 players on the team. What is the probability that your brother's line-up lists the same 5 players as the coach's line-up for the next game?

3. Writing Explain the difference between a permutation and a combination.

Calculator **Use a calculator to evaluate.**

4. $_6C_6$ **5.** $_6C_5$ **6.** $_6C_4$ **7.** $_6C_3$ **8.** $_6C_2$ **9.** $_6C_1$

10. $_{15}C_{11}$ **11.** $_{15}C_4$ **12.** $_8C_5$ **13.** $_8C_3$ **14.** $_7C_4$ **15.** $_7C_3$

16. a. Describe any patterns you see in the answers to Exercises 4–15.

   b. Critical Thinking Explain why the pattern you described is true.

   c. Open-ended Write two more combinations that have the pattern you described in part (a).

17. a. Geometry Draw four points on your paper like those in Figure 1. Draw line segments so that every point is joined with every other point.

   b. How many segments did you draw?

   c. Now find the number of segments you need for the drawing using combinations. You are joining four points, taking two at a time.

   d. How many segments would you need to join each point to all the others in Figure 2?

Figure 1

Figure 2

18. A famous problem, known as the Handshake Problem asks, "If ten people in a room shake hands with everyone else in the room, how many different handshakes occur?"

   a. Karen thinks that the Handshake Problem is a permutation problem while Tashia thinks it is a combination problem. What do you think? **Justify** your answer.

   b. Solve the problem.

   c. Critical Thinking Is the Handshake Problem similar to the problem in Exercise 17 (d)? Explain.

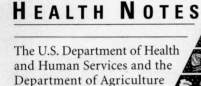

HEALTH NOTES

The U.S. Department of Health and Human Services and the Department of Agriculture guidelines recommend that

daily food intake should include at least 3–5 servings of vegetables, at least 2–4 servings of fruit, 6–11 servings of grains, 2–3 servings of milk or cheese, and 2–3 servings of meat or poultry.

14

19. Math in the Media Suppose you want to have the highest number of recommended daily servings of fruit without repeating a fruit. Find how many different combinations of these products you can have.

Classify each of the following as a permutation or a combination problem. Explain your choice.

20. A locker contains eight books. You select three books at random. How many different sets of books could you select?

21. You rent three videos to watch during spring vacation. In how many different orders can you view the three videos?

22. The security guard at an auto plant must visit 10 different sections of the building each night. He varies his route each evening. How many different routes are possible?

23. A committee of four people needs to be formed from your homeroom of 25 students. How many four-person committees are possible?

One Serving of Fruit	
apple	1
apple juice	1 cup
banana	1
cherries	10
grapefruit	$\frac{1}{2}$
orange	1
orange juice	1 cup
raisins	1 cup
strawberries	1 cup

24. Standardized Test Prep Compare the quantities in Columns A and B.

Column A	Column B
$_{10}C_7$	$_7P_4$

A. The quantity in Column A is greater.
B. The quantity in Column B is greater.
C. The quantities are equal.
D. The relationship cannot be determined from the given information.

Find the number of combinations of letters taken three at a time from each set of letters.

25. A B C D E   **26.** P Q R   **27.** E F G H I J K   **28.** M N O P

29. Open-ended Write and solve two problems: one that can be solved using permutations and one that can be solved using combinations.

30. For your birthday you received a gift certificate from a local music store for three CDs. There are eight that you would like to have. In how many different ways can you select your CDs?

31. Manufacturing Twelve computer screens are stored in a warehouse. The warehouse manager knows that three of the screens are defective, but the report telling him which ones are defective is missing. He selects five screens to begin testing.
 a. How many different choices of five screens does the manager have?
 b. In how many ways could he select five screens that include the defective ones?
 c. What is the probability that he finds the three defective screens when he tests the first five screens?

32. a. A committee of three people is to be selected from three boys and five girls. How many different committees are possible?
 b. How many committees could have all boys?
 c. What is the probability that a committee will have all boys?
 d. Critical Thinking What is the probability that the committee will have no boys?

33. The letters A, B, C, D, E, F, G, H, I, and J are written on slips of paper and placed in a hat. Two letters are drawn from the hat.
 a. What is the number of possible combinations of letters?
 b. How many combinations consist only of the vowels A, E, or I?
 c. What is the probability the letters chosen consist only of vowels?
 d. What is the probability the letters chosen consist only of B, C, D or F?

34. Research Find the number of members in your state legislature. Find how many ways a committee of ten people may be formed from the members of the legislature.

Chapter Project ▽ **Find Out by Communicating**

Every musical instrument has a part that vibrates to make different pitches. Choose an instrument and find out how it works. Make a poster that describes what vibrates and how different pitches are produced.

Exercises   MIXED REVIEW

Evaluate.

35. $_4P_2$ **36.** $_8P_3$ **37.** $_7P_6$

38. $_8P_6$ **39.** $_9P_1$ **40.** $_7P_4$

Express each sum or difference in simplest form.

41. $\dfrac{4x^2}{3x} + \dfrac{5}{3x}$ **42.** $\dfrac{5c}{8m} - \dfrac{7m}{c}$ **43.** $\dfrac{9x}{x^2 - 4} + \dfrac{4}{x + 2}$

44. $\dfrac{9}{z} + \dfrac{10}{3z}$ **45.** $\dfrac{12}{5n} - \dfrac{15}{4n}$ **46.** $\dfrac{8w^2}{3 - w} - \dfrac{5w}{18 - 2w^2}$

47. a. Weather After a heavy snowfall, a homeowner had to clear about four tons of snow off a 20 ft by 20 ft driveway. A full shovel of snow weighs about 7 lb. How many times would the homeowner have to fill his shovel to clear the driveway?
 b. How many tons of snow would be on a 20 ft by 30 ft driveway?

PORTFOLIO

Select one or two items from your work for this chapter. Consider:
• corrected work
• diagrams, graphs, or charts
• a journal entry
Explain why you have included each selection you make.

GOOD VIBRATIONS

Questions on pages 514, 526, 531, 536, and 547 should help you to complete your project. Plan a presentation of what you have learned for your classmates. Include graphs, charts, illustrations, and demonstrations on homemade or professional instruments.

Reflect and Revise

Share your presentation with a small group of your classmates. Were your explanations clear and accurate? How does your musical instrument sound? Were you able to describe its pitch? If necessary, make any changes in your work.

Follow Up

In Western culture, C and C# are consecutive pitches in the chromatic scale. The ratio of their frequencies is about 1:1.06. Find out about the scales used in Asian cultures. How might their scales affect the design of their instruments?

For More Information

Haak, Sheila. "Using the Monochord: A Classroom Demonstration on the Mathematics of Musical Scales." *Applications of Secondary School Mathematics.* Reston, Virginia: National Council of Teachers of Mathematics, 1991.

Macaulay, David. *The Way Things Work.* Boston: Houghton Mifflin, 1988. Software Version: Dorling Kindersley Multimedia, 1994.

Wilkinson, Scott R. *Tuning In: Microtonality in Electronic Music: A Basic Guide to Alternate Scales, Temperaments, and Microtuning Using Synthesizers.* Milwaukee, Wisconsin: H. Leonard Books, 1988.

Wrap Up

Key Terms

asymptote (p. 516)
combination (p. 543)
constant of variation (p. 510)
domain (p. 522)
inverse variation (p. 510)
multiplication counting
   principle (p. 539)

$_nC_r$ (p. 543)
$_nP_r$ (p. 540)
permutation (p. 539)
rational equation (p. 532)
rational expression
   (p. 522)
rational function (p. 516)

How am I doing?

- State three ideas from this chapter that you think are important. Explain your choices.
- Explain the importance of restrictions on the variable in rational expressions.

Inverse Variation 11-1

When two quantities are related so that their product is constant, they form an **inverse variation.** An inverse variation can be written $xy = k$, where k is the **constant of variation.**

Find the constant of variation for each inverse variation.

1. $m = 6$ when $n = 1$ **2.** $g = 90$ when $h = 0.1$ **3.** $s = 88$ when $t = 0.05$

For each table, tell whether it represents an inverse variation. If so, write an equation to model the data.

4.

x	1	1.4	3	7
y	4	5.6	12	28

5.

x	4	1	2	2.5
y	2.65	10.6	5.3	4.24

Rational Functions 11-2

A **rational function** can be written in the form $f(x) = \frac{\text{polynomial}}{\text{polynomial}}$. The graph of a rational function may have asymptotes. An **asymptote** is a line that a graph approaches, but does not cross.

Graph each function. Use a dashed line for each asymptote.

6. $y = \frac{8}{x}$ **7.** $y = \frac{20}{x}$ **8.** $y = \frac{6}{x - 5}$ **9.** $y = \frac{3}{x} + 2$

10. Open-ended Write the equation of a rational function with a graph that is in three quadrants only.

11. Writing Explain why the function $f(x) = \frac{5}{x + 3}$ has asymptotes.

Rational Expressions

A **rational expression** can be written in the form $\frac{\text{polynomial}}{\text{polynomial}}$ where a variable is in the denominator. The **domain** of a variable is all real numbers excluding the values for which the denominator is zero. A rational expression is in simplest form when the numerator and denominator have no common factors other than 1.

You can multiply and divide rational expressions.

$\frac{a}{b} \cdot \frac{c}{d} = \frac{ac}{bd}$, where b and d are nonzero

$\frac{a}{b} \div \frac{c}{d} = \frac{a}{b} \cdot \frac{d}{c}$, where b, c, and d are nonzero

Simplify each expression and state any restrictions on the variable.

12. $\frac{x^2 - 4}{x + 2}$ **13.** $\frac{5x}{20x + 15}$ **14.** $\frac{-3t}{t^3 - t^2}$ **15.** $\frac{z + 2}{2z^2 + z - 6}$

Find each product or quotient.

16. $\frac{8}{m - 3} \cdot \frac{3m}{m + 1}$ **17.** $\frac{2e + 1}{8e - 4} \div \frac{4e^2 + 4e + 1}{4e - 2}$ **18.** $\frac{5c + 3}{c^2 - 1} \cdot \frac{c + 1}{2c}$ **19.** $\frac{4n + 8}{3n} \div \frac{4}{9n}$

Operations with Rational Expressions

You can add and subtract rational expressions. Restate each expression with the LCD as the denominator, then add or subtract the numerators.

Add or subtract.

20. $\frac{5}{k} + \frac{3}{k}$ **21.** $\frac{8x}{x - 7} - \frac{4}{x - 7}$ **22.** $\frac{9}{3x - 1} + \frac{5x}{2x + 3}$ **23.** $\frac{7m}{(m + 1)(m - 1)} - \frac{10}{m + 1}$

24. Standardized Test Prep What is the LCD of $\frac{1}{4}$, $\frac{2}{x}$, $\frac{5x}{3x - 2}$, and $\frac{3}{8x}$?

A. $96x^3 - 64x^2$ **B.** $12x + 2$ **C.** $24x^2 - 16x$ **D.** $27x^2 - 6x - 8$ **E.** $6x + 2$

Solving Rational Equations

You can use the least common denominator (LCD) to solve **rational equations.** Check possible solutions in the original equation to make sure that they do not make the denominator equal to zero.

Solve each equation.

25. $\frac{1}{2} + \frac{3}{t} = \frac{5}{8}$ **26.** $\frac{3}{m - 4} + \frac{1}{3(m - 4)} = \frac{6}{m}$ **27.** $\frac{2c}{c - 4} - 2 = \frac{4}{c + 5}$

28. Business A new photocopier can make 72 copies in 2 min. When an older photocopier is working, the two photocopiers can make 72 copies in 1.5 min. How long does it take the older photocopier working alone to make 72 copies?

You can find a number of different outcomes using the **multiplication counting principle.** If there are m ways to make a first selection and n ways to make a second selection, there are $m \times n$ ways to make the two selections.

A **permutation** is an arrangement of objects in a definite order. To calculate $_nP_r$, the number of permutations of n objects taken r at a time, use the formula

$$_nP_r = n(n-1)(n-2)\ldots \quad \longleftarrow r \text{ factors starting with } n$$

Evaluate.

29. $_5P_3$ **30.** $_8P_4$ **31.** $_6P_4$ **32.** $_5P_2$ **33.** $_9P_4$ **34.** $_7P_2$

35. a. Telephones Before 1995, three-digit area codes could begin with any number except 0 or 1. The middle number was either 0 or 1, and the last number could be any digit. How many possible area codes were there?

   b. Beginning in 1995, area codes were not limited to having 0 or 1 as the middle number. How many new area codes became available?

A **combination** is an arrangement of objects without regard to order. The number of combinations $= \dfrac{\text{number of permutations}}{\text{number of times the objects in each group are repeated}}$.
To find $_nC_r$, the combinations of n objects taken r at a time, use the formula

$$_nC_r = \frac{_nP_r}{_rP_r} = \frac{n(n-1)(n-2)\ldots}{r(r-1)(r-2)\ldots} \quad \begin{array}{l} \longleftarrow r \text{ factors starting with } n \\ \longleftarrow r \text{ factors starting with } r \end{array}$$

Evaluate.

36. $_6C_5$ **37.** $_{10}C_4$ **38.** $_9C_2$ **39.** $_{11}C_3$ **40.** $_5C_4$ **41.** $_6C_4$

42. Nutrition You want to have three servings of dairy products without repeating a food. Milk, yogurt, cottage cheese, and cheddar cheese are in the refrigerator. How many different combinations can you have?

43. Ten friends go to an amusement park. A roller-coaster car holds eight people. Find how many different groups from the ten friends can ride in one car.

44. You subscribe to eight monthly magazines. Two are news magazines, three are on sports, two are on health and fitness, and one is about gardening. What is the probability that the next two magazines you receive in the mail are sports magazines?

Find the constant of variation for each inverse variation.

1. $y = 5$ when $x = 6$

2. $y = 2.4$ when $x = 10$

3. $y = 78$ when $x = 0.1$

4. $y = 5.3$ when $x = 9.1$

5. Standardized Test Prep Which point is *not* on the same graph of an inverse variation as the others?

   A. $(3, 12)$ **B.** $(9, 4)$ **C.** $(6, 6)$
   D. $(16, 2)$ **E.** $(2, 18)$

6. It took you 1.5 h to drive to a concert at 40 mi/h. How long will it take you to drive back driving at 50 mi/h?

Graph each function. Include a dashed line for each asymptote.

7. $y = \dfrac{6}{x}$

8. $y = \dfrac{15}{x}$

9. $y = \dfrac{1}{x} + 3$

10. $y = \dfrac{4}{x} + 3$

11. Writing Explain how direct variations and inverse variations are similar and different. Include an example of each.

Find each product or quotient.

12. $\dfrac{3}{x - 2} \cdot \dfrac{x^2 - 4}{12}$

13. $\dfrac{5x}{x^2 + 2x} \div \dfrac{30x^2}{x + 2}$

14. $\dfrac{4w}{3w - 5} \cdot \dfrac{7}{2w}$

15. $\dfrac{6c - 2}{c + 5} \div \dfrac{3c - 9}{c}$

16. Open-ended Write a rational expression for which 6 and 3 are restricted from the domain.

Solve each equation.

17. $\dfrac{v}{3} + \dfrac{v}{v + 5} = \dfrac{4}{v + 5}$

18. $\dfrac{16}{x + 10} = \dfrac{8}{2x - 1}$

19. $\dfrac{2}{3} + \dfrac{t + 6}{t - 3} = \dfrac{18}{2(t - 3)}$

20. If three people can clean an apartment working two hours each, how long will it take a crew of four people?

Simplify.

21. $\dfrac{5}{t} + \dfrac{t}{t + 1}$

22. $\dfrac{9}{n} - \dfrac{8}{n + 1}$

23. $\dfrac{2y}{y^2 - 9} - \dfrac{1}{y - 3}$

24. $\dfrac{4b - 2}{3b} + \dfrac{b}{b + 2}$

Classify each of the following as a combination or permutation problem. Explain your choice. Then solve the problem.

25. The 30-member debate club needs a president and treasurer. How many different pairs of officers are possible?

26. How many different ways can you choose two books from the six books on your shelf?

27. You have enough money for two extra pizza toppings. If there are six possible toppings, how many different pairs of toppings can you choose?

Find the number of combinations of letters taken four at a time from each set.

28. A E I O U Y

29. E Q U A T I O N

30. L E A R N

Evaluate.

31. $_4C_3$ 32. $_8P_6$ 33. $_{10}P_7$ 34. $_5C_2$

35. You have 5 kinds of wrapping paper and 4 different colored bows. How many different combinations of paper and bows can you have?

36. There are 15 books on your summer reading list. Three of them are plays, one is poetry, and the rest are novels. What is the probability that you will choose three novels if you choose the books at random?

Part I

1 Suppose you buy two items that cost d dollars each. You give the cashier $10. Which expression models the change you should receive?
(1) $10 - d$ (3) $10 + 2d$
(2) $10 - 2d$ (4) $d - 10$

2 Evaluate $2y + 7$ for $y = 4$.
(1) 31   (3) 13
(2) 11   (4) 15

3 Which of the following expressions has a value of 48?
(1) $[8 + (2 \cdot 4)] \cdot 3$ (3) $(8 + 2) \cdot 4 \cdot 3$
(2) $8 + 2 \cdot 4 \cdot 3$ (4) $(8 + 2) \cdot (4 \cdot 3)$

4 If $y - x > 0$, what does $|x - y|$ equal?
(1) $y - x$ and $|y - x|$
(2) $|y - x|$ and $x - y$
(3) $y - x$ and $x - y$
(4) $|y - x|$ only

5 A relation exists between an electronic store's profit and the number of computers it sells. In this relation, what is the dependent variable?
(1) store's profit
(2) price of each computer
(3) number of computers sold
(4) number of customers

6 Which equation is represented by the graph?
(1) $f(x) = |x| + 1$
(2) $f(x) = (x + 1)^2$
(3) $f(x) = x - 1$
(4) $f(x) = |x| - 1$

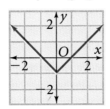

7 A baker can form two loaves of bread in 5 min. How many loaves can the baker form in an hour?
(1) 24   (3) 22
(2) 150   (4) 6

8 What is the solution of $|k + 2| = 13$?
(1) 11 only   (3) -11 and 15
(2) -15 and 11   (4) no solution

9 Which is *not* a solution of $5x - 4 < 12$?
(1) 3   (3) 4
(2) 0   (4) -2

10 Which compound inequality represents the set of numbers shown on the number line?

(1) $3 \le x < 2$ (3) $-2 < x \le 2$
(2) $3 \ge x$ and $x < 2$ (4) $-2 \le x \le 2$

11 Which of the following is an equation of a line passing through $(5, 1)$ and $(3, -3)$?
(1) $y = \frac{3}{2}x - 2$ (3) $y = 2x - 9$
(2) $y = 2x - \frac{3}{2}$ (4) $y = 2x + 9$

12 A scatter plot shows a positive correlation. Which of the following could be an equation of the line of best fit?
(1) $y = -5x + 1$ (3) $2x + 3y = 6$
(2) $x = 16$ (4) $y = 2x - 1$

13 What is the minimum value of the function $f(x) = x^2 + x + 4$?
(1) $\frac{15}{4}$ (3) $\frac{17}{4}$
(2) 4   (4) -2

14 Which of the following points is *not* a solution of $y \le 2x^2 - 5x + 3$?
(1) $(3, 6)$ (3) $(-1, 4)$
(2) $(0, -2)$ (4) $(2, 18)$

15 If $x^2 = 36$ and $y^2 = 16$, what is the least possible value for $y - x$?
(1) 2   (3) 10
(2) -2 (4) -10

16 Suppose you deposit $1000 in an account paying 5.5% interest, compounded annually. Which expression represents the value of the investment after 10 years?

(1) $1000 \cdot 1.55^{10}$ (3) $1000 \cdot 0.055^{10}$

(2) $1000 \cdot 1.055^{10}$ (4) $1000 \cdot 10^{1.055}$

17 Which expression is in simplest form and is equivalent to $-3a^8 \cdot cb^{-3} \cdot b^{12} \cdot 9c^5$?

(1) $-27a^8b^9c^6$ (3) $-27a^8b^9c^5$

(2) $6a^9b^5c^6$ (4) $-27a^8b^{15}c^6$

18 Which number has the least value?

(1) $2.8 \cdot 10^{-5}$ (3) $7.04 \cdot 10^{-8}$

(2) $8.3 \cdot 10^{-7}$ (4) $1.6 \cdot 10^{-8}$

19 A support wire from the top of a tower is 100 ft long. It is anchored at a spot 60 ft from the base of the tower. What is the height of the tower?

(1) 80 ft   (3) 800 ft

(2) 40 ft   (4) 160 ft

20 Which expression is equal to $8x^3 - 12x^2 + 4x$?

(1) $2x(4x^2 + 6x + 2)$

(2) $x(8x^3 - 12x + 4)$

(3) $4x(2x^2 - 3x + 1)$

(4) $4x(4x^2 - 3x + 1)$

21 The value of x varies inversely with y, and $x = 2$ when $y = 5$. What is x when $y = 10$?

(1) 4   (2) 5   (3) 7   (4) 1

22 What is the restriction on the variable in $\frac{x-8}{x-10}$?

(1) $x \neq 8$ (3) $x \neq 10$

(2) $x \neq 9$ (4) $x \neq 11$

23 What is the LCD of $\frac{1}{2}, \frac{3}{10x}, \frac{4x}{2x+3}$, and $\frac{5}{x}$?

(1) $40x^2 + 60x$ (3) $20x^2 + 30x$

(2) $10x + 6$ (4) $4x^2 + 6x$

24 What is the quotient $\frac{x-4}{x^2+2x} \div \frac{x^2-16}{x^2-x}$?

(1) $\frac{x-1}{x^2+6x+8}$ (3) $\frac{x^2-6x+4}{x^2+x-4}$

(2) $\frac{1}{x^2+x-4}$ (4) $\frac{x^2+6x+8}{x^2-1}$

Part II

25 What is the solution set for $5h < 20$ if the replacement set is $\{1, 2, 3, 4, 5\}$?

26 Suppose your test scores are 88, 78, 81, 83, and 90. What score do you need on your next test to raise your median score to 85?

27 Suppose you toss three coins. What is the probability of getting 2 heads and 1 tail?

28 Translate the following mathematical sentence into an equation. Then solve the equation. Seventeen more than three times a number is 32.

29 A bag contains 10 red marbles and 20 white marbles. You draw a marble, keep it, and draw another. What is the probability of drawing two red marbles?

30 A bag contains 6 blue marbles and 4 yellow marbles. You draw a marble, replace it, and draw another marble. Make a probability distribution table showing the chances of getting 0, 1, or 2 blue marbles.

31 A new company employed 12 people. Two years later it employed a total of 20 people.

  a What was the percent of increase?

  b If one of the 20 people retires, what would be the percent of decrease?

32 The sides of a square are measured as $8\frac{1}{2}$ in. each.

  a What is the greatest possible error in the calculation of the perimeter of the square?

  b Write the greatest possible error in the calculation of the perimeter as a percent. Round to the nearest tenth of a percent.

33 Solve the system using elimination.

$x + y = 34$

$x - y = 16$

34 In triangle ABC, $\angle C$ is a right angle, $\overline{AB} = 7$ units, and $m\angle B = 28°$. What are the lengths of $\overline{BC}$ and $\overline{AC}$ to the nearest hundredth unit?

35 What is the simplest form of $\frac{3x-9}{x^2-6x+9}$?

Part III

36 What is the solution of $4x^2 - 4x - 3 \leq 0$?

37 Suppose you earn a commission of 6% on your first $500 of sales and 10% on all sales above $500. If you earn $130 in commissions, what are your total sales?

38 Write an equation of the line that passes through $(2, -3)$ and is perpendicular to the graph of $y = \frac{2}{5}x - \frac{7}{8}$.

39 The slopes of four different lines are: $\frac{3}{5}$, $-\frac{10}{6}$, $-\frac{5}{3}$, and $\frac{9}{15}$. Fully describe the closed figure formed by these lines.

40 A manufacturing company spends $1200 each day on plant costs plus $7 per item for labor and materials. The items sell for $23 each. How many items must the company sell in one day to equal its daily costs?

41 Find the x-intercepts of the function $y = 4x^2 - 9x + 2$. Then graph the function.

42 Find the x-intercept and the y-intercept of the graph of $y = \frac{5}{x-2} + 1$.

43 Simplify: $\frac{3}{s-1} + \frac{2}{s^2 + s - 2}$.

44 Suppose you have 12 coins that total $1.95. Some coins are dimes and some are quarters. How many of each coin do you have?

Part IV

45 A truck traveling 45 mi/h and a car traveling 55 mi/h cover the same distance. The truck travels 4 h longer than the car. How far did they travel?

46 Workers at a local charity worked the following numbers of hours: 3, 5, 9, 5, 8, 4, 2, 10, 7, 3, 4, 6.
 a Find the mean.
 b Find the range of the data.
 c Graph the data in a cumulative frequency histogram.

47 A box is 2 cm wide, 5 cm long, and 4 cm high. To the nearest tenth of a centimeter, what is the distance between the most distant pair of corners?

48 A rectangle was originally twice as long as it is wide. Its sides have each been increased by 10 cm. The area of the new rectangle is 252 cm². Find the dimensions of the original rectangle.

49 A group of people reported watching a certain television show. The table shows their ages, rounded to the nearest year.
 a Compute the percentiles for each interval in the table. Round to the nearest tenth of a percent.
 b Make a histogram for the data that shows percentiles on the vertical axis.
 c What percent of the viewers are 20–39 years old?

Ages	Cumulative Frequency
0–9	27
10–19	79
20–29	165
30–39	235
40–49	300
50–59	364
60+	400

50 One baker can shape 24 bagels in 15 min. When the baker works with an apprentice, they can shape 24 bagels in 10 min. How long does it take the apprentice to shape 24 bagels working alone?

51 Solve: $\frac{-2}{x-3} = \frac{x+4}{2(x-3)} + \frac{1}{4}$.

52 There are 20 people in the art club.
 a The club needs a president, vice president, secretary, and treasurer. How many different groups of officers are possible?
 b The club needs a publicity committee of four people. How many different ways can the committee be chosen?

Challenge Problems

CHAPTER 1

1-1 Six students received scores of 83, 93, 97, 99, 91, and 88 on an algebra test. One of the original scores was incorrect. After correction, the median increased 2 points. The corrected data produced a mode of 97. What was the mean for the corrected data? Justify your answer.

1-2 Write an equation that models the relationship in the table.

Hours	Pay
1	$5.75
2	$9.50
3	$13.25
4	$17.00

1-3(1) *Open-ended* Using operation symbols and parentheses as needed, write an expression using five 3's that has the value 11.

1-3(2) Determine which expression, I or II, equals the given expression. Support your answer with numerical examples.

a. $(d \div e) \div f$
  I. $d \div (e \div f)$ **II.** $(d \div f) \div e$

b. $\dfrac{m - n}{p - q}$
  I. $\dfrac{n - m}{q - p}$ **II.** $\dfrac{m - n}{q - p}$

1-4 Order $|x + y|, |x - y|, |x| - |y|,$ and $x - y$ from least to greatest for $x = -8$ and $y = -10$.

1-5 For what integer values of n will the expression $(-n)^3$ be positive and have a 2 in the ones place?

1-6 Evaluate $\dfrac{\left(\frac{5}{3} - (-\frac{2}{3})\right)\left(\frac{4}{9} - (-\frac{1}{9})\right)^2}{-\frac{4}{3} \div \frac{8}{5}}$.

1-7 Use the random number table below to conduct a simulation to find the experimental probability of obtaining a sum less than 7 when two number cubes are rolled. (*Hint*: First cross out the digits for impossible outcomes.)

23948	71470	12573	05954
65628	22310	09311	94864
41261	09943	34078	79481

1-8 The coordinates of the vertices of a rectangle are $(0, 1)$, $(1, 3)$, $(5, 1)$, and $(4, -1)$. They are shown in matrix A.

$$A = \begin{bmatrix} 0 & 1 \\ 1 & 3 \\ 5 & 1 \\ 4 & -1 \end{bmatrix}$$

a. Write a matrix B that when added to matrix A would add -3 to every x-coordinate and 1 to every y-coordinate.
b. Find the sum of matrices A and B.
c. Graph the original rectangle and the rectangle represented by $A + B$. Describe how the new rectangle is related to the original rectangle.

1-9 The spreadsheet below shows test scores and mean test scores for an algebra student. The student enters each test score in column A, and the spreadsheet computes the rest. Write the formulas for cells B4, C4, and D4.

	A	B	C	D
1	Test score	Total score	Number of tests	Mean score
2	89	89	1	89
3	95	184	2	92
4	98	282	3	94

CHAPTER 2

2-1 *Open-ended* Marie services vending machines at the locations shown on the map below. If necessary, Marie could move her warehouse from Seventh and B Streets to cut delivery time and cost. Recommend a warehouse location for each of the following delivery routes. Explain your reasoning.
  a. Marie makes one continuous trip from the warehouse, stopping at each location and returning to the warehouse.
  b. Marie makes a round trip from the warehouse to each of the locations.

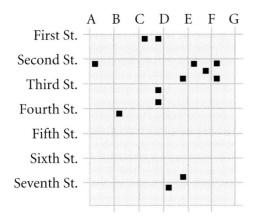

2-2 *Open-ended* The graph below represents the speed of a vehicle over a certain period of time. Draw a graph that could represent the distance the vehicle traveled over the same period of time.

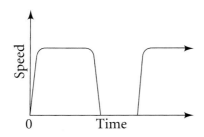

2-3 **a.** For this pattern of blocks, copy and complete the table below.

Number of Blocks High	Number of Blocks
1	
2	
3	
4	
5	

  b. Graph the data in the table.

2-4 The function $y = [x]$ is called the greatest integer function. $[x]$ is the greatest integer less than or equal to x. For example, $[2.99] = 2$ and $[-2.3] = -3$.
  a. Evaluate each of the following:
     $[0.5]$ $[-0.1]$ $[-1.99]$ $[-5.2]$
  b. The domain of the function $y = [x]$ is all real numbers. What is the range?

2-5 The function $s(x)$, which is sometimes called the signum function, is defined as follows:

$$s(x) = \begin{cases} 1 \text{ if } x > 0 \\ 0 \text{ if } x = 0 \\ -1 \text{ if } x < 0 \end{cases}$$

For example, $s(17) = 1$, $s(0) = 0$, and $s(-32) = -1$.
  a. Evaluate each of the following.
     $s(3.77)$ $s(0.003)$ $s(-1.5)$ $s(-2300)$
  b. If the domain of the function is all real numbers, what is the range?
  c. Do you think $s(a + b) = s(a) + s(b)$ for all real numbers? First, test some values of a and b. Then, if your answer is yes, justify your answer. If your answer is no, give a counterexample by showing values of a and b for which the statement is *not* true.

2-6 a. Complete the table of values for the function $y = x^3$.

x	y
-2	
-1.5	
-1	
-0.5	
0	
0.5	
1	
1.5	
2	

b. Use the table to graph the function.
c. Will any points that satisfy $y = x^3$ lie in Quadrant II or IV? Explain.

2-7 Make a table of values and graph each of the following absolute value functions. Then describe how the graphs are similar and how they are different.
a. $y = |x - 2|$ **b.** $y = 2|x|$
c. $y = |x| - 2$ **d.** $y = -|x|$
e. $y = |x + 1| - 1$

2-8 You can use the formula
$$\text{odds} = \frac{\text{number of favorable outcomes}}{\text{number of unfavorable outcomes}}$$
to compute the odds in favor of any event. A gardener is planting tulip bulbs in a variety of colors. For the bulbs she plans to plant, the odds that a randomly chosen bulb is for a pink tulip are $\frac{3}{20}$. What is the least possible number of bulbs the gardener is planting?

CHAPTER 3

3-1 a. Solve each equation.

$22 = 23 + a$ $\frac{s}{4} = \frac{1}{16}$

$-a = 0.1$ $2T = -33$

$f + 10 = 11$ $\frac{5}{8} + t = -\frac{1}{8}$

$80h = -1288$ $\frac{1}{5}u = 4$

$9 + n = 33$ $w - 1\frac{1}{6} = -1\frac{5}{6}$

b. Order the ten solutions from part (a) from least to greatest. Use this order to spell a sentence or phrase with the corresponding variables.

3-2 a. Solve each equation.

$16a - 22 = 106$ $5\frac{3}{4} + \frac{b}{8} = 6\frac{1}{2}$

$5c - 23 = -38$ $17.2 - \frac{d}{3} = 15.45$

b. Use the solutions in part (a) to find the perimeter of this figure.

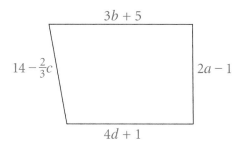

$3b + 5$

$14 - \frac{2}{3}c$ $2a - 1$

$4d + 1$

3-3 A triangle has perimeter 165 cm. The first side is 65 cm less than twice the second side. The third side is 10 cm less than the second side. Write and solve an equation to find the length of each side of the triangle. (*Hint:* Let $x =$ length of the second side.)

3-4 A collection of 33 coins is worth 5 dollars. The coins are nickels, dimes, and quarters. There are three times as many dimes as nickels. How many of each type of coin are there?

3-5 a. Elsa biked a certain distance at 12 mi/h. Then she walked twice as far at 4 mi/h. Her total time was $3\frac{1}{2}$ h. What was the total distance Elsa traveled? (*Hint:* Use the formula time $= \frac{\text{distance}}{\text{rate}}$.)

b. Sketch a graph to describe the distance Elsa traveled over time.

3-6 At a community college, 80 students are incoming freshmen. Of these, 72 are enrolled in mathematics, 70 are enrolled in an English class, and 3 are enrolled in neither. This information is shown in the following Venn diagram.

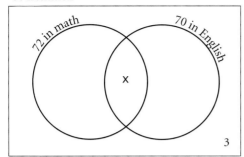

80 freshmen

a. How many students x are enrolled in both mathematics and English? In mathematics but not English? In English but not mathematics?

b. If one freshman is chosen at random, what is the probability that the student is enrolled in both mathematics and English?

c. If one freshman is chosen at random, what is the probability that the student is enrolled in mathematics and not English?

d. If two freshmen are chosen at random, what is the probability that the first student is enrolled in mathematics and English, and the second is enrolled in mathematics and not English?

3-7 Since percent is a ratio that compares a number to 100, $a\% = \frac{a}{100} = 0.01a$.

a. What is $n\%$ of $\frac{6}{n}$?

b. $2k$ is $k\%$ of what?

c. What percent of $0.75x$ is $3x$?

3-8 *Open-ended* Find a rate of speed and a distance that will make the following statement true.

If I increase my rate of speed by 20%, I can get to my destination one hour earlier than I usually do.

CHAPTER 4

4-1 Solve each equation.

a. $\frac{3x - 5}{24} = \frac{8}{3}$

b. $\frac{2}{x - 3} = \frac{8}{9}$

c. $\frac{3x + 5}{12} = \frac{5}{4}$

4-2 At 9:00 A.M., your friends begin a hike, walking at 4 mi/h. Starting late, you begin from the same place at 9:45 A.M. If you run at 10 mi/h, when will you catch your friends?

4-3 Solve each equation. (*Hint:* Check each solution in the original equation.)

a. $|x + 4| = 3x$

b. $|4x - 5| = 2x + 1$

c. $8|2x + 3| = 4x$

4-4 a. The formula for the area A of a trapezoid is $A = \frac{1}{2}(b_1 + b_2)h$, where b_1 and b_2 represent the lengths of the parallel sides and h represents the height. Solve for b_1.

b. The area of this trapezoid is 30 cm². Use your answer to part (a) to find b_1.

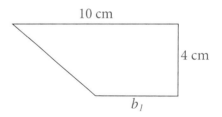

4-5 Decide if each statement is true for all real numbers. If the statement is not true, give a counterexample by showing real numbers for which the statement is false.

a. $a - b < a + b$.

b. If $a \geq b$, then $a + c \geq b + c$.

c. If $c > d$, then $a - c < a - d$.

d. If $a < b$, then $a < b + c$.

4-6 If a, b, and c are real numbers, for which values of a are the following statements true? (*Hint:* Test each statement replacing a with a positive number, a negative number, and 0.)
   a. If $c < 0$, then $ac < a$.
   b. If $b > c$, then $ab > ac$.
   c. If $b > c$, then $a^2b > a^2c$.
   d. If $b > c$, then $ab = ac$.
   e. If $b > c$, then $\frac{b}{a} < \frac{c}{a}$.

4-7 Solve each inequality. Graph the solutions on a number line.
   a. $\frac{3}{4}x - \frac{3}{2}(\frac{1}{6} + 3x) \le \frac{1}{2} - x$
   b. $2 - a \ge -[4a + 6 - 3(a - 3)]$

4-8 Graph the solutions of each absolute value inequality on a number line.
   a. $|x - 2| < \frac{1}{2}$ **b.** $|x - 1| < 2$
   c. $|x - \frac{1}{2}| \le 2$ **d.** $|x - 2| \le 1$
   e. Are there values of x that make all four inequalities true? If so, describe them by writing an absolute value inequality.

4-9 **a.** Graph $|3x - 6| \le 12$ using the set of negative integers as the replacement set.
   b. Write an inequality that models your graph.

CHAPTER 5

5-1 Find the slope of $\overleftrightarrow{PQ}$. Then find the values of x and y so that point R will lie on $\overleftrightarrow{PQ}$.
   a. $P(12, 1)$, $Q(-6, 25)$, $R(x, 9)$
   b. $P(-15, 4)$, $Q(-15, -5)$, $R(x, -8)$
   c. $P(7, -5)$, $Q(9, -1)$, $R(3, y)$

5-2 The table shows a linear function. Find the value of y when $x = 120$.

x	y
4	14
8	15.5
12	17
16	18.5

5-3 Suppose a car gets 24 mi/gal. Then the number of gallons g of gas used varies directly with the number of miles m traveled. The equation is $g = \frac{1}{24}m$.
   a. Suppose the price of gas is \$1.14/gal. Write an equation for the cost c for g gallons of gas. Is this a direct variation?
   b. Write a direct variation equation that relates the cost of gas to the number of miles traveled. What is the constant of variation?

5-4 Write an equation of a line that has the same slope as the line $3x - 5y = 7$ and the same y-intercept as the line $2y - 9x + 1 = 9x$.

5-5 **a.** Write an equation in slope-intercept form for the line that passes through the points $(0, h)$ and (c, d).
   b. Use your answer to part (a) to write an equation for the line through the points $(0, 3)$ and $(2, 2)$.

5-6 The number of participants taking a national college entrance test are shown for the years 1988 through 1997.

Year	Participants (thousands)
1988	842
1989	855
1990	817
1991	796
1992	832
1993	875
1994	892
1995	945
1996	925
1997	959

   a. Divide the data into two groups: 1988–1992 and 1993–1997. For each group find the ordered pair (mean of years, mean of participants).

b. Plot the points in the table and graph the line through the two ordered pairs found in part (a). The line approximates the line of best fit. Is its correlation coefficient closest to $-1, 0,$ or 1? Explain.

c. Write an equation of the line you drew in part (b).

d. Predict the number of participants taking the entrance test in the year 2010.

5-7 a. Graph $2x + 3y = 6$ and $2x + 3y = 18$.

b. What is the slope of each line?

c. Compare the x-intercepts of the two lines. How are they related? How are the y-intercepts related?

5-8 A quadrilateral with two pairs of parallel sides and with diagonals that are perpendicular is a rhombus. Quadrilateral $ABCD$ has vertices $A(-2, 2)$, $B(1, 6)$, $C(6, 6)$, and $D(3, 2)$. Show that $ABCD$ is a rhombus.

5-9 You want to go into business making earrings. With plan A, you would spend $200 on materials and charge $9.20 for each pair of earrings. With plan B, you would spend $236 on materials and charge $10.40 for each pair of earrings.

a. With which plan would you break even selling fewer earrings? Explain why.

b. Suppose you can make up to 100 pairs of earrings with the materials you buy for either plan. If you hope to stay in business long past the break-even point, which plan is the better choice? Explain.

CHAPTER 6

6-1 The slope of the line joining point $P(x, y)$ to the origin is $\frac{2}{9}$. The slope of the line joining P to $(-4, 3)$ is 1. Find the values of x and y.

6-2 Use the substitution method to solve for the variables $t, r,$ and s.

$t + r + s = 20$
$r = t + 3$
$t + 5r + 10s = 129$

6-3 Solve each system for x and y.

a. $\dfrac{6}{x} - \dfrac{4}{y} = -4$
$\dfrac{3}{x} + \dfrac{8}{y} = 3$

b. $ax + y = c$
$ax + by = 0$

6-4 An artist sells original hand-painted greeting cards. He makes $2.50 profit on a small card and $4.00 profit on a large card. He generally sells 5 large cards for every 2 small cards. He wants a profit of $10,000 from large and small cards this year.

a. Write an equation showing the total profit from both types of cards that will equal the desired profit.

b. Write an equation showing the relationship between the number of large cards and small cards the artist generally sells.

c. Solve the system of equations to determine how many of each kind of card he needs to have available.

d. The artist can create a card every 12 minutes. How many hours will he need to complete his annual requirement?

e. What is the artist's hourly rate of pay based on your answer in part (d)?

6-5 The following two statements describe the solution of a linear inequality.
The points $(0, -3)$ and $(8, 5)$ lie on the boundary of the solutions, but neither point is a solution.
The point $(1, 1)$ is not a solution.

a. Graph the solution described.

b. Write an inequality that has the solution described.

6-6 a. Graph the system.

$|x| - y \le 4$
$|x| + y \le 4$

b. Describe the geometric shape formed by the solution.

c. Write another system whose solution has the same shape.

6-7 **a.** *Open-ended* Write a system of restrictions that forms a triangular region that lies in Quadrant I.

b. Find the maximum and minimum values of $K = 2x + y$ using the restrictions from part (a).

6-8 Solve the system by graphing.

$$y = \tfrac{1}{2}(x - 1)^2$$
$$y = |x - 1|$$

CHAPTER 7

7-1 Consider the graphs of $y = ax^2$ and $y = (ax)^2$. Assume $a \neq 0$.

a. For what values of a will both graphs lie in the same quadrants?

b. For what values of a will the graph of $y = ax^2$ be wider than the graph of $y = (ax)^2$?

7-2 Complete each statement. Assume $a \neq 0$.

a. The graph of $y = ax^2 + b$ intersects the x-axis in two places when _____.

b. The graph of $y = ax^2 + b$ does not intersect the x-axis when _____.

7-3 The points $(0, 2)$, $(-1, -1)$, and $(3, -1)$ lie on the graph of a parabola.

a. Write an equation of the parabola in the form $y = ax^2 + bx + c$.

b. Find the vertex of the parabola.

7-4 Find the value of each radical expression when $x = 4$. Round irrational numbers to the nearest hundredth.

a. $\sqrt{3x^2 + 1}$

b. $\sqrt{x^2 - 7}$

c. $\sqrt{2x^2 - x - 3}$

d. $\sqrt{\dfrac{9x}{x + 2}}$

e. $\sqrt{x^4}$

7-5 Solve each equation.

a. $(x - 1)^2 = 25$

b. $(x + 7)^2 = 49$

c. $(4x - 3)^2 - 5 = 31$

7-6 In a rectangular garden, the longer sides are 9 ft longer than twice the length of the shorter sides. The area of the garden is 180 ft². Find the dimensions of the garden.

7-7 Solve for x if $ax^2 + 9x + 12 = 0$ and the value of the discriminant is 225.

CHAPTER 8

8-1 Solve for x. (*Hint:* In each equation, the variable x represents an exponent.)

a. $3^x = 9$

b. $3^x = 243$

c. $2^x = 64$

d. $2 \cdot 3^x = 162$

e. $5 \cdot 2^x - 152 = 8$

8-2 *Open-ended* The expression $\frac{72}{r}$ approximates the number of years needed for an investment to double when $r\%$ is the annual interest rate. Approximate the doubling times for three different interest rates. Check your approximations by finding the actual balance if $1000 is invested for the indicated number of years at interest rates you chose.

8-3 On January 1, 2000, Chessville had a population of 40,000 people. Its population increases 7% each year. On the same day, Checkersville had a population of 60,000 people. Its population decreases 4% each year. During what year will the population of Chessville exceed that of Checkersville?

8-4 **a.** For what values of n is $n^{-3} = \left(\frac{1}{n}\right)^5$?

b. Describe n if $n^x < 1$ and $x > 0$. Assume $n > 0$.

8-5 Write each number in scientific notation. Then order the results from least to greatest.

$130{,}000 \times 10^{-11}$ 204×10^2

$32{,}910{,}000 \times 10^{-4}$ 0.0611×10^7

0.0905×10^{-4}

8-6 Simplify each expression.
  a. $3^x \cdot 3^{2-x} \cdot 3^2$
  b. $2^n \cdot 2^{n+2} \cdot 2$
  c. $3^x \cdot 2^y \cdot 3^2 \cdot 2^x$

8-7 Solve each equation.
  a. $3^{2x} = 9^4$ **b.** $4^x = \dfrac{1}{32}$

8-8 Simplify each expression.
  a. $n^{x+2} \div n^x$
  b. $n^{5x} \div n^x$
  c. $\left(\dfrac{x^m}{x^{m-2}}\right)^2$

CHAPTER 9

9-1 Find the perimeter of $\triangle ABC$.

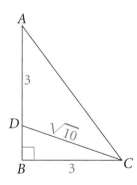

9-2 Use the steps that follow to find the distance between the parallel lines ℓ and m.

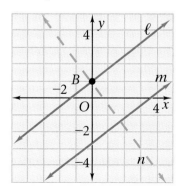

  a. An equation for line ℓ is $y = \dfrac{3}{4}x + 1$; an equation for line m is $y = \dfrac{3}{4}x - \dfrac{11}{4}$. Write an equation for line n, which is perpendicular to line ℓ at point B.
  b. Use the equations for lines m and n to find their point of intersection, C.
  c. Find the distance between points B and C.

9-3 At a certain point in a large level park, the angle of elevation to the top of an office building is 30°. If you move 400 ft closer to the building, the angle of elevation is 45°. To the nearest ten feet, how tall is the building?

9-4 Simplify each expression. Assume that all variables represent positive numbers.
  a. $(3\sqrt{x})^2$
  b. $\sqrt{24} \cdot \sqrt{2x} \cdot \sqrt{3x}$
  c. $2b(\sqrt{5b})^2$
  d. $\sqrt{45a^7} \cdot \sqrt{20a}$

9-5 Simplify each radical expression.
  a. $\sqrt{288} + \sqrt{50} - \sqrt{98}$
  b. $\dfrac{\sqrt{27} + \sqrt{48} + \sqrt{75}}{\sqrt{3}}$
  c. $2\sqrt{5}(3\sqrt{20} - \sqrt{5})$

9-6 Solve each equation.
  a. $\sqrt{x^2 - 6x} = 4$
  b. $\sqrt{2x^2 + 8x} = x$
  c. $\sqrt{x^2 + 4x + 5} = x$
  d. $\sqrt{3x - 5} = \sqrt{5x - 3}$

9-7 Solve this system algebraically. Verify by graphing.
$$y = 2\sqrt{x}$$
$$y = \sqrt{5 - x}$$

9-8 Open-ended Create a set of integer data, with at least five data items, where the mean and median have different values, and the standard deviation is less than 3.

CHAPTER 10

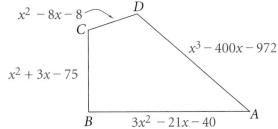

10-1

a. Find the perimeter of the figure in terms of x.

b. Solve for x if AB is twice BC.

c. Use the value you found for x to find CD.

d. Find the perimeter of the figure.

10-2 Find the area of the yellow region. Leave your answer in factored form.

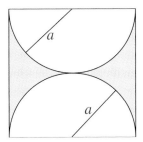

10-3 Two sides of a rectangle have lengths $(5x - 8)$ and $(5x + 8)$. The area of the rectangle is 336 cm². Find the perimeter of the rectangle.

10-4(1) Factor each expression.

Sample:
$$a^2 - 4ab - 5b^2 = (a - 5b)(a + b)$$

a. $x^2 - 8xy + 15y^2$

b. $r^2 - 4rt - 12t^2$

c. $5a^2 - 17ab + 6b^2$

d. $2m^2 - 11mn - 21n^2$

10-4(2) **a.** A box that is a rectangular prism has a volume of $6c^3 + 14c^2 + 4c$. The length, width, and height are represented by monomial and binomial factors of the volume. Find possible expressions for each dimension.

b. Suppose $c = 5$ in. Find the dimensions and the volume of the box.

10-5 Factor each expression.

a. $x^4 + 6x^2 + 9$

(*Hint:* Fill in the ■'s so that
$■^2 + 6■ + 9 = (■ + 3)^2$.)

b. $x^4 - 4$

c. $x^4 - 5x^2 + 6$

10-6 Solve for x. (*Hint:* See the sample problem after Exercise 34 on page 494.)

a. $x^3 = 256x$

b. $4x^4 = 5x(4x^2 - 5x)$

10-7 Solve for x.
$$x^3 - 5x^2 + 7x = 0$$

CHAPTER 11

11-1 The intensity of a sound s varies inversely as the square of the distance d from the sound. This can be modeled by the equation $sd^2 = k$. If you move half the distance closer to the source of a sound, by what factor will the intensity of the sound increase? Explain your reasoning.

11-2 Graph each function. Include a dashed line for each asymptote.

a. $f(x) = \dfrac{x - 1}{x + 1}$

b. $f(x) = \dfrac{2}{(x - 2)(x + 2)}$

c. $f(x) = \dfrac{1}{(x - 1)^2}$

11-3 Simplify each expression.

a. $\dfrac{x^2 + x - 6}{x^2 - x - 6} \div \dfrac{x^2 + 5x + 6}{x^2 + 4x + 4}$

b. $\left(\dfrac{x^2 - 25}{x^2 - 4x}\right)\left(\dfrac{x^2 + x - 20}{x^2 + 10x + 25}\right)$

c. $\dfrac{\dfrac{3x}{x^2 - 1}}{\dfrac{6}{x^2 - x - 2}}$

Hint: To divide by a fraction, multiply by its reciprocal.

11-4 a. Simplify.
$$\frac{x}{x^2 - 9} - \frac{x}{x^2 + 6x + 9}$$
b. Simplify.
$$\frac{7x - 10}{x^3 + x^2 - 20x} + \frac{1}{x + 5}$$

11-5 Solve.
$$\frac{x - 6}{x + 3} + \frac{2x}{x - 3} = \frac{4x + 3}{x + 3}$$

11-6 A three-digit number is formed by randomly selecting from the digits 1, 2, 3, 4, and 5 without replacement.
  a. How many different 3-digit numbers can be formed?
  b. How many different numbers with three odd digits can be formed?
  c. Find the probability that the number formed has 3 different odd digits.
  d. Find the probability that the number formed has at least one even digit.

11-7 On a particular test, you must answer 7 out of 10 questions. You also must answer at least 4 of the first 6 questions.
  a. In how many ways can you choose 4 questions from the first 6 questions?
  b. How many questions are left after you have answered 4 of the first 6 questions? How many must still be answered?
  c. In how many ways can you choose questions to finish the test?
  d. In all, how many different ways are there of completing the test, meeting all its requirements?

Extra Practice

Find the mean, median, and mode for each set of data.   ■ **Lesson 1-1**

1. 36, 42, 35, 40, 35, 51, 41, 35   **2.** 1.2, 0.9, 0.7, 1.1, 0.8, 1.3, 0.6   **3.** 5, 8, 6, 8, 3, 5, 8, 6, 5, 9

4. A student surveyed the members of the drama club. She included a
question about age. Her results are at the right.
  a. Make a line plot for the data.
  b. What is the median age of the drama club members?

Ages of Drama Club Members
14 18 16 15 17 14 15 18 15
13 14 15 18 14 17 16 14 16

5. Write an equation to model each situation.   ■ **Lesson 1-2**
  a. The length of three cars is 24 feet.
  b. The weight of two books equals 39 pens.

6. a. Write a sentence and an equation to describe the relationship
between the number of notebooks and the price.
  b. If you have $5, can you buy a notebook for each of your classes?
Explain.

Notebooks	Price
1	$.99
2	$1.98
3	$2.97

Simplify each expression.   ■ **Lessons 1-3 to 1-6**

7. $4 + 3 \cdot 8$ **8.** $2 \cdot 3^2 - 7$ **9.** $6 \cdot (5 - 2) - 9$ **10.** $2 - 12 \div 3$

11. $\left(\frac{1}{3}\right)^2 + 8 \div 2$ **12.** $\frac{1}{2} \div \frac{4}{3}$ **13.** $-6 \cdot 4.2 - 5 \div 2$ **14.** $9 - (3 + 1)^2$

15. $\frac{1}{3} - \frac{5}{6}$ **16.** $-4 + 9 \div 3 - 2$ **17.** $(8 - 1.5) \cdot -4$ **18.** $\frac{3}{4} \cdot 6 - \frac{1}{2}$

Evaluate each expression for $a = 8$, $b = -3$, and $c = \frac{1}{2}$.

19. $a - b - c$ **20.** $c - a^2$ **21.** $8c + ab$ **22.** $c(a - 2c)$

23. $9b - 4a$ **24.** $\frac{1}{2}b - ac$ **25.** $(2b)^2 - 2b^2$ **26.** $\frac{1}{a} + \frac{1}{c}$

The results of rolling a number cube 54 times are at the right.   ■ **Lesson 1-7**
Use the results to find each experimental probability.

27. $P(3)$ **28.** $P(4)$ **29.** $P(\text{not } 5)$

30. $P(7)$ **31.** $P(\text{even number})$ **32.** $P(\text{not } 1)$

6 3 4 5 1 1 5 5 3 6 3 2 1 3 3 3 2 1
2 3 6 3 3 4 5 1 2 2 6 3 3 6 5 4 5 3
2 5 1 4 5 2 6 2 5 2 1 2 5 3 2 4 6 3

Find the sum or difference.   ■ **Lesson 1-8**

33. $\begin{bmatrix} -3 & 0 \\ 11 & -5 \end{bmatrix} + \begin{bmatrix} -4 & 6 \\ -8 & 13 \end{bmatrix}$ **34.** $\begin{bmatrix} 6 & 12 \\ -9 & 7 \end{bmatrix} - \begin{bmatrix} 8 & -6 \\ 15 & 0 \end{bmatrix}$ **35.** $\begin{bmatrix} 4.2 & 0.6 \\ 1.7 & 9.5 \end{bmatrix} - \begin{bmatrix} 5.8 & -3.5 \\ 0.2 & 4.9 \end{bmatrix}$

36. You can find the surface area of a cube using the formula $A = 6s^2$,   ■ **Lesson 1-9**
where s is the length of a side.
  a. Write a spreadsheet formula for cell B2.
  b. Find the values for cells B2, C2, and D2.
  c. Write a spreadsheet formula to find the sum of
the surface areas of the three cubes.

	A	B	C	D
1	Side Length	3	5.2	9
2	Surface Area			

Extra Practice

Use the table for Exercise 1.　　　　　　　　　　　　　■ Lesson 2-1

Cover Price and Number of Pages of Some Magazines

Cover Price	$2.25	$2.50	$3.75	$3.00	$4.95	$1.95	$2.95	$2.50
Number of Pages	208	68	122	124	234	72	90	90

1. a. Draw a scatter plot of the data.
b. Draw a trend line on the scatter plot. What is the relationship between the cover price and the number of pages in a magazine?
c. How many pages would you expect a $2.00 magazine to have? Explain.

Sketch a graph to describe each situation. Explain the activity in each section of the graph.　　　■ Lesson 2-2

2. the amount of milk in your bowl as you eat cereal　　**3.** the energy you use in a 24-h period

4. your distance from home plate after your home run　　**5.** the number of apples on a tree over one year

Graph the data. Then write a function rule for each table of values.　　■ Lessons 2-3, 2-5, 2-6

6.

x	$f(x)$
−3	−1
−1	1
1	3
3	5

7.

x	$f(x)$
0	0
3	6
6	12
9	18

8.

x	$f(x)$
21	14
25	18
29	22
33	26

9.

x	$f(x)$
−8	−4
−6	−3
−4	−2
−2	−1

Find the range of each function when the domain is {−4, −1, 0, 3, 8}. Each equation belongs to what family of functions?　　■ Lessons 2-4, 2-7

10. $y = 6x - 5$　　**11.** $y = |x| - 2$　　**12.** $y = x^2 + 3x + 1$　　**13.** $y = \frac{1}{2}x + 8$

14. $y = -x^2 - x$　　**15.** $y = \frac{2}{3}x$　　**16.** $y = |x - 2|$　　**17.** $y = 2x^2 - 5x$

18. $y = |4 - x|$　　**19.** $y = x + 5$　　**20.** $y = \frac{4}{9}x^2$　　**21.** $y = \left|\frac{3}{5}x\right|$

Find each theoretical probability for one roll of a number cube.　　■ Lesson 2-8

22. P(an odd number)　　**23.** P(a negative number)　　**24.** P(an integer)　　**25.** P(a factor of 6)

At the Sock Hop, socks are sold in three sizes and six colors. The sizes are small, medium, and large. The color selection consists of white, gray, blue, red, black, and purple. Find the probability of choosing each kind of sock randomly.

26. P(large and gray)　　**27.** P(blue or red)　　**28.** P(small and purple)　　**29.** P(medium)

30. Make a tree diagram to show all the kinds of socks.

Extra Practice

Solve each equation. ■ Lesson 3-1 to 3-5

1. $h - 4 = 10$
2. $8p - 3 = 13$
3. $8j - 5 + j = 67$
4. $6t = -42$
5. $-n + 8.5 = 14.2$
6. $6(t + 5) = -36$
7. $m + 9 = 11$
8. $\frac{1}{2}(s + 5) = 7.5$
9. $\frac{s}{3} = 8$
10. $7h + 2h - 3 = 15$
11. $\frac{7}{12}x = \frac{3}{14}$
12. $3r - 8 = -32$
13. $8g - 10g = 4$
14. $-3(5 - t) = 18$
15. $3(c - 4) = -9$
16. $\frac{3}{8}z = 9$
17. $0.1(h + 20) = 3$
18. $\frac{3m}{5} = 6$
19. $4 - y = 10$
20. $8q + 2q = -7.4$

Write an equation to solve each problem.

21. **School** Your test scores for the semester are 87, 84, and 85. Can you raise your test average to 90 with your next test?

22. You spend $\frac{1}{2}$ of your allowance each week on school lunches. Each lunch costs $1.25. How much is your weekly allowance?

You pick two balls from a jar. The jar has five blue, three yellow, six green, and two purple balls. Find each probability. ■ Lesson 3-6

23. P(purple and blue), with replacement
24. P(yellow and purple), without replacement
25. P(green and yellow), with replacement
26. P(green and blue), without replacement
27. P(purple and green), without replacement
28. P(green and blue), with replacement
29. P(blue and yellow), without replacement
30. P(blue and purple), with replacement

Write and solve an equation to answer each question. ■ Lesson 3-7

31. What is 10% of 94?
32. What percent of 10 is 4?
33. 147 is 14% of what?
34. What percent of 1.2 is 6?
35. 13.2 is 55% of what?
36. What is 0.4% of 800?
37. What is 75% of 68?
38. 5 is 200% of what?
39. What percent of 54 is 28?
40. 114 is 95% of what?
41. What percent of 20 is 31?
42. What is 35% of 15?

Find each percent of change. Describe each as a percent of increase or decrease. Round to the nearest percent. ■ Lesson 3-8

43. $4.50 to $5.00
44. 56 in. to 57 in.
45. 18 oz to 12 oz
46. 1 s to 3 s
47. 8 lb to 5 lb
48. 6 km to 6.5 km
49. 39 h to 40 h
50. 7 ft to 2 ft
51. 0.2 mL to 0.45 mL
52. $\frac{1}{2}$ tsp to $\frac{1}{8}$ tsp
53. 18 kg to 20 kg
54. 55 min to 50 min

55. In 1988, the average resident of the United States ate about 2.4 lb of bagels per year. In 1993, bagel consumption had increased to about 3.5 lb annually. What percent increase is this?

Extra Practice

Solve each proportion. ■ Lesson 4-1

1. $\frac{3}{4} = \frac{-6}{m}$ **2.** $\frac{t}{7} = \frac{3}{21}$ **3.** $\frac{9}{j} = \frac{3}{16}$ **4.** $\frac{2}{5} = \frac{w}{65}$ **5.** $\frac{s}{15} = \frac{4}{45}$ **6.** $\frac{9}{4} = \frac{x}{10}$

7. $\frac{10}{q} = \frac{8}{62}$ **8.** $\frac{3}{2} = \frac{18}{y}$ **9.** $\frac{5}{9} = \frac{t}{3}$ **10.** $\frac{6}{m} = \frac{3}{5}$ **11.** $\frac{c}{8} = \frac{13.5}{36}$ **12.** $\frac{7}{9} = \frac{35}{x}$

13. Architecture A blueprint scale is 1 in. : 4 ft. On the plan, the garage is 2 in. by 3 in. What are the actual dimensions of the garage?

Solve and check. If the equation is an identity or if it has no solution, write *identity* or *no solution*. ■ Lessons 4-2, 4-3

14. $|t| = 6$ **15.** $5m + 3 = 9m - 1$ **16.** $8d = 4d - 18$ **17.** $4h + 5 = 9h$

18. $|k| - 4 = -7$ **19.** $7t = 80 + 9t$ **20.** $|w - 9| = 4$ **21.** $|m + 3| = 12$

22. $-b + 4b = 8b - b$ **23.** $8 - |p| = 3$ **24.** $|h + 17| = -8$ **25.** $6p + 1 = 3p$

26. $10z - 5 + 3z = 8 - z$ **27.** $3(g - 1) + 7 = 3g + 4$ **28.** $17 - 20q = -13 - 5q$

29. Transportation A bus traveling 40 mi/h and a car traveling 50 mi/h cover the same distance. The bus travels 1 h more than the car. How many hours did each travel?

Solve each equation for the given variable. ■ Lesson 4-4

30. $A = lw; w$ **31.** $c = \frac{w + t}{v}, t$ **32.** $h = \frac{r}{t}(p - m); r$ **33.** $P = 2l + 2w; l$

34. $v = \pi r^2 h; h$ **35.** $m = \frac{t}{b - a}; t$ **36.** $y = bt - c; b$ **37.** $g = 1.9\frac{m}{r^2}; m$

Solve each inequality and graph the solutions on a number line. ■ Lessons 4-5 to 4-8

38. $-8w < 24$ **39.** $9 + p \le 17$ **40.** $\frac{r}{4} > -1$ **41.** $7y + 2 \le -8$

42. $t - 5 \ge -13$ **43.** $9h > -108$ **44.** $|8w + 7| > 5$ **45.** $\frac{s}{6} \le 3$

46. $\frac{6c}{5} \ge -12$ **47.** $-8l + 3.7 \le 31.7$ **48.** $9 - t \le 4$ **49.** $|m + 4| \ge 8$

50. $y + 3 < 16$ **51.** $|n - 6| \le 8.5$ **52.** $12b - 5 > -29$ **53.** $4 - a > 15$

54. $6m - 15 \le 9$ or $10m > 84$ **55.** $9j - 5j \ge 20$ and $8j > -36$ **56.** $37 < 3c + 7 < 43$

57. The booster club raised $102 in their car wash. They want to buy $18 soccer balls for the soccer team. How many can they buy?

Solve and graph each inequality. The replacement set is the positive integers. ■ Lesson 4-9

58. $t - 5 \le -3$ **59.** $-6m + 2 > -19$ **60.** $|3c + 1| \ge 7$ **61.** $8 - w < 8$

62. $2b + 3 < 7$ **63.** $-c - 5 \le 6$ **64.** $|n| + 4 \le 5$ **65.** $\frac{3}{5}t > 6$

66. You are solving a problem involving weight. Find the replacement set.

Extra Practice

Find the slope of the line passing through each pair of points. Then write the equation of the line.   ■ Lessons 5-1, 5-5

1. $(2, 5)$ and $(4, 8)$ **2.** $(1, 6)$ and $(7, 3)$ **3.** $(-2, 4)$ and $(3, 9)$ **4.** $(1, 6)$ and $(9, -4)$

5. $(-5, -7)$ and $(-1, 3)$ **6.** $(7, 0)$ and $(3, -4)$ **7.** $(0, 0)$ and $(-7, 1)$ **8.** $(10, -5)$ and $(-2, 7)$

Write an equation for a line through the given point with the given slope. Then graph the line.

9. $(4, 6); m = -5$ **10.** $(3, -1); m = 1$ **11.** $(8, 5); m = \frac{1}{2}$ **12.** $(0, -6); m = \frac{4}{3}$

13. $(-2, 7); m = 2$ **14.** $(-5, -9); m = -3.5$ **15.** $(4, 0); m = 7$ **16.** $(6, -4); m = -\frac{1}{5}$

Find the rate of change for each situation.   ■ Lesson 5-2

17. growing from 1.4 m to 1.6 m in one year **18.** bicycling 3 mi in 15 min and 7 mi in 55 min

19. walking 3 blocks in 10 min and 12 blocks in 55 min **20.** reading 8 pages in 9 min and 22 pages in 30 min

Draw the graph of a direct variation that includes the given point. Write the equation of the line.   ■ Lesson 5-3

21. $(5, 4)$ **22.** $(7, 7)$ **23.** $(-3, -10)$ **24.** $(4, -8)$ **25.** $(-2, 9)$ **26.** $(11, 1)$

27. $(8, -2)$ **28.** $(-5, 9)$ **29.** $(6, 8)$ **30.** $(1, -4)$ **31.** $(-3, 3)$ **32.** $(1, 12)$

Find the slope and *y*-intercept. Then graph each equation.   ■ Lessons 5-4, 5-7

33. $y = 6x + 8$ **34.** $3x + 4y = -24$ **35.** $-2y = 5x - 12$ **36.** $6x + y = 12$

37. $y = \frac{-3}{4}x - 8$ **38.** $2y = 8$ **39.** $y = \frac{1}{2}x + 3$ **40.** $y = -7x$

41. a. Graph the ages and grade levels of some students in a school below.   ■ Lesson 5-6
  b. Draw a trend line.
  c. Find the equation of the line of best fit.

$(10, 6), (16, 10), (15, 10), (18, 12), (17, 11),$
$(17, 12), (19, 12), (16, 11), (11, 7), (15, 9), (13, 8)$

Write an equation that satisfies the given conditions.   ■ Lesson 5-8

42. parallel to $y = 4x + 1$, through $(-3, 5)$ **43.** perpendicular to $y = -x - 3$, through $(0, 0)$

44. perpendicular to $3x + 4y = 12$, through $(7, 1)$ **45.** parallel to $2x - y = 6$, through $(-6, -9)$

46. perpendicular to $y = -2x + 5$, through $(4, -10)$ **47.** parallel to $2y = 5x + 12$, through $(2, -1)$

Solve each equation by graphing.   ■ Lesson 5-9

48. $x + 5 = 3x - 7$ **49.** $-4x + 1 = 2x - 5$ **50.** $9x - 2 = 7x + 4$ **51.** $6x + 1 = 3x - 5$

52. $8x - 2 = 7x + 9$ **53.** $12x + 4 = x - 29$ **54.** $-x - 4 = x + 18$ **55.** $5x = 6x - 19$

Extra Practice

Choose your own method to solve each system. ■ Lessons 6-1 to 6-3

1. $x - y = 7$
$3x + 2y = 6$

2. $x + 4y = 1$
$3x - 2y = -25$

3. $4x - 5y = 9$
$-2x - y = -29$

4. $x - y = 13$
$y - x = -13$

5. $3x - y = 4$
$x + 5y = -4$

6. $x + y = 4$
$y = 7x + 4$

7. $x + y = 19$
$x - y = -7$

8. $-3x + 4y = 29$
$3x + 2y = -17$

9. $4x - 9y = 61$
$10x + 3y = 25$

10. $6x + y = 13$
$y - x = -8$

11. $3x + y = 3$
$-3x + 2y = -30$

12. $4x - y = 105$
$x + 7y = -10$

Write a system of equations to solve each problem. ■ Lesson 6-4

13. Suppose you have 12 coins that total \$.32. Some of the coins are nickels and the rest are pennies. How many of each coin do you have?

14. Your school drama club will put on a play you wrote. Royalties are \$50 plus \$.25 for each ticket sold. The cost for props and costumes is \$85. The tickets for the play will be \$2 each.
a. Write an equation for the expenses.
b. Write an equation for the income. What is the break-even point?
c. How much will the club earn if 200 tickets are sold?

Graph each linear inequality. ■ Lesson 6-5

15. $y \geq 4x - 3$

16. $y < x - 4$

17. $y > -6x + 5$

18. $y \leq 14 - x$

19. $x < -8$

20. $2x + 3y \leq 6$

21. $y \leq 12$

22. $y > -3x + 1$

Graph each system. ■ Lessons 6-6, 6-8

23. $y \leq 5x + 1$
$y > x - 3$

24. $y > 4x + 3$
$y \geq -2x - 1$

25. $y = |2x| - 3$
$y = x + 4$

26. $y < -2x + 1$
$y > -2x - 3$

27. $y = |6x| - 2$
$y = x^2 - 2$

28. $y = 4x^2 - 5$
$y = x$

29. $y \leq 8$
$y \geq |-x| + 1$

30. $y \leq 5x - 2$
$y > 3$

31. $y = -2x - 7$
$y = |x + 3|$

32. $y > -3x - 9$
$y < 5x + 7$

33. $y = x^2 + 2$
$y = |\frac{1}{2}x| + 4$

34. $y \geq x$
$y \leq x + 1$

Graph each system of restrictions. Find the coordinates of each vertex. Evaluate the equation to find the maximum and minimum values of B. ■ Lesson 6-7

35. $x \geq 0$
$y \geq 0$
$x \leq 5$
$y \leq 4$
$B = 2x + 5y$

36. $x \geq 2$
$x \leq 6$
$y \geq 1$
$y \leq 4$
$B = x + 3y$

37. $x \geq 2$
$y \geq 1$
$x + y \leq 10$

$B = 3x + 2y$

38. $x \geq 0$
$y \geq 0$
$y \leq -2x + 10$
$y \leq 4x + 2$
$B = x + y$

Extra Practice

Without graphing, describe how each graph differs from the graph of $y = x^2$.

■ Lessons 7-1 to 7-3

1. $y = 3x^2$

2. $y = -4x^2$

3. $y = -0.5x^2$

4. $y = 0.2x^2$

5. $y = x^2 - 4$

6. $y = x^2 + 1$

7. $y = 2x^2 + 5$

8. $y = -0.3x^2 - 7$

Graph each quadratic function. Label the axis of symmetry, the vertex, and the y-intercept.

9. $y = 3x^2$

10. $y = -2x^2 + 1$

11. $y = 0.5x^2 - 3$

12. $y = -x^2 + 2x + 1$

13. $y = 3x^2 + 5x$

14. $y = \frac{3}{4}x^2$

15. $y = 2x^2 - 9$

16. $y = -5x^2 + x + 4$

17. $y = x^2 - 7x$

18. $y = x^2 - 3x + 8$

19. $y = -x^2 + x + 12$

20. $y = -\frac{1}{2}x^2 + x - 3$

Graph each quadratic inequality.

21. $y > x^2 - 4$

22. $y \geq -x^2 + 3x + 10$

23. $y < 2x^2 + x$

24. $y \leq 2x^2 + 5$

25. $y > -\frac{1}{2}x^2 - 3x$

26. $y \leq x^2 + x - 2$

Find the square roots of each number.

■ Lesson 7-4

27. 25

28. $\frac{4}{9}$

29. 64

30. $\frac{25}{36}$

31. 0.81

32. 900

33. 2.25

34. 16

35. $\frac{1}{25}$

36. 169

37. $\frac{4}{36}$

38. 289

Solve each equation. Round solutions to the nearest hundredth when necessary. If the equation has no real solution, write *no real solution*.

■ Lessons 7-5, 7-6

39. $x^2 = 36$

40. $x^2 + x - 2 = 0$

41. $c^2 - 100 = 0$

42. $9d^2 = 25$

43. $(x - 4)^2 = 100$

44. $3x^2 = 27$

45. $2x^2 - 54 = 284$

46. $7n^2 = 63$

47. $h^2 + 4 = 0$

48. $x^2 + 6x - 2 = 0$

49. $x^2 - 5x = 7$

50. $x^2 - 10x + 3 = 0$

51. $2x^2 - 4x + 1 = 0$

52. $3x^2 + x + 5 = 0$

53. $\frac{1}{2}x^2 - 8 = 3x$

54. $x^2 + 8x - 5 = -9$

55. $2x^2 - 5x = x^2 - 3x + 6$

56. $-3x^2 + x - 2 = 5$

Evaluate the discriminant. Determine the number of real solutions of each equation.

■ Lesson 7-7

57. $x^2 - x + 5 = 0$

58. $3x^2 + 4x = -3 - 2x$

59. $-2x^2 - x + 7 = 0$

60. $3x^2 + 8x = 9$

61. $3x^2 + 5 = 6x$

62. $6x^2 + 11x - 4 = 0$

63. $-x^2 + x - 4 = 3$

64. $6x - x^2 = 4$

65. $x^2 = 5x - 1$

Graph each function. Label each graph as *exponential growth* or *exponential decay*.

■ **Lessons 8-1 to 8-3**

1. $y = 3^x$

2. $y = \left(\frac{3}{4}\right)^x$

3. $y = 1.5^x$

4. $y = \frac{1}{2} \cdot 3^x$

5. $y = 3 \cdot 7^x$

6. $y = 4^x$

7. $y = 3 \cdot \left(\frac{1}{5}\right)^x$

8. $y = 2^x$

9. $y = 2 \cdot 3^x$

10. $y = (0.8)^x$

11. $y = 2.5^x$

12. $y = 4 \cdot (0.2)^x$

Identify the growth factor or decay factor for each exponential function.

13. $y = 8^x$

14. $y = \frac{3}{4} \cdot 2^x$

15. $y = 9 \cdot \left(\frac{1}{2}\right)^x$

16. $y = 4 \cdot 9^x$

17. $y = 0.65^x$

18. $y = 3 \cdot 1.5^x$

19. $y = \frac{2}{5} \cdot \left(\frac{1}{4}\right)^x$

20. $y = 0.1 \cdot 0.9^x$

Write an exponential function to model each situation. Find each amount after the specified time.

21. $200 principal
   4% compounded annually
   5 years

22. $1000 principal
   3.6% compounded monthly
   10 years

23. $3000 investment
   8% loss each year
   3 years

Simplify each expression. Use only positive exponents.

■ **Lessons 8-4, 8-6 to 8-8**

24. $(2t)^{-6}$

25. $5m^5m^{-8}$

26. $(4.5)^4(4.5)^{-2}$

27. $(m^7t^{-5})^2$

28. $(x^2n^4)(n^{-8})$

29. $(w^{-2}j^{-4})^{-3}(j^7j^3)$

30. $(t^6)^3(m^2)$

31. $(3n^4)^2$

32. $\dfrac{r^5}{g^3}$

33. $\dfrac{1}{a^{-4}}$

34. $\dfrac{w^7}{w^{-6}}$

35. $\dfrac{6}{t^{-4}}$

36. $\dfrac{a^2b^{-7}c^4}{a^5b^3c^{-2}}$

37. $\dfrac{(2r^5)^3}{4t^8t^{-1}}$

38. $\left(\dfrac{a^6}{a^7}\right)^{-3}$

39. $\left(\dfrac{c^5c^{-3}}{c^{-4}}\right)^{-2}$

Evaluate each expression for $m = 2, t = -3, w = 4,$ and $z = 0.$

40. t^m

41. t^{-m}

42. $(w \cdot t)^m$

43. $w^m \cdot t^m$

44. $(w^z)^m$

45. w^mw^z

46. $z^t(m^t)^z$

47. $w^{-t} \cdot t^t$

Write each number in scientific notation.

■ **Lesson 8-5**

48. 34,000,000

49. 0.000 63

50. 1500

51. 0.0002

52. 360,000

53. 6,200,000,000

54. 0.05

55. 0.000 000 000 891

56. 910,000,000,000

57. 0.38

58. 0.000 000 07

59. 5,070,000,000,000

Write each number in standard notation.

60. 8.05×10^6

61. 3.2×10^{-7}

62. 9.0×10^8

63. 4.25×10^{-4}

Could each set of three numbers represent the lengths of the sides of a right triangle? Explain your answers.

■ Lesson 9-1

1. 4, 5, 7
2. 6, 8, 10
3. 6, 9, 13
4. 10, 13, 17

5. 15, 36, 39
6. 3, 7, 10
7. 8, 15, 17
8. 9, 12, 15

Find the length of the diagonal of a rectangle with sides of the given lengths a and b. Round to the nearest tenth.

9. $a = 6, b = 8$
10. $a = 5, b = 9$
11. $a = 4, b = 10$
12. $a = 9, b = 1$

Find the distance between the endpoints of each segment. Round your answers to the nearest tenth. Then find the midpoint of each segment.

■ Lesson 9-2

13. $A(1, 3), B(2, 8)$
14. $R(6, -2), S(-7, -10)$
15. $G(4, 0), H(5, -1)$

16. $A(-4, 1), B(3, 5)$
17. $G(11, 7), H(-7, -11)$
18. $R(1, -6), S(4, -2)$

19. $R(-8, -4), S(5, 7)$
20. $A(0, 6), B(-2, 9)$
21. $G(5, 10), H(0, 0)$

Use $\triangle ABC$ to evaluate each expression.

■ Lesson 9-3

22. $\sin A$
23. $\cos A$
24. $\tan A$

25. $\sin B$
26. $\cos B$
27. $\tan B$

Simplify each radical expression.

■ Lessons 9-4, 9-5

28. $\dfrac{\sqrt{27}}{\sqrt{81}}$
29. $\sqrt{\dfrac{25}{4}}$
30. $\sqrt{\dfrac{50}{9}}$
31. $\dfrac{\sqrt{72}}{\sqrt{50}}$

32. $\sqrt{75} - 4\sqrt{75}$
33. $\sqrt{5}(\sqrt{20} - \sqrt{80})$
34. $\sqrt{25} \cdot \sqrt{4}$
35. $\sqrt{6}(\sqrt{6} - 3)$

36. $3\sqrt{300} + 2\sqrt{27}$
37. $5\sqrt{2} \cdot 3\sqrt{50}$
38. $\sqrt{8} - 4\sqrt{2}$
39. $\sqrt{27} \cdot \sqrt{3}$

Solve each radical equation. Check your solutions.

■ Lesson 9-6

40. $\sqrt{3x + 4} = 1$
41. $6 = \sqrt{8x - 4}$
42. $2x = \sqrt{14x - 6}$

43. $\sqrt{2x + 5} = \sqrt{3x + 1}$
44. $2x = \sqrt{6x + 4}$
45. $\sqrt{5x + 11} = \sqrt{7x - 1}$

Find the domain of each function. Then graph the function.

■ Lesson 9-7

46. $y = \sqrt{x + 5}$
47. $y = \sqrt{x - 2}$
48. $y = \sqrt{x + 1}$

49. $y = \sqrt{x - 4}$
50. $y = \sqrt{x - 3}$
51. $y = \sqrt{x + 6}$

Find the standard deviation of each set of data to the nearest tenth.

■ Lesson 9-8

52. 11, 14, 10, 13, 15
53. 2, 4, 3, 5, 3, 7
54. 21, 20, 26, 18, 30

55. 15, 13, 10, 20, 17
56. 32, 33, 30, 37
57. 7, 10, 4, 8, 2, 11

Extra Practice

Find each sum or difference. Write in standard form.   ■ Lesson 10-1

1. $(5x^3 + 3x^2 - 7x + 10) - (3x^3 - x^2 + 4x - 1)$ **2.** $(x^2 + 3x - 2) + (4x^2 - 5x + 2)$

3. $(4m^3 + 7m - 4) + (2m^3 - 6m + 8)$ **4.** $(8t^2 + t + 10) - (9t^2 - 9t - 1)$

5. $(-7c^3 + c^2 - 8c - 11) - (3c^3 + 2c^2 + c - 4)$ **6.** $(6v + 3v^2 - 9v^3) + (7v - 4v^2 - 10v^3)$

7. $(s^4 - s^3 - 5s^2 + 3s) - (5s^4 + s^3 - 7s^2 - s)$ **8.** $(9w - 4w^2 + 10) + (8w^2 + 7 + 5w)$

Find each product.   ■ Lessons 10-2, 10-3

9. $4b(b^2 + 3)$ **10.** $(5c + 3)(-c + 2)$ **11.** $(3t - 1)(2t + 1)$

12. $9c(c^2 - 3c + 5)$ **13.** $8m(4m - 5)$ **14.** $(w - 1)(w^2 + w + 1)$

15. $5k(k^2 + 8k)$ **16.** $(3t + 5)(t + 1)$ **17.** $(2n - 3)(2n + 4)$

18. $5r^2(r^2 + 4r - 2)$ **19.** $(b + 3)(b + 7)$ **20.** $2m^2(m^3 + m - 2)$

21. Geometry A rectangle has dimensions $3x - 1$ and $2x + 5$. Write an expression for its area as a product and in standard form.

Find the greatest common factor of each expression.

22. $t^6 + t^4 - t^5 + t^2$ **23.** $3m^2 - 6 + 9m$ **24.** $16c^2 - 4c^3 + 12c^5$ **25.** $8v^6 + 2v^5 - 10v^9$

26. $6n^2 - 3n^3 + 2n^4$ **27.** $5r + 20r^3 + 15r^2$ **28.** $9x^6 + 5x^5 + 4x^7$ **29.** $4d^8 - 2d^{10} + 7d^4$

30. $5t^2 + 3t - 8t^4$ **31.** $4m^2 + 16m - 20$ **32.** $7n + 14n^2 + 21n^3$ **33.** $5w - 8w^2 + 2w^3$

Factor each polynomial.   ■ Lessons 10-4, 10-5

34. $x^2 + 6x + 9$ **35.** $x^2 - 25$ **36.** $4t^2 + t - 3$ **37.** $9c^2 - 169$

38. $2c^2 - 5c - 3$ **39.** $t^2 - 6t + 9$ **40.** $x^2 - 8x + 16$ **41.** $4d^2 - 12d + 9$

42. $4m^2 - 121$ **43.** $3v^2 + 10v - 8$ **44.** $4g^2 + 4g + 1$ **45.** $w^2 + 3w - 4$

46. $9t^2 + 12t + 4$ **47.** $12m^2 - 5m - 2$ **48.** $36s^2 - 1$ **49.** $c^2 - 10c + 25$

Solve each quadratic equation. Round answers to the nearest hundredth, if necessary.   ■ Lessons 10-6, 10-7

50. $x^2 + 5x + 6 = 0$ **51.** $d^2 - 144 = 0$ **52.** $c^2 + 6 = 2 - 4c$

53. $x^2 + 4x = 2x^2 - x + 6$ **54.** $3x^2 + 2x - 12 = x^2$ **55.** $r^2 + 4r + 1 = r$

56. $d^2 + 2d + 10 = 2d + 100$ **57.** $3c^2 + c - 10 = c^2 - 5$ **58.** $t^2 - 3t - 10 = 0$

59. $4x^2 - 5x - 5 = 2x^2 + 4x$ **60.** $4m^2 + 6m + 1 = 6m + 82$ **61.** $d^2 - 5d = 3d^2 + 1$

62. Agriculture You are planting a rectangular vegetable garden. It is 5 feet longer than 3 times its width. The area of the garden is 250 ft². Find the dimensions of the garden.

Extra Practice

Find the constant of variation for each inverse variation. ■ Lesson 11-1

1. $y = 10$ when $x = 7$

2. $y = 8$ when $x = 12$

3. $y = 0.2$ when $x = 4$

4. $y = 4$ when $x = 5$

5. $y = 0.1$ when $x = 6$

6. $y = 3$ when $x = 7$

Each pair of points is from an inverse variation. Find the missing value.

7. $(5.4, 3)$ and $(2, y)$

8. $(x, 4)$ and $(5, 6)$

9. $(3, 6)$ and $(9, y)$

10. $(100, 2)$ and $(x, 25)$

11. $(6, 1)$ and $(x, 2)$

12. $(8, y)$ and $(2, 4)$

13. $(7, 35)$, and $(49, y)$

14. $(x, 32)$ and $(16, 1)$

Graph each function. Include a dashed line for each asymptote. ■ Lesson 11-2

15. $y = \dfrac{6}{x}$

16. $y = \dfrac{8}{x + 2}$

17. $y = \dfrac{4}{x} - 3$

18. $y = \dfrac{5}{x + 1} + 3$

19. $y = \dfrac{-1}{x}$

20. $y = \dfrac{5}{x} - 1$

21. $y = \dfrac{-2}{x - 3}$

22. $y = \dfrac{2}{x - 1}$

23. $y = \dfrac{3}{x} + 4$

24. $y = \dfrac{5}{x}$

25. $y = \dfrac{2}{x + 1} - 1$

26. $y = \dfrac{x - 3}{x + 3}$

Simplify each expression and state any values restricted from the domain. ■ Lessons 11-3, 11-4

27. $\dfrac{4t^2}{16t}$

28. $\dfrac{c - 5}{c^2 - 25}$

29. $\dfrac{4m - 12}{m - 3}$

30. $\dfrac{a^2 + 2a - 3}{a + 3}$

31. $\dfrac{4}{x} - \dfrac{3}{x}$

32. $\dfrac{6t}{5} + \dfrac{4t}{5}$

33. $\dfrac{6}{c} + \dfrac{4}{c^2}$

34. $\dfrac{6}{3d} - \dfrac{4}{3d}$

35. $\dfrac{5s^4}{10s^3}$

36. $\dfrac{4n^2}{7} \cdot \dfrac{14}{2n^3}$

37. $\dfrac{8b^2 - 4b}{3b} \div \dfrac{2b - 1}{9b^2}$

38. $\dfrac{v^5}{v^3} \cdot \dfrac{4v^{-1}}{v^2}$

39. $\dfrac{5}{t + 4} + \dfrac{3}{t - 4}$

40. $\dfrac{8}{m^2 + 6m + 5} + \dfrac{4}{m + 1}$

41. $\dfrac{3y}{4y - 8} \div \dfrac{9y}{2y^2 - 4y}$

42. $\dfrac{4}{d^2} - \dfrac{3}{d^3}$

Solve each equation. Check your answers. ■ Lesson 11-5

43. $\dfrac{1}{4} + \dfrac{1}{x} = \dfrac{3}{8}$

44. $\dfrac{4}{m} - 3 = \dfrac{2}{m}$

45. $\dfrac{1}{b - 3} = \dfrac{1}{4b}$

46. $\dfrac{4}{x - 1} = \dfrac{3}{x}$

47. $\dfrac{4}{n} + \dfrac{5}{9} = 1$

48. $\dfrac{x}{x + 2} = \dfrac{x - 3}{x + 1}$

49. $t - \dfrac{8}{t} = \dfrac{17}{t}$

50. $\dfrac{x + 2}{x + 5} = \dfrac{x - 4}{x + 4}$

51. $\dfrac{4}{c + 1} - \dfrac{2}{c - 1} = \dfrac{3c + 6}{c^2 - 1}$

52. $\dfrac{4}{m + 3} = \dfrac{6}{m - 3}$

53. $\dfrac{4}{t + 5} + 1 = \dfrac{15}{t^2 - 25}$

Evaluate. ■ Lessons 11-6, 11-7

54. $_6C_4$

55. $_7P_2$

56. $_{10}C_5$

57. $_8C_7$

58. $_{12}P_6$

59. $_9C_7$

60. $_6P_4$

61. $_9C_3$

62. $_5P_2$

63. $_{12}P_3$

64. $_8C_3$

65. $_7P_6$

66. You are choosing a personal identification number using the digits 1, 3, 5, and 6 exactly once each. How many different numbers can you choose from?

67. The 18 members of the debate team need to form a committee of five people. How many different five-person committees are possible?

Problem Solving Strategies

You may find one or more of these strategies helpful in solving a word problem.

STRATEGY	WHEN TO USE IT
Draw a Diagram	The problem describes a picture or diagram.
Guess and Test	The needed information seems to be missing.
Look for a Pattern	The problem describes a relationship.
Make a Table	The problem has data that need to be organized.
Solve a Simpler Problem	The problem is complex or has numbers that are too cumbersome to use at first.
Use Logical Reasoning	You need to reach a conclusion using given information.
Work Backward	You need to find the number that led to the result in the problem.

Problem Solving: Draw a Diagram

■Example   **Two cars started from the same point. One traveled east at 45 mi/h, the other west at 50 mi/h. How far apart were the cars after 5 hours?**

Draw a diagram:

West ◄————— 50 mi/h • 5 ————— Start ————— 45 mi/h • 5 —————► East

The first car traveled: 45 • 5 or 225 mi. The second car traveled: 50 • 5 or 250 mi.

The diagram shows that the two distances should be added:
225 + 250 = 475 mi

After 5 hours, the cars were 475 mi apart.

EXERCISES

1. Jason, Lee, Melba, and Bonnie want to play each of the others in tennis. How many games will be played?

2. A playground, a zoo, a picnic area, and a flower garden will be in four corners of a new park. Straight paths will connect each of these areas to all the other areas. How many pathways will be built?

3. Pedro wants to tack 4 posters on a bulletin board. He will tack the four corners of each poster, overlapping the sides of each poster a little. What is the least number of tacks that Pedro can use?

Problem Solving: Guess and Test

When you are not sure how to start, guess an answer and then test it. In the process of testing a guess, you may see a way to revise your guess to get closer to the answer or to get the answer.

■Example **Maria bought books and CDs as gifts. Altogether she bought 12 gifts and spent $84. The books cost $6 each and the CDs cost $9 each. How many of each gift did she buy?**

Guess:	6 books	Test:	$6 \cdot \$6 =$	$36
	6 CDs		$6 \cdot \$9 =$	+$54
				$90

Revise your guess. You need fewer CDs to bring the total cost down.

Guess:	7 books	Test:	$7 \cdot \$6 =$	$42
	5 CDs		$5 \cdot \$9 =$	+$45
				$87

The cost is still too high.

Guess:	8 books	Test:	$8 \cdot \$6 =$	$48
	4 CDs		$4 \cdot \$9 =$	+$36
				$84

Maria bought 8 books and 4 CDs.

EXERCISES

1. Find two consecutive odd integers whose product is 323.

2. Mika bought 9 rolls of film to take 180 pictures on a field trip. Some rolls had 36 exposures and the rest had 12 exposures. How many of each type did Mika buy?

3. Tanya is 18 years old. Her brother Shawn is 16 years younger. How old will Tanya be when she is 3 times as old as Shawn is then?

4. Steven has 100 ft of fencing and wants to build a fence in the shape of a rectangle to enclose the largest possible area. What should be the dimensions of the rectangle?

5. The combined ages of a mother, her son, and her daughter are 61 years. The mother is 22 years older than her son and 31 years older than her daughter. How old is each person?

6. Kenji traveled 40 mi in a two-day bicycle race. He biked 8 mi farther on the first day than he did on the second day. How many miles did Kenji travel each day?

Problem Solving: Look for a Pattern and Make a Table

Some problems describe relationships that involve regular sequences of numbers or other things. To solve the problem you need to be able to recognize and describe the *pattern* that gives the relationship for the numbers or things. One way to organize the information given is to *make a table*.

■Example **A tree farm is planted as shown at the right. The dots represent trees. The lot will be enlarged by larger squares. How many trees will be in the fifth square?**

Make a table to help find a pattern.

Square position	1st	2nd	3rd	4th	5th
Number of trees	4	12	20	▒	▒

Pattern: 8 more trees are planted in each larger square.

The fourth square will have 28 trees. The fifth square will have 36 trees.

EXERCISES

1. Kareem made a display of books at a book fair. One book was in the first row and the other rows each had two more books than the row before it. How many books does Kareem have if he has nine rows?

2. Chris is using green and white tiles to cover her floor. If she uses tiles in the pattern, G, W, G, G, W, G, G, W, G, G, what will be the color of the twentieth tile?

3. Jay read one story the first week of summer vacation, 3 the second week, 6 the third week, and 10 the fourth week. He kept to this pattern for eight weeks. How many stories did he read the eighth week?

4. Jan has 6 coins, none of which is a half dollar. The coins have a value of $.85. What coins does she have?

5. Sam is covering a wall with rows of red, white, and blue siding. The red siding is cut in 1.8-m strips, the white in 2.4-m strips, and the blue in 1.2-m strips. What is the shortest length that Sam can cover by uncut strips to form equal length rows of each color?

6. A train leaves a station at 8:00 A.M. and averages 40 mi/h. Another train leaves the same station one hour later and averages 50 mi/h traveling in the same direction. At what time will the second train catch up with the first train? How many miles would each train have traveled by that time?

7. The soccer team held a car wash and earned $200. They charged $7 per truck and $5 per car. In how many different ways could the team have earned the $200?

Problem Solving: Solve a Simpler Problem

By solving one or more simpler problems you can often find a pattern that will help solve a more complicated problem.

■Example **How many different rectangles are in a strip with 10 squares?**

Begin with one square, then add one square at a time. Find out whether there is a pattern.

Squares in the strip:	1	2	3	4	5
Number of rectangles:	1	3	6	10	15

| Pattern: | | $1 + 2 = 3$ | $3 + 3 = 6$ | $6 + 4 = 10$ | $10 + 5 = 15$ |

Now continue the pattern.

Squares in the strip:	6	7	8	9	10
Number of rectangles:	21	28	36	45	55

Pattern: $15 + 6 = 21$ $21 + 7 = 28$ $28 + 8 = 36$ $36 + 9 = 45$ $45 + 10 = 55$

There are 55 rectangles in a strip with 10 squares.

EXERCISES

1. Lockers in the east wing of Hastings High School are numbered 1–120. How many contain the digit 8?

2. What is the sum of all of the numbers from 1 to 100? (*Hint:* What is 1 + 100? What is 2 + 99?)

3. Suppose your heart beats 70 times per minute. At this rate, how many times had it beaten by the time you were 10?

4. For a community project you have to create the numbers 1 through 148 using large glittered digits, which you have to make by hand. How many glittered digits do you have to make?

5. There are 63 teams competing in the state soccer championship. If a team loses a game it is eliminated. How many games have to be played in order to get a single champion team?

6. You work in a supermarket. Your boss asks you to arrange oranges in a pyramid for a display. The pyramid's base should be a square with 25 oranges. How many layers of oranges will be in your pyramid? How many oranges will you need?

7. Kesi has her math book open. The product of the two page numbers on the facing pages is 1056. What are the two page numbers?

Problem Solving: Use Logical Reasoning

Some problems can be solved without the use of numbers. They can be solved by the use of logical reasoning, given some information.

■ **Example**   **Joe, Melissa, Liz, and Greg each play a different sport. Their sports are running, basketball, baseball, and tennis. Liz's sport does not use a ball. Joe hit a home run in his sport. Melissa is the sister of the tennis player. Which sport does each person play?**

Make a table to organize what you know.

	Running	Basketball	Baseball	Tennis
Joe	✗	✗	✓	✗
Melissa				✗
Liz	✓	✗	✗	✗
Greg				

←— A home run means Joe plays baseball.
←— Melissa cannot be the tennis player.
←— Liz must run, since running does not involve a ball.

Use logical reasoning to complete the table.

	Running	Basketball	Baseball	Tennis
Joe	✗	✗	✓	✗
Melissa	✗	✓	✗	✗
Liz	✓	✗	✗	✗
Greg	✗	✗	✗	✓

←— The only option for Greg is tennis.

Greg plays tennis, Melissa plays basketball, Liz runs, and Joe plays baseball.

EXERCISES

1. Juan has a dog, a horse, a bird, and a cat. Their names are Bo, Cricket, K.C., and Tuffy. Tuffy and K.C. cannot fly or be ridden. The bird talks to Bo. Tuffy runs from the dog. What is each pet's name?

2. A math class has 25 students. There are 13 students who are only in the band, 4 who are only on the swimming team, and 5 who do both activities. How many students are not in either activity?

3. Annette is taller than Heather but shorter than Garo. Tanya's height is between Garo's and Annette's. Karin would be the shortest if it weren't for Alexa. List the names in order from shortest to tallest.

4. The Colts, Cubs, and Bears played each other two games of basketball. The Colts won 3 of their games. The Bears won 2 of their games. How many games did each team win and lose?

5. The girls' basketball league has a calling chain when it needs to cancel its games. The leader takes 1 min to call 2 players. These 2 players take 1 min to call 2 more players, and so on. How many players will be called in 6 min?

Problem Solving: Work Backward

To solve some problems you need to start with the end result and work backward to the beginning.

■Example **On Monday, Rita withdrew $150 from her savings account. On Wednesday, she deposited $400 into her account. She now has $1000. How much was in her account on Monday before she withdrew the money?**

Money in account now: $1000

Undo the deposit:
$$\begin{array}{r} -\ \$400 \\ \hline \$600 \end{array}$$

Undo the withdrawal:
$$\begin{array}{r} +\ \$150 \\ \hline \$750 \end{array}$$

Rita had $750 in her account on Monday before the withdrawal.

EXERCISES

1. Ned gave the following puzzle to Connie: I am thinking of a number. I doubled it, then tripled the result. The final result was 36. What is my number?

2. Fernando gave the following puzzle to Maria: I am thinking of a number. I divided it by 3. Then I divided the result by 5. The final result was 8. What is my number?

3. This week Sandy withdrew $350 from her savings account. She made a deposit of $125, wrote a check for $275, and made a deposit of $150. She now has $225 in her account. How much did she have in her account at the beginning of the week?

4. Jeff paid $12.50 for a taxi fare from his home to the airport including a $1.60 tip. City Cab charges $1.90 for the first mile plus $.15 for each additional $\frac{1}{6}$ mile. How many miles is Jeff's home from the airport?

5. Ben sold $\frac{1}{4}$ as many tickets to the fund-raiser as Charles. Charles sold 3 times as many as Susan. Susan sold 4 fewer than Tom. If Tom sold 12 tickets, how many did Ben sell?

6. Two cars start traveling towards each other. One car is averaging 30 mi/h and the other 40 mi/h. After 4 h the cars are 10 mi apart. How far apart were the cars when they started?

7. Nina has a dentist appointment at 8:45 A.M. She wants to arrive 10 min early. Nina needs to allow 25 min to travel to the appointment and 45 min to dress and have breakfast. What is the latest time Nina could get up?

Prime Numbers and Composite Numbers

A *prime number* is a whole number greater than 1 that has exactly two factors, the number 1 and itself.

Prime number:	2	5	17	29
Factors:	1, 2	1, 5	1, 17	1, 29

A *composite number* is a number that has more than two factors. The number 1 is neither prime nor composite.

Composite number:	6	15	26	48
Factors:	1, 2, 3, 6	1, 3, 5, 15	1, 2, 13, 26	1, 2, 3, 4 , 6, 8, 12, 16, 24, 48

■**Example 1**   **Is 51 prime or composite?**

$51 = 3 \cdot 17$ ◄——Try to find factors other than 1 and 51.

51 is a composite number.

Every composite number can be factored into prime factors using a factor tree. When all the factors are prime numbers, it is called the *prime factorization* of the number.

■**Example 2**   **Use a factor tree to write the prime factorization of 28.**

The order of listing the factors may be different, but the end result is the same.

The prime factorization of 28 is $2 \cdot 2 \cdot 7$.

EXERCISES

Is each number prime or composite?

1. 9	**2.** 16	**3.** 34	**4.** 61	**5.** 7	**6.** 13
7. 12	**8.** 40	**9.** 57	**10.** 64	**11.** 120	**12.** 700
13. 39	**14.** 23	**15.** 63	**16.** 19	**17.** 522	**18.** 101

List all the factors of each number.

19. 46	**20.** 32	**21.** 11	**22.** 65	**23.** 27	**24.** 29

Use a factor tree to write the prime factorization of each number.

25. 18	**26.** 20	**27.** 27	**28.** 54	**29.** 64	**30.** 96
31. 100	**32.** 125	**33.** 84	**34.** 150	**35.** 121	**36.** 226

Factors and Multiples

A common factor is a number that is a factor of two or more numbers. The *greatest common factor* (GCF) is the greatest number that is a common factor of two or more numbers.

■ **Example 1**   **Find the GCF of 14 and 42.**

Factors of 24: 1, 2, 3, 4, 6, 8, 12, 24   Find the common factors: 1, 2, 4, 8
Factors of 64: 1, 2, 4, 8, 16, 32, 64   ⟵ The greatest common factor is 8.
GCF (24, 64) = 8

Another way to find the GCF is to first find the prime factors of the numbers.

$24 = 2 \cdot 2 \cdot 2 \cdot 3$ ⟵ Multiply the common prime factors.
$64 = 2 \cdot 2 \cdot 2 \cdot 2 \cdot 2 \cdot 2$
$GCF = 2 \cdot 2 \cdot 2 = 8$ ⟵ Use the factor the number of times it appears as a common factor.

A common multiple is a number that is a multiple of two or more numbers. The *least common multiple* (LCM) is the least number that is a common multiple of two or more numbers.

■ **Example 2**   **Find the LCM of 12 and 18.**

Multiples of 12: 12, 24, 36,...   List a number of multiples until you find
Multiples of 18: 18, 36,...   the first common multiple.
LCM = (12, 18) = 36

Another way to find the LCM is to first find the prime factors of the numbers.
$12 = 2 \cdot 2 \cdot 3$
$18 = 2 \cdot 3 \cdot 3$
$LCM = 2 \cdot 2 \cdot 3 \cdot 3 = 36$ ⟵ Use each prime factor the greatest number of times it appears in either number.

EXERCISES

Find the GCF of each set of numbers.

1. 12 and 22
2. 7 and 21
3. 24 and 48
4. 17 and 51

5. 9 and 12
6. 10 and 25
7. 21 and 49
8. 27 and 36

9. 14 and 42
10. 20 and 30
11. 27 and 15
12. 12 and 28

13. 10, 30, and 25
14. 56, 84, and 140
15. 42, 63, and 105
16. 20, 28, and 40

Find the LCM of each set of numbers.

17. 16 and 20
18. 14 and 21
19. 11 and 33
20. 8 and 9

21. 5 and 12
22. 54 and 84
23. 48 and 80
24. 25 and 36

25. 54 and 80
26. 75 and 175
27. 10 and 25
28. 24 and 28

29. 10, 15, and 25
30. 6, 7, and 12
31. 5, 8, and 20
32. 18, 21, and 36

Simplifying Fractions

A *fraction* can name a part of a group or region. This region is divided into 10 equal parts and 6 of the equal parts are shaded.

$\dfrac{6}{10}$ ← Numerator Read: *six tenths*
 ← Denominator

A fraction can have many names. Different names for the same fraction are called *equivalent fractions*. You can find an equivalent fraction for any given fraction by multiplying the numerator and denominator of the given fraction by the same number.

■ Example 1 Write five equivalent fractions for $\frac{3}{5}$.

$\dfrac{3}{5} = \dfrac{3 \cdot 2}{5 \cdot 2} = \dfrac{6}{10}$ $\dfrac{3}{5} = \dfrac{3 \cdot 3}{5 \cdot 3} = \dfrac{9}{15}$ $\dfrac{3}{5} = \dfrac{3 \cdot 4}{5 \cdot 4} = \dfrac{12}{16}$ $\dfrac{3}{5} = \dfrac{3 \cdot 5}{5 \cdot 5} = \dfrac{15}{25}$ $\dfrac{3}{5} = \dfrac{3 \cdot 6}{5 \cdot 6} = \dfrac{18}{30}$

The fraction $\frac{3}{5}$ is in *simplest form* because its numerator and denominator are *relatively prime*, that is, their only common factor is the number 1. To write a fraction in simplest form, divide its numerator and denominator by their greatest common factor (GCF).

■ Example 2 Write $\frac{6}{24}$ in simplest form.

First find the GCF of 6 and 24.

$6 = 2 \cdot 3$ ← Multiply the common prime factors.

$24 = 2 \cdot 2 \cdot 2 \cdot 3$ ← GCF $= 2 \cdot 3 = 6$

Then divide the numerator and denominator of $\frac{6}{24}$ by the GCF, 6.

$\dfrac{6}{24} = \dfrac{6 \div 6}{24 \div 6} = \dfrac{1}{4}$ ← simplest form

EXERCISES

Complete.

1. $\dfrac{3}{7} = \dfrac{\blacksquare}{21}$

2. $\dfrac{5}{8} = \dfrac{20}{\blacksquare}$

3. $\dfrac{11}{12} = \dfrac{44}{\blacksquare}$

4. $\dfrac{12}{16} = \dfrac{\blacksquare}{4}$

5. $\dfrac{50}{100} = \dfrac{1}{\blacksquare}$

6. $\dfrac{5}{9} = \dfrac{\blacksquare}{27}$

7. $\dfrac{3}{8} = \dfrac{\blacksquare}{24}$

8. $\dfrac{5}{6} = \dfrac{20}{\blacksquare}$

9. $\dfrac{12}{20} = \dfrac{\blacksquare}{5}$

10. $\dfrac{75}{150} = \dfrac{1}{\blacksquare}$

Which fractions are in simplest form?

11. $\dfrac{4}{12}$

12. $\dfrac{3}{16}$

13. $\dfrac{5}{30}$

14. $\dfrac{9}{72}$

15. $\dfrac{11}{22}$

16. $\dfrac{24}{25}$

Write in simplest form.

17. $\dfrac{8}{16}$

18. $\dfrac{7}{14}$

19. $\dfrac{6}{9}$

20. $\dfrac{20}{30}$

21. $\dfrac{8}{20}$

22. $\dfrac{12}{40}$

23. $\dfrac{15}{45}$

24. $\dfrac{14}{56}$

25. $\dfrac{10}{25}$

26. $\dfrac{9}{72}$

27. $\dfrac{45}{60}$

28. $\dfrac{20}{35}$

29. $\dfrac{27}{33}$

30. $\dfrac{18}{72}$

31. $\dfrac{45}{85}$

32. $\dfrac{63}{126}$

33. $\dfrac{125}{150}$

34. $\dfrac{256}{320}$

Fractions and Decimals

Fractions can be written as decimals.

■Example 1   **Write $\frac{3}{5}$ as a decimal.**

$$\begin{array}{r} 0.6 \\ 5\overline{)3.0} \\ -3.0 \\ \hline \end{array}$$

Divide the numerator by the denominator.

The decimal for $\frac{3}{5}$ is 0.6.

■Example 3   **Write $\frac{3}{11}$ as a decimal.**

Divide the numerator by the denominator. →

Notice that the remainders 8 and 3 keep
repeating. Therefore 2 and 7 will keep →
repeating in the quotient.

So, $\frac{3}{11} = 0.2727\ldots = 0.\overline{27}$

Decimals can be written as fractions.

■Example 2   **Write 0.38 as a fraction.**

$0.38 = 38 \text{ hundredths} = \frac{38}{100} = \frac{19}{50}$

A fraction for 0.38 is $\frac{38}{100}$ or $\frac{19}{50}$.

$$\frac{3}{11} = 11\overline{)\begin{array}{l} 0.2727 \\ 3.0000\ldots \\ \end{array}}$$
$$\begin{array}{r} -2\,2 \\ \hline 80 \\ -77 \\ \hline 30 \\ -22 \\ \hline 80 \\ -77 \\ \hline 3 \end{array}$$

■Example 4   **Write 0.363636 . . . as a fraction.**

Let $x = 0.363636\ldots$
Then $100x = 36.363636\ldots$ ← When 2 digits repeat, multiply by 100.
          $99x = 36$ ← Subtract the first equation from the second.
            $x = \frac{36}{99}$ or $\frac{4}{11}$ ← Divide each side by 99.

■Example 5   **Write 0.42222 . . . as a fraction.**

Let $x = 0.42222\ldots$
Then $10x = 4.22222\ldots$ ← When 1 digit repeats, multiply by 10.
          $9x = 3.8$ ← Subtract the first equation from the second.
            $x = \frac{3.8}{9}$ or $\frac{38}{90}$ or $\frac{19}{45}$

EXERCISES

Write as a decimal.

1. $\frac{3}{10}$ **2.** $\frac{1}{5}$ **3.** $\frac{4}{20}$ **4.** $\frac{25}{75}$ **5.** $\frac{2}{3}$ **6.** $\frac{12}{6}$

7. $\frac{7}{100}$ **8.** $\frac{3}{2}$ **9.** $4\frac{3}{25}$ **10.** $\frac{13}{12}$ **11.** $\frac{3}{11}$ **12.** $\frac{5}{7}$

Write as a fraction in simplest form.

13. 0.3   **14.** 0.25   **15.** 2.37   **16.** 0.07   **17.** 0.875

18. 0.4545 . . .   **19.** 6.333 . . .   **20.** 7.2626 . . .   **21.** 0.15151 . . .   **22.** 0.123123 . . .

Adding and Subtracting Fractions

You can add and subtract fractions when they have the same denominator.
Fractions with the same denominator are called *like fractions*.

■Example 1   Add $\frac{4}{5} + \frac{3}{5}$.

$\frac{4}{5} + \frac{3}{5} = \frac{4+3}{5} = \frac{7}{5} = 1\frac{2}{5}$ ←——Add the numerators and keep the same denominator.

■Example 2   Subtract $\frac{5}{9} - \frac{2}{9}$.

$\frac{5}{9} - \frac{2}{9} = \frac{5-2}{9} = \frac{3}{9} = \frac{1}{3}$ ←——Subtract the numerators and keep the same denominator.

Fractions with unlike denominators are called *unlike fractions*. To add or
subtract fractions with unlike denominators, find the least common
denominator (LCD) and write equivalent fractions with the same
denominator. Then add or subtract the like fractions.

■Example 3   Add $\frac{3}{4} + \frac{5}{6}$.

$\frac{3}{4} + \frac{5}{6} =$ ←—— Find the LCD. The LCD is the same as the least common multiple (LCM). The LCD(4, 6) is 12.

$\frac{9}{12} + \frac{10}{12} = \frac{9+10}{12} = \frac{19}{12}$ or $1\frac{7}{12}$ ←——Write equivalent fractions with the same denominator.

■Example 4   Subtract $\frac{5}{12} - \frac{2}{9}$.

$\frac{5}{12} - \frac{2}{9} =$ ←——Find the LCD. The LCD (12, 9) is 36.

$\frac{15}{36} - \frac{8}{36} = \frac{15-8}{36} = \frac{7}{36}$ ←——Write equivalent fractions with the same denominator.

To add or subtract mixed numbers, add or subtract the fractions. Then add
or subtract the whole numbers. Sometimes when subtracting mixed
numbers you may have to regroup.

■Example 5   Subtract $5\frac{1}{4} - 3\frac{2}{3}$.

$5\frac{1}{4} - 3\frac{2}{3}$ ←——Write equivalent fractions with the same denominator.

$5\frac{3}{12} - 3\frac{8}{12} =$ ←——Write $5\frac{3}{12}$ as $4\frac{15}{12}$ so you can subtract the fractions.

$4\frac{15}{12} - 3\frac{8}{12} = 1\frac{7}{12}$ ←——Subtract the fractions. Then subtract the whole numbers.

EXERCISES

Add. Write each answer in simplest terms.

1. $\frac{2}{7} + \frac{3}{7}$ **2.** $\frac{3}{8} + \frac{7}{8}$ **3.** $\frac{6}{5} + \frac{9}{5}$ **4.** $\frac{4}{9} + \frac{8}{9}$ **5.** $6\frac{2}{3} + 3\frac{4}{5}$

6. $1\frac{4}{7} + 2\frac{3}{14}$ **7.** $4\frac{5}{6} + 1\frac{7}{18}$ **8.** $2\frac{4}{5} + 3\frac{6}{7}$ **9.** $4\frac{2}{3} + 1\frac{6}{11}$ **10.** $3\frac{7}{9} + 5\frac{5}{27}$

Subtract. Write each answer in simplest terms.

11. $\frac{7}{8} - \frac{3}{8}$ **12.** $\frac{9}{10} - \frac{3}{10}$ **13.** $\frac{17}{5} - \frac{2}{5}$ **14.** $\frac{11}{7} - \frac{2}{7}$ **15.** $\frac{5}{11} - \frac{4}{11}$

16. $8\frac{5}{8} - 6\frac{1}{4}$ **17.** $3\frac{2}{3} - 1\frac{8}{9}$ **18.** $8\frac{5}{6} - 5\frac{1}{2}$ **19.** $12\frac{3}{4} - 4\frac{5}{6}$ **20.** $17\frac{2}{7} - 8\frac{2}{9}$

Multiplying and Dividing Fractions

To multiply two or more fractions, multiply the numerators, multiply the denominators, and simplify the product, if necessary.

■Example 1   Multiply $\frac{3}{7} \cdot \frac{5}{6}$.

$$\frac{3}{7} \cdot \frac{5}{6} = \frac{3 \cdot 5}{7 \cdot 6} = \frac{15}{42} = \frac{15 \div 3}{42 \div 3} = \frac{5}{14}$$

Sometimes you can simplify before multiplying.

$$\frac{^1\cancel{3}}{7} \cdot \frac{5}{\cancel{6}_2} = \frac{5}{14} \longleftarrow \text{Divide a numerator and a denominator by a common factor.}$$

To multiply mixed numbers, change the mixed numbers to improper fractions and multiply the fractions. Write the product as a mixed number.

■Example 2   Multiply $2\frac{4}{5} \cdot 1\frac{2}{3}$.

$$2\frac{4}{5} \cdot 1\frac{2}{3} = \frac{14}{{}_1\cancel{5}} \cdot \frac{\cancel{5}^{\,1}}{3} = \frac{14}{3} = 4\frac{2}{3}$$

To divide fractions, change the division problem to a multiplication problem. Remember that $8 \div \frac{1}{4}$ is the same as $8 \cdot 4$.

■Example 3   Divide $\frac{4}{5} \div \frac{3}{7}$.

$$\frac{4}{5} \div \frac{3}{7} = \frac{4}{5} \cdot \frac{7}{3} \qquad \longleftarrow \text{Multiply by the reciprocal of the divisor. Simplify the answer.}$$
$$= \frac{4}{5} \cdot \frac{7}{3} = \frac{28}{15} = 1\frac{13}{15}$$

To divide mixed numbers, change the mixed numbers to improper fractions and divide the fractions.

■Example 4   Divide $4\frac{2}{3} \div 7\frac{3}{5}$.

$$4\frac{2}{3} \div 7\frac{3}{5} = \frac{14}{3} \div \frac{38}{5} = \frac{14}{3} \cdot \frac{5}{38} = \frac{70}{114} = \frac{35}{57}$$

EXERCISES

Multiply. Write your answers in simplest form.

1. $\frac{2}{5} \cdot \frac{3}{4}$ 2. $\frac{3}{7} \cdot \frac{4}{3}$ 3. $\frac{5}{4} \cdot \frac{3}{8}$ 4. $\frac{6}{7} \cdot \frac{9}{2}$ 5. $\frac{7}{3} \cdot \frac{4}{7}$

6. $2\frac{3}{4} \cdot \frac{5}{8}$ 7. $1\frac{1}{2} \cdot 5\frac{3}{4}$ 8. $3\frac{4}{5} \cdot 10$ 9. $12 \cdot 1\frac{2}{3}$ 10. $5\frac{1}{4} \cdot \frac{2}{3}$

Divide. Write your answers in simplest form.

11. $\frac{3}{5} \div \frac{1}{2}$ 12. $\frac{4}{5} \div \frac{9}{10}$ 13. $\frac{4}{7} \div \frac{2}{3}$ 14. $\frac{5}{8} \div \frac{7}{3}$ 15. $\frac{4}{7} \div \frac{4}{3}$

16. $1\frac{4}{5} \div 2\frac{1}{2}$ 17. $2\frac{1}{2} \div 3\frac{1}{2}$ 18. $3\frac{1}{6} \div 1\frac{3}{4}$ 19. $9\frac{1}{2} \div 4\frac{1}{4}$ 20. $6\frac{3}{5} \div 2\frac{3}{5}$

Fractions, Decimals, and Percents

Percent means *per hundred*. 50% means 50 per hundred. $50\% = \frac{50}{100} = 0.50$

You can use a shortcut to write a decimal as a percent and a percent as a decimal.

■Example 1   **Write each number as a percent.**

  a. 0.47   **b.** 0.8   **c.** 2.475

Move the decimal point two places to the right and write a percent sign.

  a. $0.47 = 47\%$ **b.** $0.80 = 80\%$ **c.** $2.475 = 247.5\%$

■Example 2   **Write each number as a decimal.**

  a. 25%   **b.** 3%   **c.** 360%

Move the decimal point two places to the left and drop the percent sign.

  a. $25\% = 0.25$ **b.** $03\% = 0.03$ **c.** $360\% = 3.6$

You can write fractions as percents by writing the fraction as a decimal first.
Then move the decimal point two places to the right and write a percent
sign.

■Example 3   **Write each number as a percent.**   **a.** $\frac{3}{5}$ **b.** $\frac{7}{20}$ **c.** $\frac{2}{3}$

  a. $\frac{3}{5} = 0.6 = 60\%$ **b.** $\frac{7}{20} = 0.35 = 35\%$ **c.** $\frac{2}{3} = 0.66\overline{6} = 66.\overline{6}\%$ or 66.7%
                                                          (rounded to the nearest tenth of a percent)

You can write a percent as a fraction by writing the percent as a fraction
with a denominator of 100 and simplifying if possible.

■Example 4   **Write each number as a fraction or mixed
                    number.**

  a. $43\% = \frac{43}{100}$ **b.** $\frac{1}{2}\% = \frac{\frac{1}{2}}{100} = \frac{1}{2} \div 100 = \frac{1}{2} \cdot \frac{1}{100} = \frac{1}{200}$ **c.** $180\% = \frac{180}{100} = \frac{9}{5} = 1\frac{4}{5}$

EXERCISES

Write each number as a percent.

  1. 0.56   **2.** 0.09   **3.** 6.02   **4.** 5.245   **5.** 8.2   **6.** 0.14
  7. $\frac{1}{5}$ **8.** $\frac{9}{20}$ **9.** $\frac{1}{9}$ **10.** $\frac{5}{6}$ **11.** $\frac{3}{4}$ **12.** $\frac{7}{8}$

Write each number as a decimal.

  13. 7%   **14.** 8.5%   **15.** 0.9%   **16.** 250%   **17.** 83%   **18.** 110%

Write each number as a fraction or mixed number in simplest form.

  19. 19%   **20.** $\frac{3}{4}\%$ **21.** 450%   **22.** $\frac{4}{5}\%$ **23.** 64%   **24.** $\frac{2}{3}\%$

Exponents

You can express $2 \cdot 2 \cdot 2 \cdot 2 \cdot 2$ as 2^5. The raised number, 5, shows the number of times 2 is used as a factor. The number 2 is the *base*. The number 5 is the *exponent*.

$$2^5 \longleftarrow \text{exponent}$$
$$\uparrow \text{base}$$

Factored Form		Exponential Form		Standard Form
$2 \cdot 2 \cdot 2 \cdot 2 \cdot 2$	$=$	2^5	$=$	32

A number with an exponent of 1 is the number itself: $8^1 = 8$.
Any number, except 0, with an exponent of 0 is 1: $5^0 = 1$.

■Example 1 Write using exponents.

a. $8 \cdot 8 \cdot 8 \cdot 8 \cdot 8$ b. $2 \cdot 9 \cdot 9 \cdot 9 \cdot 9 \cdot 9 \cdot 9$ c. $6 \cdot 6 \cdot 10 \cdot 10 \cdot 10 \cdot 6 \cdot 6$

Count the number of times the number is used as a factor.

a. 8^5 b. $2 \cdot 9^6$ c. $6^4 \cdot 10^3$

■Example 2 Write each product.

a. 2^3 b. $8^2 \cdot 3^4$ c. $10^3 \cdot 5^2$

Write in factored form and multiply.

a. $2 \cdot 2 \cdot 2 = 8$ b. $8 \cdot 8 \cdot 3 \cdot 3 \cdot 3 \cdot 3 = 5184$ c. $10 \cdot 10 \cdot 10 \cdot 5 \cdot 5 = 25{,}000$

In powers of 10, the exponent tells how many zeros are in the standard form.

$10^1 = 10$
$10^2 = 10 \cdot 10 = 100$
$10^3 = 10 \cdot 10 \cdot 10 = 1000$
$10^4 = 10 \cdot 10 \cdot 10 \cdot 10 = 10{,}000$
$10^5 = 10 \cdot 10 \cdot 10 \cdot 10 \cdot 10 = 100{,}000$

You can use exponents to write numbers in *expanded form*.

■Example 3 Write 739 in expanded form using exponents.

$739 = 700 + 30 + 9 = (7 \cdot 100) + (3 \cdot 10) + (9 \cdot 1) = (7 \cdot 10^2) + (3 \cdot 10^1) + (9 \cdot 10^0)$

EXERCISES

Write using exponents.

1. $6 \cdot 6 \cdot 6 \cdot 6$ 2. $7 \cdot 7 \cdot 7 \cdot 7 \cdot 7$ 3. $5 \cdot 2 \cdot 2 \cdot 2 \cdot 2$ 4. $3 \cdot 3 \cdot 3 \cdot 3 \cdot 3 \cdot 14 \cdot 14$

Write in standard form.

5. 4^3 6. 9^4 7. 12^2 8. $6^2 \cdot 7^1$ 9. $11^2 \cdot 3^3$

Write in expanded form using exponents.

10. 658   11. 1254   12. 7125   13. 83,401   14. 294,863

Angles

An *angle* is a geometric figure formed by two rays with a common endpoint. The rays are *sides* of the angle and the endpoint is the *vertex* of the angle. An angle is measured in degrees. The symbol for an angle is ∠.

The angle pictured at the right can be named in three different ways: ∠A, ∠BAC, or ∠CAB.

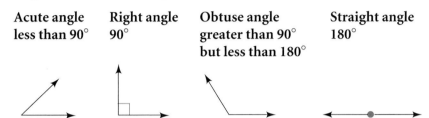

Angles can be classified by their measures.

Acute angle   **Right angle**   **Obtuse angle**   **Straight angle**
less than 90°   **90°**   **greater than 90°**   **180°**
                                 but less than 180°

■**Example**   **Measure the angle and tell if it is *acute, right, obtuse,* or *straight*.**

Line up side *DF* through 0° with the vertex at the center of the protractor. Read the scale number through which side *DE* passes.

The measure of the angle is 140°. The angle is obtuse.

EXERCISES

Measure each angle and tell whether it is *acute, right, obtuse,* or *straight*.

1.   **2.**   **3.**   **4.**

Draw an angle with the given measure.

5. 45°   **6.** 95°   **7.** 120°   **8.** 170°

9. Open-ended Draw a triangle. Use a protractor to find the measure of each angle of your triangle.

Perimeter, Area, and Volume

The *perimeter* of a figure is the distance around the figure. The *area* of a figure is the number of square units contained in the figure. The *volume* of a space figure is the number of cubic units contained in the space figure.

■Example 1   **Find the perimeter of each figure.**

a.
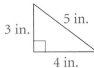

Add the measures of the sides.
$3 + 4 + 5 = 12$
The perimeter is 12 in.

b.

Use the formula $p = 2\ell + 2w$.
$p = 2(3) + 2(4)$
$\qquad = 6 + 8 = 14$
The perimeter is 14 cm.

■Example 2   **Find the area of each figure.**

a.

Use the formula $A = lw$.

$A = 3 \cdot 5 = 15 \text{ cm}^2$

b.

Use the formula $A = bh$.

$A = 6 \cdot 5 = 30 \text{ in.}^2$

c.

Use the formula $A = \frac{1}{2}(bh)$.

$A = \frac{1}{2}(7 \cdot 6) = 21 \text{ in.}^2$

■Example 3   **Find the volume of each figure.**

a.

$V = e^3$
$V = 5^3 = 125 \text{ cm}^3$

b.

$V = Bh \ (B = \text{area of the base})$
$V = 3 \cdot 5 \cdot 6 = 90 \text{ in.}^3$

c.

$V = \pi r^2 h$
$V = 3.14 \cdot 2^2 \cdot 5$
$\qquad = 3.14 \cdot 4 \cdot 5 = 62.8 \text{ in.}^3$

EXERCISES

Find the perimeter of each figure.

Find the area of each figure.

1.

2.

2 in.
1 in.
2 in.
1 in.
4 in.
5 in.

3.

10 cm
6 cm
8 cm

4.

8 in.
7 in.

Find the volume of each figure.

5.

6 cm
6 cm
6 cm

6.
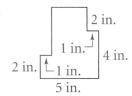
2 in
4 in.
6 in.

7.

7 cm
4 cm

New York Lessons

Contents

New York Lessons

What You'll Learn

- Determining the truth value of mathematical sentences
- Finding the solution set of an open sentence

...And Why

To use the language of mathematics

PROBLEM SOLVING

Look Back What phrases indicate inequalities in word problems?

Open and Closed Sentences

THINK AND DISCUSS

Writing Mathematical Sentences

A view of the Hudson River Valley painted by Frederic Church

Language Is the caption under the picture a sentence? No, the caption is not a sentence, because it does not include a verb. (Insert the word *was* before *painted* and you'll have a sentence.)

In the same way that sentences in English must have a verb, a mathematical sentence must also have a verb. Here are examples of how symbols are used as verbs in mathematical sentences. Notice that a slash through a symbol creates a **negation.**

Symbol	Meaning	Negation	Meaning
$=$	is equal to	$\neq$	is *not* equal to
$>$	is greater than	$\not>$	is *not* greater than
$\geq$	is greater than or equal to	$\not\geq$	is *not* greater than or equal to
$<$	is less than	$\not<$	is *not* less than
$\leq$	is less than or equal to	$\not\leq$	is *not* less than or equal to

The symbol $=$ is used to express an *equality.* Each of the other symbols is used to express an *inequality.*

A phrase such as $2xy - 3x$ is an *expression,* not a mathematical sentence, since it does not contain a symbol of equality or inequality.

Example 1 Relating to the Real World

Jobs A student found that she could earn up to $13 an hour working part-time for the local park district. State whether each of the following is an expression, an equation, or an inequality.

a. $13h$ The maximum amount earned for h hours of work
b. $e = 13h$ Amount earned e equals 13 times the number of hours h.
c. $e \leq 13h$ Amount earned e is less than or equal to 13 times the number of hours h.

a. $13h$ is an expression. It has no equal sign or inequality symbol.
b. $e = 13h$ is an equation, since it has an equal sign.
c. $e \leq 13h$ is an inequality, since it has an inequality symbol.

1. **Try This** State whether each of the following is an expression, an equation, or an inequality.
   a. $5c \neq 20 + 1$ **b.** $4ab - 11$ **c.** $3 + 6x = 2$

Mathematical sentences can be true or false. To determine the **truth value** of an equation, check whether the value of one side of the equation equals the value of the other side. For inequalities, check whether the comparison or negation is correct.

$$14 \div 4 \neq 3 \qquad\qquad 17 \cdot (0.1) > 17$$
$$\frac{14}{4} \neq 3 \qquad\qquad\qquad 1.7 > 17 \; \textit{false}$$
$$3\tfrac{1}{2} \neq 3 \;\; \textit{true}$$

2. **Mental Math** State whether each mathematical sentence is true or false.
   a. $-4 + 2 \not> 0$ **b.** $5 \cdot (0.5) = 1.5$ **c.** $10 < 27 \div 3$

Finding Solution Sets

Mathematical sentences can be *closed* or *open*. A **closed sentence** does not contain a variable. $6 + 2 > 1 - 4$ is an example of a closed sentence. An **open sentence** contains one or more variables. $8 + x = 7$ and $3a + b < 7 + 2$ are examples of open sentences.

Most open sentences are neither true nor false until you replace each variable with a specific value. The set of values from which to choose is called the **replacement set.** If the replacement set is not specified, assume that it includes all real numbers.

A value that makes an open sentence true is a solution of that sentence. An open sentence has one solution, no solution, or many solutions.

The **solution set** for an open sentence is the set of all the values from the replacement set that makes the sentence true. The solution set can change depending on the replacement set used.

QUICK REVIEW

An equation or inequality has a solution of all real numbers if it simplifies to a true statement. An equation or inequality has no solution if it simplifies to a false statement.

Example 2

Find the solution set of $c - 3 \geq 5$ for the replacement set $\{6, 7, 8, 9\}$.

c	$c - 3$	$c - 3 \geq 5$	Truth Value
6	3	$3 \geq 5$	false
7	4	$4 \geq 5$	false
8	5	$5 \geq 5$	true
9	6	$6 \geq 5$	true

The solution set is $\{8, 9\}$.

3. Try This What is the solution set for $3 + y < 6$ if the replacement set is $\{0, 1, 2, 3, 4, 5\}$?

Exercises   ON YOUR OWN

State whether each is an expression, an equation, or an inequality.

1. $-14 + 2g$

2. $7 + w \neq 13$

3. $3(7 - 0.2)$

4. $5 \geq 2 - 8c$

5. $22 \div 2 < -3t$

6. $17 + 21 = 3 \cdot 14$

7. Copy and complete the table. Then write the solution set of $x + 2 < 7$ for the replacement set $\{1, 3, 5, 7\}$.

x	$x + 2$	$x + 2 < 7$	Truth Value
1	3	$3 < 7$	true
3	▨	▨	▨
5	▨	▨	▨
7	▨	▨	▨

8. What is the solution set for $6x + 2 > 20$ if the replacement set is $\{0, 1, 2, 3, 4, 5\}$?

State the truth value of each sentence.

9. $14 + 2 > 3 \cdot 5$

10. $7(2 - 1) = 24 \div 4$

11. $6 \cdot 2 \not< 20 - 5$

12. $3 - 14 \leq -3 \cdot -5$

13. $6 + 29 = 5 \cdot 7$

14. $17 - 20 = -3 \cdot 0$

State whether each sentence is open or closed.

15. $5 + 3 = 8$

16. $x + 3 = 8$

17. $y - 4 > x + 2$

18. $37 - 9 > 3$

19. $7 < 8$

20. $y \geq 9$

21. $m + 17 \geq 25$

22. $137 \leq y + 14$

23. $37 + 8 + 3 \geq 29$

Write the negation of each sentence. Determine the truth value of the original sentence and its negation.

24. $18 - 3 = 10$

25. $14 \leq 4 \cdot 3$

26. $2 + 9 < 11$

State whether each sentence is true or false for the given value of the variable.

27. $18 - 3w > 15$ for $w = -1$

28. $8 - 2b = b + 5$ for $b = 1$

29. $2 + k \not< 5k$ for $k = 2$

30. $15 \div e = e + 2$ for $e = 3$

31. **Entertainment** A student has $22.50 to buy three movie tickets. She wrote the inequality $3t \leq 22.50$ to show that the cost of three movie tickets has to be less than or equal to the money she has. If each ticket costs $7, is her inequality true? Explain.

Find the solution set for each replacement set.

32. $8 - x > 2$ for $\{5, 6, 7, 8\}$

33. $3d = 14$ for {all whole numbers}

34. $2n \neq 12$ for {all real numbers}

35. $12 \leq f + 1$ for $\{10, 11, 12, 13, 14, 15\}$

State whether each open sentence is always true, sometimes true, or never true. Use the real numbers for the replacement set.

36. $2x = x + x$

37. $5 - n = 11$

38. $a + 0 = a \cdot 1$

39. $3g = 3(g - g)$

40. $3 + w = 2 + w$

41. $p + 1 = 5 - p$

State whether each mathematical sentence has one solution, more than one solution, or no solutions. Use the real numbers for the replacement set.

42. $2r \geq 10$

43. $5d + 2 = 12$

44. $8a = 6a$

45. $2y + 1 = 2 + 2y$

46. $3 - m < -2 + m$

47. $4(a + b) \neq 4a + 4b$

48. **Fitness** Refer to the photo.
   a. Explain how the equation $C = 25m + 50$ represents the cost of club membership.
   b. What is a reasonable replacement set for the variable m?
   c. During a special promotion, Glennhill Fitness Club will waive the $50 fee if you sign up for more than 10 months. Write a new equation to describe the cost of membership. Give a replacement set for the variable m.

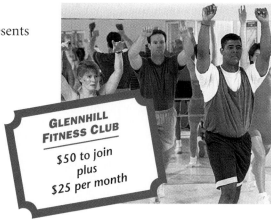

GLENNHILL FITNESS CLUB

$50 to join
plus
$25 per month

Cumulative Frequency and Percentiles

<u>W</u>hat You'll Learn

• Representing cumulative frequency with tables and histograms

• Showing percentiles with cumulative frequency histograms

...<u>And Why</u>

To analyze recreation data

THINK AND DISCUSS

Finding Cumulative Frequency

Recreation The frequency table shows the results of a survey of the users of a bike path. The users' ages have been rounded to the nearest year and grouped into intervals of 20 years.

Ages of Bike Path Users

Age Range	Frequency (Number of Users)
0–19	189
20–39	254
40–59	185
60–79	105
80–99	40

You might want to know how many people in the survey were under a certain age. You can add frequencies for the intervals to create a *cumulative frequency table*. The **cumulative frequency** for an interval is the sum of the interval's frequency and the frequencies of all previous intervals. For example, the cumulative frequency of all bike path users under the age of 40 is 189 + 254, or 443.

Example 1

Use the data above to create a cumulative frequency table.

Ages of Bike Path Users, Cumulative Frequency

Age Range	Frequency	Cumulative Frequency
0–19	189	**189**
20–39	254	**443**
40–59	185	**628**
60–79	105	**733**
80–99	40	**773**

Add the first two frequencies to get 443.

Add the next frequency to 443 to get 628, and so forth.

The cumulative frequency for an interval is the total number of all bike path users up through the given interval.

1. Explain how to find the cumulative frequency for the interval 60−79.

2. What does 773, the last entry in the third row, represent?

3. *Critical Thinking* Why is 189 the first entry in both the second and the third row?

A **cumulative frequency histogram** is a graph of the data in a cumulative frequency table.

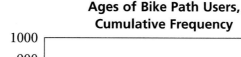

Draw a cumulative frequency histogram for the table in Example 1.

Since the largest number is 773, you can use a vertical scale numbered in intervals of 100.

4. Which bar in the histogram shows the number of bike path users who are less than 60 years old?

5. Why do the bars get taller even though the number of users decreases after age 39?

6. How can you tell the number of people in the survey from this type of graph?

Finding Percentiles

The cumulative frequency histogram in Example 2 shows that more than half of the people in the survey are younger than age 40. Another way to show this is to use cumulative percents, or **percentiles.**

Example 3

Use the table in Example 1 to draw a cumulative frequency histogram with percentiles on the vertical scale.

Step 1 Compute the percentiles for each interval in the age data table. Since 773 people were surveyed, let 773 equal 100%. Find the percents for the other intervals by dividing the cumulative frequency by 773. Round to the nearest whole percent.

Ages of Bike Path Users, Percentiles

Ages	Cumulative Frequency	Percentile
0–19	189	24
20–39	443	57
40–59	628	81
60–79	733	95
80–99	773	100

Step 2 Draw a histogram. Use a vertical scale from 0% to 100% with intervals of 10%.

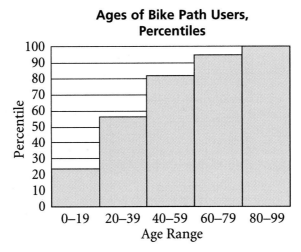

Ages of Bike Path Users, Percentiles

7. What age group would you be in if you were in the 60th percentile?

8. How old are the people in the bottom 10%?

Exercises   ON YOUR OWN

Test Scores **A group of students took a test. There were 5 questions, each worth 5 points. The table at the right shows the test results. Use the table for Exercises 1–7.**

Test Scores

Score	Frequency
0	2
5	5
10	8
15	15
20	15
25	17

1. Make a cumulative frequency table for the data.

2. How many students took the test?

3. How many students scored 20 points or less?

4. Make a cumulative frequency histogram for the data.

5. What does the height of the final bar show?

6. Critical Thinking If a score of 20 or better allowed students to start the next chapter, how many students could start the next chapter?

7. If you were a student in the class that took this test and you got a score of 20, how many of your classmates got a lower score?

Tourism **A travel agency took a survey of visitors to New York City to find out how many historical sites they visited. The table shows the survey results. Use the table for Exercises 8–13.**

Number of Historical Sites Visited	Frequency
0	143
1	175
2	72
3	86
4 or more	24

8. How many people were surveyed?

9. Copy the table.
  a. Add a third column to show cumulative frequencies.
  b. Add a fourth column to show percentiles.

10. If you visited two historical sites, what percentile would you be in?

11. How many historical sites would you need to visit to be in the top 50%?

12. Critical Thinking Why is it easy to compute percentiles for this group of visitors?

13. Draw a histogram for the data that shows percentiles on the vertical scale.

Camping **The table below shows the ages of children who signed up for a summer camp. Use the ages for Exercises 14–17.**

Ages of Campers

10	12	12	12	14	14	13	12	12	10
11	11	13	10	12	13	11	12	14	10
10	10	11	12	13	12	11	10	11	14
10	10	13	13	12	12	11	12	14	10

14. Make a cumulative frequency table from the data in the table.

15. Make a cumulative frequency histogram.

16. Compute the percentiles for each age and then make a cumulative frequency histogram with percentiles on the vertical scale.

17. What percent of the children are 13 years old or younger?

Probability Distributions

What You'll Learn

• Representing probability distributions with tables and histograms

...And Why

To solve problems involving decision making and coin tosses

THINK AND DISCUSS

A group of 10 friends are trying to make plans for next Saturday. They can't decide whether to go to the zoo, take a canoe trip, visit the natural history museum, or have a picnic. Each person votes for one activity, with these results:

zoo: 1   canoe trip: 2   museum: 5   picnic: 2

The friends decide to let chance make the decision for them. They create a spinner with 10 sectors. They code the sectors to be proportional to the results of the vote.

Example 1   Relating to the Real World

Decision Making Find the probability of choosing each activity. Show the results in a table.

Use the probability formula to find the probability of each event.

$$P(\text{event}) = \frac{\text{number of favorable outcomes}}{\text{number of possible outcomes}}$$

Probabilities of Activities

Event	Probability
Zoo	$\frac{1}{10}$ or 0.1
Canoe Trip	$\frac{2}{10}$ or 0.2
Museum	$\frac{5}{10}$ or 0.5
Picnic	$\frac{2}{10}$ or 0.2

Since only one activity will be chosen, the activities are **mutually exclusive events.** The sum of the probabilities of mutually exclusive events is 1.

In Example 1,

$$\frac{1}{10} + \frac{2}{10} + \frac{5}{10} + \frac{2}{10} = \frac{10}{10} = 1$$

A table or a graph of the probabilities of mutually exclusive events shows the **probability distribution** of the events.

1.   These letters are written on slips of paper: E N E O N R R N T T R R. One slip is drawn at random.
   a. Make a probability distribution table showing the probability of drawing each letter.
   b. Show that the sum of the probabilities equals 1.

2. Critical Thinking A probability distribution table shows six different events. The probability of one event equals 1. What are the probabilities of the other five events? Why?

Example 2 **Relating to the Real World**

Coin Tossing Three coins are tossed. The table shows the probability distribution for tossing different numbers of heads. What is the probability of tossing two or more heads?

Tossing Three Coins

Event	Probability
0 heads	$\frac{1}{8}$ or 0.125
1 head	$\frac{3}{8}$ or 0.375
2 heads	$\frac{3}{8}$ or 0.375
3 heads	$\frac{1}{8}$ or 0.125

Add P(2 heads) and P(3 heads). The sum is $\frac{4}{8}$ or 0.5. The probability of getting 2 or more heads is 0.5.

3. List the possible outcomes for tossing two coins.

You can use a histogram to display a probability distribution.

Example 3 **Relating to the Real World**

Decision Making Draw a histogram for the probability distribution in Example 1.

Use the vertical scale to show frequencies as probabilities.

4. a. Try This Draw a histogram for the probability distribution shown in the table in Example 2.

b. Draw a histogram that uses percentiles to show the cumulative probability of tossing heads in three coin tosses.

5. Critical Thinking What is the probability of tossing three coins and getting tails once? How can you find the answer using your histogram from Question 4(a)?

Contestants in a game spin the spinner shown at the right to win $10, $100, or $1000.

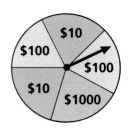

1. Draw a histogram showing the probability distribution of the prizes.

2. Is the chance of winning more than $10 in one spin greater than 50%? Explain.

3. Eight people are planning a family reunion picnic. They can't decide on the main dish. Each person writes his or her choice on a slip of paper, and one slip is drawn. The table shows the number of votes for each dish. Draw a histogram showing the probability distribution of the main dishes.

Main Dish	Hot Dogs	Fish	Chicken	Steak
Number of Votes	1	2	3	2

4. *Critical Thinking* Three people compete in a race. Helen is twice as likely to win as Josh. Josh is twice as likely to win as Vicki. Write and solve an equation to find each person's probability of winning.

Twenty people are taking a trip to a forest in New York State. Each person writes his or her favorite forest on a slip of paper. The histogram shows the probability of randomly drawing each of four forests. Use the histogram to answer Exercises 5 and 6.

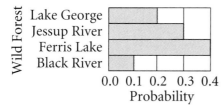

Favorite NY Wild Forest

5. How many people wrote Black River on their slips of paper?

6. What is the probability that the group will go to Ferris Lake?

The histogram shows the probability distribution of the ages of spectators at a sporting event.

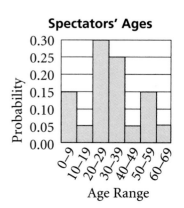

Spectators' Ages

7. Show that the sum of the probabilities equals 1.

8. Draw a histogram that uses percentiles to show cumulative probability.

9. What is the probability that a person chosen at random is younger than 20?

10. *Critical Thinking* If you choose 30 people at the event at random, how many would you expect to be younger than 20? Explain.

Connections Packaging Design . . . *and more*

Percent of Error

What You'll Learn

- Identifying the greatest possible error in measurements
- Expressing the error in measurements as percents

...And Why

To solve problems involving collectibles and packaging design

---

THINK AND DISCUSS

Finding Error in Measurement

Think about the last time you measured with a ruler. Perhaps you measured to the nearest inch, centimeter, or millimeter. Because no measurement is exact, you always measure to the nearest "something." The **greatest possible error** in a measurement is one half of the measuring unit.

Example 1 **Relating to the Real World**

Collectibles What is the height of the magnet to the nearest millimeter? What is the greatest possible error of the measurement?

The height is about 41 mm. Since the measuring unit is 1 mm, the greatest possible error is one half of 1 mm, or 0.5 mm.

1. If you measure the magnet to the nearest centimeter, what is the greatest possible error?

2. **Try This** Find the greatest possible error for each measurement.
    a. 3 mL
    b. $1\frac{1}{2}$ in.
    c. 2.2 kg

Example 2 **Relating to the Real World**

Packaging Design A packaging designer wants to know how much area is available on the inside face of a CD box, not including the area used by the CD. The diagram shows the designer's measurements. Find the minimum and maximum possible values of the shaded area.

Step 1 Find the minimum area. Since the measurements are to the nearest 0.1 cm, the greatest possible error for each is 0.05 cm.

$$A = bh - \pi r^2 \quad \longleftarrow \text{Write an expression for the difference between the areas of the rectangle and the circle.}$$

$$= 13.95(11.95) - \pi(6.05)^2 \quad \longleftarrow \text{Substitute the appropriate values.}$$

$$= 51.7123549 \quad \longleftarrow \text{Use a calculator.}$$

The minimum area is about 51.7 cm^2.

Step 2 Find the maximum area.

$$A = bh - \pi r^2$$

$$= 14.05(12.05) - \pi(5.95)^2 \quad \longleftarrow \text{Substitute the appropriate values.}$$

$$= 58.08226608 \quad \longleftarrow \text{Use a calculator.}$$

The maximum area is about 58.1 cm^2.

PROBLEM SOLVING HINT

To find the minimum area, subtract the largest possible inner area from the smallest possible outer area. To find the maximum area, subtract the smallest possible inner area from the largest possible outer area.

3. **Try This** Measure the dimensions of the figure below to the nearest tenth of a centimeter. Find the minimum and maximum possible values of the area of the shaded region. Round your answers to the nearest tenth.

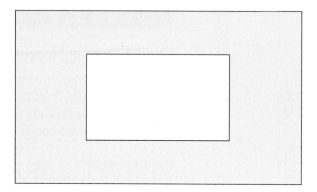

4. *Critical Thinking* Why do you subtract the largest possible inner area from the smallest possible outer area to find the minimum possible value of the shaded area?

Finding Percent of Error

You can represent error in measurements by the *percent of error*.

> ### Percent of Error
>
> **percent of error** $= \dfrac{\text{amount of error}}{\text{measurement}}$

Example 3

Find the percent of error in a measurement of 12.7 cm.

Since the measurement is to the nearest 0.1 cm, the greatest possible error is 0.05 cm.

$$\text{percent of error} = \frac{\text{amount of error}}{\text{measurement}} \quad \longleftarrow \text{Use the formula.}$$

$$= \frac{0.05}{12.7} \quad \longleftarrow \text{Substitute.}$$

$$= 0.003937009 \quad \longleftarrow \text{Divide.}$$

$$\approx 0.4\% \quad \longleftarrow \text{Round and write as a percent.}$$

The percent of error is about 0.4%.

5. **Try This** Find the percent of error for each measurement.

   a. $2\frac{1}{2}$ yd   **b.** 10.0 L   **c.** 2 kg

6. Suppose you measure the length of a book to the nearest inch and to the nearest centimeter. Which measurement involves a greater percent of error? Explain.

Errors in measurements will affect the results of computations using those measurements.

Example 4 ···

6 in.

3 in.

The diagram gives meaurements of the dimensions of a cylinder. Find the greatest possible percent of error in calculating the volume of the cylinder.

The measurements are to the nearest 1 in., so the greatest possible error is 0.5 in.

Volume without error:	Maximum volume:	Minimum volume:
$V = \pi r^2 h$	$V = \pi r^2 h$	$V = \pi r^2 h$
$= \pi \cdot 3^2 \cdot 6$	$= \pi \cdot 3.5^2 \cdot 6.5$	$= \pi \cdot 2.5^2 \cdot 5.5$
≈ 169.6	≈ 250.1	≈ 108.0
$V = 169.6$ in.^{3}	$V = 250.1$ in.^{3}	$V = 108.0$ in.^{3}

The greatest amount of error will result from the difference between the maximum volume and the volume without error.

$$\text{Percent of error} = \frac{\text{amount of error}}{\text{measurement}}$$

$$= \frac{250.1 - 169.6}{169.6}$$

$$= \frac{80.5}{169.6} \approx 47\%$$

The greatest possible percent of error is about 47%.

7. **Try This** Find the greatest possible percent of error in calculating the volume of a cube with edges measured as 3 cm. Round to the nearest whole percent.

Exercises   ON YOUR OWN

Write the greatest possible error for each measurement.

1. 42 in.

2. 13.0 mg

3. 12,012 mi

4. $16\frac{1}{8}$ gal

5. 75.25 m

6. 43 mL

Using the given measurements for each polygon, find the greatest possible perimeter and area. Round each answer to the nearest tenth.

7.

12.5 m

18.0 m

8.

$6\frac{1}{2}$ ft

$6\frac{1}{2}$ ft

9.

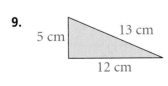

5 cm   13 cm

12 cm

Using the given measurements, find the greatest and least possible circumferences and areas for each circle. Use $\pi \approx 3.14$. Round answers to the nearest hundredth.

10.

4 cm

11.

5.5 in.

12.

2.6 m

13. Biology A biologist measures frogs and tadpoles to the nearest tenth of a centimeter. What is the greatest possible error in millimeters?

14. Graphic Arts An artist measured a poster as $28\frac{1}{8}$ in. long. What is the greatest possible error in the artist's measurement?

15. Landscape Architecture An architect is creating a scale drawing for a garden. His measurements are accurate to the nearest tenth of a centimeter.
 a. What is the greatest possible error in a calculation of the perimeter of a drawing of a rectangular flower bed?
 b. If the scale of the drawing is 100 : 1, what is the greatest possible error in a calculation of the perimeter of the actual flower bed?

Write the greatest possible error for each measurement as a percent. Round to the nearest tenth of a percent.

16. $2\frac{1}{4}$ qt, measured to the nearest $\frac{1}{8}$ qt

17. 18 km, measured to the nearest 0.5 km

18. 0.6 g

19. $25\frac{1}{2}$ in.

20. 45 mL

Find the greatest possible percent of error to the nearest tenth of a percent.

21. Without error:
 $P = 18$ cm
 Greatest possible perimeter:
 $P = 20$ cm
 Least possible perimeter:
 $P = 16$ cm

22. Without error:
 $A = 24$ ft^2
 Greatest possible area:
 $A = 29.75$ ft^2
 Least possible area:
 $A = 18.75$ ft^2

23. Without error:
 $V = 30$ in.^{3}
 Greatest possible volume:
 $V = 48.13$ in.^{3}
 Least possible volume:
 $V = 16.88$ in.^{3}

24. Sports After a fishing trip in the Catskills, a fisherman reported the length of a $6\frac{1}{2}$ in. salmon as 7 in. A second fisherman reported the length of a $36\frac{1}{2}$ in. salmon as 36 in. Compare the percents of error.

25. Critical Thinking For a given set of measurements, why is the percent of error greater for a calculation of area than for a calculation of perimeter or circumference?

26. Find the greatest possible percent of error to the nearest tenth of a percent for a calculation of the volume of the cone at the right. Use a calculator.

9 m

4 m

Tables

Measures

United States Customary	Metric

Length

12 inches (in.) = 1 foot (ft)
36 in. = 1 yard (yd)
3 ft = 1 yard
5280 ft = 1 mile (mi)
1760 yd = 1 mile

10 millimeters (mm) = 1 centimeter (cm)
100 cm = 1 meter (m)
1000 mm = 1 meter
1000 m = 1 kilometer (km)

Area

144 square inches (in.^{2}) = 1 square foot (ft^2)
9 ft^2 = 1 square yard (yd^2)
43,560 ft^2 = 1 acre (a)
4840 yd^2 = 1 acre

100 square millimeters (mm^2) = 1 square centimeter (cm^2)
10,000 cm^2 = 1 square meter (m^2)
10,000 m^2 = 1 hectare (ha)

Volume

1728 cubic inches (in.^{3}) = 1 cubic foot (ft^3)
27 ft^3 = 1 cubic yard (yd^3)

1000 cubic millimeters (mm^3) = 1 cubic centimeter (cm^3)
1,000,000 cm^3 = 1 cubic meter (m^3)

Liquid Capacity

8 fluid ounces (fl oz) = 1 cup (c)
2 c = 1 pint (pt)
2 pt = 1 quart (qt)
4 qt = 1 gallon (gal)

1000 milliliters (mL) = 1 liter (L)
1000 L = 1 kiloliter (kL)

Mass

16 ounces (oz) = 1 pound (lb)
2000 pounds = 1 ton (t)

1000 milligrams (mg) = 1 gram (g)
1000 g = 1 kilogram (kg)
1000 kg = 1 metric ton (t)

Temperature

32°F = freezing point of water
98.6°F = normal body temperature
212°F = boiling point of water

0°C = freezing point of water
37°C = normal body temperature
100°C = boiling point of water

Time

60 seconds (s) = 1 minute (min)
60 minutes = 1 hour (h)
24 hours = 1 day (da)
7 days = 1 week (wk)
4 weeks (approx.) = 1 month (mo)

365 days = 1 year (yr)
52 weeks (approx.) = 1 year
12 months = 1 year
10 years = 1 decade
100 years = 1 century

Symbols

$=$	equals	p. 5	$\angle A$	angle A	p. 111
$\approx$	is approximately equal to	p. 5	$\%$	percent	p. 139
$\cdot$	multiplication sign, times ($\times$)	p. 5	$a:b$	ratio of a to b	p. 158
$(\ )$	parentheses for grouping	p. 15	$\neq$	is not equal to	p. 159
a^n	nth power of a	p. 15	$\triangle ABC$	triangle ABC	p. 159
$[\ ]$	brackets for grouping	p. 17	AB	length of $\overline{AB}$; distance between points A and B	p. 159
$\ldots$	and so on	p. 19			
$\|a\|$	absolute value of a	p. 20	$\leq$	is less than or equal to	p. 179
$-a$	opposite of a	p. 22	$\geq$	is greater than or equal to	p. 179
$^\circ$	degree(s)	p. 23	$\{\ \}$	set braces	p. 202
$<$	is less than	p. 28	$\overleftrightarrow{AB}$	line through points A and B	p. 218
$>$	is greater than	p. 28	m	slope of a linear function	p. 231
π	pi, an irrational number, approximately equal to 3.14	p. 30	b	y-intercept of a linear function	p. 231
$\frac{1}{a}$	reciprocal of a	p. 32	$\sqrt{x}$	nonnegative square root of x	p. 332
$P(\text{event})$	probability of the event	p. 36	$\pm$	plus or minus	p. 332
$\begin{bmatrix} 1 & 2 \\ 3 & 4 \end{bmatrix}$	matrix	p. 40	a^{-n}	$\frac{1}{a^n}, a \neq 0$	p. 380
$\wedge$	raised to a power (in a spreadsheet formula)	p. 46	$\overline{AB}$	segment with endpoints A and B	p. 420
$\star$	multiply (in a spreadsheet formula)	p. 46	$\sin A$	sine of $\angle A$	p. 425
$/$	divide (in a spreadsheet formula)	p. 46	$\cos A$	cosine of $\angle A$	p. 425
			$\tan A$	tangent of $\angle A$	p. 425
(x, y)	ordered pair	p. 58	$m\angle A$	measure of angle A	p. 429
$f(x)$	f of x; the function value at x	p. 79	$\bar{x}$	mean of data values of x	p. 452
x_1, x_2, etc.	specific values of the variable x	p. 89	$n!$	n factorial	p. 539
y_1, y_2, etc.	specific values of the variable y	p. 89	$_nP_r$	permutations of n things taken r at a time	p. 540
$\stackrel{?}{=}$	is the statement true?	p. 109	$_nC_r$	combinations of n things taken r at a time	p. 543

CHAPTER 1

Order of Operations

1. Perform any operation(s) inside grouping symbols.
2. Simplify any terms with exponents.
3. Multiply and divide in order from left to right.
4. Add and subtract in order from left to right.

The Identity Property

For every real number a:

$$a + 0 = a \quad \text{and} \quad 0 + a = a$$
$$a \cdot 1 = a \quad \text{and} \quad 1 \cdot a = a$$

The Commutative Property

For all real numbers a and b:

$$a + b = b + a \qquad a \cdot b = b \cdot a$$

The Associative Property

For all real numbers a, b, and c:

$$(a + b) + c = a + (b + c)$$
$$(a \cdot b) \cdot c = a \cdot (b \cdot c)$$

Property of Opposites

The sum of a number and its **opposite,** or **additive inverse,** is zero. $\quad a + (-a) = 0$

Property of Reciprocals

The **reciprocal,** or **multiplicative inverse**, of a nonzero number $\frac{a}{b}$ is $\frac{b}{a}$. $\quad a \cdot \frac{1}{a} = 1$

CHAPTER 2

The Probability Formula

$$P(\text{event}) = \frac{\text{number of favorable outcomes}}{\text{number of possible outcomes}}$$

CHAPTER 3

Properties of Equality

For all real numbers a, b, and c:

Addition: If $a = b$, then $a + c = b + c$.

Subtraction: If $a = b$, then $a - c = b - c$.

Multiplication: If $a = b$, then $a \cdot c = b \cdot c$.

Division: If $a = b$, and $c \neq 0$, then $\frac{a}{c} = \frac{b}{c}$.

Probability of Two Events

If A and B are independent events, then
$$P(A \text{ and } B) = P(A) \cdot P(B).$$
If A and B are dependent events, then
$$P(A \text{ and } B) = P(A) \cdot P(B \text{ after } A).$$

The Distributive Property

For all real numbers a, b, and c,

$$a(b + c) = ab + ac \qquad (b + c)a = ba + ca$$
$$a(b - c) = ab - ac \qquad (b - c)a = ba - ca$$

CHAPTER 4

Properties of Inequality

For all real numbers a, b, and c:

Addition: If $a > b$, then $a + c > b + c$.
If $a < b$, then $a + c < b + c$.

Subtraction: If $a > b$, then $a - c > b - c$.
If $a < b$, then $a - c < b - c$.

Multiplication: $c > 0$: If $a > b$, then $ac > bc$.
If $a < b$, then $ac < bc$.

$c < 0$: If $a > b$, then $ac < bc$.
If $a < b$, then $ac > bc$.

Division: $c > 0$: If $a < b$, then $\frac{a}{c} < \frac{b}{c}$.
If $a > b$, then $\frac{a}{c} > \frac{b}{c}$.

$c < 0$: If $a < b$, then $\frac{a}{c} > \frac{b}{c}$.
If $a > b$, then $\frac{a}{c} < \frac{b}{c}$.

CHAPTER 5

Slope-Intercept Form of a Linear Equation

The slope-intercept form of a linear equation is $y = mx + b$, where m is the slope and b is the y-intercept.

CHAPTER 7

Quadratic Formula

If $ax^2 + bx + c = 0$ and $a \neq 0$, then

$$x = \frac{-b \pm \sqrt{b^2 - 4ac}}{2a}.$$

Property of the Discriminant

For the quadratic equation $ax^2 + bx + c = 0$, where $a \neq 0$, the value of the discriminant $b^2 - 4ac$ tells you the number of solutions.

$b^2 - 4ac > 0$	two solutions
$b^2 - 4ac = 0$	one solution
$b^2 - 4ac < 0$	no solution

CHAPTER 8

Zero as an Exponent

For any nonzero number a, $a^0 = 1$.

Negative Exponents

For any nonzero number a and any integer n:
$$a^{-n} = \frac{1}{a^n}$$

Multiplying or Dividing Powers

For any nonzero number a and any integers m and n:
$$a^m \cdot a^n = a^{m+n}$$
$$\frac{a^m}{a^n} = a^{m-n}$$

Raising a Power to a Power

For any nonzero number a and any integers m and n:
$$(a^m)^n = a^{mn}$$

Raising a Product or a Quotient to a Power

For any nonzero numbers a and b and any integer n:
$$(ab)^n = a^n b^n$$
$$\left(\frac{a}{b}\right)^n = \frac{a^n}{b^n}$$

CHAPTER 9

Properties of Square Roots

For any numbers $a \geq 0$ and $b \geq 0$,
$$\sqrt{ab} = \sqrt{a} \cdot \sqrt{b}.$$
For any numbers $a \geq 0$ and $b > 0$, $\sqrt{\frac{a}{b}} = \frac{\sqrt{a}}{\sqrt{b}}.$

The Pythagorean Theorem

In a right triangle, the sum of the squares of the lengths of the legs is equal to the square of the length of the hypotenuse.
$$a^2 + b^2 = c^2$$

The Converse of the Pythagorean Theorem

If a triangle has sides of lengths a, b, and c, and $a^2 + b^2 = c^2$, then the triangle is a right triangle with hypotenuse of length c.

The Distance Formula

The distance d between any two points (x_1, y_1) and (x_2, y_2) is
$$d = \sqrt{(x_2 - x_1)^2 + (y_2 - y_1)^2}.$$

The Midpoint Formula

The midpoint M of a line segment with endpoints $A(x_1, y_1)$ and $B(x_2, y_2)$ is
$$\left(\frac{x_1 + x_2}{2}, \frac{y_1 + y_2}{2}\right).$$

Trigonometric Ratios

$$\text{sine of } \angle A = \frac{\text{length of side opposite } \angle A}{\text{length of hypotenuse}}$$

$$\text{cosine of } \angle A = \frac{\text{length of side adjacent to } \angle A}{\text{length of hypotenuse}}$$

$$\text{tangent of } \angle A = \frac{\text{length of side opposite } \angle A}{\text{length of side adjacent to } \angle A}$$

CHAPTER 10

Factoring Special Cases

For all real numbers a and b:
$$a^2 - b^2 = (a + b)(a - b)$$
$$a^2 + 2ab + b^2 = (a + b)(a + b) = (a + b)^2$$
$$a^2 - 2ab + b^2 = (a - b)(a - b) = (a - b)^2$$

Zero-Product Property

For all real numbers a and b, if $ab = 0$, then $a = 0$ or $b = 0$.

CHAPTER 11

Multiplication Counting Principle

If there are m ways to make a first selection and n ways to make a second selection, there are $m \cdot n$ ways to make the two selections.

Properties of Equality

For all real numbers a, b, and c:

Reflexive Property: $a = a$

Symmetric Property: If $a = b$, then $b = a$.

Transitive Property: If $a = b$ and $b = c$, then $a = c$.

Formulas from Geometry

You will use a number of geometric formulas as you work through your algebra book. Here are some perimeter, area, and volume formulas.

$$P = 2\ell + 2w$$
$$A = \ell w$$

Rectangle

$$P = 4s$$
$$A = s^2$$

Square

$$C = 2\pi r \quad \text{or} \quad C = \pi d$$
$$A = \pi r^2$$

Circle

$$A = \tfrac{1}{2}bh$$

Triangle

$$A = bh$$

Parallelogram

$$A = \tfrac{1}{2}(b_1 + b_2)h$$

Trapezoid

$$V = Bh$$
$$V = lwh$$

Rectangular Prism

$$V = \tfrac{1}{3}Bh$$

Pyramid

$$V = Bh$$
$$V = \pi r^2 h$$

Cylinder

$$V = \tfrac{1}{3}Bh$$
$$V = \tfrac{1}{3}\pi r^2 h$$

Cone

$$V = \tfrac{4}{3}\pi r^3$$

Sphere

Tables

Squares and Square Roots

Number n	Square n^2	Positive Square Root $\sqrt{n}$	Number n	Square n^2	Positive Square Root $\sqrt{n}$	Number n	Square n^2	Positive Square Root $\sqrt{n}$
1	1	1.000	51	2601	7.141	101	10,201	10.050
2	4	1.414	52	2704	7.211	102	10,404	10.100
3	9	1.732	53	2809	7.280	103	10,609	10.149
4	16	2.000	54	2916	7.348	104	10,816	10.198
5	25	2.236	55	3025	7.416	105	11,025	10.247
6	36	2.449	56	3136	7.483	106	11,236	10.296
7	49	2.646	57	3249	7.550	107	11,449	10.344
8	64	2.828	58	3364	7.616	108	11,664	10.392
9	81	3.000	59	3481	7.681	109	11,881	10.440
10	100	3.162	60	3600	7.746	110	12,100	10.488
11	121	3.317	61	3721	7.810	111	12,321	10.536
12	144	3.464	62	3844	7.874	112	12,544	10.583
13	169	3.606	63	3969	7.937	113	12,769	10.630
14	196	3.742	64	4096	8.000	114	12,996	10.677
15	225	3.873	65	4225	8.062	115	13,225	10.724
16	256	4.000	66	4356	8.124	116	13,456	10.770
17	289	4.123	67	4489	8.185	117	13,689	10.817
18	324	4.243	68	4624	8.246	118	13,924	10.863
19	361	4.359	69	4761	8.307	119	14,161	10.909
20	400	4.472	70	4900	8.367	120	14,400	10.954
21	441	4.583	71	5041	8.426	121	14,641	11.000
22	484	4.690	72	5184	8.485	122	14,884	11.045
23	529	4.796	73	5329	8.544	123	15,129	11.091
24	576	4.899	74	5476	8.602	124	15,376	11.136
25	625	5.000	75	5625	8.660	125	15,625	11.180
26	676	5.099	76	5776	8.718	126	15,876	11.225
27	729	5.196	77	5929	8.775	127	16,129	11.269
28	784	5.292	78	6084	8.832	128	16,384	11.314
29	841	5.385	79	6241	8.888	129	16,641	11.358
30	900	5.477	80	6400	8.944	130	16,900	11.402
31	961	5.568	81	6561	9.000	131	17,161	11.446
32	1024	5.657	82	6724	9.055	132	17,424	11.489
33	1089	5.745	83	6889	9.110	133	17,689	11.533
34	1156	5.831	84	7056	9.165	134	17,956	11.576
35	1225	5.916	85	7225	9.220	135	18,225	11.619
36	1296	6.000	86	7396	9.274	136	18,496	11.662
37	1369	6.083	87	7569	9.327	137	18,769	11.705
38	1444	6.164	88	7744	9.381	138	19,044	11.747
39	1521	6.245	89	7921	9.434	139	19,321	11.790
40	1600	6.325	90	8100	9.487	140	19,600	11.832
41	1681	6.403	91	8281	9.539	141	19,881	11.874
42	1764	6.481	92	8464	9.592	142	20,164	11.916
43	1849	6.557	93	8649	9.644	143	20,449	11.958
44	1936	6.633	94	8836	9.695	144	20,736	12.000
45	2025	6.708	95	9025	9.747	145	21,025	12.042
46	2116	6.782	96	9216	9.798	146	21,316	12.083
47	2209	6.856	97	9409	9.849	147	21,609	12.124
48	2304	6.928	98	9604	9.899	148	21,904	12.166
49	2401	7.000	99	9801	9.950	149	22,201	12.207
50	2500	7.071	100	10,000	10.000	150	22,500	12.247

Trigonometric Ratios

Angle	Sine	Cosine	Tangent	Angle	Sine	Cosine	Tangent
1°	0.0175	0.9998	0.0175	46°	0.7193	0.6947	1.0355
2°	0.0349	0.9994	0.0349	47°	0.7314	0.6820	1.0724
3°	0.0523	0.9986	0.0524	48°	0.7431	0.6691	1.1106
4°	0.0698	0.9976	0.0699	49°	0.7547	0.6561	1.1504
5°	0.0872	0.9962	0.0875	50°	0.7660	0.6428	1.1918
6°	0.1045	0.9945	0.1051	51°	0.7771	0.6293	1.2349
7°	0.1219	0.9925	0.1228	52°	0.7880	0.6157	1.2799
8°	0.1392	0.9903	0.1405	53°	0.7986	0.6018	1.3270
9°	0.1564	0.9877	0.1584	54°	0.8090	0.5878	1.3764
10°	0.1736	0.9848	0.1763	55°	0.8192	0.5736	1.4281
11°	0.1908	0.9816	0.1944	56°	0.8290	0.5592	1.4826
12°	0.2079	0.9781	0.2126	57°	0.8387	0.5446	1.5399
13°	0.2250	0.9744	0.2309	58°	0.8480	0.5299	1.6003
14°	0.2419	0.9703	0.2493	59°	0.8572	0.5150	1.6643
15°	0.2588	0.9659	0.2679	60°	0.8660	0.5000	1.7321
16°	0.2756	0.9613	0.2867	61°	0.8746	0.4848	1.8040
17°	0.2924	0.9563	0.3057	62°	0.8829	0.4695	1.8807
18°	0.3090	0.9511	0.3249	63°	0.8910	0.4540	1.9626
19°	0.3256	0.9455	0.3443	64°	0.8988	0.4384	2.0503
20°	0.3420	0.9397	0.3640	65°	0.9063	0.4226	2.1445
21°	0.3584	0.9336	0.3839	66°	0.9135	0.4067	2.2460
22°	0.3746	0.9272	0.4040	67°	0.9205	0.3907	2.3559
23°	0.3907	0.9205	0.4245	68°	0.9272	0.3746	2.4751
24°	0.4067	0.9135	0.4452	69°	0.9336	0.3584	2.6051
25°	0.4226	0.9063	0.4663	70°	0.9397	0.3420	2.7475
26°	0.4384	0.8988	0.4877	71°	0.9455	0.3256	2.9042
27°	0.4540	0.8910	0.5095	72°	0.9511	0.3090	3.0777
28°	0.4695	0.8829	0.5317	73°	0.9563	0.2924	3.2709
29°	0.4848	0.8746	0.5543	74°	0.9613	0.2756	3.4874
30°	0.5000	0.8660	0.5774	75°	0.9659	0.2588	3.7321
31°	0.5150	0.8572	0.6009	76°	0.9703	0.2419	4.0108
32°	0.5299	0.8480	0.6249	77°	0.9744	0.2250	4.3315
33°	0.5446	0.8387	0.6494	78°	0.9781	0.2079	4.7046
34°	0.5592	0.8290	0.6745	79°	0.9816	0.1908	5.1446
35°	0.5736	0.8192	0.7002	80°	0.9848	0.1736	5.6713
36°	0.5878	0.8090	0.7265	81°	0.9877	0.1564	6.3138
37°	0.6018	0.7986	0.7536	82°	0.9903	0.1392	7.1154
38°	0.6157	0.7880	0.7813	83°	0.9925	0.1219	8.1443
39°	0.6293	0.7771	0.8098	84°	0.9945	0.1045	9.5144
40°	0.6428	0.7660	0.8391	85°	0.9962	0.0872	11.4301
41°	0.6561	0.7547	0.8693	86°	0.9976	0.0698	14.3007
42°	0.6691	0.7431	0.9004	87°	0.9986	0.0523	19.0811
43°	0.6820	0.7314	0.9325	88°	0.9994	0.0349	28.6363
44°	0.6947	0.7193	0.9657	89°	0.9998	0.0175	57.2900
45°	0.7071	0.7071	1.0000	90°	1.0000	0.0000	

Tables

A

Examples

Absolute value (p. 20) The distance that a number is from zero on a number line.

−7 is 7 units from 0, so $|-7| = 7$.

Absolute value function (p. 92) Function whose graph forms a "V" that opens up or down.

$y = |x - 3|$

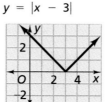

Addition Property of Inequality (p. 180) For all real numbers $a, b,$ and c: if $a > b$, then $a + c > b + c$ and if $a < b$, then $a + c < b + c$.

$4 > -2$, so $4 + 3 > -2 + 3$.
$5 < 9$, so $5 + 2 < 9 + 2$.

Additive inverses (p. 20) A number and its opposite. Additive inverses have a sum of 0.

5 and −5 are additive inverses because $5 + -5 = 0$.

Angle of elevation (p. 426) Used to measure heights indirectly. An angle from the horizontal up to a line of sight.

Associative Properties of Addition and Multiplication (p. 35) Changing the grouping of the addends or factors does not change the sum or product. $(a + b) + c = a + (b + c)$ and $(a \cdot b) \cdot c = a \cdot (b \cdot c)$

$(9 + 2) + 3 = 9 + (2 + 3)$.
$(5 \cdot 8) \cdot 2 = 5 \cdot (8 \cdot 2)$.

Asymptote (p. 516) A line the graph of a function gets closer and closer to, but does not cross.

Example: The y-axis is a vertical asymptote for $y = \frac{1}{x}$. The x-axis is a horizontal asymptote for $y = \frac{1}{x}$.

Axis of symmetry (p. 318) The line about which you can reflect a parabola onto itself.

B

Examples

Bar graph (p. 6) A bar graph is used to compare amounts.

Example: The bar graph compares the number of students for grades 9, 10, and 11 over a three-year period.

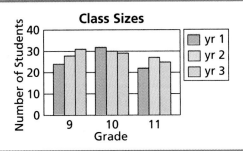

Base (p. 15) In an expression of the form x^n, x is the base.

$4^5 = 4 \cdot 4 \cdot 4 \cdot 4 \cdot 4$. The base 4 is used as a factor 5 times.

Binomial factors (p. 481) Some quadratic trinomials are the products of two binomial factors.

$$(x + 2)(x + 1) = x^2 + 3x + 2$$

↑ ↑ ↑

binomial factors   quadratic trinomial

C

Cell (p. 45) A cell is a box where a row and a column meet in a spreadsheet.

A2 is the cell where row 2 and column A meet. The entry 1.50 is in cell A2.

	A	B	C	D	E
1	0.50	0.70	0.60	0.50	2.30
2	1.50	0.50	2.75	2.50	7.25

Certain event (p. 96) A certain event always happens, and has a probability of 1.

Rolling an integer less than 7 on a number cube is a certain event.

Coefficient (p. 119) The numerical factor when a term has a variable.

In the expression $2x + 3y + 16$, 2 and 3 are coefficients.

Combination (p. 543) An arrangement of some or all of a set of objects without regard to order. The number of combinations

$$= \frac{\text{total number of permutations}}{\text{number of times the objects in each group are repeated}}$$

You can use the notation $_nC_r$ to write the number of combinations of n objects chosen r at a time.

The number of combinations of 10 things taken 4 at a time is:

$$_{10}C_4 = \frac{_{10}P_4}{_4P_4} = \frac{10 \cdot 9 \cdot 8 \cdot 7}{4 \cdot 3 \cdot 2 \cdot 1} = 210$$

Common factors (p. 471) Numbers, variables, and any products formed from the prime factors that appear in all the terms of an expression.

x, 2, and $2x$ are common factors of $2x^2 + 4x$.

Glossary/Study Guide

Commutative Properties of Addition and Multiplication (p. 35)
Changing the order of the addends or factors does not change
the sum or product. For all real numbers *a* and *b:*
$a + b = b + a$ and $a \cdot b = b \cdot a$.

$5 + 7 = 7 + 5$ and $9 \cdot 3 = 3 \cdot 9$.

Complement of an event (p. 96)   All possible outcomes that are
not in the event.
$P(\text{complement of event}) = 1 - P(\text{event})$

The complement of rolling a 1 or a 2 on a
number cube is rolling a 3, 4, 5, or 6.

Compound inequality (p. 195)   Two inequalities that are joined
by *and* or *or.*

$5 < x$ and $x < 10$
$x < -14$ or $x \geq 3$

Constant of variation (p. 225) The constant *k* in a direct
variation.

For the function $y = 24x$, 24 is the
constant of variation.

Constant term (p. 119)   A term that has no variable factor.

In the expression $4x + 13y + 17$,
17 is a constant term.

Continuous data (p. 65)   Have measurements that change
between data points, such as temperature, length, and weight.

The height of a tree changes between
annual measurings.

Converse of the Pythagorean Theorem (p. 416)   If a triangle
has sides of lengths *a*, *b*, and *c*, and $a^2 + b^2 = c^2$, then the
triangle is a right triangle with hypotenuse of length *c*.

Conversion factors (p. 219)   Used to change from one unit of
measure to another.

Convert 2 h to minutes.
Since 60 min $= 1$ h, $\frac{60 \text{ min}}{1 \text{ h}} = 1$.
Use $\frac{60 \text{ min}}{1 \text{ h}}$ to convert 2 h to minutes.
$\frac{2 \text{ h}}{1} \cdot \frac{60 \text{ min}}{1 \text{ h}} = 120$ min

---

Coordinate plane (p. 58)   Formed when two number lines
intersect at right angles. The *x*-axis is the horizontal axis and
the *y*-axis is the vertical axis. The two axes meet at the
origin, $O(0, 0)$.

Correlation (p. 60)   A trend between two sets of data. A trend
shows positive, negative, or no correlation.

Positive   Negative   No Correlation

Correlation coefficient (p. 242)   Tells how well the equation of best fit models the data. The value r of the correlation coefficient is in the range $-1 \leq r \leq 1$.

Example: The correlation coefficient for the data points (68, 0.5), (85, 0.89), (100, 0.9), (108, 1.1) is approximately 0.94.

```
LinReg
  y=ax+b
  a=.0134039132
  b=-.3622031627
  r=.9414498267
■
```

Cosine (p. 425)   In $\triangle ABC$ with right $\angle C$,

$$\text{cosine of } \angle A = \frac{\text{length of side adjacent to } \angle A}{\text{length of hypotenuse}}, \text{ or } \cos A = \frac{b}{c}.$$

$\cos A = \frac{4}{5}$

Cross products (p. 159)   In a proportion, the product of the numerator of the first ratio and the denominator of the second ratio; also the product of the denominator of the first ratio and the numerator of the second ratio. These products are equal.

$\frac{3}{4} = \frac{6}{8}$

The cross products are $3 \cdot 8$ and $4 \cdot 6$.
$3 \cdot 8 = 24$ and $4 \cdot 6 = 24$

Cubic equation (p. 494)   An equation in the form $ax^3 + bx^2 + cx + d = 0$, where $a, b, c,$ and d are real numbers and $a \neq 0$.

$14x^3 + 2x^2 - 8x - 2 = 0$

D

Degree of a polynomial (p. 465)   The highest degree of any of its terms.

The degree of $3x^2 + x - 9$ is 2.

Degree of a term (p. 465)   For a term that has only one variable, the degree is the exponent of the variable. The degree of a constant is zero.

The degree of $3x^2$ is 2.

Dependent events (p. 135)   When the outcome of one event affects the outcome of a second event, the events are dependent events.

If you pick a marble from a bag and pick another without replacing the first, the events are dependent events.

Dependent variable (p. 69)   A variable is dependent if it relies on another variable.

In the equation $y = 3x$, the value of y depends upon the value of x.

Difference of two squares (p. 487)   A quadratic binomial of the form $a^2 - b^2$.

$x^2 - 16$

Dimensional analysis (p. 219)   The process of analyzing units to decide which conversion factors to use to solve a problem.

$0.5 \text{ mi} = \frac{0.5 \text{ mi}}{1} \cdot \frac{5280 \text{ ft}}{1 \text{ mi}} = 2640 \text{ ft}$

Direct variation (p. 225) A linear function that can be expressed in the form $y = kx$, where $k \neq 0$.

$y = 18x$ is a direct variation.

Discrete data (p. 65) Involves a count of data items, such as number of people or objects.

the number of books on a shelf in the library

Discriminant (p. 349) The quantity $b^2 - 4ac$ for a quadratic equation of the form $ax^2 + bx + c = 0$.

The discriminant of $2x^2 + 9x - 2 = 0$ is $9^2 - 4(2)(-2) = 97$.

Distance Formula (p. 420) The distance d between any two points (x_1, y_1) and (x_2, y_2) is
$$d = \sqrt{(x_2 - x_1)^2 + (y_2 - y_1)^2}.$$

The distance between $(-2, 4)$ and $(4, 5)$ is
$$d = \sqrt{(4 - (-2))^2 + (5 - 4)^2}$$
$$= \sqrt{(6)^2 + (1)^2}$$
$$= \sqrt{37}$$

Distributive Property (p. 124) For all real numbers a, b, and c:
$a(b + c) = ab + ac$ $(b + c)a = ba + ca$
$a(b - c) = ab - ac$ $(b - c)a = ba - ca$

$3(19 + 4) = 3(19) + 3(4)$
$(19 + 4)3 = 19(3) + 4(3)$
$7(11 - 2) = 7(11) - 7(2)$
$(11 - 2)7 = 11(7) - 2(7)$

Division Property of Inequality (p. 187) For all real numbers a and b, and for
$c > 0$: If $a < b$, then $\frac{a}{c} < \frac{b}{c}$.
       If $a > b$, then $\frac{a}{c} > \frac{b}{c}$.
$c < 0$: If $a < b$, then $\frac{a}{c} > \frac{b}{c}$.
       If $a > b$, then $\frac{a}{c} < \frac{b}{c}$.

$2 < 8$, so $\frac{2}{4} < \frac{8}{4}$.

$5 > 1$, so $\frac{5}{2} > \frac{1}{2}$.

$-2 < 6$, so $\frac{-2}{-3} > \frac{6}{-3}$.

$-2 > -4$, so $\frac{-2}{-5} < \frac{-4}{-5}$.

Division Property of Square Roots (p. 431) For any numbers $a \geq 0$ and $b > 0$, $\sqrt{\frac{a}{b}} = \frac{\sqrt{a}}{\sqrt{b}}$.

$\sqrt{\frac{4}{9}} = \frac{\sqrt{4}}{\sqrt{9}} = \frac{2}{3}$

Domain (p. 74) The set of all possible input values.

In the function $f(x) = x + 22$, the domain is all real numbers.

E

Elimination (p. 280) A method for solving a system of linear equations. You add or subtract the equations to eliminate a variable.

$3x - y = 19$
$2x - y = 1$
$\overline{x + 0 = 18}$ ← Subtract the second equation from the first.
$x = 18$ ← Solve for x.
$2(18) - y = 1$ ← Substitute 18 for x in the second equation.
$36 - y = 1$
$y = 35$← Solve for y.
The solution is (18, 35).

Examples

Entry (p. 40) An item in a matrix.

2 is an entry in the matrix $\begin{bmatrix} 9 & 2 \\ 5.3 & 1 \end{bmatrix}$.

Equation (p. 11) An equation shows that two expressions are equal.

$x + 5 = 3x - 7$

Equivalent equations (p. 109) Equations that have the same solution.

$a = 3$ and $3a = 9$ are equivalent equations.

Equivalent inequalities (p. 180) Equivalent inequalities have the same set of solutions.

$n < 2$ and $n + 3 < 5$ are equivalent inequalities.

Event (p. 36) In probability, any group of outcomes.

When rolling a number cube, there are six possible outcomes. Rolling an even number is an event with three possible outcomes: 2, 4, and 6.

Experimental probability (p. 36) The ratio of the number of times an event actually happens to the number of times the experiment is done.

$$P(\text{event}) = \frac{\text{number of times an event happens}}{\text{number of times the experiment is done}}$$

A baseball player's batting average shows how likely it is that a player will get a hit based on previous times at bat.

Exponent (p. 15) In an expression of the form x^n, n is the exponent.

$3^4 = 3 \cdot 3 \cdot 3 \cdot 3$
The exponent 4 indicates that 3 is used as a factor four times.

Exponential decay (p. 373) For $a > 0$ and $0 < b < 1$, the function $y = ab^x$ models exponential decay. b is the decay factor.

$y = 5(0.1)^x$

Exponential function (p. 363) A function that repeatedly multiplies an initial amount by the same positive number. You can model all exponential functions using $y = ab^x$ where $b > 0$ and $b \neq 1$.

$y = 4.8(1.1)^x$

Exponential growth (p. 368) For $a > 0$ and $b > 1$, the function $y = ab^x$ models exponential growth. b is the growth factor.

$y = 100(2)^x$

Extraneous solution (p. 443) An apparent solution of an equation that does not satisfy the original equation.

$\dfrac{b}{b + 4} = 3 - \dfrac{4}{b + 4}$
Solving the equation by multiplying by $(b + 4)$ gives b as -4. Replacing b with -4 in the original equation makes the denominator 0, so -4 is an extraneous solution. The equation has no solution.

Glossary/Study Guide

Examples

Families of functions (p. 92)   Similar functions can be grouped into families of functions. Some families of functions are linear functions, quadratic functions, and absolute value functions.

$y = 3x^2$, $y = -9x^2$, and $y = \frac{3}{4}x^2$ belong to the quadratic family of functions.

Favorable outcomes (p. 95)   In a probability experiment, favorable outcomes are the possible results that you want to happen.

In a board game you advance more spaces if you roll an even number on a number cube. The favorable outcomes are 2, 4, and 6.

Function (p. 73)   A relation that assigns exactly one value of the dependent variable to each value of the independent variable.

Earned income is a function of the number of hours worked. If you earn $4.50/h, then your income is expressed by the function $f(n) = 4.5n$.

Function notation (p. 79)   To write a rule in function notation, you use the symbol $f(x)$ in place of y.

$f(x) = 3x - 8$ is in function notation.

Function rule (p. 74)   An equation that describes a function.

$y = 4x + 1$ is a function rule.

Histogram (p. 4)   A bar graph that shows the frequency of data. The height of the bars shows the number of items in each interval.

The histogram shows the birth months of 27 students in one math class.

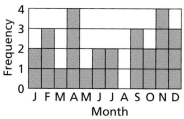

Birth Months of Students

Hypotenuse (p. 414)   In a right triangle, the side opposite the right angle. It is the longest side in the triangle.

c is the hypotenuse.

Identity (p. 166)   An equation that is true for every value of the variable.

$5 - 14x = 5(1 - \frac{14}{5}x)$ is an identity because it is true for any value of x.

Identity Property of Addition (p. 35)   The sum of any number and 0 is that number. For every real number *a: a* + 0 = *a*, 0 + *a* = *a.*

$9 + 0 = 9, 0 + 9 = 9$

Identity Property of Multiplication (p. 35)   The product of any number and 1 is that number. For every real number *a:* *a* · 1 = *a*, 1 · *a* = *a.*

$7 \cdot 1 = 7, 1 \cdot 7 = 7$

Impossible event (p. 96)   An impossible event never happens, and has a probability of 0.

Getting a decimal when rolling a number cube is an impossible event.

Independent events (p. 134)   Events are independent when the outcome of one does not affect the other.

Picking a colored marble from a bag, replacing it, and picking another are two independent events.

Independent variable (p. 69)   A variable is independent if it does not depend on another variable.

In the function $y = -2x$, the value of x does not depend on the value of y.

Integers (p. 19)   The whole numbers and their opposites.

$\ldots -3, -2, -1, 0, 1, 2, 3, \ldots$

Inverse operations (p. 108)   Operations that undo one another are called inverse operations.

Addition and subtraction are inverse operations. Multiplication and division are inverse operations.

Inverse variation (p. 512)   A function that can be written in the form $xy = k$ or $y = \frac{k}{x}$. The product of the quantities remains constant, so as one quantity increases, the other decreases.

The length x and the width y of a rectangle with a fixed area vary inversely. If the area is 40, $xy = 40$.

Irrational number (p. 30)   A number that cannot be written as a ratio of two integers. Irrational numbers in decimal form are nonterminating and nonrepeating.

$\sqrt{11}$ and 3.141592653. . . are irrational numbers.

L

Legs of a right triangle (p. 414)   The sides that form the right angle.

a and *b* are legs.

Like terms (p. 119)   Terms with exactly the same variable factors in a variable expression.

$4y$ and $16y$ are like terms.

Glossary/Study Guide

Line graph (p. 7)   A graph that shows how a set of data changes over time.

Radio Station KXXX

The line graph at the left shows the change in the number of listeners to station KXXX during the day.

Line of best fit (p. 242)   The most accurate trend line showing the relationship between two sets of data. One way to find the line of best fit for two sets of data is to enter the data into a graphing calculator and then use the linear regression feature.

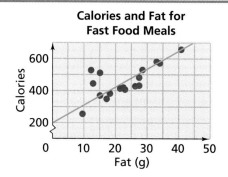

Calories and Fat for Fast Food Meals

Line plot (p. 4)   A graph that shows the number of times a data item appears.

Birth Month Line Plot

The line plot at the left shows the data collected on birth months for 20 people.

Jan Feb Mar Apr May Jun Jul Aug Sep Oct Nov Dec

Linear function (pp. 92, 221)   A function whose graph forms a straight line. Its rule is an equation that has 1 as the greatest power of x.

$y = 2x + 1$

Linear inequality (p. 290)   Describes a region of the coordinate plane that has a boundary line. Each point in the region is a solution of the inequality. A sign of $\leq$ or $\geq$ is represented by a solid boundary line. A sign of $<$ or $>$ is represented by a dashed boundary line.

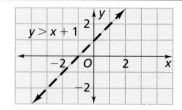

$y > x + 1$

Linear programming (p. 300)   A process that involves maximizing or minimizing a quantity. The quantity is expressed as the equation. Limits on the variables in the equation are called restrictions.

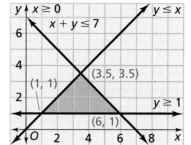

Example: Restrictions: $y \geq 1$, $x + y \leq 7$, and $y \leq x$
Equation: $B = 2x + 4y$
Graph the restrictions and find the coordinates of each vertex.
Evaluate $B = 2x + 4y$ at each vertex.
$B = 2(1) + 4(1) = 6$
$B = 2(3.5) + 4(3.5) = 21$
$B = 2(7) + 4(0) = 14$
The minimum value of B occurs at (1, 1).
The maximum value of B occurs at (3.5, 3.5).

Literal equation (p. 176)   An equation involving two or more variables.

$ax + b = c$ is a literal equation.

Matrix (p. 40)   A rectangular arrangement of numbers. The number of rows and columns of a matrix determines its size. Each item in a matrix is an entry.

$$\begin{bmatrix} 2 & 5 & 6.3 \\ -8 & 0 & -1 \end{bmatrix}$$ is a 2 × 3 matrix.

Maximum value (p. 320)   If a parabola opens downward, the y-coordinate of the vertex is the function's maximum value.

Example: Since the parabola opens downward, the y-coordinate of the vertex (0, −2) is the function's maximum value. The maximum value is −2.

Mean (p. 5)   To find the mean of a set of numbers, find the sum of the numbers and divide the sum by the number of items.
mean is $\frac{\text{sum of the data items}}{\text{number of data items}}$

In the set 12, 11, 12, 10, 13, 12, and 7, the mean is
$$\frac{12 + 11 + 12 + 10 + 13 + 12 + 7}{7} = 11.$$

Median (p. 5)   The middle value in an ordered set of numbers.

In the set 7, 10, 11, 12, 15, 19, and 27, the median is 12.

Midpoint (p. 422)   The point that divides a segment into two congruent segments.

M is the midpoint of $\overline{XY}$.

Glossary/Study Guide

Midpoint Formula (p. 422)   The midpoint M of a line segment with endpoints $A(x_1, y_1)$ and $B(x_2, y_2)$ is $\left(\dfrac{x_1 + x_2}{2}, \dfrac{y_1 + y_2}{2}\right)$.

The midpoint of a segment with endpoints $A(3, 5)$ and $B(7, 1)$ is $(5, 3)$.

Minimum value (p. 320)   If a parabola opens upward, the y-coordinate of the vertex is the function's minimum value.

Example: Since the parabola opens upward, the y-coordinate of the vertex $(0, 1)$ is the function's minimum value. The minimum value is 1.

Mode (p. 4)   The data item that occurs in a data set the greatest number of times. A data set may have no mode, one mode, or more than one mode.

In the data set 7, 7, 9, 10, 11, and 13, the mode is 7. The data set 5, 3, 2, 1.5, 9, 3, 6, 3, 2, 1, 4, 2 has two modes: 2 and 3.

Multiplicative inverse (p. 32)   The multiplicative inverse, or reciprocal, of a nonzero number $\frac{a}{b}$ is $\frac{b}{a}$. The product of a nonzero number and its multiplicative inverse is 1.

$\frac{3}{4}$ is the multiplicative inverse of $\frac{4}{3}$ because $\frac{3}{4} \times \frac{4}{3} = 1$.

Multiplication Property of Inequality (p. 185)   For all real numbers a and b, and for $c > 0$:
If $a > b$, then $ac > bc$.
If $a < b$, then $ac < bc$.
For all real numbers a and b, and for $c < 0$:
If $a > b$, then $ac < bc$.
If $a < b$, then $ac > bc$.

$5 > 1$, so $5(2) > 1(2)$.
$2 < 4$, so $2(3) < 4(3)$.
$-2 > -4$, so $-2(-5) < -4(-5)$.
$-2 < 6$, so $-2(-3) > 6(-3)$.

Multiplication Property of Square Roots (p. 430)   For any numbers $a \geq 0$ and $b \geq 0$, $\sqrt{ab} = \sqrt{a} \cdot \sqrt{b}$.

$\sqrt{54} = \sqrt{9 \cdot 6} = \sqrt{9} \cdot \sqrt{6}$
$= 3 \cdot \sqrt{6} = 3\sqrt{6}$

N

Negative square root (p. 332) $-\sqrt{b}$ is the negative square root of b.

$-\sqrt{49} = -7$ is the negative square root of 49.

O

Opposites (p. 19)   Two numbers are opposites, or additive inverses, if they are the same distance from zero on the number line. The sum of two opposites is 0.

-3 and 3 are opposites.
$-a$ is the opposite of a.

Order of operations (p. 15) 1. Perform any operation(s) inside grouping symbols. 2. Simplify any terms with exponents. 3. Multiply and divide in order from left to right. 4. Add and subtract in order from left to right.	$6 - (4^2 - [2 \cdot 5]) \div 3$ $= 6 - (4^2 - 10) \div 3$ $= 6 - (16 - 10) \div 3$ $= 6 - 6 \div 3$ $= 6 - 2$ $= 4$

Ordered pair (p. 58) An ordered pair of numbers identifies the location of a point on the coordinate plane.

The ordered pair $(4, -1)$ identifies the point 4 units to the right and 1 unit down from the origin.

Origin (p. 58) The axes of the coordinate plane intersect at the origin.

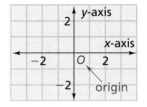

Outcomes (p. 95) The possible results of a probability experiment.

The outcomes of rolling a number cube are 1, 2, 3, 4, 5, and 6.

Parabola (p. 318) The graph of a quadratic function is a parabola.

Parallel lines (p. 250) Two lines that are always the same distance apart. The lines do not intersect and have the same slope.

Example: Lines ℓ and m are parallel.

Percent of change (p. 146) The percent an amount changes from its original amount.
$$\text{percent of change} = \frac{\text{amount of change}}{\text{original amount}}$$

The price of a meal at a restaurant was $7.95 last week; this week it is $9.95.
$$\text{percent of change} = \frac{9.95 - 7.95}{7.95} = \frac{2.00}{7.95}$$
$$\approx 0.25 \text{ or } 25\%.$$

Percent of decrease (p. 147) When a value decreases from its original amount, you call the percent of change the percent of decrease.

The number of oranges in the bag decreased from 12 to 9.
$$\text{percent of decrease} = \frac{3}{12} = 0.25 \text{ or } 25\%$$

Percent of increase (p. 146) When a value increases from its original amount, you call the percent of change the percent of increase.

The average class size will increase from 30 to 33.
$$\text{percent of increase} = \frac{3}{30} = 0.1 \text{ or } 10\%$$

Glossary/Study Guide

Perfect square trinomial (p. 487)   A trinomial whose factors are two identical binomials.

$$x^2 + 6x + 9 = (x + 3)(x + 3)$$
$$= (x + 3)^2$$

Perfect squares (p. 333)   Numbers whose square roots are rational numbers.

The numbers 1, 4, 9, 16, 25, 36, . . . are perfect squares because they are the squares of integers.

Permutation (p. 539)   An arrangement of some or all of a set of objects in a definite order. You can use the notation $_nP_r$ to express the number of permutations, where n equals the number of objects available and r equals the number of selections to make.

How many ways can 5 children be arranged three at a time?
$_5P_3 = 5 \cdot 4 \cdot 3 = 60$ arrangements

Perpendicular lines (p. 251)   Lines that form right angles. Two lines are perpendicular if the product of their slopes is -1.

Lines ℓ and m are perpendicular.

Point-slope form (p. 248)   The point-slope form of a linear equation is $\frac{y - y_1}{x - x_1} = m$ where m is the slope and the point (x_1, y_1) is on the line.

Polynomial (p. 465)   A polynomial is one term or the sum or difference of two or more terms.

$2x^2$, $3x + 7$, 28, and $-7x^3 - 2x^2 + 9$ are all polynomials.

Power (p. 391)   Any expression in the form a^n.

5^4

Principal square root (p. 332)   For $b > 0$, the expression $\sqrt{b}$ is called the principal square root of b.

$\sqrt{25} = 5$ is the principal square root of 25.

Probability of two dependent events (p. 135)   If A and B are dependent events, then
$P(A \text{ and } B) = P(A) \cdot P(B \text{ after } A)$.

You have 4 red marbles and 3 white marbles. The probability that you select one red marble, and then, without replacing it, randomly select another red marble is $P(\text{red and red}) = \frac{4}{7} \cdot \frac{3}{6} = \frac{2}{7}$.

Probability of two independent events (p. 134)   If A and B are independent events, you multiply the probabilities of the events to find the probability of both events occurring.
$P(A \text{ and } B) = P(A) \cdot P(B)$

The probability of rolling a 1 on a number cube is $\frac{1}{6}$. The probability of rolling an even number on a number cube is $\frac{1}{2}$. The probability of rolling a 1 and then an even number is
$P(1 \text{ and even number}) = \frac{1}{6} \cdot \frac{1}{2} = \frac{1}{12}$.

Properties of Equality (pp. 109, 110)   For all real numbers a, b, and c:

Addition: If $a = b$, then $a + c = b + c$.

Subtraction: If $a = b$, then $a - c = b - c$.

Multiplication: If $a = b$, then $a \cdot c = b \cdot c$.

Division: If $a = b$, and $c \neq 0$, then $\frac{a}{c} = \frac{b}{c}$.

Since $\frac{2}{4} = \frac{1}{2}$, then $\frac{2}{4} + 5 = \frac{1}{2} + 5$.

Since $\frac{9}{3} = 3$, then $\frac{9}{3} - 6 = 3 - 6$.

Since $\frac{10}{5} = 2$, then $\frac{10}{5} \cdot 15 = 2 \cdot 15$.

Since $6 + 2 = 8$, then $\frac{6 + 2}{4} = \frac{8}{4}$.

Proportion (p. 158)   A statement that two ratios are equal.

$\frac{2}{3} = \frac{10}{15}$ is a proportion.

Pythagorean theorem (p. 414)   In a right triangle, the sum of the squares of the lengths of the legs is equal to the square of the length of the hypotenuse. $a^2 + b^2 = c^2$.

$3^2 + 4^2 = 5^2$

Q

Quadrants (p. 58)   The coordinate plane is divided by its axes into four quadrants.

Quadratic equation (p. 337)   An equation you can write in the form $ax^2 + bx + c = 0$, where a, b, and c are real numbers and $a \neq 0$.

$4x^2 + 9x - 5 = 0$

Quadratic Formula (p. 343)   If $ax^2 + bx + c = 0$ and $a \neq 0$, then $x = \frac{-b \pm \sqrt{b^2 - 4ac}}{2a}$.

$2x^2 + 10x + 12 = 0$

$x = \frac{-b \pm \sqrt{b^2 - 4ac}}{2a}$

$x = \frac{-10 \pm \sqrt{10^2 - 4(2)(12)}}{2(2)}$

$x = \frac{-10 \pm \sqrt{4}}{4}$

$x = \frac{-10 + 2}{4}$ or $\frac{-10 - 2}{4}$

$x = -2$ or $x = -3$

Quadratic function (pp. 92, 319)   A function with an equation of the form $y = ax^2 + bx + c$, where $a \neq 0$. The graph of a quadratic function is a parabola, which is a U-shaped curve that opens up or down.

$y = 5x^2 - 2x + 1$

R

Radical equation (p. 440)   An equation that has a variable under a radical.

$\sqrt{x} - 2 = 12$

Range (p. 74)   The set of all possible output values of a function.

In the function $f(x) = |x|$, the range is the set of all positive numbers and 0.

Rate of change (p. 220)   Allows you to see the relationship between two quantities that are changing. The rate of change is also called slope.

Rate of change $= \dfrac{\text{change in dependent variable}}{\text{change in independent variable}}$

Video rental for 1 day is \$1.99. Video rental for 2 days is \$2.99.

rate of change $= \dfrac{2.99 - 1.99}{2 - 1}$

$= \dfrac{1.00}{1} = 1$

Ratio (p. 158)   A comparison of two numbers by division.

$\frac{5}{7}$ and $7 : 3$ are ratios.

Rational expression (p. 522)   An expression that can be written in the form $\frac{\text{polynomial}}{\text{polynomial}}$. The value of the variable cannot make the denominator equal to 0.

$\dfrac{3}{x^2 - 4}$, $x \neq 2, -2$.

Rational function (p. 520)   A function that can be written in the form $f(x) = \frac{\text{polynomial}}{\text{polynomial}}$. The value of the variable cannot make the denominator equal to 0.

$y = \dfrac{x}{x - 5}, x \neq 5$

Rational number (p. 30)   A real number that can be written as a ratio of two integers. Rational numbers in decimal form are terminating or repeating.

$\frac{2}{3}$, 1.548, and 2.292929. . . are all rational numbers.

Rationalize the denominator (p. 432)   Make the denominator of a fraction a rational number without changing the value of the expression.

$\dfrac{2}{\sqrt{5}} = \dfrac{2}{\sqrt{5}} \cdot \dfrac{\sqrt{5}}{\sqrt{5}} = \dfrac{2\sqrt{5}}{\sqrt{25}} = \dfrac{2\sqrt{5}}{5}$

Real number (p. 30)   A number that is either rational or irrational.

$5, -3, \sqrt{5}, 9.2, -0.666. . . , 5\frac{4}{11}, 0, \pi$, and $\frac{15}{2}$ are all real numbers.

Reciprocal (p. 32)   The reciprocal, or multiplicative inverse, of a nonzero number $\frac{a}{b}$ is $\frac{b}{a}$. The product of a nonzero number and its reciprocal is 1. Zero does not have a reciprocal.

$\frac{2}{5}$ and $\frac{5}{2}$ are reciprocals because $\frac{2}{5} \times \frac{5}{2} = 1$.

Relation (p. 73)   Any set of ordered pairs.

$\{(0, 0), (2, 3), (2, -7)\}$ is a relation.

Replacement set (p. 202)   The set of possible values for the variable in an inequality.

When the replacement set is all integers, the solution of the inequality $x > -2.5$ is $\{-2, -1, 0, 2, . . . \}$.

Sample space (p. 97)   The set of all possible outcomes of an event.

When tossing two coins one at a time, the sample space is (H,H), (T,T), (H,T), (T,H).

Scatter plot (p. 59)   A graph that relates data of two different sets. The two sets of data are displayed as ordered pairs.

Example: The scatter plot displays the amounts various companies spent on advertising versus product sales.

Scientific notation (p. 385)   A number expressed in the form $a \times 10^n$, where n is an integer and $1 \leq a < 10$.

3.4×10^6

Similar figures (p. 159)   Figures that have the same shape, but not necessarily the same size.

$\triangle DEF$ and $\triangle GHI$ are similar.

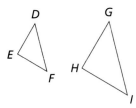

Simple interest (p. 141)   Calculated using the formula $I = prt$, where p is the principal, r is the rate of interest per year, and t is the time in years.

The simple interest on $200 with an annual rate of interest of 4% for 3 years is $I = prt = 200 (0.04) (3) = 24$. The simple interest is $24.

Simulation (p. 37)   A simulation is a model of a real-life situation.

A random number table can be used to simulate many situations.

Sine (p. 425)   In $\triangle ABC$ with right $\angle C$,

$$\text{sine of } \angle A = \frac{\text{length of side opposite } \angle A}{\text{length of hypotenuse}}, \text{ or } \sin A = \frac{a}{c}.$$

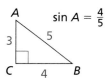

$\sin A = \frac{4}{5}$

Slope (p. 220)   The measure of the steepness of a line. The ratio of the vertical change to the horizontal change.

$$\text{Slope} = \frac{\text{vertical change}}{\text{horizontal change}} = \frac{y_2 - y_1}{x_2 - x_1}, \text{ where } x_2 - x_1 \neq 0$$

The slope of the line is $\frac{2 - 0}{4 - 0} = \frac{1}{2}$.

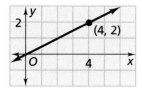

Slope-intercept form (p. 231)   The slope-intercept form of a linear equation is $y = mx + b$ where m is the slope and b is the y-intercept.

$y = 8x + 2$

Solution of an equation (p. 108)   Any value or values that make the equation true.

For the equation $y + 22 = 11$, the solution is -11.

Solution, no (pp. 165, 192, 271)   (1) An equation has no solution if no value makes the statement true.
(2) An inequality has no solution if it is false for all values of the variable.
(3) A linear system has no solution if the graphs of the equations in the system are parallel.

$2a + 3 = 2a + 5$

$4n + 1 > 4n + 7$

$y = 3x + 9$ and $y = 3x + 28$

Solution of an inequality (p. 179)   Any value or values of a variable in the inequality that makes an inequality true.

The solution of the inequality $x < 9$ is all numbers less than 9.

Solutions, infinitely many (p. 271)   A linear system has infinitely many solutions when the equations are equivalent.

$2y = x + 7$ and $6y = 3x + 21$

Spreadsheet (p. 45)   A table used in computer programs that contains numbers, text, or formulas in its cells.

In the spreadsheet, column C and row 2 meet at the shaded box, cell C2. The value in cell C2 is 2.75.

	A	B	C	D	E
1	0.50	0.70	0.60	0.50	2.30
2	1.50	0.50	2.75	2.50	7.25

Square root (p. 332)   If $a^2 = b$, then a is a square root of b. $\sqrt{b}$ is the principal (positive) square root. $-\sqrt{b}$ is the negative square root.

-3 and 3 are square roots of 9. $\sqrt{9} = 3$; $-\sqrt{9} = -3$.

Standard deviation (p. 452)   Shows how spread out a set of data is from the mean.

The standard deviation for the data set $\{2, 12, 6, 10, 9\}$ is about 3.49.

Standard form of a polynomial (p. 465)   When the degree of the terms in a polynomial decrease from left to right, it is in standard form, or descending order.

$15x^3 + x^2 + 3x - 9$

Standard form of a quadratic equation (p. 319)   When a quadratic equation is in the form $ax^2 + bx + c = 0$.

$-x^2 + 2x + 9 = 0$

Stem-and-leaf plot (p. 10) A stem-and-leaf plot displays data items in order. A leaf is a data item's last digit on the right. A stem represents the digits to the left of the leaf.

This stem-and-leaf plot displays recorded times in a race. The stem records the whole number of seconds. The leaves represents tenths of a second. So, 27|7 represents 27.7 seconds.

```
       27 | 7
       28 | 5 6 8
stem → 29 | 6 9 ← leaves
       30 | 8

       stem   leaves
```

Subtraction Property of Inequality (p. 181) For all real numbers a, b, and c, if $a > b$, then $a - c > b - c$ and if $a < b$, then $a - c < b - c$.

$5 > 2$, so $5 - 4 > 2 - 4$.
$9 < 13$, so $9 - 3 < 13 - 3$.

System of linear equations (p. 269) Two or more linear equations for which a common solution is sought.

$y = 5x + 7, y = \frac{1}{2}x - 3$

System of linear inequalities (p. 295) Two or more linear inequalities for which common solutions are sought.

$y \leq x + 11, y < 5x$

Tangent (p. 425) In $\triangle ABC$ with right $\angle C$,

tangent of $\angle A = \dfrac{\text{length of side opposite } \angle A}{\text{length of side adjacent to } \angle A}$, or $\tan A = \dfrac{a}{b}$.

$\tan A = \frac{4}{3}$

(triangle ABC with A at top, C at bottom-left right angle, B at bottom-right; legs 3 and 4, hypotenuse 5)

Term (p. 11) A number, variable, or the product of numbers and variables.

The expression $5x + \frac{1}{2}y - 8$ has three terms: $5x$, $\frac{1}{2}y$, and -8.

Theoretical probability (p. 95) If each outcome has an equally likely chance of happening, you can find the theoretical probability of an event using the ratio of the number of favorable outcomes to the number of possible outcomes.

$P(\text{event}) = \dfrac{\text{number of favorable outcomes}}{\text{number of possible outcomes}}$

In tossing a coin the chance of getting heads or tails is equally likely. The probability of getting heads is $P(\text{heads}) = \frac{1}{2}$.

Glossary/Study Guide

Tree diagram (p. 97) A diagram that shows all possible outcomes in a probability experiment.

Example: The tree diagram shows the 4 possible outcomes for tossing two coins one at a time: (H,H), (H,T), (T,H), (T,T).

Trend line (p. 60) A line on a scatter plot that can be drawn near the points. It shows a correlation between two sets of data.

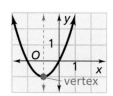

Positive   Negative   No Correlation

Trigonometric ratios (p. 425) See cosine, sine, and tangent.

Two-step equation (p. 114) An equation that has two operations.

$5x - 4 = 1$ is a two-step equation.

Variable (p. 11) A letter used to stand for one or more numbers.

x is a variable in the expression $9 - x$.

Variable expression (p. 11) A mathematical phrase that contains at least one variable.

$7 + x$ is a variable expression.

Vertex (p. 320) The highest point of a parabola that opens downward and the lowest point of a parabola that opens upward. The vertex is the point where the axis of symmetry intersects the parabola.

The vertex of the parabola is $(-1, -1)$.

Vertical-line test (p. 75) A method used to determine if a relation is a function or not. If a vertical line passes through a graph more than once, the graph is not the graph of a function.

Vertical motion formula (p. 344) When an object is dropped or thrown straight up or down, you can use the vertical-motion formula to find the height of the object.

$h = -16t^2 + vt + s$, where h is the height of the object in feet, t is the time the object is in motion in seconds, v is the initial velocity in feet per second, and s is the starting height in feet.

An object is thrown straight up with a starting velocity of 36 ft/s. It is thrown from a height of 10 ft. The formula $h = -16t^2 + 36t + 10$ describes the height h of the object after t seconds.

W | *Examples*

Whole numbers (p. 19) Whole numbers are the nonnegative integers. | 0, 1, 2, 3, . . .

X

x-axis (p. 58) The horizontal axis of the coordinate plane.

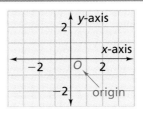

x-coordinate (p. 58) The first number of an ordered pair; indicates the distance left or right from the *y*-axis. | In the ordered pair (4, −1), 4 is the *x*-coordinate.

x-intercept (p. 246) The *x*-coordinate of the point where a line crosses the *x*-axis. | The *x*-intercept of $3x + 4y = 12$ is 4.

Y

y-axis (p. 58) The vertical axis of the coordinate plane.

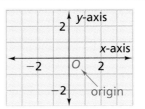

y-coordinate (p. 58) The second number of an ordered pair; indicates the distance above or below the *x*-axis. | In the ordered pair (4, −1), −1 is the *y*-coordinate.

y-intercept (p. 230) The *y*-coordinate of the point where a line crosses the *y*-axis. | The *y*-intercept of $y = 5x + 2$ is 2.

Z

Zero pairs (p. 20) ▢ ■ is a zero pair.

Zero-product property (p. 491) For all real numbers *a* and *b*, if $ab = 0$, then $a = 0$ or $b = 0$. |
$$x(x + 3) = 0$$
$$x = 0 \text{ or } x + 3 = 0$$
$$x = 0 \text{ or } x = -3$$

Glossary/Study Guide

Selected Answers

CHAPTER 1

ON YOUR OWN   **1a.**

1b. 1.96; 2; 2
3. D   **5.** 10; 10; 10
7. 25; 25; 25
9. 38.6; 37.9; 41.0
11a. 10
13b. English:
4.7; 4, 3;
Spanish: 5.1, 5, 2

MIXED REVIEW   **19.** 0.4; $\frac{2}{5}$ **21.** $\frac{1}{4}$; 0.25
23. 1.8; 180%   **25.** 7, 9, 11   **27.** 108, 324, 972

1. 27 students   **3.** 8 students   **5a.** 1.9, 2.0, 2.1, 2.2, 2.3, 2.4, 2.5   **5b.** Sample: 2.2 | 5 means $2.25

5c.

1.9	5 7 9
2.0	0 5 9
2.1	6
2.2	1 5 9
2.3	6
2.4	0 9
2.5	0 0 7

5d. $2.23; $2.50

ON YOUR OWN   **1.** 3   **3.** 2   **7.** c = cost, n = number of cans; $c = 0.7n$ **9.** r = amount of rope, t = number of tents; $r = 60t$ **11.** $d = 50h$
13. $g = 0.165d$ **15.** $r = 13w$ **17.** $e = 0.4s$
21a. Sample: Statement (a) is better because it indicates that each lawn takes 2 h to mow.
21b. 1 lawn: 2 hours; 2 lawns: 4 hours; 5 lawns should take 10 hours.   **23.** s = height of second bounce; $s = \frac{1}{4}d$ **25a.** n = number of quarters, m = money in bag (in dollars); $m = 0.25n$
25b. $3.25

MIXED REVIEW   **27.** Complete list: 23, 29, 31, 37, 41, 43, 47   **29.** 8   **31.** 7   **33.** 11

ON YOUR OWN   **1.** 23   **3.** 1   **5.** 64   **7.** 50.43   **9.** 75
11. 14   **15.** 1   **17.** 12.8   **19.** 104.58   **21.** 26
23. 2.4   **25.** $14 - (2 + 5) - 3 = 4$ **29.** F; simplify the power before multiplying.   **31.** F; simplify within parentheses first.

MIXED REVIEW   **33.** $\frac{2}{3}$ **35.** $4\frac{1}{2}$ **37.** $\frac{4}{5}$ **39.** 2 units
41. 3 units

ON YOUR OWN   **1.** $-227 + 319$ is greater because the sum is positive and $227 + (-319)$ is negative.
3. positive   **5.** negative   **7.** positive   **9.** 15   **11.** 5
13. -35 **15.** 11   **17.** -28 **19.** 4   **21.** -43.9
23. 1.5   **25.** -26.9 **27.** 45.7   **29.** 0   **31.** Q; it is the farthest point from the midpoint between R and T.   **33.** Yes; $3 - 4 = -1, 4 - 3 = 1; |-1| = |1|$. So $a - b$ and $b - a$ are opposites. Absolute values of opposites are equal.   **37.** $-11,331$ ft   **39.** 8
41. -9 **43.** -2 **45.** 1   **47.** -5 **49.** 14   **51.** 7
53. -1 **55.** B

MIXED REVIEW   **57b.** A line graph shows change over time.   **59.** 4   **61.** $\frac{1}{4}$ **63.** $\frac{1}{3}$ **65.** $-3, -6, -9$
67. $0, -2, -4$

ON YOUR OWN   **1.** -120 **3.** -81 **5.** -6 **7.** -4
9. -1 **11.** 30   **13.** 44   **15.** $5\frac{1}{2}$ **17a.** The product is positive when a and b have the same sign.
17b. The product is negative when a and b have different signs.   **19.** -12 **21.** -15 **23.** -8
25. -64 **27.** $-1\frac{1}{3}$ **29.** -27 **33.** positive; even number of factors   **35.** negative; odd number of negative factors   **37.** negative; $(-3)^2$ is positive. Its opposite is negative.   **39.** negative; 5^{10} is positive. Its opposite is negative.   **47a.** odd   **47b.** even

MIXED REVIEW   **49.** 5 people   **51a.** 2.8; 2.5; 1
51b. Sample: The median is the most useful because it is not affected by extreme values.   **53.** $\frac{1}{4}$ **55.** $\frac{1}{3}$

CHECKPOINT **1.** 20 **2.** 4 **3.** 6 **4.** 7 **5.** 7 **6.** 49
7. -3 **8.** 11 **9.** 11 **11.** $-0.4; -3; -4$
12. $t = 175b$

Lesson 1-6 pages 30–34

ON YOUR OWN **1.** $>$ **3.** $>$ **5.** $>$ **7.** $>$ **9.** $\frac{5}{3}$
11. $\frac{8}{7}$ **13.** -2 **15.** $\frac{2}{3}$ **17.** 1 **19.** $-6\frac{3}{4}$ **21.** $2\frac{1}{6}$
23. $-2\frac{1}{12}$ **25.** $-\frac{2}{3}, -\frac{1}{2}, \frac{1}{4}$ **27.** $-9\frac{3}{4}, -9.7, -9\frac{7}{12}$
29a. $-44°F$ **29b.** $-4°F$ **31.** $-\frac{9}{16}$ **33.** $-\frac{5}{48}$
37. $2\frac{3}{5}$ **39.** -4.5 **41.** $-\frac{1}{10}$ **43.** false; $-\frac{3}{4}$
45. true; since integers are real numbers, some real numbers are integers.

MIXED REVIEW **47.** c = change, p = purchase;
$c = 10 - p$ **49.** \$1,290,000

Toolbox page 35

1. identity prop. of mult. **3.** associative prop. of mult. **5.** commutative prop. of mult. **7.** 830
9. 7400 **11.** $9m + 15$ **13.** 13 **15.** $72pqr$

Lesson 1-7 pages 36–39

ON YOUR OWN **3.** $\frac{8}{15}$ **5.** $\frac{7}{15}$ **7.** 8.3% **9.** 62.5%
11. $P(\text{test}) \approx 0.04\%$; $P(\text{control}) \approx 0.08\%$; control group children were about twice as likely to develop polio. **13.** $\frac{1}{9}$ **15.** $\frac{7}{18}$ **17.** $\frac{7}{9}$ **19.** 0.04, 4%

MIXED REVIEW **23.** -19 **25.** -49 **27.** 53.6

Lesson 1-8 pages 40–43

ON YOUR OWN **1.** 2×3 **3.** 3×2 **5.** 3×4

7. $\begin{bmatrix} 0 & 0 \\ 0 & 0 \end{bmatrix}$ **9.** $-6; 5; 0$

11. $\begin{bmatrix} 81 & -32 \\ 27 & 100 \end{bmatrix}; \begin{bmatrix} 3 & -40 \\ -47 & 8 \end{bmatrix}$ **13.** $\begin{bmatrix} 8.3 & -5.8 \\ -2.6 & 2.9 \\ 13.0 & -7.8 \end{bmatrix};$

$\begin{bmatrix} -1.5 & 10 \\ -10.2 & 8.5 \\ 4.6 & -10.8 \end{bmatrix}$ **15.** $\begin{bmatrix} 1\frac{1}{6} & 1\frac{1}{5} \\ \frac{7}{8} & 1\frac{1}{6} \end{bmatrix}; \begin{bmatrix} \frac{1}{6} & \frac{2}{5} \\ -\frac{5}{8} & -\frac{5}{6} \end{bmatrix}$

17. $\begin{bmatrix} 2.5 & 0.3 \\ -8.1 & 2.7 \end{bmatrix}; \begin{bmatrix} 4.5 & -0.7 \\ 8.1 & -16.7 \end{bmatrix}$ **21.** $\begin{bmatrix} 1\frac{1}{4} & -6\frac{1}{2} \\ 2\frac{1}{2} & 0 \end{bmatrix}$

23a. $\begin{bmatrix} 13 & 5 & 6 & 2 \\ 18 & 4 & 2 & 2 \\ 6 & 2 & 0 & 2 \end{bmatrix}$ **23b.** 4 employees

25. $\begin{bmatrix} -350 & -150 & 50 \\ -400 & -100 & 250 \end{bmatrix}$

MIXED REVIEW **27.** -7.9 **29.** 17.4 **31.** 24 in.^{2}
33. 68.08 m^2

CHECKPOINT **1.** $\frac{5}{8}$ **2.** 12.1 **3.** $\frac{25}{32}$ **4.** $\begin{bmatrix} 3\frac{1}{2} & -1 \\ 4 & -9 \end{bmatrix}$

5. $\begin{bmatrix} 5.6 & -6.8 & 11.5 \\ -5.8 & 3.3 & -15.7 \end{bmatrix}$

Toolbox page 44

1. $\begin{bmatrix} 4.9 & 0.7 \\ 2.1 & 0.7 \\ -3.1 & 2.7 \end{bmatrix}; \begin{bmatrix} 2.7 & 3.5 \\ 0.9 & -2.3 \\ 0.3 & 1.1 \end{bmatrix}$

3. $\begin{bmatrix} 0 & 4 & 20 & -25 \\ 8 & 2 & -3 & 15 \\ -9 & -1 & -14 & 9 \end{bmatrix}; \begin{bmatrix} 10 & -12 & -6 & -1 \\ 0 & -20 & -17 & -5 \\ 21 & -13 & 2 & 15 \end{bmatrix}$

5a. $\begin{bmatrix} 4.9 & 0.7 \\ 2.1 & 0.7 \\ -3.1 & 2.7 \end{bmatrix}; \begin{bmatrix} -2.7 & -3.5 \\ -0.9 & 2.3 \\ -0.3 & -1.1 \end{bmatrix}$

Lesson 1-9 pages 45–49

ON YOUR OWN **3.** 4 * A2 ^ 2; 2 * A2 − 5; 3 * A2 + 7 **5.** 16, −9, 1 **7a.** -3 **7b.** -1.9 **9a.** A2 * B2 * C2 **9b.** D2: 1920; E2: 725.2; F2: 5334
11a. C2/B2 **11b.** D2: \$18,569.23; D3: \$24,259.50; D4: \$27,702; D5: \$30,861.03 **13a.** 1.766 or 1.76625
13b. 1562.665 **15a.** 52 **15b.** 118.72 **17a.** Jan.: \$1136.65; Feb.: \$1557.30; March: \$1396.20
17b. Jan.: \$279.40; Feb.: \$382.80; March: \$343.20
19. C

MIXED REVIEW **21.** -3 **23.** 2 **25.** 26 **27.** 3
29. -71

Wrap Up pages 51–53

1. 30.6; 27; 24 **2.** 84.3; 83; 80 and 87 **3.** 2.3; 2.3; 2.3 **4.** 4 recorders **5.** March **6.** 4.7 recorders; 8 recorders **7.** 8 **8.** 64 **9.** 4 **10.** 9
12a. $r = 140d$ **12b.** 2940 records; 4200 records
13. -17 **14.** -12 **15.** 9.9 **16.** 24.9 **17.** -5
18. -12 **19.** 15 **20.** 13 **21.** 2 **22.** -1 **23.** 0

Selected Answers

24. -18 **25.** -40 **26.** -8 **27.** 2 **28.** B
29. $2\frac{5}{6}$ **30.** $5\frac{1}{6}$ **31.** $-3\frac{1}{3}$ **32.** $-1\frac{1}{4}$ **33.** $1\frac{5}{18}$
34a. $\frac{3}{14}$ **34b.** $\frac{5}{14}$ **34c.** $\frac{3}{7}$ **34d.** $\frac{4}{7}$
35. $\begin{bmatrix} 7 & 7 \\ -2 & -10 \end{bmatrix}$; $\begin{bmatrix} -3 & -13 \\ 20 & 8 \end{bmatrix}$
36. $\begin{bmatrix} 4.3 & 0.6 \\ 1.0 & -0.3 \\ -1.7 & 1.2 \end{bmatrix}$; $\begin{bmatrix} -1.9 & -2.8 \\ 4.4 & 6.1 \\ -4.7 & -3.4 \end{bmatrix}$ **37.** $\begin{bmatrix} \frac{1}{8} \\ -\frac{7}{20} \end{bmatrix}$; $\begin{bmatrix} -1\frac{1}{8} \\ 1\frac{3}{20} \end{bmatrix}$
39. 5.6 **40.** -11 **41.** 80 **42.** $0; -4; 4; -8$
43. $2; 0; 0; 0$ **44.** $6; 8; 16; 64$

| Preparing for the Math A Exam | page 55 |

1. 2 **3.** 3 **5.** 4 **7.** 4

CHAPTER 2

| Toolbox | page 58 |

1. H **3.** E **5.** $(4, 5)$ **7.** $(-5, 0)$ **13.** II **15.** IV
17a.

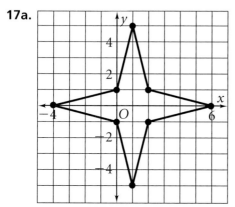

17b. It looks like a four-pointed star.

| Lesson 2-1 | pages 59–63 |

ON YOUR OWN **1.** Negative; with each class taken, you need to study more, so the amount of free time decreases. **3.** Positive; you expect to sell more shovels as the amount of snow increases.
5. Negative; as the temperature rises, people use less oil for heating. **7.** No correlation; shoes are not priced by size. **9a.** Negative correlation; everything else being equal, voters are more likely to stay home in bad weather. **9b.** Sample: Yes; a low voter turnout may favor the candidates whose supporters

feel strongly about the issues in the campaign and the turnout may be low because of bad weather.
11a.

How Big Is a Bird Egg?

11b. There is a positive correlation between the length and the mass of a bird egg, because the larger eggs are heavier. **11c.** Sample: The egg is about 5.7 cm long. From the graph, its weight should be about 52 g. **13.** positive correlation
15. positive correlation
17a.

Calories and Fat in Common Foods

17b. positive correlation **19.** Each data point represents the total toll charged (y-coordinate) for a vehicle that traveled a specified number of miles (x-coordinate). **21a.** The corresponding points have the same y-coordinate.

MIXED REVIEW **23.** 0 **25.** -9 **27.** $\frac{3}{10}$ **29.** 33
31. Mode; the mean and the median need to be computed. You can read the mode off the plot.
33. 1981–1989 and 1991–1995

| Lesson 2-2 | pages 64–68 |

ON YOUR OWN
1. Sample:

Height While Jumping Rope

3. Sample:

Pulse Rate During a Scary Movie

5. The graph is continuous but data are discrete. To fix the graph, you must remove all lines connecting data points.   **7.** Sample: Continuous; between any two weights you measure, any value is possible.

Weight from Birth to Age 14

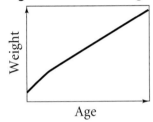

9. Sample: Discrete; there is only one time for each morning.

Getting-up Time

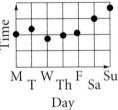

11. Sample: Discrete; you cannot have half a book.

Bringing Books Home

13. Sample: Continuous; walking speed can be measured at all times.

Walking Speed from Class to Locker

15a. blue; red   **15b.** Growing at a steady rate, a puppy becomes heavier than a baby but stops growing soon after that. A baby's weight gain increases with time, so it outgrows the puppy.
17. Graph II; graph I; at constant speed, distance increases with time.

MIXED REVIEW   **21.** $\begin{bmatrix} -14 & 11 \\ -2 & -51 \end{bmatrix}$

23a. f = amount of fruit used per day; $f + 200$
23b. 15,400 lb

CHECKPOINT   **1a–b.**

Average Low Temperatures at Different Latitudes

There is a negative correlation.   **1c.** Sample: about 70°F   **3.** C; this is the only graph where the distance from home drops back to 0, indicating that you came home.

Lesson 2-3   pages 69–72

ON YOUR OWN   **1a.** Sample: Horizontal axis from 0 to 200 with a line of the graph every 25 lb; vertical axis 0 to 30 with a line of the graph every 5 lb.

1b.   **Weight on Earth and Moon (pounds)**

1c. Find the point on the graph that corresponds to your weight on Earth. Use this point to identify the coordinate for the moon. This is your weight on the moon.   **3.** dependent; independent
5. independent; dependent   **7.** B   **9.** C

11a.

High School Dance

11b. Sample: The horizontal range is 0 to 120 with the scale marked every 20 min on the axis. The vertical range is 0 to 6 with the scale marked at every dollar on the axis.

MIXED REVIEW **15.** Sample:

Marching in a Parade

Marching at normal speed

Going around a corner

A temporary halt

17a.
```
        X
        X        X
   X  X    X  X
   ─────────────
   32 33 34 35 36
```

17b. 33   **19.** −1   **21.** 108   **23.** 3   **25.** 9

Lesson 2-4   pages 73–78

ON YOUR OWN **1.** 4   **3.** 9   **5.** 18   **7.** $-\frac{3}{4}$ **9.** No; graph fails the vertical-line test.   **11.** Yes; graph passes the vertical-line test.   **13.** function; amount of money, number of tickets   **15.** function; monthly payment, number of years   **17.** function; time, speed   **19.** no   **21.** yes   **25.** {4, 5, 11}   **27.** {−225$\frac{1}{2}$, −220, −187}   **29.** {−11, −7, 17}   **31.** {6, 0, 216}   **33.** {7, 6, −210}   **35.** {2, 0, 30}   **37a.** dependent variable   **37b.** Input value is to output value as domain is to range.   **39.** 2.13   **41.** −4.3   **43.** 0.04   **45.** 0.84   **47.** {0.25, 121}   **49.** {25, 1, 0, 4, 100}   **51.** The same y-value may correspond to any number of x-values.   **53.** D

MIXED REVIEW **55.** 6   **57.** 80   **59.** $-\frac{1}{10}$ **61.** $s = \frac{1}{3}e$

Lesson 2-5   pages 79–83

ON YOUR OWN **1.** 16   **3.** 28   **5.** 2   **7.** 21
9a. amount of water; number of loads   **9b.** $w(n) = 42n$ **9c.** 294 gal   **9d.** 13 loads; you divide 546 gal by 42 gal/load.   **13.** A   **15a.** $T(a) = 10a + 1$
15b. $31   **19.** {18, 15, 13.8, 10}   **21.** {−9, 0, −1.44, −25}   **23.** {10, 1, 2.44, 26}   **25.** {−22, −4, 3.2, 26}
27. $y = 4x$ **29.** $f(x) = x^3$ **31.** $R(K) = 8 - K$; {0, 1, 2, 3, 4, 5, 6, 7, 8}; {8, 7, 6, 5, 4, 3, 2, 1, 0}
33. $e(h) = 4.25h$

MIXED REVIEW **35.** 23   **37.** 10   **39.** −2.5

41.

43.

CHECKPOINT **1a.** number of minutes; number of words
1b.

Reading Speed

The x-value range is from 0 to 20. It is easiest to label every 4 minutes, to correspond to the given data. The y-value range is from 0 to 5500 with labels every 1100 words.

3. You multiply 3 by 4, then subtract 12 from the result.   **4.** $p(r) = 0.3r$ **5.** $c(d) = 1.15d$ **6.** {−120, −36, −24, 0}   **7.** {−40, 9, 8, 0}   **8.** {−25.5, 2.5, 6.5, 14.5}   **9.** {−3, 4, 5, 7}

ON YOUR OWN

1. Sample table:

x	y
−2	6
−1	3
0	0
1	−3
2	−6

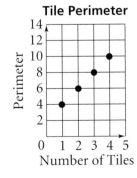

3. Sample table:

x	f(x)
0	−7
1	−5
2	−3
3	−1
4	1

5. Sample table:

x	f(x)
−3	−1
−1	−$\frac{1}{3}$
0	0
1	$\frac{1}{3}$
3	1

7. Sample table:

x	f(x)
−2	2
−2	−1
0	−2
1	−1
2	2

9a. C   **9b.** 9   **9c.**

Tile Perimeter

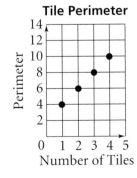

11a. $s(t) = 6t$ **11b.** $w(t) = 3t$ **11c.** 55.2 gal

11d.

Water Use in Shower

Sample: The graph shows that the difference in water use between the two shower heads grows quickly over time.

13.

15.

17.

19.

21.

23.

25.

27.

Selected Answers

29. Sample table:

x	y
−2	2
0	2
2	2
4	2

31a. $.71

31b. Sample table:

a	C(a)
0	$.27
1	$.38
2	$.49
3	$.60
4	$.71
5	$.82

Cost of Call (Boston to Worcester)

31c. at most 12 min   **33.** B

MIXED REVIEW   **39.** {3, 7, 9, 15}   **41.** {4, 2, 1, −2}
43. −20   **45.** 4   **47.** −1

1.

3.

5.

7.

ON YOUR OWN   **1.** Linear function family; the highest power of the variable is 1.   **3.** Absolute value family; there is a variable expression inside the absolute value symbol.   **5.** Quadratic family; the highest power of the variable is 2.   **7.** Quadratic family; the highest power of the variable is 2.
9. Absolute value family; there is a variable expression inside the absolute value symbol.
11. Absolute value; the graph forms a "V" that opens up or down.   **13.** Quadratic; the highest power of the variable is 2.   **15.** Sample: A family of functions is a collection of functions whose graphs and equations are alike.   **17.** No; it fails the vertical line test so it is not a function.   **19.** U-shaped curve
21. V-shape
23. linear

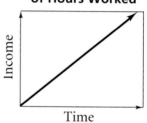

Income as a Function of Hours Worked

25. line; slants down from left to right

27. V-shaped; opens up   **29.** V-shaped; opens down

31. U-shaped; opens up **33.** V-shaped; opens up

35. Quadratic family; the curve is U-shaped, opening down. **37.** Absolute value family; the path of the ball is V-shaped, opening up. **39a.** V-shaped; opens up

39b.

MIXED REVIEW

41. **43.**

45. **47.**

49a. -116 **49b.** Square -8; multiply by -2; add 12 to the result. **51.** $\frac{5}{16}$ **53.** $\frac{15}{16}$ **55.** $\frac{11}{16}$

ON YOUR OWN **1.** $\frac{1}{2}$ **3.** $\frac{1}{6}$ **5.** $\frac{2}{3}$ **7.** $\frac{1}{2}$ **9.** 0

11. Sample: For theoretical probability, you know all the possible outcomes and you want to find out how likely a specific event is to happen. For experimental probability, you know the results of an experiment and you want to find out how frequently a specific event has happened.

13b. $\frac{1}{12}$ **13c.** $\frac{1}{2}$ **13d.** $\frac{1}{4}$ **15.** $\frac{1}{2}$ **17.** 0 **19.** $\frac{4}{9}$

21b. $\frac{1}{12}$ **21c.** $\frac{1}{6}$ **23.** $\frac{1}{6}$ **25.** $\frac{17}{18}$ **27.** $\frac{1}{3}$ **29.** 0

31. $\frac{3}{8}$ **33.** $\frac{11}{16}$ **35.** $\frac{1}{4}$ **37.** 0 **39.** B **41.** $\frac{2}{6}$

MIXED REVIEW **45.** 5 **47.** 0.6 **49.** $-\frac{1}{9}$

1. Positive correlation; people drink more cold drinks in warm weather. **2.** Negative correlation; a better-trained swimmer takes less time to swim 100 m. **4.** Sample: A computer rental costs $2.50 per hour. If you start with a fixed amount of money, the longer you plan to work on the computer, the less money you will have left. **5.** Sample: A residential thermostat senses when the temperature in the room falls below the set level, turns the heater on until the temperature reaches 3°F above the set level, then turns the heater off. The graph shows the air temperature rising while the heater is working and then falling after the heater is turned off.
6. Sample: An elevator is on the second floor. Someone gets in, goes to the eleventh floor, and gets off.

Selected Answers

7. Sample:

Height of a Sunflower Over a Summer

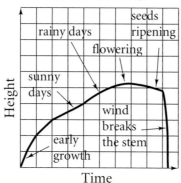

8.

Number of People in a Restaurant

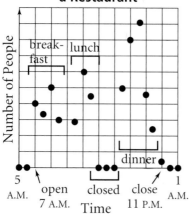

9a. year; price

9b.

Cost of a Median-Priced Home

9c. Sample: Years from 1985 to 1994 on the *x*-axis with labels every 3 years; amounts from $0 to $110,000 with a break from $0 to $70,000 on the *y*-axis with labels every $10,000; this graph accurately represents all the data without taking too much space.   **10.** {−23, −7, −3, 13}   **11.** {1, 3, 3.5, 5.5}
12. {17, 1, 2, 26}   **13.** not a function   **15.** $f(x) = x + 1$ **16.** $f(x) = -x$ **17.** $f(x) = x + 3.5$
18. Sample table:

x	$f(x)$
−1	1
0	−3
1	1

19. Sample table:

x	$f(x)$
−6	1
−5	0
−2	3
0	5

20. Sample table:

x	$f(x)$
−2	−3
−1	−1
0	1
1	3

21. Sample table:

x	$f(x)$
−2	−5
−1	−6
0	−7
1	−6
2	−5

22. quadratic, highest power of x is 2; absolute value; linear, highest power of x is 1; absolute value
23. $\frac{1}{6}$ **24.** $\frac{5}{6}$ **25.** $\frac{1}{3}$ **26.** 0 **27a.** $\frac{1}{4}$ **27b.** P(not 3 heads) means the chances of getting 0, 1, 2, or 4 heads.
28. E **29.** 8 **30.** -3 **31.** 6 **32.** $\frac{1}{2}$ **33.** 5
34. -1.2 **35.** -1 **36.** 7 **37.** 4.5 **38.** $5\frac{1}{4}$

1. 3 **3.** 1 **5.** 3

CHAPTER 3

Lesson 3-1 pages 108–113

ON YOUR OWN **1.** Kendra's method is better; it needs only one operation and Ted's needs two. **3.** 6
5. 8 **7.** 14 **9.** 500 **11.** C **13.** $B + 109 = 180$; 71°
15. $38\frac{3}{4} + g = 41\frac{1}{2}$; $2\frac{3}{4}$ in. **17.** -1 **19.** -1.57
21. -196 **23.** -4.5 **25.** -20 **27.** $-5\frac{5}{6}$ **29.** $4\frac{1}{4}$
31. -245 **33.** subtraction property **39.** 31.5
41. -99 **43.** 13 **45.** $16\frac{1}{2}$ **47.** $-1\frac{1}{4}$ **49.** 11.5
51. $330 = 280 + x$; \$50 **53a.** $3L = 166.5$; \$55.50
53b. $1.5r = 55.5$; \$37 **55.** -18 **57.** -8 **59.** $-3\frac{3}{4}$
61. -262 **63.** -4.5 **65.** $-\frac{3}{8}$ **67.** 5.12 **69.** $-\frac{1}{24}$
71. $5s = 1.6$; 0.32 km

MIXED REVIEW **73.** 8 **75.** about 500,000 **77.** 42.3
79. 31 **81.** 28

Lesson 3-2 pages 114–118

ON YOUR OWN **1.** $3x + 2 = 5$ **3.** $3x + 1 = -2$
5. -1 **7.** -2 **9.** 1 **11.** -2 **13.** 21 **15.** 7
17. -6 **19.** 27 **21.** 0.382 **23.** -60 **25.** $18 + 2t = 60$; 21 min **27.** -6 **29.** 4.5 **31.** 16 **33.** 30
35. -6 **37.** 75 **39.** 0 **41.** -19 **43.** 2.2
45. 3.864 **47a.** Yes; with this estimate, the total bill is \$55, which is close to \$60. **47b.** 125 mi
49. 14 bulbs **51.** Multiplying by 100 changes all the numbers in the equation to integers and it might be easier to work with integers. **53.** $r = (2.8 - 1.34) \cdot 2$; 2.92 **55.** $n = (8 + 0.5) \div 0.05$; 170

57. $n = (7 - 5.3) \div (-0.8)$; -2.125
59. $t = (-7.06 - 3)(-2.5)$; 25.15

MIXED REVIEW **63.** 12 **65.** -9 **67.** 9 **69.** -20
71. 3

Lesson 3-3 pages 119–123

ON YOUR OWN

1.

$2y + 1$; **3.** $-n$ **5.** $8b - 2$ **7.** $-4x + 8n$ **9.** $-6x + m + 8$ **11.** $2x - x = 4$; 4 **13.** $-x - 2 + 3x + 1 = 3$; -1 **15.** 8 **17.** 3 **19.** 7 **21.** 2 **23.** \$6.50
27. 6 **29.** -4 **31.** $5\frac{1}{2}$ **33.** $5\frac{4}{7}$ **35.** -0.48 **37.** 2.4
39. 7 **41.** $4\frac{1}{4}$ in. **43.** 1986, 1987, 1988 **45.** 60
47. 50 **49.** 50

MIXED REVIEW **51.** $y = -2x$
53. Sample:

Speed While Walking to School

walking
speed up near school
stop at intersection
Time
school yard
Speed

55. -9 **57.** -48

Lesson 3-4 pages 124–128

ON YOUR OWN **1.** $2(t - 2) = -6$; -1
3. $4(z + 1) = 4$; 0 **5.** No; $2a \cdot 2b = 4ab$. You cannot use the distributive property because ab is a product, not a sum. **7.** $-2n + 12$ **9.** $2b - \frac{8}{5}$ **11.** $4y + 6$
13. $18n - 42$ **15.** $-b$ **17.** $-11n$ **19.** 900° **21.** 3
23. 9 **25.** 1 **27.** -1 **29.** 8 **31.** -2 **33.** -1
35. 1 **37.** 380 mi; 280 mi **39.** 9 aluminum bats and 6 wooden bats **43.** \$3.96 **45.** \$29.55
47. \$98.97

MIXED REVIEW **49.** $-\frac{2}{3}$ **51.** -7 **53a.** B2/250
53b. 2.9; 0.9; 0.5 **53c.** \$504 million **55.** -17

Selected Answers

CHECKPOINT **1.** 1 **2.** 33 **3.** 20 **4.** $2\frac{1}{2}$ **5.** 120
6. -2 **7.** -2 **8.** 10 **9.** $18\frac{1}{3}$ **10.** -2.7 **11.** -16
12. 2 **13.** 63 in. by 83 in. **14.** B

Lesson 3-5 — pages 129–132

ON YOUR OWN **1.** 12 **3.** -10 **5.** -1 **7.** -48
9. In using the distributive property, the student did not multiply 1 by 8. **11.** A **13.** \$4/yd **15.** -45
17. -3 **19.** 15 **21.** -7 **23.** $-14\frac{1}{7}$ **25.** -10
27. 32 **29.** $\frac{6}{13}$ **31.** -60 **33.** 54 **35.** about 61.5 mi/h **37.** 33.7 h/wk **39.** -21 **41.** 5 **43.** -33
45. -1 **47.** $\frac{3}{5}$ **49.** -9 **51.** $1\frac{5}{6}$ **53.** $1\frac{1}{14}$
55. about \$141 million **57.** $2\frac{1}{2}$ h

MIXED REVIEW **59.** -7 **61.** $\frac{1}{2}$ **63.** 12 **65.** 1
67. $\frac{1}{5}$ **69.** $\frac{2}{5}$

Toolbox — page 133

1. Spain—gold; Poland—silver; Ghana—bronze
3. Coretta lives in New York; David lives in Houston; Nando lives in Dallas; Helen lives in Chicago.

Lesson 3-6 — pages 134–138

ON YOUR OWN **1.** independent **3.** dependent
5. $\frac{1}{6}$ **7.** $\frac{1}{12}$ **9.** $\frac{5}{12}$ **11.** $\frac{3}{50}$ **13.** $\frac{3}{20}$ **15.** $\frac{1}{10}$ **17.** $\frac{1}{6}$
19. $\frac{1}{9}$ **21.** 0 **23.** D **27.** about 1.2% **29.** 0.0036
31. $\frac{1}{5}$ **33.** $\frac{3}{5}$ **35.** $\frac{4}{5}$ **37.** $\frac{3}{4}$ **39.** A

MIXED REVIEW **41.** -60 **43.** 10 **45.** 45%
47. 32.8% **49.** 100%

Lesson 3-7 — pages 139–144

ON YOUR OWN **1.** $n = 0.04 \times 150$ **3.** $24 = 1.5 \times n$
5. $0.1 \times n = 8$; 80 **7.** $0.06 \times n = 36$; 600
9. $n \times 45 = 18$; 40% **11.** \$62.40 **15.** \$20
17. 50% **19.** 39.2 **21.** 4.5% **23.** 330 **25.** 60%
27. \$84 **29.** \$320 **31.** about 12.6% **33.** 40%

35. The number of people 65 and over is projected to be 80 million, which is 20% of the total population, so the projected population is 400 million people.
37. \$1250 **39.** 2 yr

MIXED REVIEW **41.** Sample table:

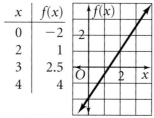

x	$f(x)$
0	-2
2	1
3	2.5
4	4

43. Sample table:

x	$f(x)$
-1	-3
0	1
1	5

45. $\{-1, -2, -3\}$ **47.** 0.75 **49.** 0.88

CHECKPOINT **1.** $-\frac{14}{5}$ **2.** 9.6 **3.** $3\frac{11}{15}$ **4.** $-11\frac{1}{4}$
5. 3 **6.** $\frac{1}{9}$ **7.** $\frac{1}{24}$ **8.** $\frac{1}{27}$ **9.** $\frac{1}{36}$ **10.** The probability increases, because the first draw is the same, but for the second the number of marbles decreases and the number of favorable outcomes stays the same.
11. 218 members

Toolbox — page 145

1.

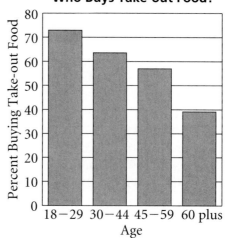

Who Buys Take-out Food?

(Bar graph — Percent Buying Take-out Food vs. Age)

3.

How Often People Misplace TV Remote Control per Week

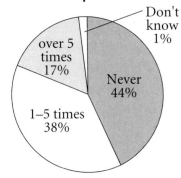

Don't know 1%
over 5 times 17%
Never 44%
1–5 times 38%

ON YOUR OWN **1.** 25% decrease **3.** 5% increase **5.** 3% decrease **7.** 29% decrease **9.** about 39% **11.** 100% **13.** 60% **15.** 33% **17.** 200% **21.** Less; the 20% you subtracted is 20% of an amount greater than the original amount, so it is greater than the 20% you added. **23.** 6% increase **25.** 22% decrease **27.** 4% increase **29.** 120% increase **31.** 22% increase **33.** 28% decrease **35a.** 100% **35b.** 100 **35c.** 50% **35d.** 50 **35e.** 100% **35f.** 100 **37.** C **39.** 60% **41.** about 14% **43.** about 50% **45a.** 25% **45b.** 20%

MIXED REVIEW **47.** 1.5 **49.** 13 **51.** 60%

1. 16 **2.** -36 **3.** 31 **4.** 24 **5.** 44 **6.** 4.25 **7.** 12 **8.** 2 **9.** $2x + 5 = 9$; 2 **10.** $3x - 2 = 7$; 3 **11.** $-4x + 2 = -6$; 2 **12.** $\frac{1}{2}$ **13.** 3 **14.** 3 **15.** 11 **16.** 18 **17.** 4 **18.** -2 **19.** -9 **21.** $4m + 3$ **22.** $b + 10$ **23.** $-5w + 20$ **24.** $36 - 27j$ **25.** -9 **26.** 4 **27.** -0.5 **28.** $1\frac{1}{2}$ **29.** -2 **30.** 1.5 **31.** 2 **32.** 1 **33.** $2[l + (l - 6)] = 72$; 15 cm $\times$ 21 cm **34.** C **35.** -45 **36.** 24 **37.** -11 **38.** -4 **39.** $40 **40.** dependent; $\frac{2}{45}$ **41.** independent; $\frac{1}{20}$ **43.** $n = 0.15 \times 86$; 12.9 **44.** $n \times 5 = 40$; 800% **45.** $1.8 = 0.72 \times n$; 2.5 **46.** 3.75% **47.** $220 **48.** about 13% increase **49.** 25% decrease **50.** about 33% decrease **51.** 27.2% **53.** -2

54. 1.4 **55.** 19 **56.** 7 **57.** 4.5 **58.** 18 **59.** $\frac{1}{4}$ **60.** $1\frac{1}{7}$ **61.** 3 **62.** $\frac{4}{9}$ **63.** -4 **64.** 5 **65.** 52 **66.** -3

1. 3 **3.** 4 **5.** 4 **7.** 4 **9.** 2

CHAPTER 4

ON YOUR OWN **1.** yes; $6 \cdot 20 = 8 \cdot 15$ **3.** yes; $-0.12 \cdot 0.5 = -0.4 \cdot 0.15$ **5.** no; $-3 \cdot 25 \neq -1 \cdot 100$ **7.** about 433 times **9.** $54 **11.** 20% **13.** 50 **15.** 27.6% **17.** 307.1 **19.** 15.6 **21.** 10 ft by 12 ft **23.** E **25.** 5 **27.** 12.5 **29.** 4 **31.** 5 **33.** 12.5 **35.** -0.864 **37a.** No; For an item that originally costs $12, $\frac{1}{3}$ off results in the price $8; 50% off results in the price $6. **39.** 9 **41.** 5.5 in. **43.** 7.1%

MIXED REVIEW **45.** $\begin{bmatrix} -1.2 & 14.6 \\ -1.4 & -5.7 \end{bmatrix}$ **47.** -11.5 **49.** 16 paperbacks **51.** -14.5

ON YOUR OWN **1.** $2x + 2 = x - 8$; -10 **3.** $2x + 3 = 3x - 7$; 10 **5.** 7 **7.** 3 **9.** no solution **11.** no solution **13.** identity **15.** You should add y, not subtract, on the third line; 5.3. **17.** 0 **19.** no solution **21.** 2 **23.** no solution **25.** -41 **27.** $-\frac{1}{2}$ **29.** identity **31.** $a = -\frac{1}{4}$; $w = -4$; $x = -1$; $y = 0$ **35.** 20 h **43.** $DF = 7$, $DE = 10$, $EF = 6$ **45.** 7 **47.** -3 **49.** -0.5 **51.** 10 **53.** C

MIXED REVIEW **55.** -28 **57.** 7.7 **59.** 15 **61.** 34 **63.** 11 **65.** -19 **67.** -2

1a. $y = 2x - 1; y = x + 1$ **1b.** 2   **1c.** 2
3. 3   **5.** 30

Intersection
X=3   Y=0

Intersection
X=30   Y=45
Xmin=−10   Ymin=−10
Xmax=50   Ymax=50
Xscl=5   Yscl=5

7. no; $-\frac{3}{4}$ **9.** no; $-\frac{2}{3}$

Intersection
X=−.75   Y=1.25

Intersection
X=−.6666667   Y=−.6666667

Lesson 4-3   pages 170−174

ON YOUR OWN   **1.** 3   **3.** 2   **5.** 6   **7.** −4   **11.** −6, 6
13. −4, 3   **15.** 3, 13   **17.** −16, 2   **19.** −9, 5
21. −0.72, 0.72   **23.** $|x| = 3$ **25.** $|x| = 0$ **29.** True;
absolute value cannot be negative.   **31.** False; $z = 0$
or $z = -6$.   **33.** −12, 12   **35.** −48   **37.** −10, 10
39. −9, 9   **41.** 39°F, 11°F   **43a.** 7.265 oz; 7.235 oz
43b. No; one coin may weigh much more than
0.18 oz, while another may weigh much less.

MIXED REVIEW   **45.** −6   **47.** −0.5   **49.** −2.5
51. Ted earns $5.50 per hour; Elio earns $7.50 per
hour.   **53.** 24 ft

Lesson 4-4   pages 175−178

ON YOUR OWN   **1.** $r = \frac{s-4}{3}$ **3.** $p = \frac{mq}{n}$ **5.** $r = \frac{C}{2\pi}$
7. $t = \frac{3m}{2} - 4$ **9a.** 5.85   **9b.** $b = 2m - a$ **9c.** 5.9
11. $n = 4m - 6$ **13.** $z = a + y$ **15.** $b = \frac{7a}{2}$
17. $b = \frac{2A}{h}$ **19.** $h = \frac{V}{lw}$ **21.** $p = \frac{b-r}{a}$ or $p = \frac{b+r}{a}$
23a. $A = \frac{s^2}{R}$ **23b.** 27 ft²   **27a.** $y = -\frac{1}{2}x + 2$

27b.

27c. $\frac{1}{2}; 0; -\frac{1}{2}$

MIXED REVIEW   **29.** 560   **31a.** $69   **31b.** Sample:
p = total pay; r = hourly rate; h = number of hours;
$p = rh$ **33.** >   **35.** >

CHECKPOINT   **1.** $n = s + 90$ **2.** $b = y - mx$
3. $a = \frac{2b^2}{L}$ **4.** $f = \frac{W}{d}$ **5.** 16.8   **6.** no solution;
$-4 \neq 4$ **7.** no solution; absolute value cannot be
negative   **8.** 0   **9.** −8, 8   **10.** $9\frac{2}{3}$ **11.** 5
12. 1.5, 7.5   **13.** $17\frac{1}{3}$ km   **14.** C

Lesson 4-5   pages 179−184

ON YOUR OWN   **1.** n = number of students; $n \leq 48$
3. a = age of applicant; $a \geq 16$ **5.** w = light bulb
wattage; $w \leq 60$ **7a.** $6 < 9$ **7b.** $10 < 13$
7c. $-1 < 2$
7d.

9. Sample: −20, −1, 0, 0.2   **11.** Sample: 1, 2, 3, 26
13. Add 4 to each side.   **15.** Add $\frac{1}{2}$ to each side.
17. b is greater than 0.   **19.** m is at most −1.
21. z is at least −4.   **23.** 40 points
25. $x > 11$

```
  +---+---+--⊕-+---+---+---+
  9  10  11  12  13  14
```

27. $h \geq -\frac{1}{4}$

```
  +---+---●---+---+---+---+
 −2  −1   0   1   2   3
```

29. $x \geq -1.7$

```
  +---+---+---●---+---+---+
 −4 −3 −2 −1   0   1
```

31. $m > 5.5$

```
  +---+---+--○+---+---+---+
  3   4   5   6   7   8
```

33. $y < 3.1$

```
  +---+---+---+○--+---+---+
  0   1   2   3   4   5
```

35. $t \geq 12.9$

```
  +---+---+---●---+---+---+
 10  11  12  13  14  15
```

37. $n < -5\frac{4}{5}$ (number line with open circle at -6, shaded left) $-8\ -7\ -6\ -5\ -4\ -3$

39. $x \neq -5.7$ (number line with open circle near -5.7) $-8\ -7\ -6\ -5\ -4\ -3$

41. $c \neq 2\frac{11}{14}$ (number line with open circle near 3) $0\ 1\ 2\ 3\ 4\ 5$

43. $g \leq -1\frac{1}{6}$ (number line with closed circle, shaded left) $-4\ -3\ -2\ -1\ 0\ 1$

45. $y < 5.5$ (number line with open circle, shaded left) $3\ 4\ 5\ 6\ 7\ 8$

47. $m \leq 5$ (number line with closed circle at 5, shaded left) $3\ 4\ 5\ 6\ 7\ 8$

51. E   **53.** $s \leq 18{,}000$ **55.** about \$5000

MIXED REVIEW   **59.** $\begin{bmatrix} -8 & 18 \\ -2 & 15 \end{bmatrix}$ **61.** $-11, -1$

63. $-12, 12$ **65.** Two quantities are equal. If you multiply (divide) both of them by a number, the products (quotients) are also equal. You cannot divide by 0.   **67.** $-\frac{2}{3}$ **69.** 6.4

Lesson 4-6   pages 185–189

ON YOUR OWN   **1a.** -1 **1b.** -1 **3.** Multiply by -1.   **5.** Sample: $-5, -1, 0, 8$ **7.** Sample: $-4, -7, -10, -20$ **9.** Sample: $-12, -3, -1, 10$ **11.** -2

13. 4   **15.** -10

17. $x \geq 4$ (number line with closed circle at 4, shaded right) $0\ 1\ 2\ 3\ 4\ 5\ 6$

19. $x > -6$ (number line with open circle at -6, shaded right) $-7\ \ -5\ \ -3\ \ -1$

21. $d > 5\frac{1}{3}$ (number line with open circle at $5\frac{1}{3}$, shaded right) $4\ \ 5\ 5\frac{1}{3}\ 6$

23. 18 h   **25.** C   **27.** $j > -6$ **29.** $s \leq -28$

31a. Kia should have divided each side by -15.
31b. 150 is a solution, but 151 is also a solution
31c. She could try any number less than -9; $(-15)(-10) \leq 135$ is false.

33. $u > 35$ (number line with open circle at 35, shaded right) $32\ 33\ 34\ 35\ 36\ 37$

35. $k \geq -30$ (number line with closed circle at -30, shaded right) $-32\ \ \ -30\ \ \ -28$

37. $t \leq -2.35$ (number line with closed circle near -2.35, shaded left) $-5\ -4\ -3\ -2\ -1\ 0$

39. $x < -8$ (number line with open circle at -8, shaded left) $-10\ -9\ -8\ -7\ -6\ -5$

41. $b < 0$ (number line with open circle at 0, shaded left) $-3\ -2\ -1\ 0\ 1\ 2$

43. $m \leq -47$ (number line with closed circle at -47, shaded left) $-49\ -48\ -47\ -46\ -45\ -44$

45a. 480 tiles   **45b.** Sample: they may need to cut some tiles.

MIXED REVIEW   **47.** $y = \frac{6 - 2x}{3}$ **49.** $y = \frac{15 - 4x}{-5}$

51a. 1750 tons   **51b.** about 0.4 oz   **53.** -4.4

55. -2.4 **57.** $-18\frac{6}{7}$

Lesson 4-7   pages 190–194

ON YOUR OWN   **1.** Subtract 5 from each side. Then divide each side by 4.   **3.** Subtract 8 from each side.
5. Subtract y from each side. Then add 5 to each side.
7. Add s to each side. Then subtract 6 from each side.
9. Multiply or divide each side by -1. Reverse the order of the inequality.   **11.** E   **13.** A   **15.** C

17. $h \geq -2$ (number line with closed circle at -2, shaded right) $-5\ -4\ -3\ -2\ -1\ 0$

19. $x > -2\frac{1}{2}$ (number line with open circle at $-2\frac{1}{2}$, shaded right) $-5\ -4\ -3\ -2\ -1\ 0$

21. $n \geq 2$ (number line with closed circle at 2, shaded right) $0\ 1\ 2\ 3\ 4\ 5$

23. $m > -8$ (number line with open circle at -8, shaded right) $-10\ -9\ -8\ -7\ -6\ -5$

25. $a < -3$ (number line with open circle at -3, shaded left) $-5\ -4\ -3\ -2\ -1\ 0$

27a. 74 boxes   **27b.** 5 trips   **29.** $k > -\frac{1}{4}$
31. all numbers   **33.** no solutions   **35.** $k \leq -33$
37. $s \geq -\frac{22}{37}$ **41.** at least \$7000   **43.** $15n - (490 + 45 + 65) \geq 1200$

MIXED REVIEW   **45.** $m > 1850$ **47.** Absolute value; variable expression is inside the absolute value symbol.   **49.** Quadratic; highest power of x is 2.
51a. about 1.125 tons   **51b.** about 10.7 million tons

53. (number line with closed circles at -5 and -2) $-6\ -5\ -4\ -3\ -2\ -1$

55. (number line with open circles at -1 and 1) $-2\ -1\ 0\ 1\ 2\ 3$

Lesson 4-8   pages 195–200

ON YOUR OWN   **1.** e = elevation anywhere in North America; $-282 \leq e \leq 20{,}320$ **3.** $-2 < x < 3$
5. $-4 \leq x \leq 3$ **7.** Sample: $x < 1$ or $x > 0$
9. $|x| < 3$ **11.** $|x - 6| > 2$
13. $-5 < j < 5$

(number line with open circles at -5 and 5) $-6\ \ -4\ \ -2\ \ 0\ \ 2\ \ 4\ \ 6$

15. $k < -5$ or $k > -1$

$-6\ -5\ -4\ -3\ -2\ -1\ \ 0$

17. $1 \le r \le 2$

$-1\ \ 0\ \ 1\ \ 2\ \ 3\ \ 4$

19. $-2 < r \le -1.5$

$-4\ -3\ -2\ -1\ \ 0\ \ 1$

21. $-1.5 < w < 3.5$

$-2\ -1\ \ 0\ \ 1\ \ 2\ \ 3\ \ 4$

23. $4 \le t \le 14$

$3\ \ 4\ \ 5\ \ 6\ \ 7\ \ 8\ \ 9\ \ 10\ \ 11\ \ 12\ \ 13\ \ 14\ \ 15$

27. $7585 \text{ cm} \le l \le 7615 \text{ cm}$
29. $f < -2.5$ or $f > 2.5$

$-4\ -3\ -2\ -1\ \ 0\ \ 1\ \ 2\ \ 3\ \ 4$

31. $n \le -13$ or $n \ge -3$

$-14\ -13\ -12\ -11\ -10\ -9\ -8\ -7\ -6\ -5\ -4\ -3\ -2$

33. $w < -2$ or $w > 2$

$-3\ -2\ -1\ \ 0\ \ 1\ \ 2\ \ 3$

35. $-6 < x < 6$

$-7\ -6\ -5\ -4\ -3\ -2\ -1\ \ 0\ \ 1\ \ 2\ \ 3\ \ 4\ \ 5\ \ 6\ \ 7$

37. $y \le 1$ or $y \ge 3$

$0\ \ 1\ \ 2\ \ 3\ \ 4\ \ 5$

39. $t \le -2.4$ or $t \ge 4$

$-4\ -3\ -2\ -1\ \ 0\ \ 1\ \ 2\ \ 3\ \ 4\ \ 5$

41. $t < -3$ or $t > 2\frac{1}{3}$

$-4\ -3\ -2\ -1\ \ 0\ \ 1\ \ 2\ \ 3\ \ 4$

43. all numbers

$-3\ -2\ -1\ \ 0\ \ 1\ \ 2$

45. $2.5 < x < 7.5$ **47.** $7 < x < 49$ **49.** $66 \le C \le 88$
51. Charlotte: $29 \le C \le 90$; Detroit $15 \le D \le 83$

MIXED REVIEW **53.** $-\frac{1}{8}$ **55.** -1 **57.** $-0.9, 0.9$
59. $-\frac{1}{4}, 1\frac{1}{4}$ **61.** $-3, -2, -1, 0, 1$ **63.** $-3, -2, -1,$
$0, 1, 2$

CHECKPOINT

1. $c > 6$

$4\ \ 5\ \ 6\ \ 7\ \ 8\ \ 9$

2. $x \le -8$

$-10\quad -8\quad -6$

3. $m \le -4$

$-7\ -6\ -5\ -4\ -3\ -2$

4. $c \ge -5$

$-8\ -7\ -6\ -5\ -4\ -3$

5. $b > \frac{1}{3}$

$-2\ -1\ \ 0\ \ 1\ \ 2\ \ 3$

6. $n \le 3$

$0\ \ 1\ \ 2\ \ 3\ \ 4\ \ 5$

7. $r \le 7$

$4\ \ 5\ \ 6\ \ 7\ \ 8\ \ 9$

8. $w \le -2$

$-5\ -4\ -3\ -2\ -1\ \ 0$

9. $h \ge -4$

$-7\ -6\ -5\ -4\ -3\ -2$

10. $0 \ge t \ge -0.5$

$-3\ -2\ -1\ \ 0\ \ 1\ \ 2$

11. $x < -27$ or $x > 4$

$-30\ -27\ -24\ -21\ -18\ -15\ -12\ -9\ -6\ -3\ \ 0\ \ 3\ \ 6$

12. $g < 1$ or $g > 5$

$-2\ -1\ \ 0\ \ 1\ \ 2\ \ 3\ \ 4\ \ 5\ \ 6$

13. $d \le -3$ or $d \ge 3$

$-4\ -3\ -2\ -1\ \ 0\ \ 1\ \ 2\ \ 3\ \ 4$

14. $-10 < x < 4$

$-10\quad -5\quad 0\quad 5$

15. $-1 < x < 4$

$-2\ -1\ \ 0\ \ 1\ \ 2\ \ 3\ \ 4\ \ 5$

16. $y \le -4$ or $y \ge 5$

$-5\ -4\ -3\ -2\ -1\ \ 0\ \ 1\ \ 2\ \ 3\ \ 4\ \ 5\ \ 6$

17. $2\frac{2}{5} \le x \le 5\frac{3}{5}$

$2\ \ 3\ \ 4\ \ 5\ \ 6\ \ 7$

18. $36 < t < 37.2$

1. 6

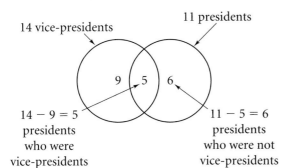

14 vice-presidents

11 presidents

9 5 6

$14 - 9 = 5$
presidents
who were
vice-presidents

$11 - 5 = 6$
presidents
who were not
vice-presidents

3a. 1   **3b.** 2   **3c.** 45

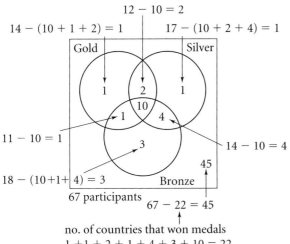

$12 - 10 = 2$

$14 - (10 + 1 + 2) = 1$ $17 - (10 + 2 + 4) = 1$

Gold   Silver

1   2   1

10

1   4

$11 - 10 = 1$

3

$14 - 10 = 4$

$18 - (10 + 1 + 4) = 3$ Bronze

45

67 participants

$67 - 22 = 45$

no. of countries that won medals
$1 + 1 + 2 + 1 + 4 + 3 + 10 = 22$

Lesson 4-9 pages 202–205

ON YOUR OWN

1. $p \leq 6$ (number line: 0 1 2 3 4 5 6 7)

3. no solutions   **5.** no solutions

7. (number line: -1 0 1 2 3 4 5 6)

9. (number line: 3 4 5 6 7 8 ...)

11. (number line: 0 1 2 3 4 5 ...)

13. (number line: $-5 -4 -3 -2 -1$ 0 1 2 3)

15. no solutions

---

17. $12 \leq a < 65$

(number line: 10 20 30 40 50 60 70)

19. $23 < c < 23.5$

(number line: 21 22 23 24 25 26)

21.

tepid   warm   hot

(number line: 80 85 90 95 100 105 110 115)

23a. 6 h   **23b.** Divide 175 by the hourly rate and subtract the hours worked so far. Round the result up to the next integer.

27. (number line: $-4 -3 -2 -1$ 0 1 2 3 4)

29. (number line: $-9 -8 -7 -6 -5 -4 -3 -2 -1$ 0 1 2 3)

MIXED REVIEW   31. 5   **33.** 50%   **35.** 150%

Wrap Up pages 207–209

1. 2   **2.** 2.3   **3.** -6 **4.** 10   **5.** -0.4 **6.** 1.5
7. 36 ft   **8.** $2x - 6 = -3x + 4$; 2   **9.** $-x + 8 = -2x - 9$; -17 **10.** -11 **11.** identity   **12.** 0
13. -2 **14.** $-5, 5$ **15.** $-12.5, 6.5$ **16.** No solution; absolute value cannot be negative.   **17.** 8
19. $c = 3m - a - b$ **20.** $d = \frac{C}{\pi}$ **21.** $x = \frac{y - b}{m}$
22. $h = \frac{2A}{b}$ **23a.** $I = \frac{E}{R}$ **23b.** 40 amperes

24. $h > -1$ (number line: $-3 -2 -1$ 0 1 2)

25. $k \leq -\frac{1}{2}$ (number line: $-3 -2 -1$ 0 1 2)

26. $b < 40$ (number line: 37 38 39 40 41 42)

27. $y \leq -168$ (number line: $-170 -169 -168 -167 -166 -165$)

28. $c \leq -2$ (number line: $-5 -4 -3 -2 -1$ 0)

29. $m < -6$ (number line: $-9 -8 -7 -6 -5 -4$)

30. $t < -5$ (number line: $-8 -7 -6 -5 -4 -3$)

31. $x \geq 9$ (number line: 7 8 9 10 11 12)

32. There is no solution because $\frac{3}{4} \leq \frac{1}{4}$ is false.

Selected Answers

33. $n \le -6$ or $n \ge 2$

34. $-2 \le z < 7$

35. $t \le -2$ or $t \ge 7$

36. $-1\frac{1}{2} \le b < 0$ **37.** $2 \le a < 4$

38. $-6\frac{1}{2} < d < 4$

39. $2 \le a < 5$ **40.** all numbers

41. C

42. $h \le -1.5$ or $h \ge 2$

43. $t \le 3\frac{1}{3}$

44. no solution

45. $-3 \le m < 0$

46. $q < 0$

47. $\frac{1}{4} \le c \le 4$

48. $l > 1000$

50.

51.

52.

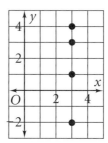

53. $f(x) = x - 5$ **54.** $f(x) = x + 9$ **55.** $f(x) = \frac{x}{2}$
56. $f(x) = 3x$

Preparing for the Math A Exam   page 211

1. 3   **3.** 2   **5.** 3   **7.** 3

CHAPTER 5

Lesson 5-1   pages 214–218

ON YOUR OWN   **1.** $1; -1$ **3.** $\frac{5}{9}$ **5.** $-\frac{6}{5}$
7. undefined

9.

11.

13.

15.

17. $y = 3, x = 4, y = 3, x = -1$ **19.** F; for example a line with slope 1 that passes through $(0, 1)$ does not pass through the origin. **21.** F; a line through any point in Quadrant III can have positive, negative, zero, or undefined slope. **23.** increase **25.** $\overleftrightarrow{AB} : 0; \overleftrightarrow{BC} : \frac{5}{6}; \overleftrightarrow{AC} : \frac{5}{3}$ **27.** $\overleftrightarrow{JK} : -\frac{1}{2}; \overleftrightarrow{KL} : 2; \overleftrightarrow{LM} : -\frac{1}{2}; \overleftrightarrow{JM} : 2$ **29.** no **31a.** About 110; the rent is $110 per hour. **31b.** 55 customers per hour **33.** E

MIXED REVIEW **35.** $\frac{1}{2}$ **37.** 1 **39.** 75%
41. independent: temperature; dependent: amount of fuel used

Toolbox   page 219

1. A **3.** B **5.** $3\frac{1}{3}$ **7.** 270 **9.** about 15.83 mi/h
11. 20,000 mi/h

Lesson 5-2   pages 220–224

ON YOUR OWN **1.** 0.9 in./mo **3.** 30 mi/h **5.** $\frac{1}{4}$; $1 buys 4 oz of oregano. **7a.** Yes; for every 6°F decline in temperature, the number of calories burned increases by 100. **7b.** Subtract 20°F. Multiply the difference by the rate of change. Then add the result to 3330 calories. The number of calories burned at 20°F is 3830. **9.** true **11.** F; the boiling temperature of water decreases as altitude increases.
13. no **15.** no **17.** yes **19a.** A: fastest; C: slowest **19b.** C; you can record more if you use less tape per unit of time.

21a.

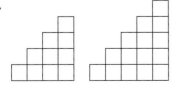

21b.

Number of Squares	Perimeter
1	4
2	8
3	12
4	16
5	20

21c. No; the number of squares increase by 1, 2, 3, etc.; but the perimeter increases 4 units with each figure.

MIXED REVIEW **25.** 4 **27.** 3 **29.** about 21%
31. Sample:

x	y
−3	−2.4
−1	−0.8
0	0
1	0.8

33. Sample:

x	y
−1	−7.2
−0.5	−3.6
0	0
0.5	3.6
1	7.2

Lesson 5-3   pages 225–229

ON YOUR OWN **1.** A; B; the graph of a direct variation must pass through the origin. **3.** no
5. yes; $\frac{1}{4}$ **7.** no **9.** yes; $y = 1.8x$ **11.** yes; $y = -1.5x$
13. $y = \frac{5}{2}x$ **15.** $y = -\frac{5}{2}x$ **17.** 52 lb **19.** False; the graph must pass through $(0, 0)$. **21.** False; a direct variation is a function. Vertical lines have more than one y-value for an x-value. **23a.** $\frac{1}{32}$; $b = \frac{1}{32}w$
25. 12 **27.** 8 **29.** 5 **31.** −2 **33a.** $d = 7p$
33b. 84 dog years

MIXED REVIEW **35.** $t > -1\frac{1}{3}$ **37.** B

39.
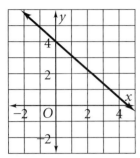

Lesson 5-4 pages 230–234

ON YOUR OWN **1.** $-\frac{3}{4}; -5$ **3.** $3; -9$ **5.** $0; 3$

7. III **9.** II **11a.** 12 in. **11b.** $h = -\frac{2}{15}t + 12$

11c.

13. **15.**

17.
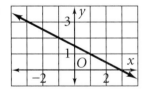

19. no; $4 \ne -2(-3) + 1$

21. $-\frac{2}{3}; 2; y = -\frac{2}{3}x + 2$ **23.** $0; 1; y = 1$

27. $y = \frac{2}{9}x + 3$ **29.** $y = -\frac{5}{4}x$

MIXED REVIEW **31.** $-\frac{9}{7}$ **33.** $-\frac{1}{5}$ **35.** 2 **37.** 1

CHECKPOINT **1.** yes; $\frac{y}{x} = m$ **2.** no; $\frac{y}{x} \ne m$ **3.** No; a vertical line cannot be a direct variation. **4.** yes; $\frac{y}{x} = m$ **5.** \$121.75 billion/yr

Toolbox page 235

1a. Divide Xmax and Ymax by the number of ticks between 0 and the edge; 5, 2 **1b.** $y = 2x + 5$

3.

5.

7.

9.

Lesson 5-5 pages 236–239

ON YOUR OWN **1.** $y = 2x - 11$ **3.** $y = \frac{4}{3}x + 3\frac{1}{3}$

5. $y = x + 3$ **7.** $y = 2$ **9.** $y = -\frac{1}{4}x + 3\frac{3}{4}$

11. $y = -\frac{3}{4}x - 3\frac{1}{2}$ **13a.** $L = 0.025M + 7.25$

13b. The y-intercept is the length of the spring when no mass is attached.   **13c.** 9 cm   **15.** $y = \frac{1}{5}x + 1\frac{3}{5}$
17. $y = \frac{1}{9}x + 2\frac{8}{9}$ **19.** $y = -2x + 150$ **21.** $y = -\frac{2}{5}x + 2\frac{4}{5}$
23a. For 86 corresponding to 1986, $r = 0.5t - 39.1$
23b. \$15.9 billion   **25.** yes; $y = -2x + 1$ **27.** yes;
$y = 3x + 25$ **29a.** $c = 2.5l + 2$ **29b.** slope:
cost/mi; y-intercept: initial cost of ride

MIXED REVIEW   31. $c < 8$ **33.** $m \le -1\frac{3}{4}$ **35.** $-1\frac{4}{7}$
37. 928.6% increase   **39.** positive   **41.** positive

Toolbox	page 240

1. positive

Lesson 5-6	pages 241–245

ON YOUR OWN   1. Sample: yes; $y = 11.25x + 200$
3. Sample: yes; $y = 0.6x + 330$ **5.** no   **9.** A
11b. Sample: $y = 6.404761905x - 392.7261905$
11c. about 280 million TV sets   **13b.** Sample: $y = 0.2278305085x - 11.71566102$ **13c.** about 12.2%

19a.

```
Xmin=0      Ymin=0
Xmax=18     Ymax=75
Xscl=2      Yscl=15
```

19b. $y = 1.206586826x + 45.71556886$ **19c.** No;
$r \approx 0.448$, which is not close to 1.

MIXED REVIEW   21. 23   **23.** -6 **25.** 3   **27.** $-\frac{8}{3}$
29. 20

Lesson 5-7	pages 246–249

ON YOUR OWN   1. A   **3.** C

5.

7.

9.

11.

15.

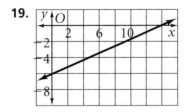 intercepts: $(0, -4)$ and $(-5, 0)$;

17.

 intercepts: $(0, 10\frac{10}{11})$ and $(-24, 0)$;

19.

 intercepts: $(0, -6)$ and $(14, 0)$;

21.
intercepts: $(0, 30)$ and $(23\frac{1}{3}, 0)$;

23. $y = \frac{A}{B}x + \frac{C}{B}$ **25.** $x + 3y = 26$ **27.** $3x + 2y = -20$ **29.** $3x + y = 7$ **31.** $x + 5y = -39$

MIXED REVIEW   **33.** $\frac{1}{36}$

35.   **37.**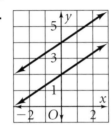

Lesson 5-8   pages 250–255

ON YOUR OWN   **1.** $\frac{1}{2}$ **3.** $-\frac{3}{4}$ **5.** 0   **7.** 2   **9.** -3
11. $\frac{5}{4}$ **13.** $-\frac{1}{2}$ **15.** $-\frac{5}{7}$ **17.** $\frac{3}{2}$ **19.** undefined
21. $-\frac{1}{2}$ **23.** $-\frac{2}{9}$ **25.** perpendicular
27. perpendicular   **29.** perpendicular   **31.** The vertical and horizontal scales use units of different length.   **33a.** Yes; they have the same slope, $-\frac{3}{5}$
33b. Since the coefficients of x and y are the same, the ratio for the slope will be the same.   **35.** No; the slopes are $\frac{5}{6}$, -2, and $\frac{1}{8}$. No pair of slopes has product -1.   **37.** The slope of $\overleftrightarrow{AD}$ and $\overleftrightarrow{BC}$ is undefined, so they are parallel. The slope of $\overleftrightarrow{AB}$ and $\overleftrightarrow{CD}$ is $\frac{1}{2}$, so they are parallel. The quadrilateral is a parallelogram.
39. The slope of $\overleftrightarrow{PQ}$ and $\overleftrightarrow{RS}$ is $-\frac{1}{2}$. The slope of $\overleftrightarrow{QR}$ and $\overleftrightarrow{SP}$ is $-\frac{3}{2}$. The quadrilateral is a parallelogram.
41. $y = 6x$ **43.** $y = -x + 10$ **45.** $y = -\frac{2}{3}x + \frac{1}{3}$
47. True; the definition of perpendicular lines says that horizontal and vertical lines are perpendicular.
49. False; two positive numbers need not be equal.
51. The slope of $\overleftrightarrow{AB}$ and $\overleftrightarrow{CD}$ is $\frac{2}{5}$. The slope of $\overleftrightarrow{BC}$ and $\overleftrightarrow{AD}$ is $-\frac{5}{2}$. The product is -1, so the

quadrilateral is a rectangle.   **53.** The slope of $\overleftrightarrow{PQ}$ and $\overleftrightarrow{RS}$ is $\frac{1}{2}$. The slope of $\overleftrightarrow{PS}$ and $\overleftrightarrow{QR}$ is -2. The product is -1, so the quadrilateral is a rectangle.

MIXED REVIEW   **55.** $m < -2$ **57.** $y > 1$ **59.** $-\frac{8}{3}$
61. 20

CHECKPOINT   **1.** $-2x + 3y = 6$ **2.** $-4x + y = -7$
3. $-\frac{1}{3}x + y = 5$ **4.** $-9x + 15y = -12$ **5.** $y = -\frac{1}{4}x + 4\frac{3}{4}$ **6.** $y = 18x - 3$ **7.** $y = \frac{5}{7}x$ **8.** $x = 5$
9. $y = 5.4x + 1.3$ **10.** $y = -6.1x + 62.7$ **15.** D

Lesson 5-9   pages 256–259

ON YOUR OWN   **1.** $y = 3x - 8$ **3.** $y = -x - 4$ **5.** A
7. $-\frac{3}{2}$ **9.** 3   **11.** $5\frac{2}{3}$ **13.** 25   **15.** 36   **17.** $7\frac{1}{4}$
19a. $15x = 100$ **19b.** $6\frac{2}{3}$ **19c.** $50   **23.** -17.5
25. 3.75   **27.** False; a vertical line has no y-intercept.
29. True; the x-intercept is the x-value for y-value 0.

MIXED REVIEW   **31.** -11.6 **33.** 4.84

Wrap Up   pages 261–263

1. Sample: $(10, 0.5)$, $(30, 1)$; $\frac{1}{40}$ **2.** Sample: $(0, 150)$, $(40, 150)$; 0   **3.** $(1, 7.5)$ $(3, 5)$; -1.25 **4.** $\frac{1}{2}$ page/min
5. $\frac{1}{22}$ mi/min   **6.** 3 goals/game   **7.** 12 pages/min
8. 6   **9.** 4   **10.** -4 **11.** $y = \frac{3}{4}x + 8$
12. $y = -7x + \frac{1}{2}$ **13.** $y = \frac{2}{5}x$ **14.** $y = -3$
15. $y = \frac{1}{3}x + 1\frac{2}{3}$ **16.** $y = -\frac{6}{5}x + 2$ **17.** $y = \frac{1}{2}x + \frac{1}{2}$
18. $y = \frac{3}{10}x + 6\frac{2}{5}$ **19.** $y = -\frac{1}{2}x - \frac{1}{2}$ **20.** $y = -3x$
21. $y = \frac{1}{4}x - 3$ **22a.** Sample: $y = 1.3x - 59$
22b. Using equation in (a): 77.5 lb/person   **23.** 2; 5
24. 8; -13 **25.** 15; -5 **26.** 13; -104
27. $y = 5x - 11$ **28.** $y = \frac{1}{3}x + 4$ **29.** $y = 9x - 5$
30. $y = -\frac{1}{8}x + 10\frac{1}{2}$ **32a.** $30x = 175$ **32b.** $5\frac{5}{6}$ lawns, or 6 lawns to make a profit   **33.** The break-even point is the amount you need to produce to make $0 profit.   **34.** C

35.

36.

37.

38.

39.

40.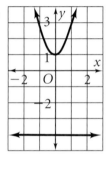

Preparing for the Math A Exam page 265

1. 2   **3.** 1   **5.** 4   **7.** 4

CHAPTER 6

Toolbox page 268

1. 4 and 8   **3a.** about 2:13 P.M.   **3b.** about 13.5 mi

Lesson 6-1 pages 269–274

ON YOUR OWN

1. no solution;

3. (1, 1);

5. infinitely many solutions;

7. yes   **9.** yes   **11a.** No; the graphs are not straight lines.   **11b.** The solution of the system is the point in time when the fear of commitment is equal to the fear of baldness.   **11c.** The solution on Lily's chart shows the point in time when the level of hope of meeting Brad Pitt is equal to the level of fear of cellulite.   **11d.** feelings; time

13. (1, 3);

15. (0, 0);

17. (3, −4);

19. no solution;

21. $(0, -1)$;

23. no solutions

25. True; the graphs of lines can intersect once, not intersect, or be the same line. **27.** False; the system may have no solutions. **29.** parallel; no solutions **31.** intersect; one solution **33.** same line; infinitely many solutions **35.** intersect; one solution **41a.** $(2, 200)$ **41b.** Both studios charge $200 rent for 2 h. **43.** $(4.5, 6.5)$ **45.** $(4, -6)$

MIXED REVIEW 47. $\frac{1}{36}$ **49.** 1 **51.** $b \le 6$ **53a.** about 138.5 mi² **53b.** about 72 million **55.** $x = 8y$ **57.** $x = \frac{3}{2}y + \frac{5}{2}$

Lesson 6-2   pages 275–279

ON YOUR OWN 1. one **3.** no solution **5.** infinitely many solutions **7.** one **9.** 12 cm by 3 cm **11.** $(2, 4)$ **13.** $(-\frac{1}{2}, -\frac{1}{2})$ **15.** $(2, \frac{1}{2})$ **17.** $(-\frac{1}{2}, 0)$ **19.** $(3, 5)$ **21.** infinitely many solutions

23. $(\frac{1}{2}, 1)$;

---

25. $(-1, 1)$;

27. no solution;

29. D **31.** C **33.** A **35.** infinitely many solutions **37.** no solution **39.** 160 acres of soybeans; 80 acres of corn **41.** $(3, -3)$ **43.** $(\frac{1}{4}, 0)$ **45.** $(12, -8)$ **47.** $(-2, -5)$

MIXED REVIEW 49. $7; -4$ **51.** $9; 0$ **53.** $y = \frac{3}{2}x$ **55.** $-7x$ **57.** $15x$

Lesson 6-3   pages 280–284

ON YOUR OWN 1. Add equations; $(5, -6)$ **3.** Multiply the first equation by 4; $(5, 4)$ **5.** Add equations; $(2, -3)$ **7.** Subtract first equation from second; $(4, 2)$ **9.** Brass parts cost $6; steel parts cost $3. **11.** $(5, 2)$ **13.** $(1, 3)$ **15.** $(-4.5, 8)$ **17.** $(14, 14)$ **19.** $(-\frac{2}{3}, 2)$ **21.** $(2, 0)$ **23.** infinitely many solutions **25.** $(2\frac{1}{2}, 3\frac{1}{2})$ **27.** 3 V, 1.5 V

29. Agree; you do not need to solve an equation for y before substituting the values. **31.** infinitely many solutions **33.** $(18, 52)$ **35.** $(3, 4)$ **37.** $(1\frac{1}{2}, -\frac{1}{2})$ **39a.** $(81.25, 8.125)$ **39b.** Room for one night costs $81.25 per person; the average cost of one meal is about $8.13.

MIXED REVIEW 41. $x = 0$ **43.** $x = 10$ **45.** $2s + d = 6.50$ **47.** $5p + 2n = 32$

CHECKPOINT 1. $(-1\frac{2}{9}, 3\frac{1}{9})$ **2.** $(3, -4)$ **3.** $(9, 10)$ **4.** $(2, -5\frac{1}{3})$ **5.** Sample: $2x - y = 3$; $\frac{1}{2}x + \frac{1}{2}y = 6$ **6a.** $(p, c) = (20, 33)$

ON YOUR OWN　1. 72.5° and 107.5°　**3.** 7 dimes and 3 nickels　**5.** $(\frac{1}{3}, 2\frac{1}{3})$　**7.** $(5, 1)$　**9.** no solution
11. $(0, 0)$　**13a.** $m = 254 + 400 + 1.2n$
13b. $m = 4n + 150$　**13c.** 180 tickets　**15.** 577 games
17. C　**19.** Sample: Substitution; at least one equation is solved for one of the variables.
21. Sample: Elimination; coefficients match well for subtraction.　**23.** Sample: Substitution; coefficients -1 and 1 make it easy to solve either equation for one of the variables.　**25a.** $2s + t = 12$　**25b.** $s = 3t$
25c. $5\frac{1}{7}, 5\frac{1}{7}, 1\frac{5}{7}$

MIXED REVIEW　27. -2　**29.** 25 or -17
31. \$130 billion

33. 　**35.**

ON YOUR OWN　1. A　**3.** B　**5.** 1 and 3
9. 　**11.**

13. 　**15.**

17. 　**19.**

21. 　**23.**

25. $y < x + 2$　**27.** $y > 2x + 1$　**29.** $y \le \frac{1}{3}x - 2$
31. $x > 0$;

33. $y \ge 0$; 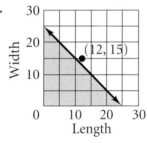　　　　**35a.** $2x + 2y \le 50$

35b.

Width vs Length graph, point (12, 15)

35d. No; $2(12) + 2(15) \le 50$ is false. On the graph, $(12, 15)$ is not in the shaded region.　**37.** yes
39. yes

MIXED REVIEW　41. 5　**43.** $\frac{8}{3}$　**45.** 1.2 h　**47.** $(3, 5)$
49. $(4\frac{2}{3}, 37\frac{1}{3})$

1.

Selected Answers

3.

5.

7.

13.

15.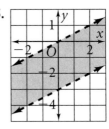

17a. $0.6f + 0.55c \leq 33; f \geq 9; c \geq 12$

17b.

17c. Sample: $(20, 20)$ **17d.** Sample: $(40, 25)$

23.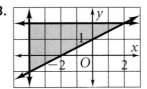

23a. triangle   **23b.** $(-4, -1), (-4, 2), (2, 2)$
23c. 9 sq. units

25.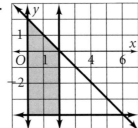

Lesson 6-6	pages 295–299

ON YOUR OWN   1. C   **3.** The point is on the boundary line of $2x + y > 2$, so it is not a solution of $2x + y > 2$.

5.

7. no solution;

9.

11.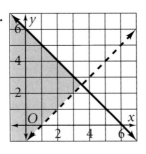

25a. trapezoid   **25b.** $(0, -4) \, (0, 2), (2, 0), (2, -4)$
25c. 10 sq. units   **27a.** $5.99x + 9.99y \leq 50; x \geq 0;$
$y \geq 1$

27b.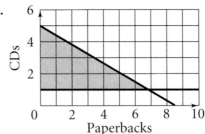

27c. 2 books and 6 CDs; $(2, 6)$ is not a solution of the system because 2 books and 6 CDs cost $71.92.
27d. 5 CDs, no books   **27e.** 8 books

MIXED REVIEW   29. 1   **31.** 4   **33.** 4   **35.** 22
37. 62   **39.** 1350

CHECKPOINT

1.

2.

3.

4.
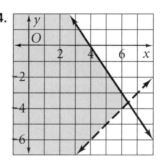

5. D   **6a.** $p = 7 + 0.75t$; $p = 8 + 0.5t$ **6b.** $(4, 10)$; a pizza with 4 toppings costs $10 in each restaurant.

Lesson 6-7   pages 300–304

ON YOUR OWN   1. 24, 32, 34, 30; $(3, 5), (8, 0)$
3. 0, 100, 400, 800; $(20, 10), (0, 0)$ **5.** $(6, 0)$
7. $(4, 0)$ **9.** 0; 36   **11.** 1; 8   **13.** $c = 8d + 20t$
15b. $N = 30x + 40y$

15c. 400 ft^2 at Location A and 100 ft^2 at Location B

MIXED REVIEW   17. $y = -\frac{1}{2}x + 2\frac{1}{2}$ **19.** $y = \frac{8}{3}x$
21. quadratic   **23.** linear

Lesson 6-8   pages 305–309

ON YOUR OWN   1. $(0, 0), (2, 4)$ **3.** $(0, 0)$
5. $(-2, -2), (2, -2)$ **7.** $(-2, 1), (2, 1)$

9. $(-1.94, 0.15),$
   $(1.94, 0.15)$

11. A; $(-1, -2), (1, -2)$ **13.** C; no solution   **15.** D
21. no solution;

23. $(-2, 3), (1, 0)$;

25. no solution;

27. $(-1, -2), (1, -2)$;

29. no solution;

Xmin=–5   Ymin=–10
Xmax=5   Ymax=10
Xscl=1   Yscl=1

31. $(-2, 1), (4, 4)$;

Intersection
X=-2   Y=1

MIXED REVIEW   **35.** 106.25%   **37.** 6.5%

39. 91,800   **41.** $\begin{bmatrix} 7-x & x-5 \\ -3x & -y \\ 8z & 0 \end{bmatrix}$

43a. 1000000*B2/C2   **43b.** D2: 1576; D3: 2423

Wrap-Up pages 311–313

1. $x = 3, y = 1; (3, 1)$ **2.** $y = -\frac{3}{2}x - \frac{3}{2}, y = \frac{3}{2}x + \frac{3}{2}$;
$(-1, 0)$ **3.** $y = x - 1, y = -x + 3; (2, 1)$
4. $x = -1, y = -x + 1; (-1, 2)$

5. $(1, 2)$;

6. $(-1, 2)$;

7. no solution;

8. $(1, -1)$;

9. $(-2, 5)$ **10.** $\left(-4\frac{1}{2}, -6\right)$ **11.** $(2, 2)$

12. $\left(-1\frac{1}{9}, -\frac{5}{9}\right)$ **14.** $(-6, 23)$ **15.** $(1, -1)$ **16.** $(6, 4)$

17. $(12, 6)$ **18.** $10\frac{2}{3}$ fl oz   **19.** 63° and 27°

20.

21.

22.

23.

24.

25.

26.

27.

29. 0; 21;

30. 3; 7.5;

31. 0; 18;

32. 7; 16;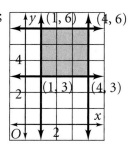

33. E

34. $(2, 0), (-3, 5)$;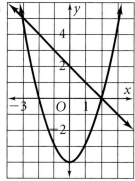

35. $(2, 1), (-\frac{2}{3}, -1\frac{2}{3})$;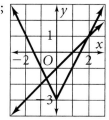

36. $(0, 3), (2, 1)$;

37. $(-1, 4), (3, 12)$

38. 0, 1, 2, 3, or 4; the number of solutions of a system with an absolute value equation and a quadratic equation correspond to the number of times the graphs of the equations intersect. It is possible for the graphs to intersect 0, 1, 2, 3, or 4 times. The graphs cannot intersect more than 4 times. **39.** 9 **40.** 49 **41.** 20.25 **42.** $\frac{1}{4}$ **43.** 121 **44.** 67.24

45.

46.

47.

48. 1   **49.** 109   **50.** 64   **51.** 17   **52.** 11   **53.** 170.24

> **Preparing for the Math A Exam** page 315

1. 1   **3.** 4   **5.** 2   **7.** 1

CHAPTER 7

> **Lesson 7-1**   pages 318–322

ON YOUR OWN   1. 1; 2; 4   **3.** −1, −3, −9
5. upward; min.   **7.** downward; max.

9.

11.

13.

15.

17. $y = x^2, y = 3x^2, y = 7x^2$ **19.** $y = -\frac{2}{3}x^2,$
$y = -2x^2, y = -4x^2$ **21.** K; L   **23.** K
29. narrower   **31.** narrower   **35.** E   **37.** F   **39.** C

MIXED REVIEW   41. 40% increase
43a. 199,980,000 Slinkies   **43b.** about 33 lb
43c. about 24,048 mi; about 7655 mi

45.

> **Lesson 7-2**   pages 323–326

ON YOUR OWN   3. maximum   **5.** maximum

7.

9.

11.

13.

15.

17.

21. E   **23.** F   **25.** C   **27.** E   **29.** E, F   **31.** G

33a.

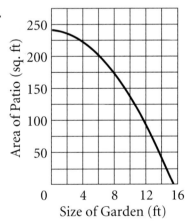

33b. $0 < x < 12$; the length of the side of the garden must be positive and shorter than 12 ft, the shorter side of the patio.   **33c.** $96 < y < 240$; the larger the garden the smaller the area of the patio. As the length of the side of the garden changes from 0 to 12 ft, the value of the function changes from 240 to 96.

MIXED REVIEW   **35.** $y = -\frac{1}{5}x + \frac{7}{5}$

37. $y = -2x - 18$ **39.** $y = -\frac{1}{4}x + 3$

41. about \$129,067   **43.** $\frac{1}{16}$

ON YOUR OWN   **1.** $x = 0$; $(0, 4)$ **3.** $x = -1$; $(-1, -7)$ **5.** $x = 0$; $(0, -3)$ **7.** $x = -2$; $(-2, -1)$ **9.** $x = 0$; $(0, 12)$ **11.** E   **13.** F   **15.** D

17.

19.

21.

23.

25.

Selected Answers

27.

29. 20 ft; 400 ft² **31.**

33. **35.**

37. **39.**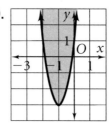

MIXED REVIEW **43.** $\frac{1}{4}$ **45.** $\frac{1}{4}$ **47a.** 10.1 mi/h
47b. 569 strokes **49.** -1 **51.** -36

Lesson 7-4 pages 332–336

ON YOUR OWN **1.** ± 13 **3.** $\pm\frac{1}{3}$ **5.** ± 0.5 **7.** ± 1.1
9. irrat. **11.** irrat. **13.** 5 and 6 **15.** -16 and -15

17. 3.46 **19.** 107.47 **21a.** about 0.93 **21b.** about
4.6 ft **23.** ± 0.6 **25.** $\pm\frac{5}{4}$ **27.** ± 20 **29.** ± 25
31. $\pm\frac{1}{9}$ **33.** ± 27 **35a.** about 8400 km
35b. about 7700 km **37.** 4 **39.** $-\frac{2}{5}$ **41.** $\frac{1}{6}$
43. -12.53 **45.** -3.61 **47.** 33 **49.** 6.40
53. irrat. **55.** rat. **57.** irrat. **59.** undefined
61. true **63.** false; $-5 < -\sqrt{17} < -4$ **65.** false;
$-17 < -\sqrt{280} < -16$ **67.** false; $-37 <$
$-\sqrt{1300} < -36$ **69.** true

MIXED REVIEW

71. $s < -2$;

73. $b < -6$;

75. $c \le \frac{1}{7}$;

77. $t > 1\frac{2}{3}$;

79. $13\frac{2}{3}$ **81.** 0

CHECKPOINT

1. $(0, 0)$; **2.** $(0, 7)$;

3. $(-1, 11)$;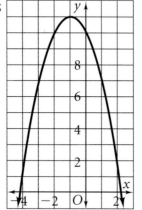

4. 2.65 **5.** -10 **6.** 4.80 **7.** 12 **8.** -12.25 **9.** $-\frac{1}{3}$

ON YOUR OWN **1.** $-2, 2$ **3.** no solution **5.** no solution **7.** $-\frac{3}{7}, \frac{3}{7}$ **9.** $-\frac{5}{2}, \frac{5}{2}$ **11.** 0 **13.** Sample: Michael used -5 and 5 as square roots of -25, which does not have a real number square root. **15.** $-2.8, 2.8$ **17.** $-1.4, 1.4$ **19.** $-4.6, 4.6$ **21.** 3.6 in. **23.** False; there are no solutions. **25.** False; there are two solutions **27.** true; $-8, 8$ **29.** true **31.** 11.2 ft **33.** 2.5 s **37.** $-2.5, 2.5$ **39.** $-2.4, 2.4$ **41.** $-2, 2$

MIXED REVIEW **43.** $(2, 3)$ **45.** $(15, -15)$ **47.** 3.16 **49.** 4.69

1. about 10.78, 13.22 **3.** $-2, 1\frac{1}{2}$ **5.** about 0.28, 17.72 **7.** $-12, 6$

ON YOUR OWN **1.** $3x^2 + 13x - 10 = 0$ **3.** $x^2 - 5x - 7 = 0$ **5.** $12x^2 - 25x + 84 = 0$ **7.** $-1.67, 0.5$ **9.** $-4.65, 4.65$ **11.** $-2.2, 3$ **13.** $0, 0.56$ **15.** $-1.78, 0.28$ **17.** $-1.5, -1$ **19b.** about 356.9 million **19c.** 2007 **21.** $-6, 6$ **23.** $-1.41, 1.41$ **25.** $-2, -3$ **27.** $-2, 3$ **29.** $-0.39, 1.72$ **31.** $-1.43, 2.23$ **35a.** 630 ft **35b.** 0 ft **35c.** about 6.3 s

MIXED REVIEW **37.** $\frac{1}{4}$ **39.** 0 **41.** 41 **43.** 24 **45.** 49

CHECKPOINT **1.** $-8.06, 8.06$ **2.** $-2, 2$ **3.** $-11, 11$ **4.** $1, 3$ **5.** $-1, 0.4$ **6.** $0.23, 3.27$ **7.** D

1. $y = x^2 + 6x + 8$ **3.** $y = 2x^2 + 6x - 8$

ON YOUR OWN **1.** C **3.** A **5.** 1 **7.** 2 **9.** 2 **11.** 0 **13.** 1 **15.** 2 **17a.** no value of x **17b.** Yes; $266 = -x^2 + 3x + 270$ transforms to $-x^2 + 3x + 4 = 0$. The discriminant is positive. **19.** A **21.** Rational; the square root of the discriminant is a positive integer. **23.** 2 **25.** 2 **27.** 0 **29.** 0 **31.** B

33. no **35.** yes; $(\frac{2}{3}, 0), (-1, 0)$ **37.** yes; $(-1, 0)$, $(2\frac{1}{2}, 0)$ **39.** no **41a.** $A2^2 - 4$; $A2^2 - 8$

41b. for integer values ≤ -2 or ≥ 2 **41c.** integer values between -2 and 2

MIXED REVIEW **43.**   **45.**

47. 3 **49.** -4

5.   **6.**

7.   **8.**

9. min. **10.** max. **11.** min. **12.** max.

13.

14.   **15.**

16.   **17.**

18.

19. irrat.   20. rat.   21. irrat.   22. rat.   23. irrat.
24. rat.   25. 3   26. -6.86 27. 0.6   28. 11.83
29. -1 30. 14   31. B   32. False; there are two
solutions.   33. true; $-3, 3$ 34. $-2, 2$ 35. $-5, 5$
36. 0   37. no solution   38. 2.3 in.   39. $-1.84, 1.09$
40. 0.5, 3   41. 0.13, 7.87   42. $-5.48, 5.48$ 43. 1.5 s
44. 49; 2   45. 112; 2   46. $-39; 0$ 48. $3^2\, 5^3$
49. $8^3\, x^4$ 50. $h^5\, w^2$ 51. 5000   52. 0   53. 80,000
54. 9   55. -720 56. 0.7   57. 36   58. 12   59. $\frac{1}{3}$

Preparing for the Math A Exam   page 359

1. 4   3. 1   5. 3   7. 2   9. 1

CHAPTER 8

Lesson 8-1   pages 362–366

ON YOUR OWN

1.

Time	Time Periods	Pattern	Number of Bacteria Cells
Initial	0	75	75
20 min	1	$75 \cdot 2$	$75 \cdot 2^1 = 150$
40 min	2	$75 \cdot 2 \cdot 2$	$75 \cdot 2^2 = 300$
60 min	3	$75 \cdot 2 \cdot 2 \cdot 2$	$75 \cdot 2^3 = 600$
80 min	4	$75 \cdot 2 \cdot 2 \cdot 2 \cdot 2$	$75 \cdot 2^4 = 1200$

There will be more than 30,000 bacteria cells after
3 h.   **3.** equal   **5.** $100x^2$ **7.** 4, 16, 64, 256, 1024;
increasing   **9.** 1, 1, 1, 1, 1; neither   **11.** 0.5, 0.25,
0.125, 0.0625, 0.03125; decreasing   **13.** 40, 400,
4000, 40,000, 400,000; increasing   **15.** B   **19.** 1.5625
21. 0.2   **23.** I: A; II: C; III. B

25a.

x	y
1	-2
2	4
3	-8
4	16
5	-32
6	64

25b. Sample: The positive and negative values alternate. The absolute values of the output are the same as the absolute values of the output of 2^x.
25c. No; the shape of the graph cannot be similar to the shape of the graph of an exponential function.

27.

29.

31.

MIXED REVIEW **33.** 1, −4   **35.** 2, 3   **37.** {2, 4, 8, 16, 32}   **39.** {1, 2, 4, 8, 16}   **41.** {6, 12, 24, 48, 96}

Lesson 8-2   pages 367–372

ON YOUR OWN   **1.** 20; 2   **3.** 10,000; 1.01
5. 50%   **7.** 4%   **9.** 1.04   **11.** 1.037   **13.** 1.005
15. x = number of years; y = population;
$y = 130{,}000 \cdot 1.01^x$ **17.** x = number of months;
y = deposit with interest; $y = 3000 \cdot \left(1 + \frac{0.05}{12}\right)^x$
19a. $355   **19b.** 8%   **19c.** about $766   **21.** E

---

23. linear   **25.** exponential

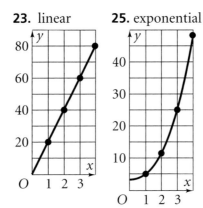

27. Linear; graph is a straight line.   **29.** Exponential; graph curves upward.   **31.** $y = 20{,}000 \cdot \left(1 + \frac{0.035}{4}\right)^{4x}$; $28,338.18   **33.** $y = 2400 \cdot (1 + 0.07)^x$; $4721.16

MIXED REVIEW   **35.** $\left(-\frac{1}{3}, -8\frac{1}{3}\right)$; minimum
37. $(0, -11)$; minimum   **39.** $\frac{1}{4}$ **41.** $\frac{3}{4}$ **43.** 0.9604

Lesson 8-3   pages 373–377

ON YOUR OWN   **1.** exponential growth
3. exponential growth   **5.** 0.5   **7.** $\frac{2}{3}$ **9.** 10%
11. 50%   **13.** 4 da   **15.** 2.5 yr

17. exponential decay   **19.** exponential decay

Xmin=0	Ymin=0
Xmax=5	Ymax=70
Xscl=1	Yscl=10

Xmin=0	Ymin=0
Xmax=3	Ymax=3.5
Xscl=1	Yscl=0.5

21. exponential decay   **23.** exponential decay

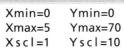

Xmin=0	Ymin=0
Xmax=3	Ymax=0.2
Xscl=1	Yscl=0.05

Xmin=0	Ymin=0
Xmax=5	Ymax=0.5
Xscl=1	Yscl=0.1

27. $y = 900 \cdot 0.8^x$; \$235.93   **29a.** $y = 161{,}000 \cdot 0.99^x$
29b. 145,606   **29c.** 119,092   **31.** 0.97   **33.** 0.974
35. 0.993   **37a.** about 4 h   **37b.** about $\frac{1}{4}$

37c. $\frac{15 \cdot 0.84^8}{15} = 0.247875891 \approx \frac{1}{4}$ **39.** 4 half-lives

MIXED REVIEW   **41.** $x < -3$ **43.** $-3, 3$ **45.** 4
47. 4; 16; $\frac{1}{4}$

CHECKPOINT   **1.** $y = 65{,}000 \cdot 1.032^x$; \$104,257.86
2. $y = 200{,}000 \cdot 0.95^x$; 71,697   **3.** $y = 300 \cdot 2^x$;
x = ten-year period; \$9600   **4.** B

5. exponential growth   **6.** exponential decay

7. exponential growth

1. $y = 13.65799901 \cdot 1.105628281^x$

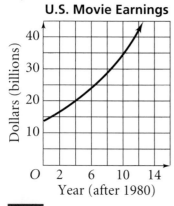

U.S. Movie Earnings

3a. Use $x = 0$ for 1970; $y = 1.040248033 \cdot 1.01999578^x$; 2.297 million

Population of New Mexico

(population in 2010)

ON YOUR OWN   **1.** -1 **3.** $-\frac{1}{5}$ **5.** 8   **7.** 9   **9.** $\frac{1}{64}$
11. 45   **13.** 6   **15.** $\frac{1}{20}$ **17.** $\frac{1}{4}$ **19a.** 5^{-2}; 5^{-1}; 5^0
or 1; 5^1; 5^2 **19b.** 5^4 **19c.** a^n **21.** x^7 **23.** $\frac{1}{625x^4}$

25. $\frac{1}{a^4}$ **27.** $\frac{12x}{y^3}$ **29.** $\frac{5a}{c^5}$ **31.** $\frac{8c^3}{a^5d^3}$ **33.** $\frac{7t^3}{5s^5}$ **35.** $\frac{a^3}{b^3}$

37. $\frac{mq^2}{n^4}$ **39.** $\frac{2}{9}$ **41.** $\frac{1}{16}$ **43.** -64

45.   **47.**

49. I

51.

a	4	0.2	$\frac{1}{3}$	6	$\frac{7}{8}$	2
a^{-1}	$\frac{1}{4}$	5	3	$\frac{1}{6}$	$\frac{8}{7}$	0.5

53. positive   **55.** negative   **57.** positive   **59.** -3
61. 0; -3 **63.** -3; -2 **65.** -2; -3 **67.** A, B, D
69a. 10^{-15} m   **69b.** 10^{-6} m   **69c.** 10^{-10} m
71. about 2 students; about 16 students; about 29 students

73.

75a. $\frac{1}{2}, \frac{1}{4}, \frac{1}{8}, \frac{1}{16}$ **75b.** $2^{-1}, 2^{-2}, 2^{-3}, 2^{-4}$
75c. $r = 2^{-n}$ **75d.** 2^{-10} or $\frac{1}{2^{10}}$

MIXED REVIEW

77.

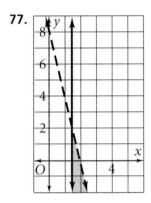

79a. $b = 31.17p$ **79b.** $124.68 **81.** 0.07
83. 0.003 **85.** 3067.85

Lesson 8-5	pages 385–389

ON YOUR OWN **1.** $10^{-3}, 10^{-1}, 10^0, 10^1, 10^5$
3. $4.1 \times 10^4, 4 \times 10^5, 4.02 \times 10^5, 4.1 \times 10^5$
5. 2.3×10^8 **7.** 2.7×10^{-7} **9.** 2.579×10^{-4}
11. 9.04×10^9 **13.** 9.2×10^{-4} **15.** 3.7×10^{11}
17. 4.18×10^{10} **19.** 6.29×10^{16} **21.** 3.3×10^{-8}
23. 8.35×10^{-5} **25.** 4.18×10^5 **27.** 1.28×10^{-2}
29. 4×10^{-6} **33.** 0.000 004 69 **35.** 50,000,000,000
37. 5.6×10^{-2} **39.** 6×10^2 **41.** 2×10^{-8}
43. about 1.5×10^{-4} **45.** about 5×10^2 s

47. 7×10^{-3} **49.** 9×10^1 **51.** 5×10^7 **53.** about
$3426 per person

MIXED REVIEW **55.** $\begin{bmatrix} -3.2 & 2.4 \\ 4.1 & -1.2 \end{bmatrix}$ **57.** t^7
59. $5^3 s^3$

Toolbox	page 390

1. 6 **3.** 3 **5.** 1.02×10^{-4} **7.** 2.53×10^5
9. 7.25×10^5

Lesson 8-6	pages 391–395

ON YOUR OWN **1.** $x^4 \cdot x^3 = x^7$ **3.** $x^{-2} \cdot x^{-5} = x^{-7}$ **5.** -4 **7.** 5 **9.** -4 **11.** $2; -3$ **13.** 8×10^5
15. 6×10^9 **17.** 4×10^3 **21.** 1 **23.** $3r^5$ **25.** $a^8 b^3$
27. $3x^4$ **29.** -0.99^3 **31.** b^3 **33.** -7 **35.** $-45a^4$
37. $\frac{b^2}{c^6}$ **39.** $12a^6 c^8$ **41.** $a^8 b$ **43.** a^5 **45.** $6a^3 + 10a^2$
47. $-8x^5 + 36x^4$ **49a.** Jerome's work; Jeremy
added exponents having different bases. **49b.** $a^3 b^6$
51. $6x^3 + 2x^2$ **53.** $4y^5 + 8y^2$ **55.** $3(-2)x^{2+4} = -6x^6$ **57.** $x^{6+1+3} = x^{10}$ **59a.** about 10^{-7} m
59b. longer

MIXED REVIEW **61.** irrational **63.** rational; $\frac{1}{2}$
65. rational; $\frac{3}{4}$ **67.** 3^6 **69.** 5^{28}

CHECKPOINT **1.** 1 **2.** $\frac{1}{9}$ **3.** $-\frac{1}{8}$ **4.** 125 **5.** -16
6. $-\frac{1}{8}$ **7.** s^3 **8.** $21ab^2$ **9.** -1 **10.** $\frac{g^3}{h^4}$ **11.** $\frac{y^6}{x^5}$
12. 1.5×10^7 **13.** 8×10^{-8} **14.** 3×10^{11}
15. 2.4×10^4 **16a.** $3 \times 10^6; 9 \times 10^4$
16b. about 462

18.

19.

20.

Lesson 8-7	pages 396–400

ON YOUR OWN   1. x^9y^9 **3.** a^6b^{12} **5.** $\frac{1}{g^{40}}$ **7.** $x^{12}y^4$
9. 16   **11.** g^{10} **13.** s^{11} **15.** $\frac{m^4}{g^4}$ **17.** 1   **19.** $64a^9b^6$
21. 1   **23.** 10,000   **25.** b^{3n+2} **27.** 1   **29a.** about
$5.15 \times 10^{14}\,\text{m}^2$ **29b.** about $3.6 \times 10^{14}\,\text{m}^2$
29c. about $1.37 \times 10^{18}\,\text{m}^3$ **31.** 8×10^{-9}
33. 3.6×10^{25} **35.** 6.25×10^{-18} **41.** 3   **43.** 4
45. 0   **47.** 6   **49.** 3   **51.** 1.1×10^{18} insects
53. $(ab)^5$ **55.** $\left(\frac{2}{xy}\right)^2$

MIXED REVIEW   57. -1 **59.** $\frac{1}{x}$ **61.** $\frac{1}{t^5}$

Lesson 8-8	pages 401–405

ON YOUR OWN   1. $\frac{1}{4}$ **3.** $\frac{9}{16}$ **5.** $\frac{1}{9}$ **7.** y **9.** a^6
11. $-\frac{27}{8}$ **13.** $5^3 = 125$ **15.** $(2c)^4 = 16c^4$
17. $x^0 = 1$ **19.** 5×10^7 **21.** 9×10^2 **23.** about
1.52×10^{-6} **25a.** about 1642 h   **25b.** about
4.5 h/da   **27.** 4   **29.** 729   **31.** $2c^6$ **33.** $\frac{a^5}{b^3}$ **35.** $\frac{d^8}{c^5}$
37. $\frac{1}{25}$ **39.** $\frac{1}{c^{12}}$ **41.** $\frac{9}{25}$ **43.** $\frac{125n^3}{m^6}$ **45.** $\left(\frac{3}{5}\right)^5$
47. d^3 **49.** $\left(\frac{3x}{2y}\right)^3$ **51a.** about \$4013   **51b.** about
\$17,846   **51c.** about 345%   **53.** division and
negative exponent properties; $\frac{1}{2^3}$ **55.** multiplication
property; $\frac{1}{2^3}$

57a.

Mercury	≈ 1.52
Venus	≈ 1.01
Earth	≈ 1.03
Mars	≈ 1.21
Jupiter	≈ 1.10
Saturn	≈ 1.12
Uranus	≈ 1.10
Neptune	≈ 1.02
Pluto	≈ 1.67

57b. Pluto; its circularity is farthest from 1; Venus; its
circularity is closest to 1.

MIXED REVIEW   59. $0.6, -0.6$ **61.** -6

63.

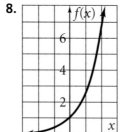

65. 3.26×10^{11} gal

Wrap-Up	pages 407–409

1. 6, 12, 24, 48   **2.** 7.5, 5.625, 4.21875   **3a.** 2430
bacteria   **3b.** about 178 min   **4.** growth; 3
5. growth; $\frac{3}{2}$ **6.** decay; 0.32   **7.** decay; $\frac{1}{4}$

8.

9.

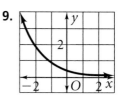

10.

[graph showing f(x)]

11.

[graph showing y]

12. 2.5% inc.   **13.** 25% dec.   **14.** 100% inc.
15. 10% dec.   **16a.** $y = 100{,}000 \cdot 1.07^x$
16a. $y = 100{,}000 \cdot 1.07^x$ **16b.** 542,743
17a. $1250.18; $1267.37   **17b.** 6%; it pays more
interest.   **18.** 2.5 mCi   **19.** $\dfrac{d^6}{b^4}$ **20.** $\dfrac{y^8}{x^2}$ **21.** $\dfrac{7h^3}{k^8}$

22. $\dfrac{q^4}{p^2}$ **23.** $\dfrac{3^4}{2^4}$ or $\dfrac{81}{16}$ **24.** Yes, if $b = 0$; no if $b \neq 0$.

25. C   **26.** 9.5×10^7 **27.** 7.235×10^9 **28.** yes   **29.**
8.4×10^{-4} **30.** 2.6×10^{-4} **31.** 2.793×10^6 **32.**
1.89×10^8 **33.** 1.606×10^8 **34.** 4.6×10^{-9} **35.**
1.4168×10^7 **36.** 1×10^{-12} **37.** $2d^5$ **38.** $q^{12}r^4$

39. $-20c^4m^2$ **40.** 1.7956   **41.** $\dfrac{243}{64}x^2y^{14}$

42. Sample: about 7.8×10^3 pores   **44.** $\dfrac{1}{w^3}$ **45.** $\dfrac{1}{64}$

46. yes   **47.** $\dfrac{n^{35}}{v^{21}}$ **48.** $\dfrac{c^3}{e^{11}}$ **49.** $s^{15}x^{45}$ **50.** 2×10^{-3}
51. 2.5×10^1 **52.** 5×10^{-5} **53.** 3×10^3 **55.** 2
56. 11   **57.** 6   **58.** $77r + 28rx$ **59.** $24m - 16mt$
60. $8b + 2b^2$ **61.** $5p + 6d$ **62.** n **63.** 61   **64.** 65
65. $13t^2$ **66.** $4y^2$ **67.** $19; about $48.86   **68.** 5 kg;
4.5 kg   **69.** 0.4 min; 1.24 min

Preparing for the Math A Exam page 411

1. 2   **3.** 3   **5.** 4   **7.** 3   **9.** 2

CHAPTER 9

Lesson 9-1   pages 414–418

ON YOUR OWN   **1.** 10   **3.** 2.2   **5.** 7.1   **7.** 5.7   **9.** 20
11. 66.1   **13a.** $6^2 + 8^2 = 100$ and $10^2 = 100$

13b.

a	b	c
3	4	5
5	12	13
7	24	25
9	40	41

13c. Sample: 8, 15, 17   **15.** 9.7   **17.** 559.9
19b. 6 in., $\sqrt{10^2 - 8^2}$; about 12.8 in., $\sqrt{10^2 + 8^2}$
21. yes; $9^2 + 12^2 = 15^2$ **23.** no; $2^2 + 4^2 \neq 5^2$
25. no; $4^2 + 4^2 \neq 8^2$ **27.** yes; $1.25^2 + 3^2 = 3.25^2$
29. yes; $14^2 + 48^2 = 50^2$ **31.** no; $1^2 + 1.5^2 \neq 2^2$
33. no; $4^2 + 5^2 \neq 6^2$ **35.** yes; $18^2 + 80^2 = 82^2$
37a. about 3610 ft   **37b.** about 180 ft/min; about
2 mi/h   **39.** 4.3 cm

MIXED REVIEW   **41.** $\dfrac{1}{2}, \dfrac{1}{2}$ **43.** 5   **45.** 8.5

Toolbox   page 419

1. yes   **3.** yes   **5.** yes   **7.** yes   **9.** no   **11.** yes
13. yes   **15.** yes

Lesson 9-2   pages 420–424

ON YOUR OWN   **1.** 10.6   **3.** 8.2   **5.** 11.3   **7.** 2.2
9. 11.2   **11.** 8.2   **13.** 14   **15.** 1.4

17a.

17b. $(0, -0.5)$ **17c.** The meeting point is 0.5 mi
south of the substation.   **19.** $(1\tfrac{1}{2}, 7\tfrac{1}{2})$ **21.** $(-2\tfrac{1}{2}, 3)$
23. $(-4, 4)$ **25.** $(8\tfrac{1}{2}, -9)$ **27.** $(7, 7)$ **29.** $(0, 0)$
31. 16   **33.** 21.6   **35.** x-coordinates are opposites;
y-coordinates are opposites.

43. $\frac{5}{13}, \frac{12}{13}, \frac{12}{5}$ **45.** 6.8 **47.** 7.28

Lesson 9-3 pages 425–429

ON YOUR OWN **1.** Sample: Kentucky and Virginia are adjacent states. **3.** $\frac{4}{5}$ **5.** $\frac{4}{5}$ **7.** $\frac{4}{3}$ **9.** 0.7660 **11.** 0.9962 **13.** $\frac{21}{29}, \frac{20}{29}, \frac{21}{20}$ **15.** $\frac{12}{13}, \frac{5}{13}, \frac{12}{5}$ **17.** 10.4 **19.** about 250 ft **21.** about 10,000 ft **23.** 78.4 **25.** 514.3

MIXED REVIEW

29. **31.**

33. 250 mi **35.** 13 **37.** -6

CHECKPOINT **1.** $c \approx 4.5$ **2.** $c \approx 5.8$ **3.** $c \approx 7.1$ **4.** $c = 5$ **5.** $b = 24$ **6.** $a \approx 8.5$ **7.** $b \approx 8.9$ **8.** $a = 15$ **10.** about 270 ft **11.** 3.2 **12.** 6.7 **13.** 9.8 **14.** 3.2 **16.** about 2.7 **17.** about 4.5

Lesson 9-4 pages 430–434

ON YOUR OWN **1.** no **3.** no **5.** no **7.** 16 **9.** 20 **11.** $10\sqrt{2}$ **13.** $875\sqrt{7}$ **15.** 72 **17.** $3\sqrt{17}$ **19.** $4\sqrt{6}$ **21.** 10 **23.** $5\sqrt{10}$ **25.** $\frac{3}{2}$ **27.** $\frac{5}{2}$ **29.** $\frac{2\sqrt{30}}{11}$ **31.** $\frac{3\sqrt{2}}{4}$ **33.** $\frac{13}{12}$ **35.** 1.2 m **37a.** $\sqrt{18} \cdot \sqrt{10} = \sqrt{180} = \sqrt{36 \cdot 5} = 6\sqrt{5}$ **39.** D **41.** $\frac{2\sqrt{a}}{a^2}$ **43.** $ab^2c\sqrt{abc}$ **45.** $2y^2$ **47.** $\frac{\sqrt{2x}}{3}$ **49.** $2\sqrt{3}$ **51.** $\frac{9\sqrt{2}}{4}$ **53.** $5\sqrt{5}$ **55.** $\frac{8\sqrt{6}}{3}$

MIXED REVIEW **57.** 3; 2 **59.** -5; 3 **61.** For c = crab and t = turkey, $5c + 3t \le 30$. **63.** -1 **65.** 10

Lesson 9-5 pages 435–439

ON YOUR OWN **1.** 42 **3.** $3\sqrt{2} + \sqrt{3}$ **5.** $6 - 2\sqrt{3}$ **7.** $3\sqrt{3} - 3\sqrt{2}$ **9.** $\sqrt{7}$ **11.** $3\sqrt{5} + 2\sqrt{3}$ **13.** $2\sqrt{3} + 2\sqrt{6} - 6$ **15.** $4 - 4\sqrt{2}$ **17.** 3.1 **19.** 15.8 **21.** 6.0 **23.** 8.5 **25.** -1.0 **27.** $2\sqrt{3} + 4\sqrt{2}$ **29.** -24 **31.** $6\sqrt{2} + 6\sqrt{3}$ **33.** $2\sqrt{17} + 17$ **37a.** $2\sqrt{6} + 4\sqrt{3}$ **37b.** Bill simplified $\sqrt{48}$ as $2\sqrt{24}$ instead of $2\sqrt{12}$ or $4\sqrt{3}$. **39.** $8\sqrt{2}$ **41.** $6\sqrt{10}$ **43.** E

MIXED REVIEW **45.** -3; 5; rational **47.** 1 **49.** 0

Lesson 9-6 pages 440–444

ON YOUR OWN **1.** 3 **3.** 27 **5.** 625 **7a.** 25 **7b.** $11\frac{1}{4}$ **9.** no solution **11.** $-\frac{1}{4}$ **13.** 0, 12 **15.** 7 **17.** 3 **19.** about 98.2 in.^{3} **21.** 2 **23.** 3, 6 **25.** no solution **27.** 4 **29.** 1, 6 **31a.** $V = 10x^2$ **31b.** $x = \frac{\sqrt{10V}}{10}$ **33.** -4 **35.** $-\frac{1}{2}$ **37.** none

MIXED REVIEW **39.** $\frac{1}{a^5b^5}$ **41.** $\frac{2}{xy^2}$ **43.** 0 **45.** 2

Lesson 9-7 pages 445–449

ON YOUR OWN **1.** $x \ge 2$ **3.** $x \ge 0$ **5.** $x \ge -7$ **7.** $x \ge -3$ **9.** $x \ge 5$ **11.** B **13.** A

15.

17.

19.

21.

23.

25.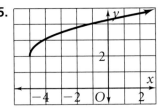

27. shift left 8   **29.** shift up 12

MIXED REVIEW

33. $(1, -1)$ **35.** 7.8   **37.** -1.8

CHECKPOINT   **1.** 9   **2.** 14   **3.** $8b^2\sqrt{b}$ **4.** $\sqrt{2}$
5. $3 + 4\sqrt{3}$ **6.** $2\sqrt{2}$ **7.** $\frac{x\sqrt{x}}{2}$ **8.** $2\sqrt{3}$ **9.** 68
10. 6   **11.** 8   **12.** 18

13.

14.

15.

16.

18. D

Toolbox	page 450

1.

3.

5.

7.

9b. 2; 33; 33   **9c.** 21 h; 23 h; both are much less than the typical 29-h week.

ON YOUR OWN

1.

x	$\bar{x}$	$x - \bar{x}$	$(x - \bar{x})^2$
5	5	0	0
3	5	−2	4
2	5	−3	9
5	5	0	0
10	5	5	25
		Sum:	38

standard deviation: about 2.8

3.

x	$\bar{x}$	$x - \bar{x}$	$(x - \bar{x})^2$
3.5	4	−0.5	0.25
4.5	4	0.5	0.25
6.0	4	2	4
4.0	4	0	0
2.5	4	−1.5	2.25
2.5	4	−1.5	2.25
5.0	4	1	1
		Sum:	10

standard deviation: about 1.2

5a. The data are spread far apart   **5b.** Most data are near 25.   **9a.** Sample: Lyman should have asked about the range and the standard deviation or the median salary and the mode. The range and the standard deviation would have told him that the salaries are widely distributed. The mode and the median, both $265, would have told him that the mean does not represent the data well.   **9b.** $1165   **9c.** Large; all the data are far from the mean.   **9d.** about 321.36 **11.** about 0.98   **13.** about 25.47   **15a.** $20 **15b.** about 5.83   **15c.** 6; 39

MIXED REVIEW   **17.** 3.47×10^{-3} **19.** 8.25×10^{-4} **21.** $(1, 2)$ **23.** $(5, 2)$ **25.** $x \geq 5$ **27.** $14,961.04

1. 5.83   **2.** 17.80   **3.** 14.76   **4.** 9.85   **6.** $(0.5, 5.5)$ **7.** $(5.5, 6)$ **8.** $(8.5, 3.5)$ **9.** $(2.5, 13)$ **11.** $BC \approx$ 6.71; $AC \approx 9.95$ **12.** $AC \approx 27.7$; $AB \approx 29.12$ **13.** $BC \approx 6.25$; $AB \approx 10.15$ **14.** C   **15.** $48\sqrt{2}$

16. $\frac{2\sqrt{21}}{11}$ **17.** $20\sqrt{6}$ **18.** $\frac{10}{13}$ **19.** $10\sqrt{2}$ cm by $70\sqrt{2}$ cm   **20.** $2\sqrt{7}$ **21.** $30\sqrt{5}$ **22.** $\sqrt{6}$ **23.** $2\sqrt{5}$ **24.** $10 - 10\sqrt{2}$ **25.** $25\sqrt{10}$ **26.** $18\sqrt{2}$ **27.** $17\sqrt{7}$ **28.** $\sqrt{29}$ in.   **29.** 2   **30.** 16   **31.** 8 **32.** 81   **33.** 2.93 in.

34. $x \geq 0$;

35. $x \geq 2$;

36. $x \geq -1$;

37. $x \geq 0$;

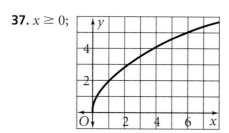

38. about 5.44   **39.** about 4.69   **40.** about 6.15   **41.** about 7.44   **42.** $0.64, -3.14$ **43.** $1.90, -1.23$ **44.** 4.70, -1.70 **45.** no solution   **46.** $2, -1.2$ **47.** $1.47, -1.75$

1. 2   **3.** 3   **5.** 4   **7.** 1

CHAPTER 10

ON YOUR OWN   **1.** C   **3.** E   **5.** A   **7.** $4x + 9$; linear binomial   **9.** $-11z^3 + 9z^2 + 5z - 5$; cubic with four terms   **11.** $c^2 + 4c - 2$; quadratic trinomial   **13.** $4q^4 + 3q^2 - 8q - 10$; fourth degree polynomial with four terms   **15.** $x^2 - 1$ **17.** $-6x^3 + 3x^2 - x - 4$ **19.** $7a^3 + 11a^2 - 4a - 2$ **21.** $6x^2 - 12$ **25.** $8y$ **27.** $28c - 16$ **31.** $5x + 18$ **33.** $6y + 2$ **35.** $-2x^2 - 7x - 11$ **37.** $2r^2 - r - 7$ **39.** $9b^4 - 3b^2 + 7b - 6$

MIXED REVIEW   **41.** 4^4 **43.** $\left(\frac{2}{3}\right)^4$ **45.** 5.0   **47.** 1.9   **49.** $2x - 6$ **51.** $15a - 21$

ON YOUR OWN   **1.** $3x + 12$ **3.** $4x^2 + 2x$ **5.** $8x^2 + 12x$

7.

$(x + 2)(3x) = 3x^2 + 6x$

9. $8x + 28$ **11.** $-54x^4 + 36x^2 - 48x$ **13.** $-12a^3 + 15a^2 - 27a$ **15.** $6p^5 - 15p^3$ **17.** $-4x^2 + 13x$ **19.** $x^2 + x$ **21.** 3   **23.** 12   **25.** 5   **27.** $3x$ **29.** $5s$ **31.** $8x^2$ **35a.** $V = 64s^3$ **35b.** $V = 48\pi s^2$ **35c.** $V = 64s^3 - 48\pi s^2$ **35d.** $V = 16s^2(4s - 3\pi)$ **35e.** about 182,071 in.^{3} **37.** $s(s^3 + 4s^2 - 2)$ **39.** $2x^2(1 - 2x^2)$ **41.** $7k(k^2 - 5k + 10)$ **43.** $3x(3 + 4x)$ **45.** $6m^2(m^4 - 4m^2 + 1)$ **47.** $m^2(5m - 7)$ **49.** $(x^2 - 7)(2x + 1)$ **51a.** 7; 4   **51b.** $n - 3$ **51c.** $\frac{1}{2}n^2 - \frac{3}{2}n$

MIXED REVIEW   **53.** $\frac{4}{5}$ **55.** $\frac{3}{5}$ **57.** $\frac{3}{4}$ **59.** $28x^3 - 48x^2 + 128x$

ON YOUR OWN   **1.** $x - 4$; $-x + 2$; $-x^2 + 6x - 8$ **3.** $x - 3$; $-x + 3$; $-x^2 + 6x - 9$ **5.** $x^2 - x - 20$ **7.** 30   **9.** 7   **11.** $x^2 + x - 42$ **13.** $2y^2 - y - 15$ **15.** $5y^2 + 12y - 32$ **17.** $a^3 - 6a^2 + 9a - 4$

19. $4t^3 - 22t^2 + 36t - 15$ **23.** $x^2 + 8x + 15$ **25.** $a^2 - 8a + 7$ **27.** $5a^2 + 13a - 6$ **29.** $-6y^2 + 20y - 14$ **33.** 1; rational   **35.** $26 + 10\sqrt{5}$; irrational

MIXED REVIEW   **37.** 2, −2   **39.** 2, −1   **41.** $(2x + 4)(3x + 5)$ **43.** $(-3x + 5)(4x + 1)$

CHECKPOINT   **1.** $3x^2 + 5x - 4$ **2.** $2a^3 + a^2 - 7$ **3.** $-2m^2 - 5m + 8$ **4.** $9x^2 - x - 8$ **5.** $-w^2 + 9$ **6.** $-6t^3 - 4t^2 + 12t$ **7.** $m^2 + m - 12$ **8.** $b^2 - 9b + 18$ **9.** $-3c(c^2 - 5c + 1)$ **10.** $5a(2a^2 + a + 1)$ **11.** $4p(2p^2 - 5p - 6)$ **12.** $x(x^2 + 4x + 7)$

1. $x^4 - x^3 + x^2$

3. $3x^2 + 2x - 1$

5. $x - 4 + \frac{7}{x + 4}$

7. $m^2 + 5m + 4$

ON YOUR OWN   **1.** $x + 3, x + 2$; $x^2 + 5x + 6$ **3.** $x + 2, x + 2$; $x^2 + 4x + 4$ **5.** No; no two numbers with product 8 can have sum 5.   **7.** Yes; $(x + 8)(x + 1) = x^2 + 9x + 8$

9.
$(x-2)(x-1)$

11.
$(x-4)(x+2)$

13.
$(x-4)(x+1)$

15.
$(x-1)(x-1)$

17. 2   **19.** -1 **21.** -3 **23a.** $x^2+15x+56$
23b. $(x+7)(x+8)$ **25.** $(a-2)(a-3)$
27. $(k+1)(k+8)$ **29.** $(r-11)(r+1)$
31. $(x+5)(x-3)$ **33.** $(x+5)(x+7)$
35. $(a-7)(a-2)$ **37.** $(y+16)(y-3)$
39. $(w-6)(w+4)$ **43.** $(2x-1)(x-7)$
45. $(2x-3)(x+1)$ **47.** $(2x+3)(x-7)$
49. $(2x-1)(x-3)$ **51.** $(7x+1)(x-3)$
53. $(3x+5)(x+4)$

MIXED REVIEW   **55.** 5   **57.** about 8.1

59.

61. 84   **63.** $4x^2+12x+9$ **65.** x^2-64
67. $4x^2-49$ **69.** $4x^2-4x+1$

Lesson 10-5   pages 486–490

ON YOUR OWN   **1.** $x^2+10x+25; x+5, x+5$
3. $9x^2+6x+1; 3x+1, 3x+1$ **5.** $(x+1)^2$
7. $(x-9)^2$ **9.** $3(x-1)^2$ **11.** $6(x+5)(x-5)$
13. $(x+7)(x-7)$ **15.** $(2x-1)^2$ **17.** $(3x+1)^2$
19. $(x+20)(x-20)$ **23a.** $3.14n^2-3.14m^2$;
$3.14(n+m)(n-m)$ **23b.** 285.74 in.^{2} **25.** 891

27. 1591   **29.** 384   **31.** 396   **33.** $\left(\frac{1}{2}m+\frac{1}{3}\right)\left(\frac{1}{2}m-\frac{1}{3}\right)$
35. $\left(\frac{1}{3}n+\frac{1}{5}\right)\left(\frac{1}{3}n-\frac{1}{5}\right)$ **37a.** $t-3; 4$
37b. $(t+1)(t-7)$
MIXED REVIEW   **39.** $5+6\sqrt{2}$ **41.** $\sqrt{41}$ **43.** 30%
45. $-\frac{4}{3}$ **47.** $\frac{5}{3}$

Lesson 10-6   pages 491–495

ON YOUR OWN   **1.** 3, 7   **3.** $-\frac{2}{7}, -\frac{4}{5}$ **5.** $-2, 7$
7. 5, 11   **9.** $-4, 3$ **11.** 0, 10   **13.** $-4, \frac{2}{5}$ **15.** $-1, 10$
17. 5 cm   **19.** $x^2-10x+24=0; 4, 6$ **21.** $2q^2+$
$22q+60=0; -6, -5$ **23.** $6n^2-5n-4=0;$
$-\frac{1}{2}, \frac{4}{3}$ **25.** $20p^2-80=0; -2, 2$ **27.** $4n^2-$
$100=0; 5, -5$ **29.** $9c^2-36=0; 2, -2$ **31.** 5 in.
33a. 10 ft base; 22 ft height   **33b.** about 24.2 ft
35. 0, 4, 6   **37.** 0, 3   **39.** 0, 1, 9   **41.** 3, 4, 5
43. 0, -1 **45.** 8 in. × 10 in.

MIXED REVIEW   **47.** $\frac{1}{3y^3}$ **49.** 1   **51.** $\frac{25}{3}$

53. 60 students   **55.** $\frac{1}{5}, -\frac{3}{2}$

CHECKPOINT   **1.** $(x-3)(x-2)$ **2.** $(n-3)^2$
3. $(g-10)(g+2)$ **4.** $(3x+7)(3x-7)$ **5.** $-3, \frac{2}{3}$
6. $6, -\frac{3}{2}$ **7.** $-7, -2$ **8.** $2, -2$ **9.** $-\frac{4}{3}$ **10.** $\frac{3}{2}, -\frac{2}{5}$
11. A

Toolbox   page 496

1. 4   **3.** 49   **5.** Sample: Divide the coefficient of
the first degree term in half and square the result.
7. $-6, -2$ **9.** $-8, 2$ **11.** $-6, 2$ **13.** $9, -5$
15. $-5 \pm \sqrt{35}$ **17.** $-4 \pm \sqrt{13}$

Lesson 10-7   pages 497–501

ON YOUR OWN   **1.** $-0.08, -13$ **3.** $1.25, -1.33$
5. no real solutions   **7.** $3, -3$ **9.** $2, -2$ **11a.** $-\frac{1}{2}, 3$
11b. $-\frac{1}{2}, 3$ **11c.** $(2x+1)(x-3)=0$, so $x=-\frac{1}{2}$ or
$x=3$.   **13.** $-4, 2$ **15.** no real solutions   **17.** no
real solutions   **19.** 4   **21.** $0, \frac{4}{5}$ **23.** $-1.85, 4.85$
25. 1.75   **27.** $\frac{13}{7}, -\frac{13}{7}$ **29.** B   **31.** about 167.7 ft

MIXED REVIEW **35.** 13; 28 **37.** the parabola $y = x^2$ shifted 2 units right, 1 unit down; $x = 2$; 3; 1 and 3.

1. $7x^3 + 8x^2 - 3x + 12$ **2.** $8g^4 - 5g^2 + 11g + 5$
3. $-b^5 + 2b^3 + 6$ **4.** $t^3 - 5t^2 + 12t - 8$
6. $-40x^2 + 16x$ **7.** $35g^3 + 15g^2 - 45g$
8. $-40t^4 + 24t^3 - 32t^2$ **9.** $5m^3 + 15m^2$
10. $-6w^4 - 8w^3 + 20w^2$ **11.** $-3b^3 + 5b^2 + 10b$
12. $3x$; $3x(3x^3 + 4x^2 + 2)$ **13.** $4t^2$; $4t^2(t^3 - 3t + 2)$ **14.** $10n^3$; $10n^3(4n^2 + 7n - 3)$ **15.** $x^2 + 8x + 15$ **16.** $15x^2 - 29x - 14$ **17.** $6x^2 + 11x - 10$ **18.** $-x^2 + 5x - 4$ **19.** $x^3 + 3x^2 + 3x + 2$ **20.** $4x^2 - 21x + 5$ **21.** $x^3 - 9x^2 + 18x + 8$ **22.** $3x^2 + 10x + 8$ **23.** $(2x + 1)(x + 4)$; $2x^2 + 9x + 4$ **24.** $(x + 2)(x + 1)$ **25.** $(y - 7)(y - 2)$ **26.** $(x - 5)(x + 3)$ **27.** $(2w - 3)(w + 1)$
28. $(-b + 4)(b - 3)$ **29.** $(2t - 1)(t + 2)$
30. $(x - 1)(x + 6)$ **31.** $2(3x + 2)(x + 1)$
32. A   **33.** $(q + 1)^2$ **34.** $(b - 4)(b + 4)$
35. $(x - 2)^2$ **36.** $(2t + 11)(2t - 11)$
37. $(2d - 5)^2$ **38.** $(3c + 1)^2$ **39.** $(3k + 5)(3k - 5)$
40. $(x + 3)^2$ **41.** The factors are equal.   **42.** -3, -4 **43.** $0, 2$ **44.** $4, 5$ **45.** $-3, \frac{1}{2}$ **46.** $-\frac{2}{3}, 1\frac{1}{2}$
47. $1, 4$ **48.** 10 ft by 17 ft   **49.** $-5, 5$
50. $-4.12, 0.78$ **51.** $0.18, 2.82$ **52.** 324 ft^2
53. $\frac{57}{10}$ **54.** $-\frac{33}{4}$ **55.** $\frac{157}{100}$ **56.** $\frac{52}{5}$ **57.** $-\frac{1849}{1000}$
58. $\frac{767}{100}$ **59.** $\frac{1}{3}$ **60.** $-1\frac{1}{2}$ **61.** $-\frac{3}{7}$ **62.** $\frac{10}{13}$ **63.** $7\frac{1}{2}$
64. $2\frac{1}{3}$ **65.** $9\frac{1}{6}$ **66.** 26

1. 1   **3.** 1   **5.** 2   **7.** 4   **9.** 2

CHAPTER 11

ON YOUR OWN   **1a.** 16 h; 10 h; 8 h; 4 h   **1b.** hourly wage and time worked   **1c.** $xy = 80$ **3.** 8   **5.** 7   **7.** 96
9. $\frac{1}{6}$ **11.** 20   **13.** 130   **15.** D   **17.** 1.1   **19.** 2.5
21. 375   **23a.** 120; distance from your house to the lake   **23b.** 3 h   **25.** 2.4 da   **27.** $y = 70x$

29. $xy = 48$ **31.** Direct; as s increases, P increases.
33. Inverse; as r increases, t decreases.

MIXED REVIEW   **37.** $(x + 5)^2$ **39.** $(x - 3)^2$ **41.** $\frac{1}{5}$
43. $\frac{3}{8}$ **45.** -1

1.

3.

5.

7.

9.

11.

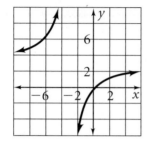

13a. The shapes of the graphs are the same, but they are in different positions along the *x*-axis. **13b.** The shapes of the graphs are the same, but they are in different positions along the *y*-axis.

Lesson 11-2   pages 516–521

ON YOUR OWN   **1.** $3; 0; \frac{1}{2}$ **3.** $\frac{1}{2}; -4; 8$ **5.** 0 **7.** -2
9. $x = 2, y = 0$ **11.** $x = 1, y = -1$

13.

15.

17.

19.

21.

23.

25a.

Xmin=0   Ymin=0
Xmax=6   Ymax=2000
Xscl=1   Yscl=200

$; d \geq 40$ **25b.** 16;
1600; 160,000

29.

31.

33.

35. **37.**

39.

41.

43.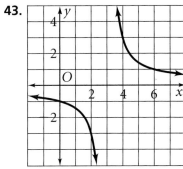

MIXED REVIEW **45.** $(g - 7)(g - 5)$
47. $(a + 7)(a - 1)$ **49.** $10 **51.** $0, 3$ **53.** $-4, 4$

CHECKPOINT **1.** 3 **2.** 2 **3.** 4

4.

5.

6.

7.

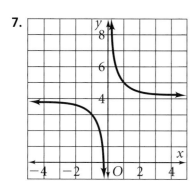

9. 91 lb

ON YOUR OWN   **1.** $\frac{a}{4}; a \neq 0$ **3.** $\frac{x-2}{x+2}; x \neq -2$

5. $\frac{2a+3}{4}$ **7.** $\frac{1}{7x}; x \neq 0$ **9.** $\frac{1}{2}; p \neq 12$ **11.** $\frac{2}{3}; x \neq 0,$

-1 **13.** $3x; x \neq 3$ **15.** $\frac{w}{w-7}; w \neq -7, 7$ **17.** $\frac{x^2-9}{x+3}$

does not have -3 in its domain.   **21.** $-\frac{125}{16}$ **23.** $\frac{12}{x}$

25. $2x$ **27.** $\frac{3x^4}{2}$ **29.** 6   **31.** $-\frac{1}{2}$ **33.** $\frac{11}{7k-15}$

35. $\frac{\frac{4}{3}\pi r^3}{\pi r^2} = \frac{r}{3}$ **37.** $\frac{5w}{5w+6}$ **39.** $\frac{3y}{4(y+4)}$

MIXED REVIEW   **41.** 3^{x+5} **43.** $-12m^4 - 18m$

45. $\frac{2}{3}$ **47.** $\frac{3}{5}$

ON YOUR OWN   **1.** $\frac{7}{5}$ **3.** $-\frac{2}{b}$ **5.** $\frac{4}{11g}$ **7.** $\frac{2}{d}$ **9.** $\frac{5n}{7}$

11. $\frac{26r}{5}$ **13.** $4x^2$ **15.** $2m^2$ **17.** $6t^5$ **19.** $46d^4$

21. $5a$ **23.** $35b^3$ **25.** $\frac{35a^3+6}{15a^4}$ **27.** $\frac{18+20x^2}{15x^8}$

29. $\frac{b^3-4}{2b^4}$ **31.** $\frac{9+2m}{24m^3}$ **33.** $-\frac{77}{36k}$ **35.** $\frac{45+36x^2}{20x^2}$

37a. $\frac{17}{7r}$ **37b.** about 0.81 h, or 49 min   **39.** $\frac{10}{m+1}$

41. $\frac{m+2}{m+3}$ **43.** $\frac{2}{t^2+1}$ **45.** $\frac{s^2+1}{2s^2+1}$ **47.** $\frac{1}{m+1}$

49. $\frac{5y-11}{(y+2)(y-3)}$

MIXED REVIEW   **53.** about 12.2   **55.** about 10.8

57. 4   **59.** 6

ON YOUR OWN   **1a.** 32   **1c.** no   **3.** 12   **5.** -1 **7.** 2

9. no solution   **11.** $-3\frac{1}{9}$ **13.** $-\frac{1}{3}$ **15.** $22\frac{1}{2}$ min

17. 2   **19.** $\frac{1}{2}$ **21.** $-2, 4$ **23.** $5\frac{1}{3}$ **25.** 6   **27.** 5

29. A   **31.** $a = 4; b = \frac{7}{27}; c = 11; d = -\frac{1}{3}$

MIXED REVIEW   **33.** $-2, 2$ **35.** -5.5 **37.** 1, 2, 3, 4,

5, 6   **39.** H1, H2, H3, H4, H5, H6, T1, T2, T3, T4,

T5, T6

CHECKPOINT   **1.** $\frac{4}{m}; m \neq 0$ **2.** $6(x-2); x \neq -2$

3. $\frac{c+3}{c-3}; c \neq 3$ **4.** $\frac{3z+12}{z^3}; z \neq 0$ **6.** $\frac{6}{7}$ **7.** -9 **8.** $\frac{5}{2}$

9. $-0.74, 10.74$ **10.** $\frac{9}{c}$ **11.** $\frac{5}{x-3}$ **12.** $\frac{2(7m-6)}{(m+2)(m-3)}$

13. $\frac{6t+3}{t^2}$ **14.** B

1. symmetric   **3.** reflexive   **5a.** division property of
equality   **5b.** distributive property   **5c.** subtraction
property of equality

ON YOUR OWN   **1.** 10 choices   **3.** 30 ways   **5a.** 24
different numbers   **5b.** 6 even numbers   **5d.** $\frac{1}{4}$

7. 210   **9.** 60   **11.** 6   **13.** 5040   **15.** 840   **17.** 7

21. 40,320 orders   **23.** $_9P_7$ **25.** C   **27a.** 2520

27b. $\frac{1}{2520}$

29.   **31.**

6.

33. campsite $20; family trail pass $5   **35.** $\frac{5}{72}$

7.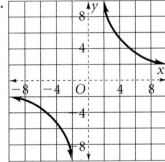

Lesson 11-7   pages 543–547

ON YOUR OWN   1a. 14,886,690 different arrangements   **1b.** about 1.94×10^{17} combinations
5. 6   **7.** 20   **9.** 6   **11.** 1365   **13.** 56

15. 35   **17a.**   **17b–c.** 6 segments

8.

17d. 45 segments   **19.** 126 different combinations
21. Permutation; the order of videos is important.
23. Combination; the order of committee members is not important.   **25.** 10   **27.** 35   **31a.** 792 different choices   **31b.** 36 ways   **31c.** $\frac{1}{22}$ **33a.** 45 possible combinations   **33b.** 3 combinations
33c. $\frac{1}{15}$ **33d.** $\frac{2}{15}$

MIXED REVIEW   35. 12   **37.** 5040   **39.** 9
41. $\frac{4x^2 + 5}{3x}$ **43.** $\frac{13x - 8}{(x + 2)(x - 2)}$ **45.** $-\frac{27}{20n}$
47a. about 1143 times   **47b.** $6\,t$

9.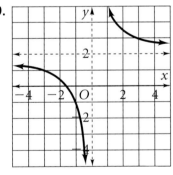

Wrap-Up   pages 549–551

1. 6   **2.** 9   **3.** 4.4   **4.** no   **5.** yes; $xy = 10.6$

12. $x - 2; x \neq -2$ **13.** $\frac{x}{4x + 3}; x \neq -\frac{3}{4}$ **14.** $\frac{-3}{t(t - 1)};$
$t \neq 0, 1$ **15.** $\frac{1}{2z - 3}; z \neq -2, 1\frac{1}{2}$ **16.** $\frac{24m}{(m - 3)(m + 1)}$
17. $\frac{1}{2(2e + 1)}$ **18.** $\frac{5c + 3}{2c(c - 1)}$ **19.** $3(n + 2)$ **20.** $\frac{8}{k}$

21. $\frac{4(2x-1)}{x-7}$ **22.** $\frac{15x^2+13x+27}{(3x-1)(2x+3)}$ **23.** $\frac{-3m+10}{(m-1)(m+1)}$

24. C   **25.** 24   **26.** 9   **27.** −14   **28.** 6 min   **29.** 60
30. 1680   **31.** 360   **32.** 20   **33.** 3024   **34.** 42
35a. 160 possible area codes   **35b.** 640 new area
codes   **36.** 6   **37.** 210   **38.** 36   **39.** 165   **40.** 5
41. 15   **42.** 4 different combinations   **43.** 45 ways

44. $\frac{3}{28}$

1. 2   **3.** 1   **5.** 1   **7.** 1   **9.** 3   **11.** 3   **13.** 1   **15.** 4
17. 1   **19.** 1   **21.** 4   **23.** 3

EXTRA PRACTICE

Chapter 1   page 566

1. 39.375; 38; 35   **3.** 6.3; 6; 5 and 8   **5a.** c = length
of a car; $3c = 24$ **5b.** b = weight of a book,
p = weight of a pen; $2b = 39p$ **7.** 28   **9.** 9   **11.** $4\frac{1}{9}$
13. −27.7   **15.** $-\frac{1}{2}$ **17.** −26   **19.** $10\frac{1}{2}$ **21.** −20
23. −59   **25.** 18
27. $\frac{7}{27}$ **29.** $\frac{22}{27}$
31. $\frac{23}{54}$ **33.** $\begin{bmatrix} -7 & 6 \\ 3 & 8 \end{bmatrix}$ **35.** $\begin{bmatrix} -1.6 & 4.1 \\ 1.5 & 4.6 \end{bmatrix}$

Chapter 2   page 567

1a.

1b. The number of pages increases as the price
increases.   **1c.** About 75 pages; you can find the
y-coordinate of the point on the line with
x-coordinate 2.00.

7. $f(x) = 2x$

9. $f(x) = \frac{1}{2}x$

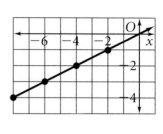

11. $\{-2, -1, 1, 2, 6\}$; absolute value   **13.** $\{6, 7\frac{1}{2}, 8,$
$9\frac{1}{2}, 12\}$; linear   **15.** $\{-\frac{8}{3}, -\frac{2}{3}, 0, 2, \frac{16}{3}\}$; linear
17. $\{0, 3, 7, 52, 88\}$; quadratic   **19.** $\{1, 4, 5, 8, 13\}$;
linear   **21.** $\{0, \frac{3}{5}, \frac{9}{5}, \frac{12}{5}, \frac{24}{5}\}$; absolute value   **23.** 0
25. $\frac{2}{3}$ **27.** $\frac{1}{3}$ **29.** $\frac{1}{3}$

Chapter 3   page 568

1. 14   **3.** 8   **5.** −5.7   **7.** 2   **9.** 24   **11.** $\frac{18}{49}$ **13.** −2
15. 1   **17.** 10   **19.** −6   **21.** n = next test score;
$\frac{87 + 84 + 85 + n}{4} = 90$; no   **23.** $\frac{5}{128}$ **25.** $\frac{9}{128}$ **27.** $\frac{1}{20}$
29. $\frac{1}{16}$ **31.** $n = 0.1 \times 94$; 9.4   **33.** $147 = 0.14 \times n$;
1050   **35.** $13.2 = 0.55 \times n$; 24   **37.** $n = 0.75 \times 68$;
51   **39.** $n \times 54 = 28$; 52%   **41.** $n \times 20 = 31$; 155%
43. about 11% increase   **45.** about 33% decrease
47. 38% decrease   **49.** about 3% increase
51. 125% increase   **53.** about 11% increase
55. about 46%

Chapter 4   page 569

1. −8   **3.** 48   **5.** $\frac{4}{3}$ **7.** $\frac{155}{2}$ **9.** $\frac{5}{3}$ **11.** 3
13. 8 ft × 12 ft   **15.** 1   **17.** 1   **19.** −40   **21.** 9, −15
23. 5, −5   **25.** $-\frac{1}{3}$ **27.** identity   **29.** The bus
traveled 5 h; the car traveled 4 h.   **31.** $cv - w$
33. $\frac{P - 2w}{2}$ **35.** $m(b - a)$ **37.** $\frac{gr^2}{1.9}$
39. $p \le 8$; ← ┼─┼─┼─┼─●─┼─→
                   −8 −4 0 4 8 12
41. $y \le -1\frac{3}{7}$; ← ┼─●─┼─┼─┼─→
                        −4 −2 0 2 4

43. $h > -12$;

45. $s \le 18$;

47. $l \ge -3.5$;

49. $m \le -12$ or $m \ge 4$;

51. $-2.5 \le n \le 14.5$;

53. $a < -11$

55. $j \ge 5$;

57. no more than five balls

59. $\{1, 2, 3\}$;

61. integers > 0;

63. integers ≥ 1;

65. integers > 10;

Chapter 5   page 570

1. $\frac{3}{2}$; $y = \frac{3}{2}x + 2$ **3.** 1; $y = x + 6$ **5.** $\frac{5}{2}$; $y = \frac{5}{2}x + 5\frac{1}{2}$

7. $-\frac{1}{7}$; $y = -\frac{1}{7}x$ **17.** 0.2 m/yr   **19.** 0.2 blocks/min

9. $y = -5x + 26$

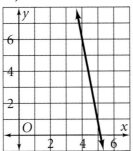

11. $y = \frac{1}{2}x + 1$

13. $y = 2x + 11$

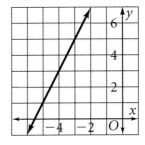

15. $y = 7x - 28$

21. $y = \frac{4}{5}x$

23. $y = \frac{10}{3}x$

25. $y = -\frac{9}{2}x$

27. $y = -\frac{1}{4}x$

29. $y = \frac{4}{3}x$

31. $y = -x$

33. 6; 8;

35. $-\frac{5}{2}$; 6;

37. $-\frac{3}{4}$; -8;

39. $\frac{1}{2}$; 3;

41a–b.

41c. $y = 0.7203196347x - 1.117579909$

43. $y = x$ **45.** $y = 2x + 3$ **47.** $y = \frac{5}{2}x - 6$

49. 1   **51.** -2 **53.** -3 **55.** 19

1. $(4, -3)$ **3.** $(11, 7)$ **5.** $(1, -1)$ **7.** $(6, 13)$
9. $(4, -5)$ **11.** $(4, -9)$ **13.** $n + p = 12$,
$5n + p = 32$

15.

17.

19.

21.

23.

25.

27.

29.

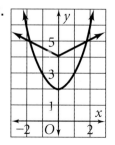

31.

33.

35. 30; 0

37. 29; 8

Chapter 7 page 572

1. narrower **3.** opens down, wider **5.** down 4
7. narrower, up 5

9.

11.

13.

15.

17.

21.

23.

25.

27. 5, −5 **29.** 8, −8 **31.** 0.9, −0.9 **33.** 1.5, −1.5
35. $\frac{1}{5}$, −$\frac{1}{5}$ **37.** $\frac{1}{3}$, −$\frac{1}{3}$ **39.** 6, −6 **41.** 10, −10
43. 14, −6 **45.** 13, −13 **47.** no real solution
49. 6.14, −1.14 **51.** 1.71, 0.29 **53.** 8, −2
55. 3.65, −1.65 **57.** −19; 0 **59.** 57; 2 **61.** −24; 0
63. −27; 0 **65.** 21; 2

Chapter 8 page 573

1. exponential growth **3.** exponential growth

5. exponential growth **7.** exponential decay

9. exponential growth   **11.** exponential growth

13. 8   **15.** $\frac{1}{2}$ **17.** 0.65   **19.** $\frac{1}{4}$ **21.** $y = 200 \cdot 1.04^x$;
$243.33   **23.** $y = 3000 \cdot 0.92^x$; $2336.06   **25.** $\frac{5}{m^3}$

27. $\frac{m^{14}}{i^{10}}$ **29.** $w^6 j^{22}$ **31.** $9n^8$ **33.** a^4 **35.** $6t^4$

37. $\frac{2r^{15}}{t^7}$ **39.** $\frac{1}{c^{12}}$ **41.** $\frac{1}{9}$ **43.** 144   **45.** 16   **47.** $-\frac{64}{27}$

49. 6.3×10^{-4} **51.** 2×10^{-4} **53.** 6.2×10^9
55. 8.91×10^{-10} **57.** 3.8×10^{-1} **59.** 5.07×10^{12}
61. 0.000 000 32   **63.** 0.000 425

1. no; $4^2 + 5^2 \neq 7^2$ **3.** no; $6^2 + 9^2 \neq 13^2$ **5.** yes;
$15^2 + 36^2 = 39^2$ **7.** yes; $8^2 + 15^2 = 17^2$ **9.** 10
11. 10.8   **13.** 5.1; (1.5, 5.5)   **15.** 1.4; (4.5, −0.5)
17. 25.5; (2, −2)   **19.** 17.0; (−1.5, 1.5)   **21.** 11.2;
(2.5, 5)   **23.** $\frac{3}{5}$ **25.** $\frac{3}{5}$ **27.** $\frac{3}{4}$ **29.** $\frac{5}{2}$ **31.** $\frac{6}{5}$
33. −10   **35.** $6 - 3\sqrt{6}$ **37.** 150   **39.** 9   **41.** 5
43. 4   **45.** 6

47. $x \geq 0$;   **49.** $x \geq 0$;

51. $x \geq 0$;

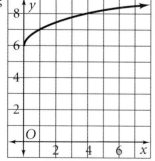

53. 1.6   **55.** 3.4   **57.** 3.2

1. $2x^3 + 4x^2 - 11x + 11$ **3.** $6m^3 + m + 4$
5. $-10c^3 - c^2 - 9c - 7$ **7.** $-4s^4 - 2s^3 + 2s^2 + 4s$
9. $4b^3 + 12b$ **11.** $6t^2 + t - 1$ **13.** $32m^2 - 40m$
15. $5k^3 + 40k^2$ **17.** $4n^2 + 2n - 12$ **19.** $b^2 +$
$10b + 21$ **21.** $(3x - 1)(2x + 5), 6x^2 + 13x - 5$
23. 3   **25.** $2v^5$ **27.** $5r$ **29.** d^4 **31.** 4   **33.** w
35. $(x + 5)(x - 5)$ **37.** $(3c + 13)(3c - 13)$
39. $(t - 3)^2$ **41.** $(2d - 3)^2$ **43.** $(3v - 2)(v + 4)$
45. $(-w + 1)(w - 4)$ or $(-w + 4)(w - 1)$
47. $(4m + 1)(3m - 2)$ **49.** $(c - 5)^2$ **51.** 12, −12
53. 2, 3   **55.** −0.38, −2.62   **57.** 1.35, −1.85
59. 5, $-\frac{1}{2}$ **61.** −0.22, −2.28

1. 70   **3.** 0.8   **5.** 0.6   **7.** 8.1   **9.** 2   **11.** 3   **13.** 5

15.   **17.**

19.   **21.**

23.   **25.**

    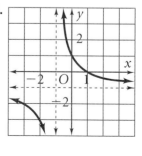

27. $\frac{t}{4}$; 0   **29.** 4; 3   **31.** $\frac{1}{x}$; 0   **33.** $\frac{6c+4}{2}$; 0   **35.** $\frac{s}{2}$; 0
37. $12b^2$; 0, $\frac{1}{2}$ **39.** $\frac{8(t-1)}{(t-4)(t+4)}$; 4, -4 **41.** $\frac{y}{6}$; 0, 2
43. 8   **45.** -1 **47.** 9   **49.** 5, -5 **51.** -12 **53.** 6, -10 **55.** 42   **57.** 8   **59.** 36   **61.** 84   **63.** 1320
65. 5040   **67.** 8568 committees

SKILLS HANDBOOK

page 577

EXERCISES   1. 6 games   **3.** 9 tacks

page 578

EXERCISES   1. 17, 19 or -19, -17 **3.** 24
5. mother 38, son 16, daughter 7

page 579

EXERCISES   1. 81 books   **3.** 36 stories   **5.** 7.2 m
7. 6 ways

page 580

EXERCISES   1. 21 lockers   **3.** about 370,000,000
times   **5.** 62 games   **7.** 32 and 33

page 581

EXERCISES   1. dog K.C., horse Bo, bird Cricket, cat
Tuffy   **3.** Alexa, Karin, Heather, Annette, Tanya,
Garo   **5.** 126 players

page 582

EXERCISES   1. 6   **3.** $575   **5.** 6 tickets   **7.** 7:25 A.M.

page 583

EXERCISES   1. composite   **3.** composite   **5.** prime
7. composite   **9.** composite   **11.** composite
13. composite   **15.** composite   **17.** composite
19. 1, 2, 23, 46   **21.** 1, 11   **23.** $2 \cdot 3 \cdot 3$ **25.** $2 \cdot 3 \cdot 3$
27. $3 \cdot 3 \cdot 3$ **29.** $2 \cdot 2 \cdot 2 \cdot 2 \cdot 2 \cdot 2$ **31.** $2 \cdot 2 \cdot 5 \cdot 5$
33. $2 \cdot 2 \cdot 3 \cdot 7$ **35.** $11 \cdot 11$

page 584

EXERCISES   1. 2   **3.** 24   **5.** 3   **7.** 7   **9.** 14   **11.** 3

13. 5   **15.** 21   **17.** 80   **19.** 33   **21.** 60   **23.** 240
25. 2160   **27.** 50   **29.** 150   **31.** 40

page 585

EXERCISES   1. 9   **3.** 48   **5.** 2   **7.** 9   **9.** 3   **11.** no
13. no   **15.** no   **17.** $\frac{1}{2}$ **19.** $\frac{2}{3}$ **21.** $\frac{2}{5}$ **23.** $\frac{1}{3}$ **25.** $\frac{2}{5}$
27. $\frac{3}{4}$ **29.** $\frac{9}{11}$ **31.** $\frac{9}{17}$ **33.** $\frac{5}{6}$

page 586

EXERCISES   1. 0.3   **3.** 0.2   **5.** $0.\overline{6}$ **7.** 0.07   **9.** 4.12
11. $1.08\overline{3}$ **13.** $\frac{3}{10}$ **15.** $2\frac{37}{100}$ **17.** $\frac{7}{8}$ **19.** $6\frac{1}{3}$ **21.** $\frac{5}{33}$

page 587

EXERCISES   1. $\frac{5}{7}$ **3.** 3   **5.** $10\frac{7}{15}$ **7.** $6\frac{2}{9}$ **9.** $6\frac{7}{33}$
11. $\frac{1}{2}$ **13.** 3   **15.** $\frac{1}{11}$ **17.** $1\frac{7}{9}$ **19.** $7\frac{11}{12}$

page 588

EXERCISES   1. $\frac{3}{10}$ **3.** $\frac{15}{32}$ **5.** $1\frac{1}{3}$ **7.** $8\frac{5}{8}$ **9.** 20
11. $1\frac{1}{5}$ **13.** $\frac{6}{7}$ **15.** $\frac{3}{7}$ **17.** $\frac{5}{7}$ **19.** $2\frac{4}{17}$

page 589

EXERCISES   1. 56%   **3.** 602%   **5.** 820%   **7.** 20%
9. 11.1%   **11.** 75%   **13.** 0.07   **15.** 0.009   **17.** 0.83
19. $\frac{19}{100}$ **21.** $4\frac{1}{2}$ **23.** $\frac{16}{25}$

page 590

EXERCISES   1. 6^4 **3.** $5 \cdot 2^4$ **5.** 64   **7.** 144   **9.** 3267
11. $(1 \cdot 10^3) + (2 \cdot 10^2) + (5 \cdot 10^1) + (4 \cdot 10^0)$
13. $(8 \cdot 10^4) + (3 \cdot 10^3) + (4 \cdot 10^2) + (1 \cdot 10^0)$

page 591

EXERCISES   1. 100°; obtuse   **3.** 180°; straight

page 592

EXERCISES   1. 22 cm   **3.** 24 cm^2 **5.** 216 cm^3
7. 351.68 cm^3

Index

Index

Acknowledgments

Staff Credits

The people who made up the Algebra team — representing editorial, design, marketing, page production, editorial services, production, manufacturing, technology, electronic publishing, and advertising and promotion — and their managers are listed below. Bold type denotes core team members.

Alison Anholt-White, Jackie Zidek Bedoya, **Barbara A. Bertell**, Bruce Bond, **Ellen Brown**, **Judith D. Buice**, **Kathy Carter**, Kerrie Caruso, Linda M. Coffey, Noralie V. Cox, Sheila DeFazio, Edward de Leon, Christine Deliee, **Gabriella Della Corte**, Robert G. Dunn, Barbara Flockhart, **Audra Floyd**, David Graham, Maria Green, Bridget A. Hadley, Joanne Hudson, Vanessa Hunnibell, Mimi Jigarjian, Linda D. Johnson, Elizabeth A. Jordan, Russell Lappa, Catherine Martin-Hetmansky, Eve Melnechuk, Cindy A. Noftle, Caroline M. Power, Roger E. Powers, Martha G. Smith, Kira Thaler, Robin Tiano, Christina Trinchero, **Stuart Wallace**, **Cynthia A. Weedel**, Jeff Weidenaar, Pearl B. Weinstein, Mary Jane Wolfe, Stewart Wood, David Zarowin

We would like to give special thanks to our National Math Consultants, Ann F. Bell, Liz Cunningham, Showyn Jackson, Sandra Mosteller, and Loretta Rector, for all their help in developing this program.

Cover Design   Sweetlight Creative Partners; Kerry Loftus Design; Suzanne Schineller

Book Design   Linda Johnson, Eve Melnechuk, Stuart Wallace, Alan Lee Associates

Technical Illustration   ANCO/Outlook

Illustration

Leo Abbett: 67

ANCO/Outlook: 16, 18, 26, 82, 87, 95, 193, 227, 230, 249, 253, 270, 274, 279, 289, 326, 399, 439

David Frazier: 116, 117, 143, 167, 170

Kathleen Dempsey: 273, 298

Dave Garbot: 161

Barbara Goodchild: 12

Fran Jarvis: Technical Illustration Manager

Keith Kasnot: 392

Ellen Korey-Lie: 3, 57, 61, 107, 157, 213, 267, 317, 361, 413, 463, 509

Seymour Levy: 107, 150, 291, 346, 371, 455, 464, 489, 490, 513, 539

Andrea G. Maginnis: 147, 221, 241, 286, 287, 292, 298, 299, 302, 369, 429, 464, 468, 529, 546

Gary Phillips: 129

Matthew Pippin: 122, 124

Pond Productions: 9

Gary Torrisi: 276-277, 306

Feature Design   Alan Lee Associates

Photography

Photo Research   Toni Michaels

Abbreviations: KO = Ken O'Donoghue; MT = Mark Thayer; JC = Jon Chomitz; TSW = Tony Stone Images; SM = Stock Market; FPG = Freelance Photographer's Guild; SB = Stock Boston; PH = Prentice Hall File Photo

Cover: Joseph Sohm; ChromoSohm Media/Corbis

Front matter: Page vii, ©Markus Amon/TSW; **viii,** KO; **ix,** MT; **x,** ©Mark Burnett/SB; **xi,** ©Paramount Studios/The Kobal Collection; **xii,** ©David Young Wolff/TSW; **xiii,** Johnny Johnson/Animals Animals; **xiv,** ©Nigel Cattlin/Photo Researchers; **xv,** ©John Gilmoure/The Stock Market; **xvi,** MT; **xvii,** ©Charles West/SM; **xix,** FPG; **xxi,** JC; **xxii,** ©John Madere/SM; **xxv,** ©Andy Sacks/TSW.

Chapter 1: Pages 2-3, O. Louis Mazzatenta/National Geographic Image Collection; **3 inset,** JC; **4,** ©David Noble/FPG; **5 t,** ©Tony Freeman/PhotoEdit; **5 b,** ©Marcel Ehrhard; **6, 8 t, 8 b,** ©Andy Sacks, Lonnie Duka, Darrell Gulin all TSW; **9,** Superstock, **12 l,** ©Markus Amon/TSW; **12 r,** KO; **14,** PH; **15,** NASA; **16,** ©Toni Michaels; **17,** KO; **19 l,** Karl Kreutz; **19 r,** ©Bruce Coleman; **20,** ©Uniphoto/Alan Lardman; **21,** ©Fotoconcept/Bertsch/Bruce Coleman; **23,** FRANK & ERNEST reprinted by permission of Newspaper Enterprise Association, Inc.; **23 t,** ©Janice Rubin/Black Star; **25,** NASA; **28,** Courtesy, Cedar Point/Photo by Dan

Feicht; **30 all,** KO; **33,** ©Nicholas Devore III/Bruce Coleman; **34,** ©Michael Holford; **37,** ©Bob Daemmrich/The Image Works; **38,** ©Toni Michaels; **41,** ©Paul Souders/TSW; **42,** PH; **46,** KO; **48,** ©Gary Geer/TSW.

Chapter 2: Pages 56-7, ©Larry Lawfer; **57 inset, 59,** JC; **61,** PH; **62,** ©Leonard Lees Rue III/Bruce Coleman; **64,** ©Richard Wood/The Picture Cube; **66,** Courtesy, Professor Bernie Phinney, University of California; **69,** Martha Cooper/Peter Arnold; **71,** NASA; **72,** PH; **74-5,** Steve Greenberg; **77,** ©JC; **80,** The Computer Museum, Boston; **82,** JC; **84,** KO; **88 t,** PH; **88 b,** UPI/Bettmann; **90-1,** JC; **93 tl, br,** ©David McGlynn, Ralph Cowan both FPG; **95,** ©Winter/The Image Works; **98,** JC.

Chapter 3: Pages 106-7, JC; **108,** MT; **112,** ©Baloo/Rothco; **114, 115 all,** KO; **117,** PH; **120,** MT; **124,** ©Kevin Morris/Allstock; **126,** Schomburg Center for Research in Black Culture, New York Public Library; **130,** ©Michael Newman/Photo Edit; **135, 137,** MT; **140,** ©M. Siluk/The Image Works; **143,** ©David Young-Wolff/TSW; **144,** ©Jose L. Pelawz/SM; **146,** Courtesy, Dr. Graciela S. Alarcon; **147,** ©Arthur C. Smith III/Grant Heilman Photography; **148,** ©Charles Krebs/SM.

Chapter 4: Pages 156-57, ©Telegraph/FPG; **157 inset,** PH; **158 t,** ©Superstock; **158 b,** ©Bonnie Kamin/PhotoEdit; **160 l,** ©Fred Whitehead/Animals Animals; **160 r,** ©Mark Burnett/SB; **163, 164 all,** KO; **167,** ©Michelle Bridwell/PhotoEdit; **170 t,** ©Bob Daemmrich; **170 b,** ©Anthony Edgeworth/SM; **171,** MT; **173,** JC; **174,** ©Bob Daemmrich; **175,** ©Bill Luster/NCAA Photos; **176 all,** The Granger Collection; **177,** ©Guido Alberto Rossi/Photo Researchers; **179 br,** JC; **179 TR,** ©David Frazier/Photo Researchers; **179 l,** JC; **182,** PH; **184,** ©George Disarid/SM; **187,** JC; **189,** ©Stephen Dalton/Animals Animals; **190,** JC; **193,** TSW; **195,** ©Melinda Berge/Bruce Coleman; **196,** ©Bob Daemmrich/SB; **199,** ©Lawrence Migdale/Photo Researchers; **203,** ©John Madere/SM; **204,** Custom Medical Stock Photo.

Chapter 5: Pages 212-13, Larry Lawfer; **213 inset,** PH; **214 l,** ©Dean Siracusa/FPG; **214 r,** ©Chris Cheadle/TSW; **215 t,** ©Valder Tormey/Picture Perfect; **215 inset,** ©John McGrail/FPG; **219,** ©E&P Bauer/Bruce Coleman; **220,** ©Gary Bigham/International Stock; **222,** ©Paul Silverman/Fundamental Photographs; **223,** ©Bruce Hands/TSW; **225,** JC; **226,** ©Telegraph/FPG; **229 tr,** ©David Madison/Bruce Coleman; **229 b,** Reprinted by permission: Tribune Media Services; **230 both,** ©Jean-Pierre/Sygma; **232,** MT; **234,** ©Peter Vanderworker/SB; **236,** ©LOL/FPG; **237,** PH; **239,** ©C. C. Lockwood/Bruce Coleman; **241,** ©Paramount Studios/The Kobal Collection; **244,** ©Chris Jones/SM; **247,** ©Nathan Bilow/Allsport; **248 l,** ©Lynn Karlin/FPG; **248 br,** Jeff Spielman/Stockphotos/The Image Bank; **250,** ©Tony Freeman/PhotoEdit; **257,** MT; **258,** ©The Granger Collection; **259,** NASA.

Chapter 6: Pages 266-67, ©David Austen/SB; **269,** ©Mary Kate Denny/TSW; **270,** ©Jose L. Pelaez/SM; **272,** Kim Barnes; **274,** ©Robert Caputo/SB; **278,** ©David Young Wolff/TSW; **279,** Courtesy, Rubber Stamps of America; **281,** JC; **283,** PH; **284,** ©Will & Deni McIntyre/TSW; **285,** ©Bob Daemmrich/The Image Works; **286 tl,** JC; **286 br,** ©Mark Burnett/SB; **286 tr,** ©David Young Wolff/PhotoEdit; **288,** ©Don Johnson/SM; **291 r,** Spencer Grant/The Picture Cube; **292,** ©D. Well/The Image Works; **296,** ©Stephen Kline/Bruce Coleman; **298 both,** PH; **300-301,** JC; **300 l,** ©Lawrence Migdale/Photo Researchers; **301 tr,** ©Bob Daemmrich; **301 b, 302,** ©John Eastcott, Frank Pedrick/The Image Works; **304,** ©Brian Smith/SB; **308,** From American Indian Design & Decoration by LeRoy H. Appleton, Dover Books; **309,** ©Charles Mercer Photography.

Chapter 7: Pages 316-17, Larry Lawfer; **317 inset,** Courtesy, Indiana Department of Motor Vehicles; **318,** ©Richard Megna/Fundamental Photographs; **321,** PH; **324,** ©Johnny Johnson/Animals Animals; **326,** ©Granitsas/The Image Works; **327 all,** JC; **328,** ©Mark Burnett/SB; **329,** ©Joe Szkodzinski/The Image Bank; **330,** ©Richard Pasley/SB; **333,** ©David Austen/TSW; **334,** NASA; **335,** Reprinted by permission: Tribune Media Services; **338,** ©Gene Peach/The Picture Cube; **340,** ©Nebraska State Historical Society; **341,** ©John Lund/TSW; **344 l, r** ©Chuck Savage, Jon Feingersh both SM; **346,** ©Hank del Espinasse/The Image Bank; **350 b,** ©Yellow Dog Productions/The Image Bank; **350 t,** ©Tony Page/TSW; **353 inset,** The Granger Collection; **353,** UPI/Corbis/Bettmann.

Chapter 8: Pages 360-61, ©Bob Daemmrich/SB; **361 inset,** ©Sidney Moulds/Science Photo Library/Photo Researchers; **363,** ©Andrew Henley/Auscape; **364,** PH; **365,** ©Chris Rogers/SM; **367,** ©Mark Burnett/SB; **371 l,** ©Alan McFee/FPG; **371 r,** ©Chip Henderson/TSW; **372,** ©Miro Vintoniv/SB; **373,** ©Corbis/Bettmann; **374** ©Grant Heilman Photography; **380 both,** ©Nigel Cattlin/Photo Researchers; **383,** ©Jack Stein Grove/Tom Stack and Assoc.; **385,** ©Bob Daemmrich/TSW; **386,** ©Telegraph/FPG; **387,** Martucci Studio; **388 tl,** Ray Ng; **388 br,** ©Paul S. Howell/Gamma Liaison; **389,** FOXTROT ©1991 Bill Amend. Reprinted with permission of UNIVERSAL PRESS SYNDICATE. All rights reserved; **390,** ©Dan McCoy/Rainbow; **392,** ©Nathan Benn/SB; **394,** ©Dr. Jeremy Burgess/Science Photo Library/Photo Researchers; **398,** The Granger Collection; **400,** Courtesy Dr. Jewel Plummer Cobb; **402 all,** MT.

Chapter 9: Pages 412-13, ©Paul Chesley/TSW; **415,** ©Spencer Jones/FPG; **417,** ©Jose Fuste Raga/SM; **418,** ©Mark Antman/The Image Works; **421,** ©Bob Daemmrich; **423,** ©Torleif Sënsson/SM; **424,** Cindy Loo/The Picture Cube; **426,** ©Joe McDonald/Bruce Coleman; **427,** T. Kevin Smyth/SM; **428,** D&J Heaton/SB; **431,** ©Dave Watters/TSW; **433,** ©Bob Daemmrich/The Image Works; **434,** PH; **436,** ©ABC/Mondrian Estate/Holtzman Trust/Haags Gemeentemuseum; **438,** Reprinted by permission: Tribune Media Services; **439 t,** ©Porterfield-Chickering/Photo Researchers; **439 b,** ©Ron Sherman/Stock Boston; **441,** ©Jim Tuten/FPG; **443,** ©Chris Jones/SM; **445,** ©John Gilmore/SM; **448,** KO; **451 tr,** ©James Shaffer/PhotoEdit; **451 bl,** ©Bob Daemmrich/SB; **453,** ©Anton Want/Allsport; **453 inset,** PH; **454,** ©Kindra Clineff/The Picture Cube; **455,** ©Jonathan Rawle/Stock Boston.

Chapter 10: Pages 462-63, ©Bob Daemmrich/TSW; **463 inset,** ©Don Mason/SM; **464 all,** MT; **472,** ©Patrick Ingrand/TSW; **476,** ©Bob Daemmrich; **479,** Courtesy, Southern Forest Products Association; **481,** ©Stacy Pick/SB; **484,** ©Kevin R. Morris/TSW; **485,** ©Tom & Pat Leeson/Photo Researchers; **486 both,** MT; **489,** ©Frank Gordon/FPG; **490,** ©Michael Newman/PhotoEdit; **492,** ©Robert Essel/SM; **493,** ©Henryk T. Kaiser/The Picture Cube; **494,** ©Michael Keller/FPG; **498,** Joachim Messerschmidt/FPG; **500,** CLOSE TO HOME copyright John McPherson. Reprinted with permission of UNIVERSAL PRESS SYNDICATE. All rights reserved; **501 t,** ©Mike Surowiak/TSW; **501 b,** ©Needham Research Institute.

Chapter 11: Pages 508-09, ©Jean-Claude Lejeune/SB; **509 inset,** ©Leonard Lessin/Peter Arnold; **510,** ©Ron Sherman/TSW; **513,** CLOSE TO HOME copyright John McPherson. Reprinted with permission of UNIVERSAL PRESS SYNDICATE. All rights reserved.; **514 r,** ©Lawrence Migdale/SB; **514 l,** ©Richard Laird/FPG; **516,** ©Michael Keller/SM; **518,** ©Michael Grecco/SB; **523,** ©Charles West/SM; **525 all,** KO; **530,** ©Bill Bachmann/PhotoEdit; **531 b,** ©Gerald Gscheidle/Peter Arnold; **531 t,** ©Greg Mancuso/Stock Boston; **533 c, l,** ©Spencer Jones/FPG; **533 r,** Lee Snider/The Image Works; **535,** Courtesy, Yield House; **540,** ©Steve Dunwell/The Image Bank; **541,** ©Christian Michaels/FPG; **544;** Ron Chapple/FPG.

New York Lessons

Page 593, Kunio Owaki/The Stock Market; **594,** *Twilight in the Wilderness* by Frederick Edwin Church. Cleveland Museum of Art, OH, USA/Bridgeman Art Library; **597,** John Henley/The Stock Market; **598,** Jonathan Nourok/PhotoEdit; **601,** Rafael Macia/Photo Researchers, Inc.; **602,** Richard Hutchings/PhotoEdit; **605,** Susan Gentry McWhinney.